T0287800

Kracauer: A Biography

Kracauer

A Biography

Jörg Später

Translated by Daniel Steuer

polity

First published in German as *Kracauer: Eine Biographie* © Suhrkamp Verlag Berlin 2016. All rights reserved by and controlled through Suhrkamp Verlag Berlin

This English edition © Polity Press, 2020

Polity Press
65 Bridge Street
Cambridge CB2 1UR, UK

Polity Press
101 Station Landing
Suite 300
Medford, MA 02155, USA

The translation of this work was funded by Geisteswissenschaften International – Translation Funding for Work in the Humanities and Social Sciences from Germany, a joint initiative of the Fritz Thyssen Foundation, the German Federal Foreign Office, the collecting society VG WORT and the Börsenverein des Deutschen Buchhandels (German Publishers & Booksellers Association).

All rights reserved. Except for the quotation of short passages for the purpose of criticism and review, no part of this publication may be reproduced, stored in a retrieval system or transmitted, in any form or by any means, electronic, mechanical, photocopying, recording or otherwise, without the prior permission of the publisher.

ISBN-13: 978-1-5095-3301-5

A catalogue record for this book is available from the British Library.

Library of Congress Cataloging-in-Publication Data

Names: Später, Jörg, 1966- author. | Steuer, Daniel, translator.
Title: Kracauer : a biography / Jörg Später ; translated by Daniel Steuer.
Other titles: Siegfried Kracauer. English
Description: Medford, MA : Polity, 2020. | Summary: "The first definitive biography of one of the twentieth-century's most important cultural theorists"-- Provided by publisher.
Identifiers: LCCN 2019050994 (print) | LCCN 2019050995 (ebook) | ISBN 9781509533015 (hardback) | ISBN 9781509533039 (epub)
Subjects: LCSH: Kracauer, Siegfried, 1889-1966. | Authors, German--20th century--Biography. | Film critics--Germany--Biography. | Philosophers--Germany--Biography. | Social scientists--Germany--Biography.
Classification: LCC PT2621.R135 Z86613 2020 (print) | LCC PT2621.R135 (ebook) | DDC 834/.912 [B]--dc23
LC record available at https://lccn.loc.gov/2019050994
LC ebook record available at https://lccn.loc.gov/2019050995

Typeset in 10.5 on 11.5pt Times
by Fakenham Prepress Solutions, Fakenham, Norfolk NR21 8NL
Printed and bound in Great Britain by TJ International Limited

The publisher has used its best endeavours to ensure that the URLs for external websites referred to in this book are correct and active at the time of going to press. However, the publisher has no responsibility for the websites and can make no guarantee that a site will remain live or that the content is or will remain appropriate.

Every effort has been made to trace all copyright holders, but if any have been overlooked the publisher will be pleased to include any necessary credits in any subsequent reprint or edition.

For further information on Polity, visit our website:
politybooks.com

For Mischa and Maxim

Contents

Contents

Figures

Acknowledgements

When the German edition of my Kracauer biography appeared in the autumn of 2016 with Suhrkamp, I had the genuine pleasure of being able to thank many colleagues and friends, both for making the book possible in the first place and for their support during the writing process. But the acknowledgements section for this English edition of the book is not the place to repeat this long list of people, for it is indebted to a different group of individuals and institutions.

I had been very pleased to see the positive responses to the appearance of the German edition: everyone seemed to welcome the fact that, at long last, someone had written a biography of this exceptionally interesting and brilliant thinker; there was a sense that he had not received the attention he deserved, that he had remained a blind passenger of intellectual history. The book's reviews were very positive, some even glowing. I received letters saying such things as: 'During my studies I read Kracauer and was fascinated. Then, I lost sight of him. And now here comes your book ...'. People who had personally known certain of the figures I discuss in the biography also got in touch with me. I would like to express my heartfelt gratitude to all of these people.

The book then had the good fortune to be nominated for the non-fiction category of the Leipzig Book Fair Prize, and I was awarded a grant from Geisteswissenschaften International, a programme of the German Publishers and Booksellers Association, which made possible this English translation, published by Polity.

I would like to thank everyone at Suhrkamp Verlag who supported me and gave me such good advice during those exciting few weeks following the book's publication, in particular Eva Gilmer and Christian Heilbronn. At Polity, I would like to thank John Thompson and Elise Heslinga for taking such good care of the translation project.

The person who has played the most important role in the creation of this English edition, however, is its translator, Daniel Steuer. To his often difficult task he brought great skill and precision. I would like to thank him for his work and for his friendly cooperation throughout the translation process.

Figure 1. Siegfried Kracauer in the 1920s (print from broken glass negative)
Copyright: DLA Marbach

1

Siegfried Kracauer – A Life

The picture shows Siegfried Kracauer. But his face looks bruised. His eyes are not quite straight; his nose seems flattened, and his lips appear to be swollen. His stereotypically Germanic first name weighs him down, while his family name indicates his Jewish ancestry. The neatly arranged bow tie is perhaps too tight. The forty-year-old's jacket restricts him. In his seemingly uncomfortable attire, he looks out sadly at the world. He does not give the impression that he is one of the leading literary names of the Weimar Republic; he rather looks like someone who has been forced to wear a suit. Perhaps the letter next to him contained some bad news, and he has just sat down, exhausted. The Nazis are coming. The broken glass is a reminder of the fragility of existence. The thought of Heine's 'torn world', in particular, comes to mind – of the modern individual whose mind is torn from the physical world and from society, and who experiences all the loneliness, absence of meaning, and alienation that follow from that separation.[1] Kracauer himself spoke of 'transcendental' and 'ideological' homelessness. But the fact that our hero appears in such a sorry shape, underneath broken glass, is purely accidental. The glass negative had broken at some point, and on the occasion of Kracauer's hundredth birthday the parts were put back together like a puzzle in order to produce a photo from the not quite complete negative. But is reality not in any case a construction – especially where contingency is involved?

Another picture shows Kracauer twenty years later, this time in America after the war. He is sitting with his back to the camera, working: he is wearing glasses, paper in front of him, a pen in his hand. He seems to be focused. The atmosphere is relaxed; the writer is sitting outside on the veranda, with the trees in front providing shade. Kracauer seems less slight than in the other picture, despite the fact that, in reality, he had neither grown taller nor put on weight. But what does that mean 'in reality'? In this photograph, we are allowed to look over the author's shoulder. It is not a typical portrait: we do not see the face of the one portrayed. And yet there is no doubt that this is Kracauer.[2] It was taken by his wife, Elisabeth, during a holiday in Stamford, New York, in 1950. It was during this year that, for the first time since 1933, financial hardship and the psychological stress of years of persecution began to abate. Kracauer had just completed *From Caligari to Hitler*, which would become a classic of the social psychology of film history and a model text for a whole generation of film critics.[3] The book did not completely do away with his financial worries, but at least he was in demand again. Film journals asked him to rank the best films, or to compile lists of his best articles from the time of the Weimar Republic, when he was senior editor of the *Frankfurter Zeitung*. On such occasions, Kracauer was also asked to provide a *curriculum vitae*. Perhaps the photograph pictures him replying to just such a request.[4] I imagine that in the line for 'Date of Birth', he would write: 'I will not give that away, as a matter of principle!'

Figure 2. Siegfried Kracauer in Stamford, New York, 1950
Copyright: DLA Marbach, Photo: Lili Kracauer

As this imagined response suggests, Siegfried Kracauer had a peculiar side, and he had various quirks – such as, for instance, insisting that no one should know how old he was. On his seventy-fifth birthday, he explained this Rumpelstiltskin attitude to his friend Theodor W. Adorno as follows:

> This is a matter that is deeply rooted in me and very personal. Call it an idiosyncrasy – but the older I get, the more everything in me revolts against the display of my chronological age. Of course, I am fully aware of the dates, which become more and more ominous, but as long as they do not confront me in public, they at least do not take on the character of an indelible inscription that everyone, myself included, is constantly forced to see. Fortunately, I am still able to ignore the chronological fatality, and that is of infinite importance for the progress of my work, for my whole inner economy. My kind of existence would literally be at stake if the dates were stirred up and attacked me from the outside.[5]

Kracauer was in a race against time. He wanted to complete a book on the writing of history before his own time came to an end. But there was even more behind this idiosyncrasy. He wanted to live extraterritorially, that is, outside of society and historical time. This was an attitude of not belonging, of shyness, the attitude of someone leading a 'non-identical existence that cannot be mediated by any generality'.[6] This need to be outside of space and time was an expression of Kracauer's experience of having been a refugee. He had escaped only by the skin of his teeth. As a survivor, he elevated extraterritoriality so that it became the ideal condition for the historian who temporarily leaves his or her own self behind in order to embark on a journey into the past. For Kracauer, it seems, homelessness and alienness were modes of being that may have resulted from compulsion and distress but nevertheless opened up new possibilities for approaching the world.[7]

If such an extraterritorial character lived outside of any contexts or personal relationships, it would be impossible to write a biography about him. But, in fact, Kracauer had a much more complex relationship to biography than his extraterritorial attitude might suggest. In an article of 1930, written during his ideology-critique years, he condemns biography as 'an art form of the new bourgeoisie' and interprets it as a 'sign of *escape*'. The more obsolete the individual becomes, the argument goes, the more important individualism becomes in literature.[8] Five years later, he wrote a biography himself – of Jacques Offenbach. At the very beginning, he assures the reader that this is not one of those biographies that depicts the private life of its protagonist but 'a biography of a society in that, along with portraying the figure of Offenbach, it allows the figure of the society that he moved and by which he was moved to arise, thereby emphasizing the relationship between the artist and a social world'.[9] The notion of a 'biography of society' was inspired by the idea of relating the individual's life to the general social totality: each side was to explain the other. Kracauer's portrait of Offenbach's life thus came to suggest the very opposite of extraterritoriality (despite the fact that the composer too was an émigré). It seems unlikely that the later Kracauer would still have written a rounded and coherent biography of the kind implied by the idea of a 'biography of society'. By that point, he considered a synthetic mediation of micro- and macro-history, of the general and the particular, to be impossible. Yet in another twist in Kracauer's relationship to biographical matters, he did recognize in himself, at the end of his life, a synthesizing continuity that he said held together all of his intellectual endeavours. He sketched a philosophy of history in which historical reality, like photographic reality, is an 'anteroom', and he thought that this philosophy – aiming 'to bring out the significance of areas whose claim to be acknowledged in their own right has not yet been recognized' – had unconsciously been the motivating force behind all of his writings.[10] In retrospect, the ego was pushing into the foreground, and this, of course, fits with the fact that Kracauer had written two semi-autobiographical fictional works – *Ginster* and *Georg* – and would have liked to write a sequel to them. Although the idea of an objective biography (including a biography of society) might be an illusion, it is nevertheless not illegitimate to attempt one – on the contrary.

The story of Kracauer's life is unusually fascinating and impressive, and it is therefore difficult to understand why no biography of him has been written before. There is only the small Rowohlt volume by Momme Brodersen and the indispensable chronicle of the *Marbacher Magazin* (1988), edited by Ingrid Belke and Irina Renz. This is all the more surprising given that there are now two editions of his collected works, each with a carefully prepared editorial apparatus, as well as countless interpretations of him in the fields of German studies and cultural studies. The reason for the absence of a biography is most likely that biographies of literary authors are written by literary scholars, those of social philosophers by sociologists or philosophers, and biographies of theorists of film by film scholars – but Kracauer did not belong to a single academic discipline, and he thus always falls between two stools. When historians write biographies (which are mostly of politicians), they are quick to claim that their protagonist is a representative of a whole age, or that the crisis of modernity is reflected in his or her works, or something of a similar magnitude. I would like to be a little bit more cautious. Kracauer, of course, did not live his life in order to become a symbol for this or that. And yet even a cursory glance at his life reveals that we are dealing with an extraordinary individual, someone about whom much more is to be related than just the details of his private life.

Kracauer was born in 1889 and grew up in Frankfurt am Main in an assimilated Jewish household he experienced as petit bourgeois and bleak. As an adolescent he felt lonely and ugly. He had a stammer, and an academic career therefore seemed unlikely. Once he had gained his university degree in architecture (during which he also studied a little sociology and philosophy under, among others, Georg Simmel), his family urged him to work as an architect to make a living, and for a short while he obeyed. But he saw himself as a writer of cultural philosophy, and in the years immediately after the First World War he went from job to job before finally becoming the literary editor of the *Frankfurter Zeitung* and a well-respected figure of the Weimar cultural scene. It was mainly because of him that film criticism came to be accepted as an intellectually respectable genre. He was a prolific writer – essays, reviews, articles on questions of philosophy and religion, of sociology and literature, on the newly formed Soviet Union, on the Bauhaus, on the Jewish renaissance, texts on his travels, on streets in Berlin, Frankfurt and Paris, on the detective novel, on hotel foyers and entertainment halls. He came to understand his times by paying attention to the things that were overlooked. In addition, he wrote two novels and an original 'ethnological' study of the social environment of Berlin employees. During this period, discussions with his peers Theodor W. Adorno, Walter Benjamin and Ernst Bloch were particularly fruitful and formative for his thinking; all three, like him, had Jewish roots.[11]

When the National Socialists came to power, Kracauer had to leave Germany. He fled overnight to Paris, where he worked as a correspondent for his newspaper. But the *Frankfurter Zeitung* then dropped him. This was the beginning of a dark period in Kracauer's life. Although he spoke fluent French and was relatively well connected, his financial situation was precarious. He kept aloof from friends and other emigrants, did not participate in anti-fascist activities, and did not even communicate with Benjamin, despite the affinities between the two, who knew each other from the Weimar period and now again found themselves in the same place, working on similar projects. They were both studying the irruption of modernity in the 'capital of the nineteenth century'[12] as a way of understanding the catastrophe that was unfolding in the present – Kracauer using Jacques Offenbach and operetta to this end, Benjamin using Charles Baudelaire and the Paris arcades. After a planned collaboration with the Institute for Social Research (ISR) on a study of Nazi propaganda fell through, Kracauer also almost fell out with his friends from Frankfurt, Adorno-Wiesengrund and Leo Löwenthal. After the French capitulation in 1940, however, these two helped him emigrate to the United States.

In the United States, Kracauer was revitalized. From the very beginning, he wrote only in English. Supported by various grants, he wrote *From Hitler to Caligari*, a history of German film which was, in fact, a history of mind and soul during the Weimar Republic. After a period of working as a freelancer, with little success, he became a research advisor at the Bureau of Applied Social Research at Columbia University and a sought-after referee for American foundations. There were new intellectual and social networks emerging, in particular around eminent authorities in visual culture such as Rudolf Arnheim, Erwin Panofsky and Meyer Schapiro (again all intellectuals of Jewish descent). Finally, Kracauer received grants that allowed him to complete two more important books, a theory of film and a theory of history. Although he did not want to return to Germany permanently, he was, towards the end of his life, drawn back to his old – lost, or perhaps never possessed – home. In the 1960s, various publishers, especially Suhrkamp, released new editions of his old texts and translations of his American books. He cultivated his precarious friendships with Adorno and Bloch, and he was a popular guest at two of the colloquia of the legendary research group 'Poetik und Hermeneutik' [poetics and hermeneutics] connected to Hans Robert Jauß and Hans Blumenberg. Kracauer died suddenly and unexpectedly in November 1966.

As we follow the life of this subtle observer, we shall travel through some important intellectual environments: we shall visit the Jewish renaissance in Frankfurt and see the workings of the editorial offices of the *Frankfurter Zeitung*; we shall stand next to the cradle of Western Marxism and come across the activities of the early Frankfurt School; we shall trace the rise and fall of film in Berlin, the capital of 1920s Europe; we shall observe the political battles of the end of the Weimar Republic and witness the catastrophe of the Nazis' persecution, expulsion and extermination of the Jews; we will see Kracauer fall on hard times while in exile in Paris, and we shall look at his attempts to explain National Socialism; we shall gain an insight into the social and psychological warfare of the Second World War, and into the social sciences in the United States during the Cold War; and we shall witness the surprisingly successful acculturation of Kracauer, then in his fifties, to America, his homesickness for Europe, as well as his perpetual ambivalence towards Germany.

This book on Kracauer is a conventional biography insofar as it deals with his 'life and work' – his work because he was a philosophical writer whose work makes his life more significant; and his life because without it his work would be unintelligible and far less meaningful. Both 'life and work' were informed by the fundamental need to cope with existence, that is, by the philosophical search for meaning; by the will to capture social reality; by the naked material and physical fight for survival; and finally, by the joy of aesthetically pleasing work.

If I had to add an adjective to the book's subtitle, it would be 'social'. This is a social biography because it tries to illuminate the social and historical contexts within which Kracauer acted. It thus traces a kind of parallel progression between these contexts and his life, in particular his intellectual life. The relationships between what would otherwise appear disparate areas should become apparent in virtue of the way in which they are linked by Kracauer, the man, himself, not as a matter of causal connection but of correspondences. The book seeks to bring objective facts, the hard facts and the less solid, porous ones, into relation with the way Kracauer grappled subjectively with these facts, a grappling sedimented in his 'experiences'. In this way, the book follows Kracauer's own advice for presenting history: the dominant perspective is at ground level, the *close-ups*, complemented occasionally by aerial views or the camera panning into *long shots*.

The 'social' aspect also relates to Kracauer's 'lifeworld'. Husserl's notion, incidentally, is at the centre of Kracauer's work in social philosophy and aesthetics, because, as the sphere that precedes actual thinking, the 'lifeworld' is what underlies philosophy. Part of the profane lifeworld I want to illuminate here is the need to secure one's livelihood, something that continually preyed on Kracauer's mind, because over long stretches of his life his material situation was precarious. Kracauer's social life is another focus of the book: his origins; family; teachers and pupils; friendships and enemies; his symbiotic relationship with his partner, 'Lili'; his professional relationships; those who shared the same fate of escape and exile; the new academic world in the US. I try to describe Kracauer in all these contexts and to reconstruct how others might have viewed him. I am particularly interested in his friendships with Adorno, Benjamin and Bloch: the book paints a portrait of a group that, around 1930, was attempting to create an avant-garde philosophy and, together, managed it – a 'revue form of philosophy', as Bloch called it, based on thought images and images of space, characterized by a broader view of the dialectic of enlightened thinking and the simultaneity of culture and barbarism, and motivated by aesthetic interests as well as by social criticism. Even after the group's erosion and diffusion, the former members remained important points of reference in one another's work, whether in agreement or disagreement.

In the final analysis, what is at stake in Kracauer's biography is our access to the world. On the one hand, this refers to Kracauer's fundamental urge to capture reality, an urge to which his 'supple thinking' and his longing for the concrete and living reality of 'this Earth which is our habitat' bear witness.[13] On the other hand, access to the world refers to the search for one's place in a world that is often hostile – and even demonic and life-threatening. In this sense, Kracauer's life encapsulates the human predicament. The second guiding theme of this social biography – after the way Kracauer coped with the demands of material existence – is thus his own analysis of his times.

This book stands in an extraterritorial relationship to research in the disciplines of German studies, literary studies, sociology and film studies. It does not ask which gaps need to be closed, which pictures need to be corrected or completed. At the same time, it stands on the shoulders of such research, especially in literary studies. Without the philological work that made Kracauer's posthumous papers available, the book would not have been possible. Thorough scholarly analysis of Kracauer's work has also left little space for new insights. The book is indebted to many ideas, but not to any single interpretive approach; rather, it follows its protagonist along his multifarious paths. Emphasis is put on those biographical elements, episodes and events which, I feel, are best suited to describing and explaining Kracauer's life. The biographical account proceeds chronologically but episodically, and thus there are numerous spaces that can be taken up by aspects from Kracauer's lifeworld and social environment. An episode is essentially a fragment: the aim is not to present a coherent (a successful or unsuccessful) life; no thesis will be attacked or defended, no puzzle deciphered.[14] Concentrated analysis and narrative passage, macro- and micro-perspectives, and close-ups and long shots all stand next to each other. Several narrative strands are intertwined, and the rope itself is held together by Kracauer, as he moves through and analyses his times, as he finds ways of coping with existence.

In writing this book, I have consulted Kracauer's complete correspondence in his posthumous papers at the German Literature Archive Marbach. With the exception of a few letters, his correspondence only begins in 1930, when the Kracauers moved to Berlin, because in 1939 Kracauer asked his mother to destroy the letters that he had left behind in Frankfurt.[15] Where copies of his letters exist in the published correspondence of other authors – Adorno, Benjamin, Bloch, Löwenthal, Panofsky, etc. – I have followed these. The correspondence with Margarete Susman is part of Susman's posthumous papers, which are also in Marbach. In addition to the correspondence, I consulted the thematic collections of papers and other materials that form part of Kracauer's posthumous papers. I spent long hours in the catacombs of the Marbach archive, which house Kracauer's library. As the biographical sources relating to the time before 1930 are fewer and further between than are those for the years thereafter, I have also drawn on the autobiographical novels *Ginster* and *Georg* in writing about the earlier period – keeping in mind, of course, that these are fictionalized.

It seemed natural to make use of these fictional documents because of their obvious autobiographical nature: among men, we are told, there *lived one of them who explored them subterraneously – Ginster*. Whenever such an italicized sentence or clause appears, it communicates Ginster's or Georg's experience. *His* [i.e. Georg's] *consciousness of being stared at like a stranger was deeply disturbing ...*[16] Even before Kracauer was driven from his homeland, Ginster and Georg were strangers in Frankfurt. This alienness was a burden for Kracauer as a private person, but it also opened up possibilities for him as an observer of his environment. Kracauer later said, in a remark about Alfred Schütz, that the stranger and exile is able to be more objective than his or her contemporaries back home because exiles are not locked into cultural patterns; they take less for granted. Further, they have had the bitter experience of having been catapulted out of their habitual orbit. As a stranger in a world that had denied him entry into its community, Kracauer discovered the possibility 'of penetrating its outward appearances, so that he may learn to understand that world from within'.[17] It was the fulfilment of this task that helped Kracauer to deal with the exigencies of his existence.

2

Early Things: Before 1918

Siegfried Kracauer was born on 8 February 1889, the same year as Charlie Chaplin and Adolf Hitler, two figures that would influence his life. His hometown, Frankfurt am Main, was *a large city on a river that had developed gradually throughout its history and lay between low mountain ranges*, as Kracauer portrayed it in his 1928 novel *Ginster*. *Like other cities, it uses its past to promote tourism. Imperial coronations, international congresses, and a national marksmen's fair took place inside the city's defensive walls, which have long since been transformed into public parks. A monument is dedicated to the gardener. Some Christian and Jewish families can trace back their ancestry. But families without ancestry have also developed successfully into banking firms with connections in Paris, London and New York. Cult sites and stock markets are separated from each other only in spatial terms. The climate is mild, the part of the population that does not live in the Westend, and Ginster belonged to it, hardly mattered. As, moreover, he grew up in F., he knew less about the city than about others that he had never seen.*[1] Kracauer wrote these words before the Jewish citizens of Frankfurt were first stigmatized and deprived of their rights – from 1933 onwards – then robbed and placed in ghettos, and finally deported and killed. Kracauer himself was no longer there at that point; he had moved to the cities where the high priests of capitalism had their connections. In Paris and New York, he didn't live in the equivalents of Frankfurt's Westend either, and he mattered even less. But now he knew some essential things about F., the place he had grown up in, that he had not known before.

Siegfried Kracauer had been forced to flee and had lost his home. After 1945, there was no homecoming, but after 1956 there was a return. A letter he received in October 1959 in New York from a lady in Frankfurt is revealing. The letter's author thought that she remembered two publications by Kracauer, from more than thirty years ago, which had left a deep impression on her: 'The Brother of the Lost Son' and 'The Crime of the Ornament'.[2] But Kracauer had never written anything bearing these titles. Maybe, after all these years, the lady had confused a few things. In 1935, Soma Morgenstern, a Jewish colleague of Kracauer at the *Frankfurter Zeitung*, had published a novel called *Der Sohn des verlorenen Sohns*.[3] And in 1908, Adolf Loos, like Kracauer an architectural critic, had written his famous essay 'Ornament and Crime'. Finally, Kracauer himself was actually the author of *The Mass Ornament* (1928). These false attributions may have been pure coincidence, yet no psychoanalyst could have dreamt up a better combination than to have mentioned, in the same breath, 'the lost son' and the 'crime' in connection with Kracauer. 'Ach! Hätte mer die Judde noch!' – 'If only we still had the Jews around!' – was a frequent lament after 1945, first when looking about bombed-out Frankfurt (implying that the bombings had been the punishment for the mass murder of the Jews), and then when thinking of the 30,000 Jews who had helped to make Frankfurt what it was and who were now no longer there.[4] Siegfried Kracauer was one of them, a 'Frankfurter Bubb', a boy from Frankfurt, who spoke the local dialect and came from a family partly of Jewish locals and partly of Jewish immigrants.[5] Adolf and Isidor Kracauer, two brothers from Silesia – the former a commercial agent, the latter a teacher – had married two sisters from Frankfurt, Hedwig and Rosette Oppenheim, the former intellectual and highly educated, the latter practically minded, but *clumsy in dealing with other people*.[6]

By German standards, Frankfurt am Main had always been a wealthy city, thanks mainly to its being a trading place, something that even many wars had failed to change. After 1240, the prosperous fair enjoyed imperial protection. There was always a very wealthy elite, which had originally developed out of the vestiges of the mediaeval land-owning nobility and then, following the Reformation, been complemented by rich French, Dutch and Italian immigrants, who became Frankfurters. 'The last addition to the citizenry of Frankfurt before 1866', writes Selmar Spier, Kracauer's childhood friend and author of a beautiful book about Frankfurt before 1914, 'were the Jews, the members of the century-old Jewish community', who lived in a quarter referred to as the 'Judde'gaß' [Jews' alley], among them Mayer Amschel Rothschild (1744–1812), founder of the Rothschild dynasty.[7] For the Untermain area of the city, the process of industrialization was neither continuous nor frictionless. Mechanical and chemical companies settled in the outer quarters, but up until the 1870s, the patriarchal ruling forces in the city fought against industrialization, which they saw as a threat to the luxurious lifestyle and trade of Frankfurt. There were also political dangers: in 1866, Frankfurt was annexed by Prussia and lost the status of an independent city state. Despite the city's conservative – even reactionary – tendencies, the second half of the nineteenth

century saw rapid modernization, mainly thanks to its democrati-
cally minded citizens, including the emancipatory-minded Jews of
Frankfurt. The *Eiserner Steg* (an iron footbridge across the Main),
the *Palmengarten* (a botanical garden), the opera, the university,
the main railway station, and the expansion of the eastern harbour
changed the face of the city into that of a modern metropolis.
Detlev Claussen summarizes this major transformation as resulting
in a 'paradoxical modernity in Wilhelminian form': an experience
of 'liberalism as a mixed social form in which the vestiges of
feudalism overlap with the forces of industrialism'.[8] That was true
in particular for the Jewish citizenry: 'There was equality before the
law, and in the empire (although not in Prussia) there was universal
suffrage regarding the parliament and freedom of the press and
trade', writes Spier, 'but apart from that all the oppositions, classes,
antipathies, and prejudices that had been produced by 1,900 years
of Christianity and 250 years of small state politics were still alive'.[9]

The *Frankfurter Zeitung*, Kracauer's later employer, symbolized
the way the Jewish citizenry was entering the bourgeoisie. It was
founded by the banker Leopold Sonnemann (1831–1909), who
was an 'Achtundvierziger' [a forty-eighter] and a supporter of the
national parliament in the Paulskirche.[10] The paper first appeared
in 1856 under the name 'Börsenblatt'; during the following decade
it bore several different names and also began to include a politics
section. In 1866, Sonnemann fled from the Prussian troops when
they marched into Frankfurt, but soon returned. From November
1866 onwards, the paper appeared as the *Frankfurter Zeitung*.[11]
Sonnemann was the prototypical Jewish member of the Frankfurt
upper bourgeoisie: he had democratic convictions, was a member
of the city council and was a patron of various city institutions,
supporting among other things the Städel Institute of the Arts and
the building of the opera house.[12] He was a social reformer who
fought a war on two fronts – against both Bismarck and Lassalle.
The paper, which he edited until his death, shared the social and
liberal orientation of the Deutsche Volkspartei [German People's
Party], without being a party organ. It was pro-capitalist, and it
rejected the skin-deep constitutionalism of the imperial German
Reich. The paper was also influenced by the peculiar, paradoxical
modernity of Frankfurt mentioned above. Paul Arnsberg, chronicler of Frankfurt's Jews after 1945, writes: 'The "Frankfurter" was
certainly considered progressive and liberal, but in line with the
local character its "infrastructure" was patrician and conservative
in an almost Baroque sense.' Sonnemann established a collegial
atmosphere at the paper's editorial offices, and his editors were
independent of him in his role as publisher. But 'despite all the
editorial "conference" democracy, the unwritten law of fixed hierarchies and authority ruled at the offices', even finding expression 'in

Early Things: Before 1918 13

the sorts of furnishings' to be found at Eschenheimer Straße 81–7.[13] As Frankfurt developed into a leading financial, commercial and industrial centre, the progressive *FZ* also blossomed, becoming Germany's most respected paper and earning an international reputation. In fact, it was probably even more highly regarded outside of Frankfurt than in the city itself.[14] This remained the case when Sonnemann put the fate of the paper in the hands of his grandchildren Heinrich and Kurt Simon.

Siegfried Kracauer's Frankfurt childhood around 1900 was apparently not a very happy one.[15] For a long time, the boy, who everyone called Friedel, knew almost nothing of his family's history; at home, no one talked about it. Only when death arrived did *the uncle* [enter] *into his childhood, his mind apparently a little mixed up. The mother, too, had had her youth, hidden childhood years of which he knew nothing, and on it went into the past, like a writing desk drawer of unfathomable depth. Ginster vainly tried to pull it open.*[16]

When Kracauer married in 1930 and sought to move to Berlin, the authorities found inconsistencies in the spelling of his name: Kracauer, Krakauer or Krackauer? They demanded information on the C and K question, and this led to some investigation.[17] It turned out that his mother's family, who were from Frankfurt, also had two versions of the family name: Oppenheim and Oppenheimer. Slowly light began to break over the family history.

According to Hedwig Kracauer, Siegfried's father, Adolf, had been born in March 1849 in Sagan (today Żagań), in Lower Silesia, a centre of cloth manufacture, wool-spinning and wool and linen weaving. The grandfather was an immigrant from Upper Silesia and a member of the synagogue's council. Adolf had a brother, three years his junior, called Isidor. Hedwig wrote of Isidor that he was allowed to attend secondary school, where he

> realized that his life's work would be dedicated to historical studies. He achieved this goal, but by way of a minor detour. Having passed his school leaving examination with flying colours, he gave in to the wishes of his mother, who wanted him to become a rabbi, and embarked on studies at the theological seminary in Breslau. Although this probably consolidated his deep interest in Judaism, he soon recognized that his talent did not push him toward a clerical but toward an academic career. He therefore soon switched to the University of Breslau, where he studied history, alongside geography and German.[18]

It was said that Adolf took up a practical profession so that his brother could pursue his studies. Initially, he became a soldier, and then a travelling commercial salesman dealing in textiles, selling the finest English materials, which he himself did not wear.[19] The companies he worked for sent him away from Sagan to France, among other places. In the meantime, his younger brother, having completed his state examination and his doctoral dissertation, had joined the Philanthropin (the Realschule of the Jewish community) in Frankfurt, first on a temporary and then, from 1876, on a permanent basis as a senior teacher.[20] At the Philanthropin, he met Hedwig Oppenheim (born 1862), the eldest daughter of Ferdinand and Frederike Oppenheim, who ran a wholesale haberdashery business. Hedwig had six sisters, among them Rosette (born 1867), the third oldest. Frederike Oppenheim died young, in 1885, aged only forty-eight, likely of bowel cancer.[21] Isidor and Hedwig married, and from 1885 they took charge of the Julius and Amalie Flersheim Foundation, an institution for the education of destitute orphaned or semi-orphaned Jewish boys. Isidor Kracauer also continued to work as a teacher and academic, and he would later write a history of the Jews of Frankfurt between 1154 and 1825.[22] Hedwig was his intellectual equal and collaborator. The hard-working couple did not have any children.

In 1888, their siblings also married. Adolf Kracauer was eighteen years Rosette Oppenheim's senior. When Siegfried was born, his father was already forty years old, and permanently away on business. On those few occasions when his father was at home, the child in *Ginster* says: *I wish you'd be gone again.* The atmosphere was suffocating. When the father came home to their modest apartment in Frankfurt Nordend, Elkenbachstraße 18, his *havelock* [shrouded] *... all of the parental home. ... Underneath lived the mother, who could hardly even lift the worn cover – she never made it out into the open.* This is not to say that Adolf Kracauer was a bad person. He sent his wife *away to summer resorts, saved every penny for her and Ginster, and if the meat turned out well for once, soft and without too much fat, he even entered into a jolly mood and told the few jokes he knew, whose punchlines he always forgot. But then, like a rain cloud, the havelock descended again ... and the living room became dark.* Adolf Kracauer must have been a very sad person, someone who was at odds with his own life. *On Sunday afternoons, he went for walks with his family, always the same walk. Ginster hated the streets on a Sunday. They walked through the Westend, where the villas and stately homes retreat behind their front gardens, so that the tarmac cannot touch them. ... The ladies and gentlemen sit behind the curtains, or are in the countryside. The father lingered in front of the villas and estimated their value.* He would have liked to have lived his life in this style, but was far from being able to afford it. Most likely, he earned even less than his brother, the teacher, whose studies he had helped to finance. *After staying in houses in which he had never set foot, he slipped back under the havelock, and Ginster would have liked to join him, and caress him, because Adolf passed the villas in such gloom.*[23] But this never happened. When Adolf Kracauer died in 1918, Siegfried's feelings were still blocked. Not a single tear flowed when his father died, even though he could be easily moved by sentimental films or sentimental novels. In fact, he was relieved. According to his sister-in-law, Adolf Kracauer enjoyed perfect physical health throughout his life, although he was a hypochondriac, something for which his family would often mock him. But towards the end of his life, his mental faculties started to fail him,[24] and this made it even harder for Siegfried's mother. It was her son's intention that she should now have a better life.

An only child, Friedel spent a lot of time alone with his mother. She too, like her husband, lacked *joie de vivre* and a strong ego. Hedwig describes her sister as hard-working, parsimonious and disciplined, strict with herself and others, conscientious, punctual and pedantic, plagued by worries, unstable and introverted, superstitious and pessimistic. She bottled everything up. Very rarely, when life was simply too much for her, she yelled and raged.[25] Ginster also speaks of the mother as living life under a depressive veil, even if not the oppressive havelock. *Sometimes she declared, for no reason, that she wanted to die: even while she was in a happy mood and laughed. When for once her laughter set in, it lasted a long time, came back*

Figure 3. Siegfried Kracauer around 1894
Copyright: DLA Marbach, Photo: Schmidt

Bleichstrasse 38 4 parf.
gegenüber der Peterskirche.

FRANKFURT a. M.

Figure 4. Siegfried and Rosette Kracauer around 1900
Copyright: DLA Marbach, Photo: H. Collischonn

repeatedly and drove an alien red flush into her cheeks. The redness could mean the beginning of an awful silence lasting several days; it glowed in cases of injustice; it was a visible language that expressed everything for which words were not enough. Ginster is worried about his ageing mother. First, she loses a tooth, then her back becomes slightly hunched and her cooking gets worse. He observes how she *dissolved; she was dismantled like a building, by unseen hands.*[26] He observes how this woman is broken by the everyday coldness of life and the insensitivity of people who joyfully and enthusiastically tumble into the madness of a war as if that were the happiness in their lives.[27] It is likely that little Friedel also felt responsible for his mother, who, in turn, constantly worried about him. They were both single parents.

Often, Friedel went to visit the boarding school of the Philanthropin in Pfingstweidstraße 14. There, he could meet other boys, but most of all it was a second home. The young Kracauer probably liked the domestic and intellectual worlds of his uncle and aunt better than his first home. In *Ginster*, there are numerous admiring passages about the practical skills of the uncle and historian who works with paper, pen, scissors, brushes and glue. As a teacher, Isidor Kracauer not only dispensed knowledge but also instilled patience. In Hedwig's judgement, he possessed an

Figure 5. Isidor Kracauer around 1900
Copyright: DLA Marbach

exceptional pedagogical talent.[28] Unlike the death of the father, the death of the uncle (the real uncle, Isidor, died in 1923) is described in great detail in the novel.

Friedel liked to roam the streets of Frankfurt. Like his later self, the grown-up flâneur, the boy sauntered through the city. Kracauer would later write about it in his feuilleton articles: 'To the boy, Frankfurt was infinite. When, as often was the case, every street lantern floated in a luminous halo of fog, he was pulled out of the house like a sleepwalker and aimlessly ambled through the intangible streets.' These forays 'were done in a state of intoxication and produced an incomparable feeling of happiness in me. What characterized them was that they always led me from darkness to light.'[29] Friedel walked every street, like a ruler visiting his provinces – incognito, like Harun al-Rashid. The train station was a particular attraction, a place for lingering, where Friedel could be among the people without having to be with them. Here, he dreamt of other places:

> Even as a child, I liked to visit *train stations*. I used to sit on a bench for hours on end and observe, unthinkingly and happily, the travellers who arrived individually and streamed out in swarms. I immersed myself in the departure and arrival boards, and felt a mysterious joy when what they promised came true. I bought platform tickets for particular trains and became excited when, suddenly, the round light on the glass skirting came on, which was the herald of the great event. I allowed myself to be jostled by the mass of people in front of the long carriages, offering no resistance, and finally I would be pushed far out into the loneliness in which the enormous locomotive, far away from the crowd, extended her body along the track.[30]

People met at this place in order to separate from one another and set off in all directions. Like the little boy observing them, they were vagabonds. They were, perhaps, also as lonely as him. Throughout his life, Kracauer was said to have something 'train station-like' [Bahnhofhaftes] about him.[31]

The Kracauer-Oppenheims were a Jewish family and members of the Jewish community. But piousness and adherence to religious rules were not exactly central to their Jewishness. Rather, they probably had that 'deep interest in Judaism' that Hedwig spoke of in her husband Isidor. What she had in mind was a feeling of historical and cultural belonging to the Jewish religion – the feeling of group belonging that, because the Jews were a persecuted minority, was somewhat different from and presumably stronger than in the case of Catholics and Protestants. Siegfried Kracauer didn't go to synagogue, nor did he celebrate his bar mitzvah. On one occasion, however, he said that he had, since his childhood, been preoccupied

Figure 6. Siegfried Kracauer, about 1907
Copyright: DLA Marbach, Photo: Wilhelm Husenbeth

with the Jewish legend of the thirty-six righteous ones.[32] Thus, he cannot have grown up entirely without some of the cultural inheritance of Jewish tradition. Isidor would have made sure of that.

Whether or not they identified with Judaism or as members of the Jewish community, the Jews of Frankfurt lived on the margins. Selmar Spier tells of the following event:

> I might have been four years old ..., when I first became acquainted with the religion into which I was born: a child, a gamin probably, as boys who were left to roam the streets without being looked after used to be called at my home, shouted ... a word after me: 'Judd' [Jew]. I did not know what that was, but felt that it was intended to be an insult and blindly protested to my ... mother. Her answer came as a surprise and triggered a feeling of complete helplessness in me: 'You are a Jew', she said.[33]

Frankfurt was a city of Jews – their influence can even be heard in the Frankfurt accent: 'Dappes', 'Zores', 'Gedibber'.[34] But public life was not Jewish but Christian; the cultivation of Jewishness remained a private matter. And so-called 'Judenriecherei' – sniffing out who was a Jew – was common: one knew who was a *Judd*.[35] And if you looked like Friedel Kracauer, there could be no doubt.

His physiognomy was often felt to be exotic, in particular because of his large flat nose and dark eyes. To Adorno he looked as if he were from the Far East, to Asja Lacis he looked like an African.[36] To the Christian natives of Frankfurt, he looked as if he were from the Orient, or rather, from the Ostend, Jewish quarter, 'Little Jerusalem'.

Up until 1880, more than 80 per cent of the Jewish population lived in Frankfurt's Ostend, and up until 1914 more than half still lived there. Before the Second World War, 44 per cent of the population in the Ostend were Jewish.[37] The most important synagogues were in Börnestraße, at the Börneplatz and in Schützenstraße. Gradually, Jewish citizens left the quarter and either moved into the Nordend (where the Kracauers lived), or, if possible, into the Westend (where the villas stood). That also had to do with the 'pollacks', as the eastern Jews were often derogatively called, who were said to bring poverty and 'un-German' customs into the city, and who the assimilated Jews shunned. Ginster was also astonished: *They wore caftans and flowing beards; two of them talked as if there were four of them – Jews who looked so genuine, they seemed to be imitations.*[38] The Jews who had left returned to the Ostend on Friday evenings and on Jewish religious holidays. Sometimes the children attended school there.

Up until 1909, the Philanthropin was at Rechneigrabenstraße 14, near today's Dominikanerplatz, at the centre of the Ostend

Figure 7. The Philanthropin: In memory of the inauguration of the
school building, 1843
Copyright: Institut für Stadtgeschichte Frankfurt (ISG FFM), ISG_
S7A_1998-19627, Lithografieanstalt Dondorf

quarter; many eastern Jewish immigrants lived on that street.[39] Isidor
Kracauer taught at the Philanthropin, and if there were ever some
ceremonial occasion, it was usually him who delivered the main
speech. (Something for which he apparently had had to overcome
a 'speech impediment'.)[40] For Adolf and Rosette Kracauer, Isidor
was reason enough to send their son to the school, which was,
according to Arnsberg, 'the symbol of the Jewish citizens' love of
their hometown, Frankfurt am Main'.[41] Formally, the school of the
Jewish community was not a Jewish school because it also accepted
teachers and pupils of other faiths. Nevertheless, it pursued the aims
of liberal German Jewry: the promotion of social equality through
education. The language of instruction was, of course, German,
and the confessional aspect was limited to classes on religious

education. True to its name, the Philanthropin sought to be a 'place for humanity'.[42] In Arnsberg's judgement, it was one of the best schools in Frankfurt.[43]

Such hymns of praise did not come from Kracauer himself, but neither did he say anything to contradict them. The boy was busy enough as it was. In the eyes of his peers, he was certainly an oddball. He would give his fellow pupils marks in his notebooks, which he also filled with scenes from everyday life at school, or with doodles.[44] The fourteen-year-old was the shortest pupil in his class, and in addition he had to cope with his conspicuous appearance. He felt that he looked ugly. But the worst thing was his speech impediment. From his diary, we can sense his utter desperation: 'Oh God, please help me and give me the strength to overcome my defect. Because when I no longer stutter, I feel the power in me to achieve something. And also let me become a good person who does his duty and is open to love his fellow human beings.'[45] Little Friedel was not only unhappy. He also saw himself as responsible for his unhappiness, and he thus put himself under a lot of pressure. God did not help him, either; rather, it was his imagination that allowed him to cope with hostile realities: 'When as a child I had to wait for a long time for a tram, I intentionally ignored the possibility of it arriving, and walked on, slowly – as if trams did not exist at all. Then, it usually came along, as if attracted by my behaviour.'[46]

In spring 1904, his time at the Philanthropin came to an end. 'In acknowledgement of his diligence and good behaviour', the 'pupil Siegfried Kracauer' received a book by Lassar-Cohn, a non-fiction author, containing 'lectures for the general public' on *Die Chemie im täglichen Leben* [Chemistry in everyday life].[47] Friedel moved on to the Obersekunda, the seventh year of secondary school, at the Klinger-Oberrealschule in Frankfurt am Main. This school was the successor institution to the Höhere Bürgerschule, which had originally been founded for the children of the 'intelligent commercial and merchant classes and civil servants'. After Gymnasien [secondary schools] and Realgymnasien or Oberrealschulen had been given equality of rank in 1901, the Klingerschule (named after the Frankfurt *Sturm und Drang* poet Friedrich Maximilian Klinger) was located in the Nordend at Hermesweg/Mauerweg, north of Friedberger Anlage and close to Bäckerweg, where the Kracauers were now living. Ernst May, who in the 1920s would become one of the leading architects and city planners of the Weimar Republic, sat his Abitur [leaving examinations] at the Klinger school around the same time. Between 1925 and 1930, he oversaw sustainable social housing projects as the head of Frankfurt's planning department. Kracauer followed his progress with interest. The spirit of progressive architecture seems to have been alive at the school. Kracauer also exhibited a talent for architecture and, in his leaving examinations of 1907, received

a 'very good' in mathematics, nature description and drawing.[48] In
foreign languages, French and English, however, he only achieved
an 'adequate'.[49] When it came to German, his examiners found that
he possessed 'a commendable flexibility in written expression, a
good knowledge of literary history and a mature understanding of
its masterpieces'.[50] Around the same time, he even managed to get a
piece of travel journalism published in the *Frankfurter Zeitung*; for
the time being, however, the article remained a one-off.[51]

The eighteen-year-old Kracauer had now passed the exam
required for him to start university, but beyond his studies his life
lacked a great deal:

> If I could find one soul, just one, tied to mine through life and
> common work in the closest friendship. Everything in me screams
> out for a friend, my whole life and longing at present amounts to one
> thing: the search for that friend. But wherever I knock, I find locked
> doors and unwilling faces. It is terribly difficult to stand alone![52]

Around 1907, Kracauer got to know Max Flesch, the son of
Frankfurt's city councillor for health, Dr Karl Flesch. Kracauer
was the same age as Max, and he went to visit Max at his home
'with feelings of great aspiration': 'a human being of great beauty
and much, much taller than me. ... Oh yes, I felt small beside him,
tiny.'[53] Friedel (or Friedrich, as he now occasionally began to call
himself) compared his vain longing for friendship with Tonio
Kröger's passionate love for Hans Hansen, the athletic, blue-eyed
boy who lives in 'happy harmony with all the world', and in
particular with the blond Inge, also worshipped by Tonio. Tonio,
however, is a 'southern' type, envious, full of yearning and gloomy;
he flees life and escapes into the world of arts.[54] In Friedel's case
it was the world of literature into which he escaped. Apart from
Thomas Mann, it was Adalbert Stifter and Hermann Hesse, in
particular, who accompanied the adolescent during these difficult
years and provided him with the solace of an imaginary world
beyond the blond and blue-eyed ones. Stifter's *Indian, Summer*
of 1857, a novel depicting utopian bliss in which nothing really
happens but the protagonist's life is nevertheless perfect and
fulfilled, was one of Kracauer's favourite books. Stifter's language,
the way the narrator almost sinks into the objects of nature,
must have had a soothing effect on a young man trying to find
direction in his life between the end of school and the beginning
of university. 'Simplicity, stability, and meaning' [Einfachheit,
Halt und Bedeutung] – these are the final three words of the novel,
and for Kracauer they were like fixed stars in the firmament in
a life that, especially when he was particularly down, he often
found difficult.[55] Apart from Stifter's hero Heinrich Drendorf,

Kracauer liked Hermann Hesse's Hans Giebenrath, a likeable but somewhat extravagant oddball, and anything but a normal pupil. Giebenrath's mother is dead (having suffered chronic poor health and depression), and his father is strict and ambitious. In the end, this exceptional boy is crushed under the weight of the uncomprehending world of the adults. Perhaps Friedel identified strongly with Hans's trips 'on his dream paths in the land of childhood'. The Giebenraths' house in *The Prodigy* is on Gerbergasse, which borders 'on the railroad embankment, which was overgrown with yellow gorse [Ginster]'.[56] These novels had 'a decisive influence' on the young Kracauer's development, as he later told Thomas Mann. And he thanked Hermann Hesse, with 'love and admiration', for 'the old wonderful paths ... that I once walked under your guidance'.[57] The young Kracauer read everything he could lay his hands on, from the small Reclam volumes, whose aesthetics he liked, to heavy philosophical tomes such as Oswald Külpes' *Einleitung in die Philosophie* [Introduction to Philosophy], whose fourth edition he worked his way through from beginning to end.[58] Kracauer was an autodidact who went about systematically closing the gaps in his own education.[59]

Kracauer's family urged him to become an architect – *because of his doodles*, as Ginster laconically remarks, although there was more

Figure 8. Georg Simmel around 1911
Copyright: Special Collections Research Center, University of Chicago Library

Figure 9. Siegfried Kracauer around 1912
Copyright: DLA Marbach

to it than that.[60] At just fourteen, Kracauer described himself to his uncle as 'thirsting for style'.[61] The pages of his diary are everywhere adorned with fantastically-shaped ornaments. And, importantly, from the very beginning 'Kracauer's gaze' on the world, on objects and on human beings had a strong spatial dimension. For him, the act of seeing was an integral, and also intuitive, aspect of appropriating and experiencing the world: 'Kracauer's thinking is in a peculiar way dependent on the illustrative [Anschaulichkeit[62]]'.[63] From early on, his engagement with architecture involved the 'primacy of the optical', and this gave his thinking its peculiar tone.[64]

In April 1907, Kracauer began to study architecture at the Großherzogliche Technische Hochschule in Darmstadt. In August, a period of practical training over the summer break led him to realize that he was not cut out for work on a construction site: it 'is the most horrible thing I can imagine at the moment. I hate the monotonous work. I count the hours until the end of the day.'[65] After work had ended, he was finally able to read – novels and biographies, Nietzsche and Dostoevsky, also philosophical books. In his second term at university, amid courses on the construction of high-rise buildings, the 'bourgeois art of building', descriptive geometry, inorganic experimental chemistry, and the 'history and theory of the ornament', Kracauer began to delve into Kant's *Critique of Pure Reason* with Felix Hentschel, who was studying physics and mathematics in Frankfurt to become a teacher and was renting a room at Pfingstweidstraße 14.[66] In Hentschel, Kracauer had at long last found someone with whom he could 'symphilosophize', as he would later refer to reading, thinking and interpreting with others.[67] But by the winter term 1907–8, Kracauer had already left Darmstadt for the Technische Hochschule in Berlin (as the TU Berlin was called before 1946).[68] There, in addition to courses in his core subject, he attended Georg Simmel's lecture on the 'problem of artistic style', in which Simmel modified Adolf Loos's critique of the ornament. Kracauer was so impressed that he went to see Simmel.[69] The cultural philosopher was not a full professor, but around 1910 he was already a cult figure in Berlin. As an outsider of Jewish descent, he knew how to have a presence in the public sphere beyond the confines of the university. He was even known outside of Germany. Simmel's preferred form was the essay, and his thought travelled down unconventional paths. His scholarly work was aimed not only at the academic world but also at society more widely; his philosophy was not just a conceptual exercise but ventured into the modern world of finance and the metropolis. He was one of the founding fathers of sociology, and his intuitive thinking enthralled Kracauer, the 'realist and visual man'.[70] But Kracauer was not his only fan: when Simmel lectured, the halls were packed. The most talented students, among them Margarete Susman, Georg Lukács and Ernst Bloch, flocked to him. The 'Lebensphilosoph' [philosopher of life] judged science, the arts, religion and morality on the basis of how well they served life. He was concerned about 'genuine' Erleben [lived experience] – 'the psychophysical unity of the living individual in the context of an immediate reality that is vividly experienced'.[71] Simmel was without doubt a philosopher of fragmented modernity who articulated the sense of a fundamental rift that runs through modern culture.[72] Kracauer's first personal contact with Simmel was apparently only brief. But their relationship intensified once Simmel, by this point already fifty-six, had finally been offered a chair and had moved to Strasbourg in 1914. Kracauer later sought him out for a conversation that took place in Frankfurt and discussed his 'future philosophical education' with him.[73]

After his preliminary examination – halfway through his diploma in architecture – Kracauer again changed university, but this time he would stay put for longer. From the summer term 1909 to the winter term 1912–13, he was enrolled at the Königlich Bayerische Technische Hochschule in Munich. In addition to courses in architecture, he was now officially signed up for lectures in philosophy and sociology. He wrote literary texts, the first of which was 'Das Fest im Frühling' [The festival in spring] (1908). The world-weary protagonist and the text's author are very much two peas in a pod. Kracauer's adolescent identity crisis also shaped his second story, 'Die Gnade' [Mercy], 'written between Easter and Whitsun 1913': a young insurance salesman is close to committing suicide when a prostitute saves him by showing him that life is worth living. Kracauer's story is the fantasy of a young man for whom the problem of life finds an erotic solution. Some 'motives, plot elements, and relations between characters'[74] are taken up again in the later *Ginster*, where, however, they are treated with more distance and irony, and where they are deployed against a social and historical background instead of as part of a narcissistic self-reflection.

In August 1911, Kracauer passed his architecture diploma, receiving an overall mark of 'good'. He worked at an architectural office in Munich and, at the same time, prepared a doctoral project on the cast-iron gates in Berlin and Mark Brandenburg, supervised by Theodor Fischer.[75] After a reunion with Felix Hentschel, he wrote: 'In my conversations with Hentschel, I noticed how much I have matured. Well, may I continue to progress.' At the same time, he still did not feel 'content in myself; I feel lonely, that is, absent from myself.'[76] In this period between university study and professional life, between the life he desired and the one he had, the young adult fell into a black hole. Existence [Dasein] seemed alienated – 'Man today has altogether lost the will to experience [Erleben]. They "are lived" ...' – but what he expected out of life was much greater: 'I cannot comprehend that I should lead a circumscribed and limited life, and that one day people will say: Friedel Kracauer was such and such a person and lived this life! Everything that exists would have to be part of my life, and there should not be a single lonely person with whom I should not have suffered and striven. I do not have enough love for my transient life, and only love for my eternal and immortal one. Each is incompatible with the other.' Often Kracauer despaired: 'Gloomy times! At certain times, I long for death. ... What is it in me that makes me alien, unfaithful and unfeeling and lonely? And clueless? And discontented with myself? Where am I headed? What is my path?' He would have preferred to listen less to his inner self, to look away from himself more: 'Philosophy as science! That would require a thorough discussion. ... Scorn and derision on these barren and weak individuals who think they practise philosophy when they solve some problems posed to them by pure understanding with the means of some understanding, and who project their bourgeois philistinism into the realm of metaphysics in the form of well-padded systems that lack vitality and strength! Who do not know that a philosophy must be lived and suffered ....'[77] Nietzsche, of course, was the hero of this life-hungry philosophy, this mixture of philosophical cultural criticism and personal anguish.

Siegfried Kracauer was twenty years of age and was afraid that his life would pass him by unlived. He was permanently preoccupied with his ego's suffering, which he sought to relate to the times in which he lived.[78] He wrote poems in which he concocted rhyming patterns around florid terms like 'Erdenleiden' [earthly suffering] or 'Sehnsuchtswogen' [waves of longing]. The writings of the young Kracauer were under the influence of dreams and tears, as for instance in a 'prayer':

You, who walks through my nights in secrecy
And stands, as a warning to my soul, before me
At every hour, in times both dark and bright
My silent friend in my loneliness, provide
relief from this sinister burden, I beg thee,
Which you once hast imposed on me,
When I wrested myself from the womb
Not knowing what confusion in this world would loom
Take from me this passion, so strong,
Which consumes me and destroys the calm for which I long
Take from me the greed to ingest man and thing,
Everything to which my eyes do cling
The flame that's glowing through my soul
And pulls me further from myself with the goal
To tear me along to the eternal unknown

To alien wonders, that will never be my own
This merciless flame of love, end its shine!
And your holy peace let instead be mine![79]

There are numerous such poems: love poems, full of longing;
sad farewell poems; words addressed to eternity; hymns to the
'Sonnenabendstunde' [The hour of the evening sun]; lines of
Nietzschean heroism, and spoonerisms ('Es sind immer wieder
Nerven/Die einen so niederwerfen...' [Again and again, the nervous
tissue/turns out to be the unsettling issue]). These verses were
of course not meant for public consumption. But the young
Kracauer also wrote substantial treatises that he presented to
others, for instance to Simmel and Max Scheler: 'Über das Wesen
der Persönlichkeit' [On the nature of personality] (1913/1914),
'Von der Erkenntnismöglichkeit seelischen Lebens' [On the possible
knowledge of psychic life] (1916), 'Das Leiden unter dem Wissen
und die Sehnsucht nach der Tat' [The suffering caused by knowledge
and the longing for the deed] (1917). The titles alone suffice to tell us
what Kracauer was trying to get off his chest in writing these texts.
There was, on the one hand, his psychologically motivated desire for
meaning, love and security; on the other hand, there was what he
considered to be the distinguishing characteristic of his times. The
texts are stories of loss and pathological discovery – typical of the
'reflective mode of modernity'.[80] Kracauer's early writings contain
Lebensphilosophie-inspired criticisms of capitalism, bemoaning its
alienating, uprooting, isolating and form-destroying effects. Modern
man is the 'man who has not "lived", because he erred in the goals he
set himself; because he did not succeed in fully expressing himself' –
'that is a tragic phenomenon peculiar to our times'.[81] In Kracauer's
view, the path towards 'life' and the escape from 'fate' had to be
sought for the most part, on the individual level, through the development of the 'personality' and, at the collective level, in a 'religious
idea' that could 'put down roots in the souls'. For Kracauer, body,
mind and soul formed a unity that was striving to unfold itself but
was prevented from doing so by the narrow rationalistic powers of
capitalism and science.[82]

'Über das Wesen der Persönlichkeit' deals with the 'need of
thought to bring order into the confused manifold of phenomena
with the help of comprehensible principles'. But in actual fact the
text is a soliloquy, the expression of an adolescent's confusion and
lack of orientation. Kracauer had not yet found his place in this
chaos, these 'manifolds'. The text is also wholly under the spell of
the bourgeois cult of the personality. It talks at length about the
ideal of projecting one's inner potential out into the world and
'mould[ing] the [inner] flowing life into a *form*', something Kracauer
associates with the demand for an organic community that enables

this process and abides by the categorical imperative that 'nothing human should be alien to the human being'. In other words, what Kracauer was seeking was personal development that meets with social recognition.[83]

Even if the young Kracauer was, when it came to the personal question of what direction he should take in life, stumbling around in the dark, and no matter how much these reflections confused the private with the philosophical, his early treatise very clearly identified 'the dramatic space' in which his later writings would move: 'the inside/outside-interface' between the individual and the world around it.[84] Although this was a depressive phase in his life, Kracauer knew very well that he had to engage with this outside world in order to lead a good life. In this first creative phase, he made a commitment: he would approach things in the world, would touch them and look at them, even if he still lamented the fact that the path to a personality and to the '*whole* man' was blocked by the social forms of capitalism and science.[85]

The treatise 'Von der Erkenntnismöglichkeit seelischen Lebens' is also characterized by this admixture of cultural criticism and desire to confront reality. On the one hand, it condemns the deracination and isolation of modern man and expresses Kracauer's longing for community.[86] On the other hand, it asks the fundamental philosophical questions that would come to define his distanced relationship to German cultural criticism and guide his work throughout his life. Kracauer's philosophical libido was directed at permeating and explaining 'the manifold of the world' – that is, the diverse, concrete reality of human beings, of the world beyond human beings, and of the relation between human beings and the world – 'with the faculties of our knowledge'. This was not meant to be an academic or ideological exercise; rather, it was an 'epistemological need' and a mode of life that aimed very firmly and directly at reality. The researcher of life behaves like a lover: 'He touches it on all sides, feels and thinks it through with all the faculties at his disposal, in order to reach the innermost ground of the phenomena that trustfully cling to him and have only one wish: to have their mystery resolved.'[87] For Kracauer, philosophy was not only necessary for leading a good life, he needed philosophy to be able to cope with existence at all. This early text's other insight, which Kracauer would hold onto throughout his life, is that the resolution of the mysteries of life's processes had to take place in an in-between space, in a space free of both dogmatism and relativism. Even at this early stage, he had already discovered that truth is not something that can be settled once and for all. But one must not give up searching for it either, for a 'relativist is only a relativist because he wants to be a dogmatic'. Truth is possible, but this truth is not an absolute and final truth elevated above all others. 'The relativist goes wrong when he despairs over truth, the dogmatist when he overestimates it and turns it into something independent ....'[88] And another keyword comes up in this early piece: 'socialization' [Vergesellschaftung] – Simmel's a priori of consciousness, that which brings the social into thinking.[89]

For this young, philosophically inclined architect, the years around 1914 were a 'time of becoming' and of struggle against the 'powers of life'.[90] He found his own 'ruminating and pondering' and 'narcissistic self-reflection' to be exceptionally burdensome.[91] From a purely practical perspective, his family was breathing down his neck: it was high time, they said, that he found a 'profession that provided him with a living' [Brotberuf]. But he wanted a 'profession to do with words' [Wortberuf], for what he dreaded more than anything else was the prospect of leading a stunted life in architectural offices and on building sites. The new friends he made confirmed him in his wish not to put up with the standard parochial bourgeois life. Towards the end of his time in Munich, while writing his dissertation on the art of forging,[92] he made the acquaintance of the student Otto Hainebach, who was also from Frankfurt and also Jewish. Hainebach had attended the Goethe-Gymnasium in Frankfurt together with Selmar Spier, who in his memoirs of Frankfurt portrays Hainebach as the unrivalled top pupil in the class, and also as a talented poet, a young man of lively temperament, full of ideas, a madcap wit. Like Friedel, who was three years their senior, Otto and Selmar lived in Nietzsche's 'Café Megalomania', and both were disappointed with the tedium of their university studies.[93] In the following years, the three young Frankfurt men formed a 'triangle'.[94] In *Ginster*, Otto appears as a serious and hugely talented philologist who diligently studies the Platonic dialogues and discusses the possibilities of knowledge and the methods of science with Ginster:

> *According to his theory, Columbus should have landed in India, but he discovered America. And any hypothesis, I presume, should prove itself in like fashion. A hypothesis is only useful to the extent that it misses the intended target and reaches another, unexpected one. ... The place to which [the broad roads] do not lead: that is precisely where we need to arrive.*[95]

This is how gay, adventurous and care-free a lively science should be. Meanwhile, the young men's personal situation was being shaped by the implacable reality around them. In August 1914, war broke out. It changed everything.

Otto volunteered for the army, although he had *just as little talent for war* as Friedel, who returned to Frankfurt after the army rejected him.[96] Indeed, it looks as if Kracauer was at first infected with an enthusiasm for the war, the prospect of which added some brightness to the bleakness of everyday life. Of his adolescent poems, one is called 'Auf der großen Reise' [On the great journey]:

> For us, who are still alive, a light does shine
> Through the bloodied alleyway
> Homeland, with you we shall forever stay
> Germany, Germany, your light for us does shine.

With these lines, Kracauer joined the soldiers in spirit. In an article published in September 1915 in the *Preußische Jahrbücher*, the then twenty-five-year-old reflected on the 'Erleben des Krieges' [On experiencing war]. He saw the emotion triggered by the war – which was not exactly 'love of country', he thought – as arising out of people's inner emptiness. War appears as liberation because it provides people with meaning where before there had been none. Serving the community, Kracauer writes, brings happiness, and provides a bond essential for living beings.[97] The young author had found an explanation for his own experience of the war, but he had also established a certain distance from that experience. He was proud of this article, his second publication after the piece in the *FZ*. He sent it to Max Scheler after he had heard Scheler's lecture on 'Ursachen des Deutschenhasses' [On the causes of the hatred of Germans] at the Frankfurter Hof in 1916, in which Scheler celebrated the war and Germanness as kindred in spirit. At the time, Kracauer was fascinated by Scheler's anti-capitalist cultural criticism and his hope for an individual and collective religious renewal, especially because Scheler's starting point was always the divided and alienated human being of modernity. Kracauer also had no objections, in principle, to Scheler's reflections on the essence of things.[98] But later, in *Ginster*, he has nothing but scorn for Scheler's attitude towards war, an attitude he puts into the mouth of his character Professor Caspari. Caspari gives a speech at the zoo on 'The Reasons for the Great War', locating these reasons in the *essence of peoples*:

> *The essence of Western peoples, Professor Caspari said, is altogether different from ours. While we cultivate militarism as an end in itself, for them it is only a means to an end; while they value political freedom, we care for inner freedom alone. ... Ginster realized that he was unwittingly trapped forever inside a particular essence which determined him just as much as did the military muster roll which contained the dates of his life. Had he grown up among the Western peoples, his essence would have been one now hostile to him. Professor Caspari alone seemed to have escaped the trap of the essence of peoples; he surveyed them all and, like a magician, manipulated them until war became inevitable.*[99]

We cannot say with absolute certainty when exactly Kracauer's judgement of the war and its proponents changed. In March 1916, Otto Hainebach was fatally wounded during the attack on Verdun and then buried in the Jewish cemetery at Rat-Beil-Straße.[100] His death preoccupied Kracauer for a long time. In *Ginster*, the lament *Otto is dead* introduces a confession: *Everyone knows how to live; I see that, in living, they pass me by, and I cannot find an access.*[101] Shortly before the horrendous battle, Ginster receives a letter from Otto:

> *If it shall be my lot to stay here, consider that a rift would probably have run through my life until the very end. The contradiction between wanting and being able to do, striving and achievement, longing and reality, the whole tragedy of semi-talented people has always worn me down. The gap I shall leave behind must close; I bless the circle of which I was allowed to be a part. Fare thee well. And keep my memory, should you receive news of my death.*[102]

His beloved friend had fallen in battle for the ideas of 1914. Friedel was left behind, in desolation, amidst the collective jingoism. The war had not dispelled the inner emptiness; on the contrary, it had deepened the unhappiness. For the time being, Friedel was left to cope on his own with the 'rift' that ran through Otto's and his own life.

In mid-September 1917, Kracauer received his call-up papers. Since July 1915, he had worked at the architectural offices of Max Seckbach, and he had even won a city council competition to design a military cemetery. The cemetery still exists, and it bears witness to the military madness of the times. It is difficult to tell whether the design is ironic, or whether the architect was genuinely motivated by the seriousness of his task. *[T]he general times of war ... demanded a layout that captured their horror.*[103] What is certain is that Kracauer's brief stint with the foot artillery in Mainz was miserable. He could not handle the rigours of the training, and he was made to peel potatoes before finally being sent home as 'fit for professional work'. 'I have had rich but somewhat depressing experiences of people and situations in the military', he reported to Simmel in December 1917, before taking up a position as an architect at the municipal planning and building department in Osnabrück, where he was tasked with building a *sweet little* estate for workers. This astounds Ginster: *First they were shot at, and now they are given gardens.*[104]

Kracauer also sought to contact Scheler, who encouraged him and even urged him to send him his writings. Scheler was generous with his compliments, but he did not shy away from the differences between them, which would have increased his credibility in the eyes of the critical young Kracauer.[105] It was obvious that Scheler was

following in the footsteps of Nietzsche, a philosopher who passionately lived what he thought – 'a human being in which chthonian
forces were inseparably linked to the powers of contemplation'.[106]
Kracauer was fascinated by the manner in which Scheler interwove
passion and knowledge.

In this early phase of Kracauer's thinking, Simmel and Scheler
were not only his philosophical points of reference but also his
career advisors. He met with them regularly whenever their paths
crossed in Frankfurt. Kracauer's desire to engage in intellectual work
was becoming ever more intense, and his two teachers supported
his ambitions through their critical commentaries on his texts.[107]
Simmel in particular encouraged Kracauer to give up the architectural profession and to risk the leap into the intellectual world. In
the final year of the war, while in provincial Osnabrück, Kracauer
felt himself more at odds with his fate than ever before. But two
deaths in the summer of 1918 changed the situation.

First, Adolf Kracauer died. 'Today, 10 July, my father died ... My
father has had a joyless life and toward the end it was lamentable.
He is redeemed.' The son did not mourn, but he dreamt that his
'father had been placed in a coffin, but at the same time he actually
lay in bed and saw the coffin standing in front of him. One tried
to keep the secret from him of just what the coffin was for. My
father slowly recovered. The whole dream was dreadful.'[108] A *post
mortem* havelock. The financial burdens grew. Rosette and Siegfried
Kracauer moved in with Siegfried's uncle and aunt in Sternstraße
29/2. The family urged Kracauer, more insistently now, to find a
profession that could provide him with a decent living. But, slowly,
Kracauer began to escape these pressures.

Two months later, Georg Simmel died. Kracauer did not dream
about him; he wrote about him – and a voluminous monograph at
that. He was not able to publish it in its entirety, but he succeeded
in finding a place for its introduction in the cultural journal *Logos*.
It expressed Kracauer's unreserved admiration for this unusual
cultural philosopher, to whom he attributed 'unusually discrimi-
nating powers of observation and unparalleled sensitivity'.[109] To
Kracauer, this intellectual stayed close to life, his thinking tracing
the features of its objects closely. Kracauer recognized himself in
someone of this – almost excessive – sensibility. He also admired the
attentiveness with which Simmel made visible 'the fabric of societal
relations' while not neglecting the individual human being and his or
her psyche.[110] Kracauer had a profound respect for the philosophical
depth of Simmel's sociology, especially for the way he provided an
epistemological grounding for the subject–object relation, that is,
the inner/outer problem that also exercised Kracauer so much. Here
was someone who investigated the 'world's manifold' at the highest
conceivable level.[111] And here was someone who wrote in a manner

that 'shaped the material' in a unique way. Simmel had put forward
an idea that Kracauer found irresistible:

> The core of mankind's essence is accessible through even the smallest
> side door.[112] ... Any individual phenomenon can serve as the point
> of departure for his philosophical examination, since all phenomena
> afford equally good entry points from which to delve into the inter-
> connections of the life totality that surrounds them all.[113]

What Kracauer learnt from Simmel is how to understand 'even the
simplest phenomenon as a symbol, as something that refers to many
other circumstances and events'.[114] Still, Simmel was no messianic
figure for Kracauer. The social world through which Simmel
journeyed had no fixed centre and no meaning: in Kracauer's eyes,
then, Simmel was a scientific relativist who was driven towards
Lebensphilosophie, which Kracauer was increasingly distancing
himself from. All in all, however, Simmel's way of philosophizing
offered itself as a model 'in the way in which it masters life'.[115] It is
interesting that, in his later work, Kracauer hardly ever mentions
Simmel explicitly, despite all the opportunities to do so. This
absence is so conspicuous that it suggests that Simmel is, in fact,
a permanent latent presence in Kracauer's work: he lurks behind
every corner; he is the foundation for every possibility in it, 'the
gateway to the world of the real' (Momme Brodersen).[116]

By the time the Great War was over, Kracauer had not yet found
the vocation for which he so longed. Life was streaming past him:

> Light and shadow; houses, paths, landscapes and cities; locomotives,
> human bodies, the bustling masses; the passion of love, lament of the
> lonely soul – in colourful arrays they whirl around manifold existence
> [Dasein], arrange it in crass oppositions; and they are allowed to do
> this because what moves them most is what forms existence's unity:
> that is, the life that pulses through it.[117]

And yet, somehow, this life hustled and bustled past Kracauer. In
1918, he thought that the main reason for this was that life had lost
its meaning, that it had lost its guiding lodestar. The long years of
maturation were not yet over, but Kracauer was now almost thirty.
One thing, at least, was certain: he would become a writer.

3

Revolution, the *Frankfurter Zeitung* and Cultural Criticism around 1920

'The German empire of the Hohenzollern collapsed. The power that played the midwife to its birth – a politics of blood and iron[1] – became its gravedigger.'[2] Thus begins Eduard Bernstein's description of the German revolution of 1918/19, published in 1921, a time when, according to Detlev Peukert, the 'period of *hope*', during the drama of 1918, and the 'period of *decisions*', during the first half of 1919, had long since been superseded by the 'period of disappointment'.[3] The empire had perished in blood and iron,[4] and the November Revolution had sprung from the war, from the experience of the worst kind of class rule and, of course, from military defeat, which rendered all the sacrifices of the patriotically minded meaningless. The Russian Revolution of 1917 had not just been unleashed by a working class reacting to its unbearable social repression either; it had also, importantly, been fuelled by the brutalities and hardship of the war and by the subtle strategic skills of the Bolsheviks.[5] In Germany, too, the collapse of the empire was more the result of the devastation of war than of the work of social revolutionaries. It is telling that the revolutionary wave Lenin hoped would follow the Russian Revolution, and which he used as a justification for his coup d'état, only reached the nations on the losing side of the war.[6]

At the beginning of 1918, a victory for the central powers was still conceivable, especially after the war in the east had ended. In March, Russia was out of the equation following the peace treaty of Brest-Litowsk, and the Western Front began to move again.[7] The language of 'victorious peace', which could often be heard before October 1918, veiled the growing exhaustion, apathy and animosity among the German population, and especially among the soldiers. Since the late summer of that year, Germany's military power had been paralysed by a covert strike of the military forces, but only at the beginning of October, and entirely out of the blue, came the acknowledgement that defeat was looming. This was an extraordinary emotional blow.[8] The October constitutional reforms, supported by the later Weimar coalition after a mostly peaceful transfer of power, were not enough to prevent the collapse of the old political order. The November Revolution was at first conducted more by the soldiers than by the workers; the call for socialism was a consequence and not a cause of the revolution.[9]

The mutiny of the sailors in Kiel, who refused to die 'honourable' deaths in a desperate battle shortly before the armistice, was the spark that caused a conflagration that spread from city to city in northern Germany. On 2 November, the workers in Kiel joined the uprising, and a workers' and soldiers' council was formed.[10] On 5 and 6 November, workers' and soldiers' councils seized power in Hamburg, Lübeck and Bremen. Wilhelmshaven, Bremerhaven, Cuxhaven, Schwerin, Rostock, Oldenburg, Lüneburg and Hanover followed. By 8 November, the revolution had spread to Brunswick, Hildesheim and Osnabrück, where Kracauer had been working as an architect at the city council's planning department since the beginning of the year. On that day, 8 October, he wrote only one word in his diary: 'Revolution!'[11]

If we believe Ginster, however, then this revolution in the east-Westphalian province was a farce. A single sailor appeared in the night and disarmed the officers, and then the whole garrison moved over to his side: *A single sailor – but presumably there had to be enough sailors for many cities, and thus only one was allocated to Q.*[12] Leaving aside Ginster's subtle irony, it is true that in many places the revolutions actually appear to have been anything but a great spectacle involving the masses. In Leipzig, Victor Klemperer wrote in his diary: 'We live in perfect peace and order; it seems strange to us to read of "revolution" ... Most things take place underground; those who are at the centre of everyday life know and see the least.'[13] If the revolution was scarcely felt even in Leipzig, then the situation would not have been much different in Osnabrück. Kracauer was suspicious of the whole affair, anyhow; he was no fervent revolutionary. Ginster observes *small indignant characters with the faces of civil servants* who want to turn the revolution into an official public holiday, and after a day of disorder are already worn out: *[n]o sooner had they started the revolution, than they wanted to restore peace and order again. ... Most people were only revolutionary during the revolution. I was not yet revolutionary at the time. I did not believe in the revolution. I found the many agitators who suddenly sprang up repellent.*[14]

But the revolutionary windbags and bourgeois adventure-seekers were not the only reasons that Kracauer was cautious. He was fundamentally sceptical of the capacity of human beings to erect a society on the basis of freedom, equality and fraternity, even though he was also convinced that the old order had to go and that the new one would have to move in the direction of socialism. He saw himself as a 'conservative revolutionary'. By this, he of course did not mean to include himself under the collective term that Armin Mohler, after 1945, used to describe right-wing movements, ranging from the Deutschnationale[15] to the National Socialists, which began to form following the Great War.[16] In 1919, the term was still innocent and did not have any of these connotations. But what did Kracauer mean by it?

He used the expression in a longer treatise on the following question: 'Are philanthropy, justice, and tolerance tied to a specific form of the state, and which form of state provides the best guarantee for their provision?'[17] His concept of the conservative revolutionary was certainly not a sharply defined one, and the whole text is composed in a meandering way, as well as displaying some learned cleverness. But the term does sum up the peculiar, almost contradictory mixture of bourgeois-conservative, socialist and anti-authoritarian elements that coalesced in Kracauer's theses and basic assumptions. It certainly fits him better than it does a Jünger, a Spengler or a Freyer, each of whom was, in his own way, a conservative (in the sense of being anti-democratic and authoritarian) and a revolutionary (in the sense of seditiously seeking something other than the existing order). But in the first instance they were, lest we forget, radically nationalistic. Kracauer was *conservative* in his assumption that the connection between ethos and institutions was fairly vague. 'Life' – by which he means empirical reality – cannot be domesticated by moral ideals or political order, and so it cannot be domesticated by 'a democracy leaning toward the side of socialism'. The real problems emerging from life, he wrote, are more difficult to solve than do-gooders and utopian thinkers would have us believe. Every naturally grown culture necessarily rests on injustice and is finally destroyed by ethical fanaticism. The *revolutionary* side of the thirty-year-old Kracauer is clear, by contrast, in his call for anti-authoritarian education: 'The old must renounce and make themselves the enemy of the young; then they serve the purposes of justice best. Revolutionaries must be bred, revolutionaries who rebel against the old order in which they grew up, human beings who are indignant, who refuse simply to continue where the previous generation has left off.'[18]

Around 1919, Daniel Kracauer was thus vacillating between authoritarianism and libertarianism. He considered the cult of power reactionary, the spirit of individualism blind to reality. The pure political realist gives in to the power of existing conditions, while the pure political idealist boldly ignores existing facts. Like Bernstein, Kracauer welcomed the events of November 1918 and abhorred the chaos that followed, which he saw caused by conflicting worldviews.[19] One might say that a battle was taking place in Kracauer between the statesman-like political views of his teachers Simmel, Scheler and Max Weber, and the utopian-socialist ideals of their pupils Susman, Bloch and Lukács. Kracauer was attached to both these intellectual milieus without identifying with either of them. Max Weber had juxtaposed an ethics of conviction with an ethics of responsibility, siding explicitly with the latter. In Kracauer's eyes, that showed him to be a follower of reason.[20] But at the same time Kracauer was drawn towards the 'dreams, love, and glowing soul' of a Margarete Susman. A utopian human being – even if bound to fail in the face of reality, even if pursuing 'delusional millenarian dreams' – had a task to fulfil: to play the role of the sage and so ensure that political leaders did not become submerged in a vile reality.

Kracauer's novel *Georg* satirizes the progressive circles of the time. In the interests of world peace, pacifist mothers do not let their somewhat wayward children play with tin soldiers, and they have their rooms decorated with pink wallpaper on which flocks of sheep graze harmoniously – while a mutilated teddy bear lies in the corner. And then there are the radical revolutionaries, who get angry at dinner over the police quashing a hunger demonstration: *the people at their table ate with gusto. The sympathy they felt for those who hungered seemed to make them only more hungry themselves.* In the novel, Susman becomes Mrs Bonnet, who displays an inner radiance and believes in the good in people. Her soul illuminates everything; dreamily, she sings of the Messiah. She deifies revolutionary female figures from history: *When they despaired, the entire world was immediately immersed in blackest night; when they loved, the very cosmos flamed and burned; if they fought for freedom, they waved a banner and led the charge of unseen crowds on behalf of all mankind.* Mrs Bonnet's smile *was of a benevolence which took in the whole of mankind. Only he – Georg – was omitted.*[21]

This was the community whose favour Kracauer tried to gain, but the abiding feeling of his Georg was that others were moving away from him. Between 1920 and 1922, Margarete Susman was Kracauer's preferred partner in correspondence for reflections on the revolutions in Russia and Germany. In the case of Russia, a key issue was not only Bolshevism but also 'West-Eastern mirrorings', that is, the mutually dependent images the West and East had of each other.[22] Like many others who admired the 'pristine' Russian soul, Kracauer bought into the cult around Dostoevsky. In an article in the pacifist journal *Vivos voco*, which was reformist and closely allied with the youth movement, he contrasted the German ethos and nature with the Russian, using Nietzsche and Dostoevsky as his examples. Nietzsche figures as the creative man, the builder of worlds, surging upwards, while Dostoevsky embodies the chaos of the Russian soul, which encapsulates all of human nature and, in brotherly spirit, delves downwards. As Kracauer saw it, the overman and the idiot stand for two worlds, each of which has emerged out of the other. And as with the oppositions between authority and individuality and between political idealism and realism, he recommended a third way – a middle ground or third realm: 'The only future for Germany that I can still see lies in our economic and intellectual interpenetration with a Russia that has overcome the present state of terror and somehow consolidated itself.'[23] In his gushing over Russia, the Kracauer of 1920 was part of a trend that included intellectuals as diverse as Rainer Maria Rilke and Oswald Spengler, intellectuals who suffered under the West: 'The mendaciousness of the people, the immorality, the lack of shame, the dissolution which spreads everywhere – oh, such a terrible musty smell emanates from this unhappy mankind to which we also belong', he wrote to Susman at the beginning of 1920. 'If I didn't know Russia, didn't know Dostoevsky, I would despair over Europe and America.'[24] We may interpret him as saying: he longed for Russia because he did not believe in Europe or America – notwithstanding the fact that he knew neither America, nor Europe, nor Russia. Nevertheless, he thought that the future lay with Russia: the 'living communal religion, the organization of existence from within' – it would happen there. If he could, he said, he would go there in order to escape the 'monotonous life and lonely philosophical work in Germany'.[25] Kracauer had no faith in the communist utopia, but nor was he actively hostile towards the October Revolution. The 'dictatorship of the proletariat' would not lead to a better society, but he found little to criticize in the fact that 'those who have been gagged for so long are now ruling'. He did not consider Lenin, whose *State and Revolution* he had acquired and studied in September 1919, a visionary dreamer; rather he saw him as an exceptional political leader. Kracauer predicted:

> In Russia, too, feuding groups will emerge, each of which will strive to become the ruling power; a bureaucracy will split off and interpersonal relations will be based in large part on coercion and discipline. At the end of the day, with the principles of brotherhood, etc., no state can be held together. ... What is Lenin other than a powerful tsar of a reversed order?[26]

That was not at all meant as a derogatory judgement. In another letter to Susman, he wrote that, just as a thinker had to be a pessimist, in political matters it was not possible to be too much of a Machiavellian, a sceptic and a man of reason. 'I myself have also lost any belief in a betterment of the world through political means, and am rather of the opinion that as long as a religious foundation is lacking, it does not matter who actually rules.'[27] At this time, Kracauer ultimately shared the image of human nature expressed by the grand inquisitor in Dostoevsky's *The Brothers Karamazov* in explaining to Jesus, upon his return, why the church had taken the path it had: freedom is terrifying for human beings and for human society; human beings are weak and unprincipled, and they need transcendence and guidance. In his first article for the *Frankfurter Zeitung* (if we ignore the one-off contribution of 1906), published on 2 June 1920, Kracauer thus expressed his commitment to the political middle ground, which for him did not represent a lukewarm compromise but a depth, maturity and insight into the limitations of humanity. In this article, he again deployed the concept of the 'conservative revolutionary' – this time with Goethe as the model – in order to sum up his attitude towards the collapse of the old order and the revolution. This article can certainly be read as an attempt to throw his hat into the ring for a post at the paper.

The *Frankfurter Zeitung* traditionally saw itself as a 'voice battling for democracy in Germany'. According to Wolfgang Schivelbusch, under the aegis of Heinrich Simon there was a shift towards a more 'calm and dignified [rather] than combative liberalism'. Before November, the paper had warned against a revolution; once it had happened, it did not shed a tear for the old regime. Now, its task was to defend the new state against the old elites, and especially against the machinations of Erich Ludendorff, but it also took aim at the members of the Spartacus League and the KPD, who were seeking to wage a class war.[28] The paper sided with the Weimar coalition, especially the Deutsche Demokratische Partei [German Democratic Party], which sought a 'democracy based on social laws' in which the state – and political attitudes generally – was democratic and based on a synthesis between liberalism and socialism, and in particular on an opposition to any reactionary tendencies. Reactionaries, especially the 'völkische Bewegung' [movement of the people], therefore tended to consider the *FZ* to be the spearhead of the 'Jewish press'.[29]

When Kracauer began to write for the paper, its daily circulation was between 60,000 and 80,000. Although this was not particularly large compared to its competitors, the *Frankfurter Zeitung* had an excellent reputation.[30] Having given up on architecture as a profession, Kracauer did not know, at first, which 'word-based profession' he wanted to pursue. In journalism he saw an opportunity to make contributions to the public debate. His character Georg, at least, is woken from his slumber and mobilized by the social gatherings at Mrs Bonnet's, despite feeling somewhat alien among the rebels:

> *There is a revolution happening and I've been off in a corner dreaming. Books, sitting rooms, the indifferent bits and bobs, and me always so preoccupied with myself. If I could put myself forward like all these people who are out doing things. … I must get myself into public life.*[31]

Kracauer's 'commitment to the political middle ground' of June 1920 further strengthened this urge. At the time, he had a somewhat rose-tinted view of the *Frankfurter Zeitung*. He praised 'the objectivity of the news reports' and 'the independence of the opinion pieces', and he saw in it 'an intellectual attitude that is well capable of satisfying the demands of an educated readership'. For Kracauer, the *FZ* meant 'factual objectivity, decency, veracity' and 'speaking out freely and courageously'.[32] He wrote regularly for the local section of the paper and also for the culture pages.

Kracauer often drew on his architectural expertise when writing for the local section. He reported on the extension of the building housing the Frankfurt stock market, on the architecture of the Frankfurt fair and on the Osthafen [Eastern harbour]. He wrote about the expansion of the Städel Museum of the Arts, the renovation of bridges across the Main, the construction of new bridges and the fate of a Dominican monastery that was to be transformed into a power station. The Opera House, Deutsche Bank, Hauptzollamt [the main customs office] – whenever there was news about such things, local reporter Kracauer was drafted in, and he weighed in on whether a building was fit for purpose without doing violence to some valuable cultural site. A few years later, Kracauer referred to this attitude as 'old objectivity' [alte Sachlichkeit].[33] He intervened in the debates over Frankfurt's planned skyscrapers, which he fervently defended, especially the building between Moltkeallee, Bismarckallee and Königstraße, opposite the Festhalle Frankfurt: the 'tower houses' were 'lasting works belonging not to a world of theatrical scenery but to the reality of our life'. Concerns over high-rise buildings mostly arose in the 'soul of the bourgeois philistine', who feared Americanization. Kracauer thought they were purposeful, made sense as office spaces and contributed to a more relaxed housing market; from an architectural perspective, they were stimulating. At the same time, he was an active member of Frankfurt's association of friends of the historic city centre.[34]

As in his childhood, the local reporter roamed the streets. He was again fascinated by the main train station, which now had an underground level for transporting luggage: '[a] new city quarter, a kind of profane catacomb city has come into existence'.[35] He was astonished about advertising columns, which 'are meant to present themselves immaculately when so many people have to walk around in extremely poor clothing'.[36] He observed the advertisements in Kaiserstraße that praised the fair and ironically spoke of the hope that the sun would 'not forget her duty to provide embellishment during the days of the fair'.[37] He attended the Schumann theatre opposite the main train station, and on Ash Wednesday visited the Astoria stage. He went to see circuses, magicians and cabarets. He reported, with some sarcasm, on the 'amusement frenzy' during the summer festivals and suspected that behind it lay a 'horrific inner emptiness that asks to be filled. The people of today neither stand in any fixed connection to each other, nor are they able to survey any connections':

> At present in Germany everyone dances as if obsessed, and the decline of the West is illuminated with Bengal lights and accompanied with the crackling of fireworks; the main reason for this is we have already been living for years *on abort*, so to speak.[38]

The decline of the West that was celebrated at the funfairs was a case for the culture pages, which was where any cultural philosopher who sought to be active as a journalist needed to get his texts published if he were to be noticed by the public.[39] But getting his articles published there proved to be more difficult for Kracauer than finding his way into the pages of the paper's local news section. The head of the culture section, Rudolf Geck, was an altogether different personality from Kracauer; according to Schivelbusch, Geck was 'the classic master of the feuilleton as a small art form' and grew 'popular with the audience on the back of columns that did not hurt anyone'.[40] Geck represented the traditional feuilleton of the generation of those born before 1890: it hosted poetic person-alities speaking in a witty, conversational tone, writers who were not blind to the superficiality of the ruling zeitgeist and who presented their educated readers with the generally agreed upon true and false values, with an ironic but never cynical smile.[41] By contrast, the language and style of the journalistic newcomer Kracauer was even more convoluted and overwrought than that of the older generation. Geck and his colleague Bernhard Diebold insisted to Kracauer that the ordinary reader had to be able to understand everything that was written in the paper.[42] Gradually, however, their new colleague estab-lished himself. From the summer of 1920 onwards, he succeeded in placing numerous reviews, conference reports and programmatic texts on expressionism, *Lebensphilosophie* and the intellectual life of the university in the culture section of the paper which he valued so highly. In August 1921, he became a permanent member of staff with a fixed annual salary. Now he could write about all the important topics of cultural criticism and occupy himself with the decline of the West and the spirit of utopia.[43]

In Germany, the war had not only brought about the collapse of the old order and the revolution; it had also aroused the interest of the philosophers of history. The events demanded an interpre-tation that was suitably comprehensive and dramatic. The war had cost more than eight million soldiers their lives. More than twenty million had been wounded. In Germany alone, several million war invalids were a daily reminder that nothing was as it had been before

August 1914, before 'Pandora's box' had been opened.[44] Europe lay in ruins; the bourgeois-liberal ideas of progress and education had been discredited, and with them the sciences and the authority of intellectual life.[45] This was the heyday of cultural criticism, and fear and existential pessimism were its distinguishing features, though they were tempered by an optimism of the will.[46] Cultural criticism was part of a 'German culture of Weltanschauung', which measured all knowledge and action against some higher sense provided by the chosen Weltanschauung.[47]

Oswald Spengler was the intellectual star of 1919, and his *Decline of the West* offered the most notable of the available Weltanschauungen.[48] The book became a point of reference for cultural criticism and was a phenomenal commercial success, seeing its fiftieth edition as early as 1924. The text became a bestseller because, in some sense, the world had indeed experienced a decline. Spengler had written the majority of it before the outbreak of the war, but only in 1918 was this 'morphology of world history' published. Spengler said that it was the result of an 'idea that is historically essential – that does not occur within an epoch but itself makes that epoch'.[49] Even Germany's defeat could not dampen this nationalist's sense of self-importance. In the preface to the 1923 edition (written in 1922), Spengler, who had spent ten years on his work, wrote that '[d]espite the misery and disgust of these years' – an allusion to the 'stab in the back' and the 'November crimes' – he was 'proud to call' what had 'taken shape in [his] hands ... a *German philosophy*'.[50] *The Decline of the West* is a sweeping universal history, comparable to Houston Stewart Chamberlain's *Foundations of the Nineteenth Century*. It aims to provide a comprehensive view of the historical universe, which it describes as 'the *last* great task of Western philosophy'.[51] By a 'morphology of history' Spengler meant an approach that treats historical phenomena as forms and mankind as an organism. His critique of the Western European thinking about history as being akin to the 'Ptolemaic system' was original and unusual at the time. Western Europeans, he thought, explained world history as a progression from pagan times to Christianity and onwards to modernity. From this occidental perspective, the eighteenth century was more important than all the sixty previous centuries taken together. But where did this leave India, Babylon, China, Egypt and Mexico? The secret purpose of world history, he argued, was not the development of the occidental spirit: '[m]ankind' – a term he always puts in inverted commas – 'has no aim, no idea, no plan, any more than the family of butterflies or orchids.'[52] Cultures emerge, grow, and – once they have reached the stage of 'civilization' – they decline. First antiquity, now the occident – something is always in decline. Spengler, a former Studienrat whose nerves had been too weak to stand the pressures of school teaching, faced the necessary course of historical events as 'a bookworm in the trenches' with an 'atavistic political aesthetics'.[53]

Kracauer was irritated by the very design of the book, by the 'know-it-all' attitude it displays towards history. He looked at it from a bird's eye view:

> We shuffle Buddhism, Confucianism and Mohammedanism the way one shuffles cards; play catch with India, China, Japan; have whole continents and cultures at our disposal ... and stride through the millennia at the speed of light. World history, nothing but world history, that is the password. Religions and political tendencies, artistic and intellectual movements, all is fitted into the pounding step of world history, until it finally pounds itself; and every here and now is blown up until it is worthy of historical consideration. This is the way in which, as the directors of a marionette theatre, we set the puppets in motion, and, as spectators, we curiously follow their creepy dance.[54]

For Kracauer, Spengler was a 'soothsayer of world history', a charlatan who had pretended to the authority of someone 'surveying the historical universe without limits and understanding it objectively' – someone who had exited the scene of real life.

Kracauer did not content himself simply with his criticisms of this culturally conservative prophet of doom. He expanded the scope of his broadside: 'Many today want to drown out the barrel organ ballads of decline with the siren song of *renewal*.' Here he had in mind both religious movements and various strains of left-wing utopian thinking. Their representatives were also 'powerful supreme commanders of history'.[55] They, too, had departed from the ground of reality and lifted off into the heavens above. They, too, played the apocalyptic melody which Spengler, the cultural critic, had intoned. Just as the revolution had followed from the military defeat, so the spirit of utopianism followed the decline of the West. Spengler had a hostile brother at the other end of the political spectrum, and that was none other than Ernst Bloch, whose *Spirit of Utopia* had been completed long before the events that secured its success took place.[56] Bloch wrote the text in 1915/16, shortly before moving to Switzerland with his seriously ill wife, Else von Stritzky.[57] Bloch sympathized with the revolutions in Eastern and Central Europe and became the 'German philosopher of the October revolution'.[58] *The Spirit of Utopia* appeared in 1918 as a communist manifesto, but a very idiosyncratic one: 'I am. We are./That is enough. Now we have to begin. Life has been put in our hands. For itself it became empty already long ago. It pitches senselessly back and forth, but we stand firm, and so we want to be its initiative and we want to be its ends.'[59] In the second edition, Bloch added the following to this expression of intent: 'The War ended, the Revolution began, and along with the Revolution, doors opened. But of course, they soon shut.'[60] This new, expressionist mode of philosophizing, which had socialist aims, took 'the comprehended darkness of the lived moment' (1923) as its compass.[61] This was a new tone, a new mixture of longing for a 'homeland' ('something which shines into the childhood of all and in which no one has yet been', as the last sentence of the *Principle of Hope* would later put it)[62] and for socialism ('the working, creating human being who reshapes and overhauls the given facts').[63] It was a matter of looking for what was 'Not-Yet-Conscious',[64] a philosophy of anticipatory consciousness and a melange of materialism and mysticism, of the 'cold and warm stream'.[65] The spirit of utopia sought religious salvation beyond any idealistic a priori philosophizing; it was a revolt against an inhumanity that had never before shown itself with such clarity as in the madness of the Great War, a revolt formulated in a categorical, uncompromising language.[66] In short, the utopian spirit was both deeply humanistic and all of a piece with the German culture of Weltanschauungen.

In Walter Benjamin's judgement, the author himself was 'ten times better than his book'.[67] Bloch was a charismatic character, full of vitality.[68] He loved to play the role of the biblical prophet and, as a raconteur, he was able to put his listeners under his spell. He looked for treasures in places that scholars did not ordinarily visit – in everyday life; in the depths of the irrational and in the spheres of the supersensory; in fairy tales; in music and in a subject-like nature. He was a member of the Wandervogel movement and a communist.[69] He was a philosopher of high spirits, a philosopher of perpetual youthfulness who yet did not shy away from the topic of death. He was an expressionist writer who lived off his images, associations and narrative powers. Last things, for Bloch, can ultimately not be captured rationally, and the arts – the path towards allegory, the indeterminable, the inconceivable – represents a possible alternative to rationalist science. For Bloch, philosophy, when not academically deformed, is the longing for infinity, for a homeland and for meaning. He understood humans as beings with wills who long for what they do not have.[70]

Thus, Bloch very much fitted in with the spirit of the *intelligenzija*.[71] And there were certainly overlaps between his work and some of the motifs in Kracauer's. But at first Bloch's alluring visions of community and solidarity, his political extremism and his rigorist apocalypticism triggered strong negative reactions in Kracauer. Between 1918 and 1925, Kracauer was – much like Bloch's 'human being' – guided by a longing for meaning, but he lacked the straightforward optimism that characterized Bloch and his thought. He was not moved by Bloch's warm stream; indeed, the war had confirmed for him his pessimistic anthropology, which assumed that humans are by their very nature inclined towards destruction.[72] Kracauer's personal and intellectual path in the world was a tortuous one.

4

Friendship (Part 1): The Jewish Renaissance in Frankfurt

The world opened up to Kracauer through his aunt and uncle, through life on the streets and through his friends.[1] His aunt and uncle represented education, the inquisitive and reflective mind. The street represented the public space, people and things, pulsating life. And friendship stood for the hope that he would escape the oppressive loneliness he felt, find a home and examine the last things in 'fruitful conversations'.[2] All these avenues, even the interpersonal ones, had to do with the intellectual life.

Between 1917 and 1923, Kracauer published three texts on friendship. The first appeared in *Logos*, a journal for philosophy and culture founded in 1910, the second in *Gabe*, a publication marking the fiftieth birthday of the rabbi of Frankfurt, Nehemias Anton Nobel (1921), and the third in the *Frankfurter Zeitung*. This trilogy on friendship demonstrates the influence of Simmel's explorations of social reality on Kracauer. Kracauer's reflections on friendship as a social phenomenon follow his teacher in centring on 'man – considered as bearer of culture and as a mature spiritual/intellectual being, acting and evaluating in full control of the powers of his soul and linked to his fellow man in collective action and feeling'.[3] Kracauer had also learned from Simmel to choose 'certain general concepts' as the basis for 'world-wide scouting trips', concepts 'that enable him to reveal the law-governed coherence of phenomena'.[4] Simmel studied the fabric of society through the concepts of 'the stranger' or 'money'; Kracauer now chose 'friendship'.

The long article of 1917 in *Logos* in particular is a peculiar hybrid: both an analysis that seeks to uncover ideal types and a text suffused with the author's own longing for life. Friendship is presented as a social phenomenon, as one of the threads between human beings 'that [is] entirely independent of the individual psychological qualities of people'.[5] The ideal is a cerebral and spiritualized friendship between free personalities; the model is the friendship between Goethe and Schiller.[6] Kracauer described friendship as a 'plant that is rooted in good soil' and needs to be

nurtured carefully; it is something natural, yet needs cultivation.[7]
Kracauer was still longing for friendship: in his own view, he
remained beset by feelings of instability, doubtful about other
people and backward in his personal and moral development. 'We
want to have a home, and be a home to others.'[8] This, for Kracauer,
was the recurrent refrain of the song of friendship, and it promised
a way out of the homelessness and coldness of the anti-social
conditions brought about by the war. That connection between an
unreliable society and the need for friendship, as later expressed
by Bloch, seemed evident: 'Where society had become suspect, the
wishful image of friendship emerged at the same time as that of
solitude, not as an escape from society but as a substitute for it, its
better garden form.'[9]

Kracauer captured the essence of friendship as follows:

> It is the community of convictions and ideals between free and
> independent human beings based on the common development of
> typical possibilities. To develop together without losing oneself to the
> others, to succumb in order to expand the possession of oneself, to
> melt into a unity and yet to maintain an independent existence: that is
> the secret of association.[10]

Such friendship seemed almost to promise immortality: 'Everyone
has the urge to pull out of the flow of time what is most valuable
about his transient existence, to establish it outside of himself and
somehow to make it eternal.'[11] According to Kracauer, this fundamental human desire is fulfilled in friendship. When he said this, he
must certainly have had in mind Otto Hainebach, his sorely missed
friend from his university days.

The now thirty-year-old Kracauer had recently made the
acquaintance of two intriguing young men – Theodor Wiesengrund-
Adorno and Leo Löwenthal. These were going to be *real* friendships,
friendships from which nothing human was to be excluded – not even
'pride, intolerance, mistrust … envy and jealousy', the obstacles to
the 'union of two souls' in ideal friendships.[12] Of course, these were
'precarious friendships',[13] especially that with Wiesengrund.

Adorno would later recall his first meeting with Kracauer – at the
time Adorno was the fifteen-year-old 'Teddie' – as follows:

> I was a student at the Gymnasium when I met him near the end of the
> First World War. A friend of my parents, Rosie Stern, had invited the
> two of us to her house. She was a tutor at the Philanthropin, where
> Kracauer's uncle, the historiographer of the Frankfurt Jews, was a
> member of the faculty. As was probably our hostess's intention, an
> intense relationship sprang up between us.[14]

Figure 10. Theodor Wiesengrund-Adorno around 1920
Copyright: DLA Marbach

Kracauer's novel *Georg* contains a scene in which the hero meets a boy called Fred, who is undoubtedly based on the young Wiesengrund. The name alone – a combination of Friedel and Teddie – suggests as much. Georg has been asked to provide Fred with private tutoring. The slim, blond boy seems to Georg like 'a prince in disguise': *Leaning against the back of his mother's chair, he proceeded to respond to the enquiries directed at him, his subdued tone contra-dicted by his great melancholy eyes and the way he would glance from beneath his long lashes. An expression in those eyes made one suspect that he held some secret, just as he was himself concealed in rough fabrics. 'You'll have to make him stick to his studies', proclaimed Frau Anders in a loud voice. 'He loves to daydream and is always veering off the subject.' Knowing that he would be permitted to be with the boy frequently from then on put Georg in a joyous mood.*
It felt to Georg as though he were undergoing a transformation, one he had long yearned for without ever having the faintest idea that such a thing could be. He had remained frozen from the war and now, to his surprise, a wonderful warmth streamed into him. The boy-figure

*was alluring; the melancholy in the eyes came out of a distant place
that he would have to reach.*[15] Nothing seemed more exciting than
the prospect of sharing in the mysteries of the association Kracauer
had rhapsodized about in his *Logos* article with this exceptional boy.

Teddie's mother appears to have been the exact opposite of
Friedel's; indeed, in the novel, Fred's mother is named 'Anders' –
or 'different'.[16] Maria Wiesengrund, born Calvelli-Adorno, was a
singer, apparently even a 'former singer at the opera of the imperial
court', something her son took pains to emphasize.[17] The family
revolved around music; Maria's sister, Agathe, who lived with the
Wiesengrund family, was a piano player.[18] Teddie's childhood was a
four-handed one:

> That music we are accustomed to call classical I came to know as
> a child through four-hand playing. There was little symphonic and
> chamber music literature that was not moved into home life with the
> help of those oblong volumes, bound uniformly green in landscape
> format by the bookbinder. They appeared as if made to have their
> pages turned, and I was allowed to do so, long before I knew the notes,
> following only memory and my ear.[19]

While Friedel, the lone wolf, was observing his environment with
suspicion and quietly assigning those fellow pupils who were
ill-disposed towards him bad grades in his secret notebook, Teddie
was devoting himself to music in the company of not just one, but
two mothers:

> If the lonesome, those who have no hope for listeners and have none
> to fear, were now and then to give four-hand playing a try, it would
> not necessarily be to their harm. In the end, a child might also be
> found to turn the pages for them.[20]

Theodor Wiesengrund's sheltered childhood was supported not
only by music and femininity but also by a generous father. Oscar
Wiesengrund was a well-to-do merchant who had taken on the
family's wine business – 'Bernhard Wiesengrund', established in
1864 and situated in Schöne Aussicht on the banks of the river Main
– when still a young man. Unlike Kracauer's parents, he did not urge
his son to choose a breadwinning profession but rather allowed him
to develop his cultural interests with his mother. This combination
of artistic leisure and indulgence was also a kind of parental four-
handed playing. There was, in this instance, no father–son conflict
over the question of 'economy or culture', the sort of conflict that
is so often observed in similar family situations and so often gives
rise to that central expressionist motif, the 'revolt of the son'.[21]
Teddie was the much-loved prodigy. Further, his parents' home was

a spacious one. The house in Seeheimer Straße 19 in the Oberrad quarter of the city, where the Wiesengrund family moved in 1914, seemed to be watched over by a lucky star, as Leo Löwenthal noted: 'It was an existence you just had to love – if you were not dying of jealousy of this protected beautiful life – and in it Adorno had gained the confidence that never left him his entire life.'[22] And Max Horkheimer recalled:

> Anyone who entered the house in Seeheimer Straße in Oberrad in which Adorno spent his youth experienced an environment to which he owed a protected childhood in the best sense of the word. The traditions that came together in his parents' house, the commercial spirit of Oscar Wiesengrund, his Jewish father from Frankfurt, and the aura of music that surrounded his mother Maria ..., the shining eyes of her sister Agathe who was like a second mother to him, are all preserved ... in Adorno's thoughts and feelings.[23]

But home was not the whole world. Oscar and Maria Wiesengrund did not spare their son the experience of attending school, including primary school. But he made sure not to waste any time; he skipped two classes before taking his leaving examinations, which he completed at the top of his year group.[24] His position as the top pupil in his class did not always earn the sensitive, talented boy who practised music with mother or aunt the sympathy of his peers. They all knew that he was a Judd, a Jew, notwithstanding the fact that he was baptized a Catholic, had received his first communion and had even been an altar boy.[25] It was not his teachers but his 'fellow pupils' who harried Teddie, 'children already equipped with Christian names like Horst and Jürgen', whose 'hallooing knew no end when the top boy blundered' and 'who could not put together a correct sentence but found all of mine too long'. In the same fragment of *Minima Moralia* from which these passages are taken, Adorno tells of the 'five patriots who set upon a single schoolfellow, thrashed him and, when he complained to the teacher, defamed him a traitor to the class'. In these children Adorno recognized, in retrospect, the future myrmidons of fascism and the national community.[26] These experiences did not dent his self-confidence, even if he might well have been this 'single schoolfellow'. But the beaten and defamed pupil could just as well have been Kracauer, of whom Adorno writes that 'as a pupil in the Klinger Upper School he had also suffered anti-Semitism, something quite unusual in the commercial city of Frankfurt'.[27] Nevertheless, such acts of aggression bounced off Wiesengrund and back on to the Horsts and Jürgens. While he made fun of the fact that the 'Deutschtümler', those who paraded their Germanness, were unable to string a German sentence together, Friedel was affected by these sorts of attacks, of which he was probably often a recipient, and he no longer felt able to speak freely. But when the Nazis really came to power, with the help of such 'patriots', the situation turned: Kracauer at once knew what he had to do, while Adorno, according to Löwenthal, 'had such an incredibly hard time finally leaving Germany (we had to drag him almost physically); he just couldn't believe that to him, son of Oscar Wiesengrund, nephew of aunt Agathe, and son of Maria, anything might ever happen'.[28] An unintended consequence of such a deep sense of security is a naïve ignorance regarding the real world.

In intellectual terms, Wiesengrund was a fatherless child, and he therefore often looked to older friends for teachers, models, mentors. Among them were, of course, Max Horkheimer, but also Walter Benjamin. Yet the first of these 'older brothers' with whom Adorno tried to identify was Siegfried Kracauer, fifteen years his senior.[29] Teddie later recalled:

> For years Kracauer read the *Critique of Pure Reason* regularly on Saturday afternoon with me. I am not exaggerating in the slightest when I say that I owe more to this reading than to my academic teachers. Exceptionally gifted as a pedagogue, Kracauer made Kant come alive for me.[30]

The words Adorno uses to describe his approach in *Minima Moralia* also serve to describe their joint reading of Kant: 'the attempt to present aspects of our shared philosophy from the standpoint of subjective experience'.[31] According to Simmel's interpretation of Kant, 'experience' refers to 'a product of sensuality and understanding', and with this concept Kant provides a new way of thinking about the relationship between the cognizing mind and the external things.[32] 'Experience' was to become a magic word for Adorno, as it became for Kracauer, Benjamin and also Bloch. And the *Critique of Pure Reason* was probably the one philosophical book whose substance and intention continued to guide Adorno's thinking.[33]

What was at stake were not just questions of philosophy but also questions of how philosophy and philosophers were to be read. According to Kracauer, the history of philosophy was more than a sequence of teachings; it was a resource that could be mined for insights into the times in which the texts were written:

> Under his guidance I experienced the work from the beginning not as mere epistemology, not as an analysis of the conditions of scientifically valid judgments, but as a kind of coded text from which the historical situation of spirit could be read, with the vague expectation that in doing so one could acquire something of truth itself.[34]

On these Saturday afternoons in Seeheimer Straße 19, the young Wiesengrund became familiar with a different Kant from the one admired by the neo-Kantians. Readings of Hegel and Kierkegaard soon followed. Wiesengrund attended a seminar that could have been named 'Critique of German Idealism', but at the same time he was cautioned not to let this critique make common cause with the forces of irrationalism and slip into a denunciation of the Enlightenment. A dialectic without totality, without sublation or synthesis – that was the perspective from which Kracauer read the history of philosophy:

> As he presented it to me, Kant's critical philosophy was not simply a system of transcendental idealism. Rather, he showed me how the objective-ontological and subjective idealist moments warred within it, how the more eloquent passages in the work are the wounds this conflict has left in the theory. From a certain point of view, the fissures and flaws in a philosophy are more essential to it than the continuity of its meaning, which most philosophies emphasize of their own accord.[35]

To think and judge independently, to stand on the shoulders of giants but still emancipate oneself from them – that was Kracauer's recommendation, and it was this which tied his ingenious pupil to him: 'Without being able to account for it fully, through Kracauer I perceived for the first time the expressive moment in philosophy: putting into words what rises in one's mind.'[36] Wiesengrund was fascinated, yet he also felt that there was something at work that threatened to become a problem between the teacher and the pupil, because

> what pressed for philosophical expression in him was an almost boundless capacity for suffering: expression and suffering are intimately related. Kracauer's relationship to truth was that suffering entered into the idea in undistorted, unmitigated form, whereas normally the idea dissipates suffering.[37]

It followed that philosophy became a paper tiger when the passion was lacking. Simmel had already written in his diary (published in *Logos* in 1919 and later as a book in 1923): 'It is surprising how little of mankind's pain has found its way into mankind's philosophy … The points where someone despairs, that is what is decisive and characteristic of a human being. … Most people only learn through suffering that life is something serious.' While Kracauer had underlined this passage in his personal copy, his friend considered this philosophical position to be more a matter of 'intuition than thinking'. All this talk of suffering and despair, all this seriousness, felt ominous to the prodigy, not least because Kracauer's passion would soon be aimed at him.[38] To read Kant with Kracauer was to read with someone who considered what was read and the social event of 'four-eyed reading and discussing' to be of an importance that affected one's very existence.[39]

Leo Löwenthal remembered his first encounter with Kracauer as follows:

> There was a little cafe kitty-corner to the Frankfurt opera, the Café Westend ..., which became an in-place for Frankfurt intelligentsia around the end of World War I. It was there we met. I forget who introduced me to Friedel, but very quickly a most intensive relationship developed. At that time, I was a student in Heidelberg on vacation in Frankfurt. Whenever we got together in Frankfurt, we would meet almost daily in that little café, only to resume the next morning by telephone the topics – ranging from juicy gossip and personal concerns to sophisticated philosophy – that had been on the agenda the previous day.[40]

At the time of this first acquaintance with Kracauer, Löwenthal was twenty years old, eleven years younger than Friedel. And he

Figure 11. Leo Löwenthal
Copyright: Goethe-Universität Frankfurt am Main

was not only young, but also radical. Following the revolution, he had founded a socialist student association in Frankfurt, together with Franz L. Neumann and Ernst Fraenkel. On 5 December 1918, after the revolutionary Workers' and Soldiers' Council had set up its headquarters at the Hotel Frankfurter Hof and the well-known social democratic lawyer and professor Dr Hugo Sinzheimer had taken charge of the police headquarters, Löwenthal noted in his diary:

> Something enormous turned into a deed, a shattering and convincing deed. Concentrated willpower exploded and condensed again into something concrete. The hour, no, the minute became fate. We were tossed around by the fierce winds produced by the spinning wheel of world history. We were scorched by the fire of time, which ran like quicksilver. We became non-persons – everyone, without exception. It was not we who acted; a something acted through us to which we listened with trepidation, something which made us tremble. Today, the highest good is at stake: the dignity of the human being.[41]

This 'Bekenntnis zur Revolution' [Pledge to the revolution] demonstrates the style in which the young Löwenthal appealed to the future, to mankind and, most of all – as this was a diary – to himself.

Like Kracauer and Wiesengrund, Löwenthal came from a Jewish family. But in the Löwenthal household Judaism had not receded into the background, where it was not really noticed. It was, instead, a stage for Oedipal struggles. Leo's grandfather was a strictly orthodox Jew and a teacher at the Samson-Raphael-Hirsch-Schule (named after the father of German-Jewish orthodoxy, who lived in Frankfurt for almost forty years). According to Selmar Spier, this school was the 'most pious [institution] a German Jew could have come up with'.[42] Löwenthal's grandfather had nine children; eight of them lived as orthodox Jews, but one went his own way: Leo Löwenthal's father, Victor, became 'not only irreligious, but decidedly anti-religious'. Leo Löwenthal described the intellectual atmosphere at home as secular, enlightened and critical of religion: 'I knew hardly anything about Judaism', he said; he did not even know the Jewish holidays.[43] Nevertheless, he was aware of being a Jew because, despite their distance from Judaism, his parents' social circle was mostly Jewish. In the case of Victor Löwenthal's home, the practical rule of the Haskalah – be a human being outside and a Jew at home – seems to have been reversed: a human being at home, and outside a Jew, even if this rule was not adopted entirely voluntarily. The Judengasse in Frankfurt, which had long since been pulled down, continued to exist within the social makeup of the city. 'Later, my closer friends at school, and also at university, were almost exclusively Jews.' Even in a place like Frankfurt, where, according to Wiesengrund and Löwenthal, there was little anti-Semitism, there was still no talk of the emancipation of the Jews.[44]

Leo Löwenthal rebelled against his father. He studied all sorts of subjects in Gießen, Frankfurt and Heidelberg – except for medicine, his father's profession. During his studies, Löwenthal developed an interest in the Jewish tradition rejected by his father. In Gießen, he was at first attracted to the neo-Kantian school centred at Marburg, and he read Hermann Cohen, who was a liberal but nevertheless cultivated an intense interest in Jewish religious philosophy. In Heidelberg, Löwenthal became involved with socialist-Zionist peers. Finally, in 1923, he married Golde Ginsburg, who came from a strict orthodox family from Königsberg. Victor Löwenthal was enraged, and he refused to attend the wedding; he was not even prepared to really get to know the bride. The newly-weds decided 'to have a Jewish household, with kosher cooking, to go to synagogue, and to obey the holy days'.[45]

After the war, extraordinary things were happening at the Frankfurt synagogue in Börneplatz, one of three synagogues in the 'Jewish Ostend'. Nehemias Anton Nobel was one of three rabbis working there. He was born in 1871 in Nagyatád, Hungary, and had been a member of the Frankfurt community since 1910. According to Jakob Rosenheim, chairman of the 'Austrittsgemeinde', the Israelite religious society of Frankfurt – a neo-orthodox association that objected to reformed Judaism and advocated leaving reform communities, and thus no ally of Nobel when it came to religious policy – Nobel was one of the 'most striking personalities of contemporary German Jewry'. In the judgement of Caesar Seligmann, the liberal rabbi of the Israelite community, Nobel seemed to be 'surrounded by a secret, mystical magic'. Nobel's sermons were impressive, even for philosophers like Cohen, who often came from Marburg just to hear him speak. Eugen Mayer, the community's syndic, described the sermons as follows:

> His sermons were often characterized by a dithyrambic flow; they were events, even for purely linguistic reasons. The words broke forth from him, like a mountain stream, they flooded his listeners and – himself. … Indeed, this speech, which seemed to flow so effortlessly, was the permanent battle of a human being with a demonic 'It' by which he was possessed, which let him speak, and spoke from out of him.[46]

Apart from his captivating rhetorical skill, it was his interest in young people that made Nobel so attractive. Although he belonged to the neo-orthodox group and thus acted in strict accordance with the laws, he was open to the world. He united multiple oppositions within himself: he was a pupil, admirer and friend of Cohen; revered Goethe, whom he called 'the master' and the 'poet of the

Germans'; and considered Samson Raphael Hirsch, the founder of the neo-orthodox secessionist community, to be his intellectual role model, despite the fact that Nobel himself promoted a uniform Jewish community and rejected separatist movements.[47] Nobel was a Zionist and a co-founder of Misrachi, an association of orthodox Zionists – and also, especially during the war, of some German patriots. Nobel showed that 'many things find their place in the soul of a *great* Jew'.[48] The cleric's house at Börneplatz 16 was always open, and young men could come and go as they pleased; when someone was in need, he was a reliable mentor. When Leo Löwenthal was suffering from a lung condition, he sent him 1,000 marks for the necessary treatment and promised further help if required.[49]

Nobel attracted a circle of pupils who saw him as both a Hasidic rabbi and philosophically trained Western Jew.[50] Löwenthal was among them. He experienced the group as a cult-like religious community, and he enjoyed the 'Jewish atmosphere': 'In a certain sense it was a cult. This man … represented a peculiar mixture of mystic religiosity, philosophical intensity, and probably also a more or less repressed homosexual love of young people.'[51] Nobel's appeal no doubt sprang in part from his charisma, but it was also a consequence of the way in which he embodied a living synthesis between Jewishness and modern existence. Nobel himself characterized his attitude towards life as follows:

> I cannot clearly express the way in which the synthesis between my religious positivism and my joyous affirmation of purely philosophical values takes place in me. I only know that the genius of religious thought rules [waltet] in me and that I bow to it. Nor can I clearly express how I am able to view distinct and even antagonistic elements together within perceptions of beauty and the artistic, something that makes me happy. But I know that in happy hours, my eyes are granted this sort of comprehensive view [Zusammenschau].[52]

Nobel was, then, an unconventional rabbi, a man of intuition and vision, and it was thus not surprising that a group of seekers and searchers, young men looking for meaning, flocked to him. It was, in any case, the era of such groups, the George Circle being the most famous of them. This trend had rubbed off on Jewish life. In Heidelberg, Salman Baruch Rabinkow led a Talmud study group and Frieda Reichmann had a private kosher psychoanalytic clinic, the 'Torapeutikum' [Torapeutic Clinic]. During the war, Siegfried Lehman, aka Salomon Lehnert, had opened the Volksheim in Berlin. Also in Berlin, various artists and intellectuals flocked to Oskar Goldberg, the 'magic Jew', fascinated by his studies of Jewish mysticism. All of them were looking, in one way or another, for the 'genuine Jewish life'.[53]

Erich Fromm joined the Nobel Circle around 1916. For him, too, the rabbi was an ally in his battle against his father. But unlike in the case of Löwenthal, Nobel helped Fromm to escape the ossified religiosity of his parental home. For Fromm, Nobel represented the renewal of religion and the opening up of the world. In a later essay, he describes this type of prophet as follows:

> Those who announce ideas ... and at the same time live them we may call *prophets*. The Old Testament prophets did precisely that: they announced the idea that man had to find an answer to his existence, and that his answer was the development of his reason, of his love; and they taught that humility and justice were inseparably connected with love and reason. They lived what they preached.[54]

They lived what they preached: in Fromm's eyes, for instance, Nobel not only dispensed ideas but united the oppositions between reason and faith, between the realm of God and the secular world, between mysticism and Enlightenment in the deeply humane and religious way in which he lived his life. Nobel was a role model, an artist of life as well as of love. Fromm also introduced the Zionist student from Heidelberg Ernst Simon into the Nobel Circle. Simon had been the editor of Martin Buber's journal, *Der Jude*, until 1924, and then, together with Löwenthal, he edited the *Jüdisches Wochenblatt*, before in 1928 emigrating to Palestine, where he became a lecturer in philosophy and theology at the Hebrew University in Jerusalem. Simon particularly appreciated Nobel's teaching of the Talmud: 'A new phenomenon. The upper classes in particular began to study the teachings again. A new form of emancipation that freed itself from the petit bourgeois aftertaste that had been associated with it in the previous generation.'[55]

Nobel's most important pupil, however, was the philosopher of religion Franz Rosenzweig, who heard him preach for the first time in spring 1919: 'He is an ingenious preacher. He speaks freely, masterfully, simply. ... I have not heard anything like it before. A free mind, of the Cohen school, with a feel for words, ... [I] am still ecstatic about it.'[56] What Rosenzweig experienced in Börnestraße was far more than just a sermon:

> The thoughts, after all, could also come to me; the flow of words may also be found in others. But there is still something else there, something ultimate, the way the whole man is enraptured; one would not be surprised were he suddenly to lift off the ground and disappear. There is no deed so audacious that he would not have risked it at such moments, and there is no word that would not be true coming from his mouth.[57]

God himself, 'something ultimate', seemed to be involved here; God had found a medium, and it was a 'whole man', body, mind and soul, with his words and deeds. It was as if God were intervening in the world, like a scene from the Old Testament right there on Börneplatz in Frankfurt am Main at the beginning of the twentieth century. Rosenzweig, who was already thirty-three at the time, decided then and there to study the Talmud with Nobel.

Thus, in the autumn of 1919, Rosenzweig moved to Frankfurt. He co-founded the Freies Jüdisches Lehrhaus [Jewish House of Free Study] and became its first director. Earlier that year, the Verein für Jüdische Volksbildung [Association for Jewish People's Education] had been established by the liberal rabbi Georg Salzberger and Erich Fromm.[58] The Freies Jüdisches Lehrhaus was to build on the Jüdische Volkshochschule [Jewish People's University], which had been set up by the community's syndic, Eugen Mayer, immediately after the Great War. Initially, Nobel could be persuaded to support the ideal of Jewish adult education, and at the opening ceremony for the first series of lectures, on 22 February 1920, Nobel spoke about a chapter from the history of the Kabbalah. In the summer of 1920, Franz Rosenzweig took over the directorship of the Lehrhaus.[59]

As Ernst Simon has noted, the alliance between Nobel and Rosenzweig was the result of a 'favourable historical moment'.[60] Rosenzweig was not simply impressed by the Talmud scholar and preacher. Like Fromm, he saw in Nobel a kind of prophet, and for Rosenzweig prophetic qualities sprang not from personal charisma but from divine intervention. The prophetic, he wrote to Kracauer, was not some special quality; it did not require genius. Rather, it involved God himself turning a human being into His mouth-piece. The prophetic 'is not part of the human being, but moves through him. It is a word, not a property.' Prophets remain human beings, but they have a 'vocation' to fulfil.[61] We can easily imagine that Rosenzweig saw not only Nobel but also himself as being surrounded by such a prophetic aura. He certainly had a 'vocation' to fulfil, namely the re-appropriation of Jewish knowledge, not in the nineteenth-century sense of Wissenschaft des Judentums [Jewish studies] but in the sense of contemporary Jewish studies – a rethinking of the old Judaism that is embedded in a Jewish philosophy of life. The circles Rosenzweig belonged to were the 'authentic' ones [die Eigentlichen], according to Adorno, who had in mind Kracauer's experiences with them.[62] Kracauer was too sceptical a mind to be acceptable to these circles.

The Freies Jüdisches Lehrhaus opened on 17 October 1920. Rosenzweig spoke about the 'new learning' that did not lead from the Torah to life but from specific points in life to the Torah. The here and now, he said, determines the questions to be asked and the areas of Jewish tradition in which the answers are to be found.

The men – and the few women – at the Lehrhaus did not intend
to revive a pre-modern Jewish community; they wanted to found
a new tradition.[63] 'A big city breeze, a breeze of the present, is
blowing about, instead of that poor man's atmosphere', Ernst Simon
joyously declared. He described what was taking place as 'the inner
emancipation of Jewishness within the Jew'.[64] The list of lecturers
was impressive. It included Leo Baeck and Nathan Birnbaum,
leading representatives of liberal and of orthodox Judaism, respectively. The rabbis in office in Frankfurt at the time participated,
and Rabinkow came from Heidelberg, Martin Buber from the
nearby Odenwald. Gershom Scholem spoke about Jewish mysticism
and the Jerusalem-based orientalist Josef Rivlin about mediaeval
Hebrew literature. The writer Josef Agnon read from his Hebrew
writings, and his non-Jewish colleague Alfons Paquet reported on
his travels in Palestine. The founder of the German-Jewish women's
movement, Bertha Pappenheim (Freud's Anna O.), and the German
nationalist Alfred Peyser gave talks on the Verband national-
deutscher Juden [Association of German Nationalist Jews]. Leo
Strauss led a seminar on Spinoza, and the friar Hermann Schafft on
Christians and the Old Testament. Chemist and chair of the recently
founded Hermann Cohen Lodge, Eduard Strauß, gave a seminar
on mysticism in the world religions, and the famous scholar of
Islam Josef Horovitz on Judaism among the world religions. Franz
Oppenheimer, professor of sociology at Frankfurt University, and
the Marxist economist Fritz Sternberg gave lectures on the organization of Palestine. Ernst Simon was among the regular lecturers,
as was Erich Fromm. Leo Löwenthal, finally, cast a spotlight on
marginal figures in Jewish history, and Siegfried Kracauer gave a
lecture on modern religious tendencies.[65]

The Jewish teaching institute was meant to be 'free', both in the
sense that everyone – Jews and Gentiles alike – was welcome to
attend and in the sense that it was committed to the democratic
idea of freedom.[66] Teachers and pupils were equals; their roles
were meant to be interchangeable. The model was the educated
layperson. But Rosenzweig discovered that these ideas were not so
easily implemented. His collaborator Nahum Glatzer later recalled:

> He did not speak their language, and they did not understand his.
> His listeners felt something of his greatness, but he did not want to
> be admired, only understood. There was something tragic about the
> situation of this man, who believed so firmly in the power of dialogue,
> and yet was condemned to deliver one-sided monologues.[67]

The new, intellectual and redemptive Judaism, which had such
grand ambitions, nevertheless confronted its limits in the worldly
mediocrity of ordinary listeners.[68]

By secular standards, however, the Lehrhaus could be counted a remarkable success. Between 1920 and 1926, it organized 90 lecture series and 180 working groups, seminars and discussions. In the first trimester, 500 of the 30,000 members of the Jewish community enrolled, although fees were set fairly high so that the lecturers could be remunerated. An audience of about 200 came to Nobel's lectures on the Halacha. In the second year, the number of students rose to 600. The fact that once the initial curiosity had ebbed away the number of attendees dropped again, so that what remained was a hard core of serious students, was nothing unusual. From an economic perspective, the Lehrhaus was ultimately unsustainable, but this does not tell us anything about its intellectual merits and influence. It provided the model for similar institutions that were set up between 1925 and 1928 in Stuttgart, Cologne, Mannheim, Wiesbaden, Karlsruhe, Munich, Breslau and Berlin. For the Jews of Frankfurt, these were exciting years, years animated by a pioneering spirit.

That spirit was part of a general 'Jewish renaissance' in Germany. Martin Buber had coined that phrase and had given it power through his collection and translation of Hasidic stories, *Tales of the Hasidim*, about the great Hasidic teachers and the life of the Jewish-Hasidic people and movement, which appeared in 1922.[69] Among Jewish intellectuals, messianism became the order of the day. One might even say that the hope for redemption was at the centre of the Jewish renaissance. Whereas Hegelian philosophies of history ascribed meaning to history – if necessary, when faced with meaninglessness, by speaking of its 'cunning' – messianic philosophies of history gave up on its meaning and found meaning instead in the not-yet. The Jewish experience of catastrophe, disappointment and failure throughout history simply discredited, in the eyes of many, the idea of a history imbued with reason. After all the mass killings, theology seemed to be the natural, inevitable heir of teleology. Standing 'on the rubble of the paradigm of historical Reason', messianism did not, however, dispense with hope as a historical category. Quite the opposite: redemption, 'as the modality of its *possible* advent at each moment of time', is the central concept of messianic historical thought.[70] Not all of those who spoke in messianic terms believed in the Messiah. Many drew on theology and the Jewish tradition from a secular position, transforming the Messiah into the messianic. Sometimes, messianism was restorationist, seeking the reconstitution of some prelapsarian ideal. Sometimes it was utopian and apocalyptic: before the new realm could be realized, the old one had to perish. In this way, Judaism produced various visions with which even non-practising Jews could identify.[71]

But, most significantly, 'elective affinities' developed between Jewish messianism and secular-libertarian utopias. Assimilated or atheist Jews like Gustav Landauer or Ernst Bloch connected messianism with anarchist and communist ideas. Neither believed that Marxism, by itself, would be able to create the realm of freedom. For Landauer, as one might expect of an anarchist, Marx was in any case merely the 'son of the steam engine'.[72] For Bloch, by contrast, Marxism's role was to forge the path to a truly free society – with the help of steam engines, if needs be – but he also felt that it lacked the inner dimension of longing, of feelings, and spirituality, a warm stream, a messianic attitude. With his *Thomas Münzer* (1921), he embarked on a tempestuous, millenarian pilgrimage from Münzer's Germany to Lenin's Russia, picking up anyone who looked vaguely like a social-revolutionary heretic along the way:

> As yet unheard of, the subterranean history of revolution awaits, having already begun in the form of the upright gait. But the Talbrüder [Valley brethren],[73] Cathars, Waldensians, Albigensians, Abbot Joachim of Calabria, the brethren of goodwill, of communal life, of full spirit, Eckart, the Hussites, Münzer and the Anabaptists, Sebastian Franck, the illuminati, Rousseau's and Kant's humanist mysticism, Weitling, Baader, Tolstoy – they all unite, and the conscience of this enormous tradition makes itself heard above fear, the state, lack of faith, and every superior authority that ignores the human being.[74]

It was then 'the world's midnight hour'; since Jesus's time the world had travelled halfway to salvation, and 'half of the realm' of a socialist church had been established, and its cathedral, at present, stood in Moscow. Ubi Lenin, ibi Jerusalem.

Although Fromm and Löwenthal sympathized with these revolutionaries, the messianism in Frankfurt was promoted by devout Jews who were, at best, lukewarm anarchists. Martin Buber, who sought a close connection between anarchism, messianism and utopia, might have been an exception.[75] Rosenzweig's messianic ideas did not imply a political project; his programme was more akin to those of the sort of religious revivalist movements that were fairly common at the time – we might think in this connection of Rudolf Steiner's anthroposophy, Max Scheler's Catholicism or the youth movement's mysticism of nature. Siegfried Kracauer observed all of these phenomena very carefully.

5

Friendship (Part 2):
The One Who Waits

On his fiftieth birthday, 30 November 1921, 'Rabbi Dr Nobel' received a Festschrift from intellectuals who were closely associated with him or admired him from afar, among them members of the community like Rudolf Hallo and Eugen Mayer, fellow travellers like Buber and Rosenzweig and disciples such as Löwenthal and Simon. Löwenthal's contribution was titled 'Das Dämonische' [The demonic] and described itself as an 'outline of a negative philosophy of religion', a synthesis of 'Marx's economics of dialectical world history' and the 'phenomenological tendency' in philosophy.[1] Löwenthal's demons played Bloch-like tunes – wild hymns making up a concert that was mystical, radical and syncretic.[2] Löwenthal was friendly with Bloch and was inspired by the *Spirit of Utopia*, and Bloch was just as enthusiastic about Löwenthal's piece for Nobel's Festschrift. Kracauer was not: he was irritated precisely by its Blochian tone, by the way Löwenthal was 'running amok' in search of God, as he put it in a letter to Löwenthal, using a phrase from Scheler:

> I find this striking expression also fits you to an extent. I would not, however, want to miss your 'running amok'; I know how much you suffer and how genuine all this is in your case (while in Bloch, despite its possible genuineness, it is nevertheless sodomy with God, spurious, lusty). This messianism, which leaves out the whole world, contains something forced within it that feels alien to me, in my very core; I should like to use your excellent phrase 'blasphemous piety' to describe it. *God himself* can never have wanted this raging anger with which he is wanted here, or else He must have created man and the world in a fit of devilish malice. To be honest: I do not believe in messianic time. ... I do not believe in *this* God, and if nothing but *this* desperado attitude is religious, then I am an altogether irreligious person and will remain so.

Kracauer was battling with Bloch over this young man: 'I was still very much impressed by the conception and the metaphysical strain

Figure 12. Ernst Bloch around
1920
Copyright: DLA Marbach

Figure 13. Margarete Susman, 1911
Copyright: DLA Marbach

in it [i.e. in the text on the 'demonic']. ... Especially because I lack
this kind of metaphysical urge and religious passion, I admire them
in you and others (in Lukács, not in Bloch).'[3]

Kracauer won the battle. To begin with, he sought to become
acquainted with Bloch, who was something of a fixed point of
reference within the circles in which Kracauer moved. Bloch was
admired not only by Löwenthal but also by Margarete Susman,
whom Kracauer had come to know, probably through Simmel in
December 1917, and whose kindness, warmth and affection were a
salve for the insecure Kracauer.[4] Susman was a student of Simmel
at the same time as Bloch and Buber. In the *Frankfurter Zeitung* she
had published an enthusiastic review of Bloch's *Spirit of Utopia*. As
Kracauer would simply have to accept, she found the charismatic
thinker a 'very sparkling, lively intellect' and was 'refreshed by his
fiery spirit'.[5] Both Löwenthal and Susman mediated the relationship
between Bloch and Kracauer. Kracauer at once noted the 'deep
differences in nature' between him and Bloch, but, as he wrote
to Susman, 'if there were not something common that unites us
[Kracauer and Bloch], then how could you accept us both and unite
us in you'.[6] Thus, he initially hoped to be able to find some common
ground. By the time the two at long last met in person, at Löwenthal's

in 1922, Kracauer had already written a damning article on Bloch's *Thomas Münzer*, and its publication would preclude any amicable relationship between them.[7] On 27 August 1922, just five weeks after their meeting, his review, titled 'Prophetentum' [Prophetism], appeared in the *Frankfurter Zeitung*. It not only rejected the substance of Bloch's chiliastic communism but also launched a personal attack on Bloch, condemning the 'Bloch phenomenon'. Kracauer discerned a pseudo-chiliasm, a pseudo-communism and an ecstatic and esoteric pseudo-philosophy at work. He simply did not buy Bloch's apocalyptic visions and revolutionary attitude; he disliked his 'roaring, frequently unintelligible torrent of words':

> Words, for this stormy, untamed character, are not holy, nor do they have an essence of their own. He becomes intoxicated as he piles them up high; he shakes them up in a rage, chases them in unbridled swarms ahead of him and away from their secret meaning. Everything comes swirling and foaming out, devours itself in its own labyrinthine movements, twists in orgiastic frenzy.

Kracauer considered Bloch a dazzler and a dreamer, a 'spirit in feverish shivers of the kind only produced by times that are unsettled in their deep foundations, equipped with an unparalleled vitality, loaded with explosives and full of sparks of insight'.[8] Bloch's character and temperament were, indeed, the exact opposite of Kracauer's sceptical and suffering spirit that conscientiously sought out life. Bloch was sure of himself and of the truth; he was passionate, and he forcefully grasped things. He did not seek but found. But Löwenthal, despite his own messianic impulses, was drawn towards his friend from Frankfurt. When Kracauer sent his text on Bloch to Margarete Susman, his advisor in all of life's matters, it was not without a 'feeling of distress', for he was afraid that his attack on her comrade-in-arms regarding this religious renaissance with a socialist face would turn her away from him. But he could be sure of Leo's support. In Kracauer's judgement, Löwenthal was 'altogether alienated' by the 'big style religious adventurer', and devoted to Kracauer 'with great love'.[9] Thus, as early as March he announced to Löwenthal that he would be unsparing in his criticism of the *Münzer* book, 'despite you (or perhaps especially because of you)'.[10]

Bloch would surely hardly have expected such a severe criticism just one month after his first meeting with Kracauer. He probably inferred a certain falseness on Kracauer's part. Nevertheless, he began his letter to Kracauer, written four days after the review had appeared, by saying: 'Your review ... essentially did not surprise me because I was familiar with the fundamentally malevolent attitude of the *Frankfurter Zeitung* as well as your own alien stance toward the tenor of my philosophy.' There was no elective affinity between them, he wrote, and what Kracauer lacked specifically was any access to Bloch's language or understanding of his 'revolutionary activity'. In Berlin – that is, at the very centre of things at the time – in the circles around Alfred Döblin, and around Lukács in Vienna, the review had caused 'a most remarkable shaking of heads'.[11] Bloch demanded 'satisfaction' and sent a rejoinder which, however, the paper did not publish. 'Thus, he who is nothing should finally stop talking. But he who is nothing but his nose should at least use it in the right way.' This was the beginning of Bloch's dispute with 'certain critics', whom he mentioned by name.[12] In the case of Kracauer,

> we see in front of us a little man who is too limited for what he wants to do, and does not notice how much he gets things wrong; who has calibrated the thermometer for his bath in philosophical seminars, puts it in geysers, and is then surprised that it shows no reading; who never got as much as a whiff of the passion and metaphysics involved in understanding existence, but nevertheless wants to be a little Kierkegaard looking for his Hegel; and ... in *Thomas Münzer*, in *The Spirit of Utopia*, he thinks he has found him. The likes of Kracauer (at first just honest mediocrity) become irritated out of wimpishness, guilty out of pure insufficiency, but methodically malicious.[13]

The usually touchy Kracauer did not show any outward signs of being impressed by Bloch's tirade. After Bloch had included the rejected text in a small volume, *Durch die Wüste* [Across the desert], in 1923, he wrote to Löwenthal: 'His polemic against me, "methodically malicious", shows all too plainly his anger over his inability to be hurtful in any way; on the contrary, we had a hearty laugh about this self-exposure of Bloch's soul.'[14] But had that laugh been genuine? Bloch had called Kracauer a whippersnapper, an average student of philosophy, an intellectual shopkeeper. Someone who has no desire to be something, does not philosophize with passion, is equipped with self-confidence and has found his place in life – such a person might be able to laugh about this. But the young Kracauer was not such a person. Both Bloch and Kracauer would later come to regret this episode.

The dispute over prophetism and messianism did not seem to wither the first tender shoots of friendship that were springing up for Kracauer. To his great relief, Susman stayed in contact with him, and Löwenthal even broke off his relationship with Bloch after the latter's counter-attack. Löwenthal had already switched from the formal 'Sie' to the informal 'Du' in letters to Kracauer, leading Kracauer to assure Löwenthal, not without a little embarrassment, that he was now 'part of his life': 'Fool that I am, I am here almost about to write you a kind of love letter – maybe it is the power of this word [i.e. the 'Du'] used for the first time that looses my tongue.'[15] And Teddie, the other young friend with whom Kracauer was on informal terms, had little interest in any of these religious matters at the time. Although the young genius had no ear for religion and, according to Kracauer, lacked philosophical Eros, Wiesengrund shared with his friends an emotional emphasis on loneliness and the experience of radical separation between ego and world, the two sources of metaphysical neediness.[16] Social loneliness could, at least, be counteracted with friendship. Thus, it made sense that Kracauer's contribution to Nobel's Festschrift was the second part of his trilogy on friendship.[17]

The text is again a sociological treatise; it sets out from the idea of friendship, and aims to capture its 'full reality' through an examination of types and processes of friendship. Particularly interesting is a passage on friendships between adult men and young men, which is obviously pertinent to Kracauer's case. Kracauer first mentions the reasons and motivations behind such uneven relationships. Young men are looking for confirmation and support. They are looking for orientation, even when they contradict the older man. Where they think they are giving, they are often taking; where they are demanding, they are often giving. The older one, by contrast, surveys the situation, and, on account of his maturity and experience, becomes an 'educator'. He therefore has to hold back, and he cannot reveal himself unreservedly. As the younger man, in turn, keeps him lively and challenges him, their friendship provides each with what he lacks. But Kracauer also identifies hurdles:

> Between different ages, communication is difficult, and the distance in years produces a strong feeling of shame which makes it difficult to get closer. ... Especially strong in the social intercourse between different age groups is sexual shame. Both parties shy away from talking about their erotic experiences.

Kracauer had in mind sexual experiences with others, not between the men themselves. In real life, and especially in his friendship with Wiesengrund, however, both possibilities were to play a role.[18]

Kracauer concludes his thoughts on friendship by mentioning an aspect that was clearly close to his heart. There are obviously personalities, he writes, that are no longer capable of friendship, and there are personalities that are more inclined towards love; and there is a third type, the 'man of works, who shuts himself off from both love and friendship' and devotes himself 'wholly to the ideas that fill him'. Kracauer knew from personal experience what price such a man had to pay:

Loneliness is his fate, but often he does not know this and becomes embittered when others do not requite his love to the same extent. And yet such demure behaviour is natural because people feel that, despite his sudden and tempestuous devotion, he only half belongs to them; they do not only want to take, but also to give, and they are jealous of the ideas to which he is invisibly chained. Thus, their souls may grant him hospitality but never the right to make his home in them.

The young Kracauer had realized that he faced just this danger. He did not want to be admired, but loved; he wanted to find a home in friendship. Friendship provided the strength one needed for life and for the search for truth. He treasured his 'symphilosophizing' with Leo Löwenthal during those years.[19]

His correspondence with Löwenthal – in which 'the "Du" that had long since been inwardly said demanded to be openly expressed' – took place in the shadow of a terrible turn of events. Shortly after his fiftieth birthday, Nobel died unexpectedly. Kracauer wrote an empathetic letter to his shocked friend, who was in the Black Forest for a stay at a health resort paid for by Nobel: 'I am also incredibly shocked by the sudden death of this man because I revered and loved him, although I only ever approached him from a distance, so to speak.' Kracauer had admired above all Nobel's 'wonderful gentleness and undemanding kindness'. He wondered whether the rabbi might have been one of the thirty tsaddiks of his generation. He published an obituary in the *Frankfurter Zeitung*, and he consoled his friend in mourning: 'In such ways, one experiences, over and over again, change and decline; nothing is spared, and in the end our soul is covered with scars.'[20]

Kracauer's relationship with Franz Rosenzweig was of an altogether different character: tetchy, tense and suffused with animosity. Rosenzweig had given Kracauer a teaching assignment for the first trimester of 1921/22 at the Jüdisches Lehrhaus, but he had done so for purely strategic reasons, namely to lure the *Frankfurter Zeitung* circles to the institute. Rosenzweig also insisted that Kracauer should, despite his speech impediment, give a public lecture. This would prove to be a debacle, just as the speaker had feared. In the end, Rosenzweig had to read Kracauer's manuscript for him, after Kracauer's efforts to carry on with the lecture had failed and he had fallen silent. Rosenzweig thought Kracauer a 'peacock' and a 'hack' who peddled just one idea, annoying everyone with it:

And then we are told for the umpteenth time that 'we' live in a broken and chaotic 'time' that has burst apart, in which a 'religious seeking' licks its lips at the prospect of this great, beautiful, harmonious one-size-fits-all cake that, in the 'Middle Ages', a benevolent confectioner delivered to the homes of a humanity that was 'close to God', as the Weltanschauung they had for dessert.

Kracauer, for his part, was no less sarcastic in his evaluation of Rosenzweig's *The Star of Redemption* (1921): 'A proper philosophy of apotheosis, which begins with nothingness and ends with a "carry the sun in your heart"',[21] 'systematic drivel that kills idealism for us, in order to resurrect it again'.[22] Kracauer also disliked the sentimentality and the 'omnipresent Talmudic glow of reason' in Rosenzweig's writing. He lacked, Kracauer said, 'holy soberness'.[23]

Although Rosenzweig's assessment of Kracauer's religious yearning as obsessive and his description of Kracauer's analysis of the times were informed by resentment, they were not, for all that, completely wrong. What Rosenzweig forgot to add, however, was that this searching for God was combined – in an exact reversal of Rosenzweig's own philosophy of religion – with a denial of the possibility of making a positive confession to God. Kracauer's position was, so to speak, based on identifying a deficiency in human existence; it was a philosophy of human unhappiness that required the adoption of a courageous attitude – or at least of a fundamentally melancholy disposition. There is, however, a letter from Kracauer to Susman that seems to contradict this. On 21 February 1920, he wrote: 'And yet, I never before felt as deeply as now' – 'now' meaning during the dark times, the times of evil people and a mindless world – 'that God is the most real thing there is; I only became truly pious in the present times.'[24] The letter is an exception, though. To the visionary Löwenthal he confessed that he had only 'a vague inkling' of God and certainly 'did not know anything about his attributes'. Kracauer believed 'that a higher being reigns [waltet] over us and that we are creatures and therefore have no access to the secrets of the creator'.[25] He felt torn: on the one hand, he was captivated by the same questions as religious thinkers; on the other, he rejected 'the brilliance of authenticity', the 'religious rose-tinted glasses'. 'The positive word is not ours ... We must be hidden, quietist, idle, a thorn to the others; we must rather let them despair (because of us) than give them hope – that appears to me the only acceptable attitude.'[26]

The young Kracauer longed to have a faith, just as he longed for truth and for a home. But he could not really believe. On balance, his scepticism towards all the offerings of faith was what dominated during the years of religious renaissance. He well understood the longing for meaning, for redemption, for God, the yearning that – in Godless times even more than in others – formed part of the *conditio humana*. But Kracauer was more interested in religion as an element of an analysis of his times and as a philosophical problem

and less as a strict matter of belief. Kracauer's analysis of his times
was suffused with cultural criticism: the human being was living in
a 'cold, rigid, soulless reality', dominated by the spirit of the natural
sciences and of capitalism. The human environment was disturb-
ingly impersonal; it had little need for humans themselves or their
souls. The spirit of the age was positivistic, and the scientific method
of thinking, in this age of the machine, spilled over into the humanities. Contemporary civilization differed from previous epochs of
high culture 'through its lack of a commonly binding body of
beliefs ... that gives meaning to the overall being of man and conse-
crates it'. 'Absolute truth' had been lost, and people longed to leave
'the sphere of relativist conditionality'.[27]

Communal movements were protests against the power of a cold
reality, an anti-social society and a civilization that was far removed
from God: in politics, this was communism; in the arts, expressionism;
in scholarship, the philosophy of life; in ordinary life, spiritualism
and occultism; and, in the public sphere, cultural criticism. Kracauer
identified a 'heroic desire for form [Gestaltwerdung]'.[28] He suspected
that this was a 'historic moment', he wrote to Susman: 'The call for
meaning can be heard louder than it has been for centuries. There are
stirrings within Catholicism, and Protestant idealism also flares up
everywhere. Settlements are founded ... which aim to begin a new life
based on Christian-communist principles.' Writing from Frankfurt,
he told Susman, who had since moved to Bad Säckingen, near the
Swiss border, that '[t]hat kind of thing happens a lot within the
Jewry. Many begin to live within "the law" again and try inwardly to
consecrate the [religious] forms.' At the same time, he insisted: 'Into
the world of orthodoxy, with its sacred forms' – that is, the world of
Rosenzweig and Nobel – 'we cannot enter. No! That, for us, would be
romanticism!'[29] Judaism was rather alien to Kracauer, but Susman was
looking to Judaism for resources to be used in political philosophy.
Kracauer wrote to her: 'Of course, I also feel the mysterious history
of the Jewish people in all its depth, but could you explain to me
once what the specifically Jewish spirit is, ... and what would remain
of Jewish religion if "the law" were subtracted from it?'[30] Kracauer
was certainly seeking to make contacts within the Jewish community
in Frankfurt. He visited Martin Buber, but he found that there was
no spark between them; they were living 'in different spheres'. Still,
Buber's religiosity meant a lot to him, 'much more than for instance
that of [Thomas] Mann, however highly I value him in other respects.
Apparently, one doesn't leave Jewishness behind, after all.'[31] But
neither, it seems, did Kracauer find a proper entry to it.

Kracauer evaluated Max Scheler's attempt to renew Catholicism
in similar terms. In a review for the *FZ* in November 1921, he
accused his former teacher of being unable to decide between
relativism and Catholicism. The 'will to believe' always becomes

an obstacle for the phenomenologist, and the diversity of natural religions becomes an obstacle for the Catholic. 'Scheler's form', he wrote, was characteristic of 'our time': 'In the present, despair over alienation from God is paired with a religious need that is markedly more intense than in previous times.'[32] This argument also applies to Protestantism, he added.[33]

Kracauer's judgement of alternative religious revivalist movements, such as anthroposophy, was scathing. In his regular reports in the *FZ* on the meetings of anthroposophical communities, he had nothing but scorn for their intuitions, for clairvoyance and the supernatural spiritual world: 'As unfortunately no one but Steiner has advanced into those spheres, we have to take what he has to say about the astral body and human reincarnation, etc., on trust.' And with characteristically mordant wit, he added: 'But we should at least mention that thanks to his clairvoyance he was able to report on a cultured people who lived twelve thousand years ago, travelled in aerial vehicles close to the earth's surface and claimed the existence of two little Jesus boys, on whom he communicated quite a few details.' Unlike Kracauer, this 'modern magician' was not practising science; his claims were unverifiable. And yet the rise of this wise teaching followed its own logic:

> With an almost ingenious instinct, Steiner has identified the defects of our time. ... Just as he knows about the harm that has resulted from the complete capitulation to a natural science that deprives self and world of their souls, so he also knows about the loss of any relationship with the fullness of the phenomena perceived by our senses that has resulted from an ever-increasing abstraction from directly experienced reality.[34]

Abstract science created the soil in which apparitions such as anthroposophy could flourish; soulless times gave birth to their own demons.

The quest for religion was not only a symptom of a time that was devoid of meaning. It was also a philosophical problem. With a colleague from the *Frankfurter Zeitung*, Hermann Herrigel, Kracauer discussed Georg Lukács's *Theory of the Novel*. The book had been written during the war and published in 1920 by Paul Cassirer. Kracauer reviewed it in the *Neue Blätter für Kunst und Literatur*, with a shorter version of the review appearing in *Weltbühne*. Seen 'from the perspective of the philosophy of history, the situation of our time' gives rise to the 'powerful need for religion', Kracauer begins. The philosophy of recent centuries had been nothing but an attempt at 'bridging the rift that runs through the world after the disappearance of any all-encompassing meaning belonging to reality'. Loneliness and homelessness are the fate of man 'in the empty space' of a 'reality without meaning'. Kracauer praised Lukács's concept of 'transcendental homelessness', of which the novel was supposed to be the expression, being the epic form of an age in which, according to Lukács, 'meaning as immanent to life has become a problem, yet whose mindset is nevertheless still one totality'. The problematic individual, in particular, suffers from nostalgia for a lost meaning. In a Godforsaken world, it is the task of philosophy to 'keep the flame of longing alive'.[35] Kracauer had previously written to Susman:

> Now I finally comprehend what this time for which I long means in metaphysical terms, that its dawn is the only possible release from the cursed relativism and subjectivism, and from the equally cursed transcendental idealism. ... Never does redemption come about by ideas, no matter how sublime they might be; only a religious genius, a great personality, a living figure can bring it about, a figure familiar with beings, and one to which fantasy attaches itself, around which a community crystallizes. Philosophy is only preparatory; pure thinking cannot give birth to a truth that becomes dogmatic and unconditional authority.[36]

Truth could no longer be established by philosophy; idealism was outdated, because historically disproven. But one could not simply ignore the last things, for this would amount to relativism.

Kracauer wanted to leave both idealism and relativism behind. The question of truth remained alive for him, as is clear from his major text from this period, 'Those Who Wait', which was published in the *Frankfurter Zeitung* in March 1922 and which summarizes his struggles:

> There are a lot of people these days who, although unaware of each other, are nevertheless linked by a common fate. Having eluded the profession of any particular faith, they have acquired their share of the cultural and educational wealth generally available today and tend to live with an alert sense of their time. These scholars, businessmen, doctors, lawyers, students, and intellectuals of all sorts spend most of their days in the loneliness of the large cities. And since they are sitting in offices, receiving clients, directing negotiations, and attending lectures, they quite often forget their actual inner being in the din of the hustle and bustle and fancy themselves free of the burden that secretly weighs upon them. But when they do pull back from the surface into the center of their being, they are overcome by a profound sadness which arises from the recognition of their confinement in a particular spiritual/intellectual [*geistige*] situation, a sadness that ultimately overruns all layers of their being. It is this metaphysical suffering from the lack of a higher meaning in the world,

a suffering due to an existence in an empty space, which makes these people companions in misfortune.[37]

Did the reasons for this author's 'profound sadness' lie solely in the lack of meaning, in the '*emptying out* of people's spiritual/intellectual space', in the '*exile* from the religious sphere', in the 'curse of *isolation and individuation*' that arose out of the dissolution of form and law, in '*relativism*', the 'fear of emptiness'?[38] Or were its causes rather his inability to love himself and the fact that he lacked a place in his society? Now in his early thirties, Kracauer had no profession, nor had he truly experienced love. At any rate, transcendental homelessness and the exigencies of worldly life certainly seemed to go hand in hand. In the face of this, Kracauer recommended to himself and his readers an attitude of waiting, a '*hesitant openness*', a tarrying 'in front of closed doors' of the kind Franz Kafka had presented in his parable of the gatekeepers, *Before the Law*.[39] Not to possess meaning meant, for Kracauer, as for Kafka, to be 'in front of the gate'. But while Kafka's man from the country sits there 'for days and years', negotiating with the gatekeeper in order, perhaps, eventually to gain access to the law, and while he studies the gatekeeper, down to the fleas on the collar of his fur coat, until the door, which is only meant for him, is shut for good – that is, while this man waits in vain, the waiting Kracauer observed all the other gatekeepers and country folk. But as he watches, his need to enter gradually disappears. At some point, he will get up from the stool that the gatekeeper has provided him, and he will let God be God. The one who waits will become the one who wanders. It is not the Castle but the shabby hut next to it that becomes important. The Trial will take a different course – certainly once Kracauer reaches America.

6

The Crisis of the Sciences, Sociology and the Sphere Theory

For now, Kracauer was still one who waited. He worked on two monographs, one on Simmel and one on sociology. If truth were not to be found in religion, then maybe the sciences could help. With sociology, there was a new discipline emerging, one that, according to Max Weber, is a science of reality – that is, something capable of providing valid statements about the profane social life of human beings. Kracauer confronted this sociology with the epistemological problem that arises in secularized modernity: how can absolute knowledge of values still be possible following the dissolution of the traditional context of meaning that had rested on God as its ultimate referent? In other words, how is such knowledge possible in Lukács's 'meaningless time'?[1]

By January 1920, Kracauer had completed a draft of a 'material epistemology' for sociology. His work on it had been interrupted by one-off assignments and jobs as an architect for his old boss, the Frankfurt architect Max Seckbach; as Kracauer put it, 'an artist may live off his art, a philosopher never'.[2] Kracauer even occasionally considered returning to his unloved 'breadwinning job' and joining an architectural bureau in Amsterdam (as there was little work in Frankfurt).[3] After Adolf Kracauer's death, the family had been forced to move in with Kracauer's aunt and uncle. Kracauer was tortured by fears for the future: 'I shall probably end up in some provincial place like Osnabrück, where I am buried alive and cannot do philosophical work, because this requires constant contact with stimulating people within an environment that esteems the intellect.'[4] To Susman, he lamented:

I am, after all, already over thirty-one years of age, age-old; this perpetually provisional existence grinds me down. All those of my generation have long since moved ahead of me; really, fate should at last satisfy the few demands I make on life. And in all this, I do not even dare think of binding a woman to me.[5]

In 1921, he occasionally worked as a private tutor in order to earn some money on the side.

The monograph on sociology was hard work for Kracauer. The first chapter alone – on the foundations of sociology – he completely redrafted seven times.[6] After he had completed an article on ideas and group individuality, which he was able to get published in the *Archiv für Sozialwissenschaft und Sozialpolitik*, he thought he needed to rewrite the foundations chapter yet again.[7] Having completed about three-quarters of the manuscript, Kracauer began to study Husserl's phenomenology, and this again changed his perspective on the subject.[8] By March 1922, he had found a publisher, but he was not satisfied with his work:

> I shall probably ..., much against my will, give ... my consent. Within the last year, I have progressed even further, and see the problems situated around phenomenology in much more depth than I did in the case of 'sociology'. Nevertheless, I can no longer change anything in this work and must publish it as it is. I shall mark my latest position in a preface and point towards the forthcoming book on phenomenology, work on which I hope soon to be able to begin.[9]

This preface begins: 'The present book is the result of purely philosophical intentions' – a sober, stiff, clumsy beginning that almost sounds like a warning to the reader, and certainly like a justification for an unusual undertaking. It prefaces what is indeed an occasionally tortuous and tedious argument. When he had completed the plan for the book, Kracauer had stated:

> My thinking gets ever closer to higher mathematics. I draw intellectual shapes, so to speak. ... My epistemology could begin thus: given two intellectual systems, x and xi, which transformations must be carried out in order to get from x to xi? These are questions and thoughts that are of interest to only a few people, and whose general importance is only recognized by a few.[10]

And this was precisely what turned out to be the case. The book treats the idea, material, foundations and problems of sociology by asking how sociology is possible; that is, it adopts the same perspective as Kant does when he asks: 'How is knowledge possible?' Can social processes be understood 'in their necessity'? 'Knowledge that is founded in necessity' requires more than the postulation of 'empirical facts, which may be confirmed by reality as things stand, but by no means need to be so confirmed'.[11] What kind of epistemological structure would a scientific edifice of a sociological sort therefore need to possess? Can the sphere of reality be penetrated by the sphere of immanence within which science moves? Or rather: is it possible 'to reach the filled space of reality, overarched by a highest transcendent meaning, from the empty space of pure thinking'? Thus, in *Soziologie als Wissenschaft* [Sociology as science] the sphere of reality is conceived as a 'space' with a 'meaning' as its roof.[12] Ultimately, then, for Kracauer the issue of the preconditions and possibilities of sociological knowledge has a religious significance, because the critique of any kind of immanent science is meant to help lead 'an expelled mankind [back] to the new-old spheres of God-filled reality'.[13] The idea of necessity itself belonged to the era of meaning. And with the end of 'the era filled with meaning', the era in which all things bore some relation to divinity and there was neither empty space nor empty time, the 'world [had] split into the manifold of beings and the subject which faces this manifold'.[14]

How does Kracauer conceive of the idea and the realm of sociology in the era devoid of meaning?

> Sociology must investigate the life of socially connected human beings to the extent that the behaviour of human beings, like all intentional expressions of this life, exhibits regularities and characteristic traits which, in some way, stand in an intelligible relation to the fact and the kind of socialization.

Following Simmel and Weber, sociology can therefore only concern itself with regularities and laws that result from socialization, that is, the social relations between individuals. This is a formal sociology, a grammar of society, a kind of mathematics of the social that extracts aspects of material reality but has no truck with the evaluation of its object – let alone with establishing its meaning. This, in Kracauer's view, is the problem with sociology.

The phenomenological method promises to help establish 'necessary knowledge'. Kracauer claims that the real foundation of sociology 'could only be provided by pure phenomenology, on which it rests and which captures it'.[15] Edmund Husserl, the founder of the phenomenological method, had set out to defend that which has timeless validity against the empirical sciences. He had tried to show that the laws of logic and the principles of philosophy are independent of all experience.[16] Back to the things themselves, to primary experience – that is phenomenology's battle cry. Reality is an appearance, and the 'phenomenon' is an intentional imagination. Knowledge is tied to a subject: 'how can we, and must we, experience the world, if our consciousness has such and such a structure?' This approach does not, however, end with the psychologism, historicism and relativism that was predominant at the time. On the contrary, Husserl insists upon an analytic and generalizing treatment of things that abstracts from the individual empirical case. This is also what interests Kracauer: 'Only pure phenomenology extracts the categorical units of consciousness from the material wealth of experience, and thus completes the series of possible de-individualizations of the subject of knowledge.' In various spaces, the ego is thus confronted with essences; these stand in a hierarchical relation to one another, with the individual reality of intentional consciousness as the base and the 'completely de-individualized essential forms' towering in the highest realms above. Through de-individualization, the concept of the pure ego re-establishes the connection with Kant, who had claimed 'that there are synthetic judgements a priori, judgements, that is, which are generally valid and apodictically necessary'.[17] Pure phenomenology reminded Kracauer also of Simmel's idea of a general, or formal, sociology. Such a sociology also rests on 'the intention of founding sociology on necessity'. The attempt to establish objective and comprehensive knowledge in a time devoid of meaning, however, had to fail: 'Phenomenology marks ... the end of a process of dissolution; it is the sign of an ultimately irremovable distance to meaning (and probably also of the longing for meaning).'[18] Sociology, by contrast, is the appropriate – although necessarily deficient – science for a complicated modern world 'after the loss of meaning', a world in which a 'generally valid and at the same time comprehensive account of individual richness' is no longer possible.

Nevertheless, Kracauer does not therefore consider sociology superfluous: 'The need to understand social existence and processes on the basis of the human spirit simply is there, and as a need of a consciousness that is not tied to meaning it is its own justification, whether it is fruitful or not.'[19] Despite his scepticism about the value of sociological knowledge and his awareness of the limited value of empirical methods, Kracauer grants the young discipline the right to 'follow a sharply delineated mission ... within established boundaries'.[20] Even if the connection with meaning has been severed and objective reality can no longer be captured, making truth impossible, this does not mean that no claims about reality can be made. The end of the book opens up a perspective from which a path from the longing for meaning to profane reality becomes visible.

But why had Kracauer charged this young science with a demand that it obviously could not meet, and then justified this demand with a sprawling, complicated argument that draws on phenomenology? By asking a Kantian epistemological question, did Kracauer impute to the historical and social sciences responsibility for dealing with a problem that is not really theirs? Is *Soziologie als Wissenschaft* ultimately based on a great misunderstanding? In a review in *Zeitschrift für Politik*, Gerhard Colm alleged that it is. Colm had studied economics in Frankfurt and worked as a consultant at the Statistisches Reichsamt in Berlin. Although he thought the book full of valuable insights, he was somewhat disappointed by its Kantian orientation and its focus on the 'recognizing I'.[21] Colm was a social policy practitioner, a student of Franz Oppenheimer with social democratic inclinations – not a disciple of Georg Simmel with an interest in epistemological problems. For Colm, the treatise on sociology simply missed the point. But what was the point of German sociology around 1920?

Sociology as a science bears some relation to modernity. It emerged at the end of the nineteenth century, a century in which 'the certainties of the life-world of early modernity ... had fallen prey to a fourfold attack: the revolutionizing of politics, the monetarization of social relations, the industrialization of work and the autonomization of the arts'.[22] Modernity was the result of the 'Great Transformation',[23] in which the old feudal order had been destroyed; new masses and classes had emerged as the result of a capitalist industrialization that did not stop at the factory gates but encompassed practically all areas of life; the emancipation of the 'productive estates' had put the world of work centre stage, at the expense of the religious and military spheres; although the wealth of the industrialized and urbanized countries was not justly distributed, there was still enough money going around; the spectre of communism haunted Europe; God seemed to be dead and emergence from self-incurred immaturity possible; one either had faith in progress, or, if that faith had been shaken or the overall situation was sufficiently dissatisfying, one practised cultural criticism.[24] 'Society' now became a topic of conversation – in Germany often in contradistinction to community or the state; just as there was 'the human being' or 'peoples', there was now 'society'. Sociology was a way such societies observed and interpreted themselves: a kind of self-knowledge. This systematic self-observation, the inclination towards an unrestrained investigation of self, which inspired not only the sciences but also modern art and culture, was something new. No age before had known such reflexivity, institutionalized in particular in the world of the media. And in the context of this intensified self-reflection, society appeared as a problem: how should the social question be solved? Where would the rise of class or mass society lead? What were the cultural costs? How did the Great Transformation change human culture in the broad sense? What were the implications of social inequality and the promise of democracy for the social order? Those talking about society after 1900 were often concerned specifically with its fault lines, and they flirted with reactionary or utopian ideas – but in doing so they had their fingers on the pulse of the times.[25]

The founding fathers of sociology in Germany were theoreticians of this so-called modernity. Prominent among them were Kracauer's teacher Georg Simmel and Max Weber, whom Kracauer also admired.

They attempted not just to describe the rapid changes taking place in industrial society but to reach a comprehensive understanding of them. Sociology was not only a new science – it was a science of what was new. It was interested in capitalism and the arts (which, around 1900, had already acquired the epithet 'modern'),[26] in processes of individualization and group formation, in law and religion, in money and metropolises. And sociology was occupied with the question of how this fast-changing society was experienced, and how society itself changed the forms of perception. Charles Baudelaire had defined *modernité* as *le transitoire, le fugitive, le contingent*. This experience of time, space and causality as transitory, fugitive and contingent was at the heart of Simmel's analyses of the times. He was the first sociologist of Baudelairean modernity.[27] With regard to society, this modernity was characterized by the objectification of relations and the dissolution of traditional ties and contexts of meaning, and these were brought about by a levelling as much as by individualization.[28] Especially for intellectuals such as Simmel, Weber and, later, Kracauer, social experience was characterized by the ambivalences of alienation and emancipation. All of Kracauer's early work is suffused with such contradictory experience.

While in France sociology developed as early as the mid-nineteenth century in the form of a positivist science of social planning that was committed to progress, German sociology was closer to cultural criticism, although it also sought to distance itself from the latter. Sociology was created out of an admixture of material from cultural history, psychology and political economy, harking back to authors such as Marx and Nietzsche, to Lebensphilosophie and to neo-Kantianism. The founding fathers of German sociology were 'reflective syncretistic thinkers who reformulated and recombined heterogeneous knowledge and material from other disciplines in accordance with the problems they approached'.[29] Cultural criticism played a decisive role in turning the perspective of sociology towards the ambiguities of modernity. As a new discipline, sociology had first to prove its legitimacy. It had to show that it could do something other disciplines could not – hence Weber's demand that sociology should be nothing less than a 'science of concrete reality'. This meant that on the one hand it was linked to the general public and on the other to the world of academic experts. For this reason, the founding fathers of sociology kept a sober disciplinary distance from cultural critics, even though they were influenced by them. Like the philosophical cultural critics, the sociologists were troubled by the gap between social being and meaning. In the beginning, German sociology was a science that argued philosophically rather than one that proceeded empirically. In the eyes of many, it provided 'philosophical compensation for those who had lost their faith in philosophy'.[30]

Although sociology was clearly on the way to becoming *the* science of modernity, it was not yet an established discipline, and it was still looking for a profile of its own. As Kracauer rightly observed, it was 'a young science still lacking agreement on its methods and object'.[31] Sociology was still waiting for its institutionalization. The 'founders' of sociology in Germany were professors of political economy, philosophy, *Völkerpsychologie*[32] and so on. The first chair dedicated explicitly to sociology was established only in 1919 in Frankfurt. The first holder was Franz Oppenheimer, whose work synthesized aspects of political economy and sociology. From April 1919 onwards, there was also the Forschungsinstitut für Sozialwissenschaften, an institute for the social sciences at the newly founded university in Cologne, where Max Scheler's work was preparing the way for the new sub-discipline of Wissenssoziologie or 'Soziologie der Erkenntnis', the sociology of knowledge. In Heidelberg, in particular, the social sciences were on the rise. The general view was that there was an urgent need to provide the young discipline with an epistemological foundation, give it a philosophical basis and define its object.[33] In 1917, in his *Grundfragen der Soziologie* [Fundamental questions of sociology], Georg Simmel had begun a debate about the question of whether sociology was a science at all, and whether the concept of 'society' referred to anything that was not also the province of other sciences. He claimed that the concept of 'society' was not enough to ground a science because it was not a 'real object beyond the individual beings and the processes associated with them'; it was an abstraction. But he also thought that 'society' was 'too much' because there was 'no science of any human matter that was not also a science of society'.[34]

In Germany, sociology was thus an elusive, vague and uncertain enterprise. At the same time, it was a science that claimed to be a kind of master discipline, the legitimate successor to philosophy. Kracauer's Kantian question – 'How is sociology possible?' – might have been a question posed by someone who stood at the margins of the discipline, but it nevertheless shows him to have been a well-informed contemporary. It was a question that was also asked in Heidelberg, in Frankfurt and Cologne, and in Leipzig. It was asked by those on the political left and by those on the political right, by academic outsiders and by established scholars.

Among the latter was Karl Mannheim, who would later, in 1930, take up the chair of sociology in Frankfurt. In 1922, he completed his Habilitation, a structural analysis of epistemology, with the cultural sociologist Alfred Weber in Heidelberg.[35] Kracauer read it and wrote to Leo Löwenthal: 'a talented work which sees problems that also exercise me very much. Thus, from all sides the same things are being worked on.'[36] During his time in Heidelberg, Mannheim, like Kracauer, struggled with philosophical questions.

In his *Beiträge zur Theorie der Weltanschauungs-Interpretation* [Contributions to a theory of the interpretation of world views], he was exercised in particular by the problem of the contradiction between meaningful totality and disconnected manifolds, between a philosophy of history that provides meaning and disparate individual research projects in the cultural sciences. Like Kracauer in his text on sociology, Mannheim thought it was necessary to ask about the 'Gegebenheitsweise', the way the object, namely a world view, is given.[37] In a similar vein, the Leipzig sociologist Hans Freyer insisted that sociology required a philosophical basis: 'This does not mean taking refuge from the facts in principles; it is not a regression of sociology into its philosophical prehistory, no evasion of the burning questions of the time. Rather, it is the inescapable duty that sociology has towards itself if it wants to move on from being an interesting "perspective" or a possible "aspect" to becoming a fully valid science.' And he continued: 'Before any science, there is always to be found the good Kantian question: how science, history, sociology "are possible."' Sociology, he claimed, had still not yet found its place among the other sciences, but it was searching for it. The question of what sociology might be and should be reached 'deep into the question of the essence, disciplinary structure and vocation of modern sciences as such'. Sociology did not simply slot into the system of the sciences; it 'practically [created] a new type of science'.[38]

Kracauer's *Soziologie als Wissenschaft* was up with the most recent debates about epistemological problems. Not without good reason did Edmund Husserl feel that it showed a 'real philosophical talent', that it presented 'fruitful thoughts' that he wished later to develop further 'in the systematic context of [his] phenomenology based on transcendental sources', thoughts he put under the heading of the 'crisis of the sciences'.[39] Kracauer had sketched this so-called crisis of the sciences in two review articles for the higher education supplement of the *Frankfurter Zeitung* in March 1923, one on Ernst Troeltsch's *Der Historismus und seine Probleme* and the other on Max Weber's *Gesammelte Aufsätze zur Wissenschaftslehre*. What was at stake were the problems of relativism in historicism and of value in the sciences: 'If they [the sciences] seek to limit themselves to gaining knowledge free of value in order to preserve their objectivity, they either end up with a conceptual formalism devoid of substance or with a boundless infinity of factual claims that can nowhere be finalized, and ultimately they become entangled in valuations after all. But if they approach their material with valuations from the very beginning, they right away lapse into a perspective on things that must be called subjective from the standpoint of today's science, because the values themselves, of course, cannot be justified in a scientific and objective way.'[40] As Kracauer saw it, Troeltsch and Weber were battling the same aporias as were Simmel and Scheler. Behind these aporias of modern science lay the same cause as lay behind the renaissance of religiosity: the loss of meaning in the age of 'transcendental homelessness'. The disenchantment and fragmentation of the world, on the one hand, and the crisis of the sciences, on the other – that, for Kracauer, constituted the present condition of existence.[41]

The search for a lost context and the preoccupation with meaning were thus not peculiar to Kracauer; they were concerns that were widespread and firmly rooted in intellectual life at the time.[42] According to Kracauer's analysis of his age, self and world, and the being and meaning of things, had become separated in the course of the transition to the epoch of lost meaning. Hannah Arendt later spoke of 'world alienation' because modern man loses not only the transcendent world but simultaneously the immanent world as well. The loss of faith does not result in him falling back on the world and immanence; rather, he falls back on himself. His measuring devices tell him no more about nature's true properties than a telephone number says about the person at the end of the line.[43] The world confronts him as contingent and relative, but the desire for unambiguity, order and the calculability of reality beyond immanent principles and regularities remain; for many, these became only more urgent after the loss of meaning.[44] To Kracauer, the split between formal and material sociology was a symptom of modernity. The loss of meaning and the epistemological antinomies were sources of suffering for him, and he considered the renaissance of religiosity and the crisis of the sciences as symptoms of the intellectual situation of the time. He was nevertheless open to the idea of sociology as a meaning-free science of social reality. At the beginning of the 1920s, the problem with modernity for Kracauer was that it was an unreal modernity: modern cultural phenomena no longer had any contact with the absolute, with that on which a genuine human existence would be grounded.

Kracauer was about to complete the book on sociology when he hinted to Löwenthal that he had already moved beyond what he had said in the book. What he was referring to was his work between 1922 and 1925 on a 'theory of spheres' and a metaphysics of the detective novel. Kracauer liked to read crime novels, and he took intellectual pleasure in them. Detective stories had existed since the mid-nineteenth century, when Edgar Allen Poe's character Auguste Dupin began his investigations. In the mid-1880s, Arthur Conan Doyle's Sherlock Holmes solved various mysteries, and around 1920 Agatha Christie created the character of Hercule Poirot with his 'little grey cells'. All three search for rational explanations for seemingly irrational events. Nothing happens within these detective novels that does not have a causal explanation. They thus follow a narrative logic that is similar to that of sociology. Both crime stories and sociology put reality to the test; they suspect that a deeper – yet not transcendent – reality lies behind the immediately visible one. In Kracauer's words, the detective, like the scholar studying society, should uncover 'the secret that lies buried between human beings', and he should practise his profession by rational means.[45]

Kracauer's metaphysics of the detective novel emerged directly from his book on sociology and overlaps with it. In the context of sociology, Kracauer had been interested in scientific explanations of the world and its aporias. Now, he descended into the realm of light fiction, but even here he was still pursuing philosophical and theoretical interests.[46] He had approached sociology from the perspective of epistemology, using Kant, and with Husserl had tried in vain to find answers to them. Now, he used Kierkegaard for his reading of crime novels and developed his theory of the spheres on the basis of the Christian existentialist's theory of 'three existential spheres': the aesthetic, the ethical and the religious. The aesthetic refers to the fine arts and the sensuous relation to the world. According to Kierkegaard, however, this is also a lack of reality, a dream-like failure to grasp reality, a mere possibility out of which nothing will come. The ethical person, by contrast, takes the decision to leave this situation, but in the process abstracts from the real by postulating general duties. The third of Kierkegaard's modes of existence is the religious one; it is the existence of the concrete individual in his or her solitude before God. This mode is superior to the other two because it is the only one that comprehends the concrete existence of the individual human being.[47]

Both the way Kracauer experienced his existence as personal torment and his analysis of contemporary times could be translated into this model of stages. He defined spheres as 'stages of being' with differing 'reality contents'. In the upper sphere he placed the existential human beings, people like Kierkegaard, 'whose behaviour is really orientated toward the unconditional' and who are thus aware of the paradoxical situation in which they find themselves. This upper sphere is still in touch with Lukács's meaningful epoch, with the law in a divine sense; it embodies moral, authentic community.[48] The lower sphere is that of immanence. It is the world of society, in which the isolated individual leads a somewhat unreal existence within the empty space of a meaningless reality. It is the sphere of the profane and of worldly law, in which 'turbid senses [get confused] within the labyrinth of distorted happenings, while no longer being aware of the distortion'.[49] The human being moves between these two spheres, as a kind of intermediary being as described by Pascal: nothing in the face of eternity; everything in the face of nothingness.[50]

In Kracauer's view, the detective novel may be interpreted as a sign of the times, as a distorted mirror image of civilization that presents a 'caricature of its dreadful non-essence'.[51] Just as Lukács had declared the novel to be a genre that characterized a whole epoch, Kracauer reflected on the compound 'detective novel' as the logical expression of an age of differentiation, fragmentation and contingency. 'Without being a work of art, the detective novel nevertheless shows a de-realized society its own face in much purer form than society is otherwise able to perceive it.'[52] The genre served Kracauer as an allegory for a world that is altogether alienated from meaning and has given itself over to a blind rationality. The detective novel, he said, is an 'allegorical painting of negativity'.[53] He interpreted the figure of the detective as embodying rationality, as a lonely, secularized priest, a lone wolf living in the no-man's land between law, intrigue and danger – in the middle sphere, so to speak, which threatens to disappear in the face of one-dimensional rationality. The detective pursues rationality's ideal of autonomy and, because he has an air of omniscience and omnipresence, he becomes God-like. But, Kracauer added, this semblance of divinity is just that – a mere semblance – because the detective solves the riddles at the level of the empirical forms he comes across, without, however, comprehending them. To the glory of rationality the detective 'celebrates his mass in hotel lobbies, a mass which is more ghostly than a Black Mass because it is dedicated to worshipping what is indifferent and even lacks the positivity of the devil'. The detective has the qualities of a monk. Standing outside of 'communal life', he lives a 'bachelorhood a priori' and is 'non-human without being divine'.[54]

The combination of detective novel and Kierkegaard probably resulted from Kracauer and Wiesengrund's joint readings. Every year between 1922 and 1925, Wiesengrund gave Kracauer a book by Kierkegaard for his birthday, and Wiesengrund was himself a lover of crime novels.[55] The idea of an allegorical interpretation of the detective novel might possibly be owed to Walter Benjamin, whom he met around the turn of 1922/23.[56]

During 1923, Benjamin's decision to embark on a Habilitation often brought him to Frankfurt for longer spells, where he hoped to make contacts at the university. The relationship between Benjamin and Kracauer soon became strained, and it almost came to an end. As in the case of Bloch, the tension had to do with Kracauer's journalism. He had offered to publish a positive review of Benjamin's translation of Baudelaire's *Tableaux Parisiens* in the *Frankfurter Zeitung*, but instead a scathing review by Stefan Zweig appeared on 1 June 1924. Benjamin was enraged. Kracauer's excuse was that there was an 'intrigue at the editorial office'; he promised to make amends and, indeed, became a dedicated supporter of Benjamin's

Figure 14. Walter Benjamin, 1926
Copyright: Süddeutsche Zeitung Photo/Alamy Stock Photo

from then on.[57] In March 1923, Benjamin decided to embark on a study of Baroque drama, which he completed and submitted to the University of Frankfurt as a Habilitation in February 1925. The focus of *The Origin of German Tragic Drama* is an attempt to rescue Baroque allegory for the present. Benjamin wanted to show that allegory was an exceptional form of artistic perception. The events surrounding the Habilitation, however, could themselves provide material for a tragedy.[58] Benjamin was advised by the faculty council to withdraw his application after Hans Cornelius, who was in charge of the proceedings, had taken the 'incomprehensible means of expression' of the author 'as betokening a lack of objective clarity', pointing out that other colleagues, among them Max Horkheimer, did not understand the arguments either.[59] As a matter of fact, Benjamin had intentionally chosen a non-scholarly format for his treatise. The candidate was unflinching in his intellectual independence, and while the positions he adopted in his text were often somewhat veiled, he did not shy away from attacking the neo-Kantians whose approval he needed.[60] Why on earth would anyone support this arrogant Berlin Jew who was no one's student? 'It is now hard to understand how he and his friends could ever have doubted that a Habilitation under a not unusual university professor was bound to end with a catastrophe', was Hannah

Arendt's retrospective view of the situation.[61] Following Cornelius's hints, Benjamin discarded his Habilitation, but the book appeared in 1928 with Rowohlt. At that point there at last appeared the first positive acknowledgements of the work, among them one from Siegfried Kracauer, who apparently found the concept of allegory useful and plausible.

Texts like Kracauer's on the detective novel and Benjamin's on tragic drama announced a new form of philosophizing. They positioned themselves against an academic philosophy that favoured concepts and systems, and against a scientific syncretism 'which weaves a spider's web between separate kinds of knowledge in an attempt to ensnare the truth as if it were something which came flying in from outside'.[62] Instead, truth and reality were to be found by way of allegory, mosaic-like representations, and thus in an indirect fashion. As early as 1925, there were clear family resemblances between Benjamin's and Kracauer's work. When Benjamin, in 1923, called his new acquaintance 'an enemy of philosophy', this was meant as a compliment.[63] He also shared Kracauer's interest in religion, although his transcendental approach tried more energetically to get to the heart of the matter; he was not someone who hesitated or waited. Adorno later wrote about him:

> Among those of his own generation, he and Franz Rosenzweig are related in the tendency to turn speculation into theological doctrine; he and the Ernst Bloch of the *Spirit of Utopia* share the conception of 'theoretical messianism', a lack of concern for the boundaries Kant set for philosophy, and the intention to interpret mundane experience as a figure of transcendental experience.[64]

Benjamin's essay 'Critique of Violence' (1921), for instance, is a tract on the philosophy of religion which locates the foundation and origin of revolutionary violence beyond human law, in the Judaeo-Christian God.[65] And Benjamin's early writings on the philosophy of language already outlined a theological paradigm for history.[66] Together with Gerhard Scholem, Benjamin attended events at the Freies Jüdisches Lehrhaus. Kracauer and his two young friends Löwenthal and Wiesengrund found 'Scholem and his brother Benjamin' extraordinarily interesting, but nevertheless too 'authentic' and tinged with the 'religious rose-colour of Buber'. 'Buberizing' or 'Scholemizing' were Kracauer's terms for sliding into the unreal and romanticism.[67] Despite these differences regarding the possibility of messianism, Benjamin and Kracauer took a liking to each other and exchanged their ideas during the planning phases of their two book projects. In March 1924, Benjamin wrote to Kracauer: 'I am curious to see the analysis of the detective. It is as rare as it is nice to hold in one's hands a work one had been told about in the planning stages. I wish my own work were already at that point.'[68]

The work on the detective novel is the last major text by Kracauer in which the longing for meaning is evident. With this text, Kracauer advanced far into the world of the profane, even to the trivial; he thus moved as far as possible from a philosophy interested in the 'last things', a move that was almost indecent. But his deep sadness over the loss of meaning, over the victory of blind rationality, over a process that leads only to nothingness and loneliness – all this is still there in the text. One need only read the juxtaposition of the house of God with the hotel lobby, 'the hall vis-à-vis de rien', the space of those 'lacking any and all relations', in which detective stories typically play out.[69] During this phase in his life, Kracauer, indeed, seems to have employed an ambiguous – partly theological, partly phenomenal – concept of reality, as Inka Mülder-Bach emphasizes. On the one hand, the profane present is 'unreal'; on the other hand, the material world can be experienced with our senses and therefore is 'real'.[70] For Kracauer the question is whether the human being is able to maintain the irresolvable tension between the profane world and the absolute in the face of the dreary rationalism of capitalism and the pseudo-solutions of philosophical idealism, religious renewal, reactionary cultural pessimism and utopian communism. The trivial detective novel was certainly kitsch; in the end the 'little grey cells' of Poirot always triumphed. But nowhere, according to Kracauer, could a greater 'kitsch of de-realized thinking' be found than in the new religious movements like messianism: 'the here and now is always surrendered and an end is stipulated which would only possess reality if given a determinate meaning'.[71] Through this unmasking of the purveyors of meaning – itself reminiscent of detective work – Kracauer came ever closer to the here and now. Theology receded into the background, without, however, disappearing altogether. Like Benjamin, he thought that theology was more likely to be found in the neglected, unconsciously perceived things of everyday life. For Kracauer, this would be, in his paradoxical expression, a 'theology in the profane' [Theologie im Profanen].[72]

7

Friendship (Part 3): Passion and the Path towards the Profane

What can be done if the sought-after absolute cannot be found? In the third part of his trilogy on friendship, Kracauer suggests that it is possible to seek a 'creative conversation'[1] which makes a virtue of necessity: 'For all those who do not live with a faith, but are seized by an insatiable desire for absolute certainty, a conversation oriented toward the last things is a process that always signifies an important stage in their development.'[2] This kind of dialogue, Kracauer held, changes those who engage in it and the way in which they seek truth. Kracauer was here again following Simmel, who had identified conversation as the 'most extensive instrument of all human common life'. Human beings may have a conversation for the sake of its material content, but they may also have one for sociability's sake, and in this latter case, talking becomes an end in itself, a 'conversing with each other'[3]:

> In order that this game may retain its self-sufficiency, the content must receive no weight on its own account; as soon as the discussion becomes centered on material questions, it is no longer social; it turns its teleological orientation around as soon as exploring a truth – which may well be its content – becomes its purpose.[4]

Thus, in Simmel's sociological perspective, the emphasis shifted from content to form, from truth to sociability, from the seriousness of philosophy to the art of conversation. Kracauer suggested a similar shift: if the sought-after absolute, the content of a conversation, were something objective, an object of knowledge, 'the conversation, strictly speaking, would have no significance whatsoever'. If truth were given – 'like a fixed star' – one could unambiguously establish who was right and who was not, 'and the two would then part without having been truly together'. Truth, Kracauer said, is complemented by the existing human individual as a concrete being with a need to enter into relationships. The age-old questions 'What is there?' and 'What is the reason for it?' are now joined by another urgent one: 'Who is the person I am talking to?' In the conversation, factual matter and essence meet. The whole human being is active, and there occur acts of *'mental creation'*, whose significance consists in the fact that they 'result from a transformation commonly undergone by those beings. Neither of the two emerges from the conversation as the same person who entered into it; something happens with both of them in the conversation, and its fruits are born out of such processes, processes of *existential connection'*.[5] The search for truth is an end in itself and, in addition, a social adventure. Profane life acquires a value of its own, in spite of the fact of transcendental homelessness.

In this third text on friendship, Kracauer describes his own transformation from a seeker of meaning into a social being. His longing for a transcendental home was increasingly coming under pressure from the desire for a sense of security in the profane here and now. One important point to note here is that Kracauer was in love; he was passionately in love, the way Georg, for instance, is in love with Fred, the disguised son of a prince with the great sad eyes. Georg is *possessed by the alien daemon of the boy.*[6] *He would have preferred to have had Fred constantly at his side; school, sports and everyone to whom he was forced to yield him periodically were personal adversaries.*[7] Fred's room becomes their cosy, sometimes uncanny cave. *The pair lived side by side as in a cell and each lay in wait for the other.*[8] Their relation is like a real, social love: *Being constantly together they grew extremely irritable. Every tiny change of expression appeared to them in manifold magnification; small movements travelled through the air as giant scratches. They argued because of provocations which were conjured out of nothing so that they could fight.*[9] Despite, or because of, these tensions, Fred repeatedly assures Georg that he wants to stay with him for the rest of his life. *Again and again they kiss each other.*[10] Georg never thinks of the future; he lives *on a small caress while waiting for the next talk.*[11] He is devastated to learn that Fred plans to leave the city to take up a job. They go travelling together before he leaves. *Georg for his part was imagining with intense excitement the various scenes that awaited them – their evening walks, how they would lock the hotel room door, get undressed, talk in bed – lingering over images of intimacy and sensing possibilities which he did not, however, mentally pursue. It was incomparably more enjoyable to sense them precisely as possibilities and to push any realization of them into the most remote future.*[12] Travelling turns out to be complicated. *As usual it was Fred who decided what they would do. ... Fred simply expressed his wishes, whereas Georg, who was always a little depressed by these forthright suggestions, tended to shrink back from his own ideas, fearing he might end up imposing on his friend.*[13] Georg always has to wait for the prince, and his anger grows. *Georg, who had retained the smaller*

*room without saying anything, was peeved to find himself being treated
so negligently by the young gentleman. And though he was deliberately
slow with unpacking, still he was long done when Fred was just starting.
Things always went like that – and Fred never even once noticed.*[14]
The two begin to torture themselves and each other. Georg always
tries to bend the younger one to his will. In the end, Fred comes to
feel that Georg is a burden. Fred, pressurized by Georg, is troubled
and unhappy. *Linguistic barricades* are erected.[15] By way of '*do you
still remember*' they return to the beginning of their friendship and
reconcile themselves to one another.[16] *The bed was narrow, and they
had difficulty avoiding physical contact. … And since they could not
just saw off the offending limbs, they continually touched each other
in spite of everything. A lively chatter that appeared senseless even to
them was meant to lessen the dangerousness of these collisions. But
the warmth of the bed soon dampened the artificially kindled talk.
Words were falling asleep even as they were exchanged, and then the
two kissed. Like once before – .*[17] Fred, however, has become involved
with a girl, Margot, unbeknownst to Georg. Georg also meets with
women, but when Fred *confesses*[18] his love affair to him, Georg is
hurt. He 'freed himself from Fred's clasp, … *It's over for good, everything is over.*[19] But bidding *farewell to Fred* takes a long time.[20] Georg
tried *to prove to Fred how wonderful things were without him.*[21] But the
daemon will continue to plague Georg for some time.

Neither the young Teddie (Wiesengrund) nor the older Teddie
(Adorno) was given a copy of *Georg* to read. In the early 1930s,
much to Teddie's chagrin, Bloch was allowed to read the novel during
its composition whereas he was not. And in the early 1960s, when
Teddie introduced Kracauer to Siegfried Unseld, he was still not
allowed to read it. The novel only appeared after both Adorno and
Kracauer had died. The prince, therefore, could not comment on the
possibilities and realities of their love relationship. In 'The Curious
Realist', he highlighted his friend's suffering, as he had experienced it
when he was still Fred. This suffering, he wrote, ruled over not only
Kracauer's philosophy of homeless life – 'Kracauer's relationship to
truth was that suffering entered into the idea in undistorted, unmiti-
gated form, whereas normally the idea dissipates suffering' – but also
over Kracauer, the man: 'To me Kracauer seemed, although not at
all sentimental, a man with no skin, as though everything external
attacked his defenceless interior, as though he could defend himself
only by giving voice to his vulnerability.' Kracauer disliked this
image of himself. And yet he had written letters to Wiesengrund that
included such passages as the following:

> During these two days I have been feeling such a tormenting love
> for you … I am in a terrible state. I fear so much the transience of
> what is the dearest thing of all to me, what is the meaning or the

consummation of my existence. Do you believe in the everlasting nature of our friendship? ... I tremble with fear it might end because of the fact that you are 19 and I am 34 – you are taking off, you must blaze your way across the world – and at 19 nobody can provide any guarantees for himself – not even you. In short, it is falling apart, and I am left prostrate. ... I am an abyss – as lost as a boy. I shall never be a mature man – I don't know what to do.[22]

That letter was written in April 1923 after Wiesengrund had informed him about his relationship with 'Gretel' – presumably his later wife, Margarete Karplus. One month later, Kracauer's 'Empfindsame Suite von der Bergstraße' [Sentimental suite about the Bergstraße],[23] which the author had hiked with his 'young companion Gianino', appeared in *Frankfurter Zeitung*. 'This was the south, the proper south': it was a miracle that the waiter in the gardens of the hotel did not speak Italian.

We walked off, and the houses, trees, gardens looked at us as we strolled along, without destination, into the uncertain. ... We thought we were in the high mountains, far away in the Dolomites; we thought we were hiking on winding passes, looked out for white mountain tops, listened to the lost sounding of bells. But no peak showed up, no strange sound enchanted us, only the rustling of forests all around and the murmuring from the brooks deep down. ... Gianino turned toward me: this is our moment, he said, and with a sigh anticipated a lot of what was to come.[24]

The peak of sentimentality was reached at this point; a valley of sensitivities was to follow. In Kracauer's passion, happiness and pain lay close to each other. 'I very rarely see my young friend Teddie Wiesengrund', he reported to Susman in January 1920.

He has so much work to do: school, piano, violin, composition and so on. I am very curious to see where all this will lead the young man. He is eminently knowledgeable; in musical theory, for instance, he knows his way around so well that his teacher, Sekles, cannot teach him anything new. He now also reads Einstein; he has put forward the most excellent arguments against Spengler. He says very thoughtful things about Wedekind and Strindberg, and all this at the age of sixteen. I would prefer it, if he fell silent more often and the path from the heart to the tongue were harder for him. Unless severe suffering befalls him, he will hardly become what could become of someone with such qualities.[25]

The same mixture of awe and possessive protectiveness is also clear in a letter to Löwenthal from the end of the same year. 'Teddie', he wrote, has 'a magnificent external existence and his character is of a wonderful naturalness'. Kracauer added that his presence made him happy. Teddie consisted 'for a good part of Lukács and myself', he wrote to Löwenthal, but he lacked 'the philosophical eros, which you possess'. In the young Wiesengrund he saw all too much intellect and will and 'not enough nature'.[26]

There can be no doubt that Kracauer and Wiesengrund spent many happy hours together – at first in their Saturday afternoon 'cave' in Seeheimer Straße, and later elsewhere. Kracauer visited his young friend in Amorbach, Adorno's childhood paradise in the Odenwald.[27] They spent a summer holiday together in Bad Überkingen, Württemberg. Finally, in August 1924, after Wiesengrund had finished his doctoral dissertation, they did travel to the Dolomites, to the white peaks, up to the 'Sella Pass, which affords the most beautiful views of the broad, snow-covered slopes of the Marmolata'.[28]

The 'serenity of the south', however, was infused with a deep sadness, as Kracauer admitted in a piece of travel writing:

> It is neither salvation nor solution; rather, its secret is *melancholy*. The happiness of the beauty of the visible, the charm of sensuality: this Romanesque *serenitas* can only be lived or experienced if the foundation of someone's being is closed and sad. ... One must have renounced and been broken in order to be allowed to linger among phenomena whose tenderness only gives itself fully to the one without hope.[29]

Kracauer and Wiesengrund's relationship involved all the emotions one might expect. But they were not a couple. Rather, the homosexual element was something latent that broke out again and again, almost as a disturbance to their friendship, something one would have preferred to remain silent. In his farewell letter to Teddie, Kracauer called his love a 'sin, a burning sin, partly born of loneliness and suffering the sense of transience'.[30] To Löwenthal he spoke of an 'unnatural passion' which he could only explain on the basis of the assumption 'that I am psychologically [geistig] homosexual after all'.[31] And Wiesengrund reported a Viennese love story to Kracauer in Frankfurt: 'About us and my commitment, she knows what, as a woman, she can know – it is unavoidable, then, that she stubbornly subsumes me under §175.[32,33] This, however, was obviously a misinterpretation. Both friends knew that the other would eventually find a female partner. That was not the issue. The reason for the heaviness in Kracauer's soul was not Margot or Gretel. For him, Teddie, the prodigy, was not human enough, and that meant: he did not suffer enough, was too much of a genius, too ambitious, too successful, too superficial, too egocentric. And too young. As the older one, Kracauer, by contrast, suffered from a peculiar kind of

Figure 15. Dolomites 1924: Siegfried Kracauer, unknown person, and Theodor Wiesengrund
Copyright: DLA Marbach

lovesickness: Teddie would 'always forget the human = the essential over one or the other important matter that is not important'.[34] Kracauer's passion was always there, and slowly his suffering came to dominate their relationship; it certainly did once Wiesengrund went to Vienna in March 1925 in order to study composition with Alban Berg.

Vienna was where the 'great revolution' in music had taken place. But the six months that Wiesengrund spent there were unhappy ones. Arnold Schönberg, the leader of the revolution, did not acknowledge him as he might have hoped, and his other projects failed.[35] The time in Vienna was like a 'desolate dream'.[36] On Soma Morgenstern he made an extremely strange impression (although we should note that Morgenstern was something of a gossip). The 'Jewish boy' from Frankfurt reminded the literary Bohemian 'in his whole demeanour of pious, tender, and awkward Jewish boys from an Eastern Yeshiva. ... And he at once began to recite a poem by Baudelaire, first in French, then in George's translation.' To Morgenstern, Wiesengrund seemed a posturing, annoying, childish show-off, someone who assumed 'that every mortal ... knew exactly what "reified", "objectified" and so on mean', someone who was more 'brain than human being', just like his friend Kracauer. To Morgenstern, the friendship between Wiesengrund and Kracauer was 'an adventure between two brains'.[37]

Nothing could be further from the truth. The intense exchange of letters between Frankfurt and Vienna shows rather how much the suffering that was part of the structure of Kracauer's personality was poisoning their relationship. The pattern ran like this: Kracauer accused the younger one of forgetting and abandoning him. The younger one defended himself by saying that Vienna was hell and that he was sad too. Wiesengrund wrote about himself; Kracauer wrote about Wiesengrund. The dominant tone was thus: he who was not unhappy cuts the common bond of melancholy that ties them together, and thus tears their friendship apart. Both were meant to be unhappy together. Wiesengrund often reassured Kracauer of his friendship, his faithfulness and his longing. He was hungry for kind words from Kracauer. Finally, he reproached him for his silence: 'I have a sense of having been pushed away by you – by *you*, the one person who could support me and will not do so, because he disdains support, even when someone is drowning; and who does not believe one is drowning, but thinks one is swimming away.'[38] Both were tormented by a fear of loss. Kracauer behaved as if the loss had already occurred, and Wiesengrund's emotions, in reaction to this, ran riot. The demons were let loose, and, 'from an instinct for self-preservation', Kracauer had to protect himself against his 'strange feelings' and his 'exaggerations'.[39] The friendship disintegrated. Both froze. Wiesengrund ultimately explained this in terms of his friend's complex affliction, a 'hypertrophy of the psychological component', an 'immoral overpowering pressure on the soul' which burdened the relationship and imposed its shape on external reality.[40] 'Oh Friedel, why does it not work with us, when it should only work with us? Again and again I bump my head against this, as you do as well, only that I bump it against the impossibility of the possible, you against the possibility of the impossible.'[41]

This platonic love – a privileged philosophical-erotic relationship between an older and a younger man, experienced as morally problematic by both of them[42] – sank Kracauer, who was unstable in any case, into a severe depression. He spoke of suicide, of numbing himself with work 'when he has no one', of 'neurasthenia', of being 'orphaned inside', of a 'sad disbelief in the possibility of ultimate, intense human relations that has recently changed and broken my whole being'.[43] Kracauer considered beginning psychoanalytic treatment with Frieda Reichmann in Heidelberg. But the plan came to nothing, and decades later he said that Reichmann refused to take him on as a patient because Kracauer knew too much Freud and was too sceptical towards Freud.[44]

Despite his existential crisis, platonic lovesickness and libidinal homelessness, a flight from reality was not an option for Kracauer. On the contrary, his suffering encouraged him to engage with the world instead of only with his inner sentiments – much like Georg, who, following his separation from Fred, throws himself into social activity, visiting a conference and other gatherings, even if these activities only serve to make his loneliness more obvious to him. Kracauer steadily continued on his path towards the profane, much as one walks 'toward one of these mountains whose contours imperceptibly stand out against the sky'.[45] This movement away from the church and towards the hotel lobby can be traced in articles written in 1924 and 1925. 'To stand amid reality': this became, for Kracauer, the aim against which to measure philosophy and theology, such as Thurneysen's, Barth's and Gogarten's Protestantism, the liturgical movement of Romano Guardini, or Ernst Michels's young Catholic group.[46] This implies paying attention to 'the limits ... that are set to the human mind', that is, to remain within the bounds of profane reality,[47] or 'to take what is conditioned fully into account', even if one strives for the unconditional.[48] It was only logical, then, that in the debate about 'society versus community', he now sided firmly with 'society'. He agreed, for instance, with Helmut Plessner's critique of 'community greed' and 'community fanaticists', and he approvingly paraphrased one of Plessner's theses: 'The *nature of society*, with its distance and its systems of mediation, is a security factor that is indispensable for human dignity.'[49] By the time of Rudolf Steiner's death in April 1925, Kracauer's distance from any religious longing had already grown so great that he thought he could historicize anthroposophy:

> The fruitful moment of the anthroposophical movement falls precisely into the revolutionary years, into those years, that is, during which large segments of the population felt they lacked anything to hold on to in either the earthly or a transcendent world. At the time, it was a foreboding more than an understanding: that the responsibility for the disaster of the war and its outcome lay with the spiritual situation in which people had existed for some time, and which they had allowed to dominate them for too long.

The 'mechanical natural sciences' had taken up residence in matter, the 'illusion' of religious renewal in the clouds – but in between those two regions lay reality, 'the intermediary realm ... in which soul, tragedy and the reflection of reconciliation exist, and which real human beings inhabit by taking it as their abode'. Kracauer had arrived in this realm, which could not really be considered to have any relation to the unconditional, and gradually he began to make himself at home there. The 'demonic formation' that was anthroposophy was thus to be condemned to history: 'Today, after these excited years have given way to a steadier everyday life', Kracauer writes, 'the gap he [Steiner] wanted to close' is still there, 'but the temptation that emanated from him has lost its power',[50] just as the longing for meaning had lost its power over Kracauer, the cultural philosopher.

The *point of no return* was reached when Kracauer went so far as to recommend engaging with Kierkegaard's 'unreal reality' because it was 'present, more real than ever'. In the Higher Education Supplement of the *FZ* of 21 August 1925, he gave the following advice:

> If the bad reality affirms itself powerfully, then one will not be able to avoid engaging with it, talking with it in its own language, or pre-language, if the aim is its liquidation. The economic evils demand an economic perspective and solution; political barbarisms must be dealt with politically. Today's realities may be ever so unreal; they nevertheless exist and continue to proliferate. In order to set effective limits to them, one must seriously focus on them and, fighting them, stay with them. ... Only through disintegration, through a *detour*, can reality be reconquered.[51]

Kracauer now accepted the plurality, relativity and fragmentary nature of reality as a problem of scientific experience. With his idea of rescuing the disintegrated through recollection, he maintained a connection with (Jewish) theological thought. The image of the detour opened up a new field: the critique of society.[52]

8

The Rebirth of Marxism
in Philosophy

In 1923, Georg Lukács's *History and Class Consciousness* was published by the Berlin Marxist publishing house Malik, owned by the Herzfelde brothers. Coming after his *Theory of the Novel*, it was another work by the cultural philosopher that would prove to have a lasting impact. Having reflected on the modern experience of a contingent world and the problematic position of the individual in the context of aesthetics and the arts, Lukács now apparently crossed the threshold into another sphere. The term 'class consciousness' alone betrayed the fact that he had changed his political allegiance – one might even say that he had betrayed his own class.[1] In December 1918, he had, in his own words, converted himself, 'from one Sunday to the next', from an aristocratic aesthete and moralist into a revolutionary Marxist, and following the revolution in Hungary he had become the People's Commissar for Education. From then on, he saw the contemporary destiny of the intelligentsia, and of himself, as lying in politics: 'we cannot continue our lives in castles defended by class privilege' while the 'dispossessed proletariat tirelessly sacrifices itself in order to liberate the mind'.[2] For Lukács – who dropped the aristocratic 'von' from his name – the revolution demanded a turn towards communism. In the preface he paid homage, on the one hand, to Rosa Luxemburg for carrying forward Marx's methods in her factual economic analyses and, on the other, to Lenin for his vigorous determination and his practical Marxism. Lukács's book thus took aim at the 'wait-and-see' Marxism of the Second International, as represented by Karl Kautsky, and also, if implicitly, at the 'scientific socialism' that had begun to take shape as a state doctrine in Soviet Russia. It was considered a problem for Marxists that Marx had left them an economic theory of the capitalist mode of production but no comparable political theory or developed theory of history. His heirs, beginning with Engels and continuing with the next generation – Mehring, Kautsky and Plechanov – had been busy trying to 'systematize historical materialism as a comprehensive theory of man and nature, capable of replacing rival bourgeois disciplines and providing the workers' movement with a broad and coherent vision of the world that could be easily grasped by its militants'.[3] Lukács raised anew the question of what Marxism – or, more precisely, 'orthodox Marxism',[4] that is, true and genuine Marxism, an 'interpretation, an exposition of Marx's theory as Marx understood it' – would actually look like.[5] The term 'orthodoxy' has a theological air, and this is even more evident in Lukács's answer to the question: he claimed that 'in Marx's theory and method the *true method* by which to understand society and history has *finally* been discovered'.[6] The dialectical consideration of the totality 'is the only method capable of under-standing and reproducing reality'.[7] 'Thou shalt have no other gods before me': this first commandment meant the end of the search for knowledge, the overcoming of relativism, the exit from the 'transcendental homelessness' which the author had, only five years earlier, described in a manner that had much impressed Kracauer.[8] The totality – the whole society – was the key to knowledge, and in the social position of the proletariat Lukács had found the position from which this totality of society could become visible. Thus, Lukács presented the proletariat as the identical subject-object of history. It needed only to become aware of its historical role and to act in accordance with its historical destiny in order to redeem mankind. Marx had revealed the secret of this history of salvation. The proletariat had to fulfil its messianic function, and it had to do so under the guidance of the revolutionary intellectuals who were the priests, so to speak, of this awakening. The place of political communism had been taken by 'communism as religion'.[9]

By using the concept of totality and emphasizing consciousness as a decisive historical factor, Lukács referred to Hegel, who had been rediscovered around the turn of the century, and to German idealism, which promised a system that smoothed over all the cracks between subject and object. Despite his epistemological absolutism, Lukács's rehabilitation of Hegel breathed fresh life into an ossified Marxism. One reason for this was that Marxism *as a method* could in principle, of course, be applied to itself to yield fruitful results as long as one pursued a dialectic that did not involve a sublation into some kind of totality. Another reason was that Lukács made Marx relevant as *a thinker* of revolution again. Contrary to the dogma of the Second International, there was no working class without class consciousness – a fact that was obvious from the war.[10] *History and Class Consciousness* finally led to Marxism being admitted into philosophy, and it meant that Marx, in turn, came to be seen as a revolutionary philosopher and not just as the author of *Capital* and the critic of political economy. The critique of political economy and the critique of idealist philosophy belonged together. And the philo-sophical core of Marx's theory was the emancipation of the worker.[11]

Young Marxist intellectuals were fascinated by Lukács's work and excited at the prospect of simultaneously being philosophically educated, artistically ambitious, firm in one's view of the world and politically radical. But Lukács's appeal was broader than the Marxist intelligentsia: his book stirred the whole Marxist and communist world. Of course, the old orthodoxy, quiescent and resting on Engels and Kautsky, did not like this new orthodoxy. There began a genuine 'Lukács debate', which in the end reached as far as Moscow, the new capital of communism. The mood there neither favoured the West nor philosophy; the pressing task was rather to fight civil war and hunger. In any case, Lukács's text seemed to be an example of what Lenin had called 'left radicalism' and described as a 'childhood disease of communism'.[12] The leader of the revolution was not the least interested in this 'Marxism of mere words'.[13] In addition, the book's publication coincided with the turn towards Bolshevism during the Third International, between 1923 and 1926, and the book was crushed under the weight of the party's power. Lukács found himself standing accused and, ultimately, submitted to the discipline of the Comintern.[14]

How did Benjamin, Bloch, Kracauer and Wiesengrund read Lukács's book? Except for Bloch, none of them had yet explicitly engaged with Marx, but they had confronted the fundamentally apocalyptic and utopian mood that arose out of the inferno of war and the electrifying revolution in Russia and the eastern parts of central Europe. The personal circumstances here are interesting: Bloch had once been a close friend of Lukács, but during the war they had lost touch; Benjamin had been a friend of Bloch's since his exile in Switzerland, and while he was impressed, from afar, with Lukács's aesthetics (without knowing Lukács personally), he was not particularly impressed by Bloch's Marxism; Kracauer, who had only just got to know Benjamin and had fallen out with Bloch, was under the spell of Lukács's phrase 'transcendental homelessness', but in 1923 he was still resisting the theory of class struggle and the materialist understanding of history;[15] and Wiesengrund, who had become familiar with Lukács's work through Kracauer, was now slowly making himself independent of his teacher and, in 1925, had the opportunity to meet the great Lukács in person in Vienna.

Walter Benjamin read *History and Class Consciousness* – after a brief delay – in May 1925, but he had already engaged intensely with the book during his time on Capri, after having read a long review by Ernst Bloch.[16] The year 1924 had been a kind of transitional period for Benjamin. He opened up to the 'problem of present-day communism'[17] while working on his book on German tragic drama (a book that would mark the distance between him and the bourgeois academic world). He met Asja Lacis, a Russian revolutionary from Riga, and fell deeply in love with her; following his conversations with her, he began to flirt with a communist ideal that went beyond the politics of the KPD, the communist party of which his brother Georg was a member. Lukács's book gave Benjamin the idea of a 'materialist aesthetics' in which Marx's dialectic would play the decisive heuristic role. Benjamin decided to rethink everything he had produced so far in the light of *History and Class Consciousness*. This, incidentally, did not lead him to reject his earlier aesthetic and theological models of history; rather, it led to a new hierarchy among the constitutive elements of his historical thinking.[18] For Benjamin, who, much like Kracauer, was tormented by the spectre of epistemological aporias, Lukács's dialectical method and his concept of 'totality' must have held out a promise of coherence that at least demanded consideration, even if, as in Gershom Scholem's judgement, 'communism in its Marxist form was the precise opposite to the anarchist convictions in which Benjamin and I politically had so far been in agreement'.[19] Benjamin's friend in Jerusalem was concerned about the 'communist signals' from Capri.[20]

Again, Benjamin came across Lukács's book through Bloch's review, which he admired very much: 'The review seems to be by far the best thing he has done in a long time and the book itself is very important, especially for me.'[21] Bloch's review of *History and Class Consciousness* appeared in *Der Neue Merkur* in 1923. It seems he saw the book as bringing his own *Spirit of Utopia* up to date for a period in which revolution was no longer on the agenda in the West. According to Bloch, Lukács had recognized this great *kairos* and had 'elevated the moment of decision and comprehension into totality', thus 'leading Marx back to Hegel again, and Hegel significantly and forcefully beyond himself'. Bloch praised the depth of Lukács's understanding of the crisis: it sees the whole capitalist economy, commodity production and circulation as separate and independent of the human being, while also being artificially rationalized and broken down into detailed individual operations. The structure of the commodity relation is the prototype for all objective forms – in particular of the intellectual forms – of bourgeois society. Abstract, quantitative thought, corresponding to exchange value, becomes the universal category of the modern world. The world of capitalism is therefore unreal, and scientific knowledge is unable to penetrate reality. But now it seemed as if a way of accessing reality, the totality of life, and of sublating the schism between subject and object had finally been found. Hegel's concept of totality provided an understanding of history in which the opposites are given a 'foundation in being' and can be dialectically sublated – as long, that is, as an identical subject-object can be discovered and theory and practice connected with each other. Lukács's construction, Bloch wrote, has nothing to do with the actual, empirical proletariat. Yet he saw the seventh day of creation approaching:

The sublation of the proletariat is the realization of philosophy, and the sublation of philosophy is the realization of the proletariat; in other words: the (sublated) proletariat is the true 'we' of history, and its material is at the same time the identical subject-object of history which finally comes to itself. ... Under these signs, and under no other signs, will the proletariat be victorious, the prehistory of mankind end and existence finally become real.[22]

Lukács must have appeared to Bloch like John the Baptist.

How did Kracauer react to Lukács's metaphysical materialism? His personal copy of the book contains a great deal of underlining but only cautious comments, suggesting a first reading that was respectful, open and driven by expectation. He stressed the importance of the 'rescue of Hegel', and he judged the dialectical method – whose central problem was '*to change reality*'[23] – to be 'interesting for [his] theory of the spheres'. Kracauer also noted Lukács's description of Simmel's *Philosophy of Money* as a superficial account of reification. But what is particularly striking is that apart from Lukács's design for a philosophy of history, Kracauer also pays attention to Marx, who is frequently quoted in the text. In the essay on reification, in particular – which would become the most influential of the book – Kracauer mostly underlined passages from Marx on the commodity form, which had become the general form of domination in society. Kracauer's first intense engagement with Marx's writings thus most likely took place through his reading of *History and Class Consciousness*, and he would only embark upon his own independent 'Marx studies' in the spring of 1926.[24] But despite the novelty of discovering Marx, the underlining in the book suggests that the intensity of his reading ebbed away significantly. Lukács's Marxism was not to be the key that opens up the truth, nor did it promise a path towards reality.

It must have been particularly disappointing for Kracauer that his erstwhile idol had, with the stroke of a pen, declared the matter of 'transcendental homelessness' obsolete. That amounted to a Kierkegaardian leap. Struggling, himself, with the Christian existential philosopher in his book on the detective novel – his 'allegorical portrait of negativity' – he wrote to Löwenthal at the end of 1924: 'But if you are standing at a limit, you can no longer go back ... Lukács did it.'[25] And in April 1925, he wrote to Wiesengrund in Vienna: 'If you would like to join Lukács, the reality of his irreality is imprisonment in jelly.'[26] Finally, in letters to Bloch dating from May and June 1926, when the two were rekindling their relationship, and after he had read Marx in the original, Kracauer formulated a clear rejection: 'His [Lukács's] concept of totality, suffering under his own formality, has more similarity with [Emil] Lask than with Marx. Instead of filling Marxism with realities he feeds it with the spirit and metaphysics of a drained-out idealism, and in addition drops, along the way, the materialist categories which would have needed to have been interpreted.' Philosophically, he says, Lukács is a reactionary who, in his use of Hegel, obscures the real source of Marx's fundamental concepts. Kracauer thought that Hegel's formal dialectics sealed Lukács's idealist fate: 'The decisive categories of Marxism, for instance his concept of "man" or of "morality", can only be understood if one [digs] a tunnel, so to speak, underneath Hegel, reaching from Marx to e.g. Helvetius', that is, to the early French enlightenment. Kracauer saw his understanding of Lukács as a 'Bruno Bauer redivivus' as confirmed by 'conversations [his] friend Wiesengrund had with him [i.e. Lukács]'.[27]

On 17 June 1925, Wiesengrund reported 'a sensation': 'Morgenstern called me and invited me to see Lukács, whom he knows through [the theoretician of film Béla] Balázs, a terrible Hungarian literatus. On Sunday, all by myself, I was out there in Hütteldorf, Istarygasse 12, where he lives in a pointedly humble room on the ground floor. My first impression was great and deep: a short, tender, clumsy, blond Eastern Jew with a Talmudic nose and wonderfully unfathomable eyes ...'. Lukács had seemed unprepossessing to Adorno, and aloof. Thus, their three-hour meeting had been more of an interview than a conversation:

> He first thoroughly disavowed the theory of the novel; it was 'idealist and mythological'. Then contrasted it with the 'substantialization' of history by Marx's dialectic. To my objection that this was also idealism (a point he did not quite get), he replied that 1) the object was 'taken along' precisely by the dialectic 'and produced in its in-and-for-itself' (something I shall never comprehend) and that 2) only in the 'classless society' would true nature be revealed.

Wiesengrund said that Lukács's dialectical madness was so complete that he had declared that, in his conflict with the Third International, his opponents were in the right.[28] This could only be a source of shock and anger to enemies of idealism and of Hegel's systematic thinking like Kracauer and Wiesengrund. For Kracauer, Lukács's dialectical materialism was 'so objectivist ... that it looks like an inverse neo-Kantianism'.[29]

Paradoxically, then, while *History and Class Consciousness* attempted to escape the impositions of a contingent modernity, to take refuge in idealistically and theologically charged constructions and in an absolute knowledge provided by a new Marxist orthodoxy, its rediscovery of the dialectical method stimulated an enormously productive period of literary activity in the second half of the 1920s, especially among cultural philosophers such as Bloch, Benjamin and Kracauer and, along with them, Wiesengrund.

Lukács's thesis of reification became the foundation of an ideology critique which did not simply evaluate intellectual and cultural products as either progressive or reactionary but instead connected them to the commodity form and unmasked them as necessarily false consciousness. This contradiction between systematic closure and dialectical-materialist creativity characterized Marxist cultural criticism generally, and it was Lukács's book that established it.

9

Kracauer Goes to the Movies: A Medium for the Masses and a Medium for Modernity

I was still a young boy when I saw my first film. The impression it made upon me must have been intoxicating, for I there and then determined to commit my experience to writing. To the best of my recollection, this was my earliest literary project. ... *Film as the Discoverer of the Marvels of Everyday Life*, the title read. ... What thrilled me so deeply was an ordinary suburban street, filled with lights and shadows which transfigured it. Several trees stood about, and there was in the foreground a puddle reflecting invisible house facades and a piece of the sky. Then a breeze moved the shadows, and the facades with the sky below began to waver. The trembling upper world in the dirty puddle – this image has never left me.[1]

We do not know in which year, in which place and under which technical conditions the young Friedel saw this, his first film. As this experience of film inspired his first literary project, it presumably was before 1906, when his first article appeared in the *Frankfurter Zeitung*, but most likely it was much earlier still. The first screenings of films in Germany took place in 1895 in the 'Wintergarten' in Berlin. The same year, the first 'living photography' could be admired in a kinetoscope exhibition in Kaiserstraße 7, Frankfurt (a year later, the first public screening took place in the 'Orpheum' at the Konstablerwache).[2] It was also in 1895 that, in Vienna, Sigmund Freud dared to undertake his first analysis of a dream. The invention of film thus coincided with the emergence of psychoanalysis, just as the discovery of the detective novel coincided with the emergence of sociology. And all of these developments were born of the modern life that began to affirm itself around 1900. There were obvious affinities between them; there were interactions and resonances which, however, remained blurred, like the sky reflected in shimmering water. Later, Kracauer would call films 'daydreams of society' and try his hand at being an interpreter of dreams. Film history and social history both speak with one voice here: film is the defining medium of modernity.[3]

Indeed, film and cinema represented a leap in the history of the media, on a par with the invention of the printing press by Johannes Gutenberg in the fifteenth century or of the internet at the end of the twentieth century. From 1900 onwards, the electronic media – first film, which was electrified in the 1910s, then from 1923 radio, and later television – took their place next to the printing media of the book, newspapers and journals, whose dominance they increasingly broke down. Thus, around 1920, the cinema was the 'most modern' medium in both the colloquial and the technical sense. And it was an urban phenomenon; its environment was the big city. As early as 1910, half of the population of the German Reich lived in urban areas, communities, that is, of at least 5,000 inhabitants. And a fifth was living in major cities of more than 100,000. Berlin had a population of 2 million. The rapid urbanization was set to continue in the 1920s.[4] The rise of film was continuous, and neither the war nor the revolution had any impact on its popularity: 'The interest in the erotic and exotic, taboos and crimes transcended politics.'[5] Yet politics also helped to create a booming film industry. The Ufa[6] was a state-born child of the war, founded by the secret dictator Erich Ludendorff and created as a means of opposing the superior Allied propaganda.[7] Nevertheless, to begin with, a relatively diverse market developed alongside this colossal corporation.[8] In 1919, 200 German film companies produced 500 films, and there were 3,000 cinemas welcoming a million visitors every day. Their doors opened in the morning, and tickets were cheap. In 1921, in Berlin alone there were 418 cinemas with 148,000 seats; by 1932, that number had risen to 189,000 (in fewer, but bigger, venues). Helped by inflation and import restrictions on foreign films, the sector had risen quickly to become the third largest branch of German industry, measured in terms of investment and unionized labour force. The year 1926 broke a record; an incredible 646 films were made. In the mid-1920s up to two million people went to the cinema every day. Berlin, which had grown to over four and a half million inhabitants, was responsible for a sixth of this figure.[9] Around 1930, there were 5,000 cinemas in Germany. Before the great economic crisis, the film industry provided work for 45,000 employees, and more films were produced in Germany than in all other European countries taken together.[10]

Film and cinema were modern not so much because they were the latest form of amusement, but because they were associated with the rise of the so-called mass culture. Film was a cultural commodity that was technically and industrially produced, and it aimed at a substantially larger audience than just the old aristocracy and educated bourgeoisie – social strata which found its entertainments in the museum, opera and theatre.[11] In contemporary parlance, the term 'mass culture', however, did not just refer to technically reproducible and affordable culture for the masses. The 'mass' was an iridescent concept which – from the sober and analytical perspective of social and political history – captured those without social status or property, those who, following the collapse of the old, pre-bourgeois forms of integration and socialization, were left without a fixed place within bourgeois society. From the perspective of the history of civilization, the mass stood for those raw and dangerous passions that were tamed and disciplined and thus excluded from the realm of civilization, or, as Freud called it, culture:[12] 'the whole sum of the achievements ... which distinguish our lives from those of our animal ancestors and which serve two purposes – namely to protect man against nature and to adjust their mutual relations'.[13] The bourgeois society of the propertied and educated, those who wanted to live in a society of free and mature individuals, was at the same time obsessed by a fear of a rebellion of those without property and of an outbreak of passions.[14] The term 'mass' was therefore often used in a pejorative sense. Those talking about the rise of mass culture often at the same time furrowed their brows and were worried about a possible decline of cultural and moral standards. Mass culture meant trash, and trash was a combination of lower instincts and the capitalist striving after profit. For Wilhelm Stapel, the 'gifted sniffer of Jews' (according to Kracauer), the cinema was almost as big a problem for the German people as the Jews were:

> Under the influence of cinema, a new psychic type is growing among the people. A human type who only flutteringly 'thinks' in rough, elementary ideas ... which no longer has the capability to make clear and convincing judgments. A human type, which during the revolution has acted disastrously enough, and which, the more generations are shaped by the cinema and its soul-corrupting apparatus, will grow and make its mark on culture (as well as on political culture). The cinema is constructing a new, spiritually and morally inferior human type: homo cinematicus.[15]

Only a few intellectuals, many of them sympathetic to socialism, saw 'culture for all' as promising a democratic cultural revolution, a liberation from the bourgeois rule over culture by way of a proletarian appropriation of it, and thus as a complement to mass democracy. Only towards the end of the 1920s did the founding of a Volksfilmverband [People's film association] and the first popular journals mark the beginning of political film initiatives by the labour movement.[16] But even in the eyes of this 'progressive' intelligentsia, popular culture that transcended class and social status was seen as a potential hindrance to the achievement of the necessary class consciousness. The old resentment of the educated bourgeoisie against cheap entertainment could also be found among social democrats: whether mass culture was – or at least had the potential to be – progressive was a question that only arose during the time of the Weimar Republic.[17]

Film was in the truest sense a 'medium of modernity' insofar as it conveyed the process of modernity's emergence. Georg Simmel had already highlighted the new forms of perception and urban life in his famous essay on 'The Metropolis and Mental Life': the 'uninterrupted change of outer and inner stimuli', the 'intensification of nervous stimulation', the quick compression of changing images.[18] Life in a metropolis was as fast as the moving pictures on the screen; the city dweller was a spectator. On buses and trams people sat for long minutes opposite each other without speaking to one another. That was a deeply unusual and disturbing experience. The relations between city dwellers were generally characterized 'by a pronounced preponderance of the activities of the eye over those of the ear'.[19] Walter Benjamin later took up this observation when he spoke of the 'daily shocks and conflicts of civilization'.[20] Of course, film is also characterized by the primacy of the visual, and it also introduces a novel form of mediated perception of reality. The reproduction of movement, the illusion of reality and the visual representation of the world amounted to a revolution in the forms of perception at the anthropological level, and a mediatization of culture at the sociological level – we need only remind ourselves of the terror caused by the Lumière brothers' locomotive rushing full steam ahead towards the audience.[21] The combination of advanced technology and magical experience was altogether uncanny, as Ernst Bloch remarked. 'Much of what the old fairy tales promised has been achieved by the latest technology: radio is able to fetch voices from afar, and television – which resulted from the application of the soberest scientific principles – comes close to embodying the concept of a magic mirror.'[22] A visit to the cinema was like a spiritualist séance, and film was a 'medium' of forces that could not be immediately seen, heard or felt. In that sense, Simmel's text might just as well have been called 'The metropolis and the life of ghosts'.[23] The rush of images provided ghost stories for adults. At the same time, as the literary journalist and radio announcer Gerhart Pohl put it, film was 'the vital power station of the city dweller', a place for recreation, distraction, amusement: a 'dream factory'.[24] The film reel was like a material realization of the modern individual's urge for excitement, suspense and fantasy, allowing people to forget the greyness of everyday life and to ward off boredom. Film was thus the centre of the mass and media culture that was beginning to affirm itself; it was the focal point of fear and a catalyst for a new regime of perception, and it was the spearhead of a developing culture industry that integrated the experience of contingency in modern life.

Along with the rise of film developed the reflection on film. Once the medium had successfully moved from travelling shows and funfairs into the cinemas, film reviews and film aesthetics emerged. Film journalism underwent a rapid development. The first specialist journal for film, *Der Kinematograph*, was founded in 1905. From 1912 onwards, journals such as *Bild und Film* [Photography and Film] published quality reviews, and by 1930 there were no fewer than 160 film journals in Germany. There were even three daily film papers. (Today, Wikipedia lists thirty-eight film journals.) In the culture sections of the large bourgeois newspapers, films that previously had only been announced as ads in the local section were now given reviews. After the Great War, reviews became a regular feature. Cultural journals provided spaces for literary authors to describe the new medium, its products and its audience. As early as 1909, Alfred Döblin, for example, defended 'Schaulust', the love and curiosity of watching, and he defended the cinematograph as 'the theatre of the ordinary people'. Four years later, the self-confessed 'admirer of the cinema' Kurt Pinthus compared the possibilities of cinema with those of the theatre. Herbert Jhering observed the mutual inspiration of expressionism and film, and Willy Haas discussed the great question that occupied everyone: whether film had the potential to be an art form.[25] Sociologists discovered the cinema – for instance Emilie Altenloh in her path-breaking study *Zur Soziologie des Kinos* (1913) [On the sociology of the cinema]. Early reflections on the theory of film concentrated on what happens *in front* of the camera, on the actors and their gestures and facial expressions.[26] In 1923, the Reichsverband der Deutschen Presse, the national press association of Germany, formulated guidelines for film journalism, a sure sign that the profession was now being taken seriously.[27]

Standing on the shoulders of this body of pioneering work, Béla Balázs's *Early Film Theory: Visible Man and the Spirit of Film* appeared in 1924: 'a comprehensive, consistent and complete aesthetic theory of the silent movie, based on rich material evidence', which already took into account the camera as an artistic means.[28] Its author was the literary writer who had introduced Wiesengrund to Lukács in Vienna, a comrade who, like Lukács, had fled to Austria following the Hungarian counter-revolution. After his arrival, he began to write screenplays, and from 1922 he was in charge of film reviews in the Viennese newspaper *Der Tag*. His book on the culture of film was a quest for it to be admitted into high culture: 'film is a new art and is as different from every other as music is different from painting and painting from literature. Film is a fundamentally new revelation of humanity.'[29] Just as the word took centre stage following the invention of the printing press, now 'visual culture' had returned.[30] It arises, he wrote, 'from our yearning for the embodied human being who has fallen silent, who has been forgotten and has become invisible'.[31] Film is a new art form: 'Not culture in the sense of the beautiful poses of statues in art galleries, but the gait and the everyday gestures of people in the street or at their work'[32] – the culture, that is, of the real human being, the social being, life. Film thus works against 'reification' by corresponding to 'the yearning for the concrete, non-conceptual, immediate experience of things'.[33] In addition, '[i]n the imagination and the emotional life of the urban population film has taken over the role formerly assumed by myth, legend and folk tales'.[34] According to Balázs, film has a social significance as well as an aesthetic dimension that distinguishes it from other art forms. These two fundamental insights – that there is a sociology of film and an aesthetics of film – the film critic Siegfried Kracauer took on board.

Kracauer wrote his first film reviews in 1921, but only from July 1923 did he write regularly about film in the *Frankfurter Zeitung*. In 1923, he published twenty articles, the annual figure rising to forty-five in 1924, fifty-five in 1925, and finally sixty-eight in 1926. He thus attended roughly one screening per week, events which consisted of the showing of the main film plus one or two short films or a vaudeville and music performance. (From 1927 onwards, his cinema attendance increased significantly.) His early film criticism exhibited a restrained tone, in stark contrast to, for instance, Joseph Roth, who, between March 1919 and April 1920, wrote on films, film-makers and cinema audiences in his very own trenchant style for various outlets in Vienna. From 1923, Roth became a collaborator at the *FZ* feuilleton and joined forces with Benno Reifenberg and Siegfried Kracauer. In his first reviews, Kracauer still allowed himself to be impressed by films he would later attack: by the historical film *Danton* (1921; director: Dimitri Buchowetzki), for instance, which, after his escape from Germany, he would come to see as anti-revolutionary and anti-democratic; and by the mountain films of Arnold Fanck, which in retrospect he considered anti-rationalistic because of their worship of nature. He also still reported very seriously and soberly, that is, without any of the pointed remarks that would later become his trademark, on the efforts of the Rhein-Main Verband für Volksbildung [Rhein-Main association for people's education] to use film for educational purposes and to fight against 'trashy films'.[35] By contrast, Roth was, during his time in Vienna, already raging against the 'schoolmasters and preachers of virtue' who mistook cinema for a 'moral institution'. The audience, he argued, should not be instructed or improved, but enlightened: 'And this with the means of film alone, which neither sweetens nor persecutes life, but merely represents it faithfully in a halfway artistic manner. Only once film contains nothing but *those* tendencies shown by life itself will the goal be reached, the goal that the so-called "Tendenzfilm" can only fail to reach.'[36] The task of film was 'to uncover what is hidden, to unveil secrets, to present the invisible', and 'to improve moral life through laughter'.[37] Another peculiar feature of Roth's writing on film was that he not only looked at the screen but also observed the audience.[38] He would insert surprising remarks which called into question the commercial aspects of film. For instance, in the midst of a discussion of dockworkers in Marseille watching a film showing robbers from the Abruzzo, he suddenly asks 'whether the robbers in the Abruzzo visit a cinema that shows the sea lions of Marseille ... That is what the film industry lives on.'[39]

According to Roth, in order to realize its aesthetic possibilities, film should pursue its tendency towards reality. This view corresponded fully with Kracauer's conviction. During those years, he was particularly impressed by two films: Karl Grune's *Die Straße* (1923) [English: *The Street*] and *Der letzte Mann* (1924) [English: *The Last Laugh*], directed by Friedrich Wilhelm Murnau, based on a screenplay by Carl Mayer. The street, we remember, had been the living space of little Friedel, and now it appeared to many of his contemporaries as a place of existential importance in modernity, as the place of the ephemeral. There, on the asphalt of great cities, the anonymous mass swirled around; there, chance ruled and the human being was subjected to processes that could not be surveyed. There, adventures were beckoning and dangers were lurking. Street films therefore were less concerned with the street as a social space, and more with the hopes, fears and dreams associated with that space. In the beginning, criminals and prostitutes held the monopoly on the streets; only once the film-makers left their studios and shot their scenes in real streets did children and old people, workers and housewives, enter into the frame.[40] Grune's *The Street*, the '*Story of a Night*', presented one such petit bourgeois fantasy, crowded with erotic promises and other sensual pleasures, a fantasy, however, that was ultimately punished, with the man returning home, full of remorse, to wife, home and hearth. Some people saw in this film a self-reflection on cinema: the magic of the street was nothing but the magic of film itself, the play of light and shadow depicting pulsating life.[41] To Kracauer, however, the street in the film rather seemed to resemble the hotel lobby he had analysed in his book on the detective novel: a space in which modern man waits, gradually forgetting what he is waiting for:

The *big city street* is a characteristic scenery for such illusory life. People cross it at random, rub against each other and disappear without greeting each other. No meeting of souls takes place, no meaningful, lasting connection ... nothing but figures bumping into each other, events taking place, and situations blindly following situations; all that without continuity or consequence, a ghostly, unreal togetherness of unreal people, which is incapable of filling the empty flow of time. An individual human who is set into this fragmented world, and who is self-aware, is nothing but alone in it.

The chaotic confusion of frenzied life, the 'hullabaloo of reified souls and pseudo-wake things', the 'hustle of larvae without existence': all this was an expression of what Kracauer identified, using Lukács's terminology, as the transcendental homelessness of modern man. And what would be better suited to representing the surface of this silent world than film?[42] Two years later, after the shift in his thinking towards the profane, Kracauer wrote again about Grune's street film, this time from the perspective of his spheres theory. The people on big city streets, he said, have no relation with what is above; they are merely an outside of the same kind as the street itself. There is an open gap between the film image and prophetic speech, an undeveloped middle ground, an empty intermediary realm. And yet, for Kracauer, the path to the heavenly kingdom – if it exists – can only be found in the big city streets, namely via the 'revelation of the negative', via 'nihilism for the sake of the potentially positive', in short via the critique of the unreal real for the sake of the real:

> People who take reality seriously, in particular, may feel all the more strongly the powers that are today remoulding [entformen] the world as a big city street.[43] And as they feel no less certain that only by taking up and transforming unreal life can reality come about ..., they strictly refuse to take part in romantic attempts at covering up the reality of technology and the economy and at preventing the process of civilization from unfolding with means that are not up to the magnitude of that process.[44]

Unlike theatre, the Torah or theosophy, film is a medium that conforms to this insight. An awake and yearning dreamer may see more in this lost reality than prophets and philosophers have access to.

Murnau's *The Last Laugh* plays exclusively in the here and now. The film tells the story of an aged hotel porter who is replaced with a younger man and demoted to the position of lavatory attendant by a ruthless manager. The last thing he can cling on to is his old Wilhelminian-style uniform, which, hiding his fate, he continues to wear at home, until his charade is discovered and he becomes the laughing stock of the poor people living in his block of flats. But there is an epilogue to this story of social decline which, as Kracauer wrote in his review, 'restores the justice that has been violated, a fairy tale epilogue that is so incredible that all one can do is believe it. It rests on a coincidence, one, however, in which there is more providence than in the accidental sequences of reality.'[45] The expelled porter inherits a large fortune from one of the customers who frequents the toilet, and he becomes a benefactor who gives generously to members of the lower social classes – and all this takes place not, of course, without an ironic intertitle informing the audience that, out of sympathy with the porter (that is, with the audience's need for a happy ending), it would be impossible to let the film end in the toilets. Kracauer praised such social irony. But he was even more impressed by the film as an artistic achievement. Emil Jannings played the last man with an almost unmoving face, his body frozen in theatrical gestures. The camera of Karl Freund was permanently moving around him – an innovation in film history that later came to be dubbed the 'unfettered camera'. The film had been made by a group of film-obsessed and experimentally minded pioneers who, for a short time around 1925, transformed the Ufa studios into a 'builder's hut of daring dreams and aesthetic utopias'.[46] Possibly the most famous among them, Carl Mayer, had thought of a plot that, in Kracauer's judgement, 'does not need first to be translated into the optical medium but is born out of it'.[47] Joseph Roth also commented on this aspect, saying 'Carl Mayer … translates the subject matter from the material, earthly, and accidental level of "existence" and the "event" onto the metaphysical, unique, valid, and necessary atmosphere'.[48] Like Kracauer in the case of street films, Roth saw *The Last Laugh* as an attempt to ask questions regarding the last things. Kracauer also assigned a metaphysical task to film, namely 'to render ironic the illusory nature of our life by exaggerating its unreality, and thus to point toward true reality'.[49] He praised *Der verlorene Schuh* [*The Lost Shoe*] (1923, directed by Ludwig Berger) for not giving a realist interpretation of the fairy tale, 'but rather, vice versa, integrating the real into the realm of the fairy tale'.[50] Kracauer did not in all cases condemn kitsch. 'As they have to entertain, their only duty is to entertain', he wrote around the same time about novels, 'and kitsch certainly is aesthetically justified as long as it serves this commitment'. The educated condemned kitsch because they used a standard that was not his, he wrote. Kracauer only rejected 'pretentious kitsch', that is, kitsch that claimed 'to represent psychological and moral reality'. And he also rejected boring novels and films.[51]

10

At the Feuilleton of the *Frankfurter Zeitung*

Kracauer's articles on film helped him to establish himself more firmly at the *Frankfurter Zeitung*. From the mid-1920s onwards he was a freelance collaborator, and in August 1921 he became an employee with his own office and a fixed annual salary. From 1924, he was in charge of the film section, and in November of the same year, Benno Reifenberg, the new chief of the feuilleton, appointed him as a full editor. From 1926 onwards, he was occasionally in charge of the literature section. Until his move to Berlin in the spring of 1930, his reputation at the newspaper and in the world of journalism at large grew continually.[1]

Kracauer spent his working day at the paper's offices in Große Eschenheimer Straße 31 (at the time of the paper's founding still Eschenheimer Gasse). The building was a 'labyrinth of corridors, pathways, and stairs' in which it was easy to get lost, a 'confusing foxhole', as the journalist and author Hans Bütow called it,

> all in all a tremendously lovable because, so to speak, humane piece of architecture that always kept the character of something accidental and improvised. The entrance, though, presented itself in grand bourgeois fashion, with marble and columns in turn-of-the-century style; the building was also fairly narrow. The lift was timidly hidden in a corner and anyhow usually did not work. The strictly separated editorial offices for economics and politics were lined up to the left and right of long corridors, one room next to another, in which the editors were housed as in a cloister, alone or in pairs, and whoever had the large letter 'L' hanging on his door was working on the lead editorial. Somewhere in the building's lower regions, the feuilleton had its physically remote existence.[2]

The 'firm', as Kracauer called the newspaper, thus externally presented itself in grand bourgeois style and as open to the world, if internally a little bit chaotic and sometimes even provincial and narrow. In this foxhole, the smell of labour and strife was in the air, but the paper that began in Eschenheimer Gasse had become a major publication reaching all of the German public.

The working day began at 8 o'clock in the morning with a conference to prepare the editions for that day, of which there were always three: one in the morning, one at midday and one in the evening. The feuilleton usually only sent one or two representatives to this men-only assembly, headed by the publisher Heinrich Simon as first among equals. It is unlikely that Kracauer attended these meetings frequently, given his speech difficulties and the sheer amount of writing he had to do. He probably sat in his 'monastery cell' from early in the morning, especially given that he would, as a rule, be visiting the cinema in the course of the day. According to Count Erik Wickenburg, who was Reifenberg's assistant from 1928 onwards, Kracauer sat 'mostly in his room, writing diligently, and doing his editorial work' for five or six hours every day, before pursuing his literary and cinematographic interests. He was an outsider, Wickenburg says, a bit inaccessible, but 'enormously agreeable and nice' once one got to know him. Wickenburg judged Kracauer's editorial work 'magnificent'.[3] Joseph Roth, who between 1923 and 1925 was a correspondent in the Berlin office of the *Frankfurter Zeitung* and later did a short stint at the offices in Große Eschenheimer Straße, reached a similar judgement on the unassuming editor in Frankfurt:

> Dr Kracauer is a poor wretch. Only once every ten years he can do what he wants, and is allowed to visit Berlin for a week or just a weekend, but unfortunately, very unfortunately – on account of his speech impediment and his un-European face – he's never allowed to represent the paper in the outside world. He has a clever and ironical mind, with no imagination, but in spite of all his awareness he remains, in a likeable way, naïve.

The advice Roth gave to his successor in Berlin, Bernhard von Brentano, in the same letter, was: 'Help him to the best of your ability, take him under your wing, and you'll be able to learn a lot from him. I myself am always learning from him, I just muster the patience to wait for half an hour while he stammers out his pearls of wisdom. It is worth it every time.'[4]

Roth, the young and very left-wing Brentano and Kracauer himself were all working for Reifenberg. So too was the George admirer and Francophile Friedrich Sieburg, who, towards the end of the decade, got close to the *Tat* circle[5] and later became a Nazi supporter.[6] Benno Reifenberg was three years older than Kracauer and grew up in a wealthier area of Frankfurt, around the Anlagenring, where Friedel's father, who was jealous of those who were better off and lived there, would bring him on Sunday walks.

In 1924, Reifenberg took over the leadership from Rudolf Geck, who had been a preserver of the old feuilleton, which catered to the requirements of the educated bourgeoisie. In the eyes of the younger collaborators, Geck was too conciliatory, too gentle and too accepting, yet they respected him and he continued to work at the paper as an editor.[7] The traditionalists were not pushed out, nor did they fight against the new direction pursued by Reifenberg. Within this arrangement Kracauer was part of the 'full-time regular staff' in Frankfurt, next to his 'leader' Reifenberg, Geck and the theatre critic Diebold. Reifenberg was the 'soul of the editorial team'.[8]

The personnel change took place at a time when the *Frankfurter Zeitung* was, for the first time in its existence, in financial trouble. During the early post-war years, its circulation declined drastically. In 1917, the figure had been a record 170,000; in 1918, this had reduced to 110,000, and from then on there was a steady decline until, in 1923, circulation had halved. The decline in advertisements was even worse, and this source of income was more important for a daily newspaper than the number of copies sold, especially in the case of a paper that aimed to be the preferred choice in the worlds of business and finance. In 1919, the *Frankfurter Zeitung* sold 2,788 pages worth of advertisements. In 1923, the year of inflation, there was a dramatic drop to just 1,032 pages. After that, there was a slight upturn again, but the number of pages of advertisements sold to business customers per year never exceeded 1,500.

Figure 16. Benno Reifenberg, 1913
Copyright: DLA Marbach

Figure 17. Joseph Roth, 1925
Copyright: GRANGER

As the production costs for three daily editions were significant, the losses mounted, not least because of the rising demand for quality content: apart from literature, there were ever more supplements on technology and higher education, for young people and for women, on travel and spas, on sport and local news. At the end of 1925, the publishing house had to ask for a loan for the first time, and by 1926 the deficit amounted to half a million marks. From then on, their annual losses stayed in that region until, at the beginning of 1928, the debt exceeded one million marks, before climbing to 1.75 million at the end of the year. The paper was facing immediate bankruptcy.[9]

The rise of film in the 1920s marked a fundamental structural transformation of the media landscape. The Weimar decade was a distinctive period within the 'axial age of mass media' in Germany.[10] On the one hand, there was the advance of images. Illustrated papers, in particular, experienced an enormous upsurge and entered into direct competition with newspapers. They catered for the needs of the masses more directly, continuously and quickly than the newspapers with their articles, set in leaden types, that made such demands on the reader's time and leisure. On the other hand, there was the invention of the radio, a technology that conquered a space in the everyday life of the people alongside, but still at the expense of, newspapers. The wireless was also a direct competitor of the serious daily press because in its early days it was conceived less as a medium for entertainment and more as a 'cultural factor' (as the promoter of the wireless and state secretary in the Reich's postal ministry, Horst Bredow, put it) in the education of the people. It also attracted a part of the literary intelligentsia, among others Walter Benjamin, because radio work paid well. The younger – speaking – brother of the silent movie was, in addition, an exciting experimental space for artists; one need only think of Bertolt Brecht's radio theory. In Frankfurt, there even existed a local radio station, Radio Frankfurt, which specialized in reports, essays, radio plays and new music; it was, in short, 'modern to its fingertips'.[11] The radio was where things were happening, and gradually it became a driving force behind the growth of the mass-media society.

The *Frankfurter Zeitung* had a difficult time in this media and press landscape, especially as it was not part of a press corporation but rather an old family business in Frankfurt, facing tough competition from large, wealthy publishing corporations such as Ullstein (*Vossische Zeitung*) and Mosse (*Berliner Tageblatt*). In the end, Mosse and Ullstein did not avoid the decline that was the fate of the bourgeois-democratic quality press, but in the short term they were better positioned and had bigger financial cushions that allowed them to adapt to the new situation. In the *Berliner Morgenpost*, which had a circulation of 400,000 copies (1930) daily, Ullstein owned a popular sister paper of the *Vossische*, whose own circulation, like that of all other quality papers, remained well below 100,000.[12] Even after the *Frankfurter Zeitung* had found a financially strong backer, the IG Farben, at the end of the 1920s, the fees it paid its writers were correspondingly lower than those paid by the Berlin-based newspapers.[13] In the words of Schivelbusch, the crisis at the *FZ* was 'a faithful measure of the decline of the bourgeois layers of society', even of that of the Weimar Republic as a whole.[14] In *Mein Kampf*, Hitler had already identified the *Frankfurter Zeitung* as the apex of the 'Jewish Press'. The paper was a favourite target of the *völkisch*-national right wing, which was engaged in a bitter war against the Weimar system. How closely the *FZ* was indeed associated with Weimar soon became clear, as the country entered the era of economic crisis, the dictatorial turn and the seizure of power by the National Socialists. These events implied a transformation of the form or structure not only of the media landscape in particular but of the public in general. This affected 'people's public use of their reason' about society and the state just as much as it affected the newspaper market.[15]

Reifenberg was a breath of fresh air at the feuilleton. Wickenburg summed it up: 'Reifenberg was of the opinion that the feuilleton must not exclusively cover the world of belles lettres, but must also report on professions, facts and circumstances.'[16] This approach turned the feuilleton into a medium that reflected the acceleration of historical time and the instability of social phenomena.[17] The narrow limits of the arts were to be transcended, and everything to do with human intellectual life was declared a part of culture and thus a potential topic for the paper's cultural section.[18] The section was also meant to be political: 'at the bottom line' a 'continuous commentary on politics', as Reifenberg himself put it.[19] This might be taken for granted today, but it was a provocation back then.[20] Reifenberg's ideas met with resistance.

On the one hand, resistance arose within the newspaper itself. The egalitarian arrangements – there was no chief editorial board – could not hide the fact that there were factions and pronounced hierarchies among the editorial offices in the foxhole of Große Eschenheimer Straße. The politics editors, especially leading editor Robert Drill, exercised a kind of supreme control over the others. This 'supreme government' was compared by some in the lower echelons with the old Austro-Hungarian k. u. k. monarchy, leaving only the question of whether, in this comparison, the feuilleton was Hungary or rather Galicia. Joseph Roth, who came from the real Galicia, rebelled openly against the rule of the politics section: 'for how much longer does the political desk (i.e., not the editorial conference) intend to supervise our feuilleton articles? If it's to be a form of censorship, then let it be according to the views of the whole board'. Roth demanded 'that the political correspondents submit their pieces to *me* for censorship'.[21] This demand was motivated not so much by disagreement over the paper's political direction but by a desire for the feuilleton to be acknowledged as an equal partner with equal rights. To others at the paper, the members of the feuilleton section insisted that they wanted more than just a jester's privilege; to the world outside, they were defending themselves against the charge, coming from the literary world, that all they were producing were flashes in the pan without lasting significance. Geck and Diebold did not mind that the great literati thought of the feuilleton articles as mere chatter about a host of random subjects, articles written by members of the educated bourgeoisie for those members of the bourgeoisie looking for educational edification – articles which the latter, having done with the politics and economics sections, could read for dessert. But this was exactly the understanding of a feuilleton that Reifenberg, Kracauer and Roth's generation decisively rejected.[22] The opinion of cultural critics that the feuilleton consists of mass-produced goods, written quickly and without a sense of responsibility – that they might have accepted as a characterization of what happened at other papers, but not at their own.

What does a feuilleton have to look like if it is neither to be designed exclusively for headmasters and eggheads nor to give itself over to commercialism, educational kitsch and pseudo-intellectual entertainment? Joseph Roth's answer to this question can be found in a review of two books by fellow reporters Alfred Polgar and Egon Erwin Kisch: 'When German journalists write books, they almost have to find an excuse for it. How did they end up doing this? Do these mayflies want to rise to the status of higher insects? Do they, who belong to the day, enter eternity?' The title of Polgar's book was *An den Rand geschrieben* [Written in the margins]; Roth commented: 'Great truths are written in the margins.'[23] Just because journalists write quickly, it does not necessarily mean that they write badly. And just because literary authors do not write in newspapers, it does not necessarily mean that they write well. Even though journalism is tied up with current affairs, it can nevertheless produce lasting and artistically valuable results. In Roth's view, a genius who turns away from the world and is a stranger to his times is no genius at all. 'In the margins' does not, after all, mean 'in passing'. Roth told Reifenberg: 'You can't write feuilleton with half a mind or one hand tied behind your back.' And he claimed: 'The feuilleton is just as important to the paper as politics. ... The modern newspaper needs a reporter more than it needs an editorial writer. I am *not* an encore, not a pudding. I am the main dish.' The reader, he wrote, bought the *FZ* in order to read the red Joseph,[24] not the editorial writer with a full beard. 'I love this paper, I serve it, I am useful to it. ... I don't write "witty glosses". *I paint the portrait of the age.* That ought to be the job of the great newspaper. I'm a journalist, not a reporter; I'm an author, not an editorial writer.'[25] Roth not only tore down the boundaries between journalism and literature. He even claimed that the genuine artistic power of creation depended on proximity to the present and facticity. The signs of the times were to be studied not in the halls where politicians assembled, no, but on the street where ordinary people hustled and bustled, amidst the things that they had created.[26]

At the end of the 1920s, Siegfried Kracauer became the leading representative of this idea of the feuilleton, of this journalistic claim to provide a sociological perspective. 'I paint the portrait of the age' was his motto and, beyond that: I practise philosophy, that is, the search for truth, by different means. He agreed with Reifenberg that the feuilleton also had to pursue a political agenda. Around 1925, however, the primary task was to investigate social reality in an empirically grounded way.

To that end, Kracauer went into the provinces – to a courtroom in Limburg, for instance.[27] There, in July 1925, the murderer Fritz Angerstein was standing trial. One day half a year earlier, Angerstein, an executive at the van der Zypen lime works, had brutally killed eight people using a hunting knife and axe. He had first killed his wife because, as he said, he loved her so much, and he wanted to release her from her illness. In the following twenty-four hours, Angerstein also killed his mother-in-law and his sister-in-law, two clerical assistants, two gardener's assistants and a domestic servant who turned up at the Angerstein home the following day. There was no apparent motive for the killing spree. In each case, Angerstein smashed the skull of his victim, and in between killings he went back to sleep until the next victim arrived. Finally, the thirty-eight-year-old killed the German shepherd, and reported a robbery to the police, before starting a fire and attempting suicide. After only two days, it had been possible to reconstruct the sequence of events and to identify the murderer, who thereupon made a complete confession. It now transpired that he had also embezzled money in his position as director. The sums involved, however, were so small that it seemed implausible that there was any connection with the murders. In order to avoid being lynched by the inhabitants of Haiger, he was transferred to the university hospital in Gießen. Before he committed his crimes, Angerstein had the reputation of a respectable, caring and agreeable fellow citizen, someone who looked after his sickly, depressive and pietistic wife with exceptional commitment. After his deeds became public, though, there were many who thought they could remember his eyes sometimes glimmering uncannily and demonically. The people also now claimed to remember that some of Angerstein's ancestors had been mentally disturbed. In Gießen, the criminal was psychiatrically examined and later transferred to the county court prison in Limburg. The homicide division of the Frankfurt police put out a statement saying that the man had been perfectly calm and composed during interrogation, and that he showed no sign of grief or remorse. In his cell, he wrote extensively and read the Bible.

On 6 July, the first day of the trial, an audience had already assembled in front of the court an hour before proceedings were due to begin. Entrance tickets were said to have been on offer for more than 300 marks. Just as at the trial of the serial killer Fritz Haarmann in Hanover, which had begun just two days after the bloody events in Haiger and had kept the public rapt, the press were there in large numbers. The publicist Theodor Lessing had called Haarmann a 'wolf man living with a radio and electricity' and had declared him the 'signature of the age in which we live'. Was Angerstein's crime also emblematic of the age? It was certainly a sensation. Even film companies had sought to attend the Limburg trial. Paul Schlesinger, a star crime reporter, followed the proceedings for the *Vossische Zeitung*. The *Frankfurter Zeitung* sent Kracauer as a special correspondent. Numerous experts were summoned, among them Richard Herbertz, from Berne, a criminal psychologist who had done pioneering work in the area of forensic psychoanalysis. He was the first of his profession to be heard by a German court, but his voice ultimately could not compete with those of the psychiatrists, whose reports declared Angerstein accountable for his actions. Like Haarmann, the perpetrator, whose motive for the multiple murders remained unclear, was convicted and executed.

Herbertz had painted a different picture of the perpetrator:

> A man who has up until now been calm, considerate, simple and pious, and who would not hurt a fly, someone who deeply loved his severely hysterical wife ... this same man kills with brutal stabs of a dagger the very same woman, murders seven more people afterwards, battering them with an axe, finally sets his house on fire and thrusts a hunting knife into his own stomach ..., and of this man the psychiatrists assure us that he was normal in the 'forensic sense' at the time of committing his deeds.[28]

The psychologist from Berne suggested that the deed should be understood as an 'impulsive cracking', an explosive, impulsive act that was preceded by years and years of 'repressive work'. Angerstein had repressed his defensive emotions towards his wife, who had made his life extremely difficult. The more these emotions morphed into hatred in his unconscious, the more he persuaded himself that he loved his wife. Finally, the perpetrator was no longer able to endure this latent and unacknowledged emotional ambivalence. The murder was a liberation that had made him a plaything of overpowering drives. What was abnormal was rather the decades-long successful work of repression, which for 99 per cent of people would have been impossible.

To Herbertz, Angerstein's bloodlust recalled prehistoric man. He interpreted his deed as a regression to pre-civilized conditions that continued to exist unrecognized, like a dark continent, in the midst of civilization. In certain individuals, especially in neurotics, the development of the species from primitive to civilized is suspended. Ever since Sigmund Freud's *Totem and Taboo* (1913), psychoanalysis had possessed a cultural theory that explained this. In his study, Freud asks why taboos, such as incest, are created by primitive peoples in the first place, before they become independent and taken for granted: 'The basis of taboo is a forbidden action for which there exists a strong inclination in the unconscious.'[29] What no one wants to do does not need to be forbidden: this is the premise of the idea that the process of civilization is based on the suppression of drives. Angerstein had contravened the age-old prohibition of killing, and from then on he had passively followed the dictates of his drives 'like a cannibal'. Now he was confronted by his deeds as something alien. He was able to give a reason only for his first murder, namely the love for his suffering wife, and thereby deny the hatred for her that became clear through his killing of her. He had broken a taboo of civilization that had been erected especially in order to rein in aggressive emotions. Angerstein felt guilty and sought to atone for his deeds with his own blood.

Schlesinger disliked the psychologist's performance: 'A few days ago, he [Angerstein] said that he no longer understood himself. Had he listened to Herbertz's exposition, he probably would have understood himself even less.' An expert testimony drawing on psychoanalysis was a novelty for a German courtroom. And it would take a long time before an expert would again cite Freud as an authority. Kracauer reported that Herbertz's expertise was met in the courtroom 'with smiles of incredulity', even though he was the only one providing clues that might help people to understand Angerstein's actions. He did not think that the thesis of a regression into instinctual violence caused by the repression of ambivalent emotions could be proven, but he considered it plausible. For Kracauer, what spoke in favour of this explanation was the complete separation of the deeds from the doer, who, immediately after having committed them, confronted them as if he were not involved in them. The arguments of depth psychology, so unusual for a courtroom, seemed more promising to him than those of the conservative psychiatrists, whose perspective did nothing to solve the puzzle of the separation of the person from his deeds. Kracauer accused the psychiatrists of having not even attempted to look for a connection between the perpetrator and the deed. Kracauer himself found the murders committed by Angerstein, this petit bourgeois man 'like a thousand others', deeply worrying (just as Lessing had found the Haarmann case); it was a question modern civilization had put to itself:

> The incident is an anomaly, fortunately. But it should therefore not be taken any less as a warning of a world in which the things and their laws assume domination over the soul. Because the more human beings become objectified in their relations to each other and the more they allow the things that are separated from them to exercise power over them, instead of pulling the things close and suffusing them with humanity, the easier it may and will happen that the humane that has been pushed off into the depths of the unconscious assumes a disfigured, goblin-like, and gruesome form, and lunges at the deserted world of things. Only in a human world does the deed have a doer.

Kracauer looked at the Angerstein case from a perspective that was critical of civilization and that brought society and the individual psyche into relation with one another. He did not envisage a perfect world in which there was no crime; what he had in mind was a world in which people are actors, masters of their own houses, and stand in a living relationship with their environment, other people and things. As he saw it, the achievement of such a world is prevented by the 'objectification of social relations' and the 'distance to things', that is, by two phenomena of alienation. He seems to have liked Freud's idea that prehistoric demons lurk underneath the patina of civilization and Freud's claim that, the less these demons are understood and the more they are separated off and ignored, the more human beings become alien to themselves, the more powerless science becomes in dealing with the objects it investigates, the more unreal civilized society becomes. According to Helmut Lethen, the Angerstein case showed that the bourgeois subject, the person of free will, accountable for his or her deeds, was still locked in a battle with the unaccountable creature.[30] The petit bourgeois could still regress into a wolf man. For Kracauer, these motiveless murders, the mechanical and primitive butchering carried out by the executive Fritz Angerstein, signalled a present that was not understood; they were a symptom of the dialectic in the process of civilization with which he would now become occupied.

Reports such as these allowed Kracauer to delve into philosophical reflection as he pursued social questions. But Reifenberg's conception of the feuilleton also permitted literary experimentation. Kracauer composed a series of articles on the world of things – choosing bourgeois accessories such as the piano, the typewriter, inkwells, monocles and braces – in which he chronicled, in a somewhat peculiar fashion, the changing times. In these texts, which, although not pessimistic, belong to the genre of cultural criticism, the West is not pictured as simply in decline. As a symbol of an epoch that was ending, umbrellas fell victim to the changing times; a new sporty, youthful and petit bourgeois generation preferred waterproofs. The umbrellas that now stood around unused were relics of the old liberal bourgeoisie that had vanished through the war and revolution. The human community, too, had lost its transcendental umbrella. Braces suffered a similar fate: they were pushed out by practical sport belts. Braces had once served to produce 'the harmony between mind and body, ideal and life, that is the sign of highest perfection', because they pulled the trousers up without losing touch with the ground. They were also invisible, thus accessories that represented inwardness and separateness. Their heyday was over: 'When the present time laments, for good reason, the decline of the personality, the horizontal positioning of the belt is the guilty party. It must be blamed for the decay of the world. In order to avoid that decay, belts would have had to stretch from below to above.'[31] There was clearly still a lot of theological substance to profane things. Kracauer's longing for meaning still haunts these articles, which are critical of their times without offering a solution to its instability. Benjamin praised such attempts at breaking new ground in the feuilleton:

> You paint the decline of the petit bourgeois class by way of a very remarkable 'loving' description of its inheritance. It is quite exceptional. The grotesque acquires a clear, legitimate political dimension, frees itself from any affinity with arbitrary mysticism and touches shoulders with theory, as it does in all outstanding examples of the genre.[32]

But what Kracauer demonstrates most of all in these feuilleton pieces on the profane is his comprehensive linguistic facility:

> In the vicinity of the big cities lie the middling mountain ranges,[33] stretching from spa to spa. For hygienic reasons, these lie at their feet, in picturesque settings. Everything lies.[34] In the course of time, the middling mountain ranges become smaller and smaller because, luckily, the speed of traffic becomes greater and greater. ... The main adornments of the middling mountain range are the cars, which could not live without a terrain of some kind, especially small cars, for the small people. Soon the whole middle class will be moving in them; they cost close to nothing. It is best to be moving in the middle ground, like the middling mountain range.[35]

Kracauer studied the misery of the middle classes at the theme parks in the lower mountain ranges, which seemed to have been invented for that purpose. Things as well as landscapes had social dimensions that were waiting to be discovered, marvelled at and charted.

11

Inflation and Journeys into Porosity

The year 1923 was the year of hyperinflation. Within a few days, prices could rise immeasurably, as they do during Georg and Fred's visit to Sulzbach in the Black Forest: *The next day when they found their way to the dining room they encountered the blackboard. Its surface was covered with a number in the billions, to which was appended the explanation that room rates were being raised in keeping with the momentary value of the dollar. After that the blackboard never returned to its first home in the ballroom. Like a menacing cloud it stood immobile on the horizon of the dining room, and not satisfied with this, proceeded to increase its billions from day to day. Soon it had become a sinister blue-black shape which outgrew the four walls of the room and, visible from every direction, weighed heavily on the entire landscape. It blotted out the sun and filled the guests with terror. Fresh masses of paper bills were always falling from it, sticky masses in every color. They could no more be done away with than the leaves advancing across the garden.*[1] Hyperinflation was more than a threatening eclipse of the sun; it was, at that point, the nadir of a catastrophic decade of monetary devaluation that began with the outbreak of the Great War.

Especially for ordinary people, for whom the economy was 'the constant force of daily life', the disintegration and destruction of the currency in 1923 felt menacing.[2] In modern capitalist societies, money plays an important role as a silent regulator of social relations. Money has risen to the status of a universal equivalent that absorbs all substantial qualities and turns all original purposes into means in order to set itself up as the ultimate end.[3] In a society hit by inflation, the decreasing value of the currency thus led, first and foremost, to a loss of trust in the values of the society. The law of the jungle was at work here; innumerable existences, marriages and families were destroyed. Hyperinflation became a collective trauma. The feeling was that of living in an 'upside-down world' in which the honest worker, diligent saver and loyal patriot lost out in the end, while speculators and black marketeers, bankers and bolshevists, foreigners and Jews were the winners.[4] With its confusing numbers and values, inflation during the disintegration of the currency seemed like a declaration of bankruptcy by the still young republic.

Inflation was in no way a surprise, and it was not the result of a conspiracy. There were utterly profane reasons for it, although these escaped most people at the time. It also had some advantages and positive effects on the economy overall. As in the case of other economic processes, there were genuine winners and losers. The decade of inflation, lasting from 1914 to 1924, can be divided into three distinct phases: wartime inflation, the inflation during demobilization, and hyperinflation. During the war, the German government had issued war bonds and increased the volume of money in circulation in order to finance the war. Following the war, mild levels of inflation served to ease social tensions because they helped to improve economic performance, thus helping in the transition to a peacetime economy and opening up a certain amount of space for social policies. The industrial labour force actually profited from inflation because it drove real-term wage increases. Owners of non-cash assets also profited, in particular industrial entrepreneurs and farmers, and also those with mortgages. Those who lost out from inflation were foreign investors and those with financial assets. While the most well-off owners could cushion their losses from the depreciation of their Reichsmarks by paying off their debts and buying new property on the cheap, the middle stratum of the bourgeoisie was heavily hit. The modest assets the members of this class had accrued simply evaporated; the war bonds defaulted. And, finally, employees and civil servants who depended on salaries, as well as pensioners and recipients of social benefits, were also among those who lost out.[5]

Inflation pulled the rug out from underneath the bourgeois forms of life of those intellectuals who lived as rentiers. That applied to Walter Benjamin and Ernst Bloch. In September 1919, Bloch returned from Switzerland, and as a freelance writer he only received irregular payments from publishers and newspapers. In 1922, he received his part of the inheritance from his deceased wife, Else von Stritzky – several thousand Reichsmarks – but inflation would have quickly diminished its value. In any case, Bloch was constantly in financial trouble.[6] Benjamin, having completed his dissertation in art history, returned to Berlin in March 1920. He, too, was tortured by severe worries about his financial prospects. He had no income, but should have been supporting a family; in addition, a collector's urge drove him to buy rare and very expensive editions of books. During the early post-war years, it was Benjamin's parents-in-law who kept the family afloat. His wife, Dora, worked as a freelance translator; the recently graduated Dr Benjamin had few opportunities to get work published. His parents demanded that the twenty-eight-year-old put himself and his family on an independent financial footing, preferably by finding some commercial profession. This was a source of continual conflict, and it would eventually destroy his relationship with his parents. They fell out shortly after Benjamin and his family had, at his parents' insistence, moved into their house in Delbrückstraße.[7]

Kracauer was also one of the losers from inflation. This was not only because he was an employee whose income in real terms was reduced by the devaluation but, in particular, because the modest inheritance he had received from his father, who had died in 1918, melted away like snow in the sun. From then on, he had also to support his mother, who had lost her assets and received no pension of her own.[8] But at least Kracauer was in employment and received a regular income. Benjamin and Bloch, by contrast, lived under the permanent threat of becoming 'proletarianized intellectuals', declassé members of the bourgeoisie, 'socially unattached intellectuals'.[9] Intellectuals like Benjamin and Bloch were 'free-floating': adrift in the labour market, without fixed employment, without social security or the security of a pension, without any financial provision. As a rule, it was not possible to earn much from writing, and from their perspective earning money was, in any case, not the purpose of their work. Thus, their financial situations remained precarious. It is telling that throughout his failed attempts to found a journal – *Angelus Novus* and *Krisis und Kritik* – Benjamin stressed to publishers and collaborators that these publications were not to attempt to win their audiences over, and that collaborators were to be chosen exclusively by the editors. Neither grubby commercialism nor the visual arts, neither politics nor educational purposes, neither fad nor irrelevant science was to provide the guiding criteria: only his personal preferences and interests, his commitment to the maxim of understanding the historical present by way of immersion in the work of art, were to count.[10] But even a genius and narcissist could not avoid thinking of money, especially once the money from his father's inheritance had dwindled almost to nothing, in May 1929 – after only three years. Between 1923 and 1933, Benjamin published about 300 articles, around 30 articles per year. But that was not nearly enough to sustain himself and his family. 'Hunger', Benjamin lamented, 'poses a most serious threat to anyone seriously engaged in intellectual pursuits in Germany'.[11] The free-floating intellectuals were part of the precariat of the day.

The cultural sociologist Alfred Weber discussed this development in a lecture at the annual meeting of the Verein für Sozialpolitik [Association for Social Policy] in Eisenach in September 1922. The modern 'intelligentsia' in the time of high capitalism, which Weber apparently thought had ended, was an 'intelligentsia of rentiers'. But now the wealth of this social stratum had disappeared. 'The distress of the intellectual worker' might expand to become the fate of an entire intellectual sphere: the educated classes. Intellectual life [das Geistige] was in danger of becoming an appendix to the economy.[12] Those who wanted to live off intellectual work and could not find a place at a university either had to find employment as editors, like Kracauer, or they had to sell their products as freelancers, like the authors Benjamin and Bloch. The most important thing, in any case, was to live cheaply.

For that reason, many of the wordsmiths would travel during times of economic and social depression. One of these refugees from inflation was Alfred Sohn-Rethel, who first, in March 1924, went with his wife and his son from Heidelberg to Capri, and then on to Positano, on the Amalfi coast. He stayed for three years and studied Marx's *Capital*, identifying the source of the transcendental subject of German idealism in the nature of commodity exchange. To put it briefly: exchange deceives consciousness.[13] For Sohn-Rethel, the causes of the economic crisis lie in the commodity form, which in capitalist societies takes hold of intellectual forms, especially through rationalism.[14] The exchange value Sohn-Rethel himself received for this particular work in cultural philosophy was a regular monthly income of 250 marks, from the publisher Martin Venzky in Oldenburg. In Germany, a family could not survive on this, but it was enough in southern Italy, especially as there were many houses there standing empty, thanks to emigration, that could be rented cheaply. For the local fishermen, fruit producers and builders, working in the area was no longer worthwhile, and they were drawn to the very countries and cities which the suffering artists and dispossessed intellectual rentiers were fleeing. For half a year in 1924, Benjamin also belonged to this, as he ironically called it, 'travelling intellectual proletariat' [intellektuelles Wanderproletariat], because 'at least here [he could] live more cheaply'.[15] He and Sohn-Rethel explored the area together; the two of them went regularly to Naples, in particular. Sometimes Asja Lacis accompanied them.

On Capri, Benjamin met Ernst Bloch, and, at a beach-side bar, they had heated, all-night discussions about Tieck's fairy tale *The Fair-Haired Eckbert* and everything to do with it.[16] Bloch led the restless life of a wandering philosopher. He 'changed countries more often than his shoes'.[17] He himself said that his 'normal condition' was the opposite of 'inhabiting'; he was looking for 'an open life in which the past remains a memory, and by all means also a support'.[18] He was not only on Capri for the low cost of living and the beautiful red sunsets. He was permanently in need of new impressions, ideas and perspectives, and he was always on the lookout for interesting partners in conversation.[19] In 1924/1925, a fair number of such partners could be found on the little island: there was Sohn-Rethel

and Benjamin; Bertolt Brecht and Caspar Neher; Asja Lacis and
her life companion, Bernhard Reich (a former senior director at
the Münchner Kammerspiele); the sociologist Gottfried Salomon;
and George's faithful follower Gundolf. For Bloch, travelling was
more than a passion. It was part of his profession as a philosophical
writer: 'A human takes himself along when he goes wandering. But
just as much he goes outside of himself, enriches himself with fields,
forests, mountains. ... To wander badly means not to change as a
human being while wandering.'[20]

In the summer of 1925, Siegfried Kracauer and Theodor
Wiesengrund embarked on a journey to Italy, Kracauer setting off
from Frankfurt, Wiesengrund from Vienna. Before this journey,
the crisis in their relationship had deepened considerably. Kracauer
had considered not travelling with his beloved younger friend but
going it alone: 'out of an instinct for self-preservation, out of the
very naked urge for wretched self-preservation'. After some back
and forth, it was decided that they would travel together after all.[21]
They met in Genoa, most likely on 8 September, in order to travel on
to Naples, Positano and Capri. Of course, he did not leave behind
his 'Friedelian suffering', his complex about the allegedly uncaring
young man; his hypertrophied soul was very much travelling with
him. On 12 September, Wiesengrund had already written to Alban
Berg: 'Being together with my friend is in every sense exciting
and important: in human terms it demands full concentration, in
factual terms it forces a revision of the very basis.'[22] The situation
was obviously taxing, but they knew why and agreed to put the
relationship on a different basis. Martin Mittelmeier called the
travellers 'a couple in crisis'.[23] That crisis, however, did not take the
form of a slow decline but of an intensification that led, ultimately,
to a turning point, at the foot of Mount Vesuvius. After their travels
there was half a year of silence between them. Then the cards were
reshuffled.

Before his departure, the *Frankfurter Zeitung* had, upon
Kracauer's suggestion, published an article on Naples by Benjamin
and Lacis that Wiesengrund thought was 'extraordinary'.[24] While
financially straitened writers longed to be in Capri, social critics
tired of civilization yearned for Naples.[25] What Benjamin and
Lacis found fascinating about this southern place, characterized
by a humane and friendly misery, was its 'porosity'. Porous was
the stone on which the city was built; porous was its architecture.
Everything seemed preliminary, improvised, anarchic. Not house
numbers, but shops, fountains and churches provide orientation;
murals of the Madonna, in the corners of inner courtyards, hold the
blocks of houses together like iron clamps; instead of department
stores, bazaars; instead of apartments with curtains, rented flats
in which cows were kept. And porous was also the social life; the

borders between house and street were permeable. The piazza was a living room, and there was no bourgeois interior. A childish delight in noisiness swept through vestibules, corridors and balconies. Everything was flooded with 'streams of communal living'; existence was a collective affair. The Neopolitans drank their coffee in political people's cafés. 'Porosity is the inexhaustible law of the life of this city, reappearing everywhere.'[26] Could that be one of those warm streams that Bloch was so eagerly looking for? Referring to the picture of Naples painted by Benjamin, Bloch did indeed declare porosity the opposite of the capitalist division of labour and of mathematically structured understanding. The concept of porosity stood for a programme that united open forms of philosophizing, perceiving and penetrating reality. Sohn-Rethel enthused over the 'ideal of the broken'. In Naples, he said, the essence of technology was the functioning of the broken; things were probably already produced as broken. Nothing worked the way it should, but everything worked well in the end.[27]

What the travelling intelligentsia saw thus corresponded to their way of thinking. Landscapes and cities could be translated into philosophy, and similarly they projected into the culture as well as nature they visited what they brought along as intellectual baggage. Kracauer and Wiesengrund first stayed on Capri ('dreaming of Greek gods and goddesses on the beach during the day, drunken from the wine and lights at night').[28] From Naples, where they were particularly captivated by the aquarium, they then travelled on to Positano, where Sohn-Rethel was living. In Sorrento, they crossed the border between porous tuff and hard limestone.[29] From there, they continued their journey on the water, passing the Sirenuse islands: 'One gets to Positano with a small steam-boat', Kracauer wrote in his travel article, 'if one gets there at all', because 'the boat is filled with the restlessness of Odysseus. ... If it does not enchant the gods of nature, Positano retreats and becomes unapproachable.'[30] To Kracauer, who only weeks before had been studying the abysses of the human soul in a courtroom in Limburg, this place seemed to be dominated by elementary forces: 'Unformed instincts, nameless desires float to the surface; unrestrained, they discharge themselves, awakened by shadowy powers whose wings cover the brightness.' Positano was a city of the dead: 'Sorcery sweeps across the place. It is the enclave of lost powers who have found a refuge in the antique landscape and now assume a bodily appearance. ... The old class of gods has vanished, hit and transformed by the word, but the old demons still skirt around. In Positano, those believed to be dead are alive.' When the tropical rain set in, Kracauer reported, the cemetery attacked the city, and from the vaults the skeletons swam into the gardens and houses.

Thus, while Benjamin cheerfully and porously explored Naples' vibrant streets with Asja Lacis, the mood in Positano was somewhat bleak and pessimistic. Upon his return, Wiesengrund told Alban Berg about an 'ongoing confrontation with [his] friend, which was in every respect a difficult matter, and which gave [him] no opportunity for repose'. He further wrote: 'In Naples we met with Benjamin shortly before our return, and engaged in a philosophical battle with him in which we were able to control the field, albeit not without finding it necessary to regroup our forces.'[31] We do not know what the battle was about, but Lukács's *History and Class Consciousness*, Marx and Hegel are potential candidates, especially as Sohn-Rethel was also taking part in the discussions. It is also not clear which intellectual positions had to be shifted, and in which way. But not one of them left Naples as he had entered it.

12

Transitional Years: Economic Upturn, Revolt, Enlightenment

At the end of November 1923, Siegfried Kracauer reported in the *Frankfurter Zeitung* that the building housing the Institute for Social Research at Viktoria-Allee, near the university, was almost ready to be opened, following half a year of construction work. The architect, Franz Roeckle, who often cooperated with Ernst May, the city council's planning officer, had chosen Franconian shell limestone for the outer façade. 'It gives the outside a serious, almost fortress-like character', Kracauer remarked, 'which, in addition, is substantially intensified by the horizontal upper line created by the flat roofs'.[1] The fact that the new institute appeared to be fortifying itself against the outside world had symbolic significance. This clearly left-wing institution made it possible, for the first time, to study and research Marxism and the labour movement at a German university, and it was regarded with suspicion by most people at the Johann-Wolfgang-Goethe University, even if its first director, Carl Grünberg, represented a more social democratic Marxism. Thanks to the large sums of money pumped into the foundation by its patron, Felix Weil, the institute opened with all the honours of an academic ceremony on 22 June 1924.[2] There were three parts to the building: one for teaching, one for research and one housing the library and administration. For the first six years, Elisabeth Ehrenreich (born 1893), 'Lili', worked in the library. She was from Strasbourg, where her father, August Ehrenreich, had moved from Rhinehessen in the 1880s because he had taken up a post as secretary of the Kaiserliche Generaldirektion der Eisenbahnen [Imperial General Directorate of the Railways] in Alsace-Lorraine. August Ehrenreich's political convictions were nationalist; Lili was brought up a Catholic. She trained as a teacher and during the war she took up a post at a secondary school for girls. In June 1919, she was dismissed by the French school authorities after Alsace had become French again. She went to Leipzig and studied the violin and piano at the university's conservatory for music and art history. But inflation did away with what remained of her inheritance and

Figure 18. Elisabeth Ehrenreich around 1926
Copyright: DLA Marbach

forced her to find gainful employment. Her sister Franziska, a pianist married to the painter Hanns Ludwig Katz, was already living in Frankfurt. The two sisters were very close. Lili probably moved to Frankfurt immediately after the institute was founded.[3]

Siegfried Kracauer must have met Elisabeth Ehrenreich sometime in 1925, between the trip to Naples and the end of year holidays. In any case, for Christmas he gave her a copy of Kafka's *A Country Doctor*. Soon after, in the late summer of 1926, the two were travelling as a couple through the south of France. This romantic relationship seems to have given Kracauer the sense of security he had been lacking for so long. His writing style changed during this time. He became more self-confident, forthcoming; the words flowed more easily, and he formulated things more incisively – sometimes with subtle irony, sometimes aggressively and sarcastically. If Kracauer had been asked to describe the relationship, he might have said: Love did not look for the one it found.

Around the end of 1925 and the beginning of 1926, Kracauer wrote the first of the programmatic critiques of mass culture that were to make him famous. One of them was about the then popular revues:

> Revues serve the purpose of keeping the members of the audience, who are engaged in existential battle with each other, busy; day after day they pursue their professional lives. The best end up as the winners, and they promote the world economy, which, in turn, promotes them. Only the weak are ruined, but work in itself is also a value. In order to regenerate from it, one enjoys the distraction of the revues.

Adopting a staccato style, Kracauer moves, sentence by sentence, to the left, without the flourishes or glitter typical of revues: 'Revues show everything that does not exist, in beautiful furnishing. Like magazines: an abundance of pictures to make sure one does not see anything. ... In the end, the audience also takes the world for a revue; both are colourful when all is taken together.'[4] Kracauer by no means despised revues; on the contrary, he loved such events. Circus Hagenbeck, the chansons of Josma Selim, the revue of the Tiller Girls, like cinema, were welcome diversions for him. They inspired him, offered distraction.[5] And distraction could be meaningful 'as improvisation' and 'as a reflection of the uncontrolled anarchy of our world'. But distraction could also be reactionary – namely if the improvisation was 'festooned with drapery and forced back into a unity that no longer exists', if, that is, distraction denied actual reality; or if film imitated the theatre, and cinemas were built in the style of ornamental theatre halls; or if distraction became an end in itself and a cult object that prevented reflection.[6]

Lili, it seems, distracted Friedel from his fear of life, spurred him on as an author, and politicized him as an intellectual. He wrote even more, went to the cinema even more often and intensified his intellectual work. All this was possible because his partner did not take up his time but shared her time with him in the pursuit of common interests. Ehrenreich became Kracauer's closest collaborator. We can assume that they watched films together, that going to the cinema was a part of their relationship just as was travelling. A love of France, especially, was something they shared. Kracauer was gaining ground: professionally, through his growing reputation as an author and editor; in terms of his world-view and politically through his turn towards the profane and material; and, most importantly, socially and emotionally through his relationship with Lili. At the end of 1926, Alfred Seidel's book *Bewußtsein und Verhängnis* [Consciousness and obscure fate] was published posthumously. Seidel had taken his own life in the late autumn of 1924. Kracauer had known him through his friends in Heidelberg, Löwenthal and Sohn-Rethel. Now Kracauer wrote:

> Seidel's rejection of science because it renders conscious life processes that can safely be kept in the unconscious is in many ways like

Nietzsche's, Spengler's and Klage's attitudes. The one who has been deprived of life finds his 'inner compensation' for this loss threatened by the 'disenchantment of the world'. He longs for what he is missing: being that rests unilluminated in itself and a religious community filled with culture.

It is almost as though, in saying farewell to his friend, Kracauer was also saying farewell to his own past, which had been deprived of life and so moved by the disenchantment of the world. That did not, however, make life good in his eyes, nor did it mean that he believed science deals with what is essential or that enchantment amounts to happiness. Yet the 'good dissatisfaction' with things as they are, and their science, should not have 'made Seidel reject the awareness provided by reason, but should have made him battle *for* reason, which, as a matter of fact, is only insufficiently realized in contemporary knowledge'.[7]

In the spring of 1926, Kracauer embarked on such a battle for reason. He attacked, both intellectually and politically, the protagonists of the Jewish renaissance in Frankfurt. It was an aggressive act that would, given the various friendly acquaintances he had in these circles, also affect him personally. Maybe he was settling scores with his own past.[8] In any case, in an article in the *Frankfurter Zeitung* Kracauer mounted a critique of Martin Buber and Franz Rosenzweig's project of a new translation of the Bible. And this was not a critique that was in solidarity with its object but a sober settlement of accounts launched from the outside, a critique that suggested his inner separation from the Jewish religious environment.

Since 1924, Buber and Rosenzweig had been working on *Die Schrift*. At the end of 1925, *Das Buch im Anfang (Genesis)* appeared.[9] As both were interested in a new Jewish form of life, promoted by the Jewish teaching institute, it made perfect sense to translate the *Tanakh*, the Hebrew Bible, into the everyday language spoken by German Jews. Luther's Bible was a Christian text, translated from Latin, not Hebrew, and it was almost 400 years old. Originally, Buber and Rosenzweig only wanted to revise and modernize Luther's translation. But they soon discarded this plan and decided to preserve the linguistic character of the original text and retain its aesthetic qualities. They did not just want to translate the Hebrew into German; rather, the German language was meant to be expanded, enriched by taking up aspects of the holy language, in a process similar to the one deployed by Hölderlin in his exemplary translations of Greek into German. The German-Hebrew Bible was meant to appeal to contemporary man and to the Jewish community in the German-speaking world, and it was ultimately intended to support a religious renewal.

Buber and Rosenzweig consciously opted not to publish it as a critical edition. This decision was what underlay Kracauer's main objection to *Die Schrift*. For him, it was a false modernization: untimely and thus untrue, unreal and, finally, archaic and reactionary. It was therefore less satisfactory than Luther's Bible, which had, in times of revolutionary protest against ecclesiastical and economic abuse, been relevant, because it had been written for the people and against the authorities. Kracauer, we should not forget, had previously criticized Rosenzweig's philosophy of religion for confusing revelation and philosophy and thus ultimately destroying both. Now, he went a step further, saying: 'today access to truth is by way of the profane.' The secular arena of economic facts was what determined actual reality, not the eternally holy word of the scripture and its reproduction. In his judgement, those who dwelled in purely spiritual spheres missed reality and stabilized the ruling social conditions. Kracauer even placed the translation of the Bible close to 'runes of a Wagnerian sort'.[10] He had become a hard-headed realist. Everything that breathed the spirit of German idealism, demanded spiritual renewal, was romanticist and spiritualist – all that fell foul of the same charge he had already levelled at rationalist, positivist and formalist thinking: that it was ideological. The measure of all things was profane reality, and reality had to be dialectically explored within the tensions between theory and experience. This had to be done in the interest of theology, but during times of attempted religious renewal it was best done against theology. And Kracauer was going to put forward proposals for how to look for and capture this reality in the hollow spaces and gaps between all the '-isms'. But first of all, he was going to experience the significant effect that his attack had had.

The *Frankfurter Zeitung* offered Buber and Rosenzweig the opportunity to respond to Kracauer's article. They used it to reject the accusation that *Die Schrift* had 'Wagnerian' traits, and used various examples referred to by Kracauer – e.g. 'Erdvolk', 'folk of the earth' or, as Kracauer understood it, 'folk of the soil' – to explain that their translation was objectively grounded.[11] The '*völkisch* fears' of the reviewer, they said, served only to show his lack of understanding. Buber and Rosenzweig assumed that Kracauer's real target was not the translation but the original. At stake was therefore a confession of faith and not aesthetic, political or philosophical questions. They countered the accusation that the religious renewal lacked a social awareness of the present simply by pointing out that every age took an 'alien, distant, and hostile' stance towards the word of God; ancient Egypt had been no different in that respect – and 'then happened what happened'.[12] Buber also thought he could detect the 'resentment of someone feeling neglected' behind Kracauer's criticisms.[13]

Kracauer's published broadsides against new religious tendencies strained his relationship with Margarete Susman. She did not like his polemic against Bloch, and she was outraged at his critique of Max Scheler's *On the Eternal in Man* (1921), saying that his article was disrespectful, misunderstood the truth of natural religion, and lacked religious seriousness and depth.[14] Following the publication of an announcement of the German-Jewish Bible in the *Frankfurter Zeitung* of 25 January 1926 whose hostile tone suggested Kracauer as its author, Susman sent her friend a kind of warning letter. She explained to Kracauer that a direct and personal critique – that is, one that addresses the author in a spirit of solidarity and friendship – was something quite different from a critique in a daily newspaper, directed at an audience that was ignorant of the matter at hand. She also stated, clearly, that 'creative achievement', no matter how flawed, meant more to her than critique. She did not think Kracauer capable of an 'objective polemic' because he had, by this point, taken up a different position.[15] With this letter she clearly sought to distance herself from Kracauer, and after the publication of his two-part review on 27 and 28 April she finally broke off their relationship.

Ernst Simon, a friend of Löwenthal's who was associated with the teaching institute, condemned Kracauer's article as 'malevolent, meaning: in the case of doubtful questions you always decided unambiguously in favour of the negative answer'. Simon also thought Buber's metaphysics lacked a sociological dimension, but he nevertheless felt that Kracauer's scathing review was disrespectful, unfair, clueless and devious. It was disrespectful because his critical judgement of the religious concept of reality had not taken into account that the seriously ill Rosenzweig, who had been suffering from motor neurone disease since 1922, was moving in a different sphere of reality and was having to cope with that sphere; unfair because his trenchant remarks about Buber failed to consider that Buber was an important opponent of nationalism within Zionism; clueless because Kracauer, being ignorant of the Hebrew language, could not see that the translation was based on objective and immanent reasons, not ideological ones; and finally devious because he did not tell his unknowing readers about his philological dilettantism.[16] Kracauer rejected these accusations. He denied that his ignorance of the Hebrew language played any role, as he had not attacked the translation as such. 'I only attacked the intention of a literal translation without commentary as such', he replied to Simon. 'Even if the language, a hundred times over, is nothing but the literal rendering of the original, its effect is no less that of a posthumous Wagnerianism. Words have their history, too, and that history must be taken into account when translating.'

Walter Benjamin's reaction was important, because he welcomed the Jewish-messianic aspirations in Frankfurt, and he was a translator himself – of Baudelaire and Marcel Proust, among other writers. Like Rosenzweig, he believed in the idea of a primordial cabalist language, and he was known to be a friend of translations that kept close to the original.[17] In the preface to his translation of the *Tableaux parisiens* (written in 1921 and published in 1923), titled 'The Task of the Translator', he had, however, said 'that no translation would be possible if in its ultimate essence it strove for likeness to the original. For in its afterlife – which could not be called that if it were not a transformation and a renewal of something living – the original undergoes a change'.[18] That statement was thoroughly in line with Kracauer's criticisms. While Benjamin shared Rosenzweig's theological paradigm of history, in particular his rejection of the idea of a historical reason and the associated axioms of continuity, causality and progress, after his turn towards Marxism he had a political perspective that covered the theological dimension. The theological dimension was only later made explicit in the arcades project and in his theses on the philosophy of history. In this later understanding of history, the emphasis was on the present. History was a question put by the present to the past, and a question of the political position adopted in the present moment.[19] It was therefore no surprise that Benjamin took sides with Kracauer, without even having looked at *Die Schrift*.

Benjamin congratulated Kracauer on the review of the German Bible from Paris, where he had been staying since spring 1926, mostly concentrating on translation:

> Something has been achieved: the matter is definitively 'classified' for us. It is not necessary to deal with it, not any longer – after you have done it in truly exemplary fashion. From the theoretical underpinning of your handling of it, to the comparison with the Lutheran translation of the Vulgate into German, to the unsparing and appropriate demonstration of the linguistic descent from Wagner, everything seems to the highest degree valid and well-formulated.

Benjamin was pleased that Kracauer had rained on the parade of the southwest German 'religious ones' and southwest German 'philosophers' and 'their shabby pied piper music'. The only thing he regretted was seeing the reputation of Rosenzweig, whose *Star of Redemption* he considered an enduring achievement, 'forever tarnished'. Rosenzweig's reply did not change Benjamin's judgement one jot, because it did not touch upon 'the only question upon which everything depends: why translate the Bible *now*, and why into *German*?' Benjamin told Kracauer that 'the Buber review ... has made a strong impression on competent Buber experts here'.[20]

The Buber expert in question was Ernst Bloch, with whom Kracauer had been at loggerheads ever since his review of Bloch's *Münzer* book. Bloch spent spring 1926 in Paris, and Benjamin had brought the controversy in Frankfurt to his attention. Bloch immediately wrote a letter to Kracauer, firstly in order to offer his support to him in the dispute, and secondly to tell him: 'now for the first time [I think] that [I understand] what your substantial point was in your review of my *Münzer* book'. At the time, he had thought that the criticism had mainly been directed at Marxism, and not in the first place against theology. Now Bloch thought he recognized 'that you have in mind precisely the narrow path of what is seemingly external, practical, without glamour, which is precisely the path of Marxism; that for you, too, all truth must stand the test of this needy, moving actuality'. This interpretation assumes that Kracauer had confused Bloch with Buber, and it was true of the Kracauer of 1926.[21] But whether Kracauer's polemic against Bloch 'running amok' towards God was indeed a 'Marxist protest against the tone of an *anarchist* manifesto, the theology still reverberating in the "Müntzer"', at the time, in 1922, as Bloch now believed, is questionable. Back then, Kracauer had not been a Marxist but an opponent of the Marxist-Hegelian dialectic of history. To that extent, Bloch may well have misunderstood his critic less than he now assumed. Kracauer wisely left Bloch in his illusory belief, especially as Bloch also hinted at the fact that he still felt hurt by the 'recourse to the authenticity or inauthenticity of [his] *person*'. Kracauer preferred to take note of the praise – 'that you caused the lifeless and contemplative educated chatter of the bourgeoisie a guilty conscience in a major bourgeois paper'[22] – and to note that he now also viewed the early dispute through different eyes: 'You interpret ... my review of your Münzer book back then more deeply and humanely than I myself would be able to, show me the connection between the past and the present which I myself did not see.' A 'meeting of [their] paths' now appeared 'very possible' to him, despite the fact that he had also been insulted as a mediocre spirit in Bloch's response at the time.[23]

In the following years, Kracauer met ever more frequently with Benjamin and with Bloch. Kracauer met Benjamin in September 1926 in southern France while travelling there with Lili. They spent their time together delighting each other with the production of literary 'Marseillana'. They watched a bullfight in Aix-en-Provence in which a boy killed the animal; Kracauer studied the geometry – the ellipses, points, planes, lines, curvatures – of the boy's movements and 'the ornaments' power' in this bloody spectacle. At night, in Marseille, they happened upon an uncanny place, a 'square without mercy', that triggered, in Kracauer, Kafkaesque fantasies of an invisible court. And they frequented the 'standing only bars of the south' in Nice in order to gain insight into the ordered and lived life from the dream landscapes of a Mediterranean city.[24] Benjamin sent Kracauer his 'religion station', a thought image about the cathedral in the harbour, the 'bleak building ... between quay and warehouse', the 'reloading point for intangible, unfathomable goods'. The 'monument' reminded Benjamin of a 'gigantic railway station ... where passengers of the first to the fourth classes (though before God they are all equal), wedged among their spiritual possessions as if between suitcases, sit reading hymnbooks that, with their concordances and cross references, look very much like international timetables'. Together, Benjamin and Kracauer watched the 'sleeping cars to eternity' set off, and they visited the suburbs, 'the docks, the inland harbours, the warehouses, the quarters of poverty, the scattered asylums of wretchedness'. At the margins, at the extremes, at the fracture points – that is where both were looking for revelations of reality.[25]

From 1926 onwards, Kracauer and Bloch engaged in an intense correspondence on the relationship between Marxism and metaphysics, and on Hegel and Lukács. Kracauer praised Bloch – in a tone he had never adopted before – for his intention 'to confront Marxism, which has become irrelevant as a philosophy and, in the hands of the official Soviet philosophers, is ruined totally, with the genuine truth contents, and thereby to turn it into a great revolutionary theory that makes the European intelligentsia tremble, the only theory that also brings about the true hour of reckoning for the church, as it does for all professions of positive convictions'. But what did Kracauer mean by 'genuine truth contents'? Truth was no longer religious truth in the traditional sense, but the ideal of a philosophically, politically and socially emancipated humanity.[26] Kracauer imagined that there are 'hidden reserves of truth' that are mythologically veiled, among other things by theological language. A truly revolutionary Marxism, he held, required a substantial philosophy of history 'that would carry out a progressive demythologization of the categories that contain the truth, a real shifting and transformation of these categories in the course of the historical process, to the point where they withstand a confrontation with the most basic needs and what is most external, because only then will demythologization have reached its end.' This Marxism thus could not be a 'badly abstract', intellectual Marxism, like that of Lukács; it had rather to be a Marxism like that of Bloch or Benjamin, which captured not only the material aspect and external life but the totality of human need. Kracauer was now able to see the advantage in Bloch's search for traces of truth in 'yet uninhabited basements and lofts': 'One would need to encounter theology in the profane, would need to show the holes and cracks into which truth has trickled down. One would need to rob religion and, once looted, leave it to its fate.'[27] Bloch liked the idea. 'The historical process of demythologization which you sketch is so close to me that, in my work in previous years, I have had intimate experience of it, in almost the same words, and want to furnish it further ...'[28] Kracauer, in turn, issued a political confession:

> I am ultimately an anarchist, even if one who is sufficiently sceptical to consider actually existing anarchism a distortion of what anarchism means. What today is understood and yearned for under the word 'community' is pure mythology that believes it can, by including nature, reach consensus, and has the form [Gestalt] as its idol. The concept of community is constructed in opposition to the concept of 'society', which dissolves the natural ties of community but does not replace it with the real human being, but instead with the reified human being. The dream, the most radical definition of genuine Marxism, is: 'association of free men' (Marx). If one uses these words with all the meaning they deserve, then they provide a norm on the basis of which the concepts of community and society can be criticized.[29]

During the years leading up to the end of 1929, Kracauer's correspondence with Bloch became more and more cordial; on Bloch's side, in particular, it sometimes became enthusiastic. In September 1929, Bloch assured Kracauer: 'As far as I am concerned, there is nothing left that would dampen our relationship.'[30] And when Bloch suggested to Kracauer that they should be on first-name terms, Kracauer was touched:

> My dear friend Ernst, I am very happy that you entrust me with your first name. For a long time I would have wanted to give you mine, but I am no longer in possession of one. The official 'Siegfried' must be ruled out from the very beginning, and the private 'Friedel' belongs to the past ... Please call me Krac.[31]

At this point, so much had changed for Kracauer that he thought he had to give up the name 'Friedel'. He had a woman at his side, 'Lili, the good, the beautiful', as Bloch described her; had found a way of entering into a relationship with reality and enduring transcendental homelessness; had found a political orientation and, with it, new friends, a circle of exceptional intellectuals. And he stood almost at the centre of this circle, in part because, working at the *Frankfurter Zeitung* and becoming an increasingly important figure in Weimar's cultural scene, he could be useful to his new friends.

It was through Kracauer that Bloch came into contact with the *FZ* – a solid, noble and important paper, in his eyes, although one that had treated him badly in the past and had denied him the recognition he was due. In a review of his *Spirit of Utopia* (8 April 1919), he had been called a 'highly eccentric spirit, wholly immersed in mythic thoughts', someone incapable 'of clear and neat thinking'. Now, Bloch received the recognition he deserved. On 17 December 1927, the *Frankfurter Zeitung* published 'Der unbemerkte Augenblick' [The unnoticed moment], his first publication in the *FZ* since the flash in the pan that was 'Ein alter Krug' [An old jug], in 1916. Bloch had requested that the editors, those guardians of purity, include a prefatory note before the piece, and it was politically significant: 'This essay is part of the new work [*Traces*] by this important philosopher.'[32] Between that point and May 1934, Bloch would publish at least sixty-one further contributions in the paper, a mixture of philosophical feuilleton articles, short narrative texts, portraits of landscapes, reviews and short pieces he called 'entrefilets'.[33]

Following the scathing review of Benjamin's *Tableaux parisiens* in 1923, Kracauer made an effort to establish Benjamin as a contributor to the paper. The article on Naples in the summer of 1925 was a first sign that his efforts were paying off. After his Habilitation had failed, Benjamin was attempting to make a living as a translator and author. His publications appeared, for the most part, in *Literarische Welt*. But the *Frankfurter Zeitung* seemed to him a better medium for shorter texts. In February 1926, he sent his new editor friend a selection of aphorisms, part of which Kracauer managed to publish in the paper under the title 'Kleine Illuminationen' [Little illuminations]; they were later incorporated into *One-Way Street*. Benjamin thanked Kracauer 'for the friendly thought of publishing my things' and also 'for persistence and the success with which you know how to find friends for them on the editorial board'. Probably upon Kracauer's initiative, he had by this point also met Roth, who was in Paris in the spring of 1926. And the new freelance collaborator was delighted by Kracauer's idea for the title: 'It is something beautiful for a writer to find himself somewhere so wonderfully complemented by philological conjecture, as is the case with this title of yours.' Benjamin thanked the editor for becoming a 'member of the "Dr Benjamin appreciation society"'. Benjamin was also pleased about Kracauer's rapprochement with Bloch and about the 'new convergences' that were resulting from the study of Marx.[34]

Kracauer's manifesto during these years of convergence was the essay 'The Mass Ornament', which appeared in the *FZ* on 9 and 10 June 1927.[35] It opens with an epistemological reflection: 'The position that an epoch occupies in the historical process can be determined more strikingly from an analysis of its inconspicuous surface-level expressions than from that epoch's judgments about itself.' Thus, if you wanted to learn something about the 'overall constitution' and 'fundamental substance' of the time around 1927, it might have been more illuminating to consider a revue of the Tiller Girls than to read Heidegger's *Being and Time*.

The phenomena that are not thought about or noticed, those that do not suggest any conscious will to create behind them, are able to illuminate an epoch because of their 'unconscious nature' and are, in turn, illuminated by that epoch. Kracauer interpreted the Tiller Girls as an ornament of mass society. They were not a simple case of 'girls' dancing for a mass audience: here, a formation performed, with the precision of Taylorism, in mathematically describable geometric patterns. The dancers were a product of industrial culture that simulated eroticism, an ornament akin to a parade, a march or a choreography performed in a sports stadium. The legs of the Tiller Girls reminded Kracauer of the hands in a factory. Their movements were synchronized and planned in detail, like those of workers on an assembly line. The legs swung in 'perfect parallel', energetically and flawlessly; despite the great physical strain, the girls were smiling. '[P]sychotechnical aptitude tests attempt to calculate dispositions of the soul as well.' Distraction during leisure time: the ladies enjoyed the dancing and the costumes; the men looked at the legs. This product was 'the aesthetic reflex of the rationality to which the prevailing economic system aspires'. Kracauer continues this materialist interpretation of the surface phenomenon with a reflection on the philosophy of history, in which he explicates the idea of a progressive domination of nature, of a battle of reason against natural powers, powers that mythological thinking, however, cannot defeat: 'After the twilight of the gods, the gods did not abdicate.' They continue to haunt Positano, but also all those places where reason rules without justice, where there are deeds without doers. The capitalist epoch with its one-sided rationality does not take account of the human being; it rests on the growth of abstract thinking or the flight towards a false concreteness. With this critique of reason Kracauer anticipated the central motif of Horkheimer and Adorno's *Dialectic of Enlightenment* (1944). Kracauer's essay on the ornament reflects on the progressive domination of nature, but it does not end with romantic lamentations about decline or with a mysticism of nature. On the contrary, Kracauer thought the process needed to be pushed even further in order to transform obscure into enlightened reason. Capitalism, he argued, did not rationalize too much but too little: 'The process leads directly through the center of the mass ornament, not away from it. It can move forward only when thinking circumscribes nature and produces man as he is constituted by reason. Then society will change. Then, too, the mass ornament will fade away and human life itself will adopt the traits of that ornament into which it develops, through its confrontation with truth, in fairy tales.' For an unsentimental and always alert realist such as Kracauer, the idea that 'we need to get through capitalism', the idea of a sudden switch from negativity into a positive utopia, was an unusual moment of optimism of a sort he had not experienced before and would not experience again. In the summer of 1927, existence was no longer under the sway of decay. Kracauer was well, was successful and was loved. Those who wait belonged to a distant past.[36]

13

The Primacy of the Optical: Architecture, Images of Space, Films

The return of the ornament in mass culture could be attributed to the cunning of history. Everywhere else in aesthetic modernity ornaments had long since been removed: 'The evolution of culture is synonymous with the removal of ornament from utilitarian objects.' That was the view of the architectural critic Adolf Loos, as expressed in his famous essay 'Ornament and Crime' (1908). Modern man was devoid of ornaments: 'Anyone who goes around in a velvet coat today is not an artist but a buffoon.'[1] Loos freed the architect from the nuisance of the ornament, as the master architect Le Corbusier acknowledged: 'Loos swept under our feet, it was a Homeric cleansing – exact, philosophical and logical'.[2] His book *Vers une architecture* (1923) contains the phrase: '*The house is a machine for living in.*'[3] Le Corbusier argued: 'In building and construction, mass production has already begun; in the face of new economic necessities, mass-production units have been created both in mass and detail.' This, he wrote, shows 'that a style belonging to our own period has come about; and there has been a revolution'.[4]

Le Corbusier was at the most extreme end of an international tendency towards objectivity. In Germany, this trend towards objectivity in the machine age was associated with the names of Ludwig Mies van der Rohe and Walter Gropius. 'Less is more' – architecture was meant to be as spare and as clear as this Mies van der Rohe slogan: no superfluous decorations or confusing details. Gropius, who was the first director of the school for the crafts and fine arts in Weimar, the so-called Bauhaus, followed the lead of cultural critics in other areas and related the new philosophy of building to the Great War: 'This is more than just a lost war. A world has come to an end. We must seek a radical solution to our problems.'[5] That solution consisted of a sober realism, the unity of art and technology, and an objectivity which, however, derived the spirit of building from the tradition of the crafts. In this, the 'hunger for wholeness' combined with manifestos for a social utopia in which class differences would cease to exist.[6]

The Bauhaus was a left-wing spin-off of the Werkbund, an association founded in 1907 that promoted the 'collaboration of art, industry and artisanship'. This amalgam of 'beauty, utility and skill' was associated with Hermann Muthesius's motto 'vernünftige Sachlichkeit' (reasonable objectivity).[7] Theodor Fischer, the supervisor of Kracauer's doctoral thesis, who was still an adherent of traditional city planning, was a founding member of the Werkbund. Overall, this association of architects, artists and entrepreneurs from the construction industry was open to aesthetic modernism but sceptical towards the ultra-modernists. Kracauer was not a member of the Werkbund, but he visited and reported on its important exhibitions and congresses between 1921 and 1927, including, for instance, the Werkbund exhibition 'Die Form' in Stuttgart in July 1924.

In his article, Kracauer proclaimed his support for objectivity, for a turn away from the traditional ornamental arts and crafts and towards an ascetic attitude in architecture and design, as well as in technology and industry as the dominant powers of modern life.[8] He praised in particular the iron stoves of the Frankfurt architect Ferdinand Kramer, and it seems that the circle that had formed around the 'Rat für künstlerische Angelegenheiten' (Council for Matters Concerning the Arts) in Frankfurt during the revolutionary days of November 1918 had generally left a strong impression on him. Here, avant-garde architects looked to join forces with Walter Gropius. These circles had long since bid farewell to the historical city of the nineteenth century, the city Theodor Fischer still wanted to protect against the excesses of uncontrolled capitalism. Regarding the question of high-rise buildings, Kracauer had already positioned himself on the side of the avant-garde, and from 1925 onwards he would also be sympathetic towards the 'socialist city planning' of his former fellow student Ernst May.[9] In his text on the exhibition of the Werkbund, however, he did not subscribe to the formula 'form without ornament' – now also adopted by the Werkbund – without reservation. On the one hand, the new ascetic artists had simply dispensed with ornament and declared 'the meagre rest to be form as such'. On the other hand, the return to form served only to lay the groundwork for a return to ornamentation. Against the Bauhaus position, he argued that the absence of ornament should not be an end in itself:

Abstinence from ornamental exuberance is neither the ultimate goal nor a lasting ideal; it is only the order of the here and now because structures otherwise lose touch with the sober facts of the day that give them substance. Today, art that designs use objects ... may be compared to a ship that is under quarantine, and the ordered retreat to form only has the meaning of a waiting that, for the time being, is also apt for those existing under negative conditions. The turn of actual life towards reality is tied to the question of whether reality's muteness will one day dissolve.[10]

Thus, Kracauer shared the criticism of quasi-organic architecture and sympathized with rational building. In times of meaninglessness, the absence of ornament was appropriate. But he did not agree with the opinion of many radical innovators, like Le Corbusier, that out of rationalization by itself would grow 'in undialectical directness the liberation of the humankind', because the new way of building and constructing was a mirror image of the economic system rather than an expression of the liberation of the human. At best, it prepared the way for 'new forms of life' while waiting for a new age to arrive, a new age perhaps filled with meaning by revolution – though he did not want to advocate the latter explicitly.[11] Kracauer was also not too fond of the concept of 'new objectivity'. He preferred 'old objectivity', as architect Gottlob Schaupp's bon mot described it. All in all, however, he thought 'the new way of building embodies tendencies that are favourable for progress and that have not yet successfully struggled to the surface in other places'.[12]

The traces of Kracauer's old profession are not only to be found in his architectural criticism. As Adorno fittingly remarked, Kracauer pursued the 'primacy of the optical', not only in philosophy but also in his metaphorical descriptions of social places: dancing clubs and other amusement places he called the 'pleasure barracks' of the New Objectivity;[13] cinemas were 'optical fairylands'.[14] Kracauer was a physiognomist who inferred from the exterior to the interior. He did not try to comprehend reality with the help of concepts but with the help of the immediate perception of phenomena. If in the modern world access to meaningful being was blocked, then one had to find detours in the profane that would allow one to establish a connection with reality. What was not possible through philosophy and its concepts might be possible through images and their social functions. The visual penetration of the world of things was a potential way to find a relation with reality. In that sense, Kracauer mapped the city as a way of reflecting on the social and its history. He adopted the stance of the literary figure of the flâneur, who, like Baudelaire's characters and Proust's *passante* in *In Search of Lost Time*, roamed the city. At Kracauer's side through Berlin, this metropolis of speed and business, ambled Franz Hessel. Hessel read 'the street like a book' and people and things became words and sentences, pages. And Benjamin – like Hessel, a translator of Proust – even constructed a text-street in his *One-Way Street*, whose aphorisms were all taken from the space of the street.[15]

'The knowledge of cities is tied to the decipherment of the dreamlike images they murmur', Kracauer stated in an article on

Berlin landscapes.[16] The interpretation of images of space was his special and original way of appropriating reality, comparable to Benjamin's thought-images. In both cases, reality is depicted in visual reflection and reflected visuality and statements of a general nature are made through concrete objects without reducing the objects to mere illustrations of a theory.[17] Kracauer's images of space are social forms with embedded temporal layers. His texts on streets from the period 1926 to 1932 contain illuminations of social spheres, attempts at interpretations of dreams and pictures of society. In the suburbs of Paris, he visited the squalid quarters of the lower classes, which stood 'under the sign of demolition'. He juxtaposed the decay of complex structures at these margins to the glorious, glittering world of the central boulevards, where 'the demon of absentmindedness reigns supreme': 'Wide streets lead from the faubourgs into the splendor of the center. But this is not the intended center. ... Nevertheless, the streets that lead to the center must be traveled, for its emptiness today is real.'[18] For Kracauer, the map of Paris was an allegory showing that the centre of modern life is vacant and that emptiness is the ruling form of existence. He was attracted by the proletarian quarters, the faubourgs, where once the revolution had begun. The peripheries of the cities were at the same time the peripheries of order. The 'oblivion' and 'abandonment' of Malakoff, a working-class suburb south of Paris, appeared to Kracauer like a 'rubbish heap' – and not only in a metaphorical sense. It was, indeed, Paris's garbage dump. And, in addition, 'the business that is called life ... had turned its back on Malakoff'. Here, the bleak emptiness was physical rather than metaphysical: 'The Paris that appears at Malakoff is a grey mass of tenement blocks which are infinitely long and much too narrow – as if its directional extensions had been warped by a gigantic concave mirror.'[19]

Kracauer roamed the streets of the metropolises as if intoxicated. In a somewhat surrealist text on his recollections of a Paris street, he describes how he saw pavements and rows of houses as if grown into each other 'like the limbs of organisms': 'The sidewalls and pavement frequently flow imperceptibly into each other, and before he knows it the dreamer moves as if on level ground over vertical walls up to the rooftops and beyond, further and further into the thicket of chimney stacks.' The street ecstasy of the flâneur took on Kafkaesque characteristics: 'I believed I had a destination, but to my misfortune I had forgotten the destination.' Or: 'A secret smuggler's path led to the area of hours and decades, whose network of streets was as labyrinthine in its design as that of the city itself.'[20]

Kracauer's dreamlike images of space are similar to Benjamin's first drafts of the *Arcades Project*, which he wrote down between mid-1927 and the autumn of 1929 as a continuation of *One-Way Street*. The *Arcades Project* had been intended as a 'dialektische

Figure 19. Postcard from Walter Benjamin to Siegfried Kracauer, Paris 1929
Copyright: DLA Marbach

Feerie', a dialectical fantasy play, as a study of the development of
capitalism in the unfolding of its phenomena, which adopted both
the perspective of historical materialism and that of the surrealist
theory of dreams. In his first drafts, 'Arcades' and 'The Arcades of
Paris', Benjamin announced that his work would treat the world of
nineteenth-century objects as if it were a world of dreamt objects,
images of collective desire. Thus, Benjamin, the interpreter of
dreams and the social critic, wanted to decipher the language of the
images of emerging modernity as a layer deep in the unconscious
that was, in the *Arcades Project*, to be awakened. At the moment of
awakening, this dream-filled slumber of the capitalist epoch could
be overcome. Benjamin described this awakening as a revolutionary
upheaval in which the past is rescued and the spell that has been cast
over the world, as over the castle of Sleeping Beauty, is broken. The
arcades were a dream image, a dialectical image, which was meant
to illuminate, at one fell swoop, the fate of all human beings, things
and works – namely the fate of becoming commodities – and thus
to dissolve the phantasmagoria.[21]

For Kracauer, by contrast, there were also streets that had no temporal layers and for that very reason had to be interpreted as images of space. On Berlin's Kurfürstendamm, for instance, many houses had had their ornaments removed, something the Kracauer of late 1932 no longer found agreeable, for it destroyed a bridge to the past: 'Now, the robbed facades stand in time without support and are a symbol of the ahistorical change that takes place behind them.'[22] The 'Farewell to the Linden Arcade' (1930), an arcade between Friedrichstraße and Unter den Linden which contained residues of Renaissance architecture and small shops selling bric-a-brac, served as a symbol of the end of a form of existence. The 'peculiar feature' of the arcades, wrote Kracauer, strikingly similar to Benjamin, was 'that they were passageways, ways that passed through the bourgeois life ... They housed the cast off and the disavowed, the sum total of everything unfit for the adornment of the facade. ... In this way the passageway through the bourgeois world articulated a critique of this world which every true passerby understood.' But now, 'under a new glass roof and adorned with marble', the character of the arcade had altogether changed: 'All the objects have been struck dumb. They huddle timidly behind the empty architecture, which, for the time being, acts completely neutral but may later spawn who knows what – perhaps fascism, or perhaps nothing at all. What would be the point of an arcade [Passage] in a society that is itself only a passageway?'[23]

Kracauer made a point of visiting certain social spaces in order to collect impressions of social reality, for instance the 'Wärmehallen' [warm shelters] for the homeless in Berlin, or the 'Arbeitsnachweise' [work registries], themselves a kind of 'passage' meant to lead the unemployed into gainful employment. It was, as Kracauer wrote, a desolate and degrading passage. Those who were waiting there in vain 'play draughts, chess, and card games, all games of fortune that are nothing but tricks of misfortune, because happiness is refused entry by the need that is here intensified to the point of fatefulness'. The space of the 'Arbeitsnachweis' had been arranged by reality itself:

> Every typical space is created by typical social conditions and these conditions find expression in it without any disturbing interventions by consciousness. Everything that is denied by consciousness, everything that usually is assiduously overlooked, takes part in its construction. Images of space are the dreams of society. Wherever the hieroglyph of some image of space is deciphered, the ground of social reality lays bare.[24]

For Kracauer, to read urban space therefore meant: to read society and its times, the *conditio humana* of modern humankind and its primordial history. The images of space were 'smugglers' paths' along which one could capture and interpret reality.[25] In this, Kracauer followed Simmel's idea of the spatial projection of social forms and distinguished himself as a 'social iconologist'.[26] Even his more surrealist expeditions served the purpose of a realism that observed what had broken free from human beings, what had only a forgotten meaning, what had become object-like, in order to make this reality, which had become separate from human beings, available for the human again. Of course, cultural philosophers perceive in the city images, in landscapes and in things precisely what corresponds to their social analyses and views of the world. The images of space were instructed by a theory. Whether demolition or departure, whether nightmare or ecstatic happiness, whether revolution or regression: the reality or possibilities seen by the flâneur depend on the shape of his or her philosophy of history. Whether an arcade is a passage to fascism or to social revolution is decided by the theory, not by the arcade. The images seen by the flâneur are also suffused with his or her own subjectivity. Ultimately, the flâneur recognizes in the image what he or she already knows. Kracauer's enormous sensitivity for the external world may have had to do with his decision to move his gaze away from himself and his own suffering. Making contact with the world was a way of coming to terms with existence.

Apart from 'The Mass Ornament', 1927 saw the publication of another landmark text asserting the primacy of the optical: 'Photography'. In this article, Kracauer notes the remarkable fact that historicism and modern photographic technology emerged at roughly the same time. Both are ways of capturing the world: photography offers a spatial continuum; historicism promises to fill the temporal continuum. 'Historicism is concerned with the photography of time. The equivalent of its temporal photography would be a giant film depicting the temporally interconnected events from every vantage point.' Memory is a different matter, as it 'encompasses neither the entire spatial appearance of a state of affairs nor its entire temporal course'. The images of memory preserve the past only to the extent that it has significance, that it means something and is meaningful to those who remember. Memory, he says, is 'full of gaps'; it distorts.[27] But it has a connection to meaning and truth that photography lacks. Kracauer's reflections on the theory of the image are directed against the positivist illusion of a perfect representation of the world. Never before, he says, has a time produced so many images of itself and yet known so little about itself. Illustrations do not automatically create insights: philosophical knowledge of something is different from seeing something. For Kracauer, the photographed world and the representation of reality in images had, just like conceptual thinking, come to a decisive point: 'The turn to photography is the *go-for-broke game* of history.'[28] For Kracauer, the relationship between realism and form-giving processes in the perception of reality can, with the help of photography, be reconfigured.[29]

Benjamin, in particular, got a great deal out of Kracauer's work on this theme, as is demonstrated by Benjamin's 'Short History of Photography', from 1931, in which he introduced the notion of the 'optical unconscious', a notion that, like the unconscious of images of urban spaces, is reminiscent of the instinctual unconscious of psychoanalysis.[30] But Kracauer's initial reflections also resembled the iconology of the Warburg circle, a fact that would later come out more clearly in his theory of film. It is not possible to say whether, or to what extent, he was already following the work of Aby Warburg, Ernst Cassirer, Erwin Panofsky, Fritz Saxl and Edgar Wind in 1927. It was only later that he actively sought out members of the Warburg circle, especially Panofsky. Yet, similarities can be detected in both the 'photography' and 'ornament' articles: physiognomy was the common methodological element in Benjamin, Kracauer and Panofsky.[31]

The primacy of the optical, finally, found expression in Kracauer's passion for film. According to Balázs, film is the medium par excellence of visual culture; it makes the human being visible again, while also, as Kracauer wrote, recording the 'small life of physical detail' and incorporating it into the world of symbols. Nevertheless, at this point Kracauer did not want to place too much of a burden on film, because the new visibility of the human being, just like the new objectivity in architecture, only confirmed 'the bad rationality of capitalist thinking'.[32] In his last three years in Frankfurt, between 1927 and 1929, Kracauer published at least 369 texts on film, about 120 each year. He visited the cinema several times each week. Why? What magic did cinema work on him? *Georg* can tell us: *This time spring made itself dreadfully at home. Buds everywhere and endless warbling. A universal burgeoning. ... To save himself from the importunings of Nature, on late sunny afternoons Georg sometimes sought shelter in a cheap cinema frequented by errand boys and shop girls – or anyone unable to afford the business of spring. Seasons were for a select public. The place smelled of unaired bodies, beer, embraces, pissoir, and coins – old entrenched odors with which one soon felt a comradeship ... Georg felt safe here. Over and over he relished that moment when it became pitch dark and the images began to live. No doubt, the same spring sun he had just fled immediately rose again, but now he reconciled himself to the blooming landscapes and went strolling blissfully through their reflection on the screen.*[33] If someone had asked Georg whether he wanted to see paradise or a film on paradise, he would have chosen the film. Film is a third reality, next to nature and human society, an as-if reality in which the spectator can participate without belonging to it. Watching a film in a cinema is a magic event: 'Let there be light!' and there is light on the screen; the images move, and reality is banished into the square of the screen. The auditorium grows dark, and the unobserved observer looks at the world through a mirror and succumbs to an illusory reality. He takes part without being directly affected. Little Friedel had already felt safe here, and here the grown-up Kracauer still enjoyed a special access to the world.

And then there were characters like Buster Keaton and Charlie Chaplin. They fascinated Kracauer – tramps, wayfarers and outsiders who stumble and waddle through life rather than taking life in their stride. They displayed a shabby elegance, with walking stick and hat, harmless vagabonds who always met with some obstacle or other, who were chased by strong men – some of them tattooed, some of them in uniform – and thereupon showed themselves to be quick, tough and smart: they ducked, dodged the punches, sometimes even struck back; they ran away and escaped – until they ended up in the next tight spot. Although they are innocent, they are always accused of something. Yet they want nothing but to be the saviours of the orphans and the blind. With a ludicrous agility they fight against modern machinery. They are always close to ruin, yet they are saved by a protective hand in the end; they keep their walking sticks and hats. They do not really achieve anything in life, but their hearts are of such goodness that, wherever they are, the sun shines. They face the mess that is life with dignity and magnanimity. Even if the tramp receives a present, or something just falls to him – a lump of gold, a good meal or even a girl who loves him – he moves on in the end, sometimes with empty hands, carrying on, along the highway of life, into the sunset. He loves, even without being loved in return; he gives presents, even though he owns nothing. 'Chaplin's main comical vehicle', wrote Georges Sadoul, 'is his dignity', while the actual 'dignitaries' appear without dignity, appear ridiculous.[34] The tramp is the hero of modern life, always close to the abyss, but never afraid. 'Hey, look here!' he seems to shout: 'Look how I escape by the skin of my teeth! Grit your teeth and leave some traces behind!'[35] This is a message every child can understand, and the grown-ups laugh and cry, cry and laugh. We should not forget that the end is, in most cases, happy after all, because this illusion, this little bit of cheating in the face of reality, is needed. The realist sees through this yet does not want to do without it.[36] In Chaplin's films, the spectator not only follows a story but feels life itself – his films are 'imbued with a poetry that everyone encounters in his life, admittedly without always being conscious of it'.[37]

Having watched *The Gold Rush* (1925), Kracauer enthused over the way the film treats the human just as it is treated in fairy tales. There is a presentiment of how the powerless might move the world.

Figure 20. Charlie Chaplin in *City Lights* (1931)
Copyright: Ullstein Bild

Chaplin's powerlessness, a moved Kracauer wrote, is dynamite; 'his comic effects conquer the laughter and rather evoke emotion because they touch upon the existence of our world'. It is also possible that Kracauer was so moved because he identified with this clumsy fellow chasing after gold. Whatever the truth of the matter, a great deal in Kracauer's portrait is redolent of the highly sensitive Friedel:

> Other people have a conscious ego and live in human relationships; he has lost his ego, which is why he cannot live along with what is generally called life. He is a hole and everything falls into it, and what is usually connected is splintered into its elements when it hits the ground in him. ... A human being without surface, without the possibility of being in touch with the world. In pathology this would be called a split ego, schizophrenia. A hole. But the purely human, unconnected, shines out of this hole.

When Kracauer (whom Adorno once called a man without a skin) watched the all-too-human battle fought by this solitary tramp against dead and living things, against rough men and heartless women, he laughed, he cried – 'one knows that the surface has been torn up'.[38] With some amusement, he followed Chaplin, in *The Circus* (1928), fleeing from a policeman into a hall of mirrors, where the images of fugitive and pursuer are multiplied a hundred times over: 'the world is torn into pieces that swirl around; it seems to have gone mad'. But he had also to accept, with sadness, that the good and gentle Chaplin is misunderstood by an environment which he, in turn, misunderstands. For Kracauer, in Chaplin's films the violence of the world and the weakness of the individual wrestle with each other, and the fact that Chaplin's humour at least makes a world that behaves with such seriousness look foolish, even if it is not able to unhinge it, is a consolation.[39] Like Chaplin in *City Lights* (1931), Kracauer walked through the social world, wide awake, as 'a friend of the weak and the woebegone' who strode 'through our social wilderness with a warm heart and a sharp eye'.[40]

When Chaplin visited Berlin on 9 March 1931, Kracauer made sure to be at Bahnhof Friedrichstraße, waiting, like a fan, for his arrival. The planned visit had preoccupied the city for weeks, and the platform was an overcrowded commotion. The SA had campaigned against the Hollywood star, whom they believed, erroneously, to be Jewish. The Nazi mob was waiting outside the station, chanting 'Down!' On the platform, by contrast, there were cheers when Chaplin alighted from the red carriage. Just as in a film, Kracauer was standing in the right place at the right time, and found himself very close to the great director and actor:

> So this is him – this short Gentleman with grey hair, who alights from the carriage without a hat and laughs. I have seen him in a thousand photographs, and yet at this moment I see him for the first time. He laughs with his mouth open, and what I never understood from the representations I now understand as in a flash: that the real Chaplin coincides exactly with the tramp in the film. That is the laughter I know from the circus film, this released laughter of happiness from a hapless one who, against all odds, for once draws the lucky number.[41]

Another of Kracauer's cinematic heroes was Sergej M. Eisenstein. Kracauer reported enthusiastically about *Battleship Potemkin* (1925): 'He has broken through that wall behind which those [American and European] films cannot penetrate. He hits upon a matter that is real, intends the truth that has to be at stake.' Eisenstein seemed to capture those genuine truth contents that Kracauer had been searching for. The Soviet director took his subject matter from social life, photographing its visible phenomena and using montage in order to turn the images into a film with a plot and a political message. For Kracauer, Eisenstein was an artist who had mastered space, who managed to create epics and to guide the spectators' thoughts purely using the means of film. At the centre of his films were not actors; the masses were their real protagonists.[42]

Critics in the Weimar Republic received the so-called 'Russenfilme' rapturously, deeming them politically and aesthetically innovative. Old and new stereotypes intermingled in this enthusiastic reception: exoticism and revolutionary sentimentalism, the Dostoevsky cult and the new objectivity.[43] Whether it was Alfred Kerr, Herbert Jhering, Bernard von Brentano or Kurt Pinthus, all were full of admiration for Soviet film, which they considered a paragon for the medium – ignoring the fact that in the Soviet Union there was only *one* Eisenstein and only *one* Pudovkin.[44] Their films, however, stunned audiences with a new aesthetic that was enthusiastically received, also by those of diverging ideological convictions. When for spurious reasons *Battleship Potemkin* was banned in Germany on 24 March 1926, this caused angry, and ultimately successful, protests from film critics. The decision was swiftly overturned by the supreme film review office. Walter Benjamin's paean for Soviet revolutionary film in the *Literarische Welt* was the most full-throated:

> Among the points of fracture in artistic formations, film is one of the most dramatic. We may truly say that with film a *new realm of consciousness* comes into being. To put it in a nutshell, film is the prism in which the spaces of the immediate environment – the spaces in which people live, pursue their avocations and enjoy their leisure – are laid open before their eyes in a comprehensible, meaningful and passionate way. In themselves, these offices, furnished rooms, saloons, big-city streets, stations and factories are ugly, incomprehensible and hopelessly sad. Or rather, they were and seemed to be, until the advent of film. The cinema then exploded this entire prison-world with the dynamite of its fractions of a second, so that now we can take extended journeys of adventure between their widely scattered ruins.[45]

Benjamin considered *Battleship Potemkin* in particular as embodying the state of the art, because it represented the moving collective in its aesthetic beauty and political significance.

Only Joseph Roth had some objections. The scene in *Battleship Potemkin* in which a naval doctor, who is reduced to ridiculously small proportions, denies the existence of the fantastically oversized maggots in the sailors' meat provisions, he declared flawed and false. He did not insist that film be revolutionary but that it show a tendency towards realism. Eisenstein may rightly have appeared a genius to the film critics, but Roth criticized him for glorifying Soviet Russia. The general line Soviet art had to toe did not suit him: it worshipped the new form of civilization, turned it into a new religion. That new religion was no longer an opium of the people, no sleeping powder, 'but a washing powder, a utilizable cleaning resource'.[46] Roth wrote this in 1930, however, and by then the general excitement over Russian film had subsided, including in Kracauer.

In 1927, Kracauer was still defending 'the tendentiousness' of Pudovkin's *Mother* (1926), describing it as 'a tendency directed against the appalling state of affairs'; judges of the artistic, he claimed, should not elevate themselves above such tendencies.[47] One year later, he was disappointed with Eisenstein's *October* (1928), which he called an 'official festival on the revolution': 'The house has been erected; its walls are being painted. ... The starving of the still subjugated population is picturesque. ... Only someone who is triumphant composes like this, someone no longer plagued by doubt.'[48] Kracauer was of the opinion that, ten years after the revolution, what was needed was less tendentiousness and more substance. With Pudovkin's *Storm over Asia* (1928) in mind, he argued that, through their rigidity and schematization, realist films become unreal: 'On one side those in power, on the other the exploited. The former recede in the end, the latter begin to triumph. ... Bolshevik Russia has turned into the Russia of today, and anyhow we have left the glorious beginnings behind. ... The primitiveness of the arguments has been overtaken by the history of recent years. It is time for the Russian art of film to catch up with reality.'[49] Kracauer nevertheless continued to praise the Russian cinematic aesthetics, while he became more and more dissatisfied with German film.

Kracauer accused German film of nostalgia, of glorifying war and of producing 'silly, rose-tinted' illusions. The war that had been lost was gloriously won, repeatedly, on the screen, and the youth, cheerful and fresh, was prepared for the next one. Instead of looking for its themes in the streets, the films used old stories, popular songs or operettas as their material. There were scores of films with powdered aristocrats and dashing lieutenants, on Frederick the Great and the great Frederick, on the cheerful sinking of ships[50] and hearty military marches, on congresses that were dancing and girls marrying their bosses. The two Harrys – Harry Liedtke and Harry Piel – were the typical faces of such films: the one was always smiling, loving, frivolous; the other knocking down a villain with his right, while holding a girl, waiting to be kissed, in his left. The only person Kracauer disliked more was the irresistible, yet insufferable Hans Albers, or perhaps Otto Gebühr, in whom the national socialist section of the audience jubilantly recognized the old Fritz, Frederick the Great.[51]

In March 1927, Kracauer, the suffering cinema-goer, had a series of articles on film and society published in the *Frankfurter Zeitung* under the title 'Film und Gesellschaft' [Film and society]. It became a classic of film criticism because it put forward a central tenet: films are a mirror of society because films have to bring in money and thus production companies have to try to satisfy the apparent tastes of the audience. Thus, '[s]tupid and unreal film fantasies' are not necessarily attempts at manipulating the audience; they are rather 'the *daydreams of society*, in which its actual reality comes to the fore and its otherwise repressed wishes take on form.'[52] In a reversal of the proletarian-communist criticism of the Ufa films as instruments of class domination, he wrote: 'There is no kitsch one could invent that life itself could not outdo ... Sensational film hits and life usually correspond to each other because the Little Miss Typists model themselves after the examples they see on the screen. It may be, however, that the most hypocritical instances are stolen from life.'[53] If you want to know how a society based on great social inequality is held together, you have to go to the cinema, because that is the place where people in need and misery are saved, or at least kindly pitied, at no cost. There, you can travel the whole beautiful world without reflecting on the world. There, the little people learn that their bosses carry gold not only in their purses but also in their hearts. There, they are told that what matters is the human being and not whether someone is rich – even if the idea of happiness without prosperity is, in truth, a fairy tale. There, tragedies lead to tears instead of revolts; love is more powerful than money; life is good, if everyone makes a bit of an effort. In short, at the cinema the desires of little shop-girls and employees, who were flocking to the film palaces in their millions, are fulfilled for ninety minutes.

Kracauer was a disappointed cinephile, and in 1928 he settled his accounts with film productions 'like an Old Testament prophet'[54]: he called them 'stupid, false, and often mean'. They lacked '[u]prightness, the gift of observation, humaneness'. But Kracauer's criticisms did not just take aim at the industry; they were also directed at the audiences who enjoyed such films. As a passionate movie-goer, he condemned the general tendency of films to distort social reality. Even in documentary films, there were flights from reality. Moreover, the films were not filmic – that is, they were not committed to the primacy of the optical; rather, the images were illustrations of a foreign text, while they themselves should have been the text to be read. In 1928, Kracauer thought that German film had gone to the dogs: it was without substance, unreal, confused – just like the society that had produced it.[55]

At that point, Kracauer had not yet developed a theory of film, but he did have fairly precise ideas about what such a theory should focus on, namely the immanent conditions of film, meaning the technical procedures and the fact that only the visible world can be represented. To Kracauer the materialist and realist, film seemed better suited than other media to let the mute world be present and to create a visual continuity that did not lead to the systemic and idealist. With the help of close-ups film is able to make things talk and to make them part of the world of meaningful symbols. It is able to disclose, maybe even to create, a world of spatial configurations, although it is not allowed to turn into an artistic end in itself in the process – it has to remain close to human reality.[56] A film on a great city has to show the human significance of the streets, squares and houses, and should not be distracted by literary ideas about these things (as did, according to Kracauer, Ruttmann's *Berlin – Symphony of a Great City* [1927]).[57] Unlike Rudolf Arnheim, for instance, Kracauer was open to talkies. If the silent movie had made the life of light and shadow accessible to human consciousness, then now the talkies could do the same for 'the unintentional roaring of the street'; that is, they could capture those noises that escape our senses and combine them with images. Of course, sound films had to respect certain limits: their philosophical limits, which were identical to those of positivist photography, and their aesthetic limits, namely that they had to remain faithful to their role of serving film as an optical medium without confusing the grammar of optical language.[58]

Kracauer demanded that films be realistic, but he was himself no naïve realist. According to him, film was an optical penetration of reality, but he did not ask of a film that it represent the visible world in just the way that everyone saw it. Quite the contrary, reality could, as Chaplin's films masterfully demonstrated, very well be distorted or take on grotesque forms. Realism and a kaleidoscopic view of the world, or surrealist fantasy – these did not contradict one another. What was decisive for Kracauer was that the 'processing' of reality be carried out by means of film, that is, strictly within the realm of the visual.[59] For him, realism did not mean representation of the visible world but a connection with natural and social reality from a humanist perspective. Films were not meant to embellish life but to illuminate it. They should not pursue some idea, but rather describe real existence. They should be able to withstand the sight of real people and their actions and openly depict injustices, 'because the strength to take in undisguised life is a precondition for genuine political action'.[60]

14

Ginster, Georg and the Salaried Masses

War has broken out. It is the continuation of peace by other means. Suddenly the people are a people. Among them lives one who investigates them subterraneously. He is a rather peculiar person, someone who does not want anything, who wants to crumble or become vaporous. He does not have a proper name, either, only a first name from his time at school: Ginster – the name of a plant, although Ginster is glad that he is not a plant. His fellow human beings are obviously more important than Ginster. They live in two-bedroom-professions, have their informers everywhere and walk around in well-fitting suits. Ginster is embarrassed when he notices that the others are not superior. The human beings observed by Ginster are, despite all their bustling, rather lifeless. Things, by comparison, are sometimes alive. Arms in uniforms move automatically. Ginster stands aside, at times without making any contact with his environment. On the one hand, that is regrettable; on the other, it is not, because it is very likely that Ginster would not gain anything through relations with his fellow human beings. Quite the opposite: he would probably lose his power of observation amidst the general bustle. Nevertheless, Ginster is oppressed by voices that are none of his business; he feels guilty for things he did not bring about. Ginster has to enter into military service, although he does not know the reasons for the war. He is astonished by his fellow human beings, who, for the sake of a little piece of occupied land, are willing to give up all the things that are no less important than war. He hates the patriotism, the glory, the flags – because they block the view. Even his family sings 'Gloria, Viktoria'. His mother longs for the mass death, by fire, of the enemy, although she would be incapable of uttering a single angry word to a stranger. His uncle, a historian who studies the wars of the Middle Ages and thereby discovers that it is especially during wartime that those at the top are glorified and those on the bottom squeezed – this uncle becomes the fatherland personified. Ginster's friend Otto even volunteers. Ginster, by contrast, is a coward. He decides that

Figure 21. Picture of the company with Ginster (in the back, standing, the fourth from the left)

Copyright: DLA Marbach

he will not give away his true views to anyone. While in military service, he learns that a properly conducted war depends on trivial things whose significance in battles he had never before considered. Thus, in the morning he is not allowed to leave the blanket rumpled on the bed, but has to fold it into a prescribed angle. And he must salute correctly, so that the whole project can flourish, and clean the windows, get up early and give himself a number; he must march behind those in front and in front of those behind, kicking his legs up in the air, eyes to the left. All this is headed up by a sergeant, with a waxed moustache whose two halves are made up of precisely the same amount of hair. Slowly it dawns on Ginster that these exercises do not serve the war; the war serves as a pretext for these exercises. He manages to shirk the front. All he does is peel potatoes against the enemy. War is something incredibly ordinary. *Ginster* tells the story of a young man without qualities, and how he does not take part in the war.

Parts of the novel appeared in April 1928 in the *Frankfurter Zeitung*. It was a decade since the end of the world war, in which time a number of war novels had been published. The most successful of them was Erich Maria Remarque's *All Quiet on the Western Front*. *Ginster* was different. It was not a novel about the front but one set in the homeland. Its reckoning with the war was of a different kind, inspired, rather, by the emptiness of everyday life. The character Ginster was like a tramp who had accidentally ended up in Imperial Germany, and the book was a picaresque novel in which the mischievous and melancholic, the grotesque and the real, were constantly bounced off each other. Any attentive reader of the *Frankfurter Zeitung* should have been capable of guessing the author – 'Ginster' was one of Kracauer's many pseudonyms and thus meant something to the readers of the culture pages. Playing hide-and-seek with pseudonyms was part of the Ginster performance, of a 'naïvety that understands and describes itself'.[1] Kracauer never tried to hide the fact that this was a quasi-autobiographical novel. Its fundamental theme – the search for life, a life from which the protagonist feels excluded – had been Kracauer's preoccupation during the decade of war and inflation. The fictional character Ginster showed all the signs of suffering that also had characterized the young Kracauer. At the same time, however, Ginster was more of a vehicle for investigations into wartime society than a representative of Kracauer's ego. The author does nothing to psychologically illuminate the character, who thus does not seem to have served the purpose of autobiographical self-assurance. He is a void, almost an 'anti-subject', although the aim is to rescue the subjectivity and individuality that had been destroyed in the war.[2] Kracauer completed *Ginster* after his 'exit from inwardness'.[3] At its centre stands a desolate world, not the ego; an irrational 'reality' is superimposed on everyday 'life'. The novel's hero does not progress towards some higher point that is to be reached at the end. Rather, the text reflects in episodic fashion on the ordinary. The world had become contingent, the individual problematic. Thus, the novel as a literary genre was also in crisis. In his article 'The Biography as an Art Form of the New Bourgeoisie', Kracauer wrote that, now that the human being had experienced its own nullity in the war, confusion had itself to take on an epic form.[4] Thus, *Ginster* was a self-portrait that distanced itself from the category of the self; it was an intentionally confusing mix of autobiography, criticism of the contemporary world and philosophical motivation that was as peculiar as its author. Kracauer's irony was on full show. One critic compared Kracauer's dry humour to the 'straight faces of the great comedians'.[5] Not even the hero of the story, Kracauer's alter ego Ginster, was safe from this tone of 'caustic resignation', as Thomas Mann called it.[6]

Kracauer had been writing literary texts ever since he began his studies in 1907. Some passages from the prose pieces 'Ein Fest im Frühling' [A celebration in spring] (1907/08) and 'Die Gnade' [Mercy] did actually find their way into *Ginster*, albeit stripped of their sophomoric world-weariness and yearning for life. There are also two short prose pieces of 1925 and 1926 that had previously been published in the *Frankfurter Zeitung*, and which anticipate motifs from *Ginster*.[7] A particular event had convinced Kracauer to decide to turn these fragments into a novel:

> One evening I told Joseph Roth in the Hotel Englischer Hof in Frankfurt, where we always met in the evenings, about my war experiences, how I peeled potatoes against the enemy, etc. He laughed and laughed and told me that I had to make a novel out of it. I objected that I had never written a novel before and that the material was good for twenty pages at the most, whereupon he advised me to make my uncle and other things part of it. And that is how it began.[8]

Kracauer certainly also used Franz Tunda, the hero from Roth's *Flight Without End* (1927), as a model. Or perhaps it was the other way around: Roth's book appeared half a year before Kracauer's, but the actual writing of the two books would have overlapped. We should probably assume that there was a mutual inspiration, especially given that each author was full of praise for the other.[9]

Tunda, who has been homeless since the war and has been gadding around between Siberia and Paris, is, in Kracauer's words, 'a human being that does not act. ... Sometimes he aimlessly floats along; sometimes he stops and does not know where to go. ... Only someone who does not join in and does not want anything can today be a vessel for the observations that matter to the heart.' Kracauer's character Ginster is also such an impassive observer. And not only were there similarities between the shy heroes of the novels. In his review, Kracauer also praises the construction of *Flight Without End*. The events, he writes, are not pressed into a closed schema; rather, the 'parallel side by side displayed by reality remains a side by side in the novel'. *Ginster* exhibits a similar episodic structure. Kracauer also liked Roth's attitude: 'a hard to define humanity', no sentimentalism, but empathy and insight into the human condition. He was also impressed by the language, for example the shifting of the emphasized meaning from the main clause to the sub-clause – a technique Kracauer liked to employ himself and even extended to the relative importance of subject and object. And finally Kracauer appreciated his colleague's tone: 'Not a protest against the times, but a grief that takes note of the facts.'[10]

Roth, in turn, was enthusiastic about *Ginster* and made efforts to interest publishers in the novel. He spoke to Kurt Wolff, to Bruno Cassirer and to Gottfried Bermann Fischer. Following the publication of the extracts in the *Frankfurter Zeitung*, Roth reported from Berlin that the literary scene was getting curious and wondering who this Ginster was. Kracauer, he recommended, should remain silent for the time being, as this would stimulate further interest in the texts. Meanwhile, Roth would negotiate with Bermann Fischer.[11] At the end of June 1928, Kracauer himself went to Berlin, met with the publisher and signed a book contract, which guaranteed him 300 marks per month (roughly £1,000 in today's money) for a year, in which time he could work on his next novel. Prosperous times seemed to lie ahead. In December, the S. Fischer Verlag announced in the *Börsenblatt*:[12] 'This, too, was the war! Just out: the new novel Ginster. Written by himself.' And below: 'Who is Ginster? Ginster in the war, that is: Chaplin in the department store.' Roth had written the text for the advertisement. Thus, in his person he united the roles of initiator, agent and promoter. And, of course, he also reviewed the book for the *Börsenblatt*: 'We have found our literary Chaplin at last.' The affinity between Ginster and Chaplin had not escaped others either, for instance Ernst Bloch, who wrote to Kracauer: 'Despite Schwejk … this is a new type. At best, there are a few traits from film characters, from Chaplin and Buster Keaton.'[13] On Kracauer's film review of Chaplin's *The Circus*, he remarked: 'Throws some light on Ginster.' Kracauer's film reviews had also highlighted the 'Ginster-like' nature of Chaplin's tramp. And in Buster Keaton he had seen personified an 'allegory of absent-mindedness' of a kind that was also typical of his novel's anti-hero.[14] Apart from Bloch and Roth, Friedrich T. Gubler also pointed out intentional and unintentional similarities in the *Neue Zürcher Zeitung*: 'Among more recent stories written in the German language, "Ginster" appears with a sensational form of inwardness that is reminiscent of Franz Kafka. Or of Charlie Chaplin.'[15] Ernst Glaeser, the author of *1902* – a pacifist novel in the style of the new objectivity – identified a parallel with Chaplin in Ginster's evasion of military service. Ginster, he said, avoided the war not for pacifistic reasons, but because he enjoyed living: 'Just as Chaplin always is the last one there, after all the great action is over, thus Ginster stands there at the end of the war, smiling, and says: everything is fine, if you can bear it.'[16] In short, 'Ginsterism' was an indictment of a society that deified rationality and opted for the madness of war, one in which only the Ginsters seemed strange.[17]

The literary critics had nothing but praise for the book. In the *Weltbühne*, Hermann Kesten applauded Kracauer the stylist and humourist, and Joachim Maass emphasized the clarity of the language and the dryness of the humour. But the highest praise came from Alban Berg, who sent Kracauer a telegram which Kracauer would treasure for the rest of his life. The composer not only acknowledged *Ginster* as a 'literary masterpiece', but also as a 'in the truest sense of the word *document humain*' – 'something that always seems to me the ideal condition of an artwork'.[18] The fact that Bloch, independently of this evaluation, compared *Ginster* to Berg's opera *Wozzeck* suggests that this was, indeed, a case of an affinity

Figure 22. Kracauer in Berlin – a photograph for the publisher S. Fischer, around 1928
Copyright: DLA Marbach

between different artistic domains. Consumer demand for the book was, however, restrained. By the end of 1928, no more than 1,673 copies had been sold. To give a figure for comparison: Remarque's novel sold 450,000 copies within the first three months. Bermann Fischer had to tell the disappointed author: 'Your book is a literary success; it will not become a great success with the audience, and it cannot be otherwise, for reasons we all know. They mainly lie in the high quality of the work, which means that it is easily accessible to only a small group of people.'[19] *All Quiet on the Western Front* was translated into twenty-six languages during the first year after its publication. For *Ginster*, Bermann Fischer could not find an American publisher, despite his hopes. But at least the Libraire Gallimard got in touch straightaway and bought the French rights. Clara Malraux, the wife of the literary star André Malraux, turned *Ginster* into *Genêt*, with the support of Bernhard Groethuysen, Kafka's editor in France. The prospect of the translation delighted Kracauer. The contract with Gallimard meant intellectual recognition and access to the literary scene in Paris. And because he had, through his travels in France since mid-1925, become something of a Francophile, the translation held out the promise of being loved by those he loved himself. His impression was that, unlike in Germany, in France, and especially in Paris, the human, the humane, had not completely disappeared, despite the material, intellectual and psychological devastation of the Great War. In France, there was a real society and a people that was committed to humanity. People were more important than principles; life was what mattered, not theories. The conservatives were not reactionary, the socialists not Marxist and the Catholics not political. In Paris, in contrast to pretentious Berlin, Kracauer saw the city's spirit tied to the human; the public sphere was home to the little people, who lived with things that resisted the evaporation into abstract objects. In Paris, he held, surfaces were essential and, despite Hausmann's avenues, improvised cavities formed.[20]

For Kracauer, Paris was a place of longing, a place where he experienced flashes of a more fulfilled life, just as he had in Naples and, in particular, in Marseille. The southern French port city is the setting for the last chapter of *Ginster*; on the Cannebière, five years after the end of the war, Ginster finds a connection to life again, and almost feels at home amidst pieces of washing and filth, the innumerable children and cats, the dirty rivulets and streams of people, the meat counters and the fish stench. In Marseille, he learns *what I never experienced during all of the war: that I have to die, that I am alone. I cannot explain it further, but back then all fear had left me. I was liberated from all dependency and judged things correctly – I had learned death.* In addition to this existentialist moment, there is an anarchic impulse in the novel – a hatred of splendid castles, of the *domination practised by people* and of an order that denies the existing misery: *These buildings should be torn down, the bad beauty, the splendour: down with it. Here, in the harbour district, nothing is encapsulated; the naked ground lies open.*[21] Kracauer drew a picture of 'Marseille' as a utopian place of decay and anarchy. In the bustle of people and things, in the unplanned collectivity of social existence, in the sensual stimuli of surfaces, a secret happiness could be found, a happiness that could no longer be felt in the blocked spaces of northern civilization and bourgeois forms of life.[22] Some readers saw this last chapter as documenting the end of Ginster's negativity. The chapter bears witness to the fact that Kracauer too had found a relation to empirical life. The lament for a world that was disintegrating in the conflagration of war was, in the mid-twenties, superseded by a passionate search for reality, for the chaotic world of real people and non-reified things.[23] Around 1930, Kracauer had found a sensual, philosophical and political connection to this reality, as a human being and as a man, as a cultural philosopher and public critic, and not least as a writer.

'Ginster' kept writing. More precisely, he worked on a 'novel from the German republic'. The first chapter, 'Salon 1920', concerned those self-confident and self-satisfied salon revolutionaries whom Kracauer had met in real life in Susman's house, the progressives who – as the novel has it – believe in the good in people and the bad in tin soldiers and, at the same time, arouse in the novel's hero, Georg, the political and professional desire to play a role 'in public'. This first chapter initially appeared in the *Frankfurter Zeitung* in 1929, and subsequently also in an anthology compiled by the busy editor of the Kiepenheuer publishing house Hermann Kesten, in which he presented what he thought were the most talented and best storytellers of the new generation. Apart from Ginster, they were Joseph Roth, Ernst Glaeser, Erich Kästner, Anna Seghers, Ödön von Horváth and Kesten himself – a colourful mix of humanist sentiment and new objectivity. Two further fragments of *Georg* appeared in 1931, again in the *FZ*. Until his flight from Germany, Kracauer had completed seven chapters, a solid half of the final book.

Georg is a continuation of *Ginster*; the two heroes of the novels are distant cousins. The panorama of society it presented concentrated on the intellectual, 'progressive' left camp, but, as in *Ginster*, yesterday's dignitaries, with their parted hair, also made their undignified entrances. The war is over; the revolution has marked the beginning of a new time. Like Ginster, Georg is embarrassed for others and is an oddball, without real orientation in life, but he wants to be in the limelight, even has a proper name and sexuality. The place of Otto is taken by Fred, but this time disaster comes not in the form of death but in the form of a relationship drama.

Through Fred's mother's connections, the sorry hero of the book gets a post at the *Morgenbote*, a newspaper which, at the beginning of the novel, is politically to his left. From this post he observes Weimar's theatre of competing world views, from occult anthroposophs, to the Dostoevsky disciples, yearning for redemption, and delightful declines of the West. He visits congresses that congratulate themselves on their existence, and salons that congratulate themselves on their discussions. Georg becomes a pawn in the political battles at the newspaper. His longing for community turns increasingly into an attitude of disgust towards it. An abyss separates him from the progressives. Unlike Ginster, Georg undergoes a development. 'Ginster' went on to write *Georg*, but Ginster only turned into Georg during his time as a migrant in Paris.

Prior to his time in Paris, Kracauer wrote another ambitious – in literary terms – book. This time it was not a story, but a text that explored his sociological interests and ventured into a social space that had hitherto been little investigated, namely the world of so-called salariat. Late in spring 1929, Kracauer went to Berlin for ten weeks in order to undertake research for this book. He visited the career centre of the central association of salaried employees and the *Berufsämter* [professional offices], which were responsible for assessing the suitability of the masses of salaried employees and candidates who wanted to become salaried employees. He also went to the bleak *Arbeitsnachweise* [work registries]. He observed the work routines at department stores and offices. He interviewed business directors, heads of personnel departments, workers' councils, typists, shorthand typists, accountants, foremen, clerks, legal assistants, cash messengers, street sweepers, apprentices, trainees and those who had been made redundant. He studied the communications from the imperial board for economic efficiency and from limited partnerships, and he examined surveys of the unemployed carried out by trade unions. He read company bulletins and employers' pamphlets, and the Act on Workers' Councils. He analysed the hierarchy in large-scale enterprises, followed labour law trials in court and watched company sports events. And he followed the salaried employees after work, taking leisurely strolls, distracting themselves and going on trips to the *Moka-Efti-Lokal* in the Leipziger Straße at the corner with Friedrichstraße, the 'Resi' (Residenz-Kasino), or the *Haus Vaterland*. Using the employees as his example, Kracauer demonstrated how human beings are economically utilized in modern capitalist society during their leisure time as well as their work time.[24]

Kracauer's brief visit to Berlin was a test run for his move to the Berlin office of the *Frankfurter Zeitung* in Potsdamer Straße, which was already being planned at that time. Kracauer was meant to replace the head of the office, Bernard von Brentano. Benno

Reifenberg also had plans for a career change, hoping to pass on the headship of the feuilleton for a spell in order to go to Paris as a political correspondent, and he supported Kracauer's project on the salariat from the very beginning. For Kracauer, it seemed almost inevitable that Berlin would be the place for his investigations; the condition of the salaried employee could be observed in its most extreme form in the capital, and, Kracauer noted in an allusion to Benjamin's book on German tragic drama, only from the extremes can reality be opened up.[25]

But who were the salaried employees? Well, they were those who were not employed in actual production and thus did not form part of the industrial labour force. They were thus defined in opposition to 'the bottom'. The first salaried employees in industry appeared between 1850 and 1890 (technicians, draughtsmen, commercial personnel, so-called *Industriebeamte* [industrial civil servants]), and they began to appear within state institutions. Then they appeared in trade, in particular in the wake of the emergence of the large department stores. They were an intermediary social stratum; some spoke of a middle stratum or of a new 'middle class'. In 1911, a law on employees' insurance determined the professional groups that were to be considered as employees. These were executive employees in general, then the more senior office employees and foremen, sea captains and officers, teachers and educators and, finally, pharmacy assistants.[26] There were salaried employees everywhere; they could only be considered as forming a unified group by setting them off against other classes and strata. The comparatively high percentage of women in such professions was striking: in 1924, a third of the 3.5 million white-collar employees were women. In big cities, the 'typical gainfully employed woman' was a salaried employee, as Susanne Suhr established in 1930 on behalf of the central association of employees. This central association belonged to the Afa-Bund [Allgemeiner freier Angestelltenbund; General Association of Independent Employees], an association with social-democratic leanings. There were also other employee associations looking out for the interests of their members, for instance the Gewerkschaftsbund der Angestellten (GdA) [Federation of Trade Unions of Salaried Employees], which was united with the liberal Hirsch-Dunckerscher Gewerkverein in the Gewerkschaftsring Deutscher Arbeiter-, Angstellten- und Beamtenverbände [Trade Union Group of German Workers, Employees, and Civil Servants Associations], or the Deutschnationaler Handlungsgehilfen-Verband (DHV) [German Nationalist Assistants Association], whose profile was corporative and nationalistic and which attracted National Socialists.[27]

Kracauer described this world of the salariat as a *terra incognita*: 'Hundreds of thousands of salaried employees throng the streets of Berlin daily, yet their life is more unknown than that of the primitive tribes at whose habits those same employees marvel in films.'[28] Kracauer was, however, not the first to engage with the world of work and the lifeworld of the 'stand-up collar proletarians' or 'drilled petit bourgeois', as they were mockingly called, depending on the perspective of one's own social class. There were already a few academic studies of this new social stratum, for instance, those of Emil Lederer, Hans Speier and Otto Suhr, and Kracauer referred to all of these. Writing in the *Neue Rundschau*, Lederer had drawn attention to the 'restructuring of the proletariat' and the 'intermediary capitalist strata'; he gave a figure of 5.2 million for the number of civil servants and salaried employees in Germany.[29] But no one really recognized the political significance of this new social stratum for the crisis-plagued republic as clearly as the salaried employee of the *Frankfurter Zeitung* Kracauer. He was worried that salaried employees could become easy prey for the National Socialists if the employee associations did not shed their anti-socialist prejudices and their conceit about their social standing and if the radical intelligentsia, and if the collectivist, anti-bourgeois party officials for their part continued to cultivate their separation from real life. With regard to salaried employees and their associations, this meant that the denial of the proletarianization of the salaried employee had to end. With regard to the communists, it meant that this new socially marginalized group should not simply be inserted between the bourgeoisie and the proletariat within the existing pattern of class struggle. With regard to the intellectuals, it meant that they should not turn their noses up at the dull mass of salaried employees; they had rather to analyse the working and living conditions that made them dull.[30]

The book, which was dedicated to Benno Reifenberg and which was eventually published with his support (after some dispute within the newspaper) by the Frankfurter Societäts-Druckerei, opened with two stories:

I. Before a Labour Court, a dismissed female employee is suing for either restoration of her job or compensation. Her former boss, a male department manager, is there to represent the defending firm. Justifying the dismissal, he explains inter alia: *'She didn't want to be treated like an employee, but like a lady.' In private life, the department manager is six years younger than the employee.*

II. One evening an elegant gentleman, doubtless a person of some standing in the clothes trade, enters the lobby of a big-city night club in the company of his girlfriend. It is obvious at first glance that the girlfriend's side-line is to stand behind a counter for eight hours. The cloakroom lady addresses the girlfriend: 'Perhaps Madam would like to leave her coat?'[31]

Each anecdote serves to comment on the other, and to illuminate the double existence of being and seeming to which salaried employees were exposed between their professional and private lives.[32] The real topic that Kracauer minutely dissected here is the discrepancy between social and economic misery and bourgeois expectations, and he does so with what is, by this point, skilful writing, as elegant as it is sharp. Kracauer was not only interested in the material proletarianization of the employees and the grey, often undignified, work routine. He was also interested in the 'employee culture' – 'i.e. a culture made by employees for employees and seen by most employees as a culture'.[33] It was the culture of the palaces of distraction and Luna Park, of the little shop-girl who goes to the movies, and knows every hit song, or 'rather the hits know her, steal up behind her and gently slay her'.[34] Kracauer interpreted the culture of employees as a form of escapism. As they were 'spiritually homeless', they were no longer proletarians with a class consciousness, but bourgeois ruins who had not yet noticed their proletarianization, like the elderly commission agent who no longer matters but 'who spices his conversation with Latin quotations' in order to assure himself of his (long since lost) importance.[35] This motif of social criticism might sound stale today: those who have been betrayed and scorned in real life flee, out of false consciousness, into manipulated, illusory worlds that numb them and keep them from reflecting on their actual situation. Following 1968, countless people have regurgitated this early critique of social coldness, stultifying consumption and a manipulating culture industry. But Kracauer's essay on employees, on the brutal selection processes in aptitude tests, combined with the 'morally pink complexion' required by the ideology of the ordinary; on the rationalized work processes that care not a jot about the human being; on heads of departments who are 'cyclists' and who 'bow down to those above them and trample those below'; on the cult of vitality in a numb, unlived life; and on the whiff of greatness available, for little money, in the Luna Park, where 'an auto-racing track gives lowly salary-earners the pleasure of feeling like amateur motorists' – all these observations conveyed new insights at the time and remain stylistic gems today.[36]

Kracauer's method, which recalls Eisenstein and Pudovkin, was also remarkable. He did not want to write reportage of the kind that had been in vogue since the mid-1920s. Egon Erwin Kisch had stated: 'Nothing is more stunning than the simple truth, nothing more exotic than our environment; nothing shows more fantasy than the new objectivity.'[37] Kracauer certainly could have signed up to that. And he too considered himself an impartial witness and shared the view that a text had to depend on the facts. But in his book on salaried employees, he distanced himself from the reporting of the new objectivity. He interpreted this approach as expressing a 'hunger for directness that is undoubtedly a consequence of the malnutrition caused by German idealism': 'A hundred reports from a factory do not add up to the reality of the factory, but remain for all eternity a hundred views of the factory. ... Certainly life must be observed for it to appear.' But, still, '[r]eality is a construction.'[38] And the right method for constructing it, for him, was montage, a mosaic of photography. A second way in which Kracauer's reportage differed from Kisch's was the element of critique. Pure reportage, Kracauer held, reproduces bad existence, with all its small daily catastrophes, while a critic's representation of reality seeks to remove the spell, to liberate human beings from their reified compulsions in the name of sincerity, empathy and humanity.[39] For this project a number of requirements had to be met: one was the Kantian a priori insight that experience without concepts (but also without theory) is blind, and concepts (or theories) without experience empty; another was the form of attention set out by Simmel, which begins with individual phenomena and, by way of induction, investigates social reality, without being guided by philosophical speculation about history. Finally, the project required a basically Marxian under-standing of capitalist society, without which one could not identify false consciousness or produce any synthetic mosaic of snippets from reality. In his exposition of the arcades project, Benjamin announced that he wanted to test the extent to which it is possible to be concrete in philosophical matters; Kracauer put to the test the idea that it is possible, from a sociological perspective, to create meaningful coherence out of splinters of reality.[40] His observations and conversations were not intended as illustrations of a theory but as examples taken from reality. According to Kracauer, the *Salaried Masses* was 'an example of material dialectics'.[41] To Wiesengrund, who had praised both the form and content of the work while also asking whether the thesis might not have been developed without the help of empirical sources, he wrote:

> It isn't that I had delivered my opinions *prima vista*, but actually my insight into the purely defensive position of capital developed out of a theoretically based view of empirical reality. Elsewhere, too, I have repeatedly had to revise my original intuitions with hindsight. I regard the work as very important in methodological terms inasmuch as it constitutes a new type of statement – one which does not, as it were, juggle between general theory and specific practice but represents an autonomously structured way of seeing.[42]

Kracauer took his bearings from Marx, although without wanting to be a Marxist. He was looking for a dialectics, without wanting to commit himself to a philosophy that claimed to grasp the totality. And he allowed space for subjective experience and intuition, without wanting to deny the general. We need not seek to answer whether the book really manages to do without any kind of overall framework. Its author was, in any case, aware that his social panorama had the character of a construction based on a solid empirical core. It was based, throughout, on Kracauer's 'urge to capture reality' [Elan zur Realität], an urge to which he felt committed.[43]

Kracauer's treatise attracted enormous attention. Even local newspapers announced its publication, and there followed an intense and heated debate over it. Emil Lederer and Hans Speier, the pioneers of sociological research into salaried employees as a professional class, defended Kracauer's book. In the *Frankfurter Zeitung*, Lederer, who was the director of the Institut für Sozial- und Staatswissenschaften [Institute for Social and State Sciences] in Heidelberg, characterized it as 'an English book' because it 'knows how to grasp the concreteness which, so far, has been closed off and unapproachable for us'. And his pupil Speier summarized the work in the *Magazin der Wirtschaft*, saying that while the existing social scientific studies on the 'new middle class' had taken the measure of the social space, Kracauer described 'the air that fills it'.[44] Karl Mannheim even suggested 'that a new method is approaching here, which may be called up at least to complement our old statistical and other scientific methods in its intuitive and at the same time constructivist fashion'.[45]

The reactions from the journals of the employees' associations were mixed. In the papers owned by the trade unions, *Beamten-Gewerkschaft* and *Arbeit und Wirtschaft*, Henrik de Man welcomed Kracauer's book as a corrective to the left's theory of class struggle. Kracauer, he said, had confronted the riddle of why the consciousness of the salaried employee becomes more and more like that of the petit bourgeois, despite their economic prole-tarianization. And Kracauer's answer was: replace the 'despite' with 'because of'. De Man, who was a social psychologist at the University of Frankfurt, supported Kracauer against accusations from trade union circles which accused the study of a purely literary radicalism that was of no use to the labour movement. In *Der freie Angestellte*, the official journal of the ZdA, Fritz Croner recom-mended 'to our colleagues to, on occasion, take a look at how their life and existence is reflected in the eyes of a mindful observer, not to be irritated by distortions and to learn from the mirror images'. The reviewer in *Der leitende Angestellte*, by contrast, did take issue with these distortions, and especially with the 'prejudice' of the author, who he said failed to recognize that there is no such thing as 'the employee' – there are only types of employee. The professional associations GdA and DHV, which Kracauer had criticized in his study, hit back. The GdA claimed to have been misquoted and subjected to 'caustic irony'. Kracauer's 'normal employee', they wrote, was not one who they recognized from their associations. In the *Deutsche Handelswacht*, no less a figure than the national revolutionary Ernst Niekisch inveighed against the 'flippant, cheeky, vengeful' ridicule of the middle class's sense of community and the 'organic structure of society'. Kracauer was, 'for obvious reasons' – one could probably see it in his nose – not interested in the fate of the German people: 'The grinning faces of those who will reap the "profits" once the self-assurance, pride and professional honour have also been extinguished among the employees hide behind his back.' Niekisch invoked the professional honour of shop assistants and the tribal consciousness of a *völkisch* people against the 'withering, big-city democracy' of the Kracauers and other Jews.[46]

These criticisms from interest groups and from the anti-Semitic enemy make it clear that Kracauer now found himself in the middle of the political battles of the late Weimar Republic, which, around 1930, were beginning to look more like a civil war. The stock market crash in New York in October 1929, shortly before Kracauer's book came out, sparked a nervous fear among all those who followed economic developments. Kracauer was all in favour of political argument; he wanted to be a part of the public sphere and to be a political writer. He was attracted by Berlin, the city of salaried employees and the heart of political and artistic life. At the time, Berlin was considered the newspaper capital of the world – well over 2,000 papers and journals were available daily at kiosks and in bookshops.[47] Berlin was where it was all happening. The more placid Frankfurt was provincial by comparison, despite the banking houses, the chemical industry, the fair, the up-and-coming university and the important newspaper in Große Eschenheimer Straße.

Financial problems at that newspaper meant that, towards the end of the 1920s, significant changes loomed. The old family business was in such financial peril that a completely new type of organization seemed the only hope. On 27 February 1929, the Imprimatur GmbH was founded.[48] The man behind it (although his hand in the firm was hidden by a middle-man) was Carl Bosch, the head of the executive board at I.G. Farben, who acquired 49 per cent of the shares for twice their nominal value, and in addition provided a loan of over 1.5 million marks at an exceptionally low interest rate. Many people suspected Bosch's involvement, and rumour spread that the once independent newspaper was now run by the corporation. When Arthur Feiler, one of the oldest serving editors and a fierce critic of monopoly capitalism, was, following serious personal and political disagreements with Heinrich Simon, handed his notice, some saw this as a sign of the paper shifting to the right. The 'great *revirement*' (Margret Boveri) in spring 1930 was also associated with the I.G. Farben.[49] There were fears that the *FZ* would now become an organ of the biggest German industrial corporation.

Kracauer's move, however, was not really connected with the change of ownership. His series of articles on the employees in the autumn of 1929 had not been well received in the chemical industry either, and within the *Frankfurter Zeitung* it had led to a conflict between the feuilleton and the business editorial office. But Kracauer, with the backing of Reifenberg and the approval of Simon, went to Berlin of his own accord in order to take over from Brentano at the editorial office of the feuilleton there. He was by no means 'driven out' (as Erich Noth believed);[50] rather, he saw better opportunities in the capital, even if Rudolf Kirchner, who succeeded the left-liberal Bernhard Guttmann as head of the Berlin office, was a political counterweight to his predecessor. Kracauer had helped to select the Swiss national Friedrich Traugott Gubler to stand in for Reifenberg during his time in Paris and had shown him the ropes in Frankfurt and befriended him. He believed that Gubler, former secretary of the Swiss Werkbund and an admirer of *Ginster*, would be his man in Frankfurt.[51] Kracauer's self-confidence had grown considerably, and the prospect of political clashes in a radicalized and politicized Berlin did not frighten him.

Figure 23. Elisabeth Kracauer, ca. 1928
Copyright: DLA Marbach

His move to Berlin also had to do with the fact that Kracauer was about to get married. Elisabeth Ehrenreich gave up her position at the Institute for Social Research and became not only his wife but also his collaborator: 'On 5 March 1930, I married Dr Siegfried Kracauer, who, in his extensive activities as an editor of the "Frankfurter Zeitung", as a social scientist, and as an author, depended on collaborators', she wrote in her application for compensation as a refugee in 1963. 'Thanks to my versatile professional training over many years, I was able to carry out all necessary work for my husband. My activities for him included research, producing excerpts of material, proofreading, dealing with an extensive correspondence, etc.'[52] But the most important point was that Kracauer could rely on her. There was nothing, either in his private or professional life, that he did not discuss with her. In all likelihood, there was scarcely an article, book or film on which he had not solicited her opinion, or with which she had not been involved in some way. Elisabeth Ehrenreich was, from then on, a part of Kracauer's intellectual life. She was, as Friedrich Gubler put it, a part of his mental existence.[53] They became a 'We, Inc.', with roles that were clearly divided up along patriarchal lines. Both sides fully entered into it and were very happy with the arrangement. Lili certainly stood in the shadow of her husband, but it would be more fitting to say: she was his shadow. The two lived in complete identification with each other, 'in a form of marriage', as Adorno would later write to Kracauer's widow, 'which those following after us will hardly be able to experience any longer'.[54]

The *Salaried Masses* was, as it were, Kracauer's inaugural lecture in big-city Berlin. For some, it was a gauntlet thrown down; others enjoyed the brisk and refreshing new tone coming from the far left. Of course, Kracauer's friends praised the polished essay because of the very political tendencies for which its author was attacked from other quarters. In the *Neue Rundschau*, Bloch wrote:

Kracauer has travelled to the very core of this way of not existing. With a single glance that penetrates where others only report, or even chatter. With a language that is able to say what it sees, that attaches itself fast to the matter under scrutiny, with a certain sober colourfulness. The starting point is several steps ahead of the usual scientific point of departure, and the study thereby ends up, across the text as a whole, just as far beyond the theoretical end, which is to say it gets there tendentiously. Here the actual situation of the salaried employees is hit on its head – or rather on the false consciousness that it has of itself. The masks which the employees put on, or allow to be put on them, are shown and exposed as masks.[55]

Benjamin spoke about the *Salaried Masses* on the radio and praised it in *Die Gesellschaft*, a journal for social-democratic and Marxist theory.[56] In Kracauer's book, he wrote, 'humanity is born from the spirit of irony'. The language cunningly follows the contours of its objects, the jargon of cold economists, of pompous employee functionaries and of the cosy ambience of pleasure domes, in order then to expose them to light of reason. Kracauer, he wrote, dialectically forces himself into his subject matter, unmasks ideologies, and he is in that sense a Marxist writer. But he 'stands alone. A malcontent, not a leader. No pioneer, but a spoilsport.' What we see is

> a ragpicker, at daybreak, picking up rags of speech and verbal scraps with his stick and tossing them, grumbling and growling, a little drunk, into his cart, not without letting one or another of those faded cotton remnants – 'humanity', 'inwardness', or 'absorption' – flutter derisively in the wind. A ragpicker, early on, at the dawn of the day of the revolution.[57]

15

The Idea as Bearer of the Group: The Philosophical Quartet

Kracauer was delighted by Benjamin's image of the rag-picker, and he felt flattered. Earlier, in July 1928, he had promoted and reviewed Benjamin's writings – the rejected Habilitation *The Origin of German Tragic Drama* and the volume of aphoristic short prose *One-Way Street*, both published by Rowohlt – in the *Frankfurter Zeitung*. Kracauer appreciated Benjamin as a thinker who was a stranger to his own times, someone who 'burrows into the material thicket in order to unfold the dialectic of the essences'. He was, Kracauer thought, driven by a peculiar theological knowledge of the world that is blocked from our view, hoping, through contemplation, to rescue and redeem what had been overlooked in 'those hidden moments and nodal points in the course of history'. Kracauer painted a portrait of his idiosyncratic friend as a kind of secret agent, in Kierkegaard's and Kafka's mould. Benjamin's interest was the trial 'that takes place, between heaven and hell, behind the backs of things and that at times visibly breaks into the world of our dreams'. 'His proper material is what has been: for Benjamin, knowledge arises out of ruins' – just as, one is tempted to add, the rag-picker gains his knowledge from the rubbish of society.[1] Kracauer's review of his friend's work was a continuation of his support for the private scholar's work, but now Kracauer's was far from a lone voice. The book on tragic drama, in particular, had gained widespread attention and acclaim, despite not being a particularly accessible read. This unexpected success heartened Benjamin, and he now set his sights on becoming the most important literary critic in Germany.[2]

Kracauer also reviewed Bloch's *Traces* (1930), 'a new treasure chest containing stories from everyday life and narrations that shine and glimmer in unfamiliar ways',[3] a book which was looking for traces that lead to the land of utopia from out of the darkness of the lived moment – the 'nowhere and everywhere land, in which human beings will have shed even the last mythological veil and finally meet with themselves as, otherwise, they only do in fairy tales'.[4] These warm remarks on Bloch's *Traces* only appeared, however, half a year after the book's publication, and even then the review was relatively short, acknowledging Bloch's status as a thinker in general more than commenting on the book in particular. The reason might have been that Reifenberg had already reviewed the book and that Kracauer originally intended to publish a review of it in the *Weltbühne*, a plan that was vetoed by the *Frankfurter Zeitung*.[5] It is also possible, though, that a political disagreement played into all this – a matter to which we shall return presently.

All this mutual reviewing and promoting of other people's work shows just how much the review business in the Weimar era was dominated by networking. Kracauer regretted this: 'Dilettante wilfulness, cliques and subjective interests dominate the field.'[6] Literary criticism, Kracauer said, had been corrupted. Still, he very much got involved in it. Benjamin, Bloch, Kracauer and Wiesengrund-Adorno formed a peer group whose members referred to and mutually supported each other. 'There were ties of friendship between us and we communicated a lot with each other', Kracauer reported towards the end of his life, although he added: 'despite all our shared characteristics we were keenly aware of our differences, including our temperamental differences.'[7] Around the same time, he wrote to Adorno: 'It is interesting that the younger critics constantly recall the affinity between you, me, Benjamin and Bloch. For them we constitute a group which is set off against the background of the times. This should be fine by us, I think. I find it enthralling and curious to learn how we, who know each other from the *inside*, appear to the outside world.'[8] In a letter Lili Kracauer wrote to Löwenthal, after the death of her husband, she noted the 'major and deep differences in the thinking and the resulting thoughts' of Adorno and Kracauer, adding, however, that these differences did not destroy their friendship, which, 'despite intense discussions', 'continued for such a long stretch of life'.[9] What kind of group was this?

We have already talked a good deal about Kracauer's friendship with Bloch and Benjamin, and especially his relationship with Wiesengrund. The relationship between Friedel and Teddie remained strained from the time of the trip to Naples in 1925 until autumn of 1929, but it was so precisely because of its intimacy. Their exhausting journey was followed by six months of silence. After that, both sides sought to make amends, but things would never be the same again. 'Too much is blocked between us, and the memory of the relationship as it was is too great to be skipped over at the outset', was the resigned analysis of a downbeat Wiesengrund after his return from Vienna. 'There is a fate overshadowing our relationship which seems to me stronger than we are.' By this point both had more or less long-term female partners, a fact that gave rise to new complications. Wiesengrund felt that Kracauer had distanced himself from him; he complained that Kracauer had not even asked him his opinion of Lili.[10] But a 'meeting à trois' was not something he could countenance either, and he himself was now looking for stability in his relationship with Gretel Karplus, despite having wanted to end it only a year earlier.[11] Following the nightmare of Vienna, he moved in a somewhat desultory manner between art, academic philosophy and music criticism. He felt as though the whole world had turned its back on him. He was particularly angry at Leo Löwenthal; the two were now in competition for a Habilitation with Hans Cornelius on which only one of them would be able to embark. Wiesengrund was particularly upset at the fact that, as he saw it, this interloper was cosying up to Horkheimer to further his cause.[12] He considered Löwenthal's claim 'rapacity' and Kracauer's neutrality in the matter as a betrayal. To his mind, in a case of a conflict that was of such importance to him, Kracauer should have come down clearly on his side; Horkheimer, he thought, must have interpreted Kracauer's neutrality as a tacit criticism.[13] The tide had turned in their relationship. Now it was the younger one who was distressed by the aloofness of the older one. And, where once he was so well loved, Wiesengrund now found himself jealous of Bloch, who had received 'large portions' of the *Ginster* manuscript from Kracauer 'while', Wiesengrund complained to Kracauer, 'you have not passed a single page on to me'. Now apparently downgraded and only of secondary or tertiary importance in Kracauer's and Bloch's eyes, Wiesengrund began somewhat to resent the new friends. He warned Kracauer against Bloch, who, he said, had intellectually robbed Kracauer 'down to the last penny', and accused Benjamin of speaking 'in quite a distant and condescending way' about Kracauer and Wiesengrund to a female friend of theirs.[14]

The first subtle signs of a change appeared in February 1928, when Wiesengrund asked his friend's forgiveness for having initially expressed some reservations about Lili Ehrenreich. Wiesengrund's contrition was prompted by the fact that he himself had been urged, by Soma Morgenstern, to abandon Gretel Karplus. Wiesengrund now felt that his way of behaving had been 'inappropriate' and promised from now on to maintain a 'reasonable' relationship to Kracauer's 'girlfriend'.[15] Kracauer admitted that he had also found Wiesengrund's relationship with Gretel difficult. There was, in principle, nothing really to object to in Gretel. Still, no one can force themselves to feel sympathy, although politeness may be a first step. From then on, the letters between Friedel and Teddie ended with greetings to Lili and Gretel, and those two, in turn, also greeted each other: Lili greeted Gretel, and Gretel Lili. The letters also became more matter-of-fact, chatty, without reproach, lament or insinuation. And suddenly, in the late summer of 1929, Wiesengrund said he was glad of the new-found tone: 'It is as if you had, for the first time, relaxed that wretched attitude of humane neutrality which had afflicted our relationship for so long, and instead finally behaved towards me in a more open and spontaneous manner again.'[16] The oppressive atmosphere that had characterized the relationship for years had dissipated. Half a year later, on the occasion of Kracauer's wedding, Wiesengrund wished him 'and Lili, sincerely and unconditionally, all the happiness that can be hoped for between two people who have chosen to share their lives together'.[17]

From April 1930 onwards, the air between them was cleared; the sun shone on their relationship. Kracauer was in Berlin, and Wiesengrund retreated to Kronberg, in the Taunus mountains, in order to write his book on Kierkegaard. The older friend, as always well informed, reverted to his former role of adviser. Wiesengrund referred to his Kierkegaard book as having to do with their 'shared philosophical past'. Wiesengrund's Habilitation was an attempt to demonstrate that even the greatest critic of idealism – Kierkegaard – had lapsed into aesthetic idealism. Wiesengrund-Adorno (the name under which he published it) called Kierkegaard's doctrine of existence a 'realism without reality'.[18] The work combined everything that Teddie and Friedel had discussed during the previous twelve years: the problem of reification and the melancholy of the bourgeois *intérieur*; the search for lost meaning and the will to reach a substantial reality; the false inwardness that isolates itself from the world of objects. Kracauer praised this sociological critique of inwardness, its concepts of existence and its aesthetic, and suggested that it was methodically related to Benjamin's philosophical work. For a short time, the Kracauer-Adorno reading group had become active again. With Kracauer's review for the *Frankfurter Zeitung*, which, in the spring of 1933, reached the typesetting stage before ultimately not being published, the Kierkegaard file was closed.[19]

Benjamin's review was published in the *Vossische Zeitung* (2 April 1933). He called Wiesengrund-Adorno's analysis of the concept of existence 'penetrating'; as a critic of Kierkegaard, Wiesengrund-Adorno was 'incorruptible': 'Here Kierkegaard is taken not forward' – as in Karl Barth's dialectical theology or in Martin Heidegger's existentialism – 'but back – back into the inner core of philosophical idealism, within whose enchanted circle the ultimately theological nature of his thought remained doomed to impotence.'[20] Ten years earlier, in 1923, Benjamin and Wiesengrund had made each other's acquaintance in the Café Westend at the Opernplatz in Frankfurt, at a meeting arranged by Kracauer. They then attended a sociology seminar by Gottfried Salomon together, and during Benjamin's time in Frankfurt they saw each other at least once a week, 'very likely more often'. Benjamin was an unusual thinker, with a tendency to reflect on 'blind, intentionless material' that others failed to notice, and he made a deep impression on the twenty-year-old Wiesengrund: 'It was as if only through this philosophy did it dawn on me what philosophy had to be if it were to fulfil the promise it makes, and does not keep.'[21] He had had similar experiences during his Saturday afternoons with Kracauer. During February 1928, Wiesengrund was in Berlin and he and Benjamin began to see each other regularly. Benjamin told their matchmaker: 'Wiesengrund and I have been together frequently and fruitfully. He has also now got to know Ernst Bloch.'[22] Up until this point, Wiesengrund had known Bloch only through his writings and as a witness to his quarrel with Kracauer. Kracauer's impression had been that the young Teddie did not think particularly highly of the *Spirit of Utopia*. Yet Adorno himself reported, in a contribution to a Festschrift on the occasion of Bloch's eightieth birthday, that he had been fascinated by the volume. Perhaps this was a fascination not limited just to Bloch but extending, rather, to all that marginal philosophy being produced at a distance to the academic world by the likes of Benjamin, Bloch and Kracauer: philosophy that 'had escaped the curse of being official' and was in fact 'one prolonged rebellion against the renunciation in thought that extends even into its purely formal character',[23] a philosophy that instead advocated a 'phenomenologically trained dialectical materialism that was committed to following the contours of its objects'.[24] Whatever the truth of the matter, in the beginning Bloch and Wiesengrund's relationship was based not only on their shared bafflement at the manner in which academic philosophy ignored a host of important subjects, but first and foremost on their shared love of music. However, like Benjamin and Kracauer, Wiesengrund was particularly impressed by the narrative skill of Bloch, the 'séducteur', by his temperament and his inner fire, by which Benjamin, as he himself once said, was able to warm his own thoughts.[25] In intellectual terms, though, Wiesengrund was much closer to Benjamin than to the enthusiastic Bloch.

Benjamin visited Wiesengrund several times in Kronberg, where the latter had retreated to write the Kierkegaard book. On one such occasion, in the autumn of 1929, he read some excerpts from his drafts for the arcades project to him, Horkheimer, Karplus and Lacis, and, in return, had Marx's idea of commodity fetishism explained to him.[26] Wiesengrund was so convinced of the importance of Benjamin's work that he read and discussed the book on German tragic drama as part of a two-term seminar on recent publications in aesthetics. That happened to constitute something of a provocation: the seminar took place in the rooms of the very institution which, seven years earlier, had rejected the book as a Habilitation. It was not intended as a provocation, though; he had not announced the seminar in the list of courses offered at the university and had selected the students individually.[27] This ambivalence on Wiesengrund-Adorno's part, between his desire to become part of the university and his admiration for Benjamin, the cultural critic and outsider, had already been apparent when he gave his inaugural lecture as a private lecturer on 8 May 1931. This lecture had caused quite some furore. It all began very well: the audience was so large that the lecture had to be moved to the university's assembly hall at the last minute. 'All of Teddie's acquaintances' were there, as Hedwig Kracauer reported.[28] Wiesengrund-Adorno lectured on the 'Actuality of Philosophy'. He criticized the idealist concept of reason by pointing to the present order, which – when viewed from a materialist standpoint – appeared unreasonable. But he also discarded the alternatives to idealism that seemed to suggest themselves: a metaphysical ontology and positivism. And although he emphasized the importance of the dialectical method, he did not accept Hegel's philosophy and its notion of identity as a possible way out of the crisis either. What the new lecturer presented amounted to a materialist and scientifically contextualized version of Benjamin's epistemo-critical prologue to the book on tragic drama, although most members of his audience would probably have failed to notice this. In any case, their responses were not what the new lecturer had hoped for:

> Wertheimer [a Gestalt psychologist] had a convulsive fit of weeping from rage and excitement; [Paul] Tillich [a theologian] thought the form was offensive because of its conclusive tone; Mannheim grumbled, and for Horkheimer (including Leo, who has developed completely into one of the tsetse flies [Tsetser] and satellites circling him), it was not Marxist enough. You can have no idea of the wrath – the flood of hatred, opposition and malice – that the lecture brought down on me.

This is how Wiesengrund-Adorno reported the event to Kracauer in Berlin:

> I don't fit in; I have no desire to forge a 'science' or 'world view', but something which is fundamentally different – something which is entirely disparate from academic categories and embitters people who basically still want to enquire into the meaning of being in Aristotelian or Hegelian terms.[29]

In short, Wiesengrund-Adorno had achieved what his older friends, Bloch, Kracauer and Benjamin, had been denied: the leap into the academic world. But these absent outsiders were his true role models at this point. He promptly sent them typescripts of the lecture.

Kracauer, the mentor, praised the first part of the lecture, which sets out a critique of contemporary philosophy, and remarked that the second part was redolent of Benjamin and Benjamin's 'very private' and 'curious' relationship with Marxism and materialism. But he judged his friend's overall approach to be a tactically unwise game of hide-and-seek: 'You wanted to express a commitment, and yet you could not.' Instead of setting out his views on philosophy as such, he would have done better to have presented 'some little genuinely dialectical examination, and broken this off precisely at the point just before the transitional break would have occurred'. In that case, the professors would not have felt affronted 'and yet you would have entered into their brains'.[30] Despite the fact that the lecture implicitly praised him, Benjamin was irritated. He had discussed it with Bloch and reached the conclusion 'that the piece as a whole succeeds in its aim, that in its very concision it presents an extremely penetrating articulation of the most essential ideas which our circle shares'.[31] As far as 'the question Bloch raised about the possible mention or otherwise of my name' was concerned, however, Benjamin, citing 'the desire to maintain [their] philosophical friendship', demanded a reference to the introduction to his book on German tragic drama.[32] Thus rebuked, Wiesengrund-Adorno assured Benjamin that he would include a citation (the piece, though, remained unpublished before 1933), but at the same time he resented the accusations from Berlin. In his defence, he wrote to Kracauer that Benjamin's essay on Kraus had at least as much to do with his own writings as his lecture had to do with Benjamin's. He was particularly annoyed by the fact that Bloch paraded himself as 'the guardian of intellectual property',[33] because both Wiesengrund and Benjamin himself often suspected him of plagiarism.[34]

But those accusations lacked substance. There was, in general, a great deal of consideration given to questions of intellectual property rights. Rarely did people simply copy, or otherwise exploit, the work of others. Rather, as Adorno would later put it when discussing his, Benjamin's, Bloch's and Kracauer's fondness for aphorisms: 'Such things seem to be in the air when it is their time.'[35] There was a thought collective at work, and ideas were circulating and moving from one person to another, gradually coming to be modified as they did so. The following sentence from a letter from Adorno to Kracauer is revealing on this score: 'Once again, then, we are *d'accord* without having discussed the matter first.'[36] There emerged among them what Ludwik Fleck calls a 'thought style', with all the risks and side effects that come with it.[37] The more closely they worked together, the more pronounced the culture of suspicion became. The more intense their exchanges, the less clear it was who had thought of what first. And the more their group broke up into cliques, the more intensely did a certain nervous irritability and jealousy flourish.[38]

Indeed, the importance of this nervous irritability cannot be overestimated. It is tempting to ascribe to the group a 'hypertrophy of the psychological component', although it took on very different forms in different members.[39] Bloch was hyper-energetic, with a 'militant optimism' that could sometimes be wearing.[40] Benjamin's outlook was fundamentally gloomy, if not depressive, and he was at times plagued by thoughts of suicide. Wiesengrund, the precocious genius, in a sense ended up playing out the drama of the gifted child. And of course there was the eccentric Kracauer, who carried his complex of hypochondriacal suffering around with him like a mark of Cain in the form of his stutter. They all were fighting their own demons, and this made commitment and relationships difficult precisely when the need for them was most acute. Kracauer and Wiesengrund, in particular, were also permanently complaining about coughs, headaches, sleeping problems, back pain, rashes, stomach upsets, depression and all manner of other gripes. It is striking that these theoreticians of modern life themselves suffered with the very same afflictions that would come to be associated with modernity. It was a nervous age, it is said; neurasthenia was a condition not only of the soul but also of the culture.[41] These intellectuals were too sceptical to derive any sense of security from the new (or the old, for that matter) certainties provided by philosophy, science and the arts. They had experienced too much to be hopeful and optimistic. And they were too intelligent to ignore the fact that their lives were in some way damaged. Their position as intellectuals outside the university, in particular, was one of permanent precarity. And the sunset of the Weimar Republic and the rise of the Nazi party did for whatever little reserves of equanimity they might have had left. Still, while this weakness and vulnerability, this hypochondriac susceptibility, make a person particularly sensitive to all of life's miseries, it also helps to reveal the things life has to offer. This connection between sensitivity and attentiveness applies in particular to Kracauer, who had taken an almost existential decision to look away from his life and be happy.[42] His opening up to the world was precisely what allowed him to become a subject. As Alexander Kluge argues in *Chronik der Gefühle* [Chronicle of Emotions], he who gives himself completely to a subject matter becomes a subject, because he is in possession of all his personal faculties. By contrast, the one who pays attention to his moods, his condition, the one who behaves like a romantic poet, is an object, because he turns himself into a thing, is not within himself, is objective.[43]

It was in his relationship with Wiesengrund, more than anywhere else, that Siegfried Kracauer developed his passions. With Teddie he enjoyed an intimacy, for better or for worse, of a kind that none of the other relationships within the group quite matched. Benjamin and Bloch, it is true, had known each other for some time, since 1918, when they met in Berne while fleeing the war, and this shared experience created a strong bond, as did their respective breaks with their teachers, Gustav Wyneken in the case of Benjamin, Georg Simmel in that of Bloch, over their glorification of the outbreak of the war as an ethical experience. Benjamin experienced Wyneken's speech on 'War and Youth' as a 'betrayal' and 'degradation' of the idea of educational reform and an 'unparalleled disgrace', taking this as a *pars pro toto* for bourgeois culture in general. And following Simmel's nationalistic outburst Bloch wrote sarcastically to him: 'You have never been looking for a definitive answer to anything, never. You were entirely suspicious of the absolute; striving for something absolute was a closed path to you. Hail, to you! Now you have found it at long last. For you, the metaphysical absolute is the German trenches!'[44] Bloch first looked towards Lukács for intellectual orientation and then, after the war, to Benjamin himself – on the beaches of Capri and on the rocks of Positano, and in Paris, where they lived 'for half a year in a true symbiosis', hanging out together 'every day, and in particular every night', as Bloch later recalled.[45] And of course they spent time together in Berlin, where they pursued their shared passion for the particulars, for the detail, for the marginal – and also experimented with hashish. Their friendship entered a period of crisis when Benjamin criticized Bloch's *Traces*, despite the fact that he had been the first to encourage him to write these 'stories from your own specific perception' ['Geschichten mit Ihrem Merke'].[46] Bloch took the criticisms as a sign of 'disloyalty', and he claimed that Benjamin himself was a difficult person, 'a bit bizarre, eccentric', sometimes 'cold and impertinent'. Yet he was inspired by him 'in a highly fruitful way'. Despite his utterly cerebral life, the friends could sense that, for Benjamin, the work of thinking, despite all its melancholic traits, was not the work of mourning but a human pleasure. Bloch confessed that they could all learn from Benjamin.[47]

Detlev Claussen emphasizes that the group formed by Benjamin, Bloch, Kracauer and Wiesengrund was a Jewish 'peer group'.[48] It consisted, however, of 'non-Jewish Jews',[49] that is, of non-believers from assimilated parental homes who nevertheless were attracted by a Judaism of which they had 'not so much knowledge as inklings'.[50] Benjamin related his connection with Jewishness when he spoke of the 'important experience of turning to the outside world with ideas and finding it was overwhelmingly Jews who came toward me'. Judaism was 'in no way an end in itself' for him, 'but the noblest bearer and representative of the spiritual [des Geistigen]'.[51] Thus, their Jewish origin did play a role – even in the case of those with absolutely no ear for religion, like Wiesengrund, who dismissed the

representatives of the Jewish revival, like Buber and Rosenzweig, as
'religious Tyrolians'. While in Prague in May 1925, for instance, he
reported that he had visited the grave of Rabbi Löw, the creator of
the Golem, and had stayed there for some time.[52] We have already
touched upon Benjamin's and Bloch's interest in old and new
Judaism in the context of messianism, if not for religious reasons.[53]
Claussen neatly sums up this ambivalence: 'The Jewish tradition
no longer seemed viable to them, but it left unmistakable traces in
the way they experienced life.'[54] Faced with an environment that
was potentially hostile to Jews, and mindful of their position as
outsiders in the eyes also of the 'Jewish Jews', a feeling of mutual
commitment emerged without it being necessary to talk explicitly
about their Jewish roots. The four of them simply did not belong
anywhere, and therefore they were looking towards each other for
a sense of belonging. They were non-identical, and therefore they
thought along similar lines. They were Jewish heretics who were
looking for the 'relevant others', German writers who were German
only for the time being.[55] What Scholem wrote about Benjamin
(and Kafka and Freud) applies also to the other three: 'They have
nothing of German phraseology; even the phrase "we Germans"
they have avoided over almost the entire productive phase of their
lives, and they wrote in the full awareness of the distance between
themselves as Jews and their German readers.'[56]

Drawing on Kracauer's early essay 'The Group as Bearer of
Ideas' (1922), one could say that the Benjamin-Bloch-Kracauer-
Wiesengrund group was essentially constituted and held together
by an idea which was 'set off against the background of the
times' – a kind of thinking against established philosophy, science
and arts, the aim of which was to capture reality dialectically, to
prevail in it, and possibly, by interpreting it, to change it in a more
humane direction. This thinking was meant to be identifiable by its
procedure of immanent critique and by negativity for the sake of
hope, and its form was the essay and the feuilleton. Kracauer once
wrote to Wiesengrund that an encounter with Benjamin was like
'meeting at a crossroads, before going off in different directions'.[57]

Indeed, the members of the group generally seemed to meet each
other this way. In the years between 1926 and 1933, the paths of
these four cultural philosophers crossed over in Frankfurt, Naples,
Paris, Marseille and, finally, in Berlin, and their jointly conceived
works formed a new kind of Marxist cultural criticism. At such
crossroads we find cafés, like the Café Westend in Frankfurt's
Opernplatz, the Café l'Odéon in Paris or the Romanisches Café in
Charlottenburg, at the corner of Tauentzien and Budapester Straße
near the Kaiser-Wilhelm-Gedächtniskirche, which, for Kracauer,
represented 'a fiery protest against the darkness of our existence'
when it was brightly illuminated at night.[58] The 'Romanisches', a

meeting place for left-wing artists and perhaps the only place where the members of our group were all present at the same time, was closed to Jews from 1933. Wolfgang Koeppen witnessed members of the Gestapo sitting at the tables: 'We saw the terrace and the coffee house being blown away, disappearing with its intellectual cargo, dissolving into nothingness ... and the visitors of the Café were scattered across the world or were captured or were killed or committed suicide.'[59] Kracauer and Wiesengrund, Benjamin and Bloch, were among those scattered across the world; the crossroads were closed.

But even before this, cracks had begun to form within the group, caused by petty jealousies and political differences. One such cause was Benjamin's friendship with Bertolt Brecht, to which the others responded with astonishment, if not outright rejection. Benjamin got to know Brecht in May 1929, and he was fascinated by the fiery, experimental artist. Although Brecht's demeanour was the exact opposite of Benjamin's – he was a cheery lover of life, not a cerebral type like Benjamin – they had a lot in common. They shared, for instance, the ambition of becoming the best in their respective fields, and they both had sympathies for communism. The latter informed their plan in November 1930 to create a journal, *Krise und Kritik* [Crisis and Critique]. They invited Bloch and Kracauer, among others, to preliminary talks about the project.[60] They thought Wiesengrund would be a contributor, alongside established cultural figures such as Alfred Döblin, Robert Musil, Erwin Piscator, Ludwig Marcuse, Paul Hindemith, Kurt Weill, Siegfried Giedion, George Grosz, Karl Korsch and Arthur Rosenberg. Kracauer was to be the editor of the journal, which was to pursue something they described as 'interventionist thinking'. But it is likely that Kracauer entered the discussions with the brakes already on. His employer was not happy with his involvement in the project, and Kracauer himself judged the preliminary talks to be 'dilettantish'; he did not really have any faith in 'Brecht's journal'. From his experience of working for a newspaper, he knew that such a broad collection of creative and idiosyncratic spirits was likely to be a hindrance, rather than a help, in founding a publication, not to mention in keeping it going. Even the usually voluble Bloch remained quiet during the meeting because he was not really convinced of the organizational powers of 'the ingenious-Alexandrian Benjamin': 'And whatever Benjamin tries to organize, he does wrong. He makes mountains out of molehills, and he then tries to thread them through the eye of a needle.' It is not quite clear why Bloch found fault with Brecht. Bloch certainly shared the general feverish enthusiasm for the *Threepenny Opera*.[61] And he also had communist leanings, had no fear of contact with pearls of wisdom coming from shrewd characters with rolled-up sleeves, and considered Brecht a 'dreaming head' who embarked on new socialist paths with his 'montaged theatre'.[62] Like Brecht, Bloch thought it was important not to forget the more mundane critique of pure unreasonableness in the pursuit of the philosophical critique of pure reason. Perhaps Bloch's reservations about Brecht had to do simply with the latter's relative lack of philosophical education. Kracauer, by contrast, simply found Brecht suspect. His Yes Sayers and No Sayers were not of interest to more complex minds, which rather sympathized with the Maybe Sayers. In a letter to Scholem, Kracauer reported a very intense dispute with Benjamin in the course of which there was talk of a 'slavish-masochist attitude toward Brecht'.[63] The reactions of Benjamin's friends to his friendship with Brecht were deeply emotional. They considered Brecht a vulgar Marxist who had lured Benjamin away from them with his blunt thinking. Others had no such reservations, however. Hannah Arendt, for example, called his friendship with Brecht 'a stroke of good fortune in Benjamin's life'.[64] For her, Benjamin was the 'most peculiar Marxist' in a movement 'which God knows has had its full share of oddities'.[65] And to her it only seemed natural that the 'greatest living German poet met the most important critic of the time'.[66] But she thought it 'peculiar and sad that the uniqueness of this encounter was never intelligible to the old friends, even after both Brecht and Benjamin had long since passed away'.[67] To them, Brecht was simply not a philosopher; he was 'only' a poet who loved agitprop and fast cars. He smoked cigars, not a pipe. He was a bon vivant in a leather jacket; he did not ruminate on transcendental homelessness and damaged life. For a melancholic character like Benjamin, such a figure was particularly fascinating precisely because of this lightness, especially given that Benjamin's life, like his thinking, moved 'between extreme positions', as he put it in a letter to Gretel Karplus.[68] What attracted Benjamin to the new world represented by Brecht repulsed those left behind. Benjamin's attention was shifting, and in this context Brecht's political stance was only one element of many.

The increasing alienation between Bloch and Kracauer, by contrast, had chiefly political explanations. The time during which Kracauer was writing *Ginster* turned out to have been the high point of their relationship. Bloch thought that they were 'moving in similar directions in almost all cases anyhow'.[69] He had never felt a 'more thrilling relaxation' when reading something than in the case of *Ginster*, Bloch assured Kracauer. He had received an advance copy of the novel, and his analysis of the book pleased his friend: 'It is fabulous how you have picked out my favourite sentences and words. Even – or perhaps in particular – your objections have made the work truly clear to me.' Kracauer felt as if 'my double had spoken'.[70] And so the letters of mutual admiration continued until Bloch, in January 1931, declared that 'at a time when trusts become more and more clearly anti-democratic (within the "framework of the constitution"), when the trinity of job losses, wage reductions, fascism is palpable', one could not afford to be harmless: that is, one should not write pleasant, topical articles for the feuilleton.[71] Three months later he accused Kracauer of having changed his political convictions:

> The man who now wants to defend culture against the barbarians, who compares Western Europe to Greece, is no longer the connoisseur of the most corroded parts of Marseille, of film ..., of improvisation. ... The man who saw the 'flight from revolution' in the salaried employees is not quite the same who today would prefer to do without a revolution. ... The man who examined Marx philosophically and read out many important passages from Marx's writings to me is not altogether the same as the man who today sees in them just a bit of socialization of the means of production and considers 'the human being' an eternal phenomenon that, in any case, will never change.[72]

The 'human being' must not be hidden 'under' the cover of the economy, Bloch explained to Wiesengrund, describing his philosophical and political differences from Kracauer: '[E]verything happens through the economy, but the economy is not identical with its content.' Bloch called his position a critique of philosophical economy.[73] In short, Bloch accused Kracauer of having become a bourgeois humanist and social democrat with a pessimistic view of human nature. After Kracauer criticized Brecht's banned film *Kuhle Wampe* in spring 1932, Bloch's patience was finally running out. Their mutual friend Fränze Herzfeld told Kracauer about a 'raging anger' in which Bloch had broken a desk lamp and said that Bloch had accused him of wickedness, betrayal and of being a reactionary.[74] A week later, the volcano was still erupting when Bloch wrote to Kracauer: 'That you gave expression to a blind, ugly hatred of Brecht in this newspaper, which has an increasingly pronounced anti-Marxist character – and *on this occasion*, arm in arm with the censors – was *hard to take*, given your *past* and *our friendship*.' For Bloch, this amounted to an 'abandonment of [their] common cause'.[75] The criticism was hard to swallow given that the accused had come out explicitly against the prohibition of the film, before criticizing the film on artistic grounds. Kracauer's reaction was calm: 'I have stood up very visibly, and more than others, for Marxism, and still do.' But he admitted he was hurt, saying that

> this criticism does not emerge from friendship, but from misrecognition of my nature and the continuity and meaning of my work. As a friend of mine, you would never present the kind of critique you actually have brought forward. You rather had to tell yourself that a

man whom you trusted for years on objective grounds will have his good reasons if for once he writes something that is not immediately plausible because it deviates from some approved slogan. And you would have enough respect for him to continue engaging with him on the basis of an unbroken trust. Instead ...[76]

Kracauer countered the accusation that he had changed his political orientation with an accusation of his own, alleging a distrust that was not appropriate to a genuine friendship. Bloch, in return, expressed his regret that Kracauer had defended 'the open word spoken from friend to friend' with 'a tightness and unconditionality' that seemed to rule out any self-criticism and to demand an 'absolute retreat' from Bloch. He was obviously not prepared to go along with that, and he upped the ante: Kracauer's criticism of the present, which previously had been 'homeless, desperate, relentless', was today embittered. Kracauer, Bloch said, was like an 'angry teacher ticking off his class'; his Marxism was no longer revolutionary but rather made central the idea of a planned economy. His 'train station' side [Bahnhofshaftigkeit] and liking for fairy tales had given way to rationalism; his aversion to Hegel was peacefully developing into a revisionism.[77] Kracauer responded by saying that he had only defended himself against the insinuation that he had allowed his private feelings to impact on the Brecht article and rejected the unreasonable demand for a 'solidarity that leads to a surveillance of knowledge'. 'If Marx had known you, he would probably have become very abusive towards you', Kracauer retaliated, because 'the connection you establish between the departure into transcendence etc. and revolutionary Marxism' is 'a personal one, without objective foundations'.[78] The old controversy over Bloch's *Thomas Münzer* surfaced again.

In the time shortly before the Nazis seized power, such political quarrels were no trivial matter. In Berlin, there was a civil war between different camps and world views. Everything was highly politicized. In light of these dramatic developments – 'the bourgeoisie turning fascist' – Bloch took the position that criticism of 'our own', that is, of communist artists such as Brecht, Pudovkin, Tretjakov, etc., should only be voiced internally, not in bourgeois fora such as the *Frankfurter Zeitung*, whereas Kracauer thought that one should not remain silent simply because such conditions prevailed.[79] He saw Bloch as once again chasing the spirit of utopia, incongruously mixing the utopian and the revolutionary. But was the Kracauer of Berlin really still the Kracauer of Frankfurt? Kracauer, who had once been interested in train stations and cinemas, in epistemological questions and the Kafkaesque, now could not avoid the political melee – and, indeed, wanted to get involved. That, after all, had been his reason for coming to Berlin. After his literary success with *Ginster*, he now considered himself a literary author. To Bernhard Guttmann, he confessed his ambitions as a writer and the political reasons behind his move to Berlin:

> The place of my earlier philosophical interests has been taken more and more by two other interests that will probably prevail: an interest in epic organization and an interest in throwing light on our social structures for political and moral purposes.[80]

The Kracauer of Berlin was someone who wanted to be a public persona, a political intellectual. He believed that it was important, for his newspaper, 'that as a writer at the crucial location I continually represent a solid position'.[81] He was looking to join the melee.

16

Berlin circa 1930: In the Midst of the Political Melee

When Siegfried Kracauer took up his new post as the head of the Berlin feuilleton on 1 April 1930, the final phase of the Weimar Republic had already begun.[1] Four days earlier, on 27 March, the last parliamentary government had collapsed, and from then on, until the National Socialists came to power, there were only minority governments ruling by emergency decree. The decline of social cohesion, the de-legitimization of the republic and the adoption of proto-authoritarian policies led to 30 January 1933, the day that Hitler's totalitarian collective movement legitimized the dictatorial regime by plebiscite, celebrated the day of 'national rising' and sparked a wave of political opponents and Jews (who were persecuted on racial grounds) to flee the new fascist dictatorship. In the spring of 1930, the government of the social democrat Hermann Müller had tumbled over a seemingly trivial matter, namely the DVP's planned cuts to unemployment benefits.[2] The global economic crisis, which had begun half a year ago with the Wall Street Crash of 1929, had already gripped Germany. This crisis was of unprecedented proportions, and its effects went beyond even those of the hyperinflation of the republic's early years. Unemployment rose from 1.9 million in 1929 to 3.7 million in 1930, and it would continue to climb to 6 million in 1933, when there were just 13 million in employment. Younger workers were especially affected, and welfare provision was insufficient. The SPD resisted the reductions in unemployment benefits, which threatened to undermine a central social policy that had been in place since 1918; instead the social democrats demanded an increase in unemployment insurance contributions. The grand coalition broke down over the issue, and the Weimar institutions in general could not withstand the gradual process of social erosion caused by impoverishment and insecurity. The democratic traditions proved not to be strong enough. The political class, and society in general, fled almost in panic from the Weimar 'system', which was no longer legitimate in the eyes of the public. Between 1928 and 1932, wages, salaries and unearned income fell by a third. During the same period, paramilitary group activity increased enormously. The terror and violence came predominantly from the political right, while the left found itself in a defensive position. Even democratic parties now had fighting units with 'leaders' and military posturing. There was fighting in the streets, in assembly halls and in Berlin's bars and pubs. There was fighting, too, behind the scenes – albeit still with a civilian demeanour – over what sort of dictatorship would succeed Weimar. It was not the economic crisis as such but the way it was dealt with that resulted in the end of the Weimar Republic and enabled the 'national revolution'. It was not just the economic order that was put in question, but, according to Ulrich Herbert, the combination of republic, democracy and capitalism, that is, the order of industrial society as such.[3] In the words of Detlev Peukert, the economic crisis 'hastened the final crisis' of the republic: 'The masses whose hopes for the future had been blighted by the crisis became radicalized; the old élites and the politicians of the right, for their part, believed that the moment had come when they could dismantle, once and for all, the structures established in 1918.'[4] In April 1930, when Siegfried and Elisabeth Kracauer moved into their first flat in Berlin W 15, Pariser Straße 24/II, the question was no longer 'democracy or dictatorship?' but simply 'what kind of dictatorship?' As Dan Diner puts it: 'The enigma of German history is not that Weimar was buried but rather *the identity* of those who dug the grave.'[5]

After only three months in Berlin, Kracauer had become consumed by foreboding. From a holiday in Brittany, where, after half a year of hard and tireless work, he had finally found time to reflect, he wrote to Wiesengrund:

> Apart from that, the horizon looks gloomy: the situation in Germany is more than serious – for the paper as well. There will be 3–4 million unemployed, and I can see no way out. There is a bad omen hanging over this country, and I know very well that it is not only that of capitalism. That capitalism is allowed to become so brutish is by no means down to economic reasons alone.[6]

Thus, for Kracauer the decline of the republic and of democracy was not only down to the capitalist economy and class society, to commodity fetishism and alienation. What, then, had doomed the country? What specifically caused Germany to develop towards a 'brutish' capitalism?

> How should I be able to formulate them? It is just that I note over and over again in France – where, no doubt, there is also plenty to criticize – how much has been destroyed back home: fundamental decency, all good nature as such and with it any trust among the people.[7]

That was a rather vague statement and one not entirely free of Francophilia. And yet this impression resulted from the unmistakeable feeling that in Germany humanity – compassion and empathy, tactfulness and respect, attentiveness and caution, trust and accountability, that is, those values that both make freedom possible and at the same time emerge from it – had been damaged so badly by war and nationalism that the next catastrophe was simply waiting to happen. Kracauer spoke of a burgeoning brutishness – not like Bloch and the Marxists of *fascistization*, a term that suggests that the maintenance of class rule, i.e. capitalism, leads to an authoritarian state, to the Nazis and to Hitler, who was himself, on this view, simply capital's lackey. For Kracauer, society was doomed to become inhuman rather because of the connection between war and nationalism, which gave rise to the madness of competing world views and militaristic posturing, and which prevented the emergence of a truly human society. That capitalism was also an obstacle to a humane society, he did not deny. He denied only that its abolition would suffice to create such a society:

> As, however, in our country a revolution would not, as perhaps in Russia, stimulate a fresh 'people' into action, I do not believe in the healing powers of a revolution either. I only see a general mess, and I would almost like it best if this muddling through could just go on.[8]

It seems from this as though Kracauer was indeed well on his way to becoming the defeatist, pessimist, the person just 'muddling through' – in a word, the very sceptical humanist Bloch had accused of betraying the cause. But Kracauer's political instincts, which recognized the increasing brutishness of society, were more developed than those of Bloch, who could sense only the more immediate 'fascistization'.

The political situation in Berlin was a mess, and professionally, too, it became more and more of a misery for Kracauer, despite the fact that, from the outside at least, a lot seemed to be going well for the Berlin editor. Kracauer fitted in well in the Berlin scene. His letter box regularly filled up with mail from his fans. In the autumn of 1930, Bloch wrote to him to say he was already well known: 'People are hearing a new voice and an unusual tone.'[9] The new arrival in Berlin had at first avoided the social scene; after office hours, he had been working ceaselessly on his *Georg*. But later he began to attend various literary social events, the receptions and 'evening circles' of the publishers, such as Cassirer, Kiepenheuer, Rowohlt and Fischer.[10]

After a year in Berlin, Kracauer reported to his predecessor that he had 'met more or less everyone who is of any importance in the literary world: Brecht, Kurt Weill, Döblin, Gottfried Benn, etc.'.[11] Spurred on by his literary successes, Kracauer had increasingly moved into the field of literary criticism and, as he had in the case of film, written programmatic articles on the topic. What was the current task of literature, of authors, of critics and, finally, of the intelligentsia as such? In spring 1930, he had engaged with the genre of biography, which was enjoying huge popularity at the time, classifying it as an 'art form of the new bourgeoisie'. Just as the novel had for Lukács and the detective novel had for the younger Kracauer, the biography now appeared to him as emblematic of the times, although it reflected these times in a kind of distorting mirror. During the war, people 'have been forced to experience their own insignificance – as well as that of others', and as a consequence the self had become a problematic concept; talk of a 'personality' had come to be regarded as empty chatter. The traditional novel, with the notion of a self at its centre, had therefore entered a period of transition; the instability and confusion needed to acquire an epic form, as in Alfred Döblin's *Berlin Alexanderplatz*.[12]

Thus, the genre of biography was an expression of the times, but in an ideologically disguised way. What, then, might be the emancipatory task of literature? In November 1930, a series of articles on contemporary writing began to appear in the literary pages of the *FZ* under the title 'What does our contemporary literature look like?' Reifenberg wrote on Bloch's *Traces*, Ernst Glaeser on film and politics in H. E. Jacob's *Blood and Celluloid* and Kracauer on Heinrich Mann's *Die große Sache* [The big deal]. Kracauer used his

Figure 24. Siegfried Kracauer, 1934
Copyright: DLA Marbach, Photo: Lili Kracauer

article to develop a criticism of the post-war literature of young left-wing radicals, which he labelled 'Zustandsliteratur' [literature of conditions]. The term suggested that this literature derived people's modes of thought from existing 'conditions', without, Kracauer thought, taking into consideration the fact that flesh-and-blood human beings produced those 'conditions'. Such a primitive base–superstructure schema, he said, was an 'unimaginative oversimplification' of Marx. The opposite position was adopted by Thomas Mann, who believed in the 'freedom of our souls', which is not dependent on the external world: 'Unlike the literature of conditions, his work is not based on the preformed material of reality; rather, he re-designs reality on the basis of concepts and intentions that stand in an oblique relation to reality.' The novel, however, lacks the dialectical moment: its hero does not engage 'with the conditions that are given'. According to Kracauer, a novel should give an aesthetic form to the dialectic between the conditions and the human being so that the individual can stand its ground in the face of reality and its collectivist tendencies. Such a dialectical art has to destroy the given material 'and use the debris from the demolition for insights from within the material'.[13]

For Kracauer, the Soviet avant-garde, which clustered around Sergej Tretjakov, who delivered a lecture on the new type of writer in April 1931 in Berlin, was dogmatic rather than dialectical. Their battle against the 'fetish of individuality' revealed the Soviets as the true fetishists. 'Sergeant Tretjakov', he wrote, was a 'fetishist of a world view that might be useful for fulfilling the Russian five-year plan, but is not up to the level of European consciousness and has hardly anything still to do with Marxism'. The collectivist command, according to Kracauer, disfigured dialectical materialism.[14] (Tretjakov, incidentally, became a victim of the Stalinist purges in July 1937.) Kracauer became ever more convinced that the 'attempts at revolutionizing society in the Eastern way' had failed. In a letter to Ferdinand Lion, editor at the Ullstein publishing house and author of *Das Geheimnis des Kunstwerks* (1932) [The secret of the artwork], he wrote:

> Thus, what will matter is to design a social revolution that befits us, that does not (as the vulgar communists did) discard everything that is proper European heritage, but takes this heritage along. The proper understanding of art is part of this.[15]

For Kracauer, one great master of the arts – and a 'magnetic field', as Karsten Witte puts it – was Franz Kafka. His posthumous papers appeared at Kracauer's initiative with Kiepenheuer in 1931. Kafka, Kracauer wrote, was unparalleled in his ability 'to discern and elaborate the confusion in the world', a world without justice or truth, a world that had been thrown off balance.[16] In Kafka's stories, all being [Dasein] is deceived. All doing is ensnared in incomprehensible circumstance. All efforts are in vain. Reality is a dark labyrinth, a dungeon, in which humans can hardly breathe; it is a bad dream that is not recognized as a dream. Kafka's guiding motif, according to Kracauer, is an awareness that the truth has been lost; his protagonists' restless quests to find answers that cannot be found therefore hit upon the stubborn silence of those creatures who take primitive life as the given. Rational insight and behaviour that apparently takes reality into account evaporate in the mad worlds of Kafka's novels. The elements of these worlds, in which couriers shuttle back and forth, following orders they know nothing about, do not make up a whole. The so-called Kafkaesque is the distorted mirror-image of a devilish reasonability, though without discarding reason proper. Kafka's stories are 'reverse adventure novels':

> instead of the hero conquering the world, the world becomes completely unhinged in the course of his wanderings. According to Kafka, Don Quixote was actually Sancho Panza's devil, who knew, however, how to render this devil harmless by distracting him from himself. Thus, the devil incessantly performed the craziest deeds, and Sancho Panza, who followed him out of a certain sense of responsibility, 'derived from them a great and useful entertainment to the end of his days'.[17]

For Kracauer, the present task of literature was to find a language and an epic form that would distract the devil and begin to tackle the fate that was hovering over the real world, so that the spell might be broken. Picture puzzles, allegories or fables were particularly suitable for this task. Kracauer related 'Kafka, the Jew from Prague' to the French-American writer Julien Green, who had been translated by Hermann Kesten and parts of whose novel *Léviathan* (1929) had appeared in the *FZ* in advance of publication. Benjamin followed the French literary scene very carefully and was also enthusiastic about this novelist, who was at this point unknown in Germany. He emphasized Green's idea of the passion [Passion], the entanglement of suffering [Leiden] and passion [Leidenschaft] within human culture. Green, he said, brought order into our earliest terrors:

> In the cleared-out home of our childhood, he sweeps together the traces left by the existence of our parents. And from the pile of suffering and horror that he has heaped up, their unburied corpses suddenly appear to us with as much force as, centuries ago, the human body appeared to the pious man, whom it stigmatized.[18]

In a similar vein, Kracauer wrote: 'In Green, too, our world crumbles, because it is seen from a place that is not situated inside it.' For Green, this place is madness, the madness that takes hold of Adrienne Mesurat in the eponymous novel of 1927; in Kafka, by contrast, the world itself is madness.[19] In Green's novels, fear reigns – the fear, Kracauer thought, *of the bourgeois world* in the face of its own emptiness and of the incursion of reality'.[20] 'Julien Green's human beings are creatures of an unredeemed and irredeemable creation.' Fate gnaws away at earthly matters until it has eliminated the last flower. But if the earth is a bad dream, then someone must be dreaming it, which means that reality is, in fact, not simply in the hands of fate: this is how Kracauer read this seemingly apolitical literary figure through a political lens. Green was anything but an 'operating' writer in the Tretjakov sense: 'There is no indication of a path that points to an outside, into the grown togetherness of *society*.' But: '[T]here is no human society that will be allowed to ignore its origins. If society does not take the whole of unredeemed creation along with it, the flood of the passions will rise and the Léviathan will devour the world.'[21] In order to come to terms with modernity, one had to work on myth.

Kracauer praised the obviously political aspects of literature in the case of those writers whose political development had been similar to his own, namely friends who had had a radical left-wing phase which, however, they had left behind; André Malraux, who had lived in Indochina, where he had studied 'post-war Europeans, adventurer types' fighting under the Soviet flag for a China they did not know, was a case in point: 'The asylum for all these homeless is the revolution', Kracauer wrote after reading *The Conquerors* (published in German as *Eroberer in Kanton* in 1929). He praised Malraux's skewering of the ideas and leaders of this impromptu International – a group of militant anarchists and nihilists who did not believe in the sacrifices that they made but who 'in truth are on a flight without end', like Franz Tunda, Roth's wayward revolutionary.[22] In Kracauer's eyes, Joseph Roth was – despite all the tall tales he told in real life – the poet, and the man, of 'authentic and credible experience', driven by a 'longing for Being in a linguistic melody of incomparable brightness' and in full awareness of the meaninglessness of life, the 'emptiness around'. Kracauer defended his friend against the accusation that the erstwhile 'red Joseph' had betrayed his criticism of the times and of society when he assumed that the Habsburg monarchy and Catholicism represented stronger counterforces to national socialism than did socialism. Kracauer thought that this belief was false, but he responded to it by saying that Roth was, after all, a

romantic, one of those who were driven out of every corner of the earth by their longing for home. His place is neither on the right nor on the left; neither radicals nor reactionaries can claim him as one of theirs. There is only one thing that is an intrinsic part of him: the sense of a more humane Being than the one we have.[23]

On this view, Roth was neither a socialist nor a monarchist; he was 'only' a humanist, but that was all right. The only tragic aspect about him was that he preferred alcohol above all else. But that was a different story.

But as a critic, Kracauer was not only interested in literature as art or in its political aspects. He was interested also in its existence as a commodity. The fate of literary art was, after all, no different to that of film, radio broadcasts or newspaper articles. The literary writer produced a commodity that was offered on the market, and the commercialization of the book market was therefore an important topic of literary criticism. In the *Frankfurter Zeitung*, Kracauer organized a series 'on successful books and their audience'. As in the case of his film criticism, he did not wish to dismiss the literature of Stefan Zweig, Erich Maria Remarque or Frank Thieß as mediocre just because one could read it on a Sunday afternoon by the lake. Rather, Kracauer believed that social tendencies could be inferred from consumer preferences and that, in this way, it was possible to uncover the 'structure of the consciousness of the new bourgeoisie'. He was interested in the 'non-public public sphere', in books which sold 660,000 copies but were not reviewed once in a feuilleton, such as for instance Richard Voß's *Zwei Menschen*, because '[a]nalyses of widely read books are an artifice to investigate social strata whose structure cannot be determined by a direct approach'.[24] The idea that it is impossible to understand the literary world without understanding the consumer was by no means taken for granted at the time, not even among those who were committed to the critique of political economy.[25]

Most of all, however, the Weimar Republic was a time in which literature became politicized and there ensued lively discussions of the social and political role of literature. Alfred Döblin, who had broken new narrative ground with his novel *Berlin Alexanderplatz*, a book Kracauer rated highly, provided the impetus for one such debate. A student, one 'Mr Hocke', had published an open letter asking Döblin for intellectual and political guidance. Döblin initially published his response in the *Tage-Buch*[26] and then turned it into a book, *Wissen und Verändern!* [To know and change!] (1931). The book advocated a socialism without class struggle, a socialism that transcended those of the Soviet Union, the KPD and the SPD, a 'true' socialism guided by the following principles: 'Freedom, spontaneous association between people, rejection of any coercion, outrage against injustice and coercion, humanity, tolerance and a peaceful attitude'. Döblin saw the intellectual labourer as entangled in a war on two fronts: against the bourgeoisie and against working-class theory. The intelligentsia, he argued, had to take the side of the worker without getting ensnared in Marxist doctrine; it had to fight against 'subjectivation' and 'depersonalization'. Döblin's views met with unanimous rejection, the mildest of which was perhaps that expressed in the *Neue Rundschau*, in which Kracauer had had a monthly column since his move to Berlin. Kracauer had sought to start a debate about *Wissen und Verändern!* in the paper, contributing a piece titled 'Minimalforderung an die Intellektuellen' [Minimal demand on the intellectuals], in which he argued that Döblin's response to Mr Hocke had not been satisfactory. Socialism was not a matter of feeling but of intellectual labour. If Döblin really wanted to promote socialism, he would need to give students the following advice: 'Intellectuals, apply your intellect!' This advice might sound curious at first – 'Manual labourers, use your hands!' 'Footballers, use your feet!' – but it concealed a particular motive. Kracauer maintained, 'on the basis of dialectical materialism', that the intellect is a productive force, and because the development of productive forces is what will lead to a classless society, all the intellectual has to do is work, hence: reflect. According to Kracauer, in reflecting, the intellectual is being critical, that is, destructive, casting everything into doubt and measuring the ideal against the actual possibility of its realization. In a word, the intellectual is a critic of ideology and, purely by virtue of his or her productive force, serves the purpose of progress – a progress in which Kracauer himself, however, no longer actually believed, just as he no longer believed in the classless society. This latter fact lends his intervention in the Döblin debate, in the summer of 1931, a certain air of mystery. But this mystery dissolves if we read his contribution strategically (for he was certainly no cynic). His rationale might have been to strengthen the self-confidence of intellectuals in a society that was characterized by a class struggle between the bourgeoisie and the workers. In that situation, the intellectuals were permanently in danger of being ground down between the two classes, for while they fought for the working class with their heads, they typically had their feet firmly on bourgeois ground.[27] Thus, while Kracauer did not want to approve of some 'true' idealist socialism à la Döblin, it is possible that he also wanted to reject the notion that intellectuals had to join some party or front.[28]

A month after the publication of his article in the *Neue Rundschau*, Kracauer himself received a letter from a student. His name was Wolfgang Höpker, a student of political economy, sociology and geopolitics at the university in Jena. The young man praised Kracauer's 'consistent work on the unveiling of our reality, on the dismantling of the layers of ideology which the "ruling system" stacks around itself'. Höpker said he had taken a similar lesson from

Ferdinand Fried's *Ende des Kapitalismus* (1931): 'Whoever wants to build something up must first dispassionately and soberly take it apart.' Since 1929, Fried had been the economic analyst for *Die Tat*, in which forum he defended a position that combined political anti-liberalism with economic autarky. *Die Tat* was the organ of the 'young conservative *Tat-Kreis*'. It was published by Eugen Diederich in Jena, and its editor was Hans Zehrer. According to the student's flattering letter, it promoted an 'amalgamation of socialism with the national idea for Germany'.[29] Unlike Döblin, who had replied to Hocke, Kracauer did not reply to Höpker's letter. Instead, he wrote an article about the *Tat-Kreis*, 'Aufruhr der Mittelschichten' [The revolt of the middle classes], which appeared in six parts in December 1931 in the *FZ*. He began by acknowledging the fact that the circle's social analyses set out from 'genuine and general experiences ... of the suffering German people' and that they did attempt to understand 'a substantial reality'. But the central concepts of the circle, 'people, state, myth', he called 'constructions born from longing'. The right's attack on the left, he ultimately judged, took aim at an unbounded rationality that was – inadmissibly – equated with reason. The *Tat-Kreis* was a romantic, anti-liberal and contradictory circle – contradictory because it was impossible to build a 'new cult of the personality' and at the same time demand an 'integrated nationalism' within a 'total state'. Kracauer thought the members of the *Tat-Kreis* would love the Nazis more than the Nazis would love them. The circle's revolt against the liberal order was, he claimed, a misdirected anti-capitalism, an authoritarian revolt:

> It is the dispossessed middle classes who rebel. ... The publications of the *Tat-Kreis* are therefore an exact reflection of the inner schism of the dispossessed middle classes that is caused by the material and ideational situation. These classes take refuge in romanticism and are thrown back and forth between violence and reason. ... Thence the desperate struggle ... against the liberalism from which they derive; thence the glorification of state, space, myth.[30]

These were, of course, battles among intellectuals for intellectuals. The public was not particularly interested in the question of whether the *Tat-Kreis* confused rationality with reason. A month after its publication, Kracauer was forced to admit that there was 'not even a small public response' to his elaborate piece of writing.[31] Such skirmishes were indeed insignificant when it came to *realpolitik*. The market share of cultural papers was small: *Die Tat* had 30,000 readers, the *Neue Rundschau* 20,000 and *Die Weltbühne* only 15,000. In 1930, the weekly circulation of illustrated newspapers printed in Germany, by comparison, was 5 million, with an estimated readership of 20 million. Kracauer's books did not sell well either.

The head of the public library in Höchst am Main told him that such works were hardly ever picked up: 'Our visitors, mostly "class-conscious proletarians", say that they experience "true life", poverty, unemployment, abandoned women, daily for themselves, and thus want to read about something different, about the rich, the happy, the nobility, etc.'[32] The proletarians read family papers, not specialist journals. In short, Kracauer's political commitment was a hugely dissatisfying and frustrating activity.

Georg also experienced all this. He had to accept that, as Fred had explained to him, *chasing after justice is madness. God knows, the world's a den of thieves … You've always been quick to change, my friend, and you certainly always thought that your momentary truth was the final one. I admire this tireless searching. A single thing troubles me, and really just for your sake: What have you achieved through it all?* And the answer Georg gives himself *was:* nothing. *He well remembered the vague childish yearning he once felt for a public role, before joining the newspaper. And now? Now, as then, he stood outside, and public life flowed by as before.*[33]

In the summer of 1931, Kracauer had not yet reached that point, but increasingly there were signs that the Berlin story would not have a happy ending. In politics, anti-democratic rule by presidential decree destroyed the republic. In the streets of Berlin, there were daily demonstrations, with simplistic arguments put forward by communists and no arguments put forward by Nazis, and, as Kracauer saw it, inhumanity was spreading. And the atmosphere at the newspaper became more and more suffocating for Kracauer. He must have sensed that his time there was running out, because in September 1932 he sent the Malrauxs the chapters of *Georg* that he had completed along with a summary of how the story would continue:

> Georg, the hero of the story, finally gets closer and closer to communism (without becoming a communist), and because of that is kicked out of the newspaper, which he had in any case joined only accidentally. In the end, he is altogether alone and radically disillusioned. What he will do remains unclear.[34]

We do know, however, what Kracauer did from October 1932 onwards: he negotiated with the *Frankfurter Zeitung* to be relocated to Paris.[35] But his position in these negotiations was not very strong. Despite all the glamour of the Berlin cultural scene, his standing within the paper had suffered since he had left Frankfurt.

Following the reshuffle of 1930, the rumours about a change of political direction had not ended. Feiler's sacking, the replacement of Guttmann with Rudolf Kircher, Brentano's departure, the alleged 'removal by promotion' of Kracauer and the 'deportation' of

Reifenberg to Paris provided a never-ending supply of material for the rumour mill. At the beginning of 1931, Wiesengrund suggested it might be wise for Kracauer to look for another employer, for instance, the Mosse publishing house, because

> I see and hear a great deal about the atmosphere at the paper here, and in very intimate detail too; believe me, I don't want to make you nervous and have not succumbed to the general Jewish psychosis, but I regard the situation as critical ... Above all, be careful of Kircher. Brentano ... has told me that Kircher hates you.

Kracauer reassured his worried friend: 'I know exactly what kind of institution and what kind of individuals I am dealing with – in Frankfurt and in Berlin. (What Brentano told you is not entirely accurate.)'[36] Nevertheless, he was worried.

The employment contract he entered into in March 1930 defined his task as that of 'organizing the entire reporting of the feuilleton, except reports on theatre; carrying out, or initiating, reports on Berlin; taking charge of film criticism in the Frankfurter Zeitung' and, further, 'supporting the editorial office in Frankfurt'. Together with Kircher, Kracauer was also supposed to cover Berlin cultural policy. He was promised a group of freelance collaborators to help in all this activity, although because of a lack of money they never materialized. Kracauer's monthly salary was set at 1,100 Reichsmark (which corresponds, roughly, to £4,000 today). His own articles for supplements were to be paid separately. He was allowed to contribute to other newspapers 'to a limited degree' and 'as long as the interests of the publisher and [Kracauer's] unambiguous position as a member of the editorial board of the Frankfurter Zeitung might not become compromised'.[37] His monthly salary was cut by 100 Reichsmark, and this was only the beginning. In October 1930, his salary was reduced by another 120 Reichsmark.[38] In November, he lost his office after two floors of the Berlin branch of the FZ were rented out to third parties in order to save money. In December, finally, Heinrich Simon announced that he was only able to pay him half his salary and recommended that he look for some additional source of income. In January 1931, Kracauer had figured out that he had to earn 300 Reichsmark on the side 'in order to survive'.[39] He was nevertheless still prohibited from publishing in Die Weltbühne. There was still the Neue Rundschau, although, from the beginning of 1932, he was no longer the sole commentator for the paper and he lost his regular monthly column.[40] Kracauer began primarily to seek to publish articles on film in the established specialist film journals.[41] But he was not able to compensate for his loss of income. Another disappointment was the slow sales of his book on the salaried masses. By the end of June 1930, only 2,010 copies had been sold; he received only 588 Reichsmark in royalties, instead of the 800 Reichsmark he had been hoping for.[42] Meanwhile, the costs of living were high. The Kracauers had moved into a 'stately' home in Sybelstraße 35 in Berlin-Charlottenburg, with high ceilings and bright rooms, and a monthly rent of 195 Reichsmark.[43] Kracauer did not want to burden his mother by reducing further the 230 Reichsmark he transferred to her every month.[44] Thus, there was nothing for it but to make savings. In March 1931, when he travelled to Paris in order to coordinate his plans with Reifenberg and prepare the translation of *Ginster* with the Malrauxs, Lili could not come along: 'pas de l'argent'.[45]

After putting out feelers to the director of the *Berliner Funkstunde*,[46] Hans Flesch, failed to yield anything positive,[47] Simon made a surprising suggestion to Kracauer, who reported it thus to Guttmann:

> Now, Dr Simon has negotiated, of all institutions, with Ufa on my behalf, and they are, under certain conditions, prepared to employ me with a salary for a year. No doubt, they would spend the money mostly to muzzle me during that time, for I have from the very beginning fought against the tendencies there, and I could of course not write any film criticism while employed by them.[48]

This hostile takeover did not materialize, however. At the beginning of February, Kracauer reported that the plans involving Ufa had 'fortunately long since come to nothing'.[49] What exactly Kracauer would have done at Ufa, and why the arrangements came to naught, we do not know. Given his financial situation, Kracauer probably would have gone along with 'the ominous project'.[50] A return to Frankfurt was also being considered, but Kracauer categorically rejected this idea.[51]

Kracauer's successor in Frankfurt, Friedrich T. Gubler, witnessed just how tense, nervous and aggressive Kracauer was during this period. Kracauer demanded that they 'agree down to the details our attitude, tactical questions, and common approach, and attune ourselves to each other'. Kracauer saw the two of them as engaged in 'enlightenment battles'; the newspaper, for instance, was meant to promote the new architecture without handing itself over to it wholesale – 'that is exactly our attitude in other areas as well'. Kracauer explained his agenda regarding cultural policy as consisting in a turn towards the 'intellectual areas that are seemingly on the far side', those that were trivialized by the Marxist and radical literary press, and to seek to highlight general problems. Such indirect political intervention had to take place within 'the framework of the newspaper (but not beyond!)'. Kracauer counted on Gubler, whom he called his 'only trusted person at the paper'.[52] But Gubler was swamped more and more by the demands of his role in Frankfurt, where savings were being sought 'in every conceivable place', and as a consequence the paper, he wrote, 'devour[ed] him'. Thus, he became ever less at the disposal of his predecessor, and Kracauer's dispatches became ever more bad-tempered.[53] When Gubler held back an article on a children's museum, Kracauer was curt:

> You should also trust me where you do not wholly agree with my intentions. Someone who has been partly responsible for the direction the feuilleton should take in times as unstable as these has developed an instinct for the right treatment of themes.

Whenever one of his articles went unpublished, he felt 'seriously harmed'. Nine months after the Frankfurt changeover, the Berlin editor levelled 'some serious and fundamental' accusations at Gubler: Gubler had failed to provide him with important answers, acted against Kracauer's advice and often did not even seek this advice; Gubler's desire for more general articles addressing questions of principle was 'unpedagogical' and would result in 'blather'; Gubler had snubbed intellectuals and writers, leading the good ones, who were paid poorly in any case, to leave. In February 1932, Kracauer gave up: 'As you do not cultivate any editorial contact with me, I unfortunately cannot do so from my side either.'[54]

Business matters became a burden to friendship. The position in Berlin had gone to Kracauer's head, and life in the melee was taking its toll. Kracauer's 'horrendous sciatica', exhaustion and 'a newly returned, old nervous bilious complaint' were all worse than ever. He complained: 'The physical problems, which are of a nervous nature and not merely physical, are primarily due to the agitation caused by the newspaper, the whole crisis that broke out again in June [1932].'[55] In August 1931, the publishing house began drastically to reduce its salaries: first by 100 marks, then in September by another 100 marks, and in October by yet another 100 marks. In addition, the lineage rate for Kracauer's articles in the literary supplement (which were paid separately) was reduced from 50 to 40 pfennig. From October 1932, his monthly salary, including all honoraria and allowances, came to 1,030 marks.[56]

The situation in Berlin appeared ever more ominous to the Kracauers. An apocalyptic atmosphere was taking hold. 'There have never been better times for medicine men', Kracauer wrote about clairvoyants and experimental psychologists, such as Erik Jan Hanussen, whose shows played on the 'receptiveness of the crowd' and its willingness to believe in miracles.[57] That was two-and-a-half weeks after the quick-change artist Hitler had entered the Reich Chancellery on 30 January 1933. He would soon have himself declared the 'leader of a thousand-year Reich'. The Kracauers had only one thought: they wanted to leave – to Paris, the city of their dreams – in order to escape the nightmare in Berlin. Thus, Kracauer urged Reifenberg to speak to Simon on his behalf and seek a reshuffle. Shortly after 30 January 1933, Reifenberg told him that Gubler was going to move to the *Vossische Zeitung* but that all else was still undecided. Simon, he added, was improvising, but Simon still expected Sieburg, the correspondent of the *Frankfurter Zeitung* in Paris, to return to Germany and Kracauer to go to Paris. Any questions regarding salaries and money would have to wait for the time being.

At the end of 1931, Reifenberg took charge of the editorial office for domestic politics, and he and Kircher became the most important political voices at the paper. He despised Hitler, that parvenu, with his primitive gangs of violent thugs, and he despised the petit bourgeois voters of his manipulative mass party. With this same bourgeois loftiness, he underestimated the party. For him, the real enemies of the Weimar Republic were the *Deutschnationale*. Until 1930, that was also the line adopted by the *Frankfurter Zeitung*. Thereafter, it was loyal to the Brüning government and supported Hindenburg's election as President of the Reich in the spring of 1932. There was a brief tactical change of tack in late summer 1932, when the *FZ*, under Reifenberg and Kircher's influence, argued that the NSDAP could be tamed if it were included within the political decision-making process. When the advance of national socialism began to falter in the parliamentary elections of 6 November 1932, Reifenberg thought that this was the turning point. Hitler's rise to power thus came as a particular shock to him. But now it was Reifenberg who took the risk of adopting an 'aggressive stance' towards the new government. Nevertheless, he still saw the *Deutschnationale* as the most dangerous political opponent.[58]

During the days following 30 January 1933, in a flurry of letters, Kracauer and Reifenberg analysed the political situation in minute detail and discussed the role of the *Frankfurter Zeitung* in the context of the decline of the republic. Reifenberg was still hopeful that someone, or something, might be able to stop Hitler: the Reichswehr; tensions within the coalition over economic policy; or a possible alliance between workers, political Catholicism and genuine bourgeois values. He did not see the role of the paper in too negative a light, but Kracauer thought that overall the *FZ* had 'treated the Nazis much too softly' in recent years: 'Hitler was coddled, and toward the mass of workers the attitude was not even one of consistent benevolent neutrality'. Reifenberg's oppositional gesture, he wrote, came too late. 'It is certain that Hitler is striving for a total dictatorship, and I am actually convinced that he will act against "Marxists" and democrats as soon as he can.' The German bourgeoisie, he said, was rotten, something 'we never wanted to believe [at the paper]'. But Kracauer did not believe that the working class had to take action. The leadership of the Social Democratic Party was sclerotic, he thought, and the Communist Party was narrow-minded; the millions of unemployed and the economic situation generally suggested that any political move was doomed to failure. What he feared most was the anti-Semitism: he considered an 'eviction of Jewish publicists' likely.[59]

In a letter of 18 February 1933, Kracauer related details of a conversation he had had with Otto Suhr, who had been secretary of the Allgemeiner Deutscher Gewerkschaftsbund (ADGB), the confederation of German trade unions, since 1922. Suhr feared that the trade unions would give in to the pressure from the government and obey, that they would renounce their ties with the Social Democratic Party and allow themselves to be incorporated into a cooperative system modelled on the Italian example. Far from isolating the ADGB from the workers, taking such a step would be in line with the wishes of the masses. The situation appeared hopeless. Without resistance from the trade unions, the path towards dictatorship was open, and down that path lay the 'worst terror', especially for Jewish journalists. A week later, Kracauer concluded that the paper now had to 'support the conservative-reactionary partner in the coalition'. It was imperative to keep Hitler within this three-party coalition and under no circumstances to allow him to govern with just one of the two, least of all with the Zentrumspartei, because in that case he could legally bring the Christian trade unions over to his side, even without violating the constitution or using coercion. The 'Deutschnationale and their entourage' were therefore at present 'the only bulwark against a Hitler dictatorship'. People at the paper had not yet begun to understand that the national socialist mass movement was far worse than anything threatened by the Papen–Hugenberg circle. If it came to it, monarchy would be preferable. Or they could hope for intrigue: the Bavarians or civil servants, perhaps. Maybe inflation would do for them. Or Hanussen … Kracauer asked whether his 'current plan to go abroad' might be accelerated.[60]

That acceleration eventually came about on 28 February 1933. The night before, the Reichstag had burned. Few believed that this had been the deed of an individual arsonist, the anarchist Marinus van der Lubbe. It was much more likely that the Nazis had wanted to destroy this symbol of the parliamentary rule they so despised. The same thoughts would surely have crossed Kracauer's mind as he surveyed the burned-out building: 'It bears the golden lantern, which has remained intact, and now resembles a triumphator who has been abandoned by his followers.' Kracauer joined an endless procession of people who silently followed a route around the lonely Reichstag – a stretch along Unter den Linden, then Neue

Wilhelm-Straße, Schiffsbauerdamm, towards the Lessing Theatre, then through Roonstraße and, via the western side of Siegesallee, back to the Brandenburg Gate. There was a ghostly atmosphere. People sensed that this had not been a normal fire:

> Silently, the pedestrians proceed on their way or stare at the Reichstag, where nothing is to be discovered. At the most, one hears an occasional whisper. ... The gazes penetrate right through this symbol, into the abyss opened up by its destruction.

The burned-out Reichstag symbolized a republic that had lost its republicans; and, indeed, the very same day, the rule of law was also suspended. Hindenburg, the President of the Reich, passed an emergency decree 'for the protection of people and state', the so-called 'Reichstagsbrandverordnung' [Reichstag fire decree], which suspended fundamental constitutional rights and introduced the 'preventive detention' of political opponents – the start of a development that would lead to the concentration camps (which began as temporary SA camps).[61]

In the morning, Kracauer had received a telegram from Simon ordering him to take a 'working holiday' in Paris, where he was to support the local office – and this despite the fact that Sieburg had suddenly decided to keep the post of Paris correspondent.[62] After he had dictated his article on the silent procession, Kracauer took the train to Frankfurt, where he discussed the situation with Simon, Reifenberg and his friend and lawyer Selmar Spier, before continuing his journey to Paris. Lili had gone there directly from Berlin. That night, police and SA units arrested thousands of communists, more than 1,500 in Berlin alone, among them members of the Reichstag. By 2 March, the Kracauers had arrived in Paris, where they first stayed in the Hotel Navigateur in the VI. arrondissement. On the same day, the article 'Rund um den Reichstag' [Around the Reichstag] appeared in the *Frankfurter Zeitung*. Kracauer's farewell to Germany ended with the words: 'Again and again fresh bands of schoolchildren join the adults. They smell the excitement and innocently enjoy the sensation. Once they grow up, they will learn what the burning of the Reichstag really meant.'[63]

17

The Trial

'On avait sûrement calomnié Joseph K., car, sans avoir rien fait de mal, il fut arrêté un matin.' I imagine Siegfried Kracauer, one morning in March 1933, wakes up in Paris with this sentence going around in his mind. 'Someone must have been telling lies about Joseph K. because, without having done anything wrong, one morning he was arrested.' Siegfried K. had escaped such an arrest by the skin of his teeth, but he had begun a trial he had done nothing to bring about nor was able to influence. The outcome is uncertain, and there is little cause for optimism. He thinks there may be no way out of this gloomy labyrinth:

> 'Alas', said the mouse, 'the whole world is growing smaller every day. At the beginning it was so big that I was afraid, I kept running and running, and I was glad when I saw walls far away to the right and left, but these long walls have narrowed so quickly that I am in the last chamber already, and there in the corner stands the trap that I am running into.' 'You only need to change your direction', said the cat, and ate it up.[1]

I imagine K. thinks that Kafka's trial has become secularized. A decade earlier, when misfortune came in the shape of transcendental homelessness, or the meaninglessness of life, the trial had been the 'perennial trial to which human beings are subjected. They do not know what they have been charged with, and the highest court that sits in judgment on them remains hidden to them'. People were fearful because the truth was veiled, justice alien, and the world wide and unintelligible. This has not changed, K. thinks: Kafka's eerie trial serves as a genuine representation of actually experienced reality. But now empirical reality, too, had increasingly come to resemble Kafka's trial. The spell had not been broken; rather, after the Jew from Prague looked at Medusa's head, reality had turned to stone. In fairy tales and other human fabrications, truth ultimately triumphs over demonic deception and blind violence. In Kafka's

world, which takes hold of the real one, demonic deception and
blind violence are reality and truth.[2]

I imagine K. looks around his hotel room, a narrow room,
sparsely furnished with two beds, a table and two chairs, a collection
of things 'torn out of their human contexts which alone gave them
their meaning'.[3] The toilet is across the corridor. But the room is
cheap, and they will not be able to afford a flat anytime soon –
maybe a room with a kitchenette, though. A hotel room is cheaper
than renting an apartment, even taking into account the costs of
storing the furniture he hopes to rescue from Germany. The price
of the hotel includes electricity. The Hôtel du Navigateur at the
Quai des Grands Augustins in the VI. Arrondissement between
Pont Neuf and Pont Saint-Michel, where K. and L. have found
their first refuge, is shabby, but at least it is cheap. K. hopes that
it is only a temporary solution, though at the moment his wallet is
almost empty. After deducting the money for his mother, and taking
into account all his additional honoraria, K. received 818.60 marks
for the month of March (roughly £3,000 today).[4] His fixed costs in
Berlin (rent, maid, health insurance), plus taxes and dentist bills,
were 428 marks, leaving 390.60 marks. Of that, 80 marks went on
Lili's train ticket to Paris and 50 marks went on his own ticket to
Frankfurt (his onward journey from Frankfurt had been paid for
by Simon). So K. and L. still have 260 marks. If they stay in Paris
for one month, then, at least to start with, they must assume total
outgoings of 600 marks, even on the assumption of the most basic
lifestyle.[5]

I imagine K. is trying to calm himself. The central location of the
hotel is an advantage, and he is better connected than most other
refugees. His *Ginster* arrived in the country under its French title,
Genêt, before even its author. Paris is the only foreign city in which
he enjoys some public recognition, and he may be able to work this
up with time.[6] K.'s French is fairly decent, and he loves Paris, whose
streets he has often before roamed on long walks. The Navigateur is
in a good location; from here, K. can reach all the most important
places on foot: the editorial offices of the *Nouvelle Revue Française*,
the famous literary paper, where his friends André Malraux and
Félix Bertaux work; the smaller papers, such as *L'Europe nouvelle*,
edited by Louise Weiss and Roger Nathan, which promotes 'Europe';
the socialist *Le Monde*, for which his friend Augustin Habaru
works; and, of course, the office of the *Frankfurter Zeitung*, where
Friedrich Sieburg is currently squatting. To Sieburg – according to
Roth, the worst hack of all the 'German-feeling, German-doubting,
German-hoping, and German-believing' publicists – K. will have
to present any proposals for articles.[7] The Bibliothèque nationale
in Rue de Richelieu lies half an hour by foot to the north, and the
Éditions Gallimard, where Bernhard Groethuysen works as an

editor, is not far away either, situated between Rue de Université and the Boulevard Saint-Germain. The cafés in which Kracauer works so well and where the Parisian scene meets are nearby too: the Deux Magots, Café Madeleine, Café de l'Univers or Café Tournon. K. is not particularly attracted towards the emigrant circles, although perhaps Leopold Schwarzschild's *Tage-Buch* might be one possible place to publish. Following the closure of its editorial offices in Munich by the SS on 11 March 1933, Schwarzschild decided to continue the journal from Paris under the title *Neues Tage-Buch*. K. is more interested in meeting people from film, the up-and-coming Jean Renoir, for instance. K. even has some connections with the world of politics: he meets Pierre Viénot, a member of the national assembly and the Parti républicain-socialiste, whose much-discussed and translated *Incertitude allemandes* (1930)[8] was published with a preface by Benno Reifenberg.[9] K. also knows the philosopher Gabriel Marcel, a recent convert to Catholicism who, as an editor at Plon and Grasset, is very familiar with the world of publishing. And through the well-connected Ilja Ehrenburg, K. has some feelers in Russian circles.[10]

I imagine K. thinks of his family and friends. He saw and spoke with his mother and aunt while passing through Frankfurt, and he had also seen Selmar Spier, his friend and lawyer, at whose place he had stayed for the night. 'The company where Lili was employed has closed overnight and moved to Geneva, without telling the employees about it', Hedwig K. reported at the time. After K.'s departure from Frankfurt, Hedwig and Rosette had moved into a small flat in Eschersheimer Landstraße, Hedwig's 'old-age nest', she thought. Leo Löwenthal was the last full-time employee of the Institute for Social Research to leave Frankfurt, on 2 March. Teddie has not been told about his flight and is staying with Gretel in Berlin. He recommends to K. that he return to Germany, where, he says, there is perfect peace and order and the situation is likely to stabilize. K. considers this evaluation of the situation to be the most curious thing he has recently been told, ignorant and somehow telling. Bloch's flat in the Berlin artists' colony, in Wilmersdorf, was searched by the SA on 28 February 1933 – almost immediately after the Reichstag Fire Decree was issued. Bloch, always on the go, was in Munich at the time, and he thence travelled directly to Zurich. Full of hope, as a matter of principle, he does not want to hear about the suffering of others; he sees the positive side of emigration, despite the darkness of the lived moment. The melancholic Benjamin is still in Berlin, but declared immediately after the burning of the Reichstag that 'the air is hardly fit to breathe anymore – a condition which of course gets less important given one is being strangled anyway'.[11] K. expects him to arrive in Paris any day: Benjamin knows that, now the Nazis are in power, his manuscripts will be returned without commentary and almost concluded negotiations will be broken off by publishers and editors in anticipatory obedience, even before the official *Gleichschaltung*. By practising the 'utmost political restraint', it might be possible to protect oneself from persecution, Benjamin said, 'but not from starvation'. He has started packing his books. Joseph Roth, finally, whose wife has succumbed to madness and he himself to alcohol, has been playing the Cassandra for quite some time already. He has burned all his bridges in Germany, leaving the day Hitler was appointed chancellor and, despite living in permanent financial hardship, even cutting his ties with his main publisher, the *Frankfurter Zeitung*, as well as with other publishers. He broke with anyone who did not break with Nazi Germany, anyone who tried to find some sort of accommodation with it.[12]

I imagine K.'s gaze moves towards Lili, still sleeping – dear Lili, who had travelled to Paris with nothing but two suitcases, and without saying her goodbyes to anyone, not even to her sister Fränzi in Frankfurt. What a bitter irony: now they are both in Paris together, the city they had so often dreamed of during the last three years, feeling they belonged here. Two years ago, when K. had visited Paris on his own, he had written to Lili: 'In four years we might be living in Paris. It is after all the city of all cities.' And only four weeks ago, Groethuysen had asked when he and Lili would come to Paris. Now they have arrived, sooner than expected – but under what circumstances! What will happen next? Lili's French is perfect. She even translated a text by Malraux for a German anthology. Maybe she can do more translation work, or do some language teaching, or teach music once her violin has arrived. Maybe she can turn her hobby, photography, into a source of income, if they manage to get all the requisite technical equipment. Maybe it was a mistake that Lili had not been there for his stopover in Frankfurt. She never gave up, and she might have paid attention to some of the minor matters he forgot in the rush. His visit to the offices in Große Eschenheimer Straße left K. with ambivalent feelings. Reifenberg had assured him that he could travel without worrying and that the paper would shoulder the expenses. His audience with Simon, however, only lasted fifteen minutes, and it left him dissatisfied. Simon had handed him 100 marks for travel, but added that his stay in Paris had to be understood, in part, as a holiday, and any holiday would have to be paid by K. himself. After all the reductions in his salary, K. had taken this as a particular affront. He has no savings whatsoever; the previous year, they had not been able to afford even the most basic purchases – his clothes are tattered. If the paper were indeed seriously threatened, K. thinks, it would not be possible to save it simply by taking him off the payroll. And if the paper stabilized again, then depriving him of his salary was wholly unnecessary.[13]

I imagine how K. is suddenly gripped by the suspicion that the newspaper wants to get rid of him. Had he himself not announced to the Malrauxs that his protagonist Georg will lose his post as an editor? K. paints the scene in his mind: the publisher Petri giving Georg his marching orders. The real reasons Georg is fired are his (alleged) communist convictions and his bad behaviour towards the progressive friends of the *Morgenbote*. But Petri assures the ousted Georg that it is because of the paper's financial difficulties. *'I almost envy you. What a liberation to be able to turn one's back on this operation and on society.' ... He beamed like a surgeon after a successful procedure. ... The remarkable thing was that Petri himself took the evasions he was always making for the unvarnished truth and would surely have been most surprised if someone had called him a liar.*[14] K.'s character Georg will really feel liberated, *blissfully happy – as if he had cast aside all superfluous baggage and were really setting out for the first time.*[15] But, earlier, the typesetter at the paper, an old hand who was sad that Georg was leaving, had given him a piece of advice: *'Learn to box ... With boxing you can get through anything. Georg loved him as the very best of comrades. He left with the feeling of always having to be leaving.*[16] But would K. be able to learn to box?

18

Europe on the Move: Refugees in France

'Man's history is the story of his wanderings.'[1] This insight belongs to Eugene M. Kulischer, who was born as Jewgeni Michailowitsch Kulischer in 1881 in Kiev. In 1920 he fled to Germany, in 1933 to Denmark; in 1936 he went to Paris, and then, like the Kracauers, in 1941 escaped from the Germans through Spain and Portugal to the US. His brother Alexander was arrested in southern France during his flight and died in the internment camp Drancy in 1942.[2] In the US, Kulischer worked for the Department of Defense and the Office of Strategic Services. Part of his brief was the issue of refugees; it was he who coined the term 'displaced person', which would after the war come to replace the expression 'stateless person'. His book *Europe on the Move* (1948) was the first scholarly monograph to place the connection between war and migration centre stage; adopting an eastern European perspective, it took the population movements in Russia after 1917 as its point of departure. Kulischer opened our eyes to the fact that, although migration is a part of the human condition, just as much as are procreation, birth and death – and thus it can be seen as a common, everyday social process – almost all historical migration has been the result of coercion. This is true, in particular, of Europe in the first half of the twentieth century.[3]

Bertolt Brecht's 1937 poetic commentary on the concept of the emigrant therefore applies not only in the German case but generally:

> I always found the name false which they gave us: Emigrants.
> That means those who leave their country. But we
> Did not leave, of our own free will
> Choosing another land. Nor did we enter
> Into a land, to stay there, if possible for ever.
> Merely, we fled. We are driven out, banned.
> Not a home, but an exile, shall the land be that took us in.[4]

In the German case, however, many emigrants did not want any temporary solutions and, following the genocide, few wanted to return, especially among the displaced Jews (Brecht, of course, was not one of them). And some would have preferred to have stayed where they had gone, just as the Kracauers would have liked to have stayed in Paris, if possible, and later liked to stay in New York, not least because that was possible. Moreover, Brecht's preferred concept of exile suggests a return to the promised land in the Biblical tradition, a happy end in the homeland after the divine punishment has been suffered. Just as the old Hebrews in Babylon were longing for Jerusalem, Brecht looked as an exile from beyond the border towards Germany. But many refugees thought that the old home had ceased to exist, even that the old feeling of home had rested on a mistake and that this home was now enemy territory. For them, after the destruction, there could be no return.[5] Brecht surely was right to maintain that the emigrants were primarily expellees and refugees. But they could also turn into immigrants if the country granting them asylum allowed for this. Given the weaknesses and blind spots of any concept, the term 'emigration' seems, in the end, appropriate, especially if one bears in mind that as a rule it was involuntary.[6]

Kulischer, and shortly after him Hannah Arendt (another emigrant in France and immigrant in the US), in her famous book on *The Origins of Totalitarianism* (1951), showed with complete clarity how the movements of flight and migration that emerged during the Great War continued after the war had ended. One reason for this was the Russian civil war and the collapse of the Habsburg monarchy, which led to new borders and to the creation of new ethnic-national minority groups, which in turn demanded self-determination or protection. In the mid-1920s, the total number of refugees and those involuntarily relocated as a consequence of war and the creation of new nation states in Europe came to an estimated 9.5 million people, of which two million came from Russia. Many of them fell through the cracks – they did not fit into the new network of nation states – and became stateless. As Arendt observed: 'Once they had left their homeland they remained homeless, once they had left their state they became stateless; once they had been deprived of their human rights they were rightless, the scum of the earth.'[7] In 1922, the League of Nations responded to the problem by establishing a High Commission for Russian refugees, headed by Fridtjof Nansen, which introduced an identity document for stateless refugees – the 'Nansen passport' – in order to create a certain amount of legal security for them.[8] Such measures did not, however, solve the refugee problem, especially once in the 1930s the flow of Jewish refugees set in, who, like all those expelled from Germany (except for refugees from the Saarland), did not receive a 'Nansen passport'.[9] On 26 October 1933, the League of

Nations again appointed a High Commissioner for 'Jewish and other refugees from Germany', although this office was separate from its own institutions. This not so 'high' commissioner, James G. McDonald, had to cover the costs for his office through private donations. Frustrated with this lack of commitment to the issue and with the relative powerlessness of his own High Commission, McDonald resigned at the end of 1935 in protest at the generally passive attitude of members of the League of Nations towards the refugee question. Shortly afterwards, Chaim Weizmann, president of the World Zionist Organization, wrote: 'The world appears split into two halves – places where Jews cannot live and places they are not allowed to enter.'[10] As soon as they became stateless persons, those seeking protection from persecution, war and other catastrophes lost all their rights. They were 'the unwanted', stripped of their supposedly inalienable human rights.[11] According to Arendt, the anomaly of the refugees' and the stateless persons' situation was that they were not represented or protected by anyone; there were no agreed international rules governing them. Their only hope was thus to be tolerated. With the outbreak of the Second World War, the refugee problem grew more acute and the misery of the refugees escalated. Between 1939 and 1943 in Europe, 30 million people were fleeing from their homelands.

Next to this figure, the number of people fleeing Germany from 1933 onwards is small, but it is nevertheless significant in itself; in retrospect, it can be seen as a sign of things to come. Before the outbreak of the war, 400,000 to 500,000 people fled from Germany, Czechoslovakia and Austria – numbers were especially high in 1938 and 1939. The majority, 225,000, were Jewish. Between 1939 and 1942 another 50,000 Jewish refugees can be added to that figure. After Jews were prohibited from leaving the country, another 8,500 still managed to escape. Wolfgang Benz estimates the number of Jewish emigrants from Germany to be 278,500. This would mean that about half of the German Jewish population was able to escape before the deportations to the death camps began.[12]

The exodus happened in waves: 37,000 Jews (and 28,000 non-Jewish refugees) left immediately in 1933, among them the Kracauers. The anti-Jewish boycotts and violence on 1 April and the Gesetz zur Wiederherstellung des Berufbeamtentums (Law for the restoration of the professional civil service) of 7 April 1933 made it clear to Jews that they had no future in Germany. Another wave of Jewish emigration followed after 15 September 1935, the day the Reichstag unanimously passed the Nuremberg Laws, which defined German Jews as a group with diminished rights. Whole families now decided to leave, in the full knowledge that they thereby renounced their citizenship. By the end of 1937, 125,000 Jews had left. Between 1933 and 1937, Jewish refugees lost 30 to 50 per cent of their wealth, of which 25 per cent alone went to the state in the form of the 'Reichsfluchtsteuer' (Reich flight tax). By the end of 1938, the number had risen to 150,000 Jewish refugees, while the non-Jewish proportion of refugees decreased significantly after 1933. The years between 1938 and the prohibition of emigration in 1941 saw the largest wave of Jewish emigration, with an additional 130,000 to 180,000 leaving Germany. They lost between 60 and 100 per cent of their wealth.[13]

In 1933, between 25,000 and 30,000 people fled from Germany to France. Germany's Western neighbour took in the largest number of refugees during the first wave: almost half. Among them were many political opponents of the regime and famous writers. Ninety-five per cent of the refugees who came to France were Jewish, and of the remaining 5 per cent many were the spouses of Jewish refugees. During the period from 1933 to 1940, 150,000 people from Germany sought asylum in France, among them increasingly more 'ordinary people'. At no point, however, were there more than 60,000 in France.[14] Many of those who had hurriedly fled the violence of the SA during the early days and weeks soon returned, including a quarter of the Jewish refugees. Family members were still moving back and forth. For most, France was a stop-off point.[15]

For many of the more politically active first-wave emigrants, France was the country of the 'ideals of 1789', the country of universal human rights that had granted asylum to Karl Marx, Ludwig Börne and Heinrich Heine.[16] On 20 April 1933, the French government passed generous special decrees which, however, were rescinded half a year later after an estimated 20,000 refugees had entered the country. The situation for asylum seekers – indeed, for foreigners generally – in France was deteriorating. The country was gripped by economic and financial crisis, and from 1933 to 1935 there were record levels of unemployment. The domestic political situation was generally unstable following the murder of the foreign minister Louis Barthou, who was killed in Marseille when King Alexander I of Yugoslavia was assassinated there. Xenophobia generally was on the rise, especially directed towards 'the Germans' – the Jewish refugees counted among them.[17] Following the assassination in Marseille, the rules governing foreigners became increasingly more restrictive. The fundamental right to asylum could be redesigned, interpreted and, ultimately, circumvented. Each refugee, for instance, had to apply for a 'carte d'identité' within eight days of arrival. The prefect of the department could reject this application without explanation, refuse to grant an extension or confiscate papers that had already been issued. Cards were often issued only months, sometimes years, after an application was submitted. The struggle to obtain one's papers was a nerve-racking exercise. By the end of 1934, identity cards were issued only rarely.

Refugees were seldom able to fulfil the conditions attached to them: they had to prove that they had entered the country legally and were able to provide for their livelihood. At the same time, a law for the 'protection of national labour', introduced in November 1934, made it more difficult for immigrants to find sources of income; in effect, they were prohibited from working. Those who violated that law were threatened with immediate deportation, usually to Belgium or Switzerland. Many immigrants went underground and stayed in the country illegally. With the government of the Popular Front under Léon Blum, the refugees' situation temporarily improved. An interim passport was introduced, which was to be issued to all Germans who had immigrated to France since 1933, including those who had been living in France illegally. Later, during the war, this 'titre de voyage' would be a crucial document for immigrants who were forced to flee again. In April 1938, under the government of Édouard Daladier, asylum policy shifted yet again. Only a month later, the deteriorating situation for refugees reached a new low with the passing of the so-called May decrees, which subjected them to a raft of control measures. There were tough punishments for refugees in the country illegally and political refugees were imprisoned (although they were at least protected against deportation). By that time, France, home to some 20,000 refugees, was only the third most important destination for those fleeing Germany, after Palestine (44,000) and the US (27,000).[18]

Flight and expulsion, asylum and exile, emigration and immigration affected (and still today affect) hundreds of thousands of people. And yet these mass phenomena were experienced by different individuals in different ways. What emigration meant to someone depended on the time, the place and, most importantly, the person. Three examples can provide us with a good impression of the diverse ways in which exile in Paris was experienced, examples which all bear in one way or another on the Kracauers' own experience of exile. In the professions of all three – Rudolf Olden, Alphons Silbermann and Ernst Feder – language played an important role and, like Kracauer, they had lost money and had their reputation diminished by their flight to Paris.

Rudolf Olden was born in 1885 in Stettin. Like Kracauer, he fled immediately after the burning of the Reichstag. He was also a public figure, a well-known journalist and lawyer. He had represented Carl von Ossietzky in the *Weltbühne* trial, when the accused stood charged with 'insulting the Reichswehr'. Olden was on the executive board of the League for Human Rights; he was thus a political refugee. Via Prague, he came to Paris, where in 1934 he published a black paper on the situation of the Jews in Germany. Together with his wife, Ika Olden, he wrote an account of one year of emigration from Germany; it was supposed to appear with Editions Du Mercure de l'Europe, a publishing house run by emigrants, but it never did. This text pursued three main aims: to promote anti-fascism, to defend emigration and to refute anti-Semitism. In 1933/34, it is worth remembering, emigrants were not necessarily anti-fascists, nor did anti-fascists necessarily emigrate. It was not taken for granted that anti-Semitism was based on delusions. Olden reported that, while the actual flight was easy, the decision to flee had been difficult. He described how people who would have never before countenanced engaging in criminal behaviour became the forgers of passports. He reminded the readers of the panic among the Jewish population after the humiliation and shock of 1 April 1933 – the violent beginning of the boycott of Jewish businesses. He mentioned the rumours that were circulating: that in Paris and Amsterdam committees financed by rich Jews were looking out for the refugees. He said the mostly destitute 'scroungers' who had acted on such rumours deserve our understanding: he was thinking here especially of those strictly political emigrants who looked down on 'scroungers' and did not want to be associated with them. Olden assured his readers that there was no 'colony' of German immigrants in France; the newly arrived refugees were too diverse a group for that. Nevertheless, there were initial attempts at forming associations, and the children of emigrants often went to the same schools (the numbers of children exceeded those of the adults). Olden looked in particular at the lot of writers: expatriation was the highest distinction they could receive from Hitler's Germany; still, exile was tough because Hitler had deprived these authors of a potential audience of 65 million. And Olden admitted that the emigrants were frequently perceived as a threat, and migration even as a disaster, because most people adopted the 'cake theory': a slice for one means a slice less for others. And those who only a moment ago were showing up asking for a slice had the most anger for the new mouths to feed. Emigration, Olden concluded, is a 'collection of misery and wretchedness and sorrow'.[19] (Olden moved on to London in 1937. In 1940, he was invited to lecture at the New School for Social Research at Columbia University in New York. He died during the Atlantic crossing, when the ship he was on was sunk by a German U-boat.)

Alphons Silbermann was born in 1909 in Cologne. In 1933, he had just completed his doctorate with Hans Kelsen and was a legal trainee at court. He went first with his Jewish parents to Amsterdam and then moved, against the will of his father, who stopped giving him money, to Paris in 1937/38. He kept his distance from the political emigrants who imagined themselves to be walking in the footsteps of Börne, Heine and Marx. Already in Paris, he suspected that, in retrospect, the experience of exile would somehow be glorified in literature. He did not see himself as a hero, but nor did he see himself as a victim. He was preoccupied with the *débrouiller* and *débrouillard*, that is, with the question of how one might make a living, how one could muddle through. The twenty-five-year-old Silbermann sold games machines on commission to bistros, and he worked in restaurants, because that meant free meals. Thanks to his knowledge of languages and to the number of tourists, he managed to rise from dishwasher to waiter. This opened the door to a further source of income: he advised guests 'in matters of intimate pleasure'. Silbermann fitted in seamlessly alongside the French; he got to know Charles, with whom he lived for the next twelve years. He became ever more French and ever more estranged from his circle of German-Jewish emigrant friends. But that did not mean that he escaped their plight: he still had to earn the money for daily living and the rent, and he still had to deal with residency and work permit matters. His commission work, which he hoped would earn him a tidy sum, became increasingly shady, and when one of his deals fell through, he found himself sitting on a stock of unsold one-armed bandits. Finally, the dream of easy money was over. Moreover, following the May decrees, the dandy lost his job at the restaurant, and finally even his residency permit. Fortunately, as his German passport was still valid, he managed to get hold of a 'permit' to Australia and found the money for two tickets by way of an insurance fraud. In August 1938, he and Charles unceremoniously left Paris. Emigration was an extreme experience for Silbermann, and he was neither willing to praise nor to lament it. His existence during his time in Paris was permanently precarious. But Silbermann was someone who always made the best of everything: he was a realist, clever and pragmatic. Although he lacked political awareness, he understood what a dangerous ground for Jewish refugees Paris was becoming in the second half of the 1930s, even if, or perhaps particularly if, they busied themselves with one-armed bandits.[20] (After another promotion, this time from dishwasher to restaurant owner, Silbermann later opened Australia's first fast-food restaurant. He also became a well-regarded sociologist of music and, from 1950 onwards, he shuttled back and forth between Australia and Europe, especially Paris, Cologne, Lausanne and Bordeaux.)

Before his flight from Germany, Ernst Feder, born in 1881 in Berlin, was the editor of the domestic politics section of the *Berliner Tageblatt*. He was a member of the German Democratic Party, and left immediately after Hitler rose to power, first to Switzerland and then on to Paris, where he helped to establish the *Pariser Tageblatt*, the most important emigrant newspaper. Feder, who was nearing sixty at the time, had an active life beyond his journalism and politics. He worked as a translator for an international law firm on cases that were related to Germany. He even looked after his own clients, something that was, however, rarely lucrative, as they were usually emigrants. In his journalistic work, he tried to develop his connections among the French press. And he worked for the Joint Distribution Committee for Jewish refugees, where his job was to persuade Jews who had emigrated to donate the money from their blocked accounts in Germany to the Reich Deputation of German Jews. When he was successful, he received a tenth of the donation. The Feders appear to have managed just fine (although it is not clear whether, like the Kracauers, they had arrived in Paris entirely without means). They had their own flat, a maid and a telephone; they paid taxes. Their average income of 3,000 francs (roughly 2,000 euros or £1,800 today)[21] placed them in the upper social stratum of emigrants in Paris. The fact that Ernst and Erna Feder led an active social life in various circles bears this out. They visited the Champs-Elysées, where the better-off emigrants socialized; they were invited to evening teas, together with French guests, where the language spoken was French. Feder not wanting to become politically active himself, they also maintained a somewhat cool relationship towards the groups of Jewish and political emigrants, for instance in the Lutetia circle, which was trying to build an anti-Nazi front among emigrants. The Feders had many French acquaintances but few genuine friends. In December 1938, Feder applied for French citizenship. This does not necessarily say too much about his sense of identity, though, because shortly before, on 25 June 1938, he had been stripped of his German citizenship; and the date of 9 November 1938, Kristallnacht, represented a further watershed for Jewish refugees.[22] (When the Germans occupied France, Feder did not receive a US visa but, with the help of Varian Fry's Emergency Rescue Committee, a Brazilian one instead. In 1941, Feder managed to make it to Brazil, where he succeeded as an executive at the Joint Distribution Committee and as a writer. He also became a close friend of Stefan Zweig. In 1957, he and Erna returned to Berlin, where, in 1964, in near obscurity, he died.)

Siegfried Kracauer, born in 1889 in Frankfurt am Main, was a high-ranking employee at the *Frankfurter Zeitung*. He was of Jewish descent, and enjoyed a public profile as a left-wing intellectual. He fled immediately following the burning of the Reichstag. His book on *The Salaried Masses* was publicly burned on 10 May 1933 in Munich, Nuremberg, Königsberg and Leipzig.[23] Like Olden, Kracauer was a political refugee, but he kept his distance from politics after his escape; he had been exposed to something of an overdose of it back in Berlin. He could not identify with political parties. He even began to withdraw from the informal group of intellectuals constituted by Bloch, Benjamin and Wiesengrund-Adorno – those

Marx-inspired, dialectical, anarchistic, artistic and theologically inclined thinkers. Apart from that, his mother and aunt were still stuck in Frankfurt, potential hostages, as it were, of the Nazis. And he had enough problems of his own: in particular, his livelihood. Disappointments and worries led to the need for a caesura in his intellectual orientation and political outlook. Like Silbermann, Kracauer was a Jewish refugee who was more interested in developing his contacts in the French scene than in the community of emigrants. But he was twenty years older than Silbermann, and he was not the easy-going type who would find his lucky breaks amid the dishes, sinks and gambling machines. He was an intellectual who depended on language and writing to survive. Like Feder, Kracauer was well-connected and had many French acquaintances who tried to help him out, albeit without achieving much. Unlike Feder, Kracauer did not succeed in securing his material existence in Paris. On the contrary, he lived hand-to-mouth, dependent on support from private individuals, some acting as creditors, some as patrons. Kracauer found his loss of prestige particularly galling. A moment ago, he had been an important editor; he had had influence and been in demand. Overnight, he had become an emigrant and supplicant who had to go from door to door. To Kracauer, the emigrant experience was one in which the ground disappeared from beneath him and an abyss swallowed him up. He found himself in free fall, incapable of steering life. The meaningless life in Frankfurt had been succeeded – after a brief interlude of huge success and a new vitality gained – by the ungrounded life in France. The para-religious and para-Marxist phase was now followed by one of paralysis. Philosophical questions about existence were replaced by questions about material existence and, in the end, of life and death. This groundless 'existence' was, for Kracauer, not one that deserved the name. It was a lonesome experience – or, in the case of the Kracauers, a loneliness à deux – that was somehow shared by hundreds of thousands. The groundlessness was a consequence of the loss of 'homeland, family', tradition and 'economic position'. It was a consequence of the loss of 'active, creative work, done out of a strong inner vocation'. According to Vilém Flusser, a Jewish refugee who lost his family in the extermination camps, living without ground under one's feet meant the loss of all faith, be it a religious or a secular faith. It even meant forgoing any kind of 'fundamental explanation'.[24] Groundless life forgoes all metaphysical considerations, all -isms and -nesses, the belief in progress and the belief that diligence will pay off one day. The groundless are well aware that one often has less luck than one has good judgement. They know that they have become flotsam and jetsam. The art of groundlessness is nothing but the art of survival. (Kracauer never stopped loving the place of his groundlessness, Paris and France. In 1941, he escaped to the US, to New York, where he experienced a third spring. The emigrant became an immigrant. The experience of emigration became one of extraterritoriality. Kracauer was now in a position where he could once again afford to harbour small illusions.)

19

The Liquidation of German Matters

On 16 March 1933, the Societäts-Verlag in Frankfurt sent a letter, signed by Heinrich Simon, to Siegfried Kracauer: 'In future, we shall be unable to enter into obligations which exceed the duration of one month, thus shall have to determine your payments from month to month.' For the month of April, the employer proposed to pay Kracauer 500 Reichsmark (around 2,100 euros or £1,900 today), plus 150 Reichsmark to support Rosette Kracauer and 100 marks for commitments in Berlin. That amounted to another pay cut – 280 marks less 'overnight, so to speak', as Kracauer complained to Benno Reifenberg. His rent in Berlin was 195 marks, and the earliest date for ending the contract was 1 October; he paid 230 marks each month to his mother, a sum he did not want to reduce any further. The remaining 305 marks, in Paris, were not enough to keep the wolf from the door. For Kracauer, the letter from the publishing house was 'the final catastrophe'. It was also a slap in the face: 'No consideration has been given to my eleven years of working for the paper, and the measures mentioned in the letter, and those kindly announced in advance in it, treat me like a wage-labourer whose pay one can reduce at will and at short notice, or who one can throw out altogether, without any concern for his future existence.' Only half a year ago, Simon had told him that he could expect to be sent to Paris sooner or later; now, in this hopeless predicament, he found himself being treated like a person without any rights. Kracauer ended by saying: 'Of course, I *cannot accept* the letter from the publishing house', before adding a personal note for Reifenberg, off the record: 'Hatred and contempt for this enterprise.'[1] A few days later, Kracauer received another letter from Frankfurt, addressed to all employees of the publishing house, announcing cost-cutting measures that had been forced on the publisher by the new and uncertain political situation. Kracauer complained to Reifenberg that the letter of 16 March seemed to have been 'a special measure against [him]' that seemed now to have been rendered superfluous by the terms of the second letter.[2] But

Kracauer was wrong: on 5 April, Heinrich Simon told Kracauer that the *Frankfurter Zeitung* could not continue to employ him on his existing terms, that his pay would be further reduced and that he should start looking for a new place of work on which to base his livelihood.[3]

The first month in Paris had not gone well. The Cassirer publishing house, which was preparing a 'street book' consisting of Kracauer's feuilleton articles on happenings and characters in and around the streets, had told him they were not clear about how to continue with their work 'mentally and materially', and that they therefore would not be pursuing the project further. The termination of the book project confirmed what Kracauer had written in the preface: 'The picture that is designed on the following pages evokes the Kurfürstendamm in Berlin only a few months ago, and yet separated from us by an abyss. This is what this world-famous, much-loved and much-mocked street looked like before Hitler's victory!'[4] Kracauer had also sought work, in vain, with the *Neue Schweizer Rundschau* and Max Rychner. And Wilhelm Hausenstein of the *Münchener Neueste Nachrichten*, who only a few weeks ago had asked whether his colleague in Berlin would be interested in writing a (likely very well-paid) serial novel, informed him that now it was altogether impossible to do anything for his ex-colleague in Paris – 'as impossible as it could possibly be'. (Two weeks later, with the police exerting pressure, Hausenstein was himself sacked.) On 1 April, to make matters worse, no money had arrived from Frankfurt. He had only 1,000 francs left (about 150 Reichsmark, roughly £580), he reported to Frankfurt, in a tone of both desperation and reproach. The publishing house transferred the rest of his salary late, on 6 April.[5]

In the meantime, Kracauer had called on his old friend Selmar Spier, a lawyer at the regional court of Frankfurt specializing in commercial property law, as well as publishing and copyright law. Spier assured his friend in Paris that he would not let him down, although his own personal situation was also grave. He, too, was confronting the possibility of a massive reduction in income, and perhaps even facing the loss of his licence to practise law, as a consequence of the Law for the Restoration of the Professional Civil Service.[6] He told his friend to hold his nerve. Compared to others, he said, his situation was not at all hopeless:

> You always found it a bit difficult to adapt to circumstances. You are in the rare and fortunate situation of not having lost all of the ground from under your feet, of rather having retained a little bit of space in which you may try to create a new life for yourself. There is a whole swathe of intellectuals to whom that does not apply and who nevertheless do not all fall into despair.[7]

Spier knew families of five or six people who had to make do with less than the Kracauers as a couple. Still, Spier's words must have stung the refugee, with his worn-out nerves: not hopeless, not groundless, not able to adapt? How dare his friend say such things! Kracauer's reply ended with a rant directed, for now at least, only at Simon and the company: 'They want to get rid of the Jew and leftist, that's all. For that I have worked for eleven years, have exposed myself and have squandered half of my life. You can imagine the feelings I have towards this gang.' Kracauer interpreted Simon's letter of 5 April as serving him his notice, and the reductions in his salary as a tactic to make his redundancy cheaper for the paper. In a moment of hysterical rage, he did not put it past the publishing house to seize his furniture in Berlin to pay the rent for the Berlin apartment.[8]

After a meeting with Reifenberg, Spier thought that Kracauer's worries were not justified and asked him to calm down. Spier reached an agreement whereby he and the paper were acting as guarantors for Kracauer's rent. With 150 Reichsmark of financial support from Oskar Wiesengrund, the furniture was removed from the apartment and put into storage, so that theoretically the place could be rented out again.[9] (This did not happen, however: in spring 1933, there were suddenly very many empty apartments in Berlin.) Spier did not see Simon's letter as a redundancy notice but as a piece of 'well-meaning advice, which, looked at objectively, I think one can only agree with. If these people wanted to get rid of you, they would today have very different means at their disposal.' At any rate, he added, Reifenberg was on Kracauer's side.[10] Spier thought that his friend in Paris had no idea about the present situation in Germany, and especially about the situation at the paper, as he tried to explain:

> Simon is certainly not the ideal negotiating partner. He is a typical publisher, always anxious he might cause upset somewhere, eager not to tie himself down in any way. He was probably ever thus. And now, imagine him in an enterprise in which the process of so-called *Gleichschaltung* progresses daily, in which buildings are searched, in which employees want to be given a certain right to control things because part of their salaries has been held back. The man does not want to compromise anyone. On the one hand, he does not want to make you redundant; on the other, he finds it a little difficult to make use of you. As a result, I believe, deep down inside he would like to get rid of you, but out of a regard for tradition … he cannot put that into practice.[11]

Given all this, Spier thought it not possible to negotiate a binding agreement on behalf of his friend; and any such agreement could, in any case, be nullified at any point by some *force majeure*.

In early May 1933, Kracauer nevertheless insisted on such a 'written, absolutely binding declaration by the publishing house'.[12] His situation had deteriorated further; his attempts at generating additional income had come to naught, and he was facing financial ruin. He had sought, in vain, a position as a cultural correspondent in Paris at the *Neuer Zürcher Zeitung*. The *Nouvelle Revue Française* (NRF), which, under the influence of André Gide, was reorientating itself towards a pro-communist position, did not want to publish his street articles. In fact, the NRF turned out to be a closed shop for German emigrants, as it concentrated almost exclusively on French literature. Walter Benjamin was also unable to publish there.[13] And Kracauer had annoyed his agent in London, Margaret Goldsmith, who had been diligently looking for a publisher for his proposed emigrant's diary, before Kracauer had suddenly decided that he did not want to write it after all because he feared that it might endanger his relatives in Frankfurt.[14] And, finally, he had met with Simon in Paris and was outraged by his manipulative behaviour:

> Pointing to my racial and intellectual weaknesses, he declares that my departure is necessary, in the same breath practically assumes that I have left already, and from this fiction derives the right to consider my inadequate payment as a relatively generous form of charity, almost morally glorifying it.[15]

Kracauer now wanted to pre-empt 'the payments fizzling out altogether', making the negotiations he instructed Spier to conduct on his behalf even more important. Their aim had to be to secure an official notice of termination, with an appropriate timeline and salary payments until the end of the year, as had been the norm at the Scherl publishing house. Alternatively, he could agree a severance payment of 6,240 Reichsmark, eight months' salary.[16]

Kracauer's aunt Hedwig was more inclined towards Spier's sober weighing of the various factors than she was towards her enraged nephew's approach. She said Spier was a 'true friend' to Kracauer. And she predicted that the paper would not be able to retain Kracauer as an employee without putting its own existence at risk. In the face of the *FZ*'s fears for its own future, their former star editor had lost his shine. She recommended to Kracauer that he should seek to settle with the company as soon as possible. But, she added suggestively, diplomacy was difficult for proud people.[17] Indeed, it soon became clear to the *Frankfurter Zeitung* that, if they wished to adapt themselves to the new situation, they could not continue to have such a prominent left-wing Jew on their payroll. And, despite various gestures of resistance, they did wish so to adapt themselves. But Simon did not simply want to show the long-standing leading editor the door. On 4 April 1933, the paper had still taken a risk by rejecting rumours that Jewish employees had been sacked.[18] It seemed preferable to wait for a while, to support their exile in Paris until such time as Kracauer – after all, a well-connected and well-known intellectual – had found some position elsewhere, perhaps an academic posting. But when Kracauer, his pride pricked, grew recalcitrant and 'ungrateful', pointing out all the contradictions 'the company' was knotting itself in, the relationship went sour. And further personal feuds ensued.

On the Societäts-Verlag side, Hans Lothar and supervisory board member Rudolf Schwander took over the negotiations from Simon. The time for hesitation had now passed. The publishing house's priority was now to get rid of the editor as quickly, cheaply and silently as possible, sometime after 9 May. 'I assume that the matter will now be dealt with on strictly legal terms', Spier reported from Frankfurt.[19] According to one of Spier's notes, Lothar made the following case at a meeting with the lawyers on 10 May: the paper, he argued, was simply not able to engage Kracauer as a writer. His writings were, at present, useless to them, maybe even dangerous. The rulings of the labour courts were on the employer's side in this, as evidenced by the case of a Jewish conductor, employed by a café in the Kaiserstraße, who had been fired, with immediate effect, because the audience demanded not to see him. The paper wished to treat Kracauer with decency; hence, it was now suggested that he would be paid 600 Reichsmark for each of the months of May, June and July – 500 Reichsmark for his upkeep and 100 Reichsmark for his mother. Should he not be able to find a new position by August, the paper might – at its discretion – provide limited financial assistance. Spier argued that as the notice period for editors was six months, 780 Reichsmark had to be paid to Kracauer each month until the end of the year. Lothar replied that this sort of demand made the negotiations more difficult. It would have been possible, and right, to have handed Kracauer his notice as early as February. That had been done by way of the letter of 16 March, to which the employee had not objected. At least, they had no record of any such objection, and thus Kracauer cannot have disputed the notice. Spier contended that it was impossible that Kracauer would not have protested against the letter of 16 March. The notary replied that a letter from Paris might have been 'confiscated' by the SA, which had paid a visit to the editorial offices on 31 March, before he had had the opportunity to read it.[20] Following this exchange, Spier advised Kracauer to concentrate on the letter of 16 March, which he did not consider to be a valid redundancy notice. He pointed out, however, that the paper might be able to dismiss him on grounds of absence. It would be wise, at present, to avoid a trial, he said. In any case, it was obvious that the FZ was no longer interested in continuing to work with Kracauer. Spier suggested seeking an out-of-court severance payment of 3,000 Reichsmark.[21] But Kracauer reiterated his original demand: eight monthly salary payments, beginning from April, amounting to a total sum of 6,240 marks; at a push, Spier could agree to 5,000 marks, but nothing lower than that.[22]

In the weeks to come, the publishing house kept a low profile and let things run their course. There was the potential prospect of a new press law coming into effect on 1 July, which might have taken matters out of their hands in any case. In May and June, the company transferred 500 Reichsmark to Kracauer, but contrary to their original offer his mother did not receive anything. Towards the end of May, Rudolf Geck and Karl Zimmermann, colleagues from the editorial offices, got in touch with Kracauer to express their regret that he was no longer sending articles from Paris and to seek some explanation.[23] They clearly had no idea what was going on. The correspondent in London, Wolf von Dewall, was in the same position; he was 'very deeply shocked' and conveyed his sympathies to his colleague, but he had no idea what best to do either.[24] Reifenberg was the only one at the editorial offices who was abreast of the situation, but he had been hurt by the series of accusations his friend had levelled against him, and he fell silent.[25] As he saw it, he had stayed to fight; he had not terminated his contract in order to try his hand at some literary work, as his ousted colleague from Munich, Hausenstein, had suggested he should. And now he had simply had enough of these accusations. Joseph Roth, whom he had never let down during all his years of trouble, had already ended his friendship with him. Roth thought that Reifenberg had sided with Sieburg, against Kracauer and Roth himself, and he thought Reifenberg was too accommodating and openly cultivated a relationship with the new regime. According to Roth, Reifenberg thought his wife being able to buy new hats was more important than his maintaining a dignified stance. Roth's inflexible attitude irritated Reifenberg; his political vocabulary, he thought, was 'as simple as a children's primer' – there were good people, and there were evil people. Whenever Roth made a political statement, the result was, in Reifenberg's view, radical and trivial. Neither the Roths nor the Kracauers, with their accusatory and hostile language, had any appreciation of how limited his possibilities were, how precarious the situation of the paper. 'What today is possible, reasonable and right in Germany cannot be judged by those outside of it, but only by us', wrote an anonymous author in July 1933 in the *FZ*, after Simon had used an editorial to cast doubt on the credibility of emigrants' views. That was the view from inside the foxes' den in Frankfurt.[26]

Truly precarious, however, was the situation of the Kracauers in Paris. They had moved to the cheaper Madison Hotel in the university quarter in mid-May. There, they lived in a room on the eighth floor; seeing the room on a visit, Aunt Hedwig said it was not exactly a 'happy place'.[27] The paper's delaying tactics were getting to them. From mid-June onwards, Kracauer was asking Spier to press on with the negotiations, and by the end of the month he said he simply wanted the conflict resolved as quickly as possible, even if it meant losses.[28] On 1 July, Kracauer wrote directly to Reifenberg, saying that he regretted not having heard personally from him, and asking him to take the legal process regarding this matter into his own hands. Reifenberg and Spier met on 7 July, and at that point Kracauer's lawyer accepted the suggested one-off severance payment of 4,000 Reichsmark.[29] But this did not complete the divorce, and the dispute was not over yet. On 8 July, an article by Kracauer appeared in Schwarzschild's *Das Neue Tage-Buch*. This gave Societäts-Verlag the legal grounds for terminating Kracauer's contract of 1930, the terms of which stipulated that Kracauer was only to engage in collaboration with other journals to a limited degree, 'as long as the interests of the publishing house' were not compromised.[30] The article in question was a review of André Malraux's *La condition humaine*. Ironically, the article said: 'No soothing certainties are being offered here, and miracles are also altogether absent. Imperturbably, like fate, the collective forces assert themselves over love, dreams and hope.'[31] Nothing could have described Kracauer's *condition d'emigration* with greater clarity. At any rate, his guest appearance in the well-known journal weakened his negotiating position still further. Even Zimmermann, a member of the editorial office and an admirer of Kracauer, thought that the article had done 'great damage' to his colleague's position. In addition, there were rumours circulating in Frankfurt that Malraux had supported Kracauer economically.[32]

On 11 July, Kracauer alerted Spier to the fact that he had not yet received the severance payment and was not able to settle his hotel bill. Spier discovered that the money appeared to be stuck at the foreign exchange office. On 14 July, Kracauer, who in the meantime had received 200 Reichsmark directly from Frankfurt (an unofficial payment organized by Sieburg), appealed to Reifenberg to intercede and persuade Simon and Lothar to circumvent the foreign exchange office. The way the company was proceeding demonstrated sheer 'malice', Kracauer thought: the payment could, like the 200 Reichsmark, simply have been made by the Paris office of the *FZ*. He feared now that it might be impossible to get the money released from the blocked account into which, according to the foreign exchange office, it had to be transferred.[33] Kracauer was now apparently also angry with his friend Selmar, who had not only failed to avert this bureaucratic mix-up but also, after a visit to the *FZ*, denied that there was 'malice' behind it. Spier reported that the regional tax office had stipulated that the outstanding sum of

2,666 Reichsmark had to be sent through a foreign exchange bank in Frankfurt and had not accepted Paris as the place of payment. Elisabeth Kracauer was particularly unhappy with the lawyer's work, and even Hedwig Kracauer, who so far had been supportive of Spier's line, noted that Spier 'was not a man with brio' and that Kracauer might want to consider finding a new lawyer. Kracauer decided to turn to Margherita de Francesco, who until the summer of 1932 had worked at the *FZ* and so knew everyone involved.[34]

Margherita de Francesco, an author, entered the fray enthusiastically, and soon she had identified a scapegoat: Spier. He, she thought, dealt with the case the way lawyers tended to deal with pro bono cases. He did not put his back into it at all, she alleged, and he always came to the defence of Simon and Reifenberg. Sometimes she called him vile, sometimes a nincompoop. In her eyes, all of the blame lay at Spier's door – especially once she had been to the *Frankfurter Zeitung* offices in person.[35] There, she learned that during the negotiations certain things had been put directly into the lawyer's mouth without him even understanding what was going on. On 19 August, she met Benno Reifenberg at the offices, judging him to have been 'very humble, very understanding and genuinely moved' when she told him about the Kracauers' plight in Paris. He insisted he could not correspond directly with Kracauer as, in this matter, he was not acting as a private person. 'Moved by his guilt', however, he immediately called a meeting for noon the same day to discuss ways to help Kracauer. 'Many people are active and do not let you down', de Francesco cheerfully reported about her seemingly successful intervention.[36] Later, however, she had to break some rather disappointing news:

> Everyone was full of sympathy, your friend [probably Reifenberg] became very forceful in defending your interest, and yet: there was a categorical refusal to do the tiniest bit more for you. The motive: fear, cowardice, call it what you like, but not avarice. Mainly fear. Dr. L[othar] sympathizes with the lawyer, whom he praised highly, and flatly rejects all of your friend's criticisms.

It was all a typical case of 'inertia of the heart', including on the part of Reifenberg, who was full of goodwill but powerless.[37] A couple of days after the meeting Rosette Kracauer was handed an anonymous donation of 200 Reichsmark by a 'lady' who was 'close to the editorial office'; that was something, at least.[38] But following the 'agreement', the publishing house drew a line under the Kracauer matter. After he had requested a written confirmation of the termination of his contract – he needed it to secure the release of the funds from the foreign exchange office – the Frankfurter Societäts-Druckerei sent a letter, dated 25 August, in which it declared the cessation of all relations with Kracauer with immediate effect, citing as justification his article in *Das Neue Tage-Buch*. The ousted Kracauer sarcastically remarked that the company, because of his oeuvre, was breaking off relations that had already been broken off: 'as if the separation had not already taken place. One wants protection for all eventualities.'[39] With de Francesco's help, Kracauer was able to find out what documents he needed to release his assets from Germany: a confirmation that he had no outstanding tax debts, an immigration and residency permit for France and confirmation that he had no other assets in France.[40]

For Kracauer, fleeing Germany not only meant the end of his economic and social existence as he had known it: 'The correspondence regarding severance payments, furniture, etc., over weeks has so worn me down that I can hardly work on my novel. Despite the fact that it is my only hope', he wrote to Julius Meier-Graefe. Being dropped by his paper was a source of deep grievance and hatred for him, and this clouded his view. Two of his friendships broke down, at least temporarily. His break with Reifenberg might have been what he needed to restore his mental equilibrium as he sat in Paris waiting for some sign of compassion and unconditional support. Reifenberg's argument that, given his position, he could not act in a private capacity was totally unacceptable to Kracauer, nor did Kracauer buy Reifenberg's alleged distress over his predicament. If anyone should have known about the situation, it was Reifenberg. When on 8 November he attempted to visit Kracauer in Paris, he felt the consequences: phoning from the lobby of the Madison Hotel, he was briskly and calmly sent away by Elisabeth Kracauer.[41] Shocked by this 'sad, barren' response, he left Paris and dedicated himself to his important work in publishing again: trying to keep the *Frankfurter Zeitung* alive under the Nazi state. (The paper soon adopted the Nazi line on major foreign policy and economic questions. Adaptation and agreement were the rule, while members of the educated bourgeoisie from Reifenberg's milieu might have been able to detect hidden forms of dissent or resistance. 'Especially in the case of the FZ', Bloch heard from Germany, 'there is a constant reading between the lines, and usually something is found even if nothing has been written there.'[42] On 1 January 1934, the Editors Law came into force, and in the summer of 1934 Heinrich Simon, who was of Jewish descent, had to give up his position as head of the editorial board and sell his family's shares in the Imprimatur GmbH. Of the eighty editors, thirteen others also had to leave. Simon emigrated via Paris, Tel Aviv and London to Washington DC, where in 1941 he died as the victim of a violent crime. For the time being, the *Frankfurter Zeitung* continued to be published. Throughout the 1930s, in Joseph Goebbels's opinion, its continued existence was still useful for bolstering the regime's image in foreign countries of the Western world. In 1937, however, Reifenberg was promptly arrested by the Gestapo after criticizing the removal of a painting by van Gogh from the Städel Museum. A year later, he was banned from writing political articles. In 1943, he was released from prison. In August 1943, Hitler finally banned the newspaper.[43])

The loss of his friendship with Selmar Spier, as a result of having chosen him as a lawyer, cost Kracauer much more than that of the friendship with Reifenberg. In the eyes of the Kracauer family, Spier's mistakes had had severe consequences. With a little more presence of mind and commitment, he might have avoided the involvement of the foreign exchange office in the payment. Under the influence of the agile – if somewhat rash – de Francesco, Kracauer got the impression that Spier 'is, in his heart, more on the side of the opponent than of his client'; he felt 'severely damaged' by him.[44] The truth of the matter is likely that Kracauer was at the end of his tether and Spier at the end of his wits, or, as Aunt Hedwig put it: 'He never missed anything out of indifference; rather, he did not understand the matters at hand.'[45] Spier's own troubles grew by the day; the problems with the authorities never ended. Finally, he became ill. When Hedwig related this to the Kracauers, they wrote to him, in October 1933. But the letter did not convey any warmth or compassion. It was terse, suggestive of anything but friendship. Half a year later, Spier thanked them for the letter in an equally curt manner, and expressed his disappointment and regret about not having heard anything more from his old friend. (And this is how things remained. The Spiers would ask Hedwig and Rosette Kracauer about 'Friedel and Lili', but there was never any direct contact. In 1936, Spier left Frankfurt together with his wife Marlene and emigrated to Palestine, where he built a new life for himself.)[46]

The liquidation of German matters also involved drafting a series of articles in which Kracauer pursued the question of why the National Socialists had been victorious and what this meant. These texts were written during his first year in Paris and mostly remained unpublished; only two of them appeared in French journals. Kracauer's analyses set out not so much from politics but from society: the stratification of the population, the youth, the Protestants and the intellectuals.[47] They were characterized by an attention to anti-Semitism and nationalism that was rare among writers with left-wing views.

In these texts, Kracauer extended the theory of the middle classes he had developed in the study on the salaried masses. He did not claim that National Socialism was a middle-class form of rule, but he assumed that the social marginalization and ideological delusion of the middle strata had provided the decisive breeding ground for it:

> If one does not appreciate the intellectual abandonment felt by the middle class, one will fail to understand the success of National Socialism. It is a reaction to the ideational impotence of the middle strata, and it transforms their resentment against a Marxism that dismisses them and a capitalism that simply leaves them to waste away, into aims that seem to be positive. Nationalism becomes the essential catalyst for the movement.[48]

Kracauer said that the fervent and mystically intensified idea of the nation sprang up after the war, out of the experience of defeat and the unhappy experience of the fragmentation of national community. He described this idea as a phantasmagoria breaking forth from the youth of Germany and seeming to open up new horizons. The victims of rationalization reject rationality: that was Kracauer's fundamental claim about the events at the end of the Weimar Republic.

This analysis obviously implies a criticism of the communists and socialists who, fixated upon the proletariat, failed to notice the processes of erosion being exerted on craftsmen, traders, employees, civil servants and representatives of independent professions by continuing economic crisis. Kracauer thought that these dispossessed and marginalized groups became the core of the Hitler movement, the anti-capitalism of which was far more appealing to them than that of Marxism. In addition, there was the rural population's deep dissatisfaction with the 'system' and the pseudo-liberal and weak haute bourgeoisie's fear of Bolshevism; both groups felt that the Nazis should get a chance to show what they could do. Finally, the army of the unemployed, especially among the youth, needed apocalyptic promises as much as their daily bread, which they did not have. The youth got high on night marches and torchlit processions. Meanwhile, although the communist party possessed the requisite revolutionary fire and fervour – as against the technocratic social democrats – it slavishly toed the Moscow line, and had begun to lose its sense of reality through its entrenched hatred of social democracy. Kracauer's prognosis was: against German socialism, which rejected the Marxist theory of class struggle, internationalist socialism did not stand a chance.[49]

Kracauer took the Nazis seriously, especially the manner in which they attempted to totally transform reality where it did not conform to their ideals. That perspective informed his evaluation of the Work Order Act, which was passed on 20 January 1934, a 'reform of the greatest magnitude' that sought to bring about a new relationship between employees and employers in accordance with the National Socialist world view. Its ambition was 'nothing less than a complete transformation of social reality'. The class struggle would be suspended by means of a romantic idea of community and

by political violence. Although Kracauer considered this a chimera
– the reality of class-based society could not simply be removed by
decree – he nevertheless recognized the effectiveness of the violent
energies mobilized by these attempts, especially where they were
conducted imperialistically towards the outside and directed against
minorities on the inside. Violence and terror, phantasmagorias and
ideology, were no longer purely functions of dictatorial rule, he
thought; they had become ends in themselves.[50]

'Anti-Semitism, something that many all-too-optimistic citizens
thought a mere blemish, is in reality a central ideological element
of the movement.'[51] Even though, in hindsight, it seems obvious
that the overriding aim of the National Socialists was the expulsion
of the Jews from the community of the people, 'redemptive anti-
Semitism',[52] this was not a widely held view in Kracauer's circles
around 1933. From the perspective of the theory of class struggle
and the critique of political economy, anti-Semitism seemed a
minor contradiction. It required a Jewish perspective to locate the
persecution of Jews at the heart of National Socialism, for only the
experience of persecution gave rise to the sort of questions Kracauer
asked: 'What was the matter with us, … that such a fate was allowed
to haunt us, and what will one day happen to us?' It is worth noting
that the one asking these questions was thus numbering himself
among that group, even if he only felt a part of it as a consequence
of his expulsion. 'Now the paths do split', he perceptively wrote,
addressing the other Jewish Germans, German Jews or Jews from
Germany. For Kracauer, separation from Germany was not only
physical and material but also intellectual and political.[53]

On 12 November 1933, Kracauer wrote to the correspondent
of the *Frankfurter Zeitung* in Spain, Fritz Wahl, who had given
him 200 pesetas (about 160 Reichsmark) after he had heard of the
Kracauers' problems, reporting that 'the liquidation of the German
matters' had been concluded. That is how the Kracauers felt about
it, but in truth the statement was somewhat premature.[54] They had
spent almost all of the severance payment from the 'company',
partly because the removal of the furniture to a storage place in
Paris alone had cost 950 Reichsmark.[55] In the following months,
Kracauer, by this point dependent on the help of a 'local friend',[56]
attempted to draw his editor's pension from the Retirement Fund of
the Reich's Association of the German Press. This cost him a great
deal of energy and time, as well as getting in the way of his writing.
And the regulations governing foreign exchange transactions had
become increasingly complex. He had to enter into another convoluted battle with bureaucracy, and to that end he had to begin an
intensive engagement with paragraphs and authorities. The goal
of this thicket of laws, regulations, ordinances and decrees was
clear enough, however: the economic coercion and exploitation of

emigrants, mainly the Jewish ones.[57] Kracauer's financial losses in
the course of transferring funds were significant. He agreed to a
lump sum payment of 8,027.35 marks from the Reich's Association
of the German Press, a figure that was – even taking into account the
deductions for early payment – far below what he was due for eleven
years of (partly) well-remunerated, professional employment.[58] The
best way to get hold of the money was to apply for emigration
in Berlin. That required certificates, declarations and confirma-
tions from police station 128 in Berlin, the residents' registry office
at Alexanderplatz, the tax office for Charlottenburg-West, the
emigration office and the charitable public emigration advice bureau
in Berlin, the office for foreign exchange control in Frankfurt and
from the Societäts-Druckerei in Frankfurt. It also meant 'the
architect' Dr Siegfried Kracauer signing a contract with Société
du Meuble in Paris agreeing that, upon payment of a deposit of
50,000 francs, he would become an associate and employee of
the company. That, however, was a ruse, Silbermann-style; it was
simply a way of being able to claim the money from Germany for
the purpose of 'beginning a business' abroad.[59] As a result, 5,000
Reichsmark from the pension scheme was released to Kracauer.
The outstanding rent and his legal costs were deducted from the
remaining 3,020 Reichsmark, and Kracauer then received a further
1,285 Reichsmark when the blocked account was closed. All told,
then, in the course of the foreign exchange transactions, Kracauer
lost half of his lump sum payment (which was already too small) to
the German state.[60]

'We are still alive, but that is the most positive thing that can
be said about us', was Kracauer's summary in March 1934, after
his first twelve months in Paris. 'We have absolutely no idea how
we have survived this year. The daily motto still is: tide ourselves
over.'[61] He was suffering from 'chronic fatigue'.[62] His prospects did
not seem promising: 'In the journalistic profession, it appears to
me, there is nothing to hope for in the coming years for someone
like me', Kracauer concluded, after his attempts to find work in the
Netherlands also came to nothing.[63] Letters to Karl Mannheim, Emil
Lederer and Hendrik de Man regarding potential academic positions
were answered politely, but in the negative.[64] Kracauer even applied
to the High Commissioner for German Emigration at the League of
Nations.[65] The Kracauers were 'at the end of [their] tether'[66] when
even more terrible news came: Franziska Katz-Ehrenreich, Lili's
sister in Frankfurt, died wholly unexpectedly of uraemia, resulting
from kidney disease. Elisabeth Kracauer would recover only very
slowly from this shock. Kracauer wrote to Bloch:

> She [Fränzi] was the only thing still connecting Lili to her childhood,
> and Lili and her were extremely close. You know Lili – you will be able

Figure 25. Kracauer at Combloux, summer 1934
Copyright: DLA Marbach

to imagine how much Lili is suffering from this loss, and how painful
it is for her that she was not able to see her sister again because of the
political situation.[67]

Because of all this turmoil, Kracauer could work on his novel
only sporadically. After all the sadness and disappointment he had
experienced in relation to the 'gang' in Frankfurt, he now decided
the title for the book would be 'Das träge Herz' (Inertia of the
Heart). The Fischer publishing house, which owned the copyright
and had already invested a lot of money in the author, felt incapable
of publishing the book.[68] In the autumn of 1934, Kracauer wrote
the novel's final line, and thus bade farewell to his German past.
With his removal from Frankfurt and Berlin, he had 'become aware
of the extent of the gap' not only between the manuscript and the
German 'Entwicklungsroman' (novel of inner development) but
also between him and the society of which the novel sought to
give an account. 'The foundation in my case is very Jewish (but

certainly not in the sense of the Zionists or even the assimilated Jews!)', he wrote to Friedrich Traugott Gubler, who had returned to Switzerland. '[A]nd', he continued, 'only from that perspective do I now recognize very clearly why this never-ending battle which for years at the paper I fought in the area of cultural politics against the dreadful German state of affairs and, in that sense, also against the paper, had to fail!'[69] This dreadful German state of affairs was the inertia of the heart. *People bumped into one another, paying no attention,*[70] it says towards the end of *Georg*; Georg *felt himself in a state of detachment which made him blissfully happy – as if he had cast aside all superfluous baggage and were really only setting out for the first time.*[71] Georg had failed, but thus was free – free of idealist illusions, of political strategies and ideologies, which blocked the path towards the humane. Kracauer was now free of all that, but he was also, still, without ground under his feet. The relief of having broken with an inhumane society did not compensate for the fact that he did not have his daily bread. His insecure – in fact, impossible – existence in Parisian exile was wearing him down. He did not have to wait long for the next disappointment to arrive. Kracauer tried to find a publisher, but his need to distance himself from 'companies', 'gangs' and 'cliques' proved to be an obstacle.

After 1933, the Amsterdam-based publishing houses Querido and Allert de Lange became centres for German exile literature. Emanuel Querido, a Dutch socialist, offered the former editor of Kiepenheuer, Fritz H. Landshoff, the opportunity to create a German-language literature programme. Alfred Döblin, Lion Feuchtwanger, Heinrich Mann, Joseph Roth, Anna Seghers and Arnold Zweig all published books with Querido. Klaus Mann was the editor of the literary journal *Die Sammlung*, which, however, only survived for two years. The Allert de Lange publishing house also created a German section in 1933. It was directed by Walter Landauer, with the support of Hermann Kesten. Although the publisher was conservative, Bertolt Brecht, Ferdinand Bruckner and Egon Erwin Kisch counted themselves among its authors. Joseph Roth published with both houses, which were more interested in cooperating than in competing with each other.[72] Kracauer, however, did not want to have anything to do with either of them. The reasons for this are not entirely clear. Later, he himself could not remember what the source of this idiosyncrasy on his part had been. In July 1933, he asked Bermann Fischer 'to write on my behalf to the Querido publishing house' in the event that Fischer rejected his novel. A year later, he told Bloch categorically that the publishers in Holland were not an option for him.[73] Perhaps this all had something to do with Klaus Mann, with whom he had had a serious disagreement in May 1932.[74] Most likely, however, his extraordinary

Figure 26. Elisabeth Kracauer-Ehrenreich in 1935, while in exile in Paris, painted by her brother-in-law, Hanns Ludwig Katz. (Lili here looks like her sister Franziska, who had died a year before.)
Copyright: Kunsthalle Emden/Stiftung Henri Nannen

sensitivity and irritability was down to frayed nerves and wounded pride, following the nasty course of previous events.

Julius Meier-Graefe and Max Tau, who warm-heartedly took care of Kracauer's interests from Berlin, drew Thomas Mann's attention to Kracauer's manuscript, and, knowing that Mann had admired *Ginster*, asked him to support *Georg*.[75] The Nobel laureate agreed to help, even though, as an embarrassed Kracauer admitted to him, Mann had made 'a less than winning impression' on him in the course of 'the cultural and political battle in Germany'. Mann, who now lived in Küsnacht, near Zurich, nevertheless praised the manuscript's 'high literary character', its 'supple style' and its almost painful 'poignancy' and immediately sent it, together with his endorsement, to Landshoff. The protégé was shocked and replied straight away: he could not 'envisage a connection with the two publishing houses in Holland', whose representatives he knew personally from his Berlin years.[76]

Kracauer would rather have preferred the publisher Julius Kittl in Mährisch-Ostrau, but Thomas Mann did not have contacts there; or Swiss publishers – Gubler unsuccessfully approached Emil Oprecht, the founder of the Europa Verlag, as well as Orell Füssli and Guggenbühl & Huber. In Austria, finally, where Bloch and Alban Berg were promoting the novel, it was turned down by the publishers Herbert Reichner and Hans Zsolnay. In the end, Kracauer gave up on a German publication of the novel, although the situation in Paris did not look any more promising. Part of the novel had been translated into French, and Malraux had composed a letter of recommendation, but nevertheless none of the publishers thought descriptions of the social milieu in the old Germany would find much success with their audiences. Thus, the liquidation of German matters was also something Kracauer was inclined towards by the circumstances. Apart from that, he had been pursuing another idea for some time.

20

Two Views on the Second Empire: Offenbach and the Arcades

Kracauer wanted to write a book on Jacques Offenbach. Offenbach was born in Cologne in 1819 as Jakob Offenbach. His father, Isaac Ben-Juda, a cantor, had moved from the Main to the Rhine. In 1833, he brought his son to Paris, where he was to receive his musical education at the conservatory. After just one year the young Offenbach left the institution to become a cello player at the Opéra Comique. He was taught composition by Jacques Fromental Halévy (1799–1862), who had made a name for himself with his opera *La Juive*. Around 1855, after almost two precarious and arduous decades in Paris, Offenbach's star began to rise. Paris was staging the first World Exhibition; Louis Napoleon Bonaparte had installed himself first as dictator, then a little later as emperor (1851/1852), and the theatre called Les Bouffes Parisiens was becoming very fashionable. Offenbach's first major operetta, *Orpheus in the Underworld* (1858), was a sensation; he followed this with further successes: *Beautiful Helen* (1864) and *The Grand-Duchess of Gerolstein* (1867), with the celebrated diva Hortense Schneider taking the lead role in both, and *Parisian Life* (1866), which Kracauer called 'the most enchanting of all songs of praise ever written on a city'.[1] The genre of *Offenbachiade* spread across Europe. Its decline began around the time of the second World Exhibition in 1867, when the Second Empire presented itself in all its glory for the last time before collapsing amid internecine battle and external war. Jacques Offenbach was no businessman; even at the height of his fame, his financial situation was perilous. Now the composer was threatened with poverty and, despite suffering from gout, was forced to embark on a trip to the US to put on guest performances, which did, at least, meet with acclaim. His last important work was the opera *The Tales of Hoffmann* (1881), whose premiere in Paris he would not get to witness. He died immediately after the work was completed, on 5 October 1880.

It is not clear what gave Kracauer the idea for his book. In Austria and, later, in Germany, there had been an Offenbach renaissance in the 1920s, sparked by Karl Kraus, Alban Berg and Ernst Křenek. The Viennese torchbearer of satire and critic of language had attested that the *Offenbachiade* displayed 'deep nonsense', as opposed to the 'shallow sense' of the typical operetta of salon music,[2] thus intellectually ennobling, so to speak, this easy-listening, catchy music. Benjamin had, in turn, published an essay on Kraus in four parts in the *Frankfurter Zeitung* and an article titled 'Karl Kraus Reads Offenbach' in the *Literarische Welt*, which highlighted the duplicitous, mocking and anarchic aspects of Offenbach's music.[3] Bloch, Wiesengrund ('a magician of parody and parodist of myth') and Soma Morgenstern also engaged with Offenbach as a musician. Offenbach was 'in the air', including in Kracauer's Paris neighbourhood.[4] But it is nevertheless surprising that Kracauer, who was not musical, became the one who picked the subject.

The first time Kracauer mentioned the idea of a book on Offenbach was to Margaret Goldsmith, his London agent, in April 1934; this fact itself suggests that the project had a fundamentally commercial motivation.[5] After one year in Paris, it was clear to Kracauer that outside of Germany he would not find a secure position at a newspaper or journal. Nor did the academic world wait for him. What, then, was an intellectual refugee to do? Well, he wrote books, because he had no other choice.[6] And a writer of books, if he was not a Feuchtwanger or a Thomas Mann, usually had no secure income. Kracauer was practically forced to bet on work as an author. And a subject connected to his new place of abode, Paris, was an advantage. At that time, the mid-1930s, historical novels that sought somehow to shed light on the present were fashionable: Heinrich Mann wrote about *Henri Quatre* (1935 and 1938), Hermann Kesten on *Ferdinand und Isabella* (1936) and Joseph Roth on Napoleon (*Die Hundert Tage* (1936) [*The Hundred Days*]). Biographies of musicians also found success, as Franz Werfel had demonstrated with his *Roman der Oper* on Verdi, which put the young Paul Zsolnay publishing house on a firm financial footing within a very short period of time. Another factor was that the person of Offenbach seemed to encapsulate Franco-German themes of contemporary relevance: a Jewish emigrant from Germany who tried to gain a foothold on the boulevard, a man whose rise and decline coincided with a dictatorship, namely that of Napoleon III. In October, Kracauer told Max Tau about his plan and ventured an initial description of the book: 'My intention is to make the book itself an *Offenbachiade*, full of anecdotes. It is meant to be easily readable and yet point towards deeper matters, without this necessarily being made explicit in every instance. All in all, a book that abounds with chances.'[7] After the first month of research and reading in the Bibliothèque nationale – in a reading room which, according to Benjamin, is reminiscent of an 'operatic set'[8] – Kracauer had a concrete plan for his book:

> Not a biography in the strict sense of the word, but rather a portrait of society on a grand scale, comprising the Second Empire and the decade after 1870. ... I am thinking of an epic form between biography and novel, with a plethora of characters, a story stylishly told, and secretly woven into it would be information on the revolutionary function of frivolity, parody and so on. The idea for this work arose out of necessity, and though it also interests me a lot it is in the first instance a work that serves a purpose.

Kracauer hoped that *Offenbach* would buy him a year of freedom, time enough for a new novel, because, as he put it, 'epic writing is my passion'.[9] Over time, however, the *Offenbach* text created a passion of its own, and in the end it came out as more of an epic piece of writing than even his novels *Ginster* and *Georg*. Kracauer developed a real love for his baby, perhaps also because there was something cinematographic about his narrative: a flowing 'motion picture treatment' emerged from it, and he hoped Metro-Goldwyn-Mayer might be interested.[10] In terms of his method he had, as he saw it, remained faithful to the approach he had adopted in *The Salaried Masses*, namely that of 'fully unfolding a theory in a construction made of concrete material'.[11] In any case, Kracauer firmly stood by his *Offenbach*, and even his expulsion from the critics' club, on account of its pseudo-critique, triviality and conformism, did not change that.

The book appeared in a well-regarded French translation by Lucienne Astruc in the spring of 1937 with Bernard Grasset, and in German with Allert de Lange – thus, in the end, with one of the Dutch publishers, Kracauer having been courted by the editor Walter Landauer, who offered him a contract with an advance (5,600 francs, roughly 700 Reichsmark). It seems that Landauer, knowing that in emigrating nothing is trampled on as much as one's pride and dignity, managed to find the right tone in approaching the fallen star of Weimar cultural life.[12] *Offenbach* was a book of resemblances. There were similarities between the protagonist and the author and analogies between the social and political developments in France between 1855 and 1870 and Germany between 1930 and 1935; there were also elements that the book shared with Walter Benjamin's *Arcades Project*, although Benjamin would prove to be the most forceful critic of the book. In his eyes, as in those of Wiesengrund, it was a spectacular failure.

The Offenbach book was based on months of research in the Bibliothèque nationale, in the course of which Kracauer compiled an extensive index on filing cards. In contrast to his novels, this book was to be based on verifiable facts and quotations, on analyses that could be open to discussion; there was a clear intention to be objective. Nevertheless, the biography of Offenbach reflected the experiences of the biographer. In it, Paris was *the only place where Jewish artists could make a name for themselves without obstacles being put in their way*.[13] Jewishness itself did not result from the faith or the thought of a nation, but in the case of Kracauer's Offenbach from a 'homesickness' for the father, that is, a longing for an unreachable or negated home that is produced by emigration in the first place. The genre of the operetta is also seen as a phenomenon of emigration; not only Offenbach but also Hortense Schneider and the librettist Ludovic Halévy had German roots. It was not difficult for Offenbach's biographer to empathize with the existential travail of the musician's first days in Paris, where Offenbach did not enjoy enough recognition for him to be able to find his feet: *so play for nothing he did. He was indefatigable. He knocked on each and every door, allowed himself to be pushed around, and walked until his feet were sore.*[14] *Offenbach had yet to learn that to be successful one must already have been a success and that one's first success is governed by a thousand incalculable factors.*[15] Paris was a gathering point for artists; there was plenty of competition. Offenbach's wife, Hérminie, was, it seems, intimately familiar with Lili's situation: she was by her husband's side through the bad times, and she was the guardian of his happiness, which lay in his work, during the good. Finally, the protagonist himself shared some traits with his biographer. Like Ginster before him, he was *a mockingbird* who made fun, chiefly, *of anything cloaked in false sanctity – [p]ompous dignity, empty authority, gratuitous violence.*[16] His music was like a Chaplin film. Offenbach, moreover, was very perceptive and sensitive: *he was taken over by compassion and the past, in peculiar fashion, held him in its grip.*[17] This made him a suitable – sensitive and attentive – observer of society. Like Georg after his dismissal, Offenbach was a sceptical person, and this scepticism was the basis of the *Offenbachiade* and its frivolity: that *scepticism was not based on contempt for humanity or on any fundamental scepticism as to the possibility of real human progress; it was based on his observation that progress is not easy and that even with the best of intentions it is not easy to do good.*[18] At the end of the day, Offenbach was *a fallen Ariel, a spirit of the air brought down to live among the haunting spirits of earth. Once upon a time he had been able to mock them and playfully skip over the obstacles with which they confronted him. But then his name had paled,*[19] and he had had to accept that it meant little, or nothing, to be counted among the most original authors or composers, or the most influential editors or theatre directors, if one simply ended up as a refugee, without power and influence. Nevertheless, Paris was a special place for asylum seekers: *the home of the homeless*, a place for extraterritorials.[20]

The second set of similarities concerns the rule of Louis Bonaparte and that of Hitler, the development towards dictatorship and the emergence of the modern world in general as the precondition of these developments.[21] Napoleon III was a phantom figure who was able to stand for diverse, even contradictory, expectations. Kracauer characterized Bonapartism as a form of rule which uses ideologies, illusions, violence and propaganda in order to declare real social conflicts – especially class antagonisms – non-existent. Hitlerism was no different in that respect: one had only to substitute the names, and one had a picture of contemporary Germany: *Joy and glamour was also the motto of Louis Napoleon* [Hitler]. *In his zeal for it he instituted a ruthless reign of terror directed against all who might disturb it. Immediately after the coup d'état tens of thousands of Socialists, republicans, and members of secret societies were summarily arrested and sent into exile or deported like criminals.*[22] Napoleon/Hitler was dependent on joy and glamour, or – in the terms of the Nazi slogan – *Kraft durch Freude* (strength through joy), because the underlying social contradictions could not be resolved: *As a man of the peasants he represented interests that deviated significantly from those of the bourgeoisie; as a man of the bourgeoisie he inevitably privileged the middle class, whose material development was going to threaten his rule. Both the bourgeoisie and the peasants desired the suppression of the proletariat, but in order to consolidate his dictatorship, Louis Napoleon* [Hitler] *was faced with the task of also winning over the workers to his side.*[23] *... The euphoria had to be perpetual, the nation had to be kept breathless, preventing it from ever having time to come to its senses.*[24] *The subjects of rule, in turn, desired to be liberated from reality and were looking for something to hold on to in the vague illusions which the great name awakened in them. Louis Napoleon* [Hitler] *had the incredible luck to hit upon a society that was looking for a phantasmagoria.*[25] One could not ask for a better description of the *völkisch* yearning for community that had allowed the National Socialists to overwhelm Germany like a tidal wave.

The fundamental material developments which led to dictatorships in France and Germany, i.e. the unfolding of industrial capitalism, were as important to Kracauer as the activities of political agents or changes in public opinion. The specific political-economic analysis of the Second Empire Kracauer took from Karl Marx's *The Eighteenth Brumaire of Louis Bonaparte* (1852), in which Marx established the connection between coups d'état and class struggles. Marx had set out to explain why the development towards communist society predicted by the *Communist Manifesto* (1848) seemed to have started to falter, or at least to have taken a detour. The spectre of communism had mobilized counter-forces opposed to freedom. And the people, who should have followed the promise of freedom, let this happen, contented as long as they had their bread and circuses. But if Bonaparte's coup d'état was the shabby farce following the great tragedy of the French Revolution, what then was the abolition of democracy by National Socialism in 1933? In Kracauer's eyes, the major world-historical facts and individuals do not appear twice, as Hegel had thought, but also appear a third time, perhaps even, the sceptical Kracauer implies, a fourth and a fifth time – maybe each time, in fact, that social reality is ripe for freedom but the people and the inertia of their hearts are not. Whether a crisis is resolved in a revolutionary or a reactionary direction is, for Kracauer, historically contingent. As opposed to other historical materialists, he assumes that reality contains contingent factors which any analysis must take into consideration. Every social and cultural phenomenon is full of ambivalence and has many latent aspects. That also applied to the *Offenbachiade*. The genre of the operetta was associated with the Bonaparte dictatorship. It prevailed because a society that was being dictated to was itself like an operetta. The music reflected the imperial era: its bogus character, its frivolity and its decadence. But it also contributed to the inner dissolution of the regime; it helped to break it up. The European potentates were sitting nervously in their boxes, watching themselves and the silly paraphernalia of their social class be caricatured on stage. As the audience howled with laughter, they managed a forced smile.

By looking at the striking similarities between Nazi Germany and Bonapartism, the book on Offenbach thus tried to gain insights at an even deeper level. According to Kracauer, the Second Empire saw modern society breaking through, the very social form which later also produced fascism. Society became industrialized, finance capital became the dominant power in society, and economic relations took on an international dimension. There was an avalanche of new inventions, which just went to prove how ephemeral and dynamic this new life was. At the same time, society was permeated by contradictions which could threaten one of two things: their revolutionary supersession or their authoritarian suppression.

An important element for this modern society was the boulevard, where the fashionable bohemians were at home. Here, newspaper culture flourished, and a new type of journalism was born: *A brisk demand arose for entertaining articles, stories and gossip*[26] ... *By making newspapers dependent on advertising revenue, he [Girardin] produced a state of affairs in which money became the smallest common denominator also in intellectual life.*[27] A free-floating intelligentsia emerged that offered its product for sale on the market, not unlike the one that later existed in the Weimar Republic: *But the money on which they depended for their livelihood sharpened their sense for what went on behind the facades. Thus, they became sceptics. The reverse side of the coin was that they allowed themselves to be bought*.[28] On the boulevard, these bohemians and journalists lived, *so to speak, extraterritorially*.[29] They were *outsiders*,[30] hidden rebels: *Materially they were utterly dependent on [the regime], and if they had openly rebelled, they would have lost their incomes, a sacrifice they were unwilling to make*.[31]

This attention to the situation of the artistic intelligentsia in modern society marks an affinity between Kracauer's book on Offenbach and a central text from Benjamin's *Arcades Project*: 'The Paris of the Second Empire in Baudelaire'. Since March 1934, Benjamin had again been working on the arcades project;[32] the text on Baudelaire was composed in the summer and autumn of 1938. In order to comprehend the catastrophe that was unfolding in the present, and to find out whether it might be overcome, Benjamin, like Kracauer, went back to the nineteenth century. Like Kracauer, Benjamin identified Paris as the capital of the emerging 'modernity', or 'high capitalism'. Like Kracauer, he put an artist, Charles Baudelaire, and his milieu – the very same bohemia – at the centre of the drama. Jacques Offenbach even makes an appearance in Benjamin's expository text 'Paris, the Capital of the Nineteenth Century': 'Offenbach sets the rhythm of Parisian life. The operetta is the ironic utopia of an enduring reign of capital.'[33] Although Benjamin did not suggest the analogies with the present quite as strongly as Kracauer, the relations between past and present were nevertheless part of the approach. The Paris of the Second Empire was the birthplace both of the authoritarian order and of the revolt against it, although it was a revolt without (class-) consciousness, wrapped up in 'the enigmatic stuff of allegory' in Baudelaire or performed by way of 'the mystery-mongering of the conspirator' in Blanqui. '[T]he alchemists of the revolution' were always conjoined, writes Benjamin. 'Blanqui's action was the sister of Baudelaire's dream.' In the end, Bonaparte buried the hopes of both.[34] Benjamin was more interested in artists' relations of production than he was in the relevance of past literature and political battles to the present; during that epoch, these relations were undergoing a fundamental transformation that, of course, affected Baudelaire and Offenbach. In the literary world, the feuilleton and the *réclame*, that is, newspaper advertising, emerged at the same time. The history of information and reasoning was thus related to business and corruption from the very beginning. The boulevard as a market became the social milieu of the literati. It was here that, according to Kracauer, Offenbach's popularity began to increase. And it was here that Baudelaire offered his flowers of evil for sale: 'Baudelaire knew the true situation of the man of letters: he goes to the marketplace as a flâneur, supposedly to take a look at it but in reality to find a buyer.'[35] The arcades of Paris were, in turn, the space of the flâneurs, for whom the boulevard became an interior. Their end came with the department store, the 'last promenade for the flâneur.[36] If in the beginning the street had become an interieur for him, now this interieur turned into a street, and he roamed through the labyrinth of commodities as he had once roamed through the labyrinth of the city.'[37] Just as the flâneur was once intoxicated by the crowd and allowed himself to be swept along by it, now he was bewildered by the fetish of the commodity. Kracauer and Benjamin both sought to trace the 'phantasmagoria of Parisian life',[38] but this led each to a different place. Kracauer found it in propaganda and in an artificial political theatrics that fostered the rise of the operetta. Benjamin located it in the commodity form of artistic production and of production in general, because the commodity is itself a phantom image, a work of deception, in which exchange value conceals use value such that the capitalist mode of production as a whole appears to human beings as a second nature.[39]

Despite, or maybe because of, these similarities, Benjamin condemned the book on Offenbach, which was intended specifically to be readable and, at times, fell into the sort of conversational tone designed to appeal to consumers. Benjamin understood from the very beginning that in commercial terms he would not survive in exile, and he therefore was not prepared to make any compromises. The easily digestible intellectual fodder served up by Kracauer also offended Benjamin aesthetically; as a materialist physiognomist, Benjamin sought to spread out his material on the dream world of the nineteenth century ascetically and to arrange it into new constellations. Kracauer kept his distance from his material, that is to say, Offenbach's music, and instead presented a mixture of stories and Marxist historical cultural analysis. He did not seek to produce dialectical images through contemplation but instead contented himself with nice anecdotes. Kracauer's book was not written for the sake of a repressed past that needed to be rescued; it was a commodity produced for the purposes of historico-political entertainment. In Benjamin's eyes, Kracauer was no longer the rag-picker sifting through the waste of social reality, no longer an interpreter of dreams confronting modern mythology; he did not see in the Bouffes-Parisiens, for instance, the primordial landscape of consumption that Benjamin found in the arcades. For Benjamin, Kracauer had not written a critique but an apologia.

In May 1937, Benjamin received a letter from Wiesengrund, who spoke of the 'extremely embarrassing situation' in which he had found himself after having read *Offenbach*: 'It sunk far below my worst expectations.' The few places where Kracauer mentioned music were 'crassly erroneous'; the 'arrangement of the whole, announced in the shameless and idiotic preface as a "biography of society"', befitted the detailed observations, which Wiesengrund considered inane, trivial and petit bourgeois:

No, if Kracauer really does identify with this book, then he has definitely erased himself from the list of writers to be taken at all seriously. And I am myself seriously considering whether or not I should break off relations with him. For to carry on as before would almost be even more of an offence: it would mean that nothing he does can move you.

Wiesengrund went on to ask whether 'a joint intervention by Ernst, you and me' might be appropriate.[40] Benjamin fully agreed: 'with this book, Kracauer has essentially resigned himself. He has composed a text that only a few years ago would have found its most ruthless critic in the author himself.'[41] If he had written the book cynically, Benjamin continues, simply for the money, then that would have been acceptable, given the dire straits he was in. But the author stands by his work; he 'wants to save the fallen maiden', namely Offenbach's operetta.[42] Benjamin now thought he understood why Kracauer 'was forced to isolate his work so totally from all our discussions during the years in which he was preparing this book.' Kracauer had abandoned the position 'which [they] all shared'.[43] But Bloch was withholding his judgement, and thus Benjamin concluded 'that nothing definite should be decided as yet'.[44] Had it been a matter solely between Benjamin and Kracauer, he wrote earlier in the letter, he would have decided 'silently to assume that Kracauer, for the time being, has to be declared partly intellectually incapacitated and, without dropping him, to await further developments in the situation'.[45] Benjamin's remarks, as we shall see, nevertheless egged Wiesengrund on to express his criticism.

The 'worst expectations' far exceeded, the shared position abandoned, 'intellectually incapacitated' – what had led to these letters, to such damning judgements?

21

The Disintegration of the Group

In the course of their political dispute in Berlin, Bloch had accused Kracauer of having abandoned their shared position. Kracauer had responded by saying that he would not tolerate Bloch's moralizing tone; Bloch's attitude, he said, was not appropriate to a friendship. This pattern – an accusation of betrayal followed by a rejection of the accusation and a counter-accusation of a lack of collegiality – would be repeated several times throughout their time in exile. At the centre of these disputes initially stood Ernst Bloch: this time, however, in the position of the accused. After his escape, he had stayed in Switzerland, where he was subsequently arrested as the 'accomplice' of an 'agent of the Comintern', namely his wife Karola Piotrkowska, and then expelled in September 1934. After that, he lived in Vienna, before visiting the anti-fascist congress of writers in Paris in June 1935. Benjamin had last seen Bloch in the autumn of 1931. Before that there had been an argument over Bloch's *Traces*, although Bloch took this dispute to be a merely 'temporary matter' relating to 'a very old relationship'.[1] Trusting in his old friend Benjamin, Bloch assured him in spring 1934: 'Even if our intellectual paths may diverge more and more ..., this apparently is not enough to alienate the marching companions from each other as long as they believe themselves committed to the "elements of the final condition".'[2] Whatever secrets may be concealed by the phrase 'final condition', what counted was the commitment to it: that is, to that shared position which the four of them had held before 1933. Benjamin agreed with this, and despite the accusation of plagiarism he counted Bloch among the four most important German members of the literary avant-garde: for the genre of the novel, it was Kafka; for the theatre, it was Brecht; for journalism Kraus; and for the essay Bloch.[3] But during his time in Switzerland and Austria, Bloch was difficult to get hold of for his friends. As an irked Benjamin remarked, he seemed to plan his travelling itineraries to involve generous distances from the locations of the other three, despite being in need of their intellectual exchanges as much as they were.[4]

Then, in the autumn of 1934, the elusive Bloch announced his new book, *Heritage of Our Times*, which was to appear with Oprecht & Helbling. The book promised a portrait of the present 'kaleidoscopic period', which he likened to a 'revue'. He called the book 'a scuffle, moreover in the midst of the susceptible, indeed in the midst of the enemy, in order to rob him if need be'. The susceptible ones were the members of a disintegrating bourgeoisie, including the salaried employees, and the romantic souls who were intoxicated by the Nazis and, out of a justified rejection of the capitalist 'ratio', had sided with the reactionary 'irratio' of 'life', 'soul' and 'Reich' – for instance, Oswald Spengler and Ludwig Klages. The concept of 'non-contemporaneity' [Ungleichzeitigkeit], which denotes an 'economic-ideological remaining existence from earlier times', stood at the centre of Bloch's interpretation. He discussed the progressive intellectuals whose experiments in 'objectivity' and 'montage' had left a heritage in which it was possible to hibernate and wait for better times. Proust, Joyce and Brecht were part of this group of progressive intellectuals; Kafka was too, of course, and likewise Benjamin and Kracauer. The book went on sale in January 1935, but some copies appear to have circulated in advance.[5]

It is not clear whether Theodor Wiesengrund had already seen one of these copies when, in December 1934, he wrote a long and presumably quite aggressive letter to Bloch (which unfortunately no longer exists), criticizing, as he referred to it in a separate letter to Benjamin, the 'sacrilege committed by our friend Ernst'.[6] In any case, Bloch dismissed the tone of the letter bluntly as that of a schoolmaster: 'Your letter erases the respect which is an ingredient of the very comradeship you invoke. ... You are no longer a good reader of mine, Teddy [sic!], but a malicious, and hence a bad reader.' Apparently, Wiesengrund had complained about the section on 'Revue form in philosophy', in which Bloch had characterized Benjamin's *One-Way Street* as surrealist. Bloch told the 'professional finger-wagger' with the 'evil eye' that this passage was a reprint of a review he had published as early as 1928, and that he had even read out to Benjamin prior to its publication: 'Neither before nor after that did the atmosphere between Benjamin and me change in the slightest.' Bloch intimated that Wiesengrund might have been aggrieved because his book omitted to mention Wiesengrund's *Kierkegaard*: 'Too much fever, dear Teddy, not enough warmth and old friendship, relation to the substance of the matter, not enough up-front credit for what one does not yet know, or for what one has forgotten.' Such were Bloch's words to his younger colleague (Teddy was seventeen years his junior), for future reference, so to speak; he was thus made to understand that he was behaving like a silly boy, someone who had neither learned how to behave in the grown-up world nor understood that world.[7] And he immediately told Benjamin about Wiesengrund's letter: 'Wiesengrund ... predicts an estrangement ending in enmity because of the paragraph on *One-Way Street.*' Bloch, however, did fear that something similar might happen with Benjamin, namely that he would consider questions of substance more important than their personal relationship. And thus, he added, should the 'finger-wagging ante rem' persist after reading, he would ask 'permission to remain in the state of the last three years'. His '*deep* collegiality', Bloch added, did not commit Benjamin to anything, 'but neither does it commit me [i.e. Bloch] to listen to what, to me, ... appeared to be an injustice and, in the light of the facts, a most un-called for estrangement.'[8]

Meanwhile, rumours about the *Heritage* book swirled. 'I only know from hearsay', Benjamin wrote to his old school friend Alfred Cohn shortly before he received Bloch's letter, 'that Bloch's new book was published by Oprecht and Helbling. ... The book is supposed to include accounts of embarrassing and malicious quarrels with me, as I was told by a source who is, to be sure, not infallible.'[9] And a week later he wrote to Scholem:

> I know only this much, that restlessness and bickering are about to break loose in the ranks of the faithful, insofar as I am both congratulated on the tribute shown me in the text and defended against the invective it directs at me – allegedly contained in the same passage.[10]

By mid-January, Benjamin had finally had the opportunity to read the book. From San Remo, where because of his financial troubles he had been living in the hotel owned by his former wife, Dora Kellner, since December, he immediately wrote to Kracauer: 'Bloch's book has arrived, like a majestic rumble of thunder following the lightning that announced its approach.' When reading the book, he wrote, one heard echoes from empty spaces, like thunder, diffuse and dispersed. 'Instead of presenting a clear profile of the matter at hand, the book again uses the old method of making a philosophical "statement" on everything and anything that has been dominant.' The book's topic – vaguely presented, in Benjamin's judgement – was 'non-contemporaneity', and its implicit addressee was 'the cultural office of the K.P. [communist party]. Thus, what had originally been a lament and an accusation has fizzled out into a series of complaints.'[11] Because of the book's valuable parts, and, as he wrote to Cohn, because of the author's 'excellent intentions' and 'considerable insight', he considered the *Heritage* book a missed opportunity; he had nothing to criticize, incidentally, regarding the remarks on him or his *One-Way Street*. To Cohn, he summarized his view of the book as follows:

The severe reproach I must level against the book (even if I will not level it against the author) is that it in no way corresponds to the circumstances under which it has appeared. Instead, it is as out of place as a fine gentleman who, having arrived to inspect an area demolished by an earthquake, has nothing more urgent to do than immediately spread out the Persian rugs that his servants had brought along and which were, by the way, already somewhat moth-eaten; set up the gold and silver vessels, which were already somewhat tarnished; have himself wrapped in brocade and damask gowns, which were already somewhat faded.[12]

In Benjamin's view, the book had come too late. The bandits that Bloch wanted to sneak up on and rob had already done their work and had safely stashed their loot. The *Heritage* book was thus, indeed, a non-contemporaneous book. That objection, however, was not quite right: Bloch had already published most of the pieces for his story of the decline of the bourgeoisie before 1933 in the form of feuilleton articles. The philosophical approach of Bloch's book was, moreover, not unlike that of the arcades project.[13] What was different – and, given recent political events, likely to be irritating – was its tone, the melody of the book, for Bloch was, as always, in good spirits. Unalloyed optimism radiated from the very first sentence: 'A broad view is taken here. The times are in decay and in labour at the same time. The situation is wretched or despicable, the way out of it crooked. But there is no doubt that its end will not be bourgeois.'[14]

No one still believed that socialism would ultimately be victorious – except for Bloch. The melancholic Benjamin, at this point, could not even believe in the continued existence of his friendship with Bloch.[15] To Bloch, he did not mention the book; he even asked Kracauer not to reveal to Bloch his negative judgement.[16] After ten weeks had passed, Bloch became impatient. Through Wiesengrund, he informed Benjamin that he did not have to be treated with kid gloves and that he would not be hurt, as he had in the case of *Traces*, were his book not to meet with his approval: 'I remain Benjamin's friend and his great admirer.'[17] Benjamin, however, shied away from any kind of contact with Bloch. In early May, he confessed to Wiesengrund:

The possibility of meeting up with Bloch ... rather weighs upon me. Since he rebuked me a couple of months ago for my written comments on his book, in a manner reminiscent of the way a teacher might demand to see his pupil's homework, I have abandoned the already painful attempt to express in letter form an opinion concerning *Heritage of Our Times*.[18]

Benjamin remained silent until Bloch came to Paris in June 1935. Relieved, he wrote to Alfred Cohn about their conversation:

> And if I was facing the difficult task of leading our relationship out of the critical condition it was in during the last few years, without leaving him in the dark about my in essence negative, and very negative, stance toward his last book, I may ... hope to have successfully accomplished that task. Of course, this required a great degree of loyalty on his part as well, and I am happy to have found that.[19]

With this peace between Benjamin and Bloch, the dispute between Bloch and Wiesengrund also came to an end.[20]

But the meeting between Benjamin and Bloch was no more than an intermezzo in the gradual disappearance of Bloch from the group's field of vision. Half a year later, he left Paris and went to Prague, where – to the chagrin of Wiesengrund in particular – he came to toe the Moscow party line, even defending Stalin's show trials.[21] In spring 1937, writing from Prague, Bloch tried in vain to persuade Benjamin to collaborate with the *Weltbühne*, for which he wrote a fortnightly column.[22] In September 1937, he congratulated 'Teddy and Gretel' on their wedding and told them of the birth of his son, Jan Robert.[23] In early January, Wiesengrund, after consulting with Horkheimer, asked Bloch for a sample from a manuscript on the problem of materialism, with a view to possible publication. In the end, the Institute for Social Research, however, never published anything by Bloch, nor did it review any of his works. In July 1938, Bloch moved to the USA, where for a short while he would receive a monthly grant of 50 dollars from the Institute.[24]

The caesuras in Bloch's life also affected Kracauer, who was the only one of the friends to have liked the *Heritage* book. With 'real passion', he and Lili had thrown themselves at the book and, like 'starved people', had 'gnawed on ... every last bone of it', he assured Bloch, concluding 'that [his] book is a genuinely great affair, and that it is written with an enchanting vitality'. Bloch's achievement was to have approached 'the overdue problem of a non-contemporaneous dialectics'.[25] To Benjamin, he offered a defence of the book, saying it was 'so much an incarnation of [Bloch's] nature that I love it for that reason alone'. Kracauer appreciated Bloch's 'boyish rebelliousness', his 'pleasure in taking hold of things', his circumspection. 'Maybe Bloch's nature will pull related spirits into movement. Nothing is more needed than that! Because, in my opinion, the human material on the left was (a[nd] is) pitiful, and one cannot talk of "natures" in that context at all.' The crucial point for Kracauer was: 'I attach *objective* importance to the mentioned personal traits.'[26] This marked a fundamental difference between Kracauer and Benjamin, who rather attached personal importance to objective things.

Wiesengrund, by contrast, did not want to separate things and persons. That put him on Benjamin's side, although Benjamin's strategy of waiting, silently, for conflicts to resolve themselves was not at all his style. Since October 1934, he had again been in close contact with Horkheimer, and he had gradually come to assume the role of the Institute's representative in Europe, a role that was finally made official in July 1937. When it came to matters concerning the Institute, he acted with zeal, even aggression, not holding back in his criticisms of Leo Löwenthal, Erich Fromm and Herbert Marcuse. He considered these colleagues to be mediocre, bourgeois intellectual Marxist fellow travellers, and thus a 'real danger', a view which, in turn, made it difficult for him not to be numbered 'amongst the grumblers and cavillers'.[27] Moreover, he did not make a secret of his rejection of the 'Brechtian motives' in Benjamin's work, especially in the essay on the work of art.[28] It would be a mistake to explain this self-confidence in his dealings with older colleagues solely on the basis of his increasing importance in Horkheimer's eyes. Ever since his inaugural lecture, Wiesengrund had had a clear idea about how philosophy and aesthetics had to be conceived in a way that was critical and dialectical, and in a way that rescued the promise of happiness. In Benjamin, he thought he had found the right partner for his approach. To some, Wiesengrund seemed to exert 'control' over Benjamin on Horkheimer's behalf. But he was also, at least to the same extent, Benjamin's advocate at the Institute. They were kindred spirits who were always growing closer to one another, and they had a relationship that, however it looked from the outside, was anything but hierarchical. On Benjamin's side, strategic and tactical considerations may have played a part. He needed the Institute for his survival, and its relocation to New York, for instance, struck him as an existential threat.[29] In intellectual terms, however, Benjamin was his own institute. By comparison, his younger friend was more passionate about their common cause, Benjamin's arcades project, which he regarded 'as part of [their] destined contribution to *prima philosophia*'.[30]

When Benjamin told him that his 'work on the Arcades [had] begun to revive', Wiesengrund's interest in it exceeded that of anyone else.[31] 'I regard your work on the "Arcades" as the centre not merely of your own philosophy, but as the decisive philosophical word which can be spoken today.'[32] In his eyes, Marxism was best served when its external features, especially its conceptuality, were renounced. He encouraged Benjamin to remain faithful to his approach and not to compromise it for the Institute's sake, insisting 'that we hold on all the more effectively to the real, the more thoroughly and consistently we remain true to the aesthetic origins, and that we only become more aesthetic, when we deny the latter'.[33] Wiesengrund's criticism of the exposé for the arcades project, 'Paris, the Capital of the Nineteenth Century', of August 1935, which Benjamin had written the previous May at the request of Friedrich Pollock, might sound cutting, but it was a confirmation of their friendship, and this was how Benjamin took it.[34] Only someone who had wholly committed himself to the project, and identified with it, could write a commentary of that sort. Previously, Benjamin had told his fellow thinker that he had captured his intentions precisely.[35] In the revised exposé, the fetish character of the commodity took centre stage, visible in the shop windows and world exhibitions of capitalism, and a happy Wiesengrund remarked upon 'just how closely our thoughts communicate in spite of our two year separation'.[36] Benjamin reciprocated, speaking of 'how enormously delighted' he was about the 'profound and spontaneous inner communication between [their] thoughts' and the 'analogy between [their] respective tasks'.[37] Almost all works from the context of the arcades project, except the essay on the work of art, demonstrate that the author had delved deeply into the interior of Wiesengrund's *Kierkegaard*, a book which, in turn, listed Benjamin's book on German tragic drama as an important reference point. Both were interested in exploding idealism from within, and they had a shared hope that their art criticism would be of furtive efficacy.[38]

Wiesengrund was similarly pleased with Benjamin's essay on Kafka, which, he thought, dissociated Kafka from the context of existentialist theology, thus, we might say, revealing him to Wiesengrund's eyes as a dialectical, not an archaic, poet: 'As for the rest, our agreement on the fundamental philosophical issues has never seemed clearer to me than it does in this work!'[39] Benjamin had had intensive discussions about the importance of Kafka with Brecht and Scholem, thus, as it were, within a force field between historical materialism and Jewish theology. He did not incline towards one or the other; rather, he played them off against one another. Benjamin's reading of Kafka aimed to retain the possibility of redemption, both of a communist *and* of a messianic kind, by establishing a connection with the ancient world and myth – it aimed at hope for the hopeless.[40] Distorted life will only disappear 'with the coming of the Messiah, who (a great rabbi once said) will not wish to change the world by force but will merely make a slight adjustment in it.'[41] According to Wiesengrund, the dialectical mediation between the archaic and the modern was the major task of the arcades project, and he had himself undertaken an interpretation of theological categories in his book on Kierkegaard.[42] Wiesengrund admired Benjamin, and there was no one by whom Benjamin felt better understood than Wiesengrund.

Walter Benjamin had taken over from Siegfried Kracauer as Wiesengrund's intellectual older brother. Following Wiesengrund and Kracauer's reading groups, the erstwhile child prodigy had gravitated towards an immanent, aesthetic and yet transcendental mode of socio-political critique, and it was this approach he had adopted in his book on Kierkegaard. In Wiesengrund's opinion, Kracauer, his former mentor and teacher, had now gone a different way. He was intellectually stagnating, if not regressing. Because they had once been so close, their personal relationship now also came under particular strain. In March 1933, Wiesengrund was still thanking Kracauer effusively for his glowing review of the Kierkegaard book: 'The review is ... the finest evidence of our togetherness that I could wish for.'[43] From May 1933 onwards, however, there followed two years of 'cruel silence' and 'bitterness' until the summer of 1935, when the new couple Benjamin–Wiesengrund temporarily made up with Bloch.[44] It is not entirely clear what the reasons for the renewed rift between Friedel and Teddie were, but it never did take much for old wounds to reopen. What is certain is that Kracauer was very annoyed with Wiesengrund's ludicrous suggestion that he should return to Germany. We can also safely assume that he resented the fact that Wiesengrund, having stayed in Germany, continued to associate closely with Reifenberg and sought to publish in the *Frankfurter Zeitung*.[45] Later, because he felt slighted by Horkheimer, Kracauer took against the Institute for Social Research as a whole. Now, it was not just Wiesengrund who had to deal with an exceptionally irritable Kracauer; everyone associated with the Institute did, including Leo Löwenthal.

It is possible that, from Wiesengrund's perspective, the reason for the split between them was Kracauer's resentful feelings. As before, Wiesengrund had been confronted with a struggling and aggrieved friend who condemned him, a friend whose sensitivities and accusations got to him. During the period of silence between them, he repeatedly asked Benjamin what news he had about Kracauer, but did not contact him directly. He described his emotional state: 'I have a very bad conscience about Kracauer, although I cannot regard my reservations as accidental.'[46] This ambivalence nourished his own aggressive resentment towards his curious friend. Wiesengrund felt persecuted by Kracauer's 'persecution fantasies', and he suffered under the weight of his 'narcissistic aggression'.[47] In the end, it was Kracauer who established contact again, with a letter of condolence after Wiesengrund's aunt Agathe Calvelli-Adorno died.

The two new Parisians Benjamin and Kracauer met regularly, albeit sometimes after lengthy intervals. In May 1934, Benjamin reported that Kracauer was 'increasingly retreating from view.'[48] After one of their rare meetings three years later, Benjamin reported that he had seemed exceptionally depressed, and that he was 'extremely difficult to get hold of'.[49] Sometimes, without explanation, Benjamin did not hear from Kracauer for weeks. Their isolation – 'from people, from news, and from the things I need to work' – got to both of them.[50]

The two lonesome friends lived in the same city, worked in the same library and worked on the same historical period. But Kracauer did not talk to Benjamin about his work, and Benjamin complained that there was no one in Paris with whom he could really communicate.[51] Kracauer's *Offenbach* only confirmed this loneliness. For Benjamin, the book was clearly born of need and misery, but it was also a declaration of intellectual bankruptcy by someone who had grown estranged from him. Still, he wanted to keep his thoughts to himself, so he was glad to learn that Wiesengrund had been unable to wait for a 'joint intervention' and had taken it upon himself to write to Kracauer. Benjamin himself received a copy of that letter, along with a request that he be 'very discreet' about the matter, including towards Bloch, who 'would be sure to mention it tactlessly on some occasion or other' if he knew that Benjamin had been made aware of Wiesengrund's letter to Kracauer.[52] Benjamin concurred. In fact, he was delighted:

> It is obvious that I would never have been able to attempt anything of the kind. But, as I can see, for you it was possible to do so, and this has also made my own position with regard to Kracauer one that can be defined, and one that is more defensible than I could have hoped (although I shall not say anything whatsoever to him to suggest that I have read your letter). At least, he may and should know that I know of your judgement.[53]

Relying on their long-standing close and intimate relationship, Wiesengrund could send Kracauer a 'most principled and extremely frank letter', as Wiesengrund himself described it. This made it possible for Benjamin to adopt the same position as in the case of Bloch: staying in the background, '*en attendant*', saying nothing definite and doing nothing definite.[54]

'However, if our relationship still exists in the present and is not merely feeding on the past, I could not take on the responsibility of remaining silent at a moment like this.' Thus Wiesengrund justified his devastating criticism of the *Offenbach* book to his friend. He discarded the idea of a 'biography of society': 'But if the period is indeed to be "reconstructed" in the work, that can only be done where both genuinely intersect with each other – i.e. in the form of the music, or, more precisely, its technical analysis.' It would have been necessary to determine the social character of music and not the harmony between the protagonist and his times. The dualism between figure and background would have had to have been sublated, instead of 'decorating' the background 'with anecdotes'. There was little difference, Wiesengrund wrote, between Kracauer's book and the biographies of Stefan Zweig or Emil Ludwig. Wiesengrund alleged, further, that Kracauer was of one mind with his protagonist – and hence with the society he represented. He condemned the 'old man's humour'; Kracauer's fascination with the glamour of society suggested to him that '[Kracauer] wanted to make up for all the banalities which [he] had not dared to utter for the last twenty years'. In short, he accused Kracauer of having become another person, a resigned conformist:

> In the book's weaknesses one can sense a terrible contempt for humanity and a frightening urge to destroy. Contempt for humanity: 'I still write quite well enough for swine like you.' Urge to destroy: directed against language and everything that you yourself have ever discovered. I know that for a long time now you have been surrounding yourself with a layer of insulation, and that it is enormously difficult to genuinely get through to you.[55]

This last statement gave the substance of the criticism of Kracauer's 'abomination'[56] a personal dimension: he had withdrawn from his circle of friends and had thus abandoned their common position.

The 'common position' was, in fact, the least of Kracauer's worries in Paris. He had set different priorities for himself. A significant gap had opened up between Kracauer and the Weimar past, including the avant-garde social and cultural criticism. He was in a very bad way, and now all his old reservations about Wiesengrund surfaced again. His response was cold:

> From my knowledge of your position this was exactly the criticism that I expected from you. It may seem destructive to you; foolish it certainly is ... I call your criticism foolish because it partly misrepresents and partly overlooks the material content of my book, because it comes from a rigid attitude, albeit one which is well known to me.[57]

Disappointed at this snub, Wiesengrund replied that he was saddened that Kracauer would not 'allow [his] attack to get through to [him] – whereas it was its sole intention to reach you and break through the layer of encrustation'. In his mind, the standard against which Kracauer was to be held up was *Ginster*, and he preferred to be a 'little hot-tempered rather than a dewy-eyed friend'. Heide Schlüpmann sums up Wiesengrund's view neatly: Kracauer had submerged himself in mass culture but had not resurfaced again 'as a critic'.[58] The *Offenbach* affair was but the first part of a severely testing period in the friendship between Kracauer and Wiesengrund. The second part would be even more dramatic.

22

Songs of Woe from Frankfurt

Back in Frankfurt, the *Offenbach* book came as a great consolation
for the Kracauer family. The life of Rosette and Hedwig Kracauer
centred on the two emigrants in Paris. The weekly letter from France
was the light in their lives, which stood otherwise under the shadow
of the National Socialists and the increasing threat it posed to the
Jewish population, elderly women not excluded. Since Kracauer
departed Frankfurt for Berlin, Hedwig Kracauer had noted and
commented upon everything her nephew had done with the greatest
pride one could imagine of an aunt – and always with a side glance
towards Maria Wiesengrund and Agathe Calvelli-Adorno. Teddie
she found 'enormously pretentious, as if he were the only impre-
sario'. She said it was almost a blessing that he was now in Oxford,
where he had landed in 1934 and stayed on and off until 1937, and
had to write in English: this, she remarked drily, might make it easier
to understand his sentences.[1] Other rather talented authors, such as
Benjamin, Bloch and Roth, as well as Kracauer's colleagues at the
Frankfurter Zeitung, among them Diebold, Sieburg and Kircher,
were also at the receiving end of her pointed remarks. She did not
want to leave any doubt as to who was the king among these writers:
her Friedel. He took, in a way, the place of her deceased husband.
His aunt and uncle, in turn, were also role models for Kracauer. In
certain respects, his marriage with Elisabeth Ehrenreich resembled
the relationship between Isidor and Hedwig Kracauer, who also
worked together as a team. In the 'institution', the boarding
school for orphaned boys run by the Julius and Amalie Flersheim
Foundation, Hedwig was the pillar holding it all up, as she herself
later put it, 'and yet with regard to the academic work the loyal
assistant, frequently also opponent' of her husband. After Isidor's
death, it was she who 'over several years prepared the manuscript'
on the history of the Jews of Frankfurt 'for publication'.[2]

Hedwig Kracauer was well capable of being obnoxious, but she
was also a keen observer, interested in the world and in society. After
Kracauer's move to Berlin, she wrote fortnightly to her nephew,

who, in turn, provided her with reading material and news from the cultural and political life of the capital. This way of participating in the life of the intellectuals kept her going, for everyday life in Frankfurt alone was not enough. 'What am I to do with all these old women? Old I am myself', she complained on one of her birthdays, when the ladies of her generation from her family and her circle of friends were about to descend upon her. She was shocked when a younger person offered her his seat on the tram. Of the Oppenheim sisters, she was the intellectual. In the household, Rosette was in command and took charge of all practical matters. Kracauer's mother brightened up when she could sew, clean and do the washing. Hedwig, by contrast, engaged with her nephew's articles, or worked on short contributions for the local section of the *FZ* or the community newspaper. While Rosette raved about the miracle invention that was the pressure cooker, the aunt read everything 'the boy' in Berlin wrote, and read the newspaper from cover to cover so she could inform him of developments in Frankfurt. She described to him the departure of the city's planning officer, and ex-pupil of May-Schüler, Eugen Kaufmann, who had gone to the Urals in order to build the city of Magnitogorsk; she reported on the performance of Alban Berg's *Wozzeck* at the opera, or about the anti-Semitic rabble-rousing of the Nazis.[3] In addition to keeping her abreast of cultural developments in Berlin, Siegfried would send her review copies he had received from publishers. He gradually became her way of accessing the external world.

Hedwig Kracauer was an incorruptible realist. As the assistant and wife of the chronicler of the Jews of Frankfurt, she knew that the Frankfurt Jews had experienced a catastrophe about once every hundred years. In the sixteenth century, more precisely in 1509, a man by the name of Johannes Pfefferkorn appeared in the city, armed with an imperial mandate, and confiscated all books in Hebrew as defamatory of Christianity. This was an attack aimed at the intellectual foundations of Judaism, thus was an existential threat, and it had an enormous effect that extended far beyond Frankfurt. In the seventeenth century (1614), the houses and shops in the Judengasse were raided and plundered by citizens led by the gingerbread baker Vinzenz Fettmilch and the guilds. They succeeded in temporarily driving the Jews out of Frankfurt. In the eighteenth century, major fires twice destroyed the densely built-up Judengasse, in 1711 and 1774: 'All houses … burnt down; the stones broke apart in the heat. Iron was bent', Isidor Kracauer noted in his *Geschichte der Juden in Frankfurt am Main* [History of the Jews in Frankfurt am Main]. The sight resembled the burning of Troy or Rome. 'Such devastation has not occurred since the destruction of the temple', said the text of a song of woe. In July 1796, the Jewish quarter was reduced to rubble and ash, for a third time, by the French cannonade when they took the city: about 140 houses were set ablaze and 1,800 of the Jewish inhabitants were made homeless. At least, however, this fire would come, in the nineteenth century, to be transformed into a symbol of freedom for the Jews.[4]

In 1933, Rosette Kracauer was sixty-six and Hedwig Kracauer seventy-one. Long before 30 January 1933, the two women had begun to save money, counting on having to 'suddenly depart one day. Possibly even without the Nazis officially taking the reins.' As Hedwig put it, 'the whole ground on which we stand is shaking'. On 8 February 1932, Friedel's birthday, his aunt wished him, prophetically, 'one more year without Hitler'.[5] And in July 1932, she had a premonition that Friedel and Lili would have to leave Berlin suddenly.[6] After the National Socialists had come to power, she registered very clearly

> that the Jews are being deprived of any possibility of maintaining their existence, that they have to leave the stock markets, that they are not allowed to run cinemas, that the retail industry demands the closure of Jewish shops, that even the trading of cattle and grain has been prohibited for them, not to mention higher professions. It is altogether unclear where the next generation will be trained, as for one percent of the population it is altogether unclear how a livelihood should be found.

She ended the letter to Paris with a sigh: 'In any case, be glad that you are gone for now, even if you have to live in want.'[7]

In March 1933, it was made very clear to every citizen of Frankfurt that the National Socialists were in power. On the Römerberg, and soon all over the city, swastika flags flew.[8] The Lord Mayor Ludwig Landmann had resigned and his position been filled on an interim basis by the National Socialist Friedrich Krebs, although he would stay in post until 1945. During the early days after 30 January, there were already incidents of assault against Jews, not to mention anti-Semitic insults. On 5 March, the SA occupied the Institute for Social Research, and it was closed on the grounds of its 'subversive tendencies against the state'. A decade after its opening, the 'Jewish-Marxist fortress' was dismantled. On 15 March, detectives from Police Section Ia entered the building and locked and sealed the rooms. The university senate immediately applied to the Prussian minister of culture to sever its ties with the Institute, 'as loose as they were', as the university found it necessary to emphasize.[9] On 1 April, students saw 'Jewish and Marxist' professors off the campus. A third of the professors and lecturers at Frankfurt University were sacked. The official boycott of Jewish shops, doctors' surgeries and law practices was effective. There were no signs of solidarity with the Jews of Frankfurt. City authorities were relentless in enforcing their radical anti-Jewish policies. Even before the Law for the Restoration of the Professional Civil Service came into effect on 7 April 1933, eighty-one Jewish employees were sacked (some of whom then had to be re-employed because of their status as veterans of the Great War). On 10 May, the day of the book burning, Jewish 'asphalt literature' was consigned to the flames on the Römerberg.[10] On the night of 26 April, the Heine monument, a bone of contention for anti-Semites since its erection on 13 December 1913, was toppled, and the plaque depicting the poet destroyed. The Philanthropin, however, saw rising numbers of pupils after 1933 – but that was only because a cap was placed on the number of Jewish pupils allowed to attend state schools, which were in any case getting increasingly unbearable places for them to be. As the head of the Israelite community wrote to its members: 'If no voice speaks up for us, then the stones of this city may bear witness for us, a city that owes its rise in good part to the achievements of Jews.'[11]

Despite her disillusionment, Hedwig Kracauer was surprised by how smoothly the Nazis took the reins of power. On 9 April 1933, she noted: 'I would never have thought ... that all of Germany would get behind the government, and that the long hoped-for unity of the Reich would be achieved in this way. We are the main victims of this revolution.'[12] These are forthright words from the initial days of the regime. Soon, the correspondents would no longer express themselves so openly when it came to political matters. It is not possible to write about what weighed so heavily on the heart, Hedwig complained in one letter, alluding to the monitoring of her mail.[13] After his escape from Germany, Kracauer's letters to Frankfurt no longer mentioned anything about the political situation, nothing about his mental state, nothing about money and nothing detailed about his work. In their correspondence with Frankfurt, Lili and Friedel skirted around anything problematic, leading the aunt and mother to complain that they were being treated like children who were not allowed to learn about and discuss the important matters.[14] From one day to the next, the intellectual exchange between Hedwig and her nephew ended. Her own correspondence was now also dominated by practical matters, by rumour and most of all by worries, worries, worries. In December 1933, for instance, Hedwig asked about a typhus epidemic that had reportedly broken out in Paris, and about a train crash near the French capital. She issued warnings, fretted about matters in Paris, prophesied doom, expressed doubt and asked question after question, until Friedel and Lili told her that this endless questioning was driving them crazy and had to stop. Hedwig and Rosette defended themselves, saying that they were concerned their relationship would grow stale if all they ever talked about were socks, coats, pyjamas and other trivialities. Not knowing was the source of their most urgent worries, they said. 'If we do not learn anything about important matters, we at least want to be kept informed about your everyday life.'[15]

The lives of the two women had become devoid of joy. They lived a frugal life; they did not go hungry, but they lacked intellectual stimulation or any desire to pursue activities outside of their home. From the spring of 1933 onwards, they no longer visited the theatre, concert hall or cinema. They no longer even enjoyed reading the *Frankfurter Zeitung*; in May 1934, the two sisters cancelled their subscription. Ultimately, Hedwig thought, 'your well-being is more important than ours'.[16] She also recognized that the Kracauer family was no isolated case. From their summer retreat in Königstein in July 1934, she reported to Paris:

> We very much kept to ourselves and avoided the other guests in the hotel (many old Jewish women). Nevertheless, we sometimes talked and got to know the fate of so many others. Most of them are in the same position as us; they have been left by their children, who have gone off to try their luck in some foreign place, and sometimes have been lucky.[17]

The old ones eventually died (among them her sister Amalie Frank, and also Agathe Calvelli-Adorno); the doctors, and, importantly, the taxpayers who financed the pension payments with their contributions to the Jewish community, went into exile: 'We are shocked by the departure of every solvent person.'[18]

After the initial woes, there were some brighter moments. Hedwig was genuinely happy to be able to undertake some research to help with the *Offenbach* book, while Rosette taught other women how to earn a little money by removing stains from clothing. From February 1934, the two women started to leave the house again, and they attended events at the recently founded Jewish Cultural Federation.[19] At the Neues Theater they attended a performance of *Nathan the Wise*; they visited concerts performed by the cultural federation's orchestra, which was founded in May. After one of these concerts, Hedwig wrote to Paris: 'You can't imagine how good this feels. Otherwise, I have nothing, no work that interests me, no books that I long to read and no people who can offer me anything intellectually.'[20] In the autumn of 1934, the two women started to relax a bit. They had laughed a lot recently, Friedel and Lili read; on one occasion, Rosette's infectious laughter spread to the whole group listening to a cabaret programme on the wireless.[21]

Hedwig and Rosette Kracauer were able to pay more attention to the outside world again. Hedwig spoke about disputes within the Jewish community: 'Even the most brutal fate does not make people cleverer.'[22] There were also disagreements at the cultural federation, where there was a lack of money and various external pressures. Hedwig did not think that the initiative would survive much longer.[23] But she also reported that the Jews were going to synagogue again: 'That is now the general intellectual attitude in the circles close to us: an escape into religion.' And she regretted that she could not take part in it, as little as in the 'adoration of the young rabbis'.[24]

But the Nuremberg Laws renewed their fear and suffering. At the end of 1935, Hedwig summed it up: 'So far, all we had feared has not only happened but been exceeded.'[25] The laws made German Jews into second-class citizens. The Jews' freedom of movement in Frankfurt was gradually limited. The city, for instance, prohibited Jews from using public swimming pools and established a 'Jewish pool' in Niederrad. After November 1938, they were not permitted to use any swimming pools or municipal sports facilities. At the regional court in Frankfurt, anti-Semitic judges defended the honour of Germany in various 'race defilement trials'. Not all citizens of Frankfurt, however, conformed to the expectations of the party and administration when it came to the hatred of Jews. In the autumn of 1935, Hedwig reported that she had 'even' been invited to an 'Aryan' social event – suggesting that this must have been the exception rather than the rule.[26]

Hedwig and Rosette Kracauer 'had become rather old in recent years'.[27] At Easter 1936, they moved from their three-room flat into a two-room flat in Kronberger Straße. They felt as though they only really existed 'in relation to' Siegfried Kracauer. He was the focus of the lives of both women.[28] Hedwig and Rosette were 'fully in the book' – that is, in the book on Offenbach, parts of which they were permitted to read and criticize as early as April 1936.[29] Rosette wondered when he would start discussing Offenbach's family; Hedwig thought there was not enough about Offenbach's music. The aunt found the preface, written by Daniel Halévy, the son of the librettist Ludovic and a famous Jewish essayist, out of place, because 'there is such little emphasis on the Jewish element in your work, that all these deliberations are somewhat distracting'. Following a critical – and, in her eyes, silly – review in the *Jüdische Rundschau*, she stressed that Kracauer had not written a 'Jewish book for the edification of Jews'. Yet Rosette and Hedwig did find consolation in it. Whenever Rosette was in low spirits, she read a few pages of *Offenbach*.[30]

The two women lived for those few occasions on which it was possible for them to see the Kracauers. At Easter 1934, they visited Friedel and Lili in Paris. In the summer of 1936, they met in South Tyrol, and in spring 1937 for Rosette's seventieth birthday in Brussels, where Siegfried's cousin Lutz Frank, who could pay for his aunts' travel, was living.[31] For spring 1938, another meeting in Brussels had been planned. Hedwig believed that this would be the 'very last time', 'a last farewell', and she therefore felt very nervous about it. It would 'probably be the last trip'. Everything had been planned and prepared – the Parisians had also organized their travel papers – when, on 10 March, Siegfried Kracauer warned them against embarking on the trip. His warning probably had to do with news about border controls between Germany and Belgium rather than with the escalating crisis in Austria. On 13 March 1938, one day after the Wehrmacht had entered Austria, Kracauer's mother and aunt declared: 'We have our information ... from competent people. ... Apart from that, the most recent events in world history are a new and unheard of confirmation that our decision was right.' The despair in Frankfurt was deep: 'So, it is true that it will be "never again". There will be no more arrangements.' After the failed journey the two sisters 'lived on, somehow, without hope and without consolation'. Hedwig refused to plan another meeting. At her age, it would simply be too much of a strain. Everyday life in Frankfurt was already too exhausting for her; every day there was something new, and every day there was some new fear. She was blunt: 'there will be no more travelling. I don't want to experience another disappointment at the last moment.'[32]

Figure 27. Rosette and Hedwig Kracauer in their flat in Frankfurt around 1938
Copyright: DLA Marbach

The *annus horribilis* for European Jewry was 1938.[33] With the *Anschluss* in March, there began a sinister new development. By order of the security service of the SS, Adolf Eichmann established the Central Office for Jewish Emigration in Vienna, which introduced practices that would only become possible in the 'Altreich' after 9 November 1938. The systematic expulsion of Austrian Jews, organized from Vienna, eliminated the already limited possibilities for regular migration for Jews within Europe and to the USA. The Polish administration reacted to the *Anschluss* by enacting a law that was designed to prevent the return of about 20,000 Polish Jews from Austria. The Polish passport law aimed at depriving all Polish Jews outside of Poland of their citizenship. In the summer, the Évian conference on the problem of refugees failed; that very much satisfied the Nazis, who could now claim that the Western democracies did not want any Jews either. The Sudeten crisis in early autumn further escalated the situation. From 5 October, German Jews living in the Reich and in Switzerland had a 'J' stamped in their passports. At the end of October, the German government tried to deport the 'Eastern Jews' from Poland in the so-called *Polenaktion*. Thousands were transported to the Polish border, where the border guards refused them entry. The deported had thus to survive in a no-man's land. Among them were the Grynszpan family, who had been brought to Zbaszyń from Hanover. The seventeen-year-old son, Herschel, was in Paris and on 7 November shot and killed the German diplomat Ernst vom Rath. This was followed by *Kristallnacht* on 9 November, the twentieth anniversary of the German Revolution which had led – as the propaganda would have it – to the 'Jews' Republic' of Weimar.[34]

For the Jews of Frankfurt, too, 1938 was a year of catastrophe. The Israelite community lost the status of a legally recognized body and the Philanthropin the status of a public school. More anti-Jewish regulations were passed. The 'Aryanization of the German economy' was stepped up – a euphemism for the theft of Jewish wealth and its transfer into Aryan hands. In April, the Jewish citizens of Frankfurt were forced to document and report all their possessions, down to the smallest detail. A policy of prohibiting Jews from the professions was almost complete – those Jewish doctors and lawyers who were still practising had their licences revoked. The repression intensified: rabbis were arrested, tortured and expelled by the Gestapo. In mid-June 1938, 1,500 'previously convicted' Jews were summarily arrested and sent to the Buchenwald and Sachsenhausen concentration camps. Efforts to publicly stigmatize Jews were also redoubled; from August onwards, all Jews in the Reich were forced to accept the name 'Sara' or 'Israel' as a second given name. The 'solution to the question of the Eastern Jews' also affected Frankfurt. In the summer of 1938, around 2,000 Polish

Jews were deported from the Main region to the borderlands with Poland; when they returned on 31 October, they found their homes had been locked and sealed. They were initially housed in mass accommodation, before, on 9 November, the authorities allowed them back into their homes. That night, mobs attacked, looted and destroyed Jewish homes, just as they had done in 1614.[35]

Among the Kracauer sisters' acquaintances, there was only one topic of discussion at get-togethers in 1938: emigration. 'Everyone practises their English', Hedwig Kracauer wrote to her nephew: 'All our acquaintances, if they can still afford it, slip off in all different directions. We are laughed at as wimps.' One always heard about the tough lives of emigrants, their inability to progress, the fact they were kept afloat by their wives, and yet all able men and women emigrated – just recently, her young doctor. 'Everyone complains.' Hedwig Kracauer wrote of some people they knew who had emigrated to South Africa and then returned to Frankfurt for a visit:

> When the visitors from Africa spoke of the lack of intellectuals in their new home country, we were very much prepared to believe them. But we would rather turn stupid there than remain part of the culture here. We are old, and what we want more than anything else is peace and quiet. But here, every day brings something new.

The seventy-six-year-old was torn between her fear of travelling – a 'terrible anxiety psychosis', as she confessed following the failed trip to Brussels – and the growing certainty that Jews could not stay in Germany. But Hedwig also knew that emigration was not a realistic prospect for her and Rosette. It was a 'castle in the sky'. For who was going to invite them, pay for it, provide for them? 'We are bad material, can hardly earn any money any more, have no wealth.' And which country would take in all the Jews?[36]

On 10 November, Hedwig Kracauer reported that the synagogue at Friedberger Anlage was ablaze: 'Even the wildest fantasy would not have imagined such things as happened in the last few days.'[37] The November pogrom was particularly brutal in Frankfurt. Apart from the synagogue of the Israelite religious community at Friedberger Anlage, the main synagogue in Börnestraße, the former Judengasse, was also burned down. Only places of worship directly adjacent to surrounding buildings were spared. The building housing the administration of the community was demolished, and Jewish shops and flats in the city centre and Ostend were set upon by the Nazi mob. Apart from the destruction, the men who were arrested in the morning of 10 November and brought to the Festhalle were also treated particularly badly before being taken to Buchenwald – 2,621 Frankfurt Jews were seen off at Südbahnhof by an enraged mob that was ready for lynching. Among those deported were all the teachers and senior pupils from the Philanthropin, including the director, Albert Hirsch. After their return from Buchenwald in January 1939, two of the teachers died as a result of the effects of their captivity, Henry Philipp (born 1896) and his colleague Ernst Marbach, who was three years his senior. (Marbach perished following the amputation of his frozen feet.) After the pogrom, Frankfurt city authorities agreed a so-called 'Judenverträge' with the Jewish community: on 3 April 1939, Jews were forced to enter into contracts to hand over parts of their real estate to the city for well below their value (a practice that was repeated for whatever real estate remained in 1942 and 1943). 'The people have given Alljuda their reply',[38] the *Frankfurter Volksblatt* reported. The November pogroms in fact marked the end of the Jewish community of Frankfurt. 'There is no longer a community here; the school will presumably close, and so will all foundations, and so on.' That was Hedwig Kracauer's sober – and correct – evaluation of the situation. Her pension would no longer be paid: 'It would really be better were we no longer alive, but we can't do anything about it.'[39] The one billion Reichsmark 'Sühnegeld' [atonement money] that the German Jews were asked to pay following the assassination of the secretary vom Rath at the German embassy in Paris not only robbed the Jewish citizens of their last remaining assets but also made it harder for them to emigrate. Hedwig and Rosette had to hand over a fifth of all of their possessions to the state, including silverware, jewellery and carpets. Annuities and pensions were also levied. In the end, they were left with nothing. The Jewish community had to tell the remaining Jews in Frankfurt: 'Whoever has relatives in countries of immigration, should remind them urgently to let family members who are still here follow them as quickly as possible.'[40]

At this point, Hedwig and Rosette Kracauer also wanted to get out of Germany.

We do not live a normal life, even if outwardly we pretend as if we do, eating at the right times, going to bed, doing the shopping, mending torn clothes, writing letters, seeing others and receiving visitors. Inwardly, we are disheartened, desperate human beings who are at their wits' end.

Despite all the unanswered questions – 'who will provide for us out there ... who wants old women?' – the two elderly ladies asked Siegfried and Elisabeth Kracauer to do all they could to get them to France. Hedwig soon understood:

Papers! Papers! Everywhere it is about papers! No matter where you go. I speak to more than enough despairing people here for whom ... it is much more important that they leave than it is for us. It just does not work.

And she realized: 'The final and most important piece of paper is the passport. For that you need to have time to wait, a character reference, a clearance certificate, and proof of acceptance from the receiving country.'[41] And they needed a sponsor; Siegfried now began the search for one, as he did not have sufficient income to act as a sponsor himself.

He wrote to the widow of Hedwig and Rosette's brother, who had emigrated to the USA; he got in touch with Robert and Sophie Hainebach, old friends of the family from Frankfurt who had emigrated to South Africa and had been able, 'miraculously', to get their parents out of Frankfurt.[42] He turned to the family of Karl Müller, who had been giving Hedwig a hundred guilders a month ever since she had been dispossessed by the state. Kracauer's cousin, Lutz Frank, might be able to contribute a small amount, but he had to support his own mother in Nuremberg and his children and separated wife Irma in Paris; Irma was willing to provide a room for the two ladies. Kracauer also asked former pupils of the Philanthropin whether they could support Hedwig, but he mostly received negative replies, including from Abraham Horovitz, who had succeeded in bringing the Julius and Amalie Flersheim Educational Institution to England but seems to have felt incapable of doing anything for the widow of its former director Isidor Kracauer, and from Paul Baerwald, whose father had been the director of the Philanthropin before 1890.[43]

In Frankfurt, meanwhile, the catastrophe continued to unfold. The husband of a friend of Rosette and Hedwig, who had been helping them out with practical matters, died unexpectedly of an infectious disease. Hedwig was dismayed: 'Rosette always said it was getting bad, but I did not want to believe it. There are so many alive who are surplus to requirements, and this man was needed so much. ... Rosette is able to scream and rage, and she actually does.'[44] Kracauer's mother was superstitious. She played patience; if she lost, it signalled disaster. She usually just bottled up whatever worry this caused her; the health of her heart was not stable.[45] Reality began to conform to her fears, and, being the meticulous and disciplined type, she began to learn French. Hedwig, for her part, tried to keep her anxieties regarding the authorities at bay, and began to study the French immigration rules. When even old Rosie Stern, who had once introduced Teddie and Friedel, moved to England in March 1939, she was fully convinced 'that a replanting is necessary'. 'Everyone who can, leaves.'[46]

Hedwig and Rosette Kracauer were not able to leave, even though Siegfried had drawn on all the connections he had in Paris, among them high-ranking civil servants.[47] On 23 June 1939, the rejection letter from the French consulate arrived: 'But nothing ever works in our family, as Rosette used to say', was Hedwig's comment on the news; 'it is probably all a question of money. And there we cannot keep up. If we have to die here, then hopefully it will be pretty soon.'[48] Of course, the Kracauers never learned why they had not been granted an immigration visa. In the village no one knows why access to the castle is prohibited. Siegfried implored the two old ladies to not lose hope. In France, he said, such rejections were never final.[49] Perhaps all one had to do was change the direction in which one was running.

The outbreak of war in September 1939 meant leaving the country was no longer an option.

23

La Vie Parisienne

The news from Frankfurt made Siegfried and Elisabeth Kracauer worry even more. Following their difficult introduction to the city, life in Paris had not become any easier. The *Offenbach* book had not changed anything about that because, despite Wiesengrund and Benjamin's allegation that it was a book intended solely to make money, it was not a commercial success. Its French publisher, Bernard Grasset, was not even able to cover his costs.[1] The German edition sold 1,111 copies during the first six months, and sales were sluggish thereafter. The advance of 5,600 francs (700 Reichsmark) turned out to be the only payment Kracauer would ever receive for the book. Landauer had assumed that he would sell 2,500 copies in the first year, but he was not wholly dissatisfied with the numbers. In commercial terms, *Offenbach* was an average book. But for a writer with no other source of income, it was not possible to live off an average book. For the American edition, Kracauer received $250 (roughly 1,200 Reichsmark) from Knopf. The book was not selling as well as expected, the publisher, Blanche Knopf, reported a year after publication. Sales in other countries – the book also appeared in Great Britain and was translated into Swedish and Polish – still only generated pocket money for the author, after agents had taken their shares. Landauer's conclusion at the end of 1937 was: 'The sales ... actually do not really reflect your exceptional literary success. I, at least, have rarely experienced such a literary response to a book as in the case of this one.'[2]

Numerous reviews had, indeed, appeared by then, and mostly they had been positive. Theodor Adorno, as he now called himself, published his critique, albeit in a toned down and non-polemical form, in the *Zeitschrift für Sozialforschung*.[3] Ernst Křenek, however, expressed an altogether different opinion. Ever since the publication of *Ginster*, he had admired Kracauer. He had also judged *The Salaried Masses* an excellently written book, even if one pulled astray by Marxist misunderstandings. Křenek followed Kracauer's work very closely, and described the effect it had on him as being 'disturbed in a most vivid sense'.[4] He praised the *Offenbach* in the *Basler National-Zeitung* and the *Wiener Zeitung*.[5] After Adorno deemed it appropriate to send him the letter he had previously sent Kracauer, Křenek replied:

> Your letter to Krac. is a very harsh criticism of his work, and that is putting it mildly. All the points to which you object concerning the practical approach also irritated me, ... but I did not want to be too severely critical on an author who appears to me as certain of what is genuinely valuable as K. for making an attempt at a 'lighter style', which he may not even have been particularly happy about having to undertake.

Křenek thought Adorno's criticisms overblown, obstinate, and far too severe. In any case, he did not share his reservations about 'the substance in terms of social theory'.[6] Křenek's review set the tone for the reception of the book in the German-speaking world. Max Brod praised it in the *Pariser Tageblatt*; the *Prager Neue Vorwärts* followed this lead, as did the *Neues Tage-Buch*. Hermann Hesse made a point of sending a letter of praise to Landauer. Following the book's translation into English as *Orpheus in Paris*, it was reviewed very positively, twice, in the *New York Times Book Review*, and reviews also appeared in the *Saturday Review of Literature* and *The Republic*, and in Great Britain in *The Times* and the *New Statesman*. In the summer of 1937, there was scarcely a French paper that failed to mention the book or to feature a review of it in a prominent position.[7] Kracauer's tales had found their way onto the boulevard and were acclaimed – but they did not earn him any money.

The Paris Kracauer got to know was, in any case, not that of the boulevard of the non-Parisians' fantasy. 'The real Paris should not be confused with the glistening surface to which the longing of people in all five parts of the world attaches itself. It is home to a broad middle class, leading a life all to itself, a life that rarely overlaps with that of the tourists.'[8] Life in Paris by day had nothing to do with life in Paris at night – with the vaudeville and dance clubs, bistros, bars and brothels that attracted the tourists. But it also had little to do with Benjamin's rag-pickers and beggars, who were not as romantic to behold in reality as one might expect from their literary representations.[9] Like many ordinary Parisians, Kracauer led a reclusive life, so much so, in fact, that he was not even part of the parallel society of migrants who were suffering the same fate as him. They escaped from their isolation into the cafés. As Hermann Kesten put it:

> In exile, the café becomes house and home, church and parliament, desert and place of pilgrimage, becomes the cradle of illusions and a cemetery. Living in exile makes one lonely and kills. However, it

also enlivens and renews. In exile, the café becomes the only place to provide continuity.[10]

Joseph Roth had certainly made the café his home. He worked there, took all his meals there and even received visitors there. He more or less lived there.[11] For Kracauer, by contrast, the café was not a space for communication; it was strictly for work. He loved to write in public spaces, amid the noise, surrounded by garçons and guests. Hotel lobbies and the concourses of railway stations were his preferred offices. Where others became distracted, he could concentrate best. As a writer he remained the street child, alone in the crowd, observing the throngs of people, noting their behaviour in a notebook. The café was for Kracauer what the Bibliothèque nationale was for Benjamin. For Benjamin, all of Paris was a great library reading room traversed by the Seine; it was a surreal place, a labyrinthine dreamscape of arcades and crystal bearing the meaning of modern life within them, which one could read like a book. When Benjamin was sitting in the library, he thought he was, as it were, in the unconscious interior of the public space. Kracauer's everyday locations, by contrast, were the public places, and he withdrew to them like the bourgeois into his living room. The library and the café were homely places for Benjamin and Kracauer, just as the whole city became their home – however much it might also have been the scene of their existential struggle.

Both Benjamin and Kracauer kept their distance from German affairs. They did not participate in the various political activities and congresses of the emigrants: the Deutsche Freiheitsbibliothek [German freedom library], a 'library of burned books, founded by Heinrich Mann, Lion Feuchtwanger and Alfred Kantorowicz in May 1934'; the anti-fascist congress of writers defending the 'culture and the ideas of 1789', held at the Mutualité in June 1935, and attended by Gide and Malraux, Bloch and Brecht; or the political efforts at establishing an anti-National Socialist 'people's front' for Germany in February 1936.[12] Kracauer turned down invitations from Hermann Budzislawski to publish in the *Weltbühne* and invitations from Wieland Herzfelde to publish in *Neue Deutsche Blätter*.[13] He did not attend the meetings of political groups that courted him,[14] such as the Internationaler Sozialistischer Kampfbund [International Socialist Militant League] or Otto Klepper's Deutsche Freiheitspartei [German Freedom Party].[15] One reason for his reluctance was that Kracauer feared for the safety of his relatives, another that he was drifting away from his left-wing political past and from Germany. Kracauer agreed with the literary critic Erich Franzen, who said of his new environment in Zurich: 'Emigrants live like fish in a bowl; glass wall – period.'[16] Pretty soon Kracauer found himself not even wanting to visit the Deux Magots, a café that, to him, conjured up 'darkest Berlin': 'You certainly do not live in Paris in order to come across the old German literary rabble and its ... problems again, who, thankfully, will not be able to spread themselves about in the atmosphere here.'[17]

Kracauer did like to go to the Rue de l'Odéon, though; the bookshop La Maison des amis des livres, run by Adrienne Monnier, was situated there:

> The bright world of books was my constant refuge during the long years of exile in Paris (which was itself a home to me). Right at the centre of that brightness was Adrienne Monnier, usually dressed in grey, but scarcely any darker than her realm. I would come at any hour of the day, but preferably in the afternoon, just before dusk would begin to settle outside. ... [I]t was as if the room was a part of her person, as if something of these tomes through which I was browsing had communicated itself to her. And yet, she was as discreet as her grey dress. ... The brightness of her appearance, of the room and also of her voice was no ordinary brightness, but the veil or form of something inward that disappeared into the darkness. Maybe it was this mysterious intertwining of foreground and background, a bright exterior and hidden substance, that attracted me so strongly to her.[18]

Monnier, who was a bookseller, a publisher and a fixture of the literary scene in Paris, reminded Kracauer of the old Françoise and the Countess de Guermantes, that mixture of peasant and aristocratic character, of practical ability and dignity, groundedness and erudition praised by Proust. Monnier seemed to encapsulate Kracauer's image of France: the social and cultural sphere of the country, he thought, enjoyed a relative autonomy from capitalist class society; there were behavioural patterns, forms of conduct and values that were not politically or economically determined.[19] As he claimed in the book on Offenbach: 'Liberty led this people; even its darkest outbursts, therefore, were still of a human kind.'[20]

In March 1938, Kracauer had to admit to himself that, whatever warmth he felt for Paris and France, he had been trying for five years to make contacts, and yet his existence was still a precarious one. As he drily commented: 'If each relationship we felt duty bound to enter into had yielded some return, we would be multi-millionaires.'[21] The Kracauers were repeatedly forced to rely on donations and loans. One day, it was Friedrich T. Gubler who helped out, another day his cousin Lutz Frank. Lady Henriette Davies, the widow of the Canadian-Jewish philanthropist Sir Mortimer B. Davis, supported Kracauer in the winter of 1935/1936 while he was working on the Offenbach book, and again in the winter of 1938/1939 with monthly payments of around 500 francs, and then yet again after they had fled to Lisbon.[22] In February 1936, he received 2,250 francs ($150) from a fund financed by voluntary self-taxation from a group of

Figure 28. The streets of Paris. A photo taken by Elisabeth Kracauer in the 1930s
Copyright: DLA Marbach

academic emigrants at the New School for Social Research in New York: the 'University in Exile'. Half a year later, he received another payment from the group.[23] From January 1938, he received 6,000 francs in monthly payments from the Institute for Social Research as an honorarium for commissioned work on the Nazi propaganda. In 1939, he finally received a three-month grant of $90 from the American Guild for German Cultural Freedom and $50 from Thomas Mann, who maintained a small fund for writers who had emigrated.[24]

When Jewish refugees from Austria began to arrive in Paris in the spring of 1938, Kracauer thought:

> This is how the Russians here must have felt about our arrival five years ago. Just like us back then, they are all still impeccably dressed, in cordial community with others sharing their fate, whom they did not even know before, huddling round in groups in cafés, where they deliberate and get things off their chests. A very elegant man can be heard proudly saying: 'My wife now cooks on a spirit burner.' Of course, they all live in hotel rooms and confront the situation with a lack of awareness that is moving. Grotesquely, we feel by comparison that we are the experienced ones who have settled, and do not envy them despite the fact that they are still materially well off; rather, we appear to ourselves as the ones to be envied.[25]

Figure 29. A new cinema diagonally across from Kracauer's room in
Avenue Mac-Mahon. Photograph by Lili Kracauer
Copyright: DLA Marbach

Paris had become a city of strangers. In 1938, 400,000 foreigners
lived there, roughly a seventh of the population.[26] The Kracauers
looked upon the new strangers almost with the eyes of a native.

Since October 1936, the Kracauers had no longer been living
in a hotel but in a furnished room with a kitchenette and washing
facilities in Avenue Mac-Mahon 3, XVII. arrondissement. The
Offenbach book had not solved their financial problems, but it had
opened up new opportunities. After their successful cooperation,
Kracauer had agreed with Landauer that he would write a book
on film for Allert de Lange, and he had received an advance of
450 guilders (roughly 650 Reichsmark).[27] What exactly the book
would be about, he did not yet know. To his relatives in Frankfurt
he wrote:

> You know from previous instances – see the book on *The Salaried
> Masses* – that the form only crystallises out of the material. For

the time being, Lili and I are carrying out some preliminary work together. A lot of reading is required because the Americans and the English have written a lot on the subject of film and I would not be particularly successful in these countries. The only thing I can already say with certainty is that a lot will be said in the book about the relationship between film and society, on which nothing exists yet.[28]

Nothing existed yet apart, of course, from his own articles in the *Frankfurter Zeitung*, which he asked his mother to send him.[29]

In June 1938, Kracauer wrote to Frankfurt about private film screenings, some of which were even 'organized especially for me'. Attendees would only be told of the location of 'the séance' shortly before it was due to begin. 'Today, for instance, it was just around the corner from us, at the home of the director of "Maternelle" [i.e. Jean Benoit-Lévy]. Of course, we take advantage of all of these opportunities.' From the perspective of Kracauer's book, this was 'very fortunate'. On another occasion, 'a very rich Frenchman' showed G. W. Pabst's *The Joyless Street* 'for his female American visitors'. Henri Langlois, a film archivist and a co-founder of the Cinémathèque Française (which opened in 1935), each week showed an old film at the Cercle du Cinéma. Lotte Eisner, a German-French writer and film critic who had moved from Berlin to Paris and, in 1936, founded the Cinémathèque Française together with Henri Langlois, was probably also present at the 'séances'. The Kracauers were friendly with both. In May 1938, Kracauer sent Langlois a list of films he would be interested in seeing.[30] In the second half of 1938, much of the Kracauers' time was spent at film screenings. Kracauer, a film critic once again, rewatched all the old Weimar films and compiled an extensive index of his notes on them. He noticed 'how the original reaction to a film changed when it was viewed again after many years'.[31] He was working on a 'peculiar memory book', as he explained to Thomas Mann, 'because in it I have to strip off layers of the life of our generation which are still very much hidden because they are only now beginning to become history'.[32] In Joinville, Kracauer watched Pabst at work in the studio and Bernard Deschamps on set. He also met Erich von Stroheim, one of the great Hollywood directors.[33]

His renewed interest in film also led to a new source of income for Kracauer. Towards the end of 1936, he finally succeeded in selling film reviews to the *Neue Züricher Zeitung*. From August 1938, he also published a monthly 'Letter on Film from Paris' in the *Basler National-Zeitung*. The series 'Wiedersehen mit alten Filmen' [Rewatching old films], which arose out of the private film screenings in Paris, also appeared in the paper. These opportunities to publish were rays of hope for Kracauer in more ways than one. We may assume that the pay in Switzerland was already higher than that in France, despite all the pay cuts mentioned in Kracauer's correspondence with editors. The paper in Basel paid 20 centimes per line; assuming an article of 200 lines, that would amount to 40 Swiss francs.[34] Kracauer's articles in the *Basler National-Zeitung* were allowed to be relatively lengthy, and he could choose his themes and the films on which he wrote as he wished. What was more, in his dealings with the editors Edwin Arnet and Fritz René Allemann, Kracauer found that he was very much valued. Allemann's letters, in particular, were respectful, even reverent; the old pioneer and master of film criticism was obviously a role model, if not an idol, for the young editor.

And yet Kracauer remained a typical emigrant, someone who, in his words, 'emigrated without money' and had to 'build an existence out of nothing', had to battle 'with the existing regulations' in his new country, had to get used to a disorderly existence without income, home or comfort, and who had always to struggle to keep his nerve.[35] Grief, worry and despair were his daily bread. Had he to name an event that typified the emigrants' situation in Paris, Kracauer might well have mentioned the funeral of Joseph Roth on 30 May 1939. His friend from his Frankfurt and Berlin days had died in hospital three days earlier, the victim of a lethal mix of alcoholism, political barbarism and misfortune. Many people gathered at his grave on the Cimetière Thiais in the banlieue to the south-east of Paris in order to bid farewell to Roth, among them Hermann Kesten, Fritz Landshoff, Soma Morgenstern, Alfred Polgar, Egon Erwin Kisch and Siegfried Kracauer. There stood assembled monarchists and communists; eastern Jews and Catholics; emigrants from Vienna, Prague, Berlin; journalists, writers and artists. 'Around the freshly dug grave there were no trees, no shrubs, only withered wreaths scattered about here and there. And over all this hung an oppressive heat.' This is how Karl Retzlaw, a veteran of the Spanish civil war, remembered the day.[36] The Kracauers were deeply moved by this mixture of hustle and hopelessness. To his mother and aunt in Frankfurt, Kracauer wrote:

For us it was an event that personally affected and shocked us deeply. A few days before, we had become very agitated over the suicide of [Ernst] Toller, which was also in a way tragic. ... It was an altogether incredibly depressing sight to see all these uprooted people from many different countries united at Roth's grave.[37]

And in a letter to Landauer, he said:

This death seriously got to my wife and to me. We saw the old times again, old times we had shared in, and we saw where we had all ended up. Maybe Roth is to be envied. When we last came across him here – it was quite a while ago – the way he looked already terrified us. But he probably knew that not much good was waiting for him or for us.[38]

Joseph Roth had once painted the portrait of his age in the pages of the *Frankfurter Zeitung*; now he himself had become the very portrait of the fate of the emigrants in Paris.

Roth's last word was *The Legend of the Holy Drinker*, a book Kracauer got hold of immediately after the funeral. The legacy Roth left in this book was that of a stubborn denial of reality. Roth's beggar in Paris, Andreas, dies an easy and beautiful death; he celebrates the last day of his life in style, after having been given money by an unknown noble donor.[39]

24

The 'Institute for Social Falsification'[1]

Siegfried Kracauer and Max Horkheimer each harboured strong reservations about the other. Kracauer's aversion might have had to do with the time when Elisabeth Ehrenreich worked at the Institute for Social Research because, when she left, Wiesengrund jokingly wrote to Kracauer that he hoped she had 'recovered from the last lingering after-effects of revolutionary Marxism'. Wiesengrund also reported that the 'pair of friends, Lenin and Trotsky' – meaning Horkheimer and Friedrich Pollock – in Kronberg were angry at Kracauer for not having sent them a copy of *The Salaried Masses*, despite the fact that they very much approved of the study.[2] But it was an incident in November 1930 that had particularly harmed the relationship. Horkheimer had sent a copy of his *Beginnings of the Bourgeois Philosophy of History* to Kracauer at the *FZ*, asking whether he could review it. But Kracauer had 'no time' for it and promised to place the book in the right hands. A clearly insulted Horkheimer wrote back to say that if Kracauer could not write the review himself, then he was to see to it 'that it is not reviewed at all'. He was indifferent, he said, towards a 'review from the pen of some stranger'. A week later, however, Horkheimer suggested Wiesengrund as a reviewer, assuring Kracauer that he had 'no intention whatsoever of exerting moral pressure' on Kracauer'.[3] Such arranged reviews were not uncommon, and Kracauer had in fact already suggested to his colleague Robert Drill that Wiesengrund write the review, but Drill had already given the book to someone else. In the end the review was forgotten.[4] Of course, Horkheimer was anything but indifferent to this matter. He was, after all, about to give his inaugural lecture on 'The Present Situation of Social Philosophy and the Task of an Institute for Social Research' (on 24 January 1931). And he had quite a few enemies in Frankfurt.[5] Kracauer, of course, was not one of them, but the now successful author was a friend and teacher to Löwenthal and Wiesengrund, who had both written their Habilitations under Horkheimer's supervision, and thus Kracauer was in a sense his rival, against whom he was competing for the sympathies of the younger ones.

Horkheimer thought the situation an injustice, and Wiesengrund agreed. Where Kracauer had initially wanted to support the book there was now the threat of a scathing review. The editor had dealt with matters 'in a "dilatory" fashion where this was inappropriate'.[6] Kracauer did not think he had done anything wrong, and he responded professionally and calmly: 'In a newspaper, other and still more important things do not always go as one wishes.'[7] In this dispute Kracauer held the upper hand, but circumstances would soon change.

Horkheimer saw the demise of the Weimar Republic coming, and he had transferred the capital financing the Institute to Switzerland in good time, before the Nazis came to power. Just a few days after 30 January 1933, he had moved to Geneva, and in February 1933 the Société Internationale de Recherches Sociales replaced the 'Gesellschaft für Sozialforschung' [Society for Social Research]. Pollock, Fromm, Marcuse and Löwenthal had followed Horkheimer to Geneva, now the official headquarters of the Institute. A little more than a year later, Horkheimer received an unexpected and tempting offer. In May 1934, the President of Columbia University, Nicholas M. Butler, invited Horkheimer to move the Institute to New York, and was willing to provide a whole building for it. Over the course of a year, the members of the Institute in Geneva moved to New York. In 1936, Franz L. Neumann joined the Institute in New York.[8] When Löwenthal one day departed suddenly to New York, an envious Kracauer could only say: 'You have done well to get out of the mess.' He asked him to keep him in mind if he heard of 'any opportunity over there' that might be an option.[9] After that, they did not correspond for four years. The reasons for this are not clear, but it is quite possible that even Löwenthal was included within the grudge Kracauer increasingly bore against the Institute. Löwenthal, however, had not forgotten about the favour he had been asked.

At the time, quite a few people wondered to themselves why Kracauer was not turning to Horkheimer and the Institute for help. Perhaps Heinrich Simon had this in mind when he told Kracauer that he should look for new opportunities beyond the *Frankfurter Zeitung*. There were reasons enough to think of this possibility: a feeling of loyalty from the common time in Frankfurt, even friends at the Institute; the political, social philosophical, academic and literary affinities between Kracauer's work and that undertaken there; a sense of solidarity shared by the victims of the National Socialist dictatorship, especially victims of anti-Semitism – why, despite all this, did Kracauer not find a place at the Institute? The question was put to Kracauer by Gertrud and Richard Krautheimer, both art historians who had been in the US since the end of 1935. Kracauer responded, in May 1936, by saying that 'this Institute' was indeed the only one 'to which in all this time we did *not* turn; although, given the shared sociological interests, it might have seemed obvious to do so'. At the Institute, he said,

> Horkheimer and Pollock managed to establish themselves as directors for life with the help of the money from the Institute founded by Hermanus Weil, and now spend their days as they please. This means that they no longer support the fighting Marxism the Institute originally was meant to serve, but rather cautiously navigate the gilded ship past all such threatening cliffs.

Now, Kracauer was many things, but a 'fighting Marxist' he certainly was no longer, and he usually had no objections against cautious navigators. Finally, to be brought ashore in America aboard a gilded ship was probably something of a dream for him. What stopped him from reaching out was the feeling 'that the people at the Institute meet me with great animosity since I am no longer at the *Frankfurter Zeitung*, but am only an emigrant'.[10]

In Kracauer's eyes, 'these people' were now exacting their revenge: Horkheimer because Kracauer had not had time to review his *Beginnings of the Bourgeois Philosophy of History*; Pollock because of Kracauer's wife, the former librarian at the Institute, who had told him some 'ugly truths'; Löwenthal because Kracauer had not found him a place at the *Frankfurter Zeitung*; and Wiesengrund, the arch-narcissist, because of all the old wounds, and the resulting anger, left from their more intimate times, which he guarded as if they were museum pieces. Kracauer was sure that he did *not* want to be saved by *these* people. Such was his wounded pride that he would not allow himself to be the first to get in touch with his 'natural allies', who, in his view, were in fact taking pleasure in harming and humiliating him. This is how it must have appeared to Kracauer, from his groundless Parisian existence. He was still living hand to mouth, dependent on others, while Horkheimer and the gang discussed problems in the sociology of language, the social conditions of psychoanalytic therapy or philosophical anthropology from soft armchairs in well-heated rooms at Columbia University. Kracauer distrusted the Frankfurt people. He envied them. Sometimes, he despised them. This, too, was one of the rotten fruits of emigration.

That despair was really what underlay his tirades against the 'Institute for Social Falsification' became clear less than half a year after his categorical declaration of 'no cooperation with these people', when he did, in fact, come to an agreement with them (although not without accompanying nervous tensions and irritability). Wiesengrund had planned it, had acted as a mediator and had seen to it that the agreement was accepted. His initial aim was to find a place for 'his' people, that is, Benjamin, Bloch and Kracauer, at the Institute's journal, or even at the Institute itself. Ever since his Kierkegaard book, his philosophical agenda had been to explode idealism from within, to put dialectical thinking at the centre of the 'critical theory' that Horkheimer had in mind and to develop an interpretive and material aesthetic theory that could somehow also accommodate the theological motifs of rescuing what has decayed or is misunderstood. In order to put these plans in train, he placed his hopes, first of all, in Benjamin, but also, given their past, in Kracauer, and – thinking ahead – in Sohn-Rethel. Bloch, however, he thought had gone politically astray.[11] In 1936, while in England, Wiesengrund tried to get in touch with the relevant parties. The easiest and simplest case was the collaboration with Benjamin, which also enjoyed the backing of Horkheimer. As early as 1935, the work on the arcades was on the list of projects supported by the Institute, and since Horkheimer's visit to Paris in February 1936, the Institute was paying Benjamin a regular salary. In October of the same year, Wiesengrund also visited Paris. He met with both Benjamin and Kracauer, but he conferred mostly with the former. After their 'days in Paris', the two were 'Walter' and 'Teddie' to one another. Benjamin summed up their meetings: 'That was a time which brought things long since prepared to mature fulfilment.'[12] They spoke at length about Kracauer, who in their eyes had abandoned the position they had shared since their Berlin days. Wiesengrund reported to Horkheimer: 'I also met with Kracauer. He is a hopelessly difficult case, and I can only adopt Benjamin's formula: one needs to consider him "intellectually incapacitated", that is, if one wants to rescue him in the literal and in the intellectual sense, it is only possible against his will.'[13] Later, he told Benjamin that he had written to Horkheimer about Kracauer and 'followed your [i.e. Benjamin's] own formulation. I hope what I have written about him will prove beneficial to him. It was no easy task to formulate the matter.'[14] When it came to matters relating to Kracauer, Benjamin was now the one whispering in Wiesengrund's ear. Both were worried about their old friend, but both had reached a negative intellectual judgement of him. The erstwhile teacher was now someone that needed to be taken care of, and, what was more, someone who was aggressive and did not hesitate to spout his conspiracy theories. Wiesengrund, however, still had enough of a belief in his nursing case's talent to secure a place for him. And he assured Horkheimer that, in view of Kracauer's situation, they could assume that he would be 'intellectually docile, all too docile':

Of course he would absolutely love to work for the Institute, but feels persecuted by all of us, including myself, and exhibits narcissistic responses, which are in his case unavoidable. ... I know your affects about Kracauer, and trust me: they are no different from mine. You will nevertheless understand that, ultimately, my pity for my old friend outweighs even these affects.

Wiesengrund had the idea of suggesting to Kracauer an investigation of propaganda, having thought that insights into the 'structure of fascism' might be gained by looking at the phenomenon of 'advertising'.[15]

Kracauer initially rejected Teddie's proposal: 'All that was discussed between us was that I was prepared to *talk* to Horkheimer, *when he is here*. After the *various* rejections which the Institute has dealt me, any initiative on my part is impossible.' Kracauer wanted to be asked politely by Horkheimer: 'I shall never ever knock on doors where I have been kicked out three or four times, or been treated in an undignified way. I shall only go in here *through the wide open main entrance*, and be received with full honours.'[16] In reality, what Kracauer perceived as 'having been kicked out', or having been treated in an undignified way, consisted of nothing more than Löwenthal once offering him a review article and, after he had turned it down, never coming back to him. Behind all this, Kracauer suspected an 'intentional humiliation' was being plotted by Horkheimer, who he thought was full of 'animosity' towards him.[17] But Kracauer soon changed his mind and became, as Wiesengrund had predicted, docile. Just two weeks later, he called his remark about the 'main entrance' 'the product of a severe depression and ... confusion' and assured Wiesengrund of his 'good will'.[18] Since Horkheimer, despite his 'affects', had already agreed to the project on propaganda, the further bumps in the road introduced by Kracauer did not lead to it faltering. In his need, Kracauer attempted to have the commissioned research project turned into a fixed position at the Institute by suggesting there was a third person interested in the project. Wiesengrund saw what Kracauer was doing, and criticized his 'system of tactical considerations, obscure relations, calculated measures'. In March 1937, Kracauer accepted the grant for his work on propaganda, which was to be 'credited solely to the Institute'.[19]

All this happened two months before Wiesengrund wrote his devastating letter on the *Offenbach* book to Kracauer, whose uncharacteristically cool reaction to that letter is explained by this prehistory. Kracauer had to control himself because he knew what was at stake. He swallowed the bitter pill because he had no alternative, apart from whatever might come from the possible commercial success of the *Offenbach* book. Thus, even though there was no guarantee that the resulting text would actually get published, he set to work, diligently, on the propaganda project. Horkheimer had made it clear at the outset that, if the article were not suitable for the journal, it would be 'stored as part of our archive, like some other important works', for future reference. 'In such projects, the likelihood that nothing comes of them is always greater than the opposite.'[20]

Kracauer's study of the genesis, character and methods of fascist and National Socialist propaganda and its relation to power and social reality turned out to be an original piece of work by any standard. His approach was partly Marxist, partly social psychological, and throughout he consistently applied, in moderate fashion, a sociological functionalism to the study of domination. On the one hand, Kracauer pursued a theory of fascism, explaining the rise of National Socialism as a consequence of the social and economic crisis of capitalism. As in his earlier work, he emphasized the role of the dispossessed middle class and its intellectual homelessness as a vehicle for National Socialism. On the other hand, as opposed to approaches based on political economy, which stressed the deactivation of class antagonisms, Kracauer took the defeat in the war as the decisive point of origin for the rise of rackets and desperados in Germany and Italy. Within this pluralistic model of the causes of fascist dictatorship, nationalism has a prominent place, and the 'will to power' is the last and 'decisive impulse which the fascist and national socialist cliques obey'.[21] Thus, when examining fascism, Kracauer did not concentrate exclusively on the effects of social forces. Unusually, for an approach based on political economy, he put the concept of the masses, and not that of class, centre stage. His exposé was titled 'Mass and Propaganda'.

He who wishes to gain power must win over the masses, by whatever means necessary. For Kracauer, this insight united the clique around Hitler, in addition to the movement's ideological basis. Kracauer described propaganda as a manipulative tool that aims at achieving domination by way of *producing the illusion of the reintegration of the masses*.[22] In this way, propaganda is a cousin of terror, the latter understood as a violent means of smothering class antagonisms within a system. But Kracauer went beyond such a conventional understanding of the purposes of propaganda in claiming that, in the context of fascism, propaganda (like terror) becomes an end in itself, develops its own social dynamic and thus creates a social reality out of itself. Propaganda is able to change the *psycho-physical structure of human beings*. Kracauer was not only interested in asking who profited from all this; he also wanted to know why people succumbed to this new form of politics. These questions had also been addressed in the studies on authority and family that the Institute in New York had produced under

Horkheimer's leadership and published in 1936.[23] Kracauer paid tribute to Horkheimer, but he did not remain inside the intellectual parameters of the Horkheimer circle. As was typical of Kracauer's approach, he was not just interested in unmasking the rulers; he was interested in the mask itself, which is one of those surface phenomena that lend themselves to the study of social reality.

The text which Kracauer submitted in January 1938 bore the title 'Die totalitäre Propaganda' [Totalitarian Propaganda]. It was a torso, unfinished, with many repetitions, and it still lacked a coherent form. The impression of incompleteness was reinforced by the fact that it pursued various approaches to the matter in parallel. The manuscript contained many brilliant ideas and excellent formulations, but it had not been given the finishing touches. One could practically still feel the author's sweat on the pages – and no small amount of it cold. Because of his plans to go to America, Kracauer was now particularly dependent on Horkheimer. The work on propaganda was no normal piece of commissioned, grant-supported research leading to a publication – potentially, Kracauer's future was riding on it.

When Kracauer sent Horkheimer the first part of the study in October 1937, he quite liked it. He had 'hardly any doubt that the article was suitable for the journal'. It is 'very likely that we shall already include your article in the first volume of next year'.[24] That statement proved to be somewhat premature. By February 1938, Horkheimer was already having to backpedal, saying that it would 'probably be impossible to find room for more than two print sheets', presumably equalling thirty-two pages. At that point, the manuscript had grown to 105 pages, with fifty pages more to follow. It was obvious that substantial changes and cuts to the text would be necessary if it were to be published in the envisaged volume. Adorno wanted to take on the task. Horkheimer wrote to Kracauer that Adorno had 'advocated our cooperation very strongly'.[25] On 5 March, Adorno presented a report on Kracauer's study which again revealed his ambivalence towards his old teacher. He wrote: 'The study is not of any real theoretical value, nor sufficiently grounded in empirical material, but at times expresses, in highly useful literary formulations, certain experiences and observations that are valid beyond the outsider position of the author.' He further noted 'that Kracauer neither definitely belongs to us as far as his theoretical attitude is concerned, nor is he to be classified as a scientific writer as such as far as his method of working is concerned'.[26] Despite thus distancing himself from the manuscript, it was Adorno's ambition to save it. The reference to Kracauer's position as an outsider provided for an implicit 'and yet' argument: precisely because Kracauer worked in such an unconventional, unsystematic and non-committal way, he managed to achieve insights which

Adorno did not necessarily expect others at the Institute to be able to come up with. What was more, Kracauer possessed exceptional literary ability, and it was clear that he was now moving away from 'commodity writing'. Adorno suggested that a 'journal article of no more than two print sheets' be created out of the material. Adorno expressed himself far less diplomatically towards Benjamin: 'Whether anything here is actually usable is still uncertain, but I am quite sure that if one does undertake to salvage any of it, this will only be possible if it is completely demolished first and then pieced together again from the smallest fragments.'[27]

Adorno's short edited version had little in common with Kracauer's original text. Together with Löwenthal and Neumann, he picked out those elements and theses that agreed with the Institute's policies.[28] He turned the main line of argument into a subordinate point, and replaced the historical genealogy with a closed and synthesizing perspective. In its literary style, the text also became Adornoesque, which is plain to anyone who is halfway familiar with the writing styles of the two. Adorno also altered the substance of certain passages. The tin might have said 'Kracauer' on the label, but it contained Adorno. The propaganda that was investigated was no longer 'totalitarian', but 'authoritarian'. As an example of the 'reproduction of stupidity', propaganda was now seen as on a par with advertising in democratic countries, while Kracauer had strongly wanted to keep the two phenomena separate.[29] Adorno had indeed treated Kracauer as 'intellectually incapacitated' and had taken on the role of his intellectual guardian. And all this he did with the clear conscience of someone who believes he is helping someone else.

Kracauer's reaction to the editing of his text was clear and controlled – there were limits even to his docility. On 20 August 1938, he told Horkheimer that he refused to give his imprimatur. He told Adorno

> that never in my entire literary career have I set eyes on editorial work which runs counter to every legitimate normal practice in such a way – not to mention the fact that in my own personal practice I should never have played around with another author's text like that. The truth is, you have not edited my manuscript but used it as the basis for a work of your own.

Kracauer also disagreed with Adorno's understanding of fascism: 'You identify it from the first with counter-revolution, set its interests in diametrical opposition to those of the majority and leave aside its ambiguous relationship with capitalism.'[30] Kracauer left it at that. He did not want to spark a major row; in his dealings with Horkheimer, in particular, he was concentrating on his move to the United States, which was being supported by several people in New York. One condition for it was to find the money for a research assignment that would make it possible for him to get an immigration visa. The Institute (even though he disliked it) and its collaborators were to play a major role in this. In the end, Kracauer had to accept that he was going to be saved by 'these people'. To begin with, however, the driving force behind the attempt to get the Kracauers to America lay elsewhere, namely with Richard and Gertrud Krautheimer and Meyer Schapiro, all of them art historians.

25

Vanishing Point: America

The grant from the Institute for Social Research and the financial help from the fund set up by emigrated social scientists from Germany at the New School for Social Research made the US, and in particular New York, the Kracauers' preferred option as a destination. At the New School, Alvin Johnson had founded a 'University in Exile' with money from the Rockefeller Foundation. This university looked particularly to employ economists and social and political scientists who had previously been supported by the Foundation while in Europe and who had researched and taught at institutions which undertook empirical research, according to European standards: that is, which by European standards had an 'American' orientation, yet, by American standards, were at the same time still part of the tradition of the European humanities. Because of this hybrid orientation, Johnson wanted to protect the researchers that he brought from Germany to New York in a 'gilded ghetto', as Lewis Coser puts it, and thus preserve the German academic tradition.[1] At the core of this group were two sociologists from Heidelberg, Emil Lederer, the first Dean of the New York faculty, and Hans Speier, his right-hand man. The fund from which Kracauer profited demonstrates the special social nature of this academic community, the Graduate Faculty that grew out of the 'University in Exile'.[2]

Lederer was not able to offer Kracauer a grant – from 1935/36 onwards, the New School received about 5,000 such requests every year.[3] But with Kracauer's enquiry, the search for some opportunity for him to come to America began – be it a research assignment, a fellowship or a teaching assignment. Richard and 'Trude' Krautheimer, who had presumably known Elisabeth Ehrenreich since their university days, had taken the initiative and presented Kracauer's case to Lederer and Speier.[4] After the faculty turned down the request for a grant, the Krautheimers kept the Kracauers' spirits up: 'America is such a strange country; you never know from which side money may suddenly be coming in again, and therefore one has to make sure that no stone is left unturned.' They also immediately wrote to Meyer Schapiro, to whom they introduced Kracauer as a friend with three 'quality labels'; he was a Jew, an art historian and a Marxist. 'He himself is a poor fellow who currently just about makes do for himself and his family – but he is richly connected and has helped us in many respects in New York.'[5]

Schapiro's parents had come to the US from Lithuania when he was still an infant. Since 1928, he had been assistant professor for art history at Columbia University. Like many other children of Eastern Jewish emigrants, he belonged to New York's radical modernist avant-garde of the 1930s. He first supported the communists and was part of the circles around Lionel Trilling, whose members looked at the fine arts through a Marxist lens. As these New York intellectuals were both looking for a revolutionary perspective and pursuing high cultural standards, it was only a question of time before they broke with Stalinist communism and with proletarian art. This point came in 1936, with the foundation of the journal *Partisan Review*. Its second edition, of which Schapiro was one of the editors, set out a programme. Schapiro moved easily in both academic and radical political circles; he was always interested in conversation, and he was refreshingly undogmatic. He was also utterly committed and reliable when it came to support for expelled intellectuals like Benjamin or Kracauer, whose works he read and held in exceptionally high regard. Adorno thought he was 'a well-informed and intellectually imaginative man' and considered him an 'active Trotskyist'.[6] Schapiro edited the art history journal *Marxist Quarterly*, and in January 1937 he contacted Kracauer asking him for an article on Jacques Offenbach.[7]

Probably still in January 1937, Richard Krautheimer had conversations with Schapiro and Alfred H. Barr, the founding director of the Museum of Modern Art and himself an art historian, to discuss plans for a research project on European or German film, to be housed at the museum's Film Library. The Film Library had existed since 1935, the work of Iris Barry, a British national, who with her book *Let's Go to the Movies* of 1926 was among the pioneers of film criticism and film studies.[8] The very name, the Film Library, was intended to emphasize its serious and non-commercial character. It was established with the help of $100,000 from the Rockefeller Foundation and $60,000 from private donors. Barry became its curator, her husband, John E. Abbott, its director.[9] Hoping to advance plans for a 'Kracauer project' further, Krautheimer spoke to Erwin Panofsky, who was an advisor to the Film Library and a Permanent Fellow at the Institute for Advanced Studies in Princeton. Panofsky was a renowned art historian, himself an emigrant, and one of the few representatives of his discipline to engage with film not only as a leisure activity. His essay 'On Movies' of 1936 (later expanded under the title 'Style and Medium in the Moving

Pictures') was an important introduction to the aesthetics of film. Panofsky's initial reaction was negative; he did not know Kracauer personally.[10] But Schapiro succeeded in securing Horkheimer's support. Horkheimer immediately reported to Kracauer that the Film Library's archive contained almost every film ever produced since the beginnings of the industry, and in particular an almost complete collection of films produced in Germany: 'Some have floated the idea of investigating the connection between the development of German society and the art of film using this material. I at once said that I knew no one who would be more competent for carrying out such a task than you.' 'The prospects', however, were 'at present still slim' – meaning that the money for the project still had to be found.[11]

Prompted by Horkheimer, Kracauer applied to the Museum of Modern Art in May 1937.[12] For half a year, nothing happened. Kracauer continued to work on his film exposé and 'intensely' on 'improving his school English', while trying to find out what life in America might be like. Trude Krautheimer showed him he could afford a room with a kitchen in Brooklyn for thirty-five dollars a month. If he earned $100 a month, she said, that would cover 'rent, food, travel and coffee'. Additional purchases and medical bills would have to be covered by other means. The Kracauers did not yet worry about such things. For them, in 1937, the 'journey to America' became the central goal, and not a day passed without the couple thinking about their move. The 'New York Museum opportunity is our only hope' was Kracauer's mantra. Wilhelm Cohnstedt, a former colleague from the *FZ* who had lived in New York since 1934, gave them exactly the right advice: 'Illusions are a dangerous nutrition for emigrants, almost as dangerous as a lack of illusions.'[13]

The update they received from the Krautheimers at the end of 1937 was depressing reading. The Film Library had failed with its application to the Rockefeller Foundation, and thus did not have the money for the project. A fellowship at Yale University that had been talked about had not materialized either. At least the film people at the Museum of Modern Art continued to be interested in Kracauer.[14] In spring 1938, Richard Krautheimer got to know John Abbott. Abbott, he told Kracauer, was 'good-natured, conceited, stiff' and 'the real spiritus rector is Mrs. Abbott [i.e. Iris Barry], who is intelligent, English, snobbish, and educated'. Abbott had suggested employing Kracauer at the Library as an assistant to the curator, with a nominal annual salary of one dollar, to pursue his own research project. This could serve as a springboard to other positions. Krautheimer recommended that his friend in Paris not be guided by a mistaken sense of pride in responding to such suggestions. Feelings and business had not to be confused. What he meant, firstly, was that Kracauer should definitely accept the help offered by Horkheimer and, secondly, that he should be mindful of his position as a jobseeker and hence supplicant. In Krautheimer's view, there was a clear advantage to the fact that the business aspect was all that mattered. For the Museum of Modern Art, Kracauer was no emigrant and the project was not a charitable act. Kracauer was needed for a project on German film.[15]

In spring 1938, Friedrich Pollock visited the French capital, and on 12 April he met with Kracauer. Kracauer had prepared himself for this conversation and, in a sign of how seriously he was taking the meeting, he had written a memorandum. The work on propaganda was one of the topics he wanted to talk about, the possibilities at the Institute another. But the most important point his notes emphasized was: 'We want to go to America' – with or without an assignment. The most important question to ask Pollock was, therefore, whether the Institute could help him obtain an immigration visa. The question specifically concerned the issuing of an affidavit, which was obligatory for immigration purposes.[16] Pollock probably reiterated what he himself and also Horkheimer had told Kracauer several times before: namely that, at the moment, they had no opportunities for him, but that if he were in dire need he could approach the Institute, even though only minor assistance could be offered.[17] Still, the conversation had a very important consequence: Kracauer and Löwenthal got in touch with each other again. It would later be Löwenthal who, together with Schapiro, would take care of the problem of affidavits and the costs of the Atlantic crossing.

Before all that, however, the Museum of Modern Art came to Paris. Between May and July 1938, it presented an exhibition on 'Trois Siècles d'Art aux États-Unis' at the Jeu de Paume in the Tuileries. Kracauer wrote an article on the exhibition for the *Neue Zürcher Zeitung* and two long reports for the Swiss journal *Das Werk*. His comments on the exhibited Americana expressed nothing but admiration and longing. They were a paean to American architecture and film. Precision, space, movement – these he identified as the basic impulses and particular skills of the Americans. America, he thought, was a country where immigrant artist builders like Walter Gropius had been able to find their feet immediately. America was, in fact, a land of film, because its history was one of movement, and film was movement and the reproduction of movement. At the exhibition, Kracauer watched Chaplin's *The Immigrant* (1917) and saw Chaplin's own arrival in New York. His 'gags and tricks' were 'the fairy-tale weapons of the weak against bad compulsion'. Kracauer praised the pioneering work of the film libraries, Henri Langlois's Cinémathèque in Paris and John E. Abbott and Iris Barry's Film Library in New York, saying:

While the Americans were forced to engage with a rich cultural heritage in all areas of the arts, in the area of film they are the conquistadores. Free of all the ballast of the theatre tradition in Europe, they have colonized this *terra nova* with a magnificent freedom that today guarantees them an outstanding position. All the more fascinating is the film section [of the exhibition], organized by the Film Library of the Museum of Modern Art.

If we trust Kracauer's Orphic song, the future of the arts lay across the Atlantic. His certainly did. Had not the director of the Museum of Modern Art himself said that the fate of American art was to be inspired by Europe without being disloyal to its native motives?[18]

Iris Barry and Kracauer met at least twice at the exhibition. Kracauer concluded from their conversations that there was no chance of a paid research assignment at present. But their exchanges were stimulating and valuable for him, because he now realized that 'the significance of the Film Library ... cannot be overestimated'. It was the 'only place in possession of all the material I need for my aesthetic and sociological investigation'. Kracauer also sensed that Barry and the director of the museum, Alfred Barr, were genuinely interested in him.[19] It seemed worthwhile, therefore, to continue pursuing the plans to move to the US. In the summer of 1938, another American who might have been able to assist him in his passage to the US also came to Paris: Henry McIlhenny, from Philadelphia. Schapiro had found him. McIlhenny was, it was said, an extraordinarily rich young man, naïve in all matters social and economic, head over heels in love with the arts, and with a soft spot for all creative people, whatever their political convictions. He came to Paris in order to prepare an exhibition on the Second Empire.[20] Kracauer had been looking forward to their meeting 'with the greatest expectations'. He would consider it an 'act of providence', he said, should the Second Empire of Jacques Offenbach turn out to be what would get him to America: that would be 'the turning point in my existence'.[21] McIlhenny was indeed prepared to let Kracauer take charge of the documentation and the catalogue if his project for an exhibition were approved by the director of the Philadelphia Museum, Fiske Kimball. When Kracauer met Kimball two weeks later, all his dreams of Orpheus in America ended at a stroke: 'The conversation with him lasted twenty minutes; it was not really a conversation but consisted of a series of notifications.'[22]

And further difficulties kept piling up. Since 1921, immigration into the US had been regulated by a quota system, under figures set out in the National Origins Law of 1924. In total, 164,667 foreigners were allowed to settle in the US every year. In 1929, the figure was adjusted downwards, slightly, to 153,879. Of that figure, 51,227 places were allocated to Germany; after the economic crisis that number was reduced to 25,957.[23] Following the *Anschluß* in 1938, the American immigration office had subsumed applications from Austria under the quota for Germany, which was already not enough to meet existing demand. Thus, the Kracauers were now competing with Jewish refugees from Austria for a visa. Kracauer calculated that this would mean half a year's wait before an application was even considered. 'The access routes to America become more and more clogged up for people in my category.' In September, the Kracauers were informed that the German quota had been exhausted, meaning that they would not be granted the right to immigrate before the end of 1939.[24] In spite of all this, McIlhenny still expressed his optimism – and then he fell silent.

Meanwhile, in New York, Schapiro was tirelessly advocating on Kracauer's behalf; and now he was seconded by Löwenthal, and advised by Adorno in the background.[25] If a full immigration visa were not on the cards, they thought perhaps a visitor's or professional visa, including the necessary guarantees, should be sought. To this end, Schapiro organized a teaching assignment for Kracauer at the Young Men's Hebrew Association (YMHA), where he was to teach a seminar on 'Problems of Modern Culture'. The event was intended to be in an informal setting so that Kracauer's speech defect would prove no obstacle for him. As the YMHA could only pay $400 for such an adult education event, Löwenthal said he was willing to contribute $600 so that the payment would be large enough to justify a visa. Like Franz L. Neumann, he was also happy to provide an affidavit for Kracauer.[26]

The difficulty with this new initiative was that the Kracauers had registered for regular immigration at the beginning of October, shortly before the suggestion for the YMHA assignment had reached them. In order to get a visitor's visa, they would need to ask for their names to be taken off the list of applicants for regular immigration. Kracauer supposed that once a visitor's visa expired, its holder would have to leave the country immediately, with no extensions or appeals. The Kracauers decided to stick with the normal immigration process. That process now had to be pushed as hard as possible: with a further affidavit, from someone with money, with a recommendation from some governmental body or ministry in Washington, with an intervention from an important US citizen at the American consulate in Paris, and, crucially, by getting the film project at the Museum of Modern Art off the ground. Perhaps that would even be enough to get hold of a non-quota visa. To Schapiro in New York he wrote: 'It would be wrong to gain the momentary advantage of a journey to America at the cost of forsaking immigration.' When he put this thought to Schapiro, he at least had some good news for Kracauer: McIlhenny was going to give a substantial sum to the Film Library for Kracauer's project. That would make it easier to receive still further funds.[27]

In fact, at the beginning of January 1939 Abbott had $1,400 for the project, and at the end of the month $2,200. He announced to Kracauer that he would send him an official invitation; Kracauer was relieved 'to feel firm ground under my feet for the first time in six years'.[28] But Abbott did not succeed in getting a non-quota visa for Kracauer. Then, in March 1939, Adorno believed he had 'finally ... found a way' to cut the Gordian knot and 'truly to rectify your [i.e. Kracauer's] situation', something that was, no doubt, very important to Adorno too. He hoped to be able to find a position for Kracauer in the form of a large research project on film funded by the Rockefeller Foundation, which also financed Lazarsfeld's Radio Research Project in Princeton, where Adorno was employed as a director of the section on music. Kracauer offered his services to Lazarsfeld but he still wanted to continue to prioritize the Film Library path.[29] He was guided by his temperament: no knee-jerk reactions, but also no hopeless scepticism – a controlled realism. And this paid off: Lazarsfeld put him off until the summer, but then the discussions about the movie project would begin.[30] Kracauer was in the waiting room again. On 19 June, he received an official offer from Abbott for a two-year post as 'special research assistant' at the Film Library of the Museum of Modern Art, with an annual salary of $2,500. His task would be to write a book on the history of German film.[31] But a 'paper wall', as David S. Wyman calls it, stood between Kracauer and this opportunity. Kracauer felt like 'Tantalus – rescue within reach, but doomed to perish'. The summer passed. Hedwig and Rosette Kracauer were unable to emigrate to Paris, and Siegfried and Elisabeth Kracauer did not book their passage to New York. In August 1939, Meyer Schapiro was in Paris, and Kracauer had the opportunity to meet his new friend and selfless supporter in person. War broke out. Schapiro had to drop everything and leave. With him, Kracauer's hopes went too: 'The world today is like the one in Kafka's novels' – a 'horrible trial that happens to us.'[32]

26

Fleeing from France, a Last Minute Exit from Lisbon

On 3 September 1939, France and Great Britain declared war on Nazi Germany, after Germany had invaded Poland. Across France there was talk of 'the spectre of the fifth column'. All German citizens in the country were declared 'enemy aliens', and all men aged between seventeen and forty-eight were asked to attend transit camps, bringing a woollen blanket, the most essential personal items and some provisions.[1] The Daladier government had already been interning foreigners who had broken any of the many laws and regulations that applied to them or were suspected of posing a threat to the country's security. With Franco beginning to gain the upper hand in the civil war in Spain, the majority of them were Spanish refugees from Spain from the Republican side. Via the 'Route Lister', a great many socialists, communists and anarchists who had joined the International Brigade came across the Pyrenees into France. The route was named after General Enrique Lister, of Spain, and was later, following the truce between Germany and France in the summer of 1940, used again, this time in the other direction, at which time it was known as the F-Route.[2] The brigadiers had once been the pride of the European left. They were the militant international avant-garde, but now they joined the 'scum of the earth', to use Arthur Koestler's pointed phrase for those without rights who had been cut off by the European nations, especially Nazi Germany, and were now awaiting their fate in French camps in the most run-down and derelict of barracks, such as the infamous Le Vernet in the French Pyrenees.[3]

Only a few days after the war with Germany had begun, France increased the age limit for internment to 55 years, meaning that around 23,000 men, and a couple of hundred women, from Germany and Austria, among them Hannah Arendt, were locked up. Kracauer was fifty years old. He was first brought to the Camp Maison Lafitte, Département Seine-et-Oise, not far from Paris, on 17 September 1939. Elisabeth Kracauer meanwhile moved into the small town of Gif-sur-Yvette, thirty kilometres to the south-west of Paris, where she stayed with a French family, the Gagets. On 11 October, Kracauer was moved on to the transit camp in Athis sur Orne in the Basse-Normandie region. These two camps could not be compared to Le Vernet, which was a *camp répressif* for *personnes indésirables*.[4] Kracauer was seen as harmless. After the declaration of war, he had immediately offered the French foreign ministry his services.[5] Benjamin, by comparison, had to report to the Stade de Colombes as early as 15 September; the commander in charge there 'would have cut a very good figure even in a German concentration camp'.[6] After a few days under the brutal conditions of the camp, Benjamin was moved to a camp in Clos St. Joseph, Château de Vernuche, Nevers (Burgundy). Although there could be no question of people being there voluntarily, it was a transit rather than a concentration camp. Only a short time later, the brutal commander of the Stade de Colombes was sentenced by a military tribunal and demoted.[7]

Daily life in the camp usually passed without any egregious repression or chicanery. No one was beaten; not even insults were dealt out. No one was struck with the butt of a rifle, and there were no lashes of the whip, as there had been at Colombes. But it was a dreary, monotonous and boring life. Brooding, making plans, passing on gossip, learning English, smoking, cleaning the barracks, slicing bread, handing out soup – with these activities the days passed so slowly that time seemed to stand still.[8] Although the captives were treated properly and with respect, there was nevertheless great fear among them – not of the guards, but of the Germans whose advance seemed to be unstoppable. Soma Morgenstern remembered the atmosphere in the camp as follows: 'Will we get out of there in time? Or will they group, sort, and inspect us … until the Germans arrive and massacre us? We all agreed that this is what the Germans would do.'[9] A colleague of Kracauer's later spoke about 'very bad vascular spasms, a nervous heart, etc.' After his release, he was confined to his bed for a very long time.[10] Despite being treated with respect, internment left its mark on almost everyone. Still, Kracauer got to know many people with whom he would still be in friendly contact many years later, for instance 'le bon père' Kahn, the father of the musician Erich Itor Kahn, whom he would later befriend in Marseille, or Herbert Levin and Egidius Streiff, both of whom also made it to America. Finally, there was a cousin of the Krautheimers there by the name of Caspari. The highlights of the day were letters and postcards to and from Lili. Kracauer wrote at least twice, sometimes three times a day. Elisabeth Kracauer was his gateway to the world. She investigated ways in which he might be able to leave the camp, examined, as far as possible, whatever truth there was to the numerous rumours her husband had heard, went from pillar to post in Paris visiting everyone her husband thought could help. A whole army of influential people was recruited to secure his release, which finally took place on 13 November. Five testimonials confirming Kracauer's exceptional intellectual capacity, moral integrity and his loyalty to France were instrumental in bringing it about. His wife had selected the declarations astutely, opting for a mixture of different voices rather than simply picking those from the most prominent individuals. Those chosen were Henri Hoppenot, a diplomat at the foreign office; the writer Daniel Halévy, who had written the preface for the *Offenbach* book and now also supported the Kracauers financially; Adrienne Monnier, the bright light of the Parisian world of books; A. P. von Seggern and A. P. J. Kroonenburg, both Paris representatives of the Amsterdam publishers Allert de Lange; and finally Lucien Gaget, Elisabeth Kracauer's landlord, a man without public credentials, but with his heart in the right place. Hoppenot and Monnier also vouched for Walter Benjamin, who was released on 16 November and returned to Paris.

After his release, Kracauer moved in with Elisabeth in Gif at the Gagets. He had to report once a week to the mayor's office, and even was granted a travel permit for Paris, which he visited two or three days each week. Kracauer's work on his film book continued unabated.[11] Meanwhile, further affidavits had arrived from Löwenthal and Neumann in New York, the old ones having expired in the meantime.[12] Early in 1940, all seemed to be proceeding as it should when, at the end of March, the American consulate informed Kracauer that his 'convocation' would not take place within the next few weeks, but only in August. The reason, he was told, was that, in the course of processing applications, the allocation of numbers from the quota had been held up by a delay in the distribution of slots for interviews – but perhaps a few obdurate bureaucrats' hands were involved in the delay too. In any case, the deportation of the undesired scum of the European intelligentsia from the old continent to the new was held up by some congestion in the allocation of numbers.[13]

This was a worrying development for Kracauer. The Wehrmacht had begun its Western offensive on 10 May 1940. On 5 June, it had reached the north of France; on 14 June, German troops marched into Paris. On 17 June, the newly appointed head of the French government, Philippe Pétain, faced a hopeless situation and was forced to ask for a truce. On 22 June, the truce of Compiègne was signed, dividing France into an occupied and an unoccupied part, the latter governed from Vichy. The agreement amounted to a capitulation. The new authoritarian Vichy state, led by Marshall Pétain, had been stunned by the so-called 'sickle cut' plan of General von Manstein, which had led to France's rapid defeat, and it now followed German orders. Instead of 'liberty, equality, fraternity', the new tune was 'work, family, fatherland'. About

15,000 immigrants who had been naturalized between 1927 and 1939 had their French citizenship revoked, among them more than 6,000 Jews. The situation also became tense for long-established Jews, who had previously been categorized as French nationals of Jewish or Mosaic faith. Numerous anti-Jewish measures were introduced, among them, on 3 October 1940, the 'Jewish statute', which marked them out as Jews.[14]

As a rule, the refugees from Germany tried to get to the unoccupied Vichy part of France. Fleeing was now the most important strategy for survival. Whoever was unable to flee was trapped.[15] But even in the unoccupied part of France, refugees feared they might be extradited to the actual sovereign, Germany. Article 19.2 of the Compiègne agreement, indeed, stipulated that such extraditions had to be carried out upon request, and in July and August 1940 the Kundt Commission inspected the camps in the unoccupied south of France, where in mid-August 11,000 to 12,000 emigrants were still, or again, detained. The commission drew up a register of the German detainees, and also noted which of them were Jewish (about 5,000). Until 1942, however, the feared extraditions took place only sporadically. There are twenty-one documented cases, all of them requests on political grounds, among them the case of the elderly grand seigneurs of social democracy Rudolf Hilferding and Rudolf Breitscheidt, who were subsequently murdered in Gestapo custody and in the Buchenwald concentration camp, respectively. The fear of extradition was omnipresent.[16]

Following the new intervention by Hoppenot, Benjamin and Kracauer did not need to fear another internment. In mid-June, Benjamin left Paris for the south. One week before the German troops marched into the French capital, the Kracauers received their immigration visa for the US from the consulate in Paris, but they still had to wait for their quota number and for the money for the journey across the Atlantic, which was to be provided by the Hebrew Sheltering and Immigrant Aid Society (HIAS).[17] On 11 June, three days before German troops arrived, they left the Paris area 'with a few pieces of hand luggage, which contained only absolute necessities'.[18] They went directly to Marseille, where Benjamin also arrived in mid-August after a stopover in Lourdes. The 'Kracauer' dossier from the consulate, however, needed more time for the 661-kilometre journey, and only arrived at the end of August – as if someone had transported it from Paris to Marseille by foot. With the exception of 1938 and 1939, the German immigration quota was not fully used up during these years. Between mid-1940 and mid-1941, not even half of the quota was filled. But the reason for this had to do with the authorities; there were certainly always more than enough refugees seeking to leave. At the end of 1941, there were still 600,000 applicants, among them 300,000 from Germany, on consulate waiting lists. In the eyes of Samuel Miller Breckinridge Long, Assistant Secretary of State in the foreign office, these applicants were mostly Jews, communists and gays.[19]

In June 1940, many refugees actually set off by foot for Marseille. 'All France was on the move', Lion Feuchtwanger recalls. 'All France was in flight, and in all directions, madly, at random. All railway lines and all highways in southern France were crowded with fugitives, Hollanders, Belgians, millions of French from the North.'[20] Most German refugees wanted to get to Marseille and then to leave France, 'numbed, blinded, starving, deadly tired and prepared to die on the flight from the German death, which rolled on toward the South behind us, next to us'.[21] Some of those interned escaped and, like Alfred Kantorowicz, tried to get to Marseille on their own. Kantorowicz had previously been transported in a 'ghost train', which aimlessly circulated from the Les Milles camp towards the west and then back again to the camp. Throughout that journey, the passengers had to stand. Lion Feuchtwanger also found himself on this train. It serves as a fitting allegory for the general confusion, chaos and panic – the *pagaye*, as the French called it. In Kantorowicz's words: 'You never knew what would come next'. Feuchtwanger spoke of the 'Devil in France'. The term was not intended to refer to any maliciousness, or sadism, or intentional roguery: no, '[t]he Devil in France was a friendly, polite Devil. The devilishness in his character showed itself solely in his genteel indifference to the sufferings of others, in his *je-m'en-foutisme*, in his inefficiency, his bureaucratic sloth.'[22]

In the summer of 1940, tens of thousands of refugees gathered in Marseille, French as well as foreigners among them. In Hans Sahl's poems on Marseille, the city was a waiting room, full of fear, where refugees were terrified by denunciations, identity checks in the early hours, searches. For Walter Mehring, Marseille was a place of doom, a realm of shadows, limbo.[23] In the old harbour, there was a flourishing trade with passports, identity cards and other papers. The passport really was now 'the noblest part of a human being', as Brecht puts it in his *Refugee Conversations*.[24] The self-appointed consuls of small Latin American states felt like kings. People's existence circled around the papers that were needed for immigration, emigration, leave to remain, travel within France, transit and proof of identity. The whole point of life in Marseille was to acquire all these papers. Even then, though, escape from hell was not guaranteed. 'Yesterday, I spoke to a young man', Kantorowicz tells us: 'He had everything. But when he wanted to board the ship, the port authorities denied him the final stamp. Thus, everything had been in vain for him.'[25] For many, Marseille was a trap.

High above Marseille, south of the Vieux Port, the basilica of Notre Dame de la Garde rises into the sky. 'La Bonne Mère', as it is called in the vernacular, guards the inhabitants of the city and all the fishermen and seamen. The symbol of the city, visible from afar, appears as a fortress, holding out against the slings and arrows of life. From up there, an impressive view opens onto Marseille, especially the old harbour and the Canebière, where in those days one would have seen refugees stepping on each other's toes, refugees who could not hope for natural or supernatural protection. Up there, Anna Seghers must have sat while working on her impressive novel *Transit*. From personal experience, she was familiar with the places frequented by the refugees: the waiting rooms at the consulates, the visa section of the prefecture, the cafés at the harbour, where some would nurse a single cup of coffee for a day. The nature of being in transit was a 'visa dance', 'consulate hocus-pocus'.[26] Visa, transit, Visa de Sortie: that was the holy trinity, provided one had a residence permit for Marseille. Seghers knew the stories about 'phantom ships' that would rescue refugees, stories that were about as probable as the Marian apparition in Lourdes.[27] The sea, however, that began at the end of the Canebière was real. For the refugees, it was the 'edge of the world'.[28] And yet it was groundless. Hardly anyone managed to leave Marseille by boat; the ships departed without the refugees. And if someone did succeed in getting hold of a ticket, the ship probably sank somewhere 'between Dakar and Martinique' – although that may 'just be a rumour'.[29] Or the passengers' papers expired shortly before the ship's arrival in Cuba, and the vessel, with its human cargo, had to return to Europe. Seghers also met those who never left, the 'newspaper boys, the fishermen's wives on the Belsunce, the shopkeepers opening their stores, the workers going to work the early shift'. Those were the majority. They stayed even after '[w]ars, conflagrations, and the fury of the powerful had passed over them'. They did the 'really important things' in the city.[30] The refugees also longed for an ordinary, settled life with three meals a day and one's own four walls, but they were not part of that majority. And above all, the refugees were fed up with 'the wailing of the fleeing hordes' of other refugees.[31]

Arthur Koestler referred to the three phases of the flight in France as 'agony', 'purgatory' and 'apocalypse'.[32] Agony referred to the time before the outbreak of war: the fear of the war, which everyone knew would be a catastrophe, as well as a fear that there would be no war, and thus everything would continue in the same horrible way in and around Germany. Purgatory referred to the internment camps. Following the occupation of France by Nazi Germany, the frantic flight, the hunger, the threats to life, finally, there came the apocalypse. War, flight and, from March 1942, deportation to 'the East': in Marseille, in the summer of 1940, refugees waited to see whether there was any way to escape this inferno, or whether the city at the end of Europe would be their final destination.

One of Anna Segher's refugee characters in *Transit* says to another:

> You know the fairy tale about the man who died, don't you? He was waiting in Eternity to find out what the Lord had decided to do with him. He waited and waited, for one year, ten years, a hundred years. He begged and pleaded for a decision. Finally he couldn't bear the waiting any longer. Then they said to him: 'What do you think you're waiting for? You've been in Hell for a long time already.'[33]

We are back with Kafka's story of the countryman trying in vain to gain access to the law. And K.? Well, the Kracauers, too, were waiting in the hell of the beautiful Mediterranean city at the feet of the Calanques, where once Ginster had found life *in the poor harbour district – almost* [a] *home*,[34] where once they had gone for their honeymoon, and where ten years ago Kracauer had walked amidst the crowd and had captured the times in his descriptions of waste and weather-beaten ornaments, the old harbour and the clogged fairground on the Canebière. 'Marseille is small. Marseille is large. A provincial town. The world.' It was only a few steps from magic to curse. 'Notre-Dame greets you from the top, and the city glows, untouched by the misery. Maybe the misery adds to its glow. It certainly veils the rags in glamour.'[35] Now, in 1940, there was no glamour left, and the misery had increased.

In the summer of 1940, fruit and vegetables were rare. Segher's characters struggle to find an onion. The Kracauers went hungry. Elisabeth lost so much weight that it took her years to fully recover. And amid all this, despite all the deprivation and nervous tension, Siegfried continued, extraordinarily, to write his exposé on film.[36] Equally extraordinary, at first sight, is the fact that the 'Marseille outline' of November 1940 puts forward more a 'film aesthetics' than a sociology of film. Kracauer thus must have taken a fundamental decision about the direction the study was going to take.[37] Had his groundless refugee existence further widened the gap between his current position and his Weimar phase of ideology critique and social criticism of film? It is a mistake, in fact, to contrast the aesthetic and the sociological approach in this way. It is more likely that Kracauer's decision was taken at the strategic level, at the level of the writing. His perspective on film was not to be a view from above or from outside of film, but an immanent perspective. That fitted well with Adorno's and Benjamin's views of aesthetics. As Miriam Hansen writes, Kracauer pitched his Marseille outline 'on a level "below", not above, the social and political dimension'.[38] The sociology was contained within the aesthetics, and the experiences in Marseille found their way into the outline. Kracauer wanted to present film as an art form that is capable of representing the 'material-dynamic world', a medium that 'addresses its viewer as a "corporeal-material being"' and 'seizes the "human being with skin and hair"'.[39] Looking at the Canebière, he recorded 'the street as marking the complex basic layer' of film: intentionless, moving, unconscious, superficial, fleeting, familiar and ordinary. But he also saw 'phenomena that demolish consciousness: material sensations and shocks, vertiginous angles and motion; horror, torture, executions, catastrophes'.[40] The transient material world – here, at the southern edge of Europe, it was right in front of his eyes: a landscape of ruins, of uncanny existence. The old harbour was an arena of modern, permanently threatened and transient life.[41] Were these not impressions of Marseille gathered by someone who was stranded and hoped to be saved, who hoped for a happy ending? Was it not this 'flow of life', within the realm of contingency (and death), that was meant to provide the material foundation of film in the context of an aesthetics that was saturated with social experience?[42] 'The face counts for nothing in film unless it includes the death's-head beneath. "Danse macabre. To which end? That remains to be seen."'[43]

The 'go-for-broke' game of history came to a head. On 15 August, an American arrived in Marseille, like an angel from heaven. After just a week, word got around that he had his pockets lined with money and passports and was able to get any visa in an instant with the help of the State Department. The man's name was Varian Fry. He had, however, neither been sent by the Mother of God nor the American government, but by the Emergency Rescue Committee (ERC), which was based in New York, a private aid organization that had been founded three days after the Germany–France truce. Among the private donors was, incidentally, Alfred Barr, the director of the Museum of Modern Art.[44] Fry was nevertheless a 'guardian angel'. The ERC, under the cloak of humanitarian aid, provided illegal aid to those wanting to escape. Fry and his helpers forged passports, identified escape routes and cooperated with smugglers.[45] The American institutions in France were at times opponents, at times partners. Eleanor Roosevelt, the American first lady, was actively involved in refugee aid, and the President himself instructed the State Department to deal with the refugee problem in a humanitarian fashion. But the assistant state secretary Breckinridge Long torpedoed these initiatives wherever possible. And there were conflicting tendencies inside the American institutions in France as well. In Marseille, for instance, Vice Consul Hiram Bingham even helped Fry and his people in getting Feuchtwanger out of the internment camp, while the American embassy in Vichy, as the higher authority, pursued a restrictive policy regarding visas and finally removed Bingham from office.[46] The reactions of the French authorities to Fry's activities also differed widely. Some looked the other way or took their time before doing anything, allowing refugees time to evade them. Sometimes they made some random arrests first, before looking for illegal refugees. But often they did neither.[47] The ERC was not interested in helping all refugees indiscriminately; it was there for the political and intellectual refugees. According to Fry, within the first eight months, some 15,000 people had turned to him. In 1,800 cases, he and his collaborators became active: 'Of these 1,800 cases, representing, in all, some 4,000 human beings, we had paid weekly living allowances to 560 and had sent more than 1,000 out of France. For the rest we had made every kind of effort, from getting them liberated from concentration camps to finding them a dentist.'[48] Among these 1,800 cases were, upon the suggestion of Meyer Schapiro, Walter Benjamin and Siegfried Kracauer.[49]

Between mid-August and mid-September 1940 – their Marseille days – Benjamin and Kracauer met almost daily. They may have got closer to each other again – the 'Marseille outline' certainly suggests as much. Elisabeth Kracauer clearly seems to have been able to get through to Benjamin. Kracauer wrote after the war: 'He believed his world had been destroyed and a fearful panic suffocated all hope in him; only Lili, to whom he was very attached, was still able to offer him some support.'[50] During the second half of September, Benjamin left Marseille for Banyuls sur Mer, with an immigration visa for the US and a transit visa for Spain and Portugal in his pocket, but without a *Visa de Sortie*, an exit visa. On 26 September, he crossed the green border to Spain via the Lister route. He was part of a small group led by Lisa Fittko, who was working with Varian Fry. In Portbou, the group was told that they would be returned to France. Benjamin, whose life had long since disintegrated, took an overdose of morphine tablets, which he carried with him for emergency situations. He fell unconscious before passing away. Before taking the tablets, he had arranged for a short note to be sent to Adorno, in which he explained his decision: 'In a situation with no way out, I have no choice but to end it. My life will finish in a little village in the Pyrenees where no one knows me.'[51] Shortly after Benjamin, the Kracauers also tried to cross the border to Spain, though presumably not illegally, by train, on the route from Narbonne to Portbou, which leads through the aptly named border station Cerbère. During those weeks, it was never clear what the Spanish would do. Sometimes the border was open; at other times it was closed. Since April 1938, the Kracauers had been in possession of a *certificat d'identité et de voyage* and affidavits in lieu of passports, as well as the necessary transit visa, but no exit visa. They tried their luck, but their attempt to leave was unsuccessful. They were sent back, 'and landed in Perpignan, where we learned that he [Benjamin] had also been refused entry, and thereupon had taken his own life. In Perpignan, we were close to doing the same; at least I was.'[52]

The French asylum policy shifted in November 1940. Until then, exit permits had not been granted; now, large numbers of undesired foreigners were to be given permission to leave the country, except for those who were on a blacklist of which nothing but its existence was known. The Kracauers had to act swiftly. They renewed their transit visa for Spain and Portugal. For this, they had to present a booking for the onward journey by ship. Löwenthal had organized part of the money for the crossing and transferred it to the HIAS. They were still $325 short, but the down payment sufficed to make the booking and Kracauer was able to apply for the transit visa for Portugal. He was still waiting for the transit visa for Spain. He was increasingly anxious: his immigration visa for the US had expired on 20 December, and Elisabeth's on 6 December. And despite the new 'freedom of movement', she had not yet been granted an exit visa for France.[53] The Kracauers were again confronting the possibility of losing everything: 'We are facing oppressive difficulties, and every day brings a new one', he wrote in French to his friends; 'every day I come to resemble this K. in Kafka's *Trial* more and am seriously surprised that I keep myself going.'[54] In this winter of 1940/41 in Marseille, K. and his wife did not have enough to eat and were bitterly cold.[55]

But then their rescue was suddenly at hand. By the end of December, with the help of the friends from New York, a third affidavit had been organized, the visa renewed, and the crossing from Lisbon secured. At the end of January, the Kracauers were informed that they would receive the visa for leaving France. For the first time since its arrival in Marseille, the ERC could send refugees to the Spanish border knowing they would be able to leave France legally. And yet, in the end, only 6,500 people left France legally in the period between the introduction of the new asylum policies in November 1940 and November 1942: little more than a tenth of all refugees from Europe to cross the border via the Pyrenees during the war.[56]

On 5 February, a new visa for the US and a transit visa for Portugal arrived, followed by the transit permission for Spain, on 15 February, and the *Visa de Sortie* on 20 February.[57] On 24 February, the Kracauers left Marseille. On 26 February, they crossed the border near Pau; via Zaragoza, Madrid and Alcántara, they reached Portugal two days later on 28 February. On 3/4 March, they arrived safely in Lisbon. But now they learned, from HICEM,[58] the central committee for the support of Jewish emigrants, that such were the numbers of refugees arriving that they would have to wait for months for a ticket across the Atlantic, even though they had already paid for their tickets. It took very strong intervention, in very urgent cases, to get around this latest obstacle, Kracauer wrote to his friend Löwenthal. Now, Löwenthal, Adorno and Schapiro took the initiative again. The Kracauers were finally allocated places on the *Nyassa*. On 15 April, the overcrowded ship set sail from Lisbon harbour.[59]

It was a rescue almost at the last minute. Those German emigrants who did not succeed in leaving France before the summer of 1941 were trapped in the country. After 20 May 1941, Jews were no longer allowed to exit France. In March 1942, the deportations began, and they lasted until autumn 1944. From November 1942 onwards, the Germans occupied all of France. Some 85,000 Jews were sent to the extermination camps in the east.[60]

Unlike Kafka's K., Kracauer survived. But what was next? While still in Lisbon, he had written to Adorno (and in a similar vein to Löwenthal): 'It is bad to arrive as we shall be doing – after eight years of an existence which isn't worthy of the name. I have grown older – in myself, too.' And: 'I could achieve so much, especially now, and yet I arrive bare of all prerequisites for the first start'. He knew very well that this 'is the last station, the last opportunity, which I must not squander, or else it is all over. And this last opportunity I can only seize, if I get a first opportunity immediately upon arriving in New York.'[61]

27

Arrival in New York

On 25 April 1941, the *Nyassa* docked in Brooklyn Harbour. There were 816 men, women and children on board the liner, well above its legal capacity of 457 passengers. Newspapers in New York reported that refugees had paid between $40 and $250 extra to middlemen for a ticket on the fully booked vessel. The thirty-five-year-old Gisela Peiper described the crossings as follows:

> More people had to be carried by the ships than planned as time seemed to be running out. The compartments which normally held luggage were now also filled with passengers. The ships moved slowly; they had to circumnavigate minefields and follow the black-out regulations that were in force for the nights. The journey from Lisbon to New York took fourteen days. ... The adults were mostly silent during the journey. There were too many memories, and no one knew what the future would hold.[1]

The *New York Herald Tribune* reported that one of the passengers on board was Siegfried Kracauer, 'the author of *Orpheus in Paris*'.[2]

Millions of immigrants had arrived at New York's harbour before Kracauer, had sailed past the Statue of Liberty and Ellis Island, where Chaplin's 'immigrant' is subjected to questioning and examination. Almost every other American today has ancestors who came to the country on this route. The hearts of the passengers on the *Nyassa*, looking at the skyline of the metropolis behind which, it must have seemed to them, urban canyons, stone deserts and masses of people lurked, were probably beating fast, out of excitement, joy – but also fear for the future. They knew America from stories and pictures. They had rescued themselves from a Europe in flames, where the Nazi beast was ravaging the continent. Here, monsters were a threat only on screen, only in the nightmare of civilization – King Kong clasping the Empire State Building as his throne.

For Kracauer, the first encounter with life in America was unforgettable. He felt as if he were in a film:

As we entered New York harbour, the strange feeling of having already seen all this began to grow upon me. Each new sight was an act of recognition. We passed such old acquaintances as the Statue of Liberty, Ellis Island and the sky-line, which, however, in the vast sky looked smaller than I had imagined it from the pictures. Then the detective-inspectors came aboard, shouting 'Take it easy!' and 'Go ahead!,' and afterwards the dock swarmed with reporters. To the passionate movie-goer it was like a dream: either he had been suddenly transplanted onto the screen or the screen itself had come into three-dimensional existence.[3]

Back in the real world, New York Harbour saw not only the arrival of ships with refugees, but also the departure of ships carrying military equipment. Since February 1941, the US had been sending weapons, ammunition, vehicles, aeroplanes, fuel and food to England. Officially neutral, the US used the Land-Lease Act to support states which fought against the Axis powers. Franklin D. Roosevelt had declared the US the 'arsenal of democracy' in a radio broadcast on 29 December 1940. The harbour was thus a transit point for both people and goods marked by the sign of the war in

Figure 30. The monster on screen. Still from *King Kong* (1933)
Copyright: SZ Photo/Süddeutsche Zeitung Photo

Europe. It did not take long before the US was at war with Nazi
Germany, and the war became a world war.

On the eve of the US entering the war, 7.5 million people lived in
New York. It was the city of immigrants *par excellence*. There were
the Irish and Italians, the Chinese and Puerto Ricans, and above all
'the wandering people', as Joseph Roth called the Jews. In quantitative terms, New York in 1940 was the capital of the Jews, who
were now more than ever – and, as Kracauer wrote, 'in an extreme
fashion' – distributed across the whole world.[4] About 30 per cent of
New Yorkers were Jewish, roughly 2.25 million people: four times
as many as lived in Palestine or Warsaw, the European city with the
largest Jewish population. Following the massive wave of Jewish
immigration between 1880 and 1920, when more than two million
Jewish refugees came to the country via Ellis Island, the Lower East
Side to the southwest of Manhattan had become a Jewish quarter.[5]
New York was an attractive safe haven. Once they had overcome the
bureaucratic hurdles and climbed the 'paper wall', the Jews coming
to the US did not have to fear the arrogance of the natives, especially
not the arrogance of the 'western Jews' that the eastern Jews met
when they came to Berlin or Vienna. The western Jews, as Joseph
Roth wrote, 'by virtue of the fact that they grew up with elevators
and flush toilets', allowed themselves 'to make bad jokes about
Romanian lice, Galician cockroaches, or Russian fleas', associating
them with the Jews from the east.[6] Rather, the immigrants often
found that, although life and the struggle for existence in the new
world were hard, Americans were 'warm and generous', 'interested
and open-minded', 'naïve, fresh, and eager to gain knowledge'. This
was not affected by the widespread anti-Semitism to be found also
in this country. And there was always some friend or relative from
the old days to be found somewhere in America.[7]

From the 1930s onwards, most Jewish New Yorkers lived in
Brooklyn, where the *Nyassa* had arrived. On the quay, Leo and
Golde Löwenthal were waiting for the Kracauers. They found the
new arrivals accommodation in the American Jewish Congress
House, between Broadway and Central Park. At the southern
end of Central Park was the Museum of Modern Art. Sauntering
through the streets of Manhattan, Kracauer entered into the same
kind of daydream that had come upon him on the ship. Everywhere
he saw types he already knew: the ice-cream man, the shoe-shiner,
the Salvation Army man. Just like the feeling that had struck
him upon seeing the great Chaplin, when he arrived at Bahnhof
Friedrichstraße in Berlin, Kracauer now saw that '[a]ll the things
that had filled in the background of hundreds of American films
proved to be true to life'. 'The steps before the brownstone houses
were as real as the furnished rooms, the miraculous drug stores and
the splendid lobbies of the apartment houses one had suspected in

Europe as mere studio settings.'[8] All this was 'a convincing proof of the realistic power with which Hollywood pictures transmit everyday American life to people abroad'.[9] Of course, no sooner had Kracauer arrived than he went to the movies. The first article he wrote in New York was a review of Orson Welles's *Citizen Kane* (1940/41), the story of a New York press baron, whose dying word, 'rosebud', a reporter attempts to decipher and, in the course of his investigations, reconstructs the dynamic but unhappy life of the media mogul. In the end, the reporter's search for meaning is unavailing. Only the audience witnesses, in a final shot that pans across Kane's material legacy, the word 'ROSEBUD' on a children's sled, which is burned along with other old junk. Kracauer gave his text the title 'An American Experiment', but he does not explain in detail what it is that makes Welles's film American.[10] Did he think that there was here an American and cinematographic echo of the Kafkaesque futility of the search for meaning in an unapproachable world, and of the Benjaminian solution to the riddle, a solution to be found in the profane, overlooked scrap heap? Kracauer's text certainly had something American about it: its language. Kracauer had decided to become an American author. From the very beginning, he wrote strictly, and without initial German drafts, in English.[11]

With his arrival in New York, there was, for the first time in a long while, a certain sense of euphoria again. The Kracauers were enthusiastic about the city, especially about the 'indescribably beautiful views' from the skyscrapers, as they told Kracauer's mother and aunt, with whom they could now resume correspondence. They wrote about the forests and lakes at the edge of the city, which were visible from the skyscrapers. They gushed about the contrast between 'often shocking ugliness and often incomparable beauty'. To friends Kracauer wrote: 'These masses of stone do not give a plump appearance, but look as delicate as lace because they are divided by rows of small windows which look like myriads of glowing points of light at night.' When Kracauer walked around Manhattan, he fell back into his old 'street rapture'. The new arrivals were also taken in by the curiosity and open-mindedness of the people. They visited the Radio City Music Hall in the middle of Manhattan, opposite the Rockefeller Center. In the largest movie theatre anywhere in the world, films were shown on a gigantic screen; Kracauer managed to organize complimentary tickets: 'You know that we are city-dwellers.'[12]

The funds for the research project on film history organized in 1939, however, were no longer available. Kracauer had learned about this from Meyer Schapiro while still in Lisbon. He had also learned that there had been a misunderstanding over the money collected by Leo Löwenthal and Alfred Schütz for the crossing, and that the money Kracauer had imagined would be available for him to make a start in New York was not there. On the contrary, their mountain of debt had risen significantly as a result of their flight around France and to America.[13] It would take the Kracauers until the 1950s to pay it all back. But the friends and benefactors of Kracauer, who was now fifty-two, continued to work on finding him his big break in his new life. Iris Barry and Hans Speier put him in touch with John Marshall, the deputy director of the humanities section of the Rockefeller Foundation, which had made the biggest contribution to the founding of the Film Library in 1935.[14] The Rockefeller Foundation now quickly, and unbureaucratically, gave Kracauer a two-month grant for his research work at the Film Library.

Marshall was a key figure in academic policy setting, and it proved to be fortunate that Kracauer got to know him. Since the second half of the 1930s, the foundation had been supporting the new discipline or field of communication studies, which consisted of four already existing research areas: propaganda research, public opinion research, media psychology and market research. In 1939, Marshall had brought together a group of experts, the 'Communications Seminar', among them the social scientists Harold D. Lasswell, Paul Lazarsfeld and Hadley Cantril, and charged them with formulating scientific standards for the new discipline: 'who says what to whom, with what effect', as Lasswell's basic formula for research on mass communication had it.[15] Between 1936 and 1941, numerous research institutions were founded: Lazarsfeld's Radio Research Project, from which the Office of Radio Research at Columbia University and later the Bureau of Applied Social Research emerged; the journal *Public Opinion Quarterly*, led by Cantril; Lasswell's department for the 'Study of War Time Communications' at the Library of Congress; a research project on 'totalitarian communication', especially on German radio propaganda, at the New School for Social Research; and, last but not least, the Film Library at the Museum of Modern Art. Kracauer was to be engaged in some way with all these institutions and projects over the coming years. Lazarsfeld and Lasswell were pioneers of communication studies, and propaganda studies in particular. All these initiatives were not only academic but at the same time served a political purpose; they had Nazi propaganda and the threat of the war in mind. Barry and Lasswell, in particular, were power players operating within a thinly knitted network of academic institutions, foundations and government agencies.[16]

Thanks to the efforts of Barry, Speier and Marshall, Kracauer was offered a post as assistant to the curator of the Museum of Modern Art, with particular responsibility for the Film Library. He took up his post on 1 July 1941, immediately after his initial two-month grant had ended.[17] Kracauer's task was to research German film propaganda for a year, for which he would receive $2,000 from the Rockefeller Foundation. Since 1 April 1941, Speier – Kracauer's 'old friend from Berlin' – had been directing the research project on radio propaganda at the New School, together with the art historian and psychoanalyst Ernst Kris. Kracauer was looking forward to their collaboration and the 'lengthy detective work' of investigating the material.[18] He was also glad to have Speier's moral support. Having asked Kracauer for a copy of his manuscript on propaganda for the Institute for Social Research, Speier praised its analytical sharpness, which was recognizable, he said, despite its unfinished form.[19] From the very beginning, Schapiro, who was studiously overseeing the coordinated activities, made the newcomer feel needed: 'And now we are all waiting for your first works in English, for we are all convinced that you have so much to give us that no American can produce.' He also gave him the advice to write only in English.[20] The Kracauer, who once stuttered as he talked, probably already spoke a free-flowing English, conversing without inhibition or fear of making mistakes. At least we know that speaking on the telephone, he liked best. The freedom of New York seems to have chased away old fears.[21]

The early days in New York were also made easier by the fact that, over the summer months, the Kracauers could live for twenty dollars a month in the Speiers' apartment in Riverdale, in the Bronx, while they were travelling. 'You will hardly be able to imagine what it means for us – and especially for my wife – after years to be in a proper flat again. Since we left Berlin, where we had a nice flat, we have had to do without that. It is like the first sign of a normalized life.'[22] While they stayed provisionally in Riverdale, Lili Kracauer would search the various quarters, house by house, to find themselves their own place there. The couple wanted to live as centrally as possible, but their financial means were limited. At the end of August, Lili found an apartment: 56 West 75th Street, between Columbus Avenue and Central Park West. From there, her husband could walk to the museum. It was, as Kracauer wrote home to Frankfurt, one of the relatively rare 'Whitestone' houses, 'which have a bright and friendly appearance, similar to a great urban villa'. The room on the second floor of the 'villa', however, cannot have been bigger than five by six metres, with a kitchen in the corner, and even a fridge. There was an anteroom with a large built-in wardrobe and a door on to a 'modern bathroom'. Lili purchased household goods, mostly from the Salvation Army, and arranged the furniture. For the first time in many years, the Kracauers owned a writing desk again. They had something like 'solid ground under their feet'.[23]

The Kracauers' first acquaintances were, of course, those who had suffered a similar fate to them and had also arrived on the *Nyassa*. Everyone tried to stay in touch. Among them were the renowned cameraman Eugen Schüfftan, with whom Kracauer made

Figure 31. Lili Kracauer, New York (1944)
Copyright: DLA Marbach

plans for a Hollywood film on Jacques Offenbach, and his wife, Marlise, and Herbert and Gertrud Levin, with whom the Kracauers spent their first New Year's Eve in New York.[24] In Aron Gurwitsch and Alfred Schütz, both of whom had been instrumental in securing the Kracauers' escape from France, they found an old and a new friend in New York.[25] Then there were the colleagues from the Film Library, especially the film historian Richard Griffith, and Barbara Deming, who worked for the National Film Library Project at the Library of Congress, which was housed at the Museum of Modern Art. These were young and creative people, around thirty years of age, and Kracauer got on well with them. He also sought to cultivate relationships with practitioners and theoreticians from the world of images. Three weeks after his arrival, he introduced himself to Erwin Panofsky, of Princeton, upon a recommendation from Rudolf Arnheim, who had been in New York since 1940, working at the Office for Radio Research at Columbia University. Arnheim was a former colleague of Kracauer's; they had known each other in Berlin. Arnheim had been at the *Weltbühne* and, like Kracauer, was a pioneer of film criticism and film theory. Also familiar from his Berlin days was Hans Richter, the experimental film-maker, who had been in the US and New York since 1940 and now headed the film institute at the City College of New York.[26] And, of course, the Kracauers had a very cordial relationship with the Krautheimers, and through them with the art historian Walter Friedlaender, now almost seventy, having taught at New York University since 1933.[27]

An important well-meaning advisor to the new arrivals was the Jewish philosopher, and co-founder of the New School, Horace M. Kallen. From the New York intellectual scene, Kracauer knew, apart from Schapiro, the writer James T. Farrell (from his time in Paris). Through Löwenthal and Speier, paths opened up to Horkheimer's Institute for Social Research, which was first located at 117th Street, and later in Morningside Heights, at the edge of the Columbia University campus, and also to the New School for Social Research in Greenwich Village. Kracauer presented his 'Marseille outline' at the Institute.[28] At the New School, he was soon participating in the weekly colloquium of the Faculty for Political and Social Sciences.

28

Define Your Enemy: What is National Socialism?

Both the New School and the Institute for Social Research were think tanks whose members consisted almost exclusively of German-speaking immigrants. It is therefore not surprising that the activities of both institutions were dominated by research and reflection on National Socialism. Hardly any of the German refugees could avoid looking back. And the topic also allowed these immigrant scholars to achieve expert profiles. Apart from their academic qualifications, they could bring to bear on the work their own experiences, or, as Kracauer fittingly put it, the capacity 'to look at familiar things from an unfamiliar angle'.[1] The 'University in Exile' at the New School was explicitly based on this special wealth of knowledge. It had been founded in 1919 by a circle of liberals and radical democrats, led by Kallen and, in particular, Alvin Johnson. The aim was to contribute to a new social order, within the framework of the American constitution, through an enlightened critique of society. In 1933, Johnson reacted immediately to the expulsion of German scientists by organizing donations and grant money for the foundation of the University in Exile. He planned to build this university within a university around Adolf Löwe, Emil Lederer and Karl Mannheim, whose institutions had previously received money from the Rockefeller Foundation. Hans Speier acted as Johnson's scout, looking for suitable academics who might join the New School. Löwe (who only arrived in 1940) and Mannheim, however, opted for exile in England. At the end of 1933, Johnson had mustered a group of twelve scholars – economists, sociologists and political scientists – with Lederer acting as the first dean. On 1 October 1933, the University in Exile was renamed the Graduate Faculty of Political and Social Science. It was part of Columbia University and yet an autonomous institution. After 1938, it had a faculty of up to twenty-five academics.[2]

The faculty members met weekly for the General Seminar, which was intended to facilitate collective research. Every year, one of the participants chose a topic that all members were to investigate.[3]

The discussions of the first General Seminar were based on an article by Paul Tillich to which all participants, presumably, could relate. It was titled 'The Totalitarian State' and was included, as a programmatic text, in the first volume of the group's journal, *Social Research*. Following his dismissal after the passing of the Law for the Restoration of the Professional Civil Service, Tillich, a philosopher of religion from Frankfurt, had found a post at the Union Theological Seminary in New York. Like many of the social scientists on the new faculty at the New School, he sympathized with a non-Marxist form of socialism. In epistemological terms, Tillich was an ecclecticist. He assumed that an event like the victory of National Socialism was in part caused by structural social forces, but he thought that history was also determined by coincidence and the actions of specific individuals. Tillich analysed the emergence of the totalitarian state on three levels. Firstly, at a global level, capitalism had led to economic uncertainty and thus competing nation states. Secondly, in east and central Europe, in particular, a militant type of nationalism and authoritarian state emerged as a consequence of the Great War. And thirdly, specifically in Germany, the idea of a totalitarian state had always been deeply engrained in the political culture – and now this idea was no longer only an idea. Tillich did not distinguish the concepts 'totalitarian', 'authoritarian', 'fascistic' sharply from each other; in fact, he did not define them at all. His panorama remained broad enough to serve as a platform for further research at the faculty: for example, Eduard Heimann's study *Communism, Fascism, or Democracy* (1938), and a collected volume with contributions from faculty members that came out in the spring of 1939 under a title that was an ironic nod at Chamberlain – *War in Our Time*. After the British prime minister had spoken about the 'peace for our time', it seemed to the German social scientists imperative to warn against the growing threat posed by a Germany that was systematically pursuing rearmament.[4]

Within the faculty, there was one piece of work in particular that stood out. Though the author had not been in touch with Kracauer, the piece agreed in several points with the latter's work on mass propaganda. In the 1930s, Emil Lederer had been working on a book on the Nazi state, and it was published posthumously in 1940, following Lederer's unexpected death in May 1939. Unlike Tillich, Lederer did not ask what had made the events of 1933 possible; he was interested in the way in which the new regime had consolidated its power and what the consequences of that were. Lederer's 'mass state' is a political order based on the shapeless mass. The new rulers of the mass state destroy the old society. Independent and spontaneous social forces are eliminated. The regime is based on the enthusiasm of the masses, which needs to be constantly fuelled by means of modern propaganda. To that end, the baser instincts are mobilized, power and violence glorified, and images of an enemy cultivated. The place of the individual is taken by the crowd, that of classes by masses, that of interests by passions, and that of ideas by instincts.[5] In his study for the Institute for Social Research, Kracauer had also spoken of the masses that National Socialist propaganda had helped to create, through the use of ornaments (mass meetings, mass parades, mass marches), radio broadcasting, and the invocation of the people and the leader as magical forces. In Kracauer's view, these pseudo-realities produced real effects in social reality. That was also the point of Lederer's study. After Kracauer had been assigned the study on the use of film in the German war propaganda, it was therefore a good idea for him to follow New School custom and participate in the weekly colloquium.[6]

At the Institute for Social Research, this characterization of state and society, especially the idea of the amorphous mass, met with some resistance. Franz L. Neumann, who was working on a book on the structure and practice of National Socialism, noted that the German economy was still capitalist, and German society still a class society. The concepts of class and mass did not compete with each other. Rather, the mass individual was the result of modern industrial capitalism and mass democracy; it was not a consequence of the negation of class society. National Socialism had completed the processes of the monopolization of the economy, the centralization of the state and the transformation of subjects into the mass, and it had ideologically equipped itself with the idea of the 'Volksgemeinschaft', the community of a people, and the 'Führerprinzip', the leader principle.

Neumann also objected to a thesis that had been developed in his own institution by Friedrich Pollock, and had a supporter in Horkheimer, namely that National Socialism was best described as a form of 'state capitalism'. Pollock had identified state capitalism as the successor of private capitalism. In state capitalism, the state takes on important functions that were previously performed by private capitalists. The profit motive continues to play an important role, but the central motivation driving economic activity becomes the desire to gain political power. According to this theory, state capitalism is not a form of socialism. In Pollock's view, the characteristic symptoms of state capitalism are processes of economic concentration, price stability, the control of banks and trade by the government, the monopoly of aligned trade unions, and a high level of state expenditure, especially on unemployment benefits. Society is kept in check by political terror and by ideological as well as material rewards. Pollock's thesis is that totalitarian state capitalism solves the economic problems of capitalism, but only at the price of enslavement under totalitarian rule.[7] Neumann, by contrast, considered the very concept 'state capitalism' a contradiction in terms. A capitalism without capitalists and markets was, for him, unimaginable.

Rather than 'state capitalism', Neumann adopts the concept of the 'Behemoth' in order to describe the political, economic and social processes then taking place in Germany. The Behemoth is contrasted with Hobbes's Leviathan, the latter representing a state that is also authoritarian but, unlike the Behemoth, still governed by reason. With this way of framing the issue, Neumann was attacking the widespread view that Hitler's Germany was just a particularly brutal dictatorship, one that, however, still remained on a continuum with other dictatorships from history. Behemoth is the name for an 'Unstaat', a state that contradicts the principles of any reasonable state, a state of chaos, lawlessness and anarchy, a state that dispenses with all traditional values and norms. The Behemoth is anti-democratic, anti-liberal and anti-rational. It is not based on any political theory. Ideology is simply a means of gaining power and facilitating mass propaganda: a technique of rule. The Behemoth is born of 'totalitarian monopoly capitalism'. Neumann no longer saw Germany as a state in which a coherent political power was at work; rather, society was dominated directly by four solid, centralized groups: economic monopolies, the party, the state administration and the military – all of them practitioners of violence. These groups, in turn, were tied together by profit, power and a fear of the repressed masses.[8]

All these studies, Marxist and non-Marxist alike, shared a fundamental assumption that societies are determined by economic processes, social structure, and by the effects these have on politics. At the centre of them thus stood the material hardware: power and domination, property and capital, and the exercise of violence. In order to explain National Socialism the question of interests had to be asked: *cui bono*? The software of a society – mentalities and myths, the music people dance to – was less important. As a consequence, not one of these researchers considered the figure of the 'Führer', the *völkisch* mythology, or the anti-Semitic world view to be crucial elements of Nazism. To the Marxists, no phenomenon could be looked at independently and on its own; everything had to be re-contextualized within the wider framework of capitalism. Neumann, for instance, did feel that his Behemoth indicated that something new, something unique, something monstrous was dawning, but he looked for it in the structures of domination, in the form of the state, and in socio-economic structures, not in events that would have lent themselves not so much to analysis but to description. He was also misled by the intellectual poverty of National Socialism. Because of his functionalism, he saw anti-Semitism simply as a justification for dispossessing the Jews and for expanding towards the east – a pressure valve, a means to an end, a substitute for class struggle, an expression of the break with tradition. He thought the German people were the least anti-Semitic in Europe, and the complete annihilation of the Jews he still considered impossible even when it had already begun. Lederer looked at the 'Volksgemeinschaft' exclusively as a phenomenon of mass psychology; his study failed to mention anywhere the fact that it was also defined in terms of a 'people' and of 'race'. Under the letter 'a', the index of his book lists 'appeasement', 'armament' and 'army', but not 'anti-Semitism'. Under 'r' we find 'reason' and 'revolution' but not 'racism'.

Max Horkheimer, however, wrote about anti-Semitism in his article 'The Jews and Europe', which appeared in the *Zeitschrift für Sozialforschung* in 1939. The article was a manifesto and a critique of the present, and he intended it to evoke Karl Marx's *On the Jewish Question* (1844). The subjects were not the actual European Jews who were discriminated against, persecuted and exiled, like Horkheimer himself, but the Jews as a social shibboleth. While Marx, in the mid-nineteenth century, had optimistically tied the emancipation of the Jews to the emancipation of society as a whole, Horkheimer was forced to resign himself to registering the utter hopelessness of the Jewish predicament. The decline of bourgeois and liberal culture meant there was no longer a future for Jews in Europe. Horkheimer's explanation of anti-Semitism was based on the economy; like Pollock, he connected it to the dismantling of the market economy. In his argument, Horkheimer confused the historical relevance of the presence of Jews in the capitalist system of circulation with the significance of the Jews for this system.[9] According to Horkheimer, in order to understand anti-Semitism, one did not listen to what Hitler said or study what the *völkisch* nationalists thought about themselves and the Jews. One had to recognize what was hidden behind anti-Semitism: 'Whoever wants to explain anti-Semitism must speak of National Socialism.' And: 'whoever is not willing to talk about capitalism should also keep quiet about fascism'.[10]

In November and December 1941, the Institute for Social Research held a series of lectures on National Socialism. Herbert Marcuse spoke about the state and the individual within the new order; Arcadius R.L. Gurland on private property; Neumann about the new rulers; Otto Kirchheimer on the legal order; and Pollock on the question of whether National Socialism was in fact a new order at all. Whether Kracauer, whose proposal for a contribution on mass propaganda had been rejected, attended any of these, we do not know. But he read Horkheimer's essay on the Jews, which was published in 1939, before the outbreak of the war. After his arrival in New York, Kracauer told Horkheimer:

[I]t seemed to me at the time that one had to commit suicide if this gloomy essay was right. I subsequently realized how much your insights correctly prophesied. And the thought of suicide was not far off during a particular period.

In Kracauer's eyes, Horkheimer's article contains a truth at its core: it anticipates the end of emancipation, even the end of the Jews in Europe. He saw the article within the context of his escape in and from France, Benjamin's suicide and his own thoughts of taking his own life:

> It was the darkest time of eight dark years. If I am now able to calm down, at least to some degree, I shall note down our experiences of the last two years under the title 'Journey to America'. I shall either succeed in outshining Kafka, or I shall have been incapable of presenting the events adequately.[11]

Alas, the hectic everyday life in America took up all of Kracauer's energy, and his plan came to naught.

The events that took place at Columbia University towards the end of 1941 were something like the Institute's farewell to New York. But they were also a watershed within the development of critical theory. Adorno and Horkheimer moved to California. Pollock kept the Institute ticking over; Kirchheimer, Marcuse and Neumann got civil service positions soon after the US had entered the war. In light of the events after 1942, substantial modifications were made to the political-economic approach to interpreting National Socialism that saw it as a kind of fascism and anti-Semitism as a symptom of capitalism. The murder of the European Jewry changed everyone's view of the world and understanding of society. Before 'Auschwitz' the central hypothesis had been that anti-Semitism could only be understood by looking at society; after 'Auschwitz', it was the assumption that society could only be understood by looking at anti-Semitism.[12]

29

Know Your Enemy:
Psychological Warfare

On 7 December 1941, Japanese fighter planes attacked the American naval base at Pearl Harbor and destroyed a large part of the American Pacific fleet, which was anchored there. One day later, the Americans entered the war. On 11 December, Hitler declared war on the United States, despite that country's overwhelming economic power. The politics and aims of the German state were determined by ideology.[1] This explains why it attacked central European neighbours, combated old and sated liberal democratic states in Europe and – after June 1941 – fought a war of annihilation against its ideological enemy, the Soviet Union, and it also explains why the US was considered a natural enemy. To the anti-Semites, Wall Street was no less under the control of the Jews than was the Kremlin. In their eyes, Roosevelt was acting as the 'benevolent God of the Jews'; in any case, this whole modern world, whether capitalist or communist, was Jewish.[2]

With the outbreak of war, the projects on media and communication studies funded by the Rockefeller Foundation suddenly acquired an urgent importance, because propaganda was a form of communication that made use of mass media. Even before Pearl Harbor, the Rockefeller discussion group around Lazarsfeld and Lasswell had thought about the possible role that research into communication could play should the US enter the war. Now, within a very short period of time, a joint enterprise of the Rockefeller Foundation, the intelligence services and the State Department was set up to conduct research into psychological warfare. Hundreds of social scientists left their academic institutions in order to work for or advise the dozens of state agencies involved in the war effort. In February 1942, Leo Löwenthal, now Leo Lowenthal, joined the broadcaster Voice of America, and began to analyse propaganda. In May 1942, Hans Speier went to Washington and headed up the analysis of German radio at the Foreign Broadcast Intelligence Service, which recorded and translated news programmes, announcements and speeches from Germany and produced a weekly digest for the agencies directly engaged in warfare. In early 1943, Franz L. Neumann, together with Otto Kirchheimer and Herbert Marcuse, took up a post at the Research & Analysis Branch of the Office of Strategic Services (OSS). During the war years, the network of contacts, acquaintances and sometimes even friends working in the area of mass communication studies grew ever tighter.[3]

Whoever wanted to win the war – and beyond that, the ensuing peace – needed to know his enemy. Dorothy Thompson, a columnist at the *New York Herald Tribune*, summarized this widely held view as follows: 'the first axiom of political warfare is: Know your enemy'.[4] For the R & A Branch, the director of the OSS, William Joseph Donovan, issued the motto: 'In a global, totalitarian war, work on information also has to be global, if not totalitarian.'[5] One consequence of this was that the intelligence services did not hesitate to contact Marxist social scientists and philosophers from Germany. The aim of the war was the unconditional victory of the Allies. *Never Call Retreat* was the title of a novel by Joseph Freeman that Kracauer considered to be one of the best books about National Socialism. The book's blurb contained the phrase: 'Books are weapons in the war of ideas.'[6] Words were weapons, and so were images. Experts in words and images, in propaganda and counter-propaganda, were thus needed. Kracauer was the right person for this work: an expert in images who had been cast out of Germany and no longer saw himself as a German.[7] His study on propaganda and Nazi war films explicitly served the purpose of psychological warfare. The study was the product of real effort on Kracauer's part. He 'camped in the projection room watching films over and over again, smoking foul cigars'.[8] His analysis of Nazi film production was intended to 'afford some insights into developments' beyond the concrete objects which the book considers.[9] That had always been his method: to put phenomena into a wider context without losing contact with them or, worse, using them as mere means for speculation.

At the end of April 1942, Kracauer submitted a preliminary report that, half a year later, was classified as 'confidential' and made available to certain government authorities, especially in the State Department and the OSS, in the form of a brochure.[10] Kracauer also sent his study to various offices whose work bore on psychological warfare and communication research. One of the addressees was Lasswell, the pioneer of scientific propaganda research and head of the research group on war communication at the Library of Congress. Lasswell charged Kracauer with undertaking an investigation into German wartime weekly newsreels from between 1939 and 1940.[11] Thanks to Barry, Kracauer was allowed to keep his office at the museum and use it to work on his new assignment.[12] Together with Marshall and Schapiro, she also supported him with an application to the Guggenheim Foundation, which meant he would finally be able to embark on the history of German film that had originally been planned. In the autumn of 1942, Kracauer worked manically on the application and the study for Lasswell in parallel.[13] In March 1943, he received the funding, and thus his new grant took up where his last left off. From today's perspective, the network of communication researchers working in the service of the war effort seems to have looked after its members very well: it appears even to have functioned like a military-intellectual complex. But if it looks like a well-oiled machine now, it was an entirely unpredictable process for those involved at the time. Kracauer lived from project to project, never knowing whether there would be a next one. Shortly before the end of each project, the question arose: what next? And then the old fear – by then quite familiar, and not at all unfounded – crept up on him: he could be left with nothing. In such moments, his thoughts turned to his debts; his toothache returned, and his nerves played up.[14] Although Kracauer had supporters and patrons, this changed nothing about the fact that, for his first five years in the US, he could not become a citizen, a fact that severely limited his opportunities, especially during wartime. And applying to foundations was, as Horace Kallen told him, 'like betting on a horse'.[15] The field of communication research was bound up with the academic policies of the foundations and with the foreign policy of the US government, but the rules of the academic game nevertheless still applied. The field was not a corrupt assemblage of secret agreements and conspiracies, with imperialist philanthropists seeking to rule the world with the 'power of knowledge'; it was a complex aggregate of coincidences and idiosyncrasies. It was based on a convergence between political and scientific conceptions of philanthropy, science and American foreign policy, but the philanthropic activities and scientific research were not themselves determined by politics.[16]

Kracauer's first study analysed the use of cinematic techniques, that is, the combination of commentary, image and sound, in films about military campaigns: *Baptism of Fire* (1940), *Victory in the West* (1941) and Leni Riefenstahl's *Triumph of the Will* (1935), which featured Adolf Hitler and the marching masses.[17] He concluded that Nazi propaganda films exhibit a preponderance of the visual, appealing directly 'to the subconscious and the nervous system'.[18] Verbal statements are often juxtaposed with images in a manner that further strengthens the weight of the latter. *Victory in the West*, in Kracauer's eyes, achieves a stronger emotional stimulus than the British documentary film of the same year, *Target for Tonight*. The aim of both is to keep 'the spectator's instincts and emotions ... alive', while starving 'his faculty of reasoning'.[19] The weekly Nazi newsreels followed the same pattern, while the Allies' newsreels were often not cinematic: the images merely illustrated a text that was being read out, or the commentary competed with the images for the spectator's strained attention. Because of the primacy of the visual, the German films appealed directly to the emotional life of the spectator: they were a means by which to conquer Europe via the screen.[20]

The study was published alongside an article by Speier on 'Nazi Propaganda and its Decline' in the same issue of *Social Research*. With this study, Kracauer had made an attempt to keep close to the material and to draw on the reflections on film aesthetics he had condensed into the 'Marseille outline'. He was also inspired by the 1937 version of Panofsky's essay 'Style and Medium in the Moving Pictures'. Kracauer was happy to find that there were so many similarities between their views on the aesthetics of film.[21] The fundamental tenet of Panofsky's film aesthetics was: 'The medium of the movies is physical reality as such.'[22]

Panofsky's tenet suggests that film is a particular way of appropriating reality. Panofsky defines the specific possibilities of film as consisting in the '*dynamization of space* and, accordingly, *spatialization of time*'.[23] The substance of film is 'a series of visual sequences held together by an uninterrupted flow of movement in space'.[24] The problem of film is artfully 'to manipulate and shoot unstylized reality in such a way that the result has style'.[25] In a passage on film theory that contains the basis for his analysis of the newsreels, Kracauer, in turn, wrote:

> The film surpasses other arts in that it reflects the visible world, to an extent hitherto unknown. Everyday life, with its infinitesimal movements, its multitude of transitory actions, could be disclosed nowhere but on the screen.[26]

These properties of film, which made it a tool for investigating reality, were, of course, not without consequence when it came to the production of cinematic propaganda that aimed to suggest a particular image of reality to viewers. Kracauer was forced to admit that the enemy had exploited the aesthetics of film effectively. In the films on military campaigns, he was particularly impressed by the 'totalitarian panoramas' – for instance the 'mass ornaments of soldiers'. The depiction of soldiers going about their everyday duties – suggesting a closeness to reality – was clever. The newsreels also used a technique of constantly cutting between shots of the totality of the mass and close-ups of individual faces. As Kracauer observed, this shifted the spectator's attention gradually from the individual to the mass. Even the triumphant figure of Hitler was never to be seen without those masses, which had become a permanent fixture of life in Nazi Germany. This was a way of expressing, staging, the unity of the people and the Führer. All these films, Kracauer claimed, 'insistently glorify Germany as a dynamic power, as dynamite'. The films helped to associate a myth with the world of the swastika: 'to give the impression that Germany's war and triumph were not accidental events, but the fulfilment of an historic mission, metaphysically justified'.

For Kracauer, the films reflected the regime's power and the total-itarian character of its propaganda. Those who watched these films could no longer be certain whether reality would not, in the end, bear out the message contained in the propaganda. This argument was trademark Kracauer: the Nazis 'counterfeited life after the manner of Potemkin; instead of pasteboard, however, they used life itself to construct their imaginary villages'. Propaganda is not just bold lies; in the Nazis' case, propaganda revealed an intention to transform reality after their own image. And if image and reality did not correspond, then so much the worse for reality. Kracauer's was an unusual perspective on the dramaturgy of the screen and of events; not content to disclose the manipulations and ideologies that characterize propaganda, Kracauer sought to make visible – as in a nightmare – the conflict between totalitarian practices and reality, and the threat this conflict posed to the latter.[27]

But the power of propaganda came up against its limits when confronted with military reality – that was the assumption shared by the propaganda studies undertaken by Kracauer, Kris and Speier. With the defeat of the German army, the Nazi nightmare and the travesty of reality would disappear. However, this meant that the military, moral and political victory over the Wehrmacht and the German home front had to be comprehensive and beyond doubt.[28] Every possible force and intellect had to be mobilized to bring this form of totalitarian rule to its knees. This insight had underlain Tillich's foreboding reflections in his 'The Totalitarian State', Lederer's thesis of the destruction of society through the mass state, Pollock's analysis of state capitalism, and Horkheimer's prophecy about the end of the Jews in Europe. Neumann presented a version of it in the form of his analysis of the Behemoth, and Hannah Arendt later declared 'totalitarian rule' the sign of the times. As much as all these analyses of National Socialism differed with regard to their political orientations and methodological tools, they shared the impression that, with the Nazis and their conquest of Europe, there had been a historical rupture that had introduced a hitherto-unknown form of rule. All authors had escaped from the National Socialists and now looked on in horror at events in Europe. For Kracauer, his support for the US military effort was not only a personal opportunity to embark on another heyday, but an existential concern. He must have been pleased, then, that Frank Capra's popular *Why We Fight* films drew on his analyses.[29]

Kracauer's area of research, film propaganda, was not the most important within the overall debate about the nature of National Socialism. Nevertheless, the responses he received from within his intellectual circle show that he had hit a nerve in the public debates over Germany and the Nazis. Who was the enemy? Only the criminal regime or all of the German people? Social elites or capitalism as a system? Was National Socialism the necessary consequence of Germanness or of its negation? Why did the Germans constantly attack their neighbours? Was it a belligerent national character – in their blood or temperament? And were these mass murderers simply psychopaths, on the model of Dr Jekyll and Mr Hyde? What was to be done with them? What was to happen to Germany, what to Europe?

The responses of Dwight Macdonald, Erwin Panofsky, Hans Richter, Meyer Schapiro and James T. Farrell to Kracauer's studies and their explicit and implicit statements on the Germans were, like their private dealings with him, friendly and complimentary, but they also raised minor differences of opinion and suggested certain misunderstandings. Some objected to the dichotomy between Nazi propaganda and American documentaries or information. Others disputed the value that Kracauer's analysis attributed to propaganda in supporting the rule of the regime, and his inclination towards explaining National Socialism on the basis of concepts like national character or other collective dispositions common among the Germans.

Dwight Macdonald, the former editor of the *Partisan Review*, with whom Kracauer had been in touch while still in Paris, expressed his doubts about the contrast between German and American film in a review, 'The Conquest of Europe on the Screen', for his new journal *Politics*. German films may rely on emotional effects and the viewer's instincts, putting image above word, but was it true, as Kracauer seemed to imply, that American films therefore 'use words because they appeal to conscious intelligence'? No, was his answer: the stereotypical use of commentary had 'as little relevance to reality as the Nazis' use of images'.[30] Macdonald, a left-wing radical, did not want to align himself with the tendency, in Kracauer's work, to paint American mass culture in a positive light. He was part of a New York intellectual scene in which praise for the products of Hollywood or defences of the American way of life were anathema, despite the rise of anti-communist sentiment across the country. Even though the Stalinization of the Soviet Union and of many of their comrades made it ever more difficult to find their political home, they nevertheless remained revolutionary and radical in outlook. Or, as Macdonald put it: they pursued a 'Neo-Non-Conservatism'.[31] Schapiro took the same line. He was irritated by what he saw as a naïve and simplistic juxtaposition of propaganda with information. Of course, it was well known that the Nazis lied, cheated, conquered and murdered. But it was also possible to tell people falsehoods by providing true information – as happened, he argued, every day in American democracy and mass culture. Like Adorno before him, Schapiro wanted to avoid drawing a sharp distinction between propaganda and advertising. Farrell also followed this line of argument, praising Kracauer's study in an article in the *New York Times*, but also pointing out that the creation of pseudo-realities was not an achievement unique to the Nazis.[32]

His American friends were right; Kracauer's enthusiasm for America was guiding his analyses. The US was a country in which it seemed possible to work as an academic or as a writer outside of universities and outside the market, and he identified with a society that was committed to freedom for all its citizens, independent of their origin. 'We are eternally grateful to America. It took us up and gave us back a dignified existence', he admitted. 'And I also believe in the enormous importance of America during the next era, and want to be part of it and contribute.'[33] As an immigrant, Kracauer admired American democracy, whose processes, he thought, had developed historically and were deeply anchored, whereas the democratic institutions in Germany were not tethered to anything and created no more than a semblance of democracy.[34] The Kracauers could hardly wait to become – as they expressed it with some self-irony in a letter – 'zittizens' (which they did, finally, in September 1946), and not just because of the practical advantages: 'Only European refugees can understand what citizenship means.'[35] He thus maintained his position in the face of his critics; simulated realities and pseudo-realities may also be found in democracies, but it was only National Socialism that depended on them for its very existence.[36]

The private opinions of Panofsky and Richter, immigrants themselves, pointed in another direction. Panofsky shared the critics' scepticism towards the idea of a fundamental opposition between German and American films when it came to the relation between their emotional and cognitive dimensions. 'For I believe – but don't tell anyone else – that a *genuine* "Documentary Film" does not exist, and that our so-called documentaries are also propaganda films, only – thank God – mostly for a better cause, and – alas – done with less skill.'[37] But he said this only off the record, because during wartime the American cause was much more important than any academic subtleties. Panofsky did not move in the New York intellectual circles, and he had no problem with the pro-American and anti-German orientation of the questionable dichotomy. In questions concerning the German problem, the Princeton art historian adopted positions that, to many, appeared hostile to Germany, positions that were rejected out of hand by American left-wing thinkers like Macdonald and Schapiro. Panofsky was convinced that, in National Socialism, the German masses had found their appropriate and desired representation.[38]

Hans Richter, a film-maker, went even further. He argued that it was a mistake to distinguish between rulers and ruled. He thought that there was too much talk of manipulation in Kracauer's propaganda studies, and he reminded him 'that the Nazi films are an expression of what the Nazis really believe, and not mere demagogy, because I do not believe at all that pure demagogy is enough to keep a people anaesthetized for longer periods of time'.[39] According to Richter, the basis of the regime was the consent of the population. Here, though, a misunderstanding was at work. Kracauer did not believe that the German population was ruled by terror and anaesthetized by propaganda alone. Just because National Socialism was rule based on a dictatorship and violence did not mean that its aims were not supported by those over which the Nazis ruled. For Kracauer, the German population was not simply a deluded mass; they were easy prey for the Nazis, who had painted themselves as singularly capable of delivering the people from an unhappy reality and an unbearable freedom.

Kracauer and his friendly critics thus waded into the public debates on the 'German problem' that had acquired an urgency with the entry of the US into the war. One of those setting the agenda was Sir Robert Vansittart, a former British under-secretary of state in the Foreign Office. In a brochure entitled *Black Record*, which was broadcast on the radio seven times and sold millions of copies, he had called the Germans 'a breed which from the dawn of history has been predatory and bellicose'.[40] Vansittart's theses had been designed specifically to be aired by the BBC Overseas Programme for the American public in order to shift the public mood and move the US towards entering the war.[41] For Vansittart, Germany was a bird of prey, constantly attacking its neighbours. National Socialism simply reflected German culture and history; the people and the Führer could not be separated from each other. There was no 'other Germany', at least no other that existed as a relevant political power.[42] Those who adopted this position were soon called 'Vansittartists', a term of abuse coined by opponents and used to stigmatize the chauvinists' reactionary hatred for the Germans.[43] Such stigmatization was possible because all talk of national character suffered, as Hadley Cantril explained, from a lack of definition, although it was highly suggestive.[44] Anyone talking about the *German nature, soul, mind*, or of any kind of a collective German mentality, was quickly labelled a Vansittartist, and the polemics against Vansittartism took on a dynamic of their own.[45] Commentators like Dorothy Thompson and Reinhold Niebuhr attacked the reverse Nazism of the Vansittartists, and they, in turn, founded bizarre but vociferous and missionary societies like the Society for the Prevention of World War III, headed by Rex Stout, an author of detective novels, and Emil Ludwig, a German-born author of bestselling biographies.

Kracauer used concepts taken from collective psychology. In his application to the Guggenheim Foundation for a grant in support of the book on German film, he wrote of his interest in 'the psychological preconditions' for the events of 1933. (He did not, however, deny the role of social and economic factors.) He wanted to investigate the 'characteristics of German life and German mentality' in the films.[46] Did he have something like a national character in mind? Kracauer's claim, in his Caligari-exposé, about the existence of a 'natural inclination' among the German people towards anti-rational and mythological thinking shocked Schapiro, in any case. In his eyes, that was ethnopsychology: National Socialist racial theory in reverse. 'Vansittartitis', as Dosio Koffler called it, had clearly proven contagious in this case.[47] But it goes without saying that Kracauer had not simply assumed a natural inclination towards anything on the part of the Germans. But he did think it necessary to reflect on the fact that it was in Germany that National Socialist ideology had been most successful. An explanation had to be found for the fact that ordinary Germans, especially the younger generation, the unemployed and the middle classes, had thrown their weight behind National Socialism, and had remained faithful to the regime even after the signs of military defeat began to appear. In that sense, Kracauer, like Panofsky, did not feel the need to distance himself from Vansittartist positions. They both read Vansittart's book *Lessons of My Life*, which was just as polemical as *Black Record* but, unlike that latter work, presented good arguments in favour of, first, comprehensively defeating Germany and, second, creating an order in Europe that secured Germany's neighbouring states. 'How right you were in your judgement of Vansittart's book', Kracauer wrote to Panofsky. 'In the meantime, I have read it and greatly enjoyed his wit and rhetorical skill. And I could not point out any essential point on which he is wrong.'[48]

Kracauer also agreed that it was necessary to re-educate the Germans. In a memorandum on the German film industry from October 1943, written for a future 'occupying army', he recommended that occupying forces show Germans documentary films portraying the suffering of civilians caused by the German war and the determined resistance mounted against it. The horror of the concentration camps was to be made visible everywhere, because 'the Germans will pretend they did not know anything about these things. They should see this with their own eyes.'[49]

30

Fear Your Enemy: Deportation and Killing of the Jews

When Kracauer was writing his memorandum on the German film industry, he did not yet know what had happened to his mother and aunt. But he braced himself for the worst. 'Very indirectly' he had learned that in August 1942 Rosette and Hedwig Kracauer had been sent to Theresienstadt 'by the Germans'. 'Poland' was also mentioned. But he knew nothing concrete. The situation affected him 'very deeply', especially as it came after his own rescue.[1] In November 1941, Kracauer had organized visas for Cuba for his relatives, but a telegram from Frankfurt said: 'Impossible to pay for passage from here.'[2] With the outbreak of war, emigration was no longer a realistic option for the two. After September 1939, only 20,000 Jews were still able to leave the territory of the German state.[3]

In 1941 and 1942, numerous regulations directed against German Jews made life for them even harder than it had already been. The stream of prohibitions seemed unstoppable. Jews were no longer allowed to own furs or woollen clothing, buy newspapers or journals, visit Aryan hairdressers, use public transport, keep pets, possess electrical or optical devices, have bicycles, typewriters or records in their household, etc. This list is by no means exhaustive. The authorities in Frankfurt demonstrated a great deal of creativity and innovation in adding further local prohibitions to these nation-wide regulations. In the winter of 1941/42, for instance, they banned Jewish households from buying coal as long as there was still unmet demand from the 'German population'. And they single-mindedly and unscrupulously seized Jewish property with a thoroughness that made even the Gestapo jealous and suspicious.[4]

Hedwig was almost eighty by then, and Rosette over seventy. The two old ladies were constantly being forced to move. In July 1941, they lived in Liebigstraße 19, in a room with a family they were friendly with.[5] In the autumn of that year they moved to Eysseneckstraße 41, where they lived with two other ladies, probably in a so-called 'Jews' house'. In December 1941, they again had to find new accommodation. Now they were allocated Seilerstraße 8 in the Ostend, near the old 'Judengasse'. Finally, they lived in a Jewish home for the elderly in Sandweg 7, again in the Ostend.[6] Since 1 September 1941, the Kracauers had had to wear the yellow star, like all Jews in Germany, and they had to adopt Sara as their second name, like all Jewish women. This was the first time since the Middle Ages that Jews in Frankfurt had been forced to wear something to indicate that they were Jews. This stigma was not only a symbolic humiliation. It also helped the Gestapo in preparing for the planned deportations.[7] In spring 1941, the Jewish community was even forced to draw up lists of Jews that were then used by the Gestapo to organize the deportations.[8]

In early or mid-September 1941, Hitler made the decision to deport the German Jews to the east. Before that, the Wehrmacht had moved into the Soviet Union in order to fight an ideologically motivated war of extermination in the hope of increasing Germany's 'Lebensraum'. From the very beginning of this campaign, 'Operation Barbarossa', physically able Jews and Bolshevists were systematically killed en masse. In the autumn of 1941, this systematic killing was extended to Jewish women and children and elderly Jews. In Bełżec, the first extermination camp was built. In Eastern Galicia, under the control of the so-called General Government, and in the Soviet Union, in particular, hundreds of thousands of Jews were shot by the 'Einsatzgruppen' – death squads made up of SS and police units.[9]

On 18 October 1941, the first train with Jews from the original territory of the Reich left Berlin. At that point, close to 73,000 Jews were still living in the city. From Sybelstraße, where Siegfried and Elisabeth Kracauer's last apartment had been located, the first Jews were taken away: Ida Weinschenk, Johanna Fabian and Elli Reich. The destinations were Łódz and Riga. More Jews were taken away from Sybelstraße on several later occasions: in September 1942, Ernst and Margarete Hesse, and Henry Isidor and Klara Henoch (from house no. 29, three houses away from the Kracauers' former apartment), and Margarete Basch and Paula Engel from no. 18. In March 1943, the Kracauers' former neighbours Josef Meier and Franziska Zelt and Erna Unger and Frieda Winter were sent to Auschwitz. The age range of these people spans from 39 to 77 years. None of them survived. One day after the deportation from Berlin, on 19 October, the first 1,000 Jews were deported from Frankfurt to the ghetto Litzmannstadt (Łódz). They had been rounded up by the SA and led in groups, in broad daylight, through the city to the market hall, before being put directly on trains.[10] At that point, about 10,500 Jews were still living in Kracauer's former home town. A year later, there were little more than 1,000.

The first phase of deportations ended on 5 November 1941. During this phase, 19,593 Jews had been sent on twenty separate trains to their certain death in the east.[11] At the time of the declaration of war on the US and the transformation of the conflict into a world war, at the latest, the decision had been taken on the 'final solution to the Jewish question': that is, the plan to kill all Jews living on German territory.[12] The Wannsee conference on 20 January 1942 only discussed the question of how the Jews could be murdered as efficiently as possible. Between January and July 1942, the next major wave of deportations was planned in detail. The victims were selected and listed; the confiscation of their property was planned, and their freedom of movement was limited even further to ensure that they could not escape.[13] Still more extermination facilities were built, among other places in Auschwitz. In Terezín (Theresienstadt), SS-Obergruppenführer and police general Reinhard Heydrich asked for an 'Old People's Ghetto' to be established, so that all Jews in the Reich over the age of sixty-five could die 'a natural death' there, as Heydrich put it.[14] Theresienstadt was an attempt by the Nazis to deceive the outside world. Propaganda films showed elderly and well-known Jews sitting contentedly in Theresienstadt coffee houses, reading the papers, listening to music. But Heydrich's '"reservation" for "old and sick Jews who could not stand the strains of reset-tlement"' was a Potemkin village.[15] Behind the façade, death ruled over everyday life. Theresienstadt also served as a transit camp for those being moved on to the extermination camps.

In the summer of 1942, dozens of trains rolled from the Reich and its protectorates to Theresienstadt. From the original territory of the Reich alone, 15,000 mostly old and infirm Jews were deported. Egon Redlich, a twenty-three-year-old Jewish teacher for the children of the ghetto, reported that the aged were often no longer strong enough to feed themselves: 'Fifty die daily.'[16] From September onwards, these older prisoners were brought to Treblinka, where 18,000 died in the gas chambers.[17] Others were transported to Auschwitz. By the end of the war, 140,000 people had been deported to Theresienstadt. A quarter of them died there; 88,000 were murdered in the extermination camps.[18]

Because of the detailed lists of Jews, the deportations from Frankfurt were organized very efficiently. The Jewish community would write to those affected and inform them of the time they would be collected. One of the deported remembers the march through the city to the market hall: 'All along the way, we were sworn at and mocked by a jeering crowd. "Why don't you beat them to death? Why waste the expensive coal on transport trains!"'[19] On 18 August 1942, 1,022 people were removed from Frankfurt am Main to Theresienstadt, more than half of them from Jewish homes for the elderly. One of them was an eighty-six-year-old lady. She was brought to the Gestapo prisons in Rechneigrabenstraße and Hermesweg, then brought to the market hall, and there put on one of the waiting wagons. The prisoners were only allowed to take with them the clothes they were wearing. It was an extremely hot day, and many of them had put on two sets of underwear, and were wearing two, or even three, layers of clothes. Eleven of them died on the first day of the journey. In Theresienstadt, the women were stripped naked, inspected and searched for valuables.[20]

Only seventeen of those deported on that transport survived the ghetto. One of them was Lina Katz, who had worked in the administration of the Jewish community. She later reported:

> Also deported on the same transport were: Mrs Hedwig Kracauer, the widow of Professor Isidor Kracauer, the chronicler of the Frankfurt Jews, and her sister, the mother of the editor at the *Frankfurter Zeitung* Dr Siegfried Kracauer. In Theresienstadt, we were lying on the same floor together for a while because there was no furniture. The two women were deported to an extermination camp (presumably Auschwitz) after some time.[21]

Or Treblinka. There are no other sources that can tell us anything about the last days of Kracauer's mother, the diligent and conscientious, often depressed, but at times also heartily jocular or uncontrollably vociferous Rosette Kracauer, née Oppenheim, or about her older sister, Hedwig Kracauer, also née Oppenheim, the intelligent, educated and curious observer of her times, the widowed assistant of the chronicler of the now annihilated Frankfurt Jews. It was the month Elul in the year of doom 5702.

Lina Katz's statement was made in 1961. For a long time, Elisabeth and Siegfried Kracauer knew nothing about the fate of their relatives. The Red Cross searched for them, but to no avail. The Kracauers were notified of their deportation from Theresienstadt 'to Poland' only in July 1945.[22] Of course, they had for some time feared the worst, without quite knowing what the worst was – perhaps there were things worse than death. The Kracauers had many friends and acquaintances whose relatives were still in Germany or Europe, and they knew enough not to harbour any illusions but not enough to extinguish the last flicker of hope. The Levins had also learned about the deportation of their mother without any further details.[23] 'Almost every family we call on has some relative who is deported or will be deported', Kracauer wrote in November 1942, in English, to Trude Krautheimer (usually, he wrote to the Krautheimers in German). Trude had just learned that her parents had attempted suicide in Holland in order to avoid extradition. 'And what may we learn after the war about all these beloved, poor, wretched existences somewhere in Theresienstadt or deep in Poland?'[24] In another letter, he said that, perhaps, it would be best 'if those poor people were no longer alive', only to correct himself in the very next sentence. The situation was obviously confusing as well as unbearable.[25] Then there were mutual friends who had got stuck in southern France or Paris, like Richard Krautheimer's sister or the composer of film music Joseph Kozma. Or comrades from the camp in Athis. Or friends who had joined the Resistance.[26] For some time now, the trains had departed for the east not only from Germany but from other occupied western European countries as well. After 23 March 1942, Jews, including French Jews, began to be deported to extermination camps from France.[27] On 22 and 25 June, trains containing more than 1,000 Jews left Drancy and Pithiviers for the east. 'My hatred of the Germans, great as it always was, is now really complete', confessed Trude Krautheimer, also writing in English. 'Those dirty swines. You ask yourself why do they do it? But I cannot think of anything reasonable to explain what is going on now in Europe with regards to the Jews.' She still had some hope that the Jews were only being collected as hostages in the concentration camps in the east, as a means to be used for some unknown purpose.[28]

This letter was written on 5 November 1942. At that point, the Allies had plenty of indications, and also proof, of the mass murder taking place in central and eastern Europe, but no one spoke, officially, about the enemy's extermination policies. In the summer of 1942, the occupied countries' governments in exile in London fed reports of the Nazis' crimes to the press; the secretary of the World Jewish Congress in Geneva, Gerhart Riegner, informed the British Foreign Office about the Führer's decision to deport all four million Jews now living under German rule to the east of Europe, and then to kill them; Vansittart spoke on the radio about the use of poison gas in the extermination camps and about the murder of hundreds of thousands of Polish Jews. But the first announcement by the Allies did not come until 17 December 1942. Only then did the British foreign minister Anthony Eden openly talk in the name of the governments in London, Washington and Moscow about the murder of the European Jews to both Houses of Parliament, declaring that the perpetrators would be punished after the war. Earlier, on 24 November 1942, the rabbi and president of the World Jewish Congress, Stephen Wise, had told a press conference in New York that more than two million Jews had already been murdered, criticizing that not one front page was reporting the news. On the same day, the Polish government in exile in London presented the 'Karski report' on 'Aktion Reinhard' [Operation Reinhard] and the murder of the Polish Jews. But it was only after the speech by Eden that the Nazis' war crimes at the eastern front and their crimes against the Jews began to be widely reported. Varian Fry, writing in the *New Republic*, described the methods of murder, ranging from working people to death or letting them starve to shooting or gassing them.[29]

At the beginning of 1943, any hopes that there would be survivors among the deported Jews from the Reich, the Netherlands or France were very dim. When Kracauer learned, in 1943, that his mother and aunt, having just arrived in Theresienstadt, had been transported on 'to Poland', he wrote: 'We pray that they were allowed to die naturally. I try not to think about it, in the interest of naked self-preservation. Many here are in the same situation. There is nothing to be said about it.'[30] Kracauer was not usually in the habit of praying. He probably did not believe that his mother and aunt were allowed to die naturally. He did not allow himself to think about it: that is, he thought about it constantly. The violent deaths suffered by the two women would make it harder for him to go on living. Many others shared his fate, but that was no consolation to him. There was nothing *to be said* about it: that is, there were no meaningful or consoling words worth uttering. There was nothing to be said *about it*: that is, there was just the brute fact of it, and any attempt at finding reasons, explanations, not to mention under-standing, was in vain. There was *nothing* to be said about it: that is, faced with this ultimate nihilism, the abandonment of all traditions and values, the murderous fanaticism of *völkisch* instincts and anti-Semitic drives, nothing was appropriate but – silence.

Between 1941 and 1945, approximately 5.7 million Jews were murdered – men, women, children and elderly people from all over Europe. They were first arrested and then deported over thousands of kilometres. From Norway and from the smallest Greek islands, from the Benelux countries and Bulgaria. They were killed manually with a bullet to the head, or industrially destroyed like vermin with Zyklon B. What would it be to say more than nothing about these facts? On the failure of the Weimar Republic and the Nazis' seizure of power, however, Kracauer had quite a lot to say. And, as in many other instances, he did so in an unusual and idiosyncratic way.

31

Fuck Your Enemy:
From Hitler to Caligari

In the expressionist silent movie *The Cabinet of Dr. Caligari* (1920), the demonic showman Caligari brings his attraction to the very ordinary German town of Holstenwall. His show involves the somnambulist Cesare, who sleeps during the day and predicts the future to the audience in the evening, after his master wakes him up. During the night, however, while the good citizens of Holstenwall are asleep, Cesare commits murder on the orders of Caligari. One evening, he even predicts the death of one of his victims. Francis, a friend of the victim, suspects Caligari and pursues him. He finds out that the showman is in fact the director of an insane asylum and is apparently living a double life. He is himself mad, and he has fallen prey to an obsession: that he will become the legendary eighteenth-century psychiatrist Caligari, who spread fear and horror through his medium, Cesare. At the end of the film, however, it emerges that Francis is a patient at an asylum, accusing its director of being Caligari. Who is the madman, the obstreperous patient or the authoritative director?

The film was directed by Robert Wiene and the screenplay was written by Carl Mayer and Hans Janowitz. Even today, it is considered an exemplar of expressionist film and a milestone in the history of cinema. As early as 1930, Paul Rotha, in his history of film, *Film Till Now*, described it as an epoch-making, experimental and creative film in which the inner life of the human soul finds external expression.[1] Not only the plot but also the visual language is expressionist. The film was shot in the studio, and the characters act as if on stage. They wear lavish costumes, pale makeup and gesture vigorously – one common facial expression the camera captures is that of eyes-wide-open with horror. As in theatre, the scenery is cardboard, and the arrangement of its elements is freighted with symbolism. The walls slant; the perspectives are distorted in a way that evokes Lionel Feininger's painting *The City at the End of the World* or Max Oppenheimer's *Weltuntergang* [End of the world].[2] There are no straight lines. Everything is bent, askew and claustrophobic. Even the actors sometimes walk around stooped. The play of light and shadow creates a nightmarish atmosphere. Violins play discordantly and ominously. The oppressive cabinet of the horrors that live in the human soul is transferred to the screen.

In Kracauer's view, the film was not only typical of early Weimar cinema but also symptomatic of the society it depicted and which had produced it. Starting in January 1943, Kracauer and Lili went through the literature on German film from 1918 onwards systematically, reading and excerpting passages.[3] In July 1943, Kracauer received a one-year grant from the John Guggenheim Memorial Foundation in New York, and this was extended twice before finally ending in September 1945. This was one of the most prestigious grants a scholar could be awarded, and it attracted the attention of Princeton University Press. In the autumn of 1944, Kracauer had a book contract. Panofsky also played a role in this, acting as shadchan, a matchmaker, by recommending the project to the publisher's director, Datus Smith.[4] The title – *From Caligari to Hitler*

Figure 32. Werner Krauß in a scene from *The Cabinet of Dr. Caligari* by Robert Wiene (1919/1920)
Copyright: Ullstein Bild

– was Kracauer's own idea. The publisher was at first hesitant about having Hitler's name in the title, fearing it could damage sales. The suggested alternatives were *Shadows of the Mass Mind: A History of the German Film* and *German Film and the German Mind*. It is possible that Kracauer's title was inspired by William McGovern's *From Luther to Hitler*, one of the various popular books to construct a long ideational ancestry from some figure – Luther, or Hegel, or Nietzsche – to Hitler.[5] But Kracauer had something else in mind: 'To concentrate directly on ideas is always a sure way of never getting to understand them ... Ideas reveal themselves rather by detours, in unobtrusive details' – such as unconscious remarks, accidental configurations of objects and bodies, little involuntary gestures, fleeting phenomena – 'which form the surface of life', and which were nowhere captured and documented better than in film. Why, then, should film not be used as a source of insight into social and historical developments? Why should it not be possible to explain Hitler's rise to power or the mentality underlying the Nazi regime through an examination of the plots and visual language of film?[6] To Kracauer, the Caligari film seemed to represent the form of the Weimar period, at least of the time immediately after the war.

In Kracauer's account, the script by Mayer and Janowitz had originally been written with a revolutionary message in mind; it was a revolt of the sons against the authoritarian Caligari fathers who had sent them, the hypnotized Cesare sons, into the slaughter of a horrific and pointless war. The authority of the Caligaris concealed an unscrupulous, madness-driven double life, which had to be unmasked. This original intention of the film was betrayed in the course of its production. From an unpublished manuscript by Janowitz, Kracauer learned that the commercially savvy Ufa producer Erich Pommer and the director Wiene added the final twist in the story and thus turned the film's revolutionary thrust into its opposite. The film, Kracauer wrote, thus 'reflects this double aspect of German life by coupling a reality in which Caligari's authority triumphs with a hallucination in which the same authority is overthrown.'[7] Caligari's crime was reinterpreted as fantasy. Now, the rebel character was the madman, and what he called murderous insanity was what protected the community against the insane. In Kracauer's reading, the Caligari motif stands for the failed revolution, which, from the perspective of those to the left of social democracy, had been betrayed. That corresponded to the standpoint Kracauer had already taken in the final chapter of *Ginster*, set in Marseille, and continued in *Georg*. His gradual retreat from left-wing positions, especially after his escape, had not changed his judgement on this matter. On the contrary, he saw his picture of the failed republic confirmed by Arthur Rosenberg's *History of the German Republic* (1935), a work he leant on for his interpretation of the immediate post-war period and his overall interpretation of Weimar. It was in the political, social and economic ruins of the Weimar Republic, a '"system" which had never been a true structure' – but rather one with sloping walls made of cardboard, with badly lit rooms that were so small people had to stoop to walk – 'that the Nazi spirit flourished'.[8]

Kracauer also interpreted the Caligari fantasy as a premonition of National Socialism. Perhaps the monstrous deeds of the Nazis and Germans corresponded to the horror story of Caligari and the hypnotized, murderous Cesare. Did they not emerge directly from the horror fantasies of Friedrich Wilhelm Murnau's *Nosferatu, A Symphony of Horror* or Fritz Lang's *Dr Mabuse the Gambler*, both of 1922? Were these cinematic daydreams not premonitions of fantastic and fanatical crimes? Did not *Metropolis* (1927) announce the idea of the *Volksgemeinschaft*, the community of a people through the reconciliation between classes and the mediation between manual and intellectual labour? Was not the ornamental pattern of *The Nibelungs* (1924) the template for the party rallies in Nuremberg, for the skilfully arranged seas of flags and people, as well as being a document of anarchic outbursts, uncontrollable drives and passions, of the compulsion of fate? And did not at present the homunculus himself roam Europe, the artificially created man who tried to destroy humankind and humanity in Terezín, in Treblinka and in all the other scenes of mass murder? And was the reason that Weimar failed not to be found in the fact that it had been impossible for democracy and a free society to put down roots in Germany? From Kracauer's social-psychological perspective on the history of film and society, *Caligari*, understood as a symptom, indicated 'an escape that amounts to an antidemocratic, antirevolutionary rebellion'.[9]

But what is a psychological history, and what does film have to do with it? By 'psychological history' Kracauer meant a 'secret history' that runs 'behind the overt history of economic shifts, social exigencies, and political machinations'.[10] This secret history was concerned 'with the psychological pattern of a people at a particular time'.[11] It disclosed 'the inner dispositions of the German people' that were at work in its secret history. Movies, according to Kracauer, reflect the mentality of a nation, its fluid, spatiotemporally mutable national character, more directly than other media, because they are collective products designed to satisfy the masses. 'What films reflect are not so much explicit credos as psychological dispositions – those deep layers of collective mentality which extend more or less below the dimension of consciousness.'[12] In both political and methodological terms, the book picked up where Kracauer's phase of ideology critique left off, albeit with a Freudian twist. The

FROM CALIGARI TO HITLER

A PSYCHOLOGICAL HISTORY

OF THE GERMAN FILM

By SIEGFRIED KRACAUER

PRINCETON UNIVERSITY PRESS · 1947

Figure 33. *From Caligari to Hitler*: front cover of the first edition
Copyright: DLA Marbach

opening statement of his essay 'The Mass Ornament' had declared that 'the position that an epoch occupies in the historical process can be determined more strikingly from an analysis of its inconspicuous surface-level expressions than from that epoch's judgments about itself'; that is, because these expressions are unconscious and intention-free, they may be interpreted as symptoms.[13] The *Caligari* book adds to this analysis the category of the unconscious, drawn, in turn, from the Institute for Social Research's *Studies on Authority and the Family* (1936) and Erich Fromm's monograph *Escape from Freedom* (1941). These works argued that, although modern man has liberated himself from the fetters of pre-individualistic society, he has, with that liberation, lost the security offered by those restrictions and destroyed all limitations he had once been subject to. The victory and independence of rationality is accompanied by a sense of fear and impotence. The burden of freedom drives the isolated individual into new dependencies and submissions. This flight from freedom could be observed, in particular, in the authoritarian character of the collective ideology of Nazism: the striving for power over individuals and the simultaneous desire to submit to an overwhelming power. The authoritarian character is thus sadomasochistic. The members of the 'master race' were driven by feelings of inferiority, hatred and envy. The expressionistic film already depicted the way in which rebellion ends in regression. Such is the chaos of collective psychological life that revolt does not end in freedom and in a stronger sense of reality on which a more reasonable way of shaping the external world could be based, but in a renewed submission to a hated tyrannical authority. These psychological and social conflicts, Kracauer thought, had made possible Hitler's rise to power. *From Caligari to Hitler* was an attempt to understand the political and social development of Germany by superimposing the cinematographic surface on to the collective soul. *Caligari*, Kracauer believed, shows the German '"Soul at Work"'.[14]

The *Caligari* book's method was problematic. It was based on an a posteriori approach that assumed an exceptionally high degree of coherence both within the film industry and between films and collective mentalities. It told the story of the history of German film from the perspective of 1933, as a kind of Freudian deferred action, and it left little room for elements that might have pointed in a direction other than that recounted in its narrative. Kracauer's argument was potentially tautological: what was assumed to be the case was found, and what was found confirmed what had been assumed. It exhibited the 'Moebius strip' effect (Thomas Elsaesser): there was no outside or inside, no above or below. Everything, and everything's opposite, pointed towards 1933. Causes had effects which, in turn, became causes. The book might as well have been called 'From Hitler to Caligari'.[15] What further irked film lovers was that the book did not treat films primarily as aesthetic phenomena but as symbolic cultural forms. The focus was not on films as artefacts but on the producers and consumers of films – or rather on what had, allegedly, separated itself off from them and assumed an independent form. The analysis of the art works, too, was one-sided, not sufficiently complex and at times simply unfair. In addition, Kracauer switched at will between the level of production and the level of reception.[16] Finally, Kracauer mounted only a weak defence of his use of the construct of a 'national character'. Although he stressed that his concept was a historically limited one, which was thus to be differentiated from naturalistic conceptions, he was still taking a rather great risk by asserting the existence of some fundamental collective pattern at all.

All of these justified objections came to be articulated by a later generation of film historians who were themselves standing on the shoulders of such pioneering texts as the *Caligari* book. One cannot deny the art historical or social scientific value of the book. *From Caligari to Hitler: A Psychological History of the German Film* is neither a film history in an art-history sense, nor is it an encyclopaedia of film. It is not a conventional sociological or historical treatise that seeks to connect '1933' and the films of the Weimar era as causes and effects. It is a long essay that puts forward a political argument, albeit tending towards polemic, and a novel idea. It is not interested in presenting a knock-down proof or in appreciating the art of film in aesthetic terms. Kracauer went on a hunt for evidence which intentionally proceeded in a selective and interpretive fashion; he analysed how the supposed fundamental conflict between freedom and authority was expressed in film. Kracauer came ultimately to be interested in refocusing people's attention, in correcting the dominant narratives about National Socialism. He wanted to explain to his American audience that simply giving the Germans bread, work and the Bible would not be enough to make them part of the civilized world again after the war. These ills had a deeper foundation, and the magic word 'capitalism' was not sufficient to capture them completely. In the important letter Kracauer had sent to Wiesengrund in 1930, he was already lamenting the 'fate' that hung over Germany. He was thinking of something amorphous: the social climate, the political culture, the intellectual mentality – something along these lines. Kracauer's search for the meaning of this fate led him into the scholarly margins, into areas hitherto unknown and uninvestigated. In the daydream of film, he thought, it might be possible to capture this spirit, which was otherwise difficult to delineate. 'National character' was merely a label for this 'fate'. Sometimes he called it a 'social climate'; another time he spoke of 'psychological processes which in those days took place, deep underneath the surface of divergent ideologies, in Germany'.[17] Kracauer was looking for something that was otherwise 'incomprehensible'.[18]

It should not be forgotten that while Kracauer was working on the book something incomprehensible actually did happen: the murder of millions of European Jews. His own mother and aunt among them, they had been transported almost a thousand kilometres to the east, like cattle, to be killed. The *Caligari* book should therefore also be read as a settling of scores.[19] Watching the old Weimar films again, Kracauer felt he was coming back to a home he had lost, perhaps to one he had never really possessed. It was a reminder of an 'existential misunderstanding'.[20] His former home had been enemy territory long before his expulsion. Writing to a friend after two years in America, Kracauer himself pointed out how much of *Caligari* is biography: 'More and more, and without my involvement, I am beset by memories of France, and for my wife it is the same. Whole sequences of episodes keep flooding back, and if I did not have too much professional work to do, I would sit down and make a book out of it.'[21] We can be sure that Kracauer digested many of these memories in the process of writing the *Caligari* book. Having completed the manuscript, he wrote to Panofsky:

> While writing I felt like a physician carrying out an autopsy who, in the course of it, also dissects a part of his own, now definitively dead, past. But, of course, some things continue to live, however transformed. It is a *tightrope walking* between and above yesterday and today.[22]

The history of German film, he said, is 'a kind of biography of our generation'. To study it is thus a kind of coming to terms with the past, 'and through film all those things flood back that are half forgotten and yet belong to the inner core of our lived lives'.[23]

The *Caligari* book is therefore a number of things at the same time: idiosyncratic and original, one-dimensional and focused, suggestive and innovative. But most of all it is an aggressive settling of scores with the evil homeland. It moves through a reverse teleology into unknown and uncertain territory. It establishes a surprising discursive connection that had not been articulated before, and it unveils a secret about whose existence no one had asked any questions. It paints a portrait of Weimar film that is no less bent, skewed and magically enchanted than the sceneries of *The Cabinet of Dr. Caligari*. Both artefacts, the film and the book – Kracauer suggests to his readers – transform the way the world is viewed. Film and book communicate with each other in the realm of shadows, the realm of the incomprehensible. Both fight against demons.

From Caligari to Hitler appeared in 1947 with Princeton University Press. The press reaction was mixed. Eric Bentley, a friend of Brecht, described the book in the *New York Times Book Review* as the 'revenge of a refugee'. This captured an important aspect of the book, albeit in pejorative terms, inasmuch as traditionally vengefulness is seen as a stereotypically Jewish trait ('an eye for an eye'), as something primitive that had been overcome by Christianity. A review by the film critic Seymour Stern in the anti-Stalinist and left-wing liberal weekly *The New Leader* was almost malicious. Stern claimed that Kracauer's *Caligari* pursued a communist agenda.[24] To many, its use of deep psychology was suspect. The unconscious of the film-maker aims at the unconscious of the movie-goer – for Franklin Fearing, writing in the *Hollywood Quarterly*, this premise was just obscure. Arthur M. Schlesinger, in *The Nation*, disliked the way in which Kracauer assigned collective traits, which he considered simplifications and exaggerations.[25] The New York film scene came to Kracauer's aid, though. Richard Griffith and Iris Barry praised the book's 'revolutionary method', which at long last succeeded in connecting the medium of film with society. Robert Warshow, himself a former editor of the *New Leader*, protested against Stern's vulgar review, and in the film journal *Sight & Sound*, Herman G. Weinberg emphasized that the book was not Marxist but humanist.[26] Opinion among the exiles was also divided. Berthold Viertel praised the way Kracauer analysed a society through its dreams of itself, and also insisted that he could not detect in it a construction of some mythical national character. But the writer Hans Sahl, who had escaped from Marseille with the help of Varian Fry, quipped that one might as well have interpreted Superman as a representation of the Truman doctrine, or Mickey Mouse as evidence of the escapist tendencies of the American employee (interpretations Kracauer might well have agreed with).[27] There were also very interesting readings of the book coming from the academic world. The art history journal *Magazine of Art* spoke of the book as a brilliant failure: its thesis was untenable, but its perspective very fruitful. And not one but two psychoanalytic journals were very much taken in by the idea of treating films as collective symbols.[28]

The most unqualified appreciation of Kracauer's book came from London. Paul Rotha, a film-maker who had written a history of film at just twenty-three years of age, listed the *Caligari* book in *The Film Today* as among the three most important books on film ever written. In Rotha's view, Kracauer's book suggested a new perspective on film according to which they are not the isolated works of individual artists but social forms within wider contexts. This perspective, he argued, could also be applied to American, British and French movies.[29] This praise from London would prove to be the beginning of a wonderful friendship. Rotha was a close friend of Richard Griffith, Kracauer's predecessor as assistant to Iris Barry, but Kracauer did not personally know Rotha. After the death of Carl Mayer, who co-wrote the screenplay for the *Caligari* film, in the autumn of 1944, Rotha sent an obituary he had written to Kracauer. Kracauer admired the manner in which Rotha had transformed from an author on film into a maker of films. And they both shared a passion for the documentary. Rotha authored a monograph, *Documentary Film* (1938), on the 'use of the film medium to interpret creatively and in social terms the life of the people as it exists in reality', as the book's subtitle has it.[30] Among the films Rotha had made himself were *Shipyard* (1935), shot in a modernist, Soviet style, a film which, over the course of a year, followed the building of a passenger ship, and *People of Britain* (1936), a three-minute film with a pacifist message and music by Benjamin Britten.[31] Following this British endorsement of his *Caligari*, Kracauer swelled with pride; Rotha, he said, he considered the highest authority in matters of film.[32] The London cineaste, who had been trained by John Grierson, the father of British documentary film, would become an important discussion partner for Kracauer when the latter came to write his *Theory of Film*.

An initial wave of interest in *Caligari* had also reached Germany. *Der Monat*, edited by Melvin Lasky and financed by the American military government, printed the book's chapter on the film in its February 1948 edition. The editorial announcement mentioned that Kracauer 'himself translated the text into German for us, without, however, fully reaching the level of stylistic subtleness of his earlier creative phase'.[33] This disclaimer may be an expression of annoyance on the part of the responsible editor, who had been forced by Kracauer to reject an earlier translation of the chapter. That translation had certainly been unusual; Kracauer had in fact complained about it to Lasky, and Lasky apologized for it.[34] From the very beginning, the reception of the *Caligari* book in the Federal Republic contained some discordant notes. The disclaimer may have been written by Lasky's co-editor Hellmut Jaesrich, who, shortly before, had already reviewed the *Caligari* book for the new cultural journal *Dionysos*. His review had explained the 'smooth and seductive thesis' of the book in terms of the fact that the author 'had, painfully, left the body of the people [Volkskörper] at the height of his publishing activities'. And, of course, following the death of the seducer [Ver-Führer][35] of the German nation, and all the experiences of 'unknown, diabolically organized powers that it is almost impossible to escape',[36] it was imperative to warn the people against seductions of the body of the people by former members who had voluntarily amputated themselves from it. And if that member then went to America, a certain stylistic impoverishment was, of course, almost unavoidable. Welcome to the Federal Republic of Germany!

Following the publication of the chapter on Caligari, Kracauer began to receive letters from Germany, some of them somewhat dubious attempts to get back in touch with him.[37] In December 1946, when Clementine Cramer had asked him whether he had received any mail from his old homeland, he had answered: 'Thank God, no'.[38] This was all going to change very rapidly now, as many who had lost sight of him learned where he was. At the beginning of 1949, he received a letter from Karl Friedrich Borée, sent from Berlin-Frohnau. In 1930, Borée had run a legal practice in Berlin and had enjoyed enormous success with a novel he had written. He recounted the years that had passed in the intervening period: he had neither emigrated nor become a victim of the Nazis, but his behaviour had been upstanding (one of the four novels he wrote after 1933 had been banned). Kracauer's reply was harsh: 'Why did you never write to us in Paris? I assume you knew that we were living there. And do you not remember my wife? You do not mention her in your letter.'[39] A letter to another correspondent in Berlin-Charlottenburg opened: 'I would like to know what you did during the Nazi period.'[40] These were the two criteria the Kracauers applied, unwaveringly, in judging whether they would re-establish contact with someone: Did the person keep in touch after their flight? Did the person have anything to do with the Nazis?[41]

Even Hermann Linden, an old friend of Joseph Roth's, who sought care packages, was first questioned about his conduct during Nazi rule.[42] Kracauer organized the packages, and slowly a correspondence with the friend of his dead friend Roth developed as well, but Kracauer's general attitude in early 1949 was: 'I cannot make up my mind to take up old relations again, at least not yet. Too much has happened in the meantime.'[43] Wolfgang Weyrauch, whom Kracauer had once trained in journalism in Frankfurt, got in touch early on, in May 1947, from Berlin. He, too, was rebuked. Weyrauch's first letter began with a minor confession:

> I was in Germany throughout the Nazi period. I also published a few books. Apart from two sentences, one from 1941 and one from April 1945, the former written out of cowardice, the latter out of confusion, and for both of which I feel very much ashamed, I have not written or done anything evil. From 1940 onwards, I was a soldier, but I never had to take aim at anyone.

After four months without a reply from Kracauer (perhaps he was no longer used to such long and winding sentences), Weyrauch wrote again. This time Kracauer did reply, saying that he was surprised that Weyrauch 'now insisted on a quick answer, after you did not think of maintaining contact with me during the time of Hitler or in the years before'.[44] After all that had happened, it was not easy to establish trust again. Weyrauch had to wait for four years before a regular correspondence could be established.[45]

Very occasionally, Kracauer sought contact with old acquaintances himself, for example in the case of Bernhard Guttmann. He had moved to Buchenbach, near Freiburg, to retreat from the world, and in 1949 he celebrated his eightieth birthday there, alone. Guttmann told Kracauer that Grete de Francesco, who had once supported him in his employment dispute with the *Frankfurter Zeitung*, had been 'taken from her flat in Milan at night by the SS and taken to various camps', before being taken 'at last to Ravensbrück'. She was seen there by someone shortly before the arrival of the Americans, 'but afterwards never again'. Guttmann reported that Frankfurt was devastated, adding: 'You might not be able to bear being here today. I feel almost estranged from the Germany of today, and never write about its current problems. That Mr. Thomas Mann comes here and delivers speeches to the Germans surprises me; he is speaking to people he cannot possibly understand.'[46] After the *Der Monat* episode, Kracauer came to believe that the German people would not understand his *Caligari* book.[47] For a long time, he therefore declined requests for a German translation, despite the fact that he could have done with the money.[48]

32

Cultural Critic, Social Scientist, Supplicant

Though it became his best-known work and a classic of film studies, the *Caligari* book did not resolve any of Kracauer's financial problems.[1] On the contrary: 'I was financially never worse off here than I am now', he admitted in 1947.[2] Additional costs arising out of Kracauer's excessive proof corrections were about as much as the payment for the first edition.[3] And for the time being a second one was not planned. It would take until 1950 before the royalties equalled the advance of $250 (roughly £1,800) and the additional costs for the corrections, which Princeton University Press had paid upfront after Mondadori had acquired the Italian rights.[4] Like its author, the book was a latecomer.

There was also no prospect of grant money to cover the planned book on the aesthetics of film or other research projects in the area of mass communication. After the failure of an application to the Rockefeller Foundation by Cantril's opinion research institute in Princeton, which would have guaranteed Kracauer a fixed income for three years, he learned from Cantril that the Foundation was now focusing on the soldiers returning home.[5] While Kracauer was putting the finishing touches to the *Caligari* book, Horkheimer, to whom Kracauer was still sending the occasional flattering letter, revealed that he had an assignment for him. The director of the Institute for Social Research had been appointed the head of the scientific department of the American Jewish Committee (AJC), and Kracauer was to advise on the production of a film on anti-Semitism. The aim of this project was to counter prejudice. Kracauer received $700 and buried himself in the literature on racial prejudice, especially against Jews. On 6 January 1945, Kracauer attended one of the regular meetings of the advisory committee, made up of Otto Klineberg, Ernst Kris, Paul Lazarsfeld, Margaret Mead, Robert Merton and Hans Richter – the usual suspects (except for Mead) from the field of mass communication research. A script for the film, signed by Kracauer and containing his hand-written comments, is dated 4 April 1945. The project, however, never moved beyond the drafting stage; the film – *Below the Surface* – was never produced.[6]

The publication of the *Caligari* book was another caesura in Kracauer's life, marking the beginning of another period of financial insecurity. A certain intellectual sluggishness blighted him. After the end of the war, he preferred 'not to think about Germany any more', although he believed that his earlier publications 'would not be uninteresting for the Germany of today – so that it may awake from its amnesia'. Nowadays, he preferred to think about 'American themes'.[7] On the occasion of the end of the war, which marked a caesura in world history, he remarked succinctly: 'A new age has begun, is what many say. We have seen many an age begin. You tire of ideologies. One gets older.'[8] But one also lacked a secure income, not to mention any pension, despite being in one's mid-fifties. Between 1941 and 1946, Kracauer earned no more than $4,500, less than $1,000 per year.[9]

Through Horace Kallen, Kracauer was put in touch with Elliot E. Cohen and Clement Greenberg, and thus with the intellectually important journal *Commentary*, for which he wrote four articles.[10] But this was not a happy affair for him. In the case of the first article, he was displeased at the editorial changes. It must also have felt strange to paraphrase Horkheimer's ideas on the eclipse of reason under the title 'The Revolt against Rationality', because these ideas were his own, from *The Mass Ornament*: the victorious rise of abstract thought and technical skill, the resurrection of primitive and repressed instincts, the right of defeated nature. Horkheimer now saw at work the very dialectic of enlightenment that Kracauer had described twenty years earlier, and Kracauer was not so much as mentioned. This would not have been noted by Kracauer without some torment on his part – and not without some anger towards the doyen of critical theory.[11] Kracauer also contributed to the journal's discussion 'On Jewish Culture'; his solicited contribution, however, was not included.[12] He wrote a longer article on the increasing popularity of psychiatry, in which, oddly, he also included psychoanalysis, though he knew very well that psychiatry and psychoanalysis are estranged and somewhat hostile cousins.[13] Finally, he wrote a review of the East German film 'Marriage in the Shadows', which, although it was silent about the fact that Hitler '*came from within*', he considered a serious attempt at self-examination.[14] Kracauer was particularly taken aback by the fact that this anti-fascist film 'tends to cast Jewish emigrants almost in the role of deserters'.[15] The articles from this period reveal that Kracauer was not enjoying his activities at the journal and newspaper very much. It began with the need for correspondence. He always had to offer himself, present himself as an interesting figure, sing his own praises. Then he had to wait, enquire again, hope anxiously for some small assignment. He had to show gratitude to self-important editors who were twenty years his junior.

The to-do list of the supplicant was a long one. Apart from *Commentary*, it contained: *The Hollywood Quarterly*, *The Kenyan Review*, *The Nassau Sovereign*, *The Nation*, *The National Board of Review*, *The New Republic*, *The New York Herald Tribune*, *The New York Times* and its literary supplement, *The New York Times Book Review*, *The Reporter*, *The Saturday Review of Literature*, *Theatre Arts*, *Time Magazine*, the music journal *Listen* and Hans Erich Noth's review paper *Books Abroad*, then *Films in Review*, *Harper's Magazine* and the *Partisan Review*. In England, Kracauer published in *Penguin Film Reviews* and *Sight & Sound*; in Switzerland, he published some film reviews in the *Neue Zürcher Zeitung*, but, despite his offer of articles, no longer in the *Basler National-Zeitung*. That was an illustrious list by anyone's standards. But although Kracauer was included in the American 1947 edition of *Who's Who*, and thus had himself become illustrious, he received only very few commissions. 'I feel a bit like a forgotten man', he once complained to an editor of the *New York Times*.[16] There was something humiliating about his insistent and mostly unsuccessful enquiring. Nor did it produce a lot of money; between 1945 and 1950, he earned between $735 and $1,338 a year, with an annual average of just above $1,000.[17]

'For each badly paid article I have to trouble myself with the editors for days, if I get a commission at all', he lamented.[18] But it was not just the editors who were making life difficult for him. It was Kracauer himself. He had become a slow writer. While as an editor of the *Frankfurter Zeitung* he had written articles almost daily, with great ease, for the 'below the line' section of the newspapers,[19] and while these sometimes even had become influential, perhaps even classics of cultural theory, he managed to write around thirty articles as a freelancer, that is, around five articles per year, between 1946 and 1951. And even those did not compare with the pieces from the Weimar period. One reason for this was certainly the new language, but the terrible years of his escape from Germany had also clearly left deep marks on Kracauer; his mordant wit and sense of humour had been blunted. Reality had taught him a humility; his sharp pen had been ground down. Where once was a dry humour there was now a sort of wisdom that at times appeared platitudinous, for example, his article on psychiatry's claim that '[c]ommercial considerations encroach on human pleasures and ends, perverting them into means to economic ends', or his complaint that the present day 'pictorial deluge' of mass media is no substitute for genuine conversation.[20] Such notes of cultural conservatism were sounded in his earlier texts too, but they were now presented without the sarcastic overtones that once provided a contrapuntal note. There had been a time when Kracauer had preferred to sit in a stuffy cinema and watch trivial and mediocre films rather than engage in an edifying conversation during a walk in the countryside. Kracauer had come to resemble one of Chaplin's aged heroes. He was a bit like Monsieur Verdoux (of the eponymous 1947 film), who knows everything about the inhumanity of the world, recognizes that murder is only the continuation of business by different means, and who, in response to the claim of conventional morality that crime does not pay, retorts: 'If committed on a small scale.' And he was very much like Calvero, the aged and old-fashioned clown of *Limelight* (1952), who is no longer funny, only tired and melancholic, who wants to make his peace with the world and so selflessly sacrifices himself for the girl he loves.[21] Chaplin became a philosopher of life. His later films are a combination of social critique and cultural conservatism. He always remained Kracauer's favourite artist.

But even the films of old age keep you young. It was in the world of films and picture houses that Kracauer had the most intellectually stimulating relationships. From the end of 1945, Kracauer moved within the lively New York film scene. Together with Hermann G. Weinberg, who earned his money mostly through subtitling and with the occasional film review, he attended screenings in the film clubs on Broadway, such as the Bonded Projection Room (where Hans Richter could often be found) and the small 5th Avenue Playhouse in Greenwich Village, where quality films often premiered.[22] For the people in this social scene, the film society Cinema 16, dedicated to documentary and experimental films, was of particular importance. Its founder and director was Amos Vogel, an admirer of Maya Deren's experimental films. It existed between 1947 and 1963, and at its height had around 7,000 members, making it the largest film society in the US. Kracauer was a member and was on the advisory board, which was chaired by the influential documentary film-maker Robert Flaherty.[23] Among the membership were also famous individuals like W. H. Auden, John dos Passos and Yehudi Menuhin; central figures from film like John Grierson, Jean Renoir and Basil Wright; New York intellectuals such as Philip Rahv and academics like Horace M. Kallen; and, finally, Kracauer's friends from the world of film, Griffith, Richter and Rotha. Parker Tyler also collaborated with Cinema 16. He had written his *Magic and Myth of the Movies* while Kracauer was working on *Caligari*, and since that point had been seen as Kracauer's psychoanalytic Doppelgänger.[24] Cinema 16 received practical support from the Film Library, but no public financial support. The *New York Times* ignored the film society with a conspicuous consistency. It was a political project directed against the entertainment industry, and it showed films that you would not find in commercial cinemas: avant-garde movies, documentary films, lengthy films, short films, politically controversial films. And all these it would screen in large, booked-out venues, usually university lecture halls, with 500, sometimes 1,500, seats. These screenings were very popular. In May 1949, *Harper's Magazine* sent a reporter to one. 'Several thousand' were present for 'two complete performances' on that evening:

> Cinema 16 is less than two years old, and since it has neither adver-
> tised extensively nor received wide publicity, not the least remarkable
> thing about the audience is its size. ... Before I first went to one of
> the programs, I remembered having heard Cinema 16 described as 'a
> few people who are interested in film', and I foolishly expected this to
> mean several hundred ... . After one evening's performance, I asked
> Siegfried Kracauer, one of the most penetrating film critics in the
> country and a mainstay of Cinema 16, what was the secret of success.
> 'Every time Hollywood makes a picture,' he said, 'more people come
> in here.'[25]

For Vogel, Kracauer wrote short introductory texts for the programmes that Cinema 16 put on at film clubs (as did Griffith and Tyler). In October 1948, he wrote a text on French films of the 1930s that had been prohibited by the censors, like *Amok* (1934) by Fjodor Otsep. Later, he also wrote a text on the Nazi film *The Eternal Jew* (1940) by Fritz Hippler; the screening of the film was highly contro-versial, and Kracauer's introductory explanations were therefore appreciated.[26] As a thank you, he received a small honorarium and, of course, free admittance to all screenings.[27]

It is no coincidence that his film reviews are the best texts of the second phase of Kracauer's New York period as a freelancer that lasted until the early 1950s. There are sometimes even flashes of the old Kracauer. He was excited about Roberto Rossellini's films *Roma, città aperta* (1945; *Rome, Open City*) and *Paisà* (1946), which treated the German occupation and the resistance and the liberation of Italy by the Allies. The former was a drama that, he said, 'really showed the principles of human integrity at grips with a deranged world',[28] a film full of the 'power of observation and compassion for ordinary people', a movie that seizes upon 'the raw material of life'.[29] The latter he described as an epic told in episodes: here, 'humanity appears as a quality of man's nature, as something that exists in him independently of his ideals and creeds'.[30] According to Kracauer, in these stories the Nazis were not to be hated because they entertained perverse ideas but because they did bad things. The Italians, in turn, were not revealed as anti-fascist heroes, nor was the liberation told as the story of a happy victory. At the end of *Rome, Open City*, a German officer shoots and kills the courageous priest, while the cavalry just looks on, uninterested, and no Zorro or similar figure comes to the rescue. And in *Paisà*, the partisans are killed alongside their American allies, who rush to help them. Yet in both films, humanity triumphs. Their emphatic assertion of the reality of the good and their apparent lack of interest in ideas corresponded to Kracauer's 'philosophy of life', as it had taken shape in the years after he had fled from Europe.[31] He now preferred Rossellini's films to Eisenstein's *Battleship Potemkin*, which he once had admired so much: '*Paisan* deals with the human assets of ordinary people; Eisenstein's *Potemkin* shows ordinary people wedded to the cause of revolution. ... Rossellini patiently observes where Eisenstein ardently constructs.'[32] The Italian neo-realist film remained in close contact with reality; Hollywood films, by contrast, even when they took a realist approach, lacked real-life experience.

Despite being revivified by film and enjoying its attendant social life, the New York years between 1945 and 1950 were not happy ones. Lili became very ill during the last phase of the work on the *Caligari* book, having been afflicted for some time by the effects of the eight months of starvation in Marseille, the stresses of the escape and 'gloomy memories'. She suffered a fall and became completely immobilized by sciatica. Within half a year, Lili – already a slim woman – had lost eight kilos, and she had seen no one except her husband. She became shy of people. No sooner had she started to get better than Friedel became unwell. He put it down to the stresses of having to write to a deadline and to fears about the future. His condition he diagnosed as a 'fatigue of the nerves'. Its symptoms were a shortness of breath when walking, a constant pressure in the back and 'vascular cramps'. He then developed 'a nervous muscular cramp between the shoulder blades'. The doctor confirmed that he was, physically, perfectly healthy, and spoke of a typical '"refugee" illness', a nervous affliction caused by anxiety, stresses and being overworked. Lili, now recovered, approached the problem with her usual optimism. She assisted her Friedel with his work as she had always done; she did the cooking and took care of practical matters.[33]

Those years were a period of jarring transition. During 1946, Kracauer received a small monthly grant of $100 from the American Committee for Refugee Scholars, Writers and Artists.[34] In addition, there were two one-off payments of $250 from a fund of the National Institute of Arts and Letters for artists and authors; Farrell had mentioned Kracauer's name to them.[35] From the autumn of 1946 onwards, Lili had a job at the United Service for New Americans, a job she held down while still performing all the domestic duties, something Friedel either did not want to do or could not learn.[36] When Leo Löwenthal suggested seeking another grant for Kracauer from the Committee for Refugee Scholars, Writers and Artists, he definitively ruled out any further 'alms'. He no longer wanted 'charity'. Instead, he analysed material for his friend's study *Prophets of Deceit* (1949), work for which he was paid $100. (The study appeared in the series *Studies in Prejudice*, co-financed by the Institute for Social Research and the American Jewish Committee.[37]) There was more pride than reason in this, for Kracauer was still dependent on support. From time to time, his 'old friend' from his Paris days, Lady Davies, sent her greetings in the form of a cheque, which Kracauer happily accepted.[38] In July 1948, he even had to borrow money again, and Löwenthal organized a one-off loan of $250 from the Social Studies Association, a fund set up by the New School.[39]

During those years, Kracauer applied for posts at many institutions. He applied to the film division at the Defense Department, to the Schocken publishing house and to a small New York film centre. He offered his services as an advisor to Warner Bros. and Twentieth Century Fox, and asked whether the Library of Congress would be interested in his expertise on film. He knocked on the door of the American Jewish Committee to see whether they had any more work for him; he had previously participated in discussions of the Hollywood movie *Crossfire* (1947), by Edward Dmytryk, which told the story of an anti-Semitic murder. He hoped that the United Nations would not only bring peace but also might have something for him to do.[40] But in all of these cases, Kracauer confronted a dilemma: 'My misfortune is that I am too well known, and no one would think of offering me a subordinate job; yet, I am not famous enough to attract the really interesting offers. I fall between two stools.'[41]

At the end of 1948, Lili took up a post at the USNA (United Service for New Americans), an organization of eighty employees that had developed out of the old National Refugee Service. The USNA helped displaced Jews and, later, Jewish immigrants in general, beginning with their immigration applications while still in Europe until their settlement in the US. The work did not make use of her qualifications, but it was satisfying, and the income was sorely needed.[42] It was, however, much more exhausting than her previous job in the US. Lili had to work overtime, rarely came home before nine o'clock and sometimes went to the office on Saturdays. At home, her cooking duties and ailing husband awaited her.[43] The social life of the Kracauers was almost non-existent. Only on Saturday nights, and sometimes on Sundays, did they meet with friends; they passed up almost all of the manifold opportunities on offer in the global city of New York. Still, even the possibility of going out, participating, seeing or speaking with interesting people had 'something intoxicating' about it, Kracauer wrote.[44] The couple loved New York, especially Manhattan, but, looked at with sober eyes, one cannot say that their life there was a good one, or even a particularly intellectually satisfying one.

It is nice to imagine – but it is not true – that here at the Hudson, the Frankfurt School, personified by the freelancer Siegfried Kracauer, intermingled with the New York intellectual scene, producing an exciting dialogue that spurred his work on further. No, in those years, New York was not a melting pot of networks, encounters and cooperation, no meeting place for the best minds of cultural critique – Jewish heretics, homeless communists, avant-garde modernists, radical social philosophers, creative artists and rebellious literary critics – to come together, to argue, to inspire each other. For Kracauer, this most modern city of modernity was not the place depicted in Dos Passos's *Manhattan Transfer*, a place where he would have been the missing link between the New York intellectuals and the Frankfurt School.[45] He simply continued to work, an ageing writer worn down by life, lacking basic material security, in order to provide for himself. Apart from the patriarchal division of labour with his wife, his was the work of a lone wolf. He had little time for intense intellectual exchange, and he had less and less energy. As a rule, he was sitting at his desk all day writing letters. Sometimes, he used the phone. It was rare that he met someone for lunch. Often he was ill. Between 1946 and 1950, this was the extent of his social life. It was not an intellectual adventure; it was, on the contrary, bleak and narrow. His correspondence was seldom concerned with the discussion of books, articles or films – never mind 'reality'. They were the letters of a supplicant, or, when writing to friends, communications of the everyday worries of private life. Kracauer asked how Levin's chickens were doing, or the Gublers' children. He enquired about the Streiffs' furniture and Schüfftan's work permit. He rarely had the opportunity or the appropriate partners for 'symphilosophizing'. On one occasion, however, he met with Löwenthal, and afterwards wrote to him:

> I will not forget these couple of afternoon hours we spent at the DuBarry and then on the Hudson. It was like old times, when we were still talking about the real things, and not about advantages and disadvantages, and careers and reputations, which go as they come, and all that useless stuff. Life is too short for that. (If in my own case what was at stake were not bare existence, the Rand Corporation and similar institutions would be as immaterial as, in reality, they are. The terrible thing about crude material worries is that they pull you down so low.)[46]

But bare existence was at stake. The thing to be done, then, was to write to the Rand Corporation, to smile and accept rejection, to offer compliments, to feign interest and passion for all the things which robbed him, the philosopher, of his time. And still he had to count the money in his wallet to see whether there was enough to pay the electricity bill. 'That is an improvised life, and I only wait for the day when a fixed employment with a normal income will come my way. So far, all doors are still closed. Well, I assiduously continue my efforts, emulating my wife.'[47] Tough they were, the Kracauers: 'And we both want to reach a good age; the will to live is strong in us', they said amid these difficult times.[48] And, so, he continued to try to blow his own trumpet, especially when it came to his expertise in the social sciences. In November 1947, he applied unsuccessfully to a navy research project, led by Margaret Mead, Ruth Benedict and Otto Klineberg, offering to analyse European film.[49] In February 1948, he turned to Clyde Kluckhohn, the director of the Russian Research Center at Harvard University Press, citing his expertise in Russian film.[50] Through Cantril, who was now the director of a research project on 'international understanding' at UNESCO in Paris, he tried in vain to get involved in a state-sponsored research project on mass communication.[51] Between June and August 1948, Kracauer wrote a UNESCO study on 'National Types as Hollywood Presents Them' for Cantril's research project, and it was published in *Public Opinion Quarterly*. Unsurprisingly, he mostly criticized Hollywood's stereotypes of the English and the Russians. The work was 'miserably paid', took a lot of time and, in the end, was no intellectual tour de force. To Kracauer, it was an investment in the future.[52] In February 1949, Kracauer also agreed to take part in a pilot study on the US's self-image and its image of others, with Adolph Lowe and the Institute of World Affairs (attached to the New School), which was to involve an analysis of articles published within the first three months following the US's entry into the war in the *New York Times* and the *Times* of London. The payment of $300 was, again, rather modest.[53] Finally, Kracauer applied to Viking Fund, Inc. for support for a project on the analysis of mass media from the perspective of cultural anthropology. His proposal to investigate entertainment movies, popular magazines and bestselling novels and look for recurring motifs as well as considering the leisure time behaviour of the consumers was, however, rejected.[54] His hopes of interesting the Carnegie Corporation or the Rockefeller Foundation in another project in this area were also disappointed.[55] In no small part because of all these activities and initiatives, all this running around, Kracauer's years as a freelancer were not good ones; they were 'one big nightmare'.[56]

33

The Aesthetics of Film as Cultural Studies

During his time as a freelancer, Kracauer was happiest when he was able to work on his book on film. He had thought about the idea for it since 1937/38. *From Caligari to Hitler* had been a political book from the perspective of social psychology, and now it was clear to Kracauer that, in order to develop further the idea he had had in Paris – a book that combined an aesthetics of film and a sociology of film – and the 'Marseille Notebooks', he had to produce an aesthetics of film: a contribution to social philosophy written with the intention of shining a light on those societies in which a culture of film had developed. Just as he had once used the young discipline of sociology or the detective novel, Kracauer wanted to cast film as a medium that embodied the culture of the times:

> I should like to show which aesthetic laws and which affinities for particular themes a medium develops in virtue of belonging to a time in which scientific interest in the connections between the smallest elements gradually 'sublates' the intrinsic force of the great ideas which embrace the whole of mankind, and our receptivity to such ideas.

Kracauer's idea was that, historically, 'the aesthetic of the film belongs to an era in which the old "long-shot" perspective, which in some way aims to hit the absolute, is being replaced by the "close-up" perspective, which sheds light on what is perhaps intended through the individual detail – the fragment'.[1]

Kracauer explained his basic ideas in two texts dating from the end of 1948, which he had written as part of his search for funds: a research application to the Bollingen Foundation and an exposé for Oxford University Press. Although economically motivated, these sketches are also all of a piece with the sorts of discussions the 'group', Adorno, Benjamin, Bloch and Kracauer, used to entertain. In much the same way that he and Benjamin had attempted in their respective works on photography, Kracauer sought to look back at the origins of the medium. Film, Kracauer's hypothesis runs, emerged out of a human interest in movement, the interest that had inspired, for instance, Eadweard Muybridge's well-known stop-motion photographs of galloping horses.[2]

Kracauer had thus adopted an anthropological and materialist approach to film theory. In its infancy, 'the cinema', however, had not been anthropocentric: 'It represented material facts, especially movements, for their own sake, instead of using them for the construction of meaningful contexts.' In most cases, early cinema was also fragmentary and appealed to the senses first, and only second to the intellect. Here, the old anti-idealist thrust is again evident. Films make use of the visible world in its entirety – both the real and the imagined. It is peculiar to this medium that, by way of camera movements, illumination and montage techniques, it 'isolates and makes available to our perception' that which exists around us.[3] Cutting between close-ups and long shots, Kracauer wrote, sharpens the viewers' perceptual capacities. The old phenomenological questions were still exercising Kracauer: how might we truly capture reality, and how can we come to terms with the subject–object dichotomy?

The accidents of life, the ceaseless movement, the things we overlook – these are the elements of film, and, to a greater extent than any other medium, they afford us an access to reality; certainly, they achieve more in this way than pure thought. Film also reflects the spirit of the times. Kracauer interpreted the world of film, or photography, by analogy with the scientific world, that is, the natural sciences, which observe and quantify. Following Panofsky, he now considered substituting the expression 'physical world' for the phrase 'material world'.[4] But Kracauer also noted that film was not the same as photography because, in most cases, films told stories. Films unavoidably involve two opposite tendencies as their basis: the tendency to tell a 'story' and the 'documentary' tendency. It is also necessary to acknowledge that films have producers: without selection and perspective, without cutting and montage, 'life' cannot be reflected. The fundamental epistemological rule implicit in this is, again, that 'reality is a construction', even where it is a reality in which humans do not figure.

After the Paris and Marseille notes, this was the third programmatic statement of Kracauer's views on film. It was guided by a utopian hope:

> Film, a medium that emerged in our technological age, may at present have the mission of making our bodies and souls familiar with our environment, enabling us to take our environment along and, by accepting it, even to rescue [it from] violence and terror.[5]

Film is not only the most important artistic form of the present – as the novel had been for the nineteenth century. It also has something of a messianic aspect: film is meant to take along, collect and even rescue elements of our environment. Kracauer's guiding idea was no longer that of a negativity turning into revolution, as in the 'Mass Ornament' and the essay on photography of 1927; rather, at work here is the idea of redemption through the arrival of a Messiah who alters the world only very slightly, but thereby changes everything. It was necessary, again, for Kracauer to have something to work his way through. This had previously been the ornaments and rationalization; now it was material reality. He had to work his way through it with body and soul. He had to move through things, and that meant 'salvation by moving through reification, oscillating between the phenomenologically concrete and theology'.[6]

Nevertheless, Kracauer was convinced there was no returning back to a state before alienation. On the contrary, to Kracauer, alienation has the status of a precondition of knowledge and of any kind of realism. A photographer is a stranger. The attitude of photography is an alienated one. Kracauer cites Marcel Proust, who describes how his first-person narrator in *The Guermantes Way* enters his grandmother's salon after a long absence and sees a stranger 'sitting on the sofa, beneath the lamp, red-faced, heavy and vulgar, sick, day-dreaming, letting her slightly crazed eyes wander over a book, an overburdened old woman whom I did not know'.[7] For a brief moment, he perceives something his old gaze of familiarity and love had not been able to see, namely that his grandmother is fragile and mortal. The effect of this is the opposite of salvation: it is the terror of the knowledge that had expelled man from paradise. It follows that photographic and scientific knowledge also have an anti-messianic side to them. In his outline for an aesthetics of film, we find both of these opposed tendencies: the messianic hope, the praise for alienation. This peculiar combination made it difficult for his contemporaries to place Kracauer. It was also strange to people that Kracauer wanted to limit his aesthetics of film to its early years. He justified this approach by saying that the fundamental aesthetic traits had not changed – even the advent of the talkies had not changed film fundamentally. That claim was certainly controversial, even around 1950.

Kracauer's application to the Bollingen Foundation, which he submitted at the end of 1948, was promptly accepted.[8] The foundation took its name from a place on Lake Zurich, where Carl Gustav Jung had bought a plot of land on which he had built a house, his 'tower'. The foundation had grown out of the Old Dominion Foundation, which, since 1937, had concentrated exclusively on the humanities. In 1943, it had launched the 'Bollingen Series', originally with the intention of making Jung's writings available in the US. But the series soon began to publish other research into religion and myth. In 1945, the Bollingen Foundation was established, with the intention that it would simply oversee the book series. In 1948, however, it began to promote literature and work in humanities subjects, especially philosophy, more widely, making donations, awarding fellowships and prizes, in addition to publishing the book series.[9] Kracauer was one of the first recipients of one of their scholarships. For two years, starting in February 1949, he received a monthly stipend of $300 (roughly £2,600). For Kracauer, this was a liberation.

Kracauer could hardly believe his luck. He now turned to his intellectual friends and colleagues in the hope of finding inspiration. He discussed his two exposés with Adorno, Arnheim and Warshow. While Kracauer and Adorno were both in the US, they seem not to have had much contact with each other. It is unlikely that they would have met frequently in New York before Adorno followed Horkheimer to Los Angeles in November 1941 given that, a year later, Adorno mentioned in a letter that they had 'once again maintained a silence towards one another for ages'.[10] Their friendship was still strained, and there were only occasional letters sent from coast to coast. It was only with a letter from Adorno on the occasion of Kracauer's sixtieth birthday (8 February 1949) that the mood between them suddenly lightened. It was a cordial, almost soppy, letter, written in the 'loyal consciousness of a friendship which has lasted thirty years'. Adorno hoped that Kracauer would find a solution to his financial insecurity and that he would 'manage to bring to fruition all that has been ripening within [his] intellectual existence'.[11] Kracauer was touched:

> I am really grateful to you for remembering and for your words, which conjured up the encapsulated life of the past. It is so comforting to know that you know what we shared and that you keep it inside yourself. It gives me a feeling of security – of not being lost – for the time being; and I know that it is like that for you too.

Kracauer used this opportunity to ask Adorno for comments on his plan for, as Kracauer called it, his 'last book about film', saying that Adorno had 'great experience in these areas'.[12] Adorno was encouraging: '[a]n authoritative theoretical work on film is of the greatest importance and, indeed, in a highly charged sense, not merely the usual sociological sense, because it is here that the deepest levels of experience, down to perception itself, have become sedimented'.[13] And after Benjamin's death, who was there left to write such a book other than Adorno's first teacher in philosophical matters, the man who had taught him that philosophy without the experiences of life is blind, meaningless and empty?

In the spring of 1949, Kracauer had some initial conversations on the aesthetics of film and issues relating to perception with Rudolf Arnheim. Arnheim's thinking was a product of his engagement, in the 1920s, with the Gestalt psychology of Max Wertheimer, Wolfgang Köhler and Kurt Lewin. Kracauer was probably drawn to Arnheim's conception of visual thinking [anschauendes Denken]; Kracauer himself had always claimed that thinking has at least as much to do with perceiving as it does with comprehension. However, what Kracauer probably found most attractive about Arnheim was that his theory of art had a strong philosophical undercurrent. Something had clearly gone wrong, Arnheim thought, when people were merely chipping away at isolated scientific problems. It was the task of the arts to enlighten human beings about the nature of their existence. Arnheim conceived of his psychology of the arts in much the same way as Kracauer did of his film aesthetics: as a science of culture on a philosophical foundation.[14] They were kindred spirits. Some biographical parallels also contributed to the elective affinity between them. Like Kracauer, Arnheim had been a pioneer of film criticism and film theory during the Weimar era, and in 1932 his important work *Film as Art* was published. He, too, eventually arrived in Manhattan in 1940, after being forced to travel to Rome and London. Like Kracauer, he had first received a grant from the Rockefeller Foundation (for a work on radio soap operas), and then a Guggenheim Fellowship. The immigrant fell in love with the directness of the English language, which led him 'from theory to the concrete', although without, of course, shedding his philosophical motives altogether. Despite Arnheim's enthusiasm for America, his thought and his activities had a 'German foundation': in philosophy, literature and the arts. But he quickly identified with his new home. He loved the country; he felt himself an American and very comfortable with it.[15] Kracauer could have said all this of himself.

Their paths most likely crossed immediately after Kracauer's arrival in New York. Arnheim had recommended Kracauer to Panofsky, and from 1942 Arnheim was teaching psychology of art at the New School, where Kracauer was participating in the weekly seminar of the Graduate Faculty. Their correspondence, beginning in 1949, was cordial. Arnheim noted their 'common background'; between Europeans in the new world, there was a kind of immediate and spontaneous mutual understanding. Arnheim and Kracauer debated the old question of Kant and Hume on knowledge; they debated natural and artistic beauty. They compared the edges of paintings with those of photographs, and they discussed psychological films. Arnheim explained the concepts of Gestalt psychology to Kracauer, such as the 'contemplative attitude' or 'reduced natural size' in photographed and naturally perceived images. Their conversations went back and forth between English and German. They met regularly in order to think about aesthetic problems or to discuss Erich Auerbach's *Mimesis*, a book about the representation of reality in European literature. It was the beginning of a wonderful friendship, especially during term-break time when Arnheim was less busy: 'He is always there for me and always interested – a good friend.'[16]

The third person Kracauer engaged as an advisor regarding matters of film theory was Robert Warshow, who had previously defended the *Caligari* book. He was no more than thirty years old, an editor at *Commentary,* and he wrote for the *Partisan Review*. Warshow was one of the left-wing New York intellectuals whose initial anti-Stalinism shifted gradually into an increasing anti-communism. Like Arnheim and Kracauer, he was a non-practising Jew, was interested in Kafka and comics, wrote excellent articles on criminals and gangsters, and on those who went to the American West, or rather on how film made these figures into heroes of modern American life. To Warshow, going to the movies was like fishing, drinking or playing baseball. It did not matter that a film was a work of art; what mattered was whether it managed to hold him, the spectator, spell-bound. He had unconventional ideas, which he put together in a book proposal for a grant application to the Guggenheim Foundation. (The book was, in the end, never written, because in 1955 Warshow died of a heart attack, at just thirty-eight.) Warshow divided film criticism into an aesthetic and a sociological branch. 'The aesthetic critic says: It is not the movies I go to see; it is art. ... The sociological critic says to us, in effect: It is not I who goes to see the movies; it is the audience.' But both miss out on something, namely 'immediate experience': 'A man watches a movie, and the critic must acknowledge that he is that man.'[17] Warshow had in mind a theory of film that would not take the form of an abstract work. It would instead express itself through essayistic texts on film. He declared Kracauer's *Caligari* book the prototype of the sociological method in film studies, and he exempted Kracauer's aesthetics of film from the charge that it impoverished experience. Warshow was familiar with Kracauer's planned aesthetics of film. He would have known, then, that Kracauer's intention was that 'experience' was not to be swallowed up by theory or pushed aside by a formal aesthetics, but that, despite its academic language, the enterprise was in fact the result of experience. Since Marseille at the latest, Kracauer had been committed 'with skin and hair',[18] with his whole existence, including his intellectual libido, to the aesthetics of film. Kracauer's plan was not, as was Warshow's intention, to explicate 'experience'; but experience permeated every sentence. The search for a material aesthetics was one element of Kracauer's enduring struggle to come to terms with existence. The analysis of film was in the service of a philosophy that investigated and appropriated reality. Kracauer wanted to write a book that illuminated film as a paradigmatic way in which we experience the world or, more precisely, experience the decay of the world, as Miriam Hansen suggests: 'Kracauer incorporates the threat of annihilation, disintegration, and mortal fear into his film aesthetics as a fundamental historical experience.'[19] Undergirding this was a belief that, after the 'vabanque game of history'[20] had been decided, after hopes for a rational and free society had been extinguished in the hotels of Paris, the embassies of Marseille and, most of all, in the death camps in the east, the time of the panorama, the long shot, the last things, was over. The lesson of history was not to prepare for the coming revolution but to gird one's loins for the struggle for mere survival. And the taking-along, the rescuing of the ephemeral, overlooked and disfigured things, was an attitude that had grown out of this experience. The task of film, according to Kracauer, was to adopt this attitude.

Adorno, Arnheim and Warshow thus formed a – rather illustrious – trio that Kracauer turned to on matters of film theory. Like the Weimar group (Bloch, Benjamin, Adorno, Kracauer), all three were, in Isaac Deutscher's phrase, 'non-Jewish Jews', and they had all once been politically radical and, of course, left-wing, before growing out of their convictions as a consequence of the usual disappointments suffered by left-wing intellectuals – without, however, having become apolitical. Their interest in aesthetics and film grew out of an interest in social philosophy, but each of them had his own approach: Adorno investigated the meaning of 'experience' in the context of the 'culture industry'; Arnheim's approach was based on Gestalt psychology and his interest in the way art is perceived; and Warshow's followed on from his passionate, politicized and emphatic relationship towards mass and popular culture. Kracauer's fourth advisor was Panofsky. He sent Panofsky a copy of his outline and named him as a referee in his application to the Bollingen Foundation. The match-maker from Princeton once again supported Kracauer, and he warmly endorsed the book to Oxford University Press: 'Kracauer's book promises to be a really exciting and fundamentally important work, and his main thesis – the intrinsic conflict between cinematic structure and story, endlessness and finiteness, episodic atomization and plot logic – strikes me as being both original and fundamentally correct.'[21] Panofsky, however, also had one suggestion: Kracauer should trace the conflict between the documentation tendency and the story-telling tendency right back to photography. Kracauer found this plausible. Panofsky might even have been the most important of his interlocutors in the aesthetics of film: his essay 'Style and Medium in the Motion Pictures' had been an important influence on Kracauer after he had arrived in New York. Further, Panofsky had been the one to introduce the concept of 'physical reality' into film theory, which was of such importance to Kracauer, and he had offered him his unconditional support. But, quite apart from these points, there was a 'distant closeness' uniting the two that went beyond their shared love of film.[22] Panofsky, the academic art historian, like Kracauer, the social philosopher-cum-writer, stood for an understanding of the humanities as neither distant from society nor hostile towards modernity. On this view, humanities subjects should neither be esoteric and narrow, nor should they allow themselves to be subsumed under the model of the natural sciences. Most of all, they should not follow any fashion that they had not invented themselves. Panofsky thought that the humanities had to be interested in reality. Yet that was not intended as a rebuff to theory. On the contrary: 'The man who is run over by an automobile is run over by mathematics, physics and chemistry.'[23] (And possibly, we may add, by an overstressed, or nervous, or aggressive driver, hence by psychology and sociology.) In April 1950, Panofsky spoke at a conference of the New School for Social Research that was attended by Kracauer.[24] His theme was method in philosophy and the sciences. As an institution that had helped to foster the development of new approaches in the humanities by drawing on European traditions, the New School was an appropriate place for a meeting of humanities scholars and social scientists who shared the experience of migration. The New School had played a role in the spread of phenomenology, Gestalt psychology, psychoanalysis, political sociology and cultural anthropology and structuralism (represented by the group of French scholars around Claude Lévi-Strauss, who had been invited to New York during the war).[25] These migrant scholars were open to the philosophical currents running in their country of exile, in particular to pragmatism and the emphasis on empirical research.

In any case, Kracauer and Panofsky met each other with open minds; they were even curious about each other. Panofsky wanted to pick Kracauer's brains about film as, 'in a technical and socio-logical sense', he knew very little about it. He was impressed by Kracauer's 'incredible understanding' of his own method, which he himself called 'pointillist' and Kracauer described as 'drilling little holes in the walls', an understanding most art historians lacked. For Kracauer, in turn, Panofsky was an absolute authority with regard to aesthetics and the arts. And both, of course, took film studies to be a part of the 'humanities'.[26] Kracauer sent Panofsky his first published article on the aesthetics of film, 'The Photographic Approach' (1951), which had appeared in the *Magazine of Arts*.[27] The 'approach' of the title referred to the attitude of the photographer towards his or her medium. As in his

Figure 34. Erwin Panofsky in 1966
Copyright: Getty Images. Photo: Fred Stein Archiv

major essay of 1927, he attempted to see photography against the background of its historical context; where before this context had been that of historicism, it was now one of positivism. For the first time, Kracauer floated the idea he had discovered with the help of Proust: that photography is a product of alienation. The associated definition of the photographer as a witness, observer and stranger – someone, one might think, who simply holds up a mirror to nature – he immediately qualified, however. By itself, that definition would amount to a naïve realism, for there was no such mirror. Through their selection of a frame, camera settings, the lighting and, of course, by turning three-dimensional, coloured phenomena into two-dimensional black-and-white pictures, photographers modify nature. Photographs contain thoughts, even feelings, as Beaumont Newhall had shown by citing the melancholy of Charles Marville's and Eugène Atget's Paris street scenes.

Following Panofsky's advice, Kracauer had indeed identified a storytelling tendency in photography. Objectivity in the strict sense was not possible; even Proust's alienated observer brought a certain order into his spontaneous impressions, raising the unconscious layers of his perception up to the level of consciousness. Nevertheless, Kracauer thought that the photographic attitude should pursue the realist tendency, and should resist the tendency of the intellect to introduce form. Only then might the right balance be achieved between an exploitation of the 'inherent abilities of the camera' and the requirement to heed the 'basic aesthetic principle' of photography as a medium.[28]

Panofsky thanked Kracauer for his article on photography, sending him, in return, the paper he had read at the New School conference, 'Meaning in the Visual Arts' (which had also appeared in *Magazine of Art* in 1951), and adding his greetings to his 'strange bedfellow'. Panofsky's iconology struggled with the same questions and problems as Kracauer's aesthetics of film. It was conceived as an interpretative method, guided by reason, but also by experience and intuition. Panofsky sought to expand a descriptive iconography by incorporating other methods – historical, psychological and sociological. On this approach, the art history of iconology is seen as a humanistic discipline that converts the chaotic diversity of human images into something that Panofsky named, in analogy to the natural cosmos of the scientists, the 'cultural cosmos'. But unlike the natural scientists, who face the task of 'arresting what otherwise would slip away', the scholar of pictures is faced with the task of 'enlivening what otherwise would remain dead'. Panofsky was not an idealist; he insisted upon a closeness to the material and a micrological way of proceeding that looked 'for God in the detail' (Aby Warburg).[29] Kracauer liked this approach because he, too, wanted

Figure 35. Charles Marville, Rue de Glatigny, Paris (1865)
Photo: Charles Marville

to learn first 'what his material had to tell him' before bringing his interpretation to bear on it. If the material was too unwieldy, then there was no point in imposing an interpretation on it. One might call Kracauer himself an iconologist working on foreign territory, and his *Caligari* book, with its search for recurring motifs in the stories and pictorial languages of Weimar film, a secret product of the iconological method.[30] In any case, Kracauer's relationship to Panofsky meant a lot to him, and the letters between the two reveal a great deal of mutual respect, even affection.

34

Two Boxes from Paris

Kracauer's rapprochement with Adorno was no less enlivening than his correspondence with Panofsky. It was further deepened when, in October 1950, the Kracauers sifted through old papers that had been packed up in two boxes and left behind in Paris for almost a decade. Shortly after having opened them, Kracauer wrote to his old friend:

> It was a real sensation: the past revisited, *le temps retrouvé*. I found a whole portfolio of your work, dear Teddie – printed essays and manuscripts. A copy of the *Detektivroman* [Detective novel] has turned up again. I was no longer aware that I had written a complete book-length manuscript about Georg Simmel. I also found a well-preserved copy of the novel which I completed in 1935, which takes place in a newspaper office during the Weimar Republic. At the time, Thomas Mann found a home for the manuscript in Holland, but – for reasons which seemed valid to me then and were probably nothing of the kind – I withdrew it from publication. ... And then I found a fine collection of my best essays about streets in the *Frankfurter Zeitung* (Berlin, Paris, Marseille, etc.), which were to have been published by Bruno Cassirer under the title *Straßenbuch*. But then along came Hitler. ... But the main thing is that this rummaging through the past, with a lot of correspondence among it, aroused in me an unbridled desire to write my memoirs ...[1]

Finding lost time again: that was another form of rescue. The boxes from Paris were Kracauer's *petite Madeleine*. Indeed, Proust became ever more important for Kracauer, first by way of a 'cold stream', his praise of the alienation inherent in the photographic gaze, and now by way of a 'warm stream', the rescue of things past. That one of the boxes contained the unpublished manuscript of *Georg*, which Adorno would, understandably, never be allowed to see, did not affect his rekindled love for Fred. Kracauer now followed the meteoric rise of his old-new friend with sympathy: from an expellee to a celebrity of post-war Germany, with breath-taking publications along the way. He was genuinely glad to see him appointed to a professorship:

> It looks as if your harvest-time is coming at last, and that fills me with deep satisfaction because of the poetic justice which it implies, for I know hardly anyone who has worked for so long, without chagrin or compromise, as you have – but of course also without financial worries, as I must add (as a gentle qualification).[2]

Adorno sent him all his new publications, which appeared in quick succession, mostly with Suhrkamp. Most of this work Adorno had written during his years in exile. Kracauer was full of admiration for his friend's productivity. And he was full of memories of the times when they met for their reading group in Seeheimer Straße 19 in Frankfurt-Oberrad, especially when reading the article by Adorno on the philosophy of Husserl. Kracauer was absorbed by *Minima Moralia* and, as Ginster had with his fellow pupils, secretly awarded each of its aphorisms a mark. He told Adorno about his reading experience:

> that when an interpretation seemed to me to be one-sided or appeared unsatisfactory for some other reason, shortly afterwards a passage would follow which revised or supplemented your initial approach so that in the end it was just as if the phenomenon had been totally incorporated into the dialectical process. Many objections which I raised while I was reading were corrected by you yourself as you completed your train of thought. At times, I felt that it was quite uncanny.[3]

Kracauer was pleased to see that Adorno sought to save Benjamin for posterity:

> The way in which you analyse Benjamin's dialectic and tease it out – a dialectic which does not progress, or never closes, and is always rekindled by the material of waste – gives a very profound insight into this unique and at the same time curious mechanism of thought.[4]

Kracauer praised Adorno's essay on Kafka as one of his best works. He liked that it did not interpret Kafka symbolically but took him literally, an approach Kracauer himself had defended in his articles in the *Frankfurter Zeitung*. Adorno's 'leitmotif of Kafka understanding the "system" from its refuse (like someone going through the rubbish and putting together beautiful figures from discarded rags and splinters all by himself)' reminded Kracauer of Benjamin's image of the rag-picker, an image he had once, of course, applied to Kracauer.[5] Of course, the correspondence between Kracauer and

Adorno from 1949 to 1954 is not entirely free of disagreement – about the relationship between dialectics, utopia and opinion, for instance, a dispute they later addressed explicitly – but throughout the tone is cordial, almost emotional; because of the reawakening of thoughts of their past life, perhaps, it is also a little sentimental.

In 1950, Flora and Max Stettiner, friends from Frankfurt who had found refuge in the Mount Carmel region near Haifa, wrote to Kracauer to speak of 'a tie that reaches far back into an almost forgotten time, to whose people we nevertheless still feel much more closely attached than to anyone we met at a later stage'.[6] Kracauer may not have felt this with the same clarity; he was living in the here and now. But for him, too, the past was becoming more important with every year that passed. Shortly before Leo Löwenthal travelled to Europe in August 1951, Kracauer wrote to him:

> The climax of your journey, insofar as it is private, will be Frankfurt. The reunion will do you good. Send greetings from us all. And do not forget to have a look around in Lisbon, if you can find the time. We spent six weeks there and became so fond of the city that we shall certainly go there again, should we go to Europe on occasion.[7]

Kracauer was particularly moved whenever friends from Paris got in touch, for instance the actor Alfred Beierle, who had left Germany in 1934 only to return in 1936, after which he was sent to the Sachsenhausen concentration camp for ten months on the grounds of having 'insulted the Führer abroad' and banned from his profession. Kracauer informed him of the death of Joseph Roth: 'We met him still in his last weeks: an unspeakable sight – his face bloated and almost paralyzed.' Beierle told 'dear Ginster' that Sieburg worked at the *Frankfurter Zeitung* again, something Kracauer described as a 'ghostly re-appearance'.[8] This reopened old wounds. Memory was ambivalent, a feeling shared by Fritz and Annemarie Wahl, friends of the Kracauers from before 1933. Fritz Wahl had worked as a correspondent for the *Frankfurter Zeitung* in Madrid and had financially supported Kracauer after he was sacked by the paper. Following Franco's victory, the Wahls had settled in Switzerland, where from 1938 they lived, for twelve years, in a single room, and prohibited from working. With the exception of his brother, his whole family was killed by the Nazis. The oldest brother, the owner of a large department store, 'died of nutritional oedema in Theresienstadt'; his wife 'lost her mind over this and in that condition was sent to Auschwitz'. Two other brothers, 'who were married to Christian wives, were liberated from a camp near Berlin by the Russians, dangerously ill'. Only one of them survived the effects of their captivity. 'It is not possible to forget these things, and we also do not want to forget them.' In early 1950, they nevertheless travelled to the 'land of ashes' to visit the surviving brother. After their return, the Kracauers received a detailed report: 'The impressions were in every respect agitating. Here and there you meet a decent person, and many, all too many, who pretend that they have been decent.' The word 'conviction' [Gesinnung] had been replaced with 'opinion', and

> yet they sit in all administrative bodies, in all editorial offices, these party members or beneficiaries of the system. The Nazis and the ones who adapted without wearing the party badge – the latter often are much worse – spread themselves everywhere and dominate public life to an extent that, again and again, makes you feel sick.

The Wahls had been to the Rhineland and saw there how, 'between the ruins', an incredible 'wealth of luxuries' was spreading. 'Wretched figures flatten their noses against the glass of the shop windows, which nearly burst with food and delicacies.' In addition to the indecency and insincerity, there was hardship and emotional chaos:

> A thin, amoral top layer of society lives a glorious and joyful life, and a depraved and confused population as poor as beggars can hardly cope with this rift. Worst off are the old people and those returning from Russia, who are so eagerly awaited, but who no one actually wants to see, because they have to be clothed and fed.

For Jews, the situation was uncanny:

> There is no overt anti-Semitism, but it creeps around the country silently, and all the more dangerously for that. That is hardly surprising because in the government bodies and in commercial and economic life the same people are in charge as in the glorious past. Every Jew, after all, reminds these people of their cowardice, if not of their crimes.

They just do not dare 'to express their opinion openly'.[9]

Such bleak reports confirmed the Kracauers in their resolve: they would stay in the US despite, or possibly because of, their 'longing for Europe'. When he was asked, ten years after his arrival in Brooklyn, why he had not returned, Kracauer responded not only by distancing himself from Germany but also by stating, simply, that he 'had put down roots here'.[10] The Kracauers also asked themselves:

> For what have we endured so much? In order to start again where all this unspeakable suffering has been caused to us (and the whole world)? The idea of returning to Germany would never enter our

heads. Not that we do not believe that there are some decent people living there, and so on, but the air there has been polluted for a long, long time, and you do not know whose hand you are shaking. Finally, we have continued living and learning in the seventeen years after we left. To move among the ghostly figures of the past again would mean denying and undoing this altogether new life.[11]

One of those ghostly figures was Benno Reifenberg. The scars Kracauer bore from his dealings with Reifenberg were still a source of pain. He had not heard from him since Paris in 1933. Now, the man who had fostered his career only to later drop him was trying to get the old editorial staff back together, and so he turned up at the Wahls' place out of the blue. He had already re-engaged the services of Friedrich Sieburg, who, despite insisting that he had not been a party member, had been prohibited from publishing between 1945 and 1948. Once his ban was lifted, and after he had given Reifenberg his 'word of honour' that, as the Wahls reported his statement, 'all the charges levelled against him were complete inventions', Reifenberg employed him at the weekly paper *Die Gegenwart*. The truth was, however, that he had been a member of the NSDAP, from 1941, and a committed National Socialist. According to the Wahls, Reifenberg had visited Zurich because he had not been able to find enough people to relaunch the *Frankfurter Zeitung* because 'the Jews are missing everywhere'. But the Jews, Wahl said, did 'well to avoid Germany and everything to do with it'. He turned down Reifenberg's offer. The events surrounding the re-establishment of the *Frankfurter Zeitung* were, of course, of particular interest to Kracauer. Since September 1945, the Kracauers had been in contact with the Gublers again, and they regularly sent them news about old friends from Frankfurt, including about Reifenberg, who, they reported, had grown old, tired and melancholic.[12] For Kracauer, Sieburg's case was a typical one. Kracauer did not want to 'breathe in an atmosphere (and perish morally), in which Sieburg's word of honour counts for something'. And at that time, around 1950, he did not want to have anything to do with Reifenberg either, and not just because of his dealings with Sieburg. 'We cannot forget what stands between us.'[13] A wooden Buddha saw to it that he would indeed never forget. It was a present from Reifenberg, given when all had still been well – Kracauer had kept it and placed it on his bookshelf.[14]

Despite all this, Frankfurt had come closer again. An elderly Bernhard Guttmann visited it ten years after the war and spoke of a 'prospering city' that was 'strongly influenced by the winds blowing from America; the old things are disappearing, and skyscrapers mark the cityscape'.[15] Kracauer's desire to visit old Europe – even if perhaps not, straightaway, the city of his birth – grew with each New

Yorker friend and acquaintance who crossed the Atlantic and sent him back postcards.[16] Plus, many of the 'old ties' had re-emerged, most of all with his beloved Paris and with Switzerland.[17] For the time being, though, the Kracauers could not afford such a journey. They did not have the money because there were still debts to pay, and they did not have the time. The Bollingen grant was going to end in 1952, and Kracauer still had to make headway on his project. The generous stipend should have spurred him on, but a new job got in the way. At the beginning of 1950, he started taking on assignments for the radio broadcaster *Voice of America*, which was financed by the State Department and whose mission was to make 'the world' (meaning, at the time, forty-five countries) familiar with the views of the White House, via short-wave radio. Kracauer took on these assignments out of caution, gripped by the fear that, once the grant ended, he might have to return to freelance work in his sixties.[18] For the time being, Kracauer's film aesthetics became an early victim of the Cold War, which, in 1950, was threatening to heat up.

35

Working as a Consultant in the Social Sciences and Humanities

In 1949, Leo Löwenthal (or Lowenthal, as he now spelled his name) became the director of a new research division at *Voice of America*. The department was tasked with investigating the effects of the broadcaster's programmes on its listeners.[1] In order to carry out this work, it contracted with university institutions, among them the Research Center for Human Relations at New York University, headed by Marie Jahoda, and the Bureau of Applied Social Research (BASR), which was founded by Paul Lazarsfeld. Since 1946, Kracauer had been attempting to find his way back into social science research, and it seemed his chance had finally come. The heyday of mass-communication research had come during the war, with all the research into propaganda, and in this context Lasswell was the central figure. Now, five years after the end of the war, there was renewed interest and increasing activity in the field. The journal *The Public Opinion Quarterly* gave Lowenthal the opportunity to present the research group's ideas on 'international communication research' and 'psychological research into politics' in a special issue. In Lazarsfeld and Lasswell, he had two well-known names among his contributors. But there were also new names, like Charles Y. Glock, who had just succeeded Lazarsfeld as the director of the BASR, Herta Herzog, Alex Inkeles, Daniel Lerner and Paul Massing, all sociologists who were associated with the BASR. And there was Kracauer, who contributed a text on qualitative content analysis. It was clear to all of the contributors that they were not just talking about a new area of sociology, a *'new enterprise'*, as Lazarsfeld had called it,[2] but also about politics. Mass-communication research was born out of the Cold War, and it was undertaken in the service of, and paid for by, the US government. 'Communications and psychological policy research in a world which is becoming increasingly bipolarized can do much to clarify the nature of the objectives and self-estimates of the free world' and so to counteract the 'Soviet leaders' emphasis on cleavages and diversity in the free world'.[3] Despite this nakedly political agenda, the special issue of the journal began a boom in 'international communication research'. Whether it was a fear of the Soviet Union or the work of Lowenthal, the research director, that was more instrumental in securing Kracauer's place in this field must remain an unanswered question. From June 1950 onwards, he analysed the programmes produced for Russian, German, Italian and Polish listeners, and from December onwards the reactions of listeners from Bulgaria, Greece, Spain and Austria. This was followed by work on the Near and Middle East. At the beginning of 1952, Kracauer was given a significant assignment involving the analysis of surveys of listeners in Poland, Hungary and Czechoslovakia. The results were only published in 1956, in the study *Satellite Mentality: Political Attitudes and Propaganda Susceptibilities of Non-Communists in Hungary, Poland and Czechoslovakia* (co-authored with Paul L. Berkman).[4]

When Kracauer began this work, the antagonism between the US and Soviet Russia was nearing its first peak. The Korean War, one of the first major proxy wars of the Cold War, was in full swing. There was even the threat of the use of nuclear weapons. The war claimed the lives of four million people, forced twenty million to flee and resulted in the division of the country, and it solidified the existence of two global blocs that had grown out of differences of policy regarding Germany.[5] The world was now divided into West and East, capitalism and communism, into the world of capital and the world of the proletariat. But the main difference was that there were republican states with civil rights and liberties on one side and dictatorships with one-party rule on the other – potentially open societies here, essentially controlled and sealed-off societies there. It is quite remarkable that not only Kracauer, but even self-described Marxists such as Kirchheimer, Löwenthal and Marcuse, all of them close to Horkheimer, and erstwhile revolutionary socialists from 'Red Vienna' like Jahoda and Lazarsfeld, did not hesitate to take the side of the West. This was not even a matter for debate but something simply taken for granted. 'Western Marxism' was not just a geographical term.

Why did these Marxist social scientists so happily put themselves in the service of the West? For one thing, over the past ten years they had all earned their livings in institutions that indirectly or directly served the purpose of psychological warfare. He who pays the piper, calls the tune. But there had also been a positive experience here: what other country would allow scholars from a foreign adversary – and Marxists and Jews to boot – to work for the country's own intelligence agencies? That seemed only to be possible in the US. Any other country would have interned them as enemy aliens. And in their work, they had found colleagues with whom they could cooperate productively. This had led to friendships, sometimes even to love affairs and marriages. The area of mass-communication research had become a familiar landscape to them. They knew each other, and they knew by now how to navigate an intellectual field that was very much interwoven with politics.[6] That the US had a different enemy now did not change much. The Soviet brand of Marxism, not to mention the way it was being implemented by the party, had never been the Marxism of these social philosophers and social scientists. By the Moscow Trials at the latest, the totalitarian practices of the Soviet Union had come to resemble those of the Nazi dictatorship far too closely for these émigré scholars not to have taken notice. Pollock's description of state capitalism essentially, and especially in the details, fitted the Soviet Union as much as it did Nazi Germany. And it goes without saying that, for intellectuals, a society with freedom of thought, opinion and research has to be preferred to one whose ruling elite believes that it is in the possession of the only valid world view. For Kracauer, who placed so much emphasis on the importance of the lifeworld, the realm of Soviet rule constituted an '"unreal" world',[7] an empire of fear, in which all personal relationships came under threat and 'normal' life seemed impossible. One of his studies puts his own stance into the mouth of intellectuals from the Soviet sphere of influence, some of whom are aware

> that freedom of thought is a prerequisite for creative activities in the fields of science, art and literature, and that the lack of it not only paralyzes the life of the spirit but deprives the individual of a right which is inalienable indeed – the right to bring out all he feels he harbors within himself.[8]

In addition to the pragmatic loyalty felt towards the United States and the Western world, there was also a political feeling of belonging, an attachment that went beyond a mere aversion to Soviet communism. For many, this feeling of loyalty was destroyed by McCarthyism, but, despite the fact that he was briefly investigated by the FBI, not for Kracauer.[9]

Astonishment at the fact that Marxists and left-wing intellectuals like Marcuse and Neumann would have worked for the American intelligence agencies, not only against Nazi Germany but also against Soviet communism, only seems reasonable in retrospect. For it depends on a world view that only really emerged in the late 1960s and solidified in the 1970s, that is, only *after* the Vietnam war, once the US had, in the eyes of many democrats, lost its innocence, and *in the course of* the formation of a world-wide anti-imperialist movement that had adopted a fairly Manichean view of the world.[10] Around 1950, Frantz Fanon's *Wretched of the Earth* had not yet identified America as the home of imperialism; most still thought first and foremost of the old colonial powers in that context. In 1956,

Washington even refused to support France and Great Britain (and Israel) against Egypt in the Suez crisis. Horkheimer later justified the unquestioned siding with the Western world as follows: 'To measure the so-called free world by its own concept, to be critical of it, and nevertheless to support its ideas, to defend it against fascism of the Hitler, Stalin, or any other variety, is the right and obligation of all thinking people. Despite the fateful potential, despite all the injustices within and without, it is still an island, geographically and chronologically, the end of which, in the ocean of tyrannies, would mean the end of the culture to which critical theory belongs.'[11] In the case of Kracauer, we need to add to this that he no longer believed that the socialist parties in Western Europe could succeed, having witnessed their failure in the interwar years.[12]

The study on *Satellite Mentality* was politically motivated, but it was also methodically ambitious (even if, as Kracauer later admitted, there was no time for a thorough elaboration of its findings).[13] Kracauer and Berkman's report was completed in 1953 on the basis of 300 interviews carried out in Austrian refugee camps with

Figure 36. Elisabeth and Siegfried Kracauer, the Americans, with an unknown third person in 1945
Copyright: DLA Marbach

inmates from Poland, Hungary and Czechoslovakia, in 1951 and 1952. What is striking is the manner in which Kracauer comments on – and, in part, criticizes – the design of the questions asked by the interviewers. Kracauer explicitly constructs plausible interpretations that present 'the interplay between the given conditions of Satellite life and the very manifestations of that life'.[14] He does not evaluate responses by adding up how many times the refugees expressed a particular opinion; rather, he reflects on what might lie behind the opinions, what might have been left out (and for what reasons) and what might be being expressed between the lines. Kracauer's method of interpretation involves creating and illuminating contexts. For instance, the study begins with a chapter explaining the relationship between the Soviet Union and the 'satellite states' (a concept not mentioned by his sources but introduced for the purpose of analysis), and providing a sketch of the social conditions of 'totalitarian' systems. That chapter is not based on the interviews. He also raises methodological questions, pointing out that the interviewee sample is far from representative of the populations of the three satellite states and that the validity of the material is limited because 'the escapees will try, consciously or not, to present the situation back home in a way which justifies their defection'.[15] The study draws more on arguments than figures, more on interpretation than statistics. Kracauer's personal experiences also played an important role in shaping the study: the assumption that, as a rule, people are more interested in securing the material conditions of life than they are in matters of ideology is not something Kracauer learned from the interviewees. In short, the study asks how a content analysis should be organized, especially regarding the relationship between qualitative and quantitative evaluation.

This question relates to an important divergence between the American and European traditions in sociology, 'the Atlantic divide' that separated the social theory of continental Europe from Anglo-American empiricism.[16] To suggest that these traditions diverged in this way is not to claim that there was simply no empirical dimension to the former and no theoretical dimension to the latter. Rather, these were two ideal types of scientific culture. The 'European' (or, better, 'German') tradition was based on the humanities; the 'Anglo-American' (or, better, 'Western', if we include the French thinkers Comte and Durkheim) took its cue from the natural sciences. One type of sociology emphasized understanding, the other observation; one was philosophical and systematic, the other positivist and pragmatic. There were, of course, approaches which mixed both types, first and foremost among them Max Weber's sociology. Indeed, in American sociology both traditions were present, but before the intellectual migration of German scholars to the US began in 1933, the two poles could always be clearly distinguished. Before the First World War, American sociologists sought theoretical inspiration from Comte and Spencer in particular, and as a consequence sociology in the US mostly applied the model of the natural sciences. Its primary goal was to discover the laws of social life, just as biology, say, discovers the laws of natural life. Descriptions of social change therefore followed the pattern of Darwin's theory of evolution. By contrast, the 'Chicago School', which took its inspiration from the work of Georg Simmel, was generally considered too speculative by many American sociologists. The Chicago School was the result of a first wave of intellectual migration. Robert Ezra Park had studied with Simmel, and Talcott Parsons studied with Max Weber. When Parsons became the leading sociologist in the US after the Second World War, elements from both traditions began to amalgamate into new approaches.[17] In between these two stages in the reception of European sociology came the migration of German social scientists, who found themselves in the role of mediators. The approach pursued by the New School and the sort of sociology practised at Columbia University played a crucial role in this process. Paul Lazarsfeld was an important influence in this context, as was the Bureau of Applied Social Research, for which Kracauer had conducted the *Satellite Mentality* study.

Apart from being a pioneer of mass-communication research, Lazarsfeld played a crucial role in the institutionalization of empirical social research in universities and related external bodies. In October 1935, he arrived in New York, penniless and jobless. But in 1936, upon a recommendation from Hadley Cantril, he received an extraordinary sum of money – $67,000 – from the Rockefeller Foundation for research into the influence of radio on its listeners. The resulting Office of Radio Research was originally based at Princeton University in Newark, New Jersey. In 1939, Lazarsfeld moved it to New York, where he became a professor in the sociological faculty of Columbia University, alongside Robert K. Merton. Merton also stood 'on the shoulders', as he himself put it, of European intellectual history. He became a co-director of the Office of Radio Research, which, in 1944, turned into the Bureau of Applied Social Research. From then on, both men, for a quarter of a century, were formative influences on sociology in the US.[18]

Methodological discussions in sociology centred on the issue of content analysis. Lazarsfeld insisted that his fellow researchers justify the way in which they formulate their questions, collect the necessary data and, finally, analyse and interpret their data. He did not want anyone simply to gather facts. The explanation of social phenomena was at least as important as description and quantification. Lazarsfeld was interested in striking a balance between qualitative and quantitative research, often within one and the same study.[19] As a European scholar who was open to the American way of doing science, Kracauer was just the right ally. The BASR hired him as a researcher and as an advisor. In the latter role, he wrote several position papers for the purpose of internal discussion. One of these became the paper for the *Public Opinion Quarterly* already mentioned: 'The Challenge of Qualitative Content Analysis'. This paper marked a significant shift in emphasis in the discussions around content analysis in empirical social research.

Kracauer was in the 'qualitative camp'. He positioned himself between Lazarsfeld's framework for theoretically guided empirical research and Adorno's critical rejection of positivism as ideological, while also distancing himself from traditional German intellectual history. Lazarsfeld advocated a pragmatic combination of herme-neutic insight and quantitative analysis of the facts. Adorno, by contrast, was far less pragmatic. As soon as empirical methods became involved, he grew suspicious. To him, a science that limited itself to counting, measuring and weighing represented the triumph of reification. As he himself admitted, however, the US had in a certain sense de-provincialized him. He had learned to adopt an external perspective on 'culture' and 'intellect', to view it from the point of view of a society which he considered essentially democratic.[20] Kracauer sympathized with Adorno's criticisms of empirical research, but he also thought that Adorno did not really have first-hand knowledge of the methods involved and was hiding behind philosophical argument.[21] That judgement was not altogether fair: Adorno had, after all, been involved in the Princeton Radio Project, later with the American Jewish Committee's *Studies in Prejudice*, investigating the authoritarian personality, and, after his return to Germany, with the 'group experiment' on authoritarian dispositions in post-fascist society. Kracauer's own position was respected by all, including Lazarsfeld and Adorno, and the latter drew his students' attention to the essay on content analysis. Merton and Schütz also praised the paper.[22]

It is easy to imagine that, had Kracauer been confronted with German sociology, he might well have championed quantitative analysis. He agreed with Löwenthal and Merton, who, returning from a sociology conference in Europe, described 'the intellectual habitus' of colleagues there as 'unbearable'. They either disap-peared 'behind a nebulous cloud' of philosophical speculation, or they 'eagerly tried to emulate what they thought was American empirical social research'.[23] It was a fact, though, that in America the predominant orientation was positivist, and therefore it was necessary to promote soft skills in the social sciences: 'a sense of history, a flair for ideological currents and experience of human behaviour, not to mention the greatest virtue of all – circum-spection in weighing and balancing against each other the various data assembled', as Kracauer put it. Where others saw an intuitive impressionism at work, he spoke of 'disciplined subjectivity'[24] or 'scientific experience'.[25]

Kracauer did not have strong reservations about the pursuit of objectivity. On the contrary, he thought that the humanities, in particular aesthetics and philology, could do with a dose of objectivity. He was therefore pleased to make the acquaintance of the literary scholar Erich Auerbach, who had come to America in 1947 following his exile in Istanbul. Kracauer had read Auerbach's 'In the Hotel de la Mole' in the *Partisan Review*,[26] an article which described the novel and unique connections between characters, attitudes and social conditions in Stendhal's work. According to Auerbach, *Le Rouge et le Noir* (1830) was the expression of a specifically modern and tragic realism. He also praised Balzac as the creator of a modern realism that attended to the genuine everyday lives of the 'little people'. Auerbach was attracted to these historically specific stories and their orientation towards ordinary life. Like Kracauer, he was obviously a scholar who was motivated by a will towards reality, someone who clearly understood his discipline as part of a broader science of culture. In the summer of 1951, Kracauer got to know Auerbach at the Krautheimers' place, and they began to discuss the concept of science together. The *Partisan Review* essay was in fact a chapter from *Mimesis*, Auerbach's great work on the representation of reality in Western – that is, European – literature. In it, Auerbach 'shows how each period reframed the realistic narrative according to its social and cultural conditions'.[27] Kracauer was impressed by 'the breadth and depth and lucidity with which you bring intellectual entities out of the thicket of history – one still feels the undergrowth out of which they grew, and all the sap of the soil that went into them'. Kracauer thought this historical aspect generally lacking in the philological disciplines and in the social sciences, 'which suffer from the fact that they reject history by pointing towards its allegedly unscientific character'. Auerbach, in turn, very much agreed with Kracauer's paper on qualitative analysis.[28]

Another natural ally in questions regarding sociology was, as might well have been expected, Leo Löwenthal. After all, Löwenthal had brought Kracauer back to the social sciences. Löwenthal's own research had begun to focus on literature, both in an artistic sense and as a medium of mass culture. He thus trooped into the field of the humanities with his sociological armour. Conversely, he expected social research to evince an understanding of literary and philosophical questions. He investigated the picture of the changing relationship between the individual human being and society as reflected in the great works of world literature. That was really a twist on the very question that Auerbach had been pursuing. Löwenthal pored over literary material for hints of alterations in the social psychology of past societies. That approach corresponded to the model put forth in the *Caligari* book. In short, Löwenthal studied the sociology of literature with an orientation towards the humanities, and he conceived this as an element of a sociology of culture.[29] Kracauer thought there was much to recommend Löwenthal's approach. From Löwenthal, he thought, sociologists could learn what qualitative analysis could achieve, especially if it delved 'deep into the aesthetic'.[30]

Adorno, Arnheim, Auerbach, Horkheimer, Jahoda, Kris, Lazarsfeld, Löwenthal, Neumann, Panofsky and Speier, these 'textual and pictorial scholars' of a variety of different disciplines, all of whom were from German-speaking Europe and of Jewish descent, constituted Kracauer's close friends and allies in matters academic. All of these individuals had found a place at some research institution or other in the US after 1933.[31] Some have described the process by which these intellectual émigrés confronted and adopted aspects of a different academic culture as one of 'acculturation'. And this term is, indeed, far more apt than 'assimilation' or 'adjustment', because they did not simply adapt, not even those who came to see themselves as Americans. Rather, the process in question was one of mutual trans-Atlantic knowledge transfer, from Europe to America and vice versa.[32] The rapid rise of sociology at Columbia University, spearheaded by Lazarsfeld and Merton, and with contributions from philosophers like Horkheimer and Adorno, is a prime example of acculturation in this sense.[33] And so is the work of the others on the list, who all went their own ways but whose work nevertheless shares the feature of combining old traditions with new experiences.[34] Kracauer, the external advisor of the BASR, was convinced that his memoranda remained 'without any effect', and that it was in any case hard to change the ways of sociology – this 'racket which provides bread for so many people'.[35] But that was only true in the short term. H. Stuart Hughes even goes as far as to speak of the 'de-provincialization' of America by the intellectuals who fled from Europe. That is certainly an exaggeration, but it shows that the influence cannot have been as insignificant as Kracauer assumed. The gap between the scientific cultures of America and Europe has definitely become smaller, if indeed it still exists at all.[36]

The Europeans not only brought particular thinkers along with them – Marx, Freud, Simmel and Weber, for instance. They also – and this, of course, applies to Kracauer, too – brought the experience of a historical catastrophe, a scar to serve as a permanent reminder of the naivety of taking anything to be incontrovertible, whether it be facts or theories. The Jewish intellectuals, academics and scientists who had fled or had been expelled mourned the loss of the humanistic culture to which German Jews, in particular, had been attached. That culture continued to live on in them all, and it found its way into conceptions of how to practise science: one needed to be theoretically versatile, empirically curious, sociologically oriented, philosophically grounded and directed towards reality – sometimes mimetically, sometimes critically, but always in a manner that is guided by life experience. This issued in a unique style that each of them could immediately recognize in the others.[37]

In the 1950s, Kracauer began to make acquaintances outside of this 'circle of acculturation'. In particular, he met with sociologists from Columbia University, often during holidays in Wilmington, Vermont, a small town in the Green Mountains. The place became a kind of summer colony of New York sociologists seeking to escape the unbearable humidity of the city, which Kracauer said 'fogs up the brain'.[38] Staying in Wilmington allowed one to meet other intellectuals, and it was conducive to work. In 1957, the Kracauers stayed in the mountains for a full seven weeks. Friedel worked on his aesthetics of film every day, and in the evening he and Lili met with colleagues from the Bureau, many of whom were there, and socialized with their families. The attendance of certain other sociologists helped to contribute to a sense that this small town was the 'centre of social life': the sociologist of medicine, and a pupil of Parsons', Henry Lennard visited the Kracauers, as did Erich Kahler (previously of the New School) and David Riesman, the author of the bestseller *Lonely Crowd* (1950). Kracauer liked Riesman because he wrote in a 'literary' rather than a sociological style, and he gave his empirical research a qualitative foundation. He was particularly fond of his article 'Suburban Sadness', which described the bleak and aimless life in suburbia.[39] A friendly rather than professional relationship was established with the anthropologist John W. Bennett and his family, who were seeking the older Kracauers' advice on private matters.[40]

Even everyday life in the office enriched Kracauer's social and intellectual life. To be sure, his work at the Bureau got in the way of the film book, but it also brought him joy. When he was talking with Lazarsfeld, Kracauer felt 'like a dog that had got the scent', itching to be released so that he could put all his experience regarding questions of method to good use.[41] 'I enjoy the collaboration with these young people very much', he reported, 'and as they learn from me, so I learn from them. The discussions and meetings are often quite heated, just the right kind of atmosphere for me.' Kracauer handed in his texts in advance and then sat down in the hot seat to be cross-examined by his colleagues and students.[42] These exchanges invigorated Kracauer, that lone wolf, and the sense of recognition that came from being assigned special tasks provided him with a deep satisfaction. Elihu Katz and Seymour M. Lipset, two of the 'young people' who still had their careers ahead of them, he even invited to his home.[43] It was almost sad to have to return to his desk and to film theory, to pick up the lost thread and delve into the material again, to continue work on fragments of text which had lain in a corner for some time. At such moments, he began to question the structure of the book, and in spring 1953 he confessed to Rotha that the book was turning into a nightmare and that he had not made any progress for a year.[44] He was in the middle of a research assignment for the BASR, and now he had yet another activity to add to the list: the Bollingen Foundation had asked him whether he could act as an advisor for them.[45]

That extra activity began at the end of 1952 with two reports, for which Kracauer received $25. From February 1952, there were weekly lunch meetings with the deputy director, Ernest Brooks Jr., where the two spoke about matters relating to the Bollingen Foundation and the Old Dominion Foundation. Kracauer was now a member of the advisory boards of both foundations, in which roles he was mostly concerned with reviewing applications. Sometimes he also had to read the draft work and reports of scholarship holders or compile dossiers on applicants. These applications came from the most diverse disciplines: anthropology, archaeology, art history, cultural history, the history of religion, literature, philosophy and sometimes also psychology. In 1954, Kracauer wrote eighty-three reports; in 1955, he wrote ninety-three; in 1956, ninety; and in 1957, finally, 114. The spring months, in particular, saw Kracauer occupied almost exclusively with the writing of reports 'three full days a week', and even at the weekends, for 'ten hours a day'.[46] But the work was interesting and, most importantly, it finally guaranteed him a secure and regular income.

36

Mail from Germany, Letters from the Past, Travels in Europe

At the end of 1953, Elisabeth Kracauer began studying for a psychology degree. Since August 1949, when the Kracauers felt, for the first time, that things were looking up again, they had wondered whether Lili should not realize this long-held desire of hers, especially after she lost her job in May 1950 when the USNA ran out of money.[1] Now that Friedel had a significantly higher level of income, this was possible. Also made possible, now, was a move to a larger apartment. With the ever-increasing stock of books it had had to house, the old one had been growing ever smaller.[2] In April 1955, Lili Kracauer found their new place, not far from their old one; they would again be living in their beloved Manhattan, 498 West End Avenue. Friedel Kracauer had thus finally made it to a 'Westend', even if it was not the Frankfurt quarter his socially envious father had always forced him to go to on their Sunday walks. The apartment was of course even smaller than those in the Nordend of Frankfurt, but it still made Kracauer happy. It was 'the first proper place since Berlin. And I have a room to work in again.'[3] To afford the apartment, the planned trip to Europe that had been gradually taking shape was put on hold. Ever since Kracauer had secured an annual grant of $4,000 from the Chapelbrook Foundation in Boston for the book on the aesthetics of film, the trip had been a possibility (the grant ran – albeit with some uncertainties over its extension – from 1 May 1954 until August 1957).[4]

The foundation was only a year old, and had been set up by the writer and Proust translator Mina Kirstein Curtiss. Curtiss and Kracauer had mutual acquaintances and friends in Paris: Adrienne Monnier, Daniel Halévy and Gabriel Marcel. That was certainly no disadvantage when it came to the awarding of grants. Meeting Curtiss was like opening one of his old boxes from Paris: times past, once thought lost, were brought back to life, particularly when it emerged that Curtiss was to write a biography of Georges Bizet (which was published in 1959). Kracauer described to his benefactor and colleague his experience of reading it: 'It was ... a real sensation', a kind of déja vu, as the Second Empire unfolded again in all its glory before his very eyes. He congratulated the biographer on having the wisdom not to put the music centre stage; Kracauer had apparently not changed his views on that matter. He also liked the fact that Curtiss did not succumb to the temptation to construct a synthesis out of life, work and society. In contrast to the Offenbach book, Curtiss had created a montage out of Bizet's ego-documents and testimonials from Bizet's friends and contemporaries. In this way, Kracauer had changed his mind: a 'biography of society' based on grand structures and panoramic views and theses, with all of this reflected in one person, now – at the end of the 1950s – appeared neither possible nor desirable to him.[5] The new French connections fuelled a longing for the old Europe, especially Paris, the beloved capital of the past.

Yet Kracauer still had no desire to go back to Germany. The old home was lost. There was little room for sentimentality – perhaps only in the remotest corners of consciousness, where memories of childhood and youth reside. After the persecution and murder of his mother and aunt, there was no possible redemption for his home country. Monetary compensation for some of the injustices suffered, at least for the loss of income, was possible, however. In February 1952, twenty years after their escape, the Kracauers applied to the Chamber of Reparation in Wiesbaden for financial compensation for the loss of his editorial post at the *Frankfurter Zeitung*. Kracauer had to name people who could confirm that, in June 1933, he had been sacked by his employer because he was a Jew and that he had lived many years in exile in Paris 'without a job and in genuine distress'.[6] He would later make further applications for compensation for the costs of emigration and the loss of pension rights.[7]

The Kracauers were in touch with the Wahls during the compensation process. Fritz Wahl's application was rejected by the authorities at first. Wahl appealed the decision at the regional court in Munich. He told Kracauer about the trial: 'I did not feel like the complainant in this court, but like the accused in a trial for tax evasion.' Reifenberg, however, was called as a witness, and following his convincing testimony the case was decided in Wahl's favour and the application referred back to the authorities. But he remained pessimistic: 'These compensation courts, and the whole law [regulating compensation claims], are designed to prevent compensation.' Initially, he seemed to be right; his case did not really get anywhere. 'They want to have compensation on paper. That makes a good impression and does not cost anything.' Finally, at the end of 1954, a decision was taken, although Wahl called it a 'malicious, tendentious decision' and disputed it: he had been awarded compensation amounting to one year's salary. Wahl appealed his case to the higher court, and in October 1955 he received an advance and a letter informing him that the maximum compensation he would receive was now set at 25,000 Deutschmark.[8] The increased level of compensation did not have anything to do with a change of heart from the court but was likely an advance sign of the new German Restitution Law, which was to come into force in June 1956. Whereas compensation claims had previously been dealt with by the states, under the 'Bundesergänzungsgesetz' of 1953, they were now to be settled at the federal level. In the end, the Wahls had to choose between a pension or a lump sum, but it was not clear how much this would be, nor when it would be paid. They decided in favour of the pension. But further financial misery was in store for the Wahls: the Swiss authorities now requested that they repay the state for the financial support they had been forced to rely on when they were prohibited from working during the war.

The Kracauers also had to wait a long time before there was any movement on their case. In April 1954, they applied for an 'urgent decision and advance of DM 5,000', but this was initially rejected on the grounds that the claim was 'not proven with sufficient credibility'. In the summer of 1954, Kracauer told Gubler that he would probably need a sworn declaration from him for the compensation authorities in Berlin, confirming that he had lived 'under economic duress' during his time in the city.[9] Kracauer solicited affidavits from three further individuals, among them one from Löwenthal (or rather from the Institute for Social Research), which confirmed that the institute had supported Kracauer financially for lengthy periods of time. Guttmann also swore under oath that the *Frankfurter Zeitung* had first sent Kracauer to Paris before ending all contractual relations with him. Shortly before Christmas 1954, Kracauer was granted an advance payment of 9,000 marks, reflecting his advancing years and the fact that the authorities had accepted, in full, his account of the damage done to his career. Kracauer was optimistic: 'It is good to know that over there are a few people ... who take care of compensation matters with such courage.' That, he wrote, 'is a consoling thought. Thus, we have some hope that our application will be successful.'[10] The Kracauers also opted to receive the compensation as an annual pension. In the summer of 1956, Kracauer received a second advance of 10,000 marks. Kracauer took it that the approval of the pension was now merely a formality, and he informed the German lawyer who had represented him that he would no longer require his services. But the pension – of 600 marks, Kracauer had calculated – never arrived. In spring 1957, he engaged the services of his lawyer again. Kracauer wrote to this old acquaintance Otto Suhr, who was now the mayor of Berlin, informing him that the decision on his compensation was still outstanding and that he, at sixty-eight and without material security, desperately needed it. Just three-and-a-half months later, the pension was finally approved, though Kracauer first had to prove that he was still alive by providing a 'life certificate' issued by the German consulate in New York. He also received 5,600 marks in outstanding payments. In April 1963, his claim for damages in relation to the termination of his pension from the newspaper was decided in his favour, and he received another monthly pension of 245 marks. Finally, only days before Siegfried's death, the Kracauers would be awarded 4,750 marks as compensation for the 'emigration costs', in particular the costs of their escape from France, via Lisbon, to New York.

Compared to many other victims of National Socialism, the Kracauers were quite lucky. As former German citizens living in the United States, a country that did not receive compensation from Germany as a lump sum, their case was dealt with on an individual basis. Most victims of National Socialism – all those from Warsaw Pact countries, and all those from Western European states that had struck general compensation agreements with the Federal Republic – received nothing or, at most, a nominal sum, much later. Kracauer was compensated for the loss of his career and his position within society, but there could be no compensation for the distress the couple suffered after 1933, the fear they had to endure or the pain that had been visited upon them. (Nor did Kracauer seek any compensation for 'professional damages after 1951'.) Although reparations were thus distributed very selectively, annual payments had reached three billion marks by 1961.[11] Some feared that the state might even go bankrupt very soon because of the mounting costs. That was a rather hysterical reaction, however, given that the total amount of annual compensation payments never exceeded 1 per cent of GDP and always stayed below 4 per cent of total state expenditure. The burden was, nevertheless, significant: almost as great as that following the so-called reunification in 1991 or the costs of the refugee crisis in 2015/16.

In the mid-1950s, Germany may have held a file on Kracauer's compensation claim, but one would not have been able to buy any of his own books in the country. Kracauer had given up hope that he might be able to republish his books in Germany.[12] He had tried in vain to find a German publisher for the *Offenbach* book.[13] When his 'old' publisher, S. Fischer, also declined, he resigned himself to the fact that he would not find a German publisher: 'The clear lack of interest in this book on the part of the German publishers is inexplicable to me. Could the resentment caused by my *Caligari* be the reason?'[14] Rowohlt might still have been a possibility. Since the summer of 1951, Wolfgang Weyrauch had been an editor there, and he had approached Kracauer in sackcloth and ashes; with his occasional angry outbursts against 'restoration' and 're-fascization', he was now practising a sort of belated resistance. Regarding the *Caligari*, however, he was sceptical, though he wondered whether this might be a reason for publishing it 'in this country of self-righteousness, forgetfulness and anti-humanity'. The *Offenbach* book was with Ernst Rowohlt, who was ill, and Heinrich Maria Ledig-Rowohlt was apparently always travelling or on holiday. Kracauer had to wait for two years before a decision was taken. During that time, Weyrauch's letters to Kracauer became increasingly sporadic. He was busy, after all; he had to fight Nazis and write *Die Mörder* [The murderers], which did not leave much time to write to Jews abroad.[15]

Some people in the German film scene did begin to show an interest in Kracauer, however. One of them was Enno Patalas, a twenty-five-year-old student who had read *From Caligari to Hitler* and, in a letter to its author, said that the book had shaped his 'critical perspective'. German film critics, Patalas said, lacked both the sociological and film aesthetic perspectives. The failure of German criticism was part, he said, of an enduring collective 'ideological twistedness'. Patalas had the idea to use his dissertation to pick up the history of film where Kracauer had left off, in 1933, using Kracauer's method. In his view, film in the 'Third Reich' was far less politically manipulated than was generally assumed; perhaps it did not need to be manipulated at all.[16] In the end, however, the young Patalas did not write that book. Instead, he founded journals: together with Wilfried Berghahn, he founded *Filmkritik*, which became the most important left-wing German film aesthetics journal after the war. For this group, Kracauer's writings on film were an important point of reference. Also important was Lotte Eisner, the principal curator at the Cinémathèque Française, who occasionally published articles in *Cahiers du Cinéma* and who had written a book on German silent movies and early talkies, *The Haunted Screen*, following the approach of Kracauer's *Caligari*. Patalas, Adorno wrote to Kracauer, considered himself his pupil (though he did not formally study under him), and he recommended that Kracauer get in touch with these film scholars: 'Everything that is decent in German film nowadays is more or less closely connected with the Oberhausen Group.'[17]

In the summer of 1956, Elisabeth and Siegfried Kracauer were finally able to embark on their trip to Europe. The Bollingen Foundation covered their flights, because Kracauer was representing the institution at the Eranos conference in Ascona at Monte Verità, which was being sponsored by the foundation. The first ten days on the trip, however, the Kracauers spent in Germany, visiting Hamburg, Berlin and Frankfurt. After holidaying in Klosters, near Davos, and the conference in Ascona, they took in Florence, Rome and Milan during their three-month tour. After that they went to

Basle, visiting Karl Jaspers, and Strasbourg, where they met up with relatives of Lili, and then on to Paris. For the Kracauers, the tour was a 'unique, wonderful, and in a certain respect redemptive experience'.[18]

He certainly could not have made that remark at the beginning of the trip. In Hamburg, the Kracauers had been guests at the 'much promising' house of Rowohlt. At first, Rowohlt had wanted to publish almost all of Kracauer's works – the *Offenbach* book, an edition of the book on the aesthetics of film in the series *Rowohlts deutsche Enzyklopädie* and an edition of *The Salaried Masses*. But none of these projects would come to fruition. Nor did plans to publish *Ginster* and a collection of essays come to anything, despite how important these were to Kracauer.[19] The *Caligari* book, the 'firelighter' as Weyrauch called it, was rejected out of hand. Ironically, it was precisely this book that would later become part of the Rowohlt programme after all, albeit in a distorted, that is, abbreviated and politically moderated, form – 'for reasons of space', was the justification given in a note to the reader, when that edition appeared in March 1958. It would have been more honest to say: 'Because of you, my dear former Volksgenossen – because we do not want to burden you unreasonably with the thesis that Hitler was a development from deep within'. A film scholar from the German Democratic Republic rightly called the first German edition an act of censorship – and he knew what he was talking about.[20]

The experience of Berlin was rather surreal. The Kracauers had to visit the 'Entschädigungsamt', the compensation authorities.[21] They also visited their old flat in Sybelstraße. Was it uncanny to confront what once had been familiar and taken for granted as something alien? Perhaps Kracauer imagined a camera shot: 'deceptively similar and yet without a human attachment to it'.[22] Their flat was now part of a hotel; guests were sleeping in their old living room.[23] The Kracauers could, in a kind of *danse macabre*, have stayed in one of these rooms. But they were not unemotional cynics, nor did they want to perform some sort of symbolic act. They were visitors and not stumbling blocks.[24] And yet they rather did stumble from place to place, as if blind: 'There was still the same crack in the wood of the entrance door; and the old shaky escalator still passed the coloured stairway windows. It was as if time had stopped, this terrible rain which murmurs and murmurs.'[25]

The 'redemptive' moment might have come when the two 'homecomers' visited Frankfurt, although in his letter to Löwenthal, Kracauer does not mention anything about the city itself, only about the 'unforgettable' but 'very ill' Peter Suhrkamp, an evening with Horkheimer, a visit to the Institute for Social Research and, most importantly, the lunch 'at the Teddies' place'. 'It was good to see them again, and we talked incessantly: about Germany, our work and our plans, about our friends and world history, as in the old times – well, you know what that is like.'[26] In Rome, an even more exciting reminder of the good old days reached 'Friedel'. After twenty-one years – 'for that is how long we have not seen each other, and hardly have heard of each other' – the general secretary of the Leo Baeck Institute in Jerusalem, his old and faithful friend Selmar Spier, sent him a postcard, writing from the Hotel National in Frankfurt. He had heard that Kracauer had been in town only shortly before he had arrived. They were both overjoyed, and they hurriedly organized a spontaneous meeting in Basle. It was a 'wonderful' reunion; nothing could unsettle this old childhood friendship.[27] Kracauer was touched when Spier gave him his memoirs about the time before 1914 to read. It was an encounter with Kracauer's youth seen through his friend's eyes, and to Kracauer it provided novel insights, enriched by later experiences 'we could not have had at the time': 'Through you, I am now much better able to see the background against which my own youth took place.' He liked the 'quiet, dry sarcasm' with which Spier wrote about 'the fatherland', a humour with a slight weariness 'that is irresistible' (and which Kracauer also possessed). Otto Hainebach, Kracauer's article on the outbreak of war in the *Preußische Jahrbücher*, his activities at the Lehrhaus: all these figured in Spier's book. It was a kind of local history from a distance, a form that spoke to Kracauer, that he felt comfortable with.[28] Most importantly, though, Kracauer had the opportunity to become reconciled with his friend, the man who once, as his lawyer, failed to achieve – and in retrospect, of course, could not have achieved – justice for Kracauer. It was lucky that this meeting came about when it did. At the end of 1962, Selmar Spier died in Ramot HaShavim (The Heights of the Homecomers), a village in central Israel that had been founded by immigrants from Germany. Following his death, Spier's son was 'exceptionally' (as the mother, Marlene Spier, put it) drawn towards Frankfurt.[29]

Or maybe Paris was the climax of the trip – the much loved and much missed lively capital of a Europe that was no more. 'It was all more beautiful than we had expected.' That is how Kracauer summarized their return. Paris was 'even more beautiful than it had been in our memory'. They met with Daniel Halévy, Gabriel Marcel and many other old friends. Nevertheless, the Kracauers were 'glad to be back home, because now that we have definitely ceased to be immigrants, this is our home'. And there was 'something else' that Kracauer told Löwenthal about their trip: 'It appears to me that people in Europe have lost the capacity to adopt new things. Somehow you feel crushed there.'[30]

And yet the spell was broken. Europe now had to be visited at least every two or three years. In the summer of 1958, a grant of $1,500 from the American Philosophical Society made a second trip possible.[31] The grant allowed Kracauer to search for material for his book in film archives in London and Paris and have discussions about problems in the aesthetics of film. Kracauer went to the British Film Academy, where the founding director, Roger Manvell, had organized a reception to welcome him, and Kracauer, through Rotha, got to know the London film circles around *Sight & Sound* and Penelope Houston. He also met with the famous documentary film-maker Basil Wright.[32] Rotha, Manvell and Wright were twenty years younger than Kracauer, but Kracauer still enjoyed a mutual understanding with that generation. Houston, however, was considerably younger and, like many of her generation, had an altogether different perspective on film. That would soon become clear in the response to Kracauer's aesthetics of film.

The former expellees spent only three days in Germany, two of them in Hamburg, with Rowohlt and as guests of the Hamburger Gesellschaft für Filmkunde [Hamburg Society of Film Studies], and one in Freiburg, where they visited Bernhard Guttmann.[33] 'That was quite enough for us', Kracauer affirmed.

> The attendant at the hotel in Hamburg must have been a devout member of the SA. But it is better one does not ask people. Apart from that, everyone was nice to us. The young people are curious (and know nothing); there is really good material. The reason we shuddered at the thought of having to be there had to do with something else: the fact that there has never been a society in Germany becomes evident in the most frightening ways. The people are without any form and unguided in their behaviour; they have no exterior (and an unstructured interior). Everything is there, but nothing has a place where it belongs. That is the cause of the insincere, artificial behaviour, the *stilted language*, the complete insecurity. The people are *not so much human beings as raw material for human beings*.[34] In short, I don't trust them. And I do not want to imagine what would happen in the case of an economic or political crisis.[35]

What did Kracauer mean when speaking of the absence of form? Firstly, he certainly had in mind the absence of a democratic and liberal society (in Ralf Dahrendorf's sense), a society that is served by the political system and the state rather than being ruled by them.[36] Secondly, he was noting the absence of a humane basis that would focus on the concrete individual – and thus on empathy, compassion and tactful behaviour – as opposed to a focus on an idea, world view or belief. Thirdly, people's evasion when it came to facing up to the crimes of the National Socialist period was also, in a sense, a lack of form, or the cause of the lack of form. 'The ignorance of things past among the young is unimaginable', Kracauer said. 'And many young intellectuals indulge in a sort of radicalism which is nothing but posturing. I am afraid the economic prosperity is not becoming to them.'[37] Friends had reported similar observations, for instance Ella Gubler (the Germans worked 'like mad' and were experiencing an 'almost oppressive upturn and frenzied activity') or Rainer Koehne, a student of Adorno's who had moved to the US. He told Kracauer that the ideal now was no longer 'the fanatically slim SA man' but 'a stout older gentleman, with inner vitality and greying temples. The padding of a mild obesity sends a message to the world: "We do not do such things any longer; we are respectable."'[38] It would have been wrong either to completely distrust this transformation or to completely trust it. When visiting Germany in 1950, Hannah Arendt observed a widespread indifference towards the fate of the refugees, an apathy about the landscape of rubble and, most of all, a brutal and unfeeling refusal to face up to what had happened. She also found a deep moral confusion, which she saw as the result of the intermingling of propaganda and reality, world view and truth, fabricated by the Nazis. Kracauer read Arendt's report on the post-war Germans' avoidance of responsibility in October 1950 in the journal *Commentary*.[39]

Kracauer was even distrustful of German cultural criticism, the representatives of which assembled, during his second European visit in the summer of 1958, at a conference in Munich. For Kracauer, this was a typically German event, even if Horkheimer and Adorno were the main speakers. There was a lot of cultural chatter, he reported to Löwenthal, an intellectual commotion that 'presents itself as radical and is devoid of consequence'.[40] Kracauer regarded all this with the utmost suspicion. It irritated him that someone like Peter Härlin, an editor at the *Frankfurter Allgemeine Zeitung*, would aim to write 'concrete' reports while lacking a capacity for abstract thought. Or, again, it irritated him when Peter von Haselberg (who was close to the Institute for Social Research) wrote about mountain climbing, reflecting, as he did so, on Hegel rather than on the physical contact with stones.[41] Whenever anyone played the upstanding, non-conformist rebel, Kracauer became downright caustic. When a student of Adorno's, Hans G. Helms, asked Kracauer whether he might contribute papers he could not publish in America to a 'subversive' journal instead, his reply was blunt: 'I do not have such papers. ... It seems to me that you are under the influence of the stereotypical image of America as a country of conformism which is so widespread in Europe. But American reality does not correspond to this image at all.'[42] (Despite this inauspicious beginning, the two would later get on well.) In Kracauer's eyes, Adorno was partly to blame for all this: 'He writes so much, and some of it that I have seen is, on a fundamental level, wrong, worn-out profundity, self-satisfied radicalness', which 'no one understands'.[43]

After another holiday in Switzerland, Kracauer and his wife visited the *Mostra* film festival in Venice, where Kracauer also met with Patalas. The most important meeting, however, was with Guido Aristarco from the journal *Cinema Nuovo*. Previously, in 1956, he had organized various meetings in Milan between Kracauer and people from the world of film, and he had now overseen Kracauer's invitation to the festival as a guest of honour. Aristarco had also edited and written an introduction for the translation of the *Caligari* book published by Mondadori.[44] He would later write a lengthy introduction to the Italian edition of Kracauer's *Theory of Film*, presenting it as an important theoretical work on cinema (*Il dissolvimento della ragione*, 1965). As well as Kracauer, Aristarco was responsible for introducing Arnheim and Rotha to the Italian public. He was an adherent of neo-realism in film and of the political philosophy of Marx, Gramsci and Lukács. Kracauer did not approve of Aristarco's references to Lukács, whom he considered 'a traitor to literature and to his past',[45] but Kracauer nevertheless warmed to the friendly young man from Milan who demonstrated such an active interest in him. Kracauer, in turn, demonstrated his solidarity with Aristarco when he and some of his colleagues at *Cinema Nuovo* were arrested following their publication of an article discussing a script on the Italian attack on Greece during the fascist years – 'at the instigation of the army' (according to Arnheim).[46] Aristarco admired Kracauer, persuading him to come to Italy by telling him that he 'enjoyed a degree of popularity [there] that he would not expect'.[47] It was true that Kracauer was, indeed, very much in demand at the *Mostra*. When journalists wanted to know which new films he was planning to watch, he replied that what he would most like to do was to look at Venice again, whatever films were shown there. Once more, films were a medium for the achievement of some other end – for seeing Europe, for instance. But this is not to say Kracauer neglected work during this trip. He continued to work on his book; to his delight, he was able to work in the manner he had in the past: in hotel lobbies, cafés or railway stations – any place where there was bustle and life; life, after all, was work.[48]

Paris was again the last stop on their journey, where this time the Cinémathèque Française, whose committee for historical research into film had elected Kracauer as a board member, played a central role. Kracauer also had conversations with Henri Langlois and the film scholar Gilbert Cohen-Séat.[49] And he met Erich Peter Neumann, who had plans to arrange a new edition of *The Salaried Masses* at the Verlag für Demoskopie, after Rowohlt had turned down the book and Suhrkamp had put the project on hold because of the publisher's illness.[50] In 1932, Neumann was writing for the radical left-wing magazine *Weltbühne* and, by 1940, for the National

Socialist weekly *Das Reich*. At the beginning of the war, he was still a member of the NSDAP. In 1941, he worked as a war reporter in the east, among other places in occupied Warsaw. In 1947, together with Elisabeth Noelle-Neumann, he founded the Institute for Public Opinion Research in Allensbach, West Germany. In 1961, he was elected to the parliament of the Federal Republic on the CDU ticket. In Neumann, Kracauer had someone with an extremely German biography interested in him. Neumann had not forgotten *The Salaried Masses*, which had been burned on 10 May 1933 'in the flames of the auto-da-fé', and were never seen again. Kracauer took a shine to this respectful, solicitous publisher; he found him polite, professional and Western in outlook. Neumann was seeking to publish important works of early European and US social research, 'ranging from Max Weber on to Paul Lazarsfeld and to George H. Gallup'. Kracauer's text was to be the first volume in this series. The publisher himself wrote a competent and historically informed preface for the new edition, which appeared with a new subtitle: instead of 'Aus dem neuesten Deutschland' [The latest on Germany], it now was 'Eine Schrift vom Ende der Weimarer Republik' [A treatise on the end of the Weimar Republic].[51] In his preface, Neumann praised Kracauer's investigation as a pioneering work of empirical social and political research. Everett C. Hughes of the Chicago School, who also considered the treatise a 'classical text of sociology', contributed an additional foreword. Surprisingly, Kracauer did not remove the book's original dedication: 'For Benno Reifenberg, as a tribute to our close friendship and our collaboration'. He also asked for a copy to be sent to his former friend.[52] The book appeared in December 1959. And it was as if nothing had ever changed. The *Deutsche Handelswacht* attacked the Weimar-era work in a lengthy review; even after thirty years, the journal for the protection of nationalistic employees was still angry at the 'Jew Kracauer'.[53]

The 1958 trip to Europe had a surprise ending. When the Kracauers returned home from Paris at the end of September, they felt like strangers. They experienced a sudden attack of claustrophobia, and seriously considered whether it was not, after all, most unnatural for them to have a fixed abode, to be *forced into a square* in order to live *the life of two-room professions*. Were not all scholars and artists, on account of their vocation, journeymen and, at the bottom of their hearts, vagabonds? After a day, though, the power of habit had reasserted itself; the Kracauers were glad to be home and happy with their life in New York.[54]

37

The Practice of Film Theory and the Theory of Film

Having taken up his Chapelbrook grant and returned to his book, Kracauer began to reorganize his entire project.[1] This process would take him one and a half years. In January 1956, he was finally ready to begin the actual writing process. His theory, he wrote to Koehne, was now 'wrapped up'.[2] During that time he would have 'long and frequent discussions' with Arnheim, Auerbach and Schapiro.[3] He also sought out Paul Rotha, inviting the London film-maker to spend an evening in Kracauer's new study, armed with plenty of tobacco and alcohol, to read Kracauer's hundred-page 'syllabus'. In matters of film, Rotha and Kracauer were natural allies. They shared a fundamental view of the medium: film should capture the anarchy of life, life as permeated by spontaneity, coincidence and indeterminacy. They also agreed, for the most part, on aesthetic questions. Rotha, a documentary film-maker and a consummate cinephile, was supportive of Kracauer's envisaged notion of a material rather than formal aesthetics of film. For Rotha, the real task of film, whether fiction or non-fiction, was to create a relationship towards reality. He despised artificiality and triviality. For Rotha, a dedication to film and a passion for film were part of a way of life. He thus agreed with Kracauer that film had to investigate the continuum of physical existence and the never-ending flow of fragmented life. When it came to feature films, and these are what Rotha had now turned to, both admired Italian neo-realism. *Umberto D.* (1952) by Vittorio De Sica was their favourite: it aimed to achieve a strictly objective recounting of events, without any symbolism or artistic bells and whistles. De Sica's work was also characterized by an acute sense for the coldness of society, especially his legendary *Ladri di biciclette* (1948; *Bicycle Thieves*). *Umberto D.* was a profane story, and touching precisely because of this profaneness. It tells the story of an old-age pensioner who is living alone with only his dog for company. When he is evicted from his flat, he decides to take his own life. But when he is unable to find a new home for his dog, he drops his suicide plans, and there the story ends.

Rotha was unable to take Kracauer up on the invitation for an alcohol- and tobacco-fuelled reading session, but in the summer of 1957 he visited the Kracauers while they were vacationing in Wilmington, Vermont. Rotha and Kracauer participated in a film seminar put on by Robert Flaherty Inc. in Brattleboro, where they watched *City of Gold* (1957), Walter Koenig and Colin Low's short film about a Canadian gold-mining community, which combines still photography from the 1890s with film footage from the 1940s. In this way, the film confirmed Kracauer's thesis that photography is the foundation of film and informs its style. Kracauer and Rotha's discussions about film left no stone unturned: everything they had ever thought or wanted to know about film, their experiences of film and their thoughts on the social purpose of film. Rotha even mentions this 'historic meeting' (as it is called in their correspondence) in one of his books. Kracauer, in turn, praised Rotha's professional participation and sympathetic understanding. The 'glorious days' in Wilmington were a highlight on the path that led towards the *Theory of Film*.[4]

Kracauer had adopted a new way of writing. He had first produced the 'syllabus', which he had now given to Rotha to read. This presented 'a guideline right through the whole book, with all the arguments and references in the right order'.[5] That had been an arduous piece of work, demanding the solution to quite a few intellectual conundrums and producing quite a few more. The published text of 1960 is still marked by the somewhat tedious work of over-organization that went into its production. Despite moments of rhetorical flourish, there is something monastic, ascetic and austere about the *Theory of Film*. As per the author's wishes, the aesthetics of film were to be unfolded within the bounds of a strict framework that leaves little room for spontaneity or for a more flowing literary text. Arnheim remarked that a less-disciplined reader would be tempted to apply the book's short and clear explications of film to other media, although the author resisted this urge.[6] Sixty-one stills provide the only ornamentation in the book, like stained-glass windows in an otherwise plain church. Kracauer planned to finish the manuscript fairly quickly once the syllabus was completed. That was the plan, at least, but in fact it sometimes took him months to complete a chapter that he had already prepared.[7]

In early 1958, Kracauer had completed two-thirds of the book. Following the contract for the American edition with Oxford University Press in 1950, he now had contracts for English, Italian and German editions.[8] In spring 1959, Kracauer began to work on the final chapter, the structure of which had, again, already been set out in the minutest detail. He still needed seven months for it. In this final act, his aim was to contextualize film historically and in relation to the present. To Rotha, he admitted that this was the most challenging part of the whole project. Days would go by without him making any progress at all: 'The bad thing is that the idea haunts me that I should write for eternity. It is a wrong idea, I know, yet there it is.' Kracauer felt like a sailing boat cast adrift in the middle of the ocean.[9] The strained writing process might have had to do with the fact that the book was charged with too much significance. He confessed to Löwenthal (now a professor at the University of California, Berkeley) that his 'true life' depended on writing this book.[10] The work of writing had apparently taken on an unprecedented significance in Siegfried Kracauer's life: 'The older I get, the more I find that work, reading and thinking are the only things that make life worth living. Lili feels the same.'[11] The difficulties he was encountering suggest that, with the writing of the last chapter, Kracauer had begun to deal with the last things before the last. He would have liked to have written a third autobiographical novel, following *Ginster* and *Georg*.[12] But this was not going to happen. Nor would he write the 'Journey to America' book he had proposed to Horkheimer. Kracauer now had to capture in writing all his experiences, whether profane or philosophical: everything that was to become his legacy, whatever might be of lasting significance. 'One grows older, and the urge to communicate pent-up insight precariously acquired sweeps away all other considerations', Kracauer says at one point in the *Theory of Film*, with Chaplin in mind. Chaplin had developed just such a 'desire to speak his mind' in his final films.[13] It is obvious that this insight applied just as much to Kracauer himself, now he was old; he liked Monsieur Verdoux and Cavalero, even if the films of which they were protagonists contained constant prattle, something Kracauer thought 'undeniably a retrogression' because less filmic.[14] He and Chaplin, the former maker of silent movies, were obviously driven by the same desire to speak their minds. It seems as though Kracauer's thought was something like this: if I could write down everything that I have learned in my struggle to come to terms with existence, then I would have had a "genuine life"'. Everything depended on that. It is easy to imagine, then, how he must have had to weigh each word, considering it from all sides, in the course of writing this philosophical epilogue, tweaking it constantly; many a stone that had been pushed up the hill in the morning would have been rolled back down again by the evening. He had been working on this book for over twenty years, since the original contract of 1938 with Allert de Lange. It tortured him, paralysed him. During these final months of writing, we cannot imagine Sisyphus as happy.

Kracauer made the 'final stroke', as noted in the manuscript, on 14 November 1959, and the book finally appeared at the end of October 1960. Its publication was marked by a lively party at the offices of Oxford University Press in New York.[15]

Theory of Film: The Redemption of Physical Reality consists of (a) a preface in which Kracauer outlines the aims and basic concepts of his aesthetics of film, (b) an introduction in which Kracauer discusses historical and phenomenological aspects of photography, with slightly more emphasis on the former, (c) the first part of the book, on 'general characteristics' (basic concepts, functions and affinities of film), (d) the second part, on 'areas and elements' (such as story, actors, language, sound, music, the spectator), and (e) a third part on 'composition' (which elaborates on types of film, like experimental film, the film of fact, the theatrical story, films based on novels, and episodes). *Last but not least*, the book has a historical and philosophical epilogue: 'Film in Our Time'.

Theory of Film is a theory of black-and-white film as it developed out of photography, a 'material aesthetics' that is 'concerned with content': 'It rests upon the assumption that film is essentially an extension of photography and therefore shares with this medium a marked affinity for the visible world around us. Films come into their own when they record and reveal physical reality', when they show, in the words of Henri de Parville, 'the ripple of the leaves stirred by the wind'.[16] Films come into their own when they correspond to the basic aesthetic principle of the medium, which, for Kracauer, in the case of photography and film, is the realistic tendency. Finally, films come into their own when they realize their affinities 'for unstaged reality',[17] the accidental, infinity, the indeterminate, hence the 'flow of life'.[18] The flow of life is the flow of material situations and events, including all they carry with them: feelings, values and ideas. While Kracauer agrees that film is a way of appropriating the world that is, above all, aesthetic, he does not see it as an art form like other traditional arts, which assimilate, use up and put to use their raw materials.[19] Film, by contrast, has the task of representing and casting a light on the ephemeral world in which we live. Film should cling to the surface of things; it should avoid inward life and intellectual matters: 'Such art as goes into cinematic films must be traced to their creators' capacity for reading the book of nature.'[20] And human beings and society are also part of that book. Kracauer calls film 'our contemporary', which, by 'exposing – for the first time, as it were – outer reality', deepens, 'in Gabriel Marcel's words, our relation to "this Earth which is our habitat."' In the last chapter, Kracauer writes, 'the cinema itself is set in the perspective of something more general – an approach to the world, a mode of human existence'.[21]

Film grew out of photography, and it inherited photography's particular attitude towards the world, our world. The book on film was therefore, from the beginning, more than a book on film: it was a book on life, on 'our life', and also on Kracauer's life.[22] Kracauer worked through some old philosophical themes: he recapped his analysis of ideological homelessness in the intuition of the world, and he reminded his readers of the empty bleakness of abstraction in the perception of the world. The 'technological age' had been characterized by the decay of common beliefs and the steadily increasing prestige accorded to the exact sciences. The situation of 'modern man' is that he 'lacks the guidance of binding norms', that he has lost all ideological certainties, and lives a life of impoverished experience, touching 'reality only with his fingertips'.[23] That is to say, he lacks 'experience': the experience of things in their concrete existence (although this is not to say there is no place for abstract thought). According to Kracauer, the world of modern man is in flux. It is transient and accidental, like Baudelaire's *modernité*.[24] This is where cinema comes in:

> Its imagery permits us, for the first time, to take away with us the objects and occurrences that comprise the flow of material life. ... In acquainting us with the world we live in, the cinema exhibits phenomena whose appearance in the witness stand is of particular consequence. It brings us face to face with the things we dread. And it often challenges us to confront the real-life events it shows with the ideas we commonly entertain about them.[25]

What Kracauer means by 'life' is not the life of the 'Lebensphilosophen' – not a substance, not a design for a totality, not a 'powerful entity'.[26] It is more akin to the lifeworld of Husserl and Schütz. Husserl's 'world in which we live intuitively' is not the world described by the objective natural sciences.[27] As the world of primordial experience, it precedes the world of science both in terms of genesis (of consciousness itself) and in the history of mankind.[28] There is a lot of evidence to suggest that this idea of the 'a priori of the lifeworld'[29] appealed to Kracauer, even if he put less stock in consciousness than Husserl and had set limits to the scope of phenomenology in his early *Soziologie als Wissenschaft* (Sociology as a Science). In his copy of Adorno's *Metakritik der Erkenntnistheorie*, Kracauer wrote 'good' next to Adorno's judgement of Husserl: 'Husserl accepts thinking in its reified shape, but he follows it so incorruptibly that it eventually surpasses itself.'[30] Kracauer adopted and expanded Husserl's formula of the 'world in which we live' in order to include within it profane everyday life, the 'stream of life' that Isaiah Berlin once identified as the focus of Tolstoy's thinking.[31] According to Kracauer, film is exceptionally well-suited to capturing this lifeworld.

Kracauer's analysis of his times was not the lament for the loss of a transcendental home that he had expressed in the early 1920s, nor was it a critique of culture that aimed at a revolutionary transition through the intensification of negativity or by means of a working through of the profane world (of the sort he proposed

in the late 1920s). Kracauer revived the perspective he had cultivated during the Weimar Republic, 'but as a lost one'. Modern
man should not mourn his expulsion from paradise, nor should he
hope for the creation of a new one, because the catastrophe had
taken place without bringing about the coming of the Messiah.[32] In
Kracauer's view, escaping from the ruins of theological certainty,
from philosophical systems and dialectical methods for mending the
rift that runs through the world, promises a gain in human opportunities, possibilities, delight in various realities. The 'increasing
difficulty for the individual to account for the forces, mechanisms,
and processes that shape the modern world, including his own
destiny', was no piece of misfortune. Kracauer had developed a
sort of serene melancholy. 'The world has grown so complex', he
admitted to himself, 'politically and otherwise, that it can no longer
be simplified. Any effect seems separated from its manifold possible
causes; any attempt at a synthesis, a unifying image, falls short.'[33]
In political terms, he had become a liberal, but a liberal of a unique
kind. Apart from the freedom of thought and action in politics and
society, in the arts and sciences, 'freedom' for Kracauer also meant
freedom from oppression and freedom from material need. The
vision of a classless society was, to Kracauer, a radical liberal vision.
Nevertheless, historical materialism was a residue of a bygone
world, a dogma whose alleged goal had been transformed into its
opposite. Without condemning reason, Kracauer had nevertheless
grown ever more sceptical towards it. Freedom was inconceivable
without reason, but under no circumstances was reason to be taken
to be a substitute for religion or science.

Something else had also changed for Kracauer since the pre-1933
years. If film were to disclose the world, it must also deal with the
things humans fear. The Kracauer of *Theory of Film* may have been
an open, cheerful, curious realist, but he also knew that fear was a
part of reality. In this context he acknowledged the contribution of
Freud, who showed how the forces of destruction – aggression and
the death drive – were just as much a part of the human as reason.
Freud, Kracauer thought, 'probes deeper than Marx into the forces
conspiring against the rule of reason'.[34] After Auschwitz, that is,
after everything that comes under that heading, the only remaining
task was the 'redemption of physical reality'. Solidarity with those
who were murdered, in the form of remembrance, was one part of
this. In *Theory of Film*, Kracauer tells the story of the Medusa. Her
face was so horrible (had become so horrible, one should add, as
she had been strikingly beautiful as a young woman) that her gaze
turned men and animals to stone. Perseus, sent by Athena to slay the
monster, was able to behead Medusa by looking at her reflection in
his shield. 'The moral of the myth', Kracauer writes, 'is, of course,
that we do not, and cannot, see actual horrors because they paralyze

us with blinding fear.' Of all media, it is cinema alone that 'holds up a mirror to nature. Hence our dependence on it for the reflection of happenings which would petrify us were we to encounter them in real life. The film screen is Athena's polished shield'.[35] And 'in experiencing ... the litter of tortured human bodies in the films made of the Nazi concentration camps, we redeem horror from its invisibility behind the veils of panic and imagination.'[36] This is a liberation because it removes one of the most powerful taboos, namely to confront the horror. Kracauer concludes: 'Perhaps Perseus' greatest achievement was not to cut off Medusa's head but to overcome his fears and look at its reflection in the shield. And was it not precisely this feat which permitted him to behead the monster?'[37] The 'redemption of physical reality' thus means, in part, a redemption through remembrance, 'as if the only world that is readable and can be experienced as a human face is the world that has been turned to stone in images'.[38]

Unlike his 1938 exposé, the *Theory of Film* does not, on the face of it, appear to adopt a sociological perspective. It also clearly distances itself from the question of the relationship between society and work in the sense of the theory of reification (i.e. film as a commodity), or in the sense of Benjamin's essay on the work of art in the age of its technological reproducibility (i.e. film as a 'power agent' in a materialist theory of art analogous to Marx's critique of the capitalist mode of production). For those left-wing German intellectuals who cultivated some interest in aesthetics and who, with Adorno's help, had discovered Benjamin and Kracauer in the 1960s, that was irritating and a disappointment. They had just become familiar with the critical sociologist of *The Salaried Masses* and the combative film historian of the *Caligari* book. But this Kracauer did not seem interested in pursuing a critical theory of film. Bernd Witte described the book as a withdrawal 'to a position of unmediated realism'.[39] Helmut Lethen's initial impression was that Kracauer's aesthetics of film was based on his 'erstwhile certainty of being' and 'a naïve understanding of a neutral technology'. Lethen summarized his impression by modifying Marx's final thesis on Feuerbach: so far the world has only been interpreted in various ways; what matters is to keep it free of interpretation in order to restore its visibility.[40] Gertrud Koch, like Adorno, detected a tendency towards substantialism in the work: 'Existential ontology forms the basis of his ideas of the thing-in-itself, and film is indeed a medium on the way to "beings."'[41] She also found certain theological niceties: 'The matter from which Kracauer draws part of his theory is the theological matter of creation; the thing-in-itself figures in this theory as the matter created by God, while the meaningful appropriation of matter corresponds to what is man-made.'[42] According to this argument, the existential ontology of the philosophy of the real had been supplemented by a redemptive aesthetics of rescue, justified in terms of the properties of the medium and based on a concept, the 'lifeworld', that ignores political and social relations of domination. For the political left of the Federal Republic, the book was a disappointment and a mystery, as Lethen recalls: 'Here, the world was not a "construction", never mind a dialectical construction.'[43] In the *Frankfurter Allgemeine Zeitung*, Enno Patalas called *Theory of Film* an apologetic text, because reality required not redemption but critique.[44]

What is the truth of the matter here? Had the erstwhile film critic who took himself to be a social critic, and the erstwhile film historian who had once, assuming the role of social historian, undertaken to offer an alternative explanation of '1933', now become a film theoretician whose only interest was aesthetics? Had he ontologically conjured up the 'things-in-themselves' and presented cosy cultural-philosophical fireside chats about 'our times' and 'us human beings within it'? It is true that the book's epilogue flies at a high altitude over its material. Kracauer asks a lot of film as a medium. In his eyes, film was meant not only to represent a whole historical epoch but to make that whole epoch, for the first time, visible, taking its surface expressions as the point of departure. Kracauer introduces confusion with his various different concepts of reality: there is 'camera-reality', then 'nature', 'physical reality', the latter being, at the same time, 'material reality'. And where was the 'perception' that precedes all rendering-visible of things? Where were the constructions of the film-makers who were to read the book of nature? If we follow Miriam Hansen, however, and read Kracauer's film aesthetics not as a theory of filmic realism but as a theory of the experience of film and, even more generally, of cinema as a sensual-perceptual experience matrix, the suspicion that Kracauer is putting forward an ontology simply evaporates. In any case, such an intention on Kracauer's part would fit ill within his overall oeuvre,[45] especially when one considers his biography and the experiences of Marseille and of 'Auschwitz'. Film is *the* 'medium of a disintegrating world', a world split between equally alienated subjects and objects, despite all the clever philosophical tricks to heal the rift, and a world from which one may be expelled.[46] Film is a symptom of a contingent modernity and a transient life. For all these reasons, film was a fitting travelling companion for Kracauer in his journey through life. He might well have called his epilogue 'Film in My Time'. The questions he put to modern existence were questions that could first and foremost be put to cinema. Kracauer's realism did not concern representation; it was realism as a particular perspective on things, a perspective characterized by experience. It was a specific relationship towards the world. Society and history were hidden in the undergrowth of his aesthetics, which, we should not forget, was intended as a material aesthetics. For Kracauer, reality was and remained a construction, and this was also true in the area of the aesthetics of film. But here he emphasized that there is also a reality that transcends construction and that is independent of human beings. Kracauer was a constructivist realist, or a constructivist with realist tendencies.

There were not many who understood this position. *Theory of Film* was accused of presenting an ontology or a naïve realism. The work seemed unwieldy and old-fashioned.[47] Dwight Macdonald thought that Kracauer's film theory was much too serious and difficult; others took issue with the 'fixed idea' that the book seemed to impose on everything, or were irritated by the book's academic style, with its 'virtual Socratic dialogues'.[48] Pauline Kael, some thirty years Kracauer's junior, and soon to become the most influential film critic in the US, even poked fun at the book's German pedantry. She was well known for her sharp pen; Chaplin's *Limelight*, for instance, she called 'Slimelight'. Kracauer was at the receiving end of even more savage mockery in an article she wrote for *Sight & Sound*. It begins thus:

> Siegfried Kracauer is the sort of man who can't say 'It's a lovely day' without first establishing that it is day, that the term 'day' is meaningless without the dialectical concept of 'night', that both these terms have no meaning unless there is a world in which day and night alternate, and so forth. By the time he has established an epistemological system to support his right to observe that it's a lovely day, our day has been spoiled.[49]

Kael, apparently, thought that Kracauer was a Hegelian. She expressed her puzzlement at the idea that an aesthetics could be founded on the accidental – on the 'ripple of the leaves'.[50] She was irritated by what she considered tautologies and arbitrary definitions, considered all the stuff about neo-realism the result of an old-fashioned know-it-all attitude. And, in any case, who was interested in whether film could do this or that, which painting or theatre cannot do? She was deeply suspicious of the idea of reading the book of nature, and irritated by his realist 'catechism'.[51] All this Teutonic philosophizing over films, for her, spoiled the fun they can bring; it killed off the fantasy, even the joy of life. Art only had one task: to astonish the spectator. In all art, 'we look and listen for what we have not experienced quite that way before'.[52] For Kael, *Theory of Film* stood in the way of such experience.

Kracauer had expected fierce controversy, but Kael's attack still took him by surprise.[53] He did not understand why New York intellectuals, in particular, had reacted so angrily.[54] There were two main reasons behind these criticisms. On the one hand, the fact that Kracauer spoke about film mainly as a medium, that is, as a technology of reproduction rather than an art form, was, in general, not well received.[55] This is clear even from the positive reviews by Herbert Read (*British Journal of Aesthetics*), Leo Steinberg (*Harper's Magazine*), George Steiner (*The Reporter*) and Charles A. Siepmann (*Public Opinion Quarterly*).[56] This was also the source of the suspicion that the book might be the work of a fastidious, narrow-minded German professor, someone lacking a sense of humour. But, what was more, a new generation had emerged in the international film scene, and the members of this younger generation no longer understood the issues that so exercised Kracauer. His problems were no longer topical. Around 1955, when the generation born around 1930 began to form the cinematic avant-garde, centred on the journal *Film Culture* and people like Jonas Mekas and Parker Tyler, Kracauer's name was no longer so important. He was still useful in getting money for projects, such as journals that fought for their survival from issue to issue, journals made by 'young people who felt that something was not right with film and with the world'. Kracauer even gave Mekas part of a chapter from *Theory of Film* for pre-publication in the journal.[57] Kracauer felt honoured when the film department of the Museum of Modern Art showed a series of films based on his 'syllabus' for the *Theory of Film* and accompanied it with a seminar in which Kracauer's ideas were discussed in relation to selected films.[58] This was the idea of Richard Griffith, who had succeeded Iris Barry as curator of the film archive in 1951. Yet it became increasingly clear that Kracauer's understanding of film belonged to a different era. He was often labelled, along with Flaherty, as a representative of 'realism without fantasy' or the 'naïve realism of the nineteenth century'.[59] One avant-garde film club advertised an event with a film-maker, almost maliciously, describing him as 'the most talented and exciting, non-Kracauerian director in the world'.[60] Younger cinephiles were simply baffled by the intermingling of film and philosophy. For them, films existed in order to be watched and to offer film-makers a realm of creative expression. Where 'reality' was invoked, it was for the purpose of political agitation, for attacks on organized amusement or disciplined work. Suicide and the fear of nuclear war: those were realist themes – not the 'ripple of leaves excited by the wind'. The redemption of physical reality was of no interest to this politicized generation; their revolt was directed against psycho-social reality.[61] For others, 'the apotheosis of realism' reached by the older generation represented not too little but too much moral, political, dogmatic and 'vaguely Marxist' baggage.[62] Either way, the new generation did not know what to do with Kracauer's theory of film.

Kracauer did not respond to the reviews – as a matter of principle, as he wrote to Aristarco, but probably also because he had put the topic of film behind him. Contemporary film criticism, he now thought, was incompetent and irrelevant.[63]

38

Talks with Teddie and Old Friends

Kracauer had said enough about film. Film had always been a medium that Kracauer had used in order to make sociological or philosophical points.[1] But he continued to search for spaces in between abstract thought and concrete things. Kracauer wanted to explore areas of reality that the established sciences overlooked and, in this way, to counteract the impoverishment of modern man's experience. The mission of film – to take up, in the form of images, the things that humans overlook – could in principle also be carried out by other modes through which the world is appropriated. At some point during the year after the completion of his book on film theory, Kracauer realized, 'in a flash', the many existing parallels between history and the photographic media, historical reality and 'camera-reality'.[2] The insights that Kracauer had presented in the 'epilogue' to the *Theory of Film* he now applied to a wider area, and this prompted a number of questions to arise: is the historian forced to move, just like the photographer, between realism and the construction of form? Does the historical universe have a hetero-geneous structure akin to that of the lifeworld through which film moves? Might historiography also be a medium through which hidden areas of reality are made visible?

In February 1959, in a letter to Adorno, Kracauer mentioned that among his plans was 'a collection of reflections about history'.[3] A year later, he asked Löwenthal for a copy of the English translation of Marc Bloch's *Apologie pour l'histoire ou métier d'historien* (1949; *The Historian's Craft*, 1954) as a birthday present, adding that he 'very much would like to write a few essays on history, of a method-ological and substantial nature. I have ideas for it, but I do not yet know whether I should lock myself into such a project.'[4] After another year, his ideas on history were beginning to take shape: 'I have made a discovery that has confirmed the choice of my topic. This essay on history, I suddenly realized, is the direct continuation of my *Theory of Film*: the historian has traits of the photographer, and historical reality resembles camera reality.[5] The similarity is really astonishing; I completely unconsciously followed this path.'[6] Kracauer also remembered that he had, in an early essay of 1927, made the connection between photography and historicism. Noting the historical coincidence of the development of photography and the rise of historical thinking and the structural analogy between them, he wrote:

> Photography presents a spatial continuum; historicism seeks to provide the temporal continuum. ... Historicism is concerned with the photography of time. The equivalent of its temporal photography would be a giant film depicting the temporally interconnected events from every vantage point.[7]

Delighted by the discovery of this unconscious and seemingly meaningful thread in his philosophical work, he wondered: 'Had I been struck with blindness up to this moment?'[8] But now the scales fell from his eyes. Everything he had done so far had, in truth, been driven by the same inner necessity. His philosophical writing – some done as a hobby, some professionally – his daydreaming in the cinema and his snapshots of unseen things, his work in sociology, with its criticism of the dearth of qualitative content analysis, all these were performed in the service of the search for areas that had been overlooked, misunderstood or not taken seriously. That was his true mission, and where before he had been pursuing it implicitly, he now understood that he had to make it explicit. Reality is a construction, and this is true also – in fact, especially – when it comes to autobiography. Intoxicated by the meaningfulness of this continuity in his own biography, Kracauer began his last enterprise. These would become the happiest years of his life.

Another lost connection was re-established around this time: Ernst Bloch reappeared. The two friends had parted in Paris a quarter of a century ago, the air between them 'not cleared, and in silence'.[9] Bloch had travelled on to Prague, and from there, as the situation for anti-fascists became ever more precarious, he fled to the US in July 1938. Unlike for Kracauer, for Bloch America never stopped being a country of exile. He was a writer who needed the German language as he needed air to breathe.[10] Not that he was not familiar with some foreign languages, but those were ancient Greek and Latin from his school days. But he struggled with speaking 'wretched English', let alone earning money writing in the language. For money, he thus had to rely on Karola Bloch, who worked as a waitress or in temporary office jobs, and on the Institute for Social Research, which, however, wanted to keep its distance from the sympathizer of the communist party. Horkheimer gave him a small start-up sum, but that was all. Bloch grew bitter, and he developed a genuine aggression towards the people at the Institute.

At the end of 1942, he fell out with Adorno, who was Horkheimer's advisor in the 'Bloch matter'. The trigger for this episode was in fact a grotesque misunderstanding. Bloch had written a letter to the Institute in which he complained that he had been forced to work as a dishwasher and a packer (this was actually false). Adorno then put an advertisement in the exile newspaper *Aufbau* asking for donations to support Bloch. Bloch felt this was 'hypocritical mercy' and a humiliation, and he cut off ties with Adorno.[11] In the autumn of 1958, however, the two met again. Adorno gave the main lecture at the congress of the International Hegel Society in Frankfurt, where Bloch was also speaking. Adorno attempted to avoid Bloch, who, he assumed, still bore a grudge. But Bloch attended Adorno's lecture and, when the speaker attempted to leave the lecture hall afterwards, blocked his way. In his characteristically jovial way, he asked: 'Well, Teddie, how are you?' And with that, the air between them was instantly cleared.[12] They did not even need to discuss their falling out. 'Spending the afternoon alone together, we got on so well that any such formal fuss would have been ridiculous', Adorno told Peter Suhrkamp (who published the work of both). 'I am very happy about that.'[13]

The 'Kracs' were also 'most sincerely' pleased about the changes that seemed to have come over Bloch. 'Something of the old affection always comes over us whenever we think of him', Kracauer responded to Adorno's news.[14] A little more than half a year later, 'Krac' himself received mail from Leipzig. But it would take until the summer of 1962 before the two met again, in Munich. To the great regret of both, it would be the only such meeting.[15] In political terms the two had, of course, moved even further away from each other. Kracauer, for instance, saw it as a bad sign that the 'young German intelligentsia' had responded so enthusiastically to Bloch's *The Principle of Hope* and to new editions of his older writings.[16] On a personal level, however, the spark between the old friends was certainly still there. 'Our extensive time together in Munich ... was wonderful.'[17] They spoke about the problem of time, a central element in Kracauer's history project. Bloch, who had coined the phrase the 'non-contemporaneity of the contemporaneous' in his *Heritage of Our Times*, was one of the few people with whom Kracauer might be able, he thought, to discuss his critique of diachronic time. Bloch had given him a copy of his *Tübinger Einleitung in die Philosophie*, which Kracauer had devoured 'with pleasure'. Bloch's 'distinctions regarding the concept of progress' bore some similarities with Kracauer's 'ideas on the antinomy involved in the chronological concept of time', which he was going to explicate in 'Time and History', his contribution to the Festschrift for Adorno's sixtieth birthday. The text would become one of the chapters in *History: The Last Things before the Last*.[18]

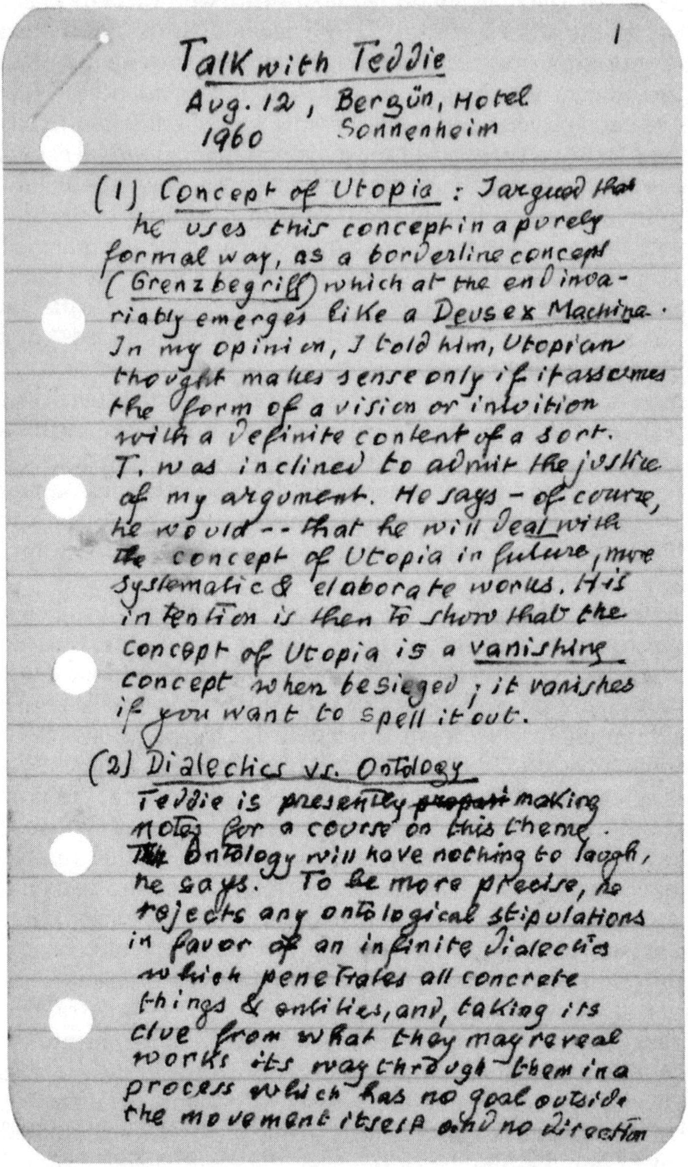

Figure 37. 'Talk with Teddie' – Kracauer's notes on his discussion with Adorno on 12 August 1960
Copyright: DLA Marbach

Meanwhile, Kracauer's exchanges with Adorno intensified, in particular after a discussion at Hotel Sonnenheim in Bergün (Canton Graubünden, Switzerland), which Kracauer recorded in notes titled 'Talk with Teddie'. Adorno had also embarked on a large book project, his *Negative Dialectics*, and they had exchanged ideas on the matter. According to Kracauer's report, the discussion focused on three areas: the concept of utopia, the opposition between dialectics and ontology, and the relationship between ideology and society. Kracauer criticized Adorno for using the concept of utopia 'in a purely formal way', as a 'borderline concept' which 'at the end invariably emerges like a *Deus ex Machina*'. According to Kracauer, utopian thought 'makes sense only if it assumes the form of a vision or intuition with a definite content of some sort'. Kracauer's notes say that Adorno accepted the 'justice' of the argument but declared that his intention was precisely to show that the concept of utopia 'is a vanishing concept when besieged; it vanishes if you want to spell it out'.[19] Kracauer then questioned Adorno's dialectical method, which, he complained, seemed arbitrary. He found particularly confusing the fact that Adorno seemed to believe that this method could operate without any content or direction. That fitted with the formality and emptiness of Adorno's concept of utopia. Adorno responded that Kracauer seemed still to be clinging to an obsolete ontological idea: namely, that thinking requires fixed points of reference – some presupposed or sought-after anchor points. The upshot of that sort of attitude would be the building of systems that, on the basis of these postulates or visions, would ignore the concrete qualities of things instead of working their way through them. Contrary to the assumptions of ontology, truth is something that hovers. Kracauer compared Adorno's dialectics to a film made exclusively from close-ups. This would be confusing and cause 'dizziness' in the spectators who need to have some spatial relation to their surrounding reality.[20] In the case of film this relation is provided by long shots. In Adorno's case, the radical immanence of the dialectical process transforms it into a pure end-in-itself. As a result, it becomes meaningless; it lacks any relation to reality. Adorno, for his part, was concerned with avoiding ontological fixations based on supposed eternal truths. But Kracauer did not think it was necessary to posit such absolute truth; all that was needed was a relation to something real outside of the dialectical movement. Kracauer here cunningly set up 'Benjamin against Teddie' by invoking the former's messianism. Finally, Kracauer was not satisfied with Adorno's sociology. He thought it far too general, and therefore incapable of capturing social reality. He mentioned Adorno's use of the adjective 'bourgeois' ('bürgerlich') in this connection. Everything was reduced to the '"bürgerliche" *Warengesellschaft* [commodity society]'; everything intellectual was a product of 'reification', whether 'specific values, abstractness in our approach to the world', or 'unjustified relativism' that led to arbitrariness.[21] Like his concepts of utopia and dialectics, Adorno's sociological concepts lacked substance and vision. 'To him', Kracauer noted down,

> dialectics is a means of maintaining his superiority over all imaginable opinions, viewpoints, trends, happenings, by dissolving, condemning or again rescuing them as he pleases. Thus he establishes himself as the master and controller of a world he has never absorbed. For had he absorbed at least segments of it, his dialectic would come to a stop, somewhere.[22]

In sum, then, Kracauer accused his friend of formalism, of an indifference towards the concrete and experiential and of 'an arrogant disregard for the internal contradictions of his position'.[23]

It seems that Kracauer thought he had emerged from this dispute the victor, for he later repeated these criticisms in his book on history.[24] In his notes on the Bergün discussion, however, one gets the sense that Adorno did not admit 'defeat' and that, in fact, he probably did not think he had lost the argument. Unfortunately, we do not have similar notes on it capturing Adorno's perspective, but *Negative Dialectics* contains traces of the conversation. There are certain passages in it that may be read as responses to Kracauer's criticisms. For instance, Adorno writes:

> We are blaming the method for the fault of the matter when we object to dialectics on the ground ... that whatever happens to come into the dialectical mill will be reduced to the merely logical form of contradiction, and that ... the full diversity of the noncontradictory, of that which is simply differentiated, will be ignored.[25]

According to Adorno, 'dialectics' does not simply refer to a method of thinking but to a real movement. Because, as he saw it, even the difference between the particular and the general is under the spell of totality, dialectics does not take up an arbitrary position in advance; rather, it is the consciousness of radical non-identity. He did not understand contradiction in formal terms, but saw it instead as 'nonidentity under the aspect of identity'.[26] The connection with the 'Talk' is revealed in the wording of yet another passage:

> A dialectics no longer 'glued' to identity will provoke either the charge that it is bottomless ... or the objection that it is *dizzying*. ... They want a bit of ontology, at least, amidst their criticism of ontology – as if the smallest free insight did not express the goal better than a declaration of intention that is not followed up. ... Unleashed dialectics is not without anything solid, no more than is Hegel. But it no longer confers primacy on it.[27]

Adorno would probably not have accepted the opposition 'Dialectics vs. Ontology' – one of the headings in Kracauer's notes from their discussion. Of course, Adorno did not think that his philosophy lacked direction any more than he thought that it put forward a system. One could not adopt some concrete idea of utopia just because it would have been good to have one. The goal of rescuing the non-identical through a critique of the autocratic mind was intended as a way of at least preserving the possibility of a domination-free society developing, while avoiding the sinister dialectic of enlightenment. The first sentence of the introduction to *Negative Dialectics* spells out the insight on which the book is based: 'Philosophy, which once seemed obsolete, lives on because the moment to realize it was missed.'[28] 'After Auschwitz', translating the Kantian goal of emerging from humanity's self-incurred immaturity into a philosophy of history required a new anti-systematic philosophy, one that took aim at all forms of domination, one that stood on the shoulders of Kant and Hegel. This was what guided Adorno's thinking.

The sense of triumph one can detect in Kracauer's notes might also be read as a sign of vindictiveness. His former pupil was always his sternest critic, and Adorno tended to assume a posture of superiority over Kracauer that the latter must have resented. In any

Figure 38. Theodor W. Adorno at Frankfurt University in 1957
Copyright: Theodor W. Adorno Archiv, Frankfurt am Main

case, Kracauer had been carrying his criticisms of Adorno around with him for quite some time. Half a year before the meeting in Bergün, he wrote to Löwenthal that 'Teddie ... is really witty and dazzling' but that he proceeded

> always according to the same principle; first he ruffles everything up, and then he smooths it out again. ... I know of no other example of a critique that attempts to make an intervention [eingreifende Kritik] that has so little purchase [Greifkraft]. In the end, everything is left as it was, and ultimately he feels very comfortable with that.

And he added: 'Keep this locked up in your heart; it would be too late now to want to change Teddie.'[29] Half a year later, though, Kracauer himself gave his disapproval a good airing. He continued to accuse his prolific friend of churning out predictable texts. Concerning the Mahler book, he told Adorno: 'the matrix from which the specific aesthetic analyses originate and against which they are set remains unchanged'. Kracauer had to get this off his chest. Looking back at the discussion in Bergün, he wrote: 'It was good to have a proper talk. Don't you think so too? I had been wishing for it very much.'[30]

To begin with, Adorno simply put up with Kracauer's attacks. From spring 1962, their correspondence even intensified, and when, on one occasion, there had been no letter from Frankfurt for six weeks, Kracauer complained that this was 'something of a breach of [their] new convention'.[31] Adorno even occasionally drew the attention of his colleagues and students to Kracauer, much in the way one might introduce members of one's family to a long-lost uncle who had disappeared to America decades ago but who was now suddenly in the frame again. In the everyday work of the Institute for Social Research and at the university Kracauer was not mentioned, but in certain specific cases Adorno would mediate between his people and Kracauer. In a letter to Kracauer, he mentioned Hermann Schweppenhäuser, a 'highly gifted student' of his who had 'written an *extraordinary* Habilitation on Kierkegaard and Hegel', praising his successful 'revision of the whole controversy' that had exercised Friedel and Teddie in their discussions in the 1920s.[32] Schweppenhäuser's study moved between the poles of a speculative Hegelian and a subjective Kierkegaardian philosophy, defending each against the other (although overall his concern was, against the philosophical trend at the time, to rescue Hegel).[33] There was much praise also for Alfred Schmidt, who had written a dissertation on the concept of nature in Marx. Both Adorno and Kracauer profited from this work. Kracauer wrote: 'It is a really excellent study of source material, with a restraint in the presentation which I esteem very highly. His exposition of the utopian motifs in Marx's writings is extraordinarily interesting – to me, at any rate.'[34] The 'dialectic of nature' that Schmidt identified in Marx would prove important for Kracauer's book on history: the idea, that is, that human relations partly belong to the realm of nature and that nature is also a part of human historicity.[35] Kracauer was interested in both Schmidt and Schweppenhäuser, but he would only end up meeting Schmidt – briefly, in the summer of 1964 in Frankfurt.[36]

Kracauer also came into contact with Rolf Tiedemann, who had written his dissertation on Benjamin with Adorno and Horkheimer. Kracauer read the chapter on 'motifs from the philosophy of history' for the *Studien zur Philosophie Walter Benjamins* (published in 1965 in the series *Frankfurter Beiträge zur Soziologie*). In a letter he told Tiedemann that he had been very impressed by the way he had presented 'Benjamin's mixed and complicated ideas on history', even navigating 'the labyrinth of the arcades [project]'. Tiedemann and Schweppenhäuser would go on to edit Benjamin's *Gesammelte Schriften* from 1970 onwards. As someone who had known him, Kracauer provided Tiedemann with the following picture of Benjamin: 'What a unique appearance he was – difficult and luminous, truly impossible and then again playing with wonderful possibilities.' Kracauer wanted to see the arcades project restored and made available: 'He spoke a lot about it, and some of it seemed to me *spleen pure and simple* – but brilliant *spleens*.'[37] Kracauer also told Tiedemann about his position in relation to Benjamin's philosophy of history. He said he liked the messianic impulse: 'that nothing should be lost; that history must be shattered so that its true contents can be found in the details'. But he always regretted that Benjamin 'did not see the dialectic between the reality in which we live and the final messianic reality (which, in my own case, only plays a negative role)'.[38]

Kracauer enjoyed being able to tell the 'young people' about their idols, being himself something of an idol to them. It was around this time that, in a letter to Adorno, Kracauer spoke of Adorno, Benjamin, Bloch and himself as constituting 'a group which is set off against the background of the times'. Kracauer was astonished that, as Adorno told him, 'people follow everything relating to us with an immense, libidinously cathected curiosity'.[39] Another one of these 'young people', at least in Kracauer's eyes, was Karl Heinz Haag. Haag sent Kracauer his *Kritik der neuen Ontologie* (1960), which Kracauer thought was 'brilliant': 'The way the quotation from Heidegger's speech of 1933 emerges as the conclusion to his doctrine (and not at all a deviation) is a superb achievement, including in literary terms.'[40] Kracauer was probably even more enthusiastic about Haag's contribution to the Festschrift for Adorno's sixtieth birthday, the essay 'Das Unwiederholbare' (1963). Haag, by then a Privatdozent,[41] handed him a copy after meeting Kracauer in Frankfurt. After reading it in New York, Kracauer told Haag that he had succeeded, in a few pages, in defining the major historical positions taken in Western philosophy with regard to the essential problem around which it circles and which it tries in vain to solve. It is precisely the problem that today faces us naked, so to speak (and that has occupied me since my early days, when I wrote *Sociology as a Science*, without me being aware of it). Over the years, I have learned to focus on this problem more and more sharply, and it is the reason why today I am working on the book on history.

This *problem* was the relation between the general and the particular within Aristotelian and nominalist thought and Haag's 'determination of the "unrepeatable" [of the particular that cannot be subsumed to anything general, due to the division between subject and object, spirit and nature], which everywhere slips through the net'. Kracauer made no secret of the fact that he did not think that a dialectical mediation between the two moments of truth was the solution, telling the Frankfurt philosopher:

> I am familiar with this dialectics; I do not believe it is a suitable method for determining what is unique. (The idea of this dialectics still belongs to the same tradition whose boundaries it wants to burst open.) It seems much more likely to me that the relation of the particular to the general under which it is subsumed must be imagined as a side-by-side – as a relation that always, or at least in most cases, must be examined and defined with a view to its specific character and structure.[42]

This theory of a side-by-side of the particular and general would prove to be one of the most important elements of Kracauer's book on history. Kracauer saw the germ of something like this idea in Benjamin. Reading Haag pushed him further along this path.

Of the other people around Adorno, Kracauer also got to know Jürgen Habermas and Peter Szondi. Habermas had already taken up Horkheimer's chair of philosophy and sociology when Kracauer met him for the first time. In intellectual terms, Kracauer thought highly of Adorno's former research assistant. In April 1965, Habermas was a guest at the Kracauers' home in New York. On Kracauer's 'unusually tidy desk lay one single piece of white paper with one handwritten sentence on it – this he showed me as the product of the day so far, and he spoke about his project'.[43] Among Kracauer's guests at West End Ave. in Manhattan was also the 'very nice and highly gifted Dr Peter Szondi', who was a visiting professor at Princeton at the time.[44] Adorno had urged Kracauer to get in touch with Szondi when Kracauer visited Zurich (the Kracauers regularly stopped over there during their trips to Europe in order to visit the Gublers and Wahls). Kracauer heeded the advice. Szondi had recently published his dissertation on the *Theory of the Modern Drama* with Suhrkamp, and Adorno now tried in vain to bring him to the University of Frankfurt.[45] Szondi in fact went to Berlin, where, in 1965, he became the chair and director of the newly founded Seminar for General and Comparative Literature at the Freie Universität. He was committed to breaking with the conventional methods of literary studies, which, by limiting themselves to the interpretation of texts, he held, were unable to understand anything about their subject matter. In the summer of 1965, Kracauer met Szondi again, in Berlin, at the philosopher Dieter Henrich's place. They were joined by Jacob Taubes, who Kracauer knew from Columbia University; the previous year, Taubes had invited Kracauer to the second colloquium of the research group Poetics and Hermeneutics.[46] Having Benjamin as a common point of reference, Kracauer's and Szondi's views converged on certain points, in particular regarding the question of what hermeneutics is and how it should be reformulated. They rejected both idealist and vulgar Marxist literary history, and they both considered literary studies without the study of history and society inconceivable – just as inconceivable as the substitution of aesthetic questions with the question of their social genesis.[47] For Kracauer, this contact with 'Adorno's children' was inspiring, even exciting; having no such 'children' of his own, nor a chair or an institution, Kracauer yet felt the need to take 'young and highly gifted' people by the hand and accompany them for a stretch along their way – and he had a talent for it.

Two artistically ambitious individuals close to Adorno made the greatest impression on Kracauer: Hans Magnus Enzensberger and Alexander Kluge. After reading Enzensberger's *Einzelheiten* [Details] (1962), which discusses, among other things, 'the consciousness industry', Kracauer wrote to Adorno that he would like 'to have a long conversation some day' with Enzensberger. 'It would be worth it – but he still has a lot to learn (and some things to unlearn).'[48] When Adorno sent Kracauer Kluge's *Lebensläufe* [Life-stories] (1962), Kracauer asked: 'Who is your friend Axel Kluge?' Adorno's response, that Kluge was 'a young, enormously talented man, in some respects comparable to Enzensberger', Kracauer had confirmed for him when he read the book. He wrote to Kluge that he had been

> deeply struck by the stylistic and factual stringency with which your book presented the experience that (today) most life-stories are not stories, and most persons are not persons. I know of no one else who has pulled this experience, which only someone who genuinely cares about humanity can have, so dramatically into the cruel limelight. (It is a light white as chalk, it seems to me.) Your dissection of the

biographical – your new form of presentation that joins together
obliquely connected fragments – and your extreme accuracy in
naming positions, situations, and places, which is fully justified, all
this leads to a shocking awareness of the condition of the things and
humans with which we are dealing. (Or especially those in Germany?
I wrote to Adorno that Benjamin might have said about this book,
too, what he said of *Ginster*: it could only have been written in
Germany.)[49]

Kracauer's more 'professional' letters were often friendly, polite and
appreciative, but he rarely wrote as enthusiastically as he did in his
letter to Kluge about the young author's first book. Kracauer saw
in it a new way of writing history, a chronicle in which 'experience'
was at the centre, and which expressed a form of historical curiosity
that was motivated by both social philosophical and literary
ambitions. Through its montages and fragments, Kluge's text
illuminated objective events and their subjective appropriation.
This method also allowed him to reflect on possible hidden dimensions to these events. Perhaps, here, Kluge had found a way of
entering the cavities and in-between spaces of human reality, into
which only a few thinkers had hitherto set foot. That Kluge was also
a film person would only have increased Kracauer's interest. There
were some resemblances here with the young Teddie Wiesengrund:
'Kluge and Enzensberger ... are two young people whom I should
like to know. In their case, the old Platonic Eros is awakening
again.'[50]

In the winter term 1961/62, Erika Lorenz, a student of Adorno's
who had previously studied with Bloch in Leipzig, wrote her final
thesis on 'the sociologist' Kracauer, even though his sociological
writings, with the exception of *The Salaried Masses*, were at that
point not available in Germany. Lorenz's boundless empathy soon
won over Kracauer, who at first had been sceptical towards the
project. With a high level of understanding, she worked her way
into the core of Kracauer's work: the 'intertwinement of theory and
practice', the 'philosophy of the anteroom' and the 'construction
out of the material'. Lorenz's primary material was mostly old,
forgotten newspaper articles from the *Frankfurter Zeitung*, which
she read at the library of the Chamber of Industry and Commerce
in Frankfurt. She wrote to Kracauer:

Whatever material you take up, one can feel that the things you say do
not serve the purpose of exemplifying a theory, and yet do not want to
do without theory, that in any case nothing is ever imputed or placed
above them, but that which seems to exceed them is nevertheless
conditioned by them. ... One has firm ground under one's feet and yet
is not stuck in one place, to the facts.[51]

She conceived of Kracauer's method of 'construction out of the material' as a partly intuitive procedure that approached the world in a sensual and concrete way, while avoiding positivism or historicism; it was a method in the service of reason. Theoretical thought is rendered concrete, and surface phenomena are analysed by means of a sensitive conceptual apparatus. Kracauer had only a few suggestions for improvements to the thesis plan. The Frankfurt student conceived of Kracauer's sociology as a form of 'critical theory of society'. Kracauer claimed that it was rather to be seen as a 'philosophy of the last things before the last'.[52] His correspondence with Lorenz reveals that Kracauer had found the perspective he would adopt in his book on history as early as October 1961. Kracauer retrospectively projected this perspective on to his early work too:

> a rehabilitation of those intermediary areas ... to which justice has never been done before, because they either were considered areas of purely impressionistic observation, or, from the opposite angle, were covered up by metaphysical speculation (e.g. in Hegel's philosophy of history).[53]

In Kracauer's self-image, he was first and foremost a philosopher, a 'philosopher of the provisional', however, who considered thoughts about the 'last things' only acceptable 'if they shine through concrete things that have been made transparent'. Kracauer did not think much of the new trend for replacing philosophy with sociology: 'Where would all those things that are not part of sociology and yet demand to be penetrated end up then?' The world, for Kracauer, was not exhausted by human society.[54] He was not even thinking primarily of nature here, but of the simple fact that in the end everyone dies by him- or herself, not in a collective. Although Lorenz's thesis was no masterpiece, Kracauer was nevertheless grateful to her. It was a 'sensation to be allowed to survey myself objectively – as if I did not really exist any longer.'[55]

Adorno also supported Kracauer in the field of literature. Where Kracauer had once been in a position to create possibilities for his friends, Adorno was now the one pulling strings for Kracauer. Adorno wanted to see the friends of his who had been expelled in 1933 return to the centre of the Federal Republic's intellectual life. He doggedly pursued the publication of Benjamin's writings – a project that, for a publisher, represented a significant economic risk – and in the end, despite all reservations, was successful. Now, he took it upon himself to act on Kracauer's behalf. He saw to it that his friend became a member of the German Sociological Society and that his writings, from *Soziologie als Wissenschaft* and *The Salaried Masses* to the works on film and the essay on content analysis, were given due recognition.[56] During the Kracauers' visit to the 'Teddies' place' in the summer of 1962, Adorno suggested he talk to Siegfried Unseld about *Ginster* and a possible essay collection. The new head of the Suhrkamp Verlag was immediately interested, especially in the essay collection, for which Adorno suggested the title *Das Ornament der Masse* (*The Mass Ornament*). It appeared a year later, in spring 1963. Kracauer was very grateful and happy, and he dedicated the book to Adorno as the mediator between him and the publisher.[57] The publication of Kracauer's *Offenbach* by the Paul List publishing house, which Weyrauch (no longer with Rowohlt) had set in train before the negotiations with Unseld, was a small hiccup – it complicated Unseld's plans to publish an edition of Kracauer's collected works – but otherwise Kracauer's admittance to the Suhrkamp club proceeded smoothly.[58] On a visit to New York, Unseld at least secured the rights for future book projects. An edition of *Ginster* was planned for summer 1963, 'the street book' for 1964. Unseld was even interested in the incomplete book on history and in *Theory of Film*, which was still being considered for publication by Rowohlt. Unseld also discussed a possible publication of *Georg* with the Kracauers. When Rowohlt decided against a publication of *Theory of Film*, Unseld took it on (the German edition came out in the autumn of 1964), and Kracauer was pleased that 'this book has now found its way home, so to speak'.[59] The year 1964, Unseld told his new author, 'had your stamp on it'.[60] 'If I were Ginster', Kracauer wrote, 'I should say that I was admiring myself with hindsight.'[61] Despite the fact that he never stopped feeling 'that [he] was in Nazi country' when he was there, the recognition of his work in Germany now became increasingly important to him.[62] Adorno continued to play the role of godfather to Kracauer's publications at Suhrkamp, his 'personal' publishing house. Together with Unseld, he suggested cutting the final chapter of *Ginster*, set in Marseille, because of its positive tone. Kracauer yielded.[63] Discussing the question of the subtitle to *Theory of Film* with Unseld, Adorno suggested 'Errettung' (rescue) as a translation of 'redemption', while Kracauer preferred 'Erlösung' (salvation). Kracauer, again, gave in, even though the 'theological sense' had been intentional. Kracauer did, however, put his foot down at one suggestion: when Adorno, Unseld and his editor Karl Markus Michel proposed omitting the final chapter, 'Film in Our Time', on the grounds that it would either be misunderstood or not understood at all in Germany, Kracauer dismissed the suggestion out of hand.[64]

Despite all this activity, the rekindled friendship between Kracauer and Adorno burned only unsteadily. Adorno had a very critical view of Kracauer and his work generally, a fact he initially kept to himself when they re-established their relationship after 1960. To Bloch, he wrote in confidence that unfortunately, I can scarcely discuss serious matters with Friedel anymore, not only because he has donned armour, as if he were a combination of Narcissus and Young Siegfried, but also because, mindful of the lime leaf, he praises my own stuff to the skies a priori, so that I do not dare any longer to say anything about his.[65]

It is, indeed, striking that Adorno did not say anything about the substance of *Theory of Film* when the American edition came out. He praised only how 'splendidly' the book had been presented with regard to its 'external form'.[66] Nor did Adorno say anything about the content of Kracauer's contribution to the publication marking Adorno's sixtieth birthday on 11 September 1963. He merely thanked him, politely, for the 'contribution on the philosophy of history' (which, however, had not been written especially for the occasion but was envisaged as a chapter of *History: The Last Things before the Last*).[67] Adorno did not pass up the opportunity to write something for Kracauer's seventy-fifth birthday, an appreciation in which Adorno emphasized how much Germany had lost with the exile of this intellectual. Adorno's abiding opinion was that the 'good a man like Kracauer could have done in a trend-setting position, as *Kulturpolitiker*, someone who deals with the politics of culture, for a large paper, for instance, cannot be overestimated'. 'Bringing back' someone like Kracauer would have been highly beneficial for post-war Germany.[68] That was a back-handed compliment. Kracauer saw himself as a cultural philosopher, and he wanted to be recognized as a philosophical writer, not as a feuilleton editor *redivivus* making fine contributions to the political culture. Adorno's remark about Kracauer having a possible place in Germany could also be read as an expression of Adorno's doubt that he had made the right decision staying in the US. This had also to do with the language in which he wrote: by living in America, Kracauer had not only decided in favour of English, but also against German, a fact that irked Adorno. He advised Kracauer to write his *Theory of Film* in German, saying: 'You know how stubborn I am on this point, despite all that has happened, which, however, should not seduce us' – as emigrants – 'into inflicting on ourselves yet again what Hitler already inflicted on us once.' And he kept reminding him 'that it is only in German that it is possible for us to say the crucial things which people like us have to say'.[69] This was an important point for Adorno, and he did not tire of making it. He could not 'shake off the belief that one can only express oneself in earnest and with full responsibility in the language in which all the associations of childhood are present, no matter how deeply buried they may lie'.[70] There was more at stake in this question than just the language one chose to write in. Adorno wanted to justify the path he had chosen, and there were also differences between their ways of thinking at issue. This became explicit when Adorno wrote the essay 'The Curious Realist' for Kracauer's birthday.

Adorno's text was broadcast as a lecture by the second channel of Hessischer Rundfunk on 7 February 1964. It was 'conceived in a truly euphoric state' during a flight to Milan and train journey to Lucca. Upon Adorno's request, Kracauer only read it once the printed version had appeared, nine months later, in *Neue Deutsche Hefte*.[71] Kracauer was, of course, 'awfully curious about what [he was] going to be learning about [himself] from [him]'.[72] What did he learn? Adorno acknowledged Kracauer as the most important philosophical teacher of his early life. He emphasized the close connection between philosophy and the capacity for suffering in Kracauer's writing. His philosophy was a medium in which 'a man with no skin' and a 'defenceless interior' asserted himself.[73] He discussed 'experience' as the medium of Kracauer's thought, a medium which he called 'more intuition than thought'.[74] Adorno mentioned the 'primacy of the optical', and he praised Kracauer's peculiar wit, the particularity, idiosyncrasy and unwieldiness of the involuntary critic of Weimar society, the '*Maybe-sayer*' who epitomized the line, 'Here you have someone on whom you can't rely.'[75] Adorno praised the 'refined silliness' of Ginster, his 'naïveté that understands and describes itself'.[76] These were acute observations and, despite a certain level of ambivalence in his evaluation, there were some warm, even cordial, formulations as well. Yet from a certain vantage point, Adorno's description of Kracauer's path through life could be seen less as an appreciation and more as an outright criticism – even as an aggressive settling of scores. All that he had repressed over the years was now given expression, and not in private conversation but on live radio. Throughout his life, Adorno said, Kracauer had pursued an 'adaptive strategy', fuelled by a mixture of resignation and cunning, in order to deal with that which was hostile and overpowering. Deeply scarred by life, Kracauer had developed an armour and had made his peace with the world. The experience of emigration and America further strengthened this conformism and 'identification with the aggressor'.[77] The result of this survival strategy in philosophical terms, Adorno claimed, was a 'reactive realism': a childlike relationship towards the world of things that ignored reification, and ended in a demand for the 'redemption of physical reality'. Adorno concluded his portrait with the words: 'so curious is Kracauer's realism'.[78]

Kracauer read the text in October 1964. It affected him deeply, and at once he realized that a lot in it was owed to the 'old affinities and antagonisms'.[79] 'The Curious Realist' was a palimpsest of the 1920s.[80] The construction of Adorno's account objectified 'things which, back then, were felt, or were half conscious' and presented them to a public that had no previous image of Kracauer. For

Kracauer, it was 'an account which did indeed come from a distant land and stemmed from [Adorno's] own mental premises rather than doing justice to the given material'.[81] Kracauer now at last began to see his friend more clearly. Adorno had frozen his picture of Kracauer in the 1920s; after he had left their philosophical quartet, Adorno denied this picture any further development. Adorno could not accept the Kracauer of Paris and New York as an equal and fully responsible philosopher in his own right. The fact that Kracauer preferred the pragmatic English to the philosophical German was, for Adorno, a symptom of adaptation. So too was the affinity for film, the desire for the concrete particular, the 'childish' attachment to things and, finally, the theory of film that believed it could do without a critique of the commodity character of film and its fate under conditions of the culture industry. Adorno criticized Kracauer for not making better use of his potential, but he simultaneously pleaded for mercy on his behalf, citing Kracauer's difficult childhood, the anti-Semitic society, the trauma of migration. Kracauer was thus partly honoured and partly dishonoured. Kracauer himself was deeply insulted by this sympathetic, but patronizing account, which, at a stroke, cast everything he had done after *Ginster* as a standing still, or even as a regression. Adorno's diagnosis of adaptation, in particular his 'attempts to depict adaptation to existing circumstances as the cause of [Kracauer's] success and [Kracauer's] success as the effect of adaptation', provoked an outraged response from Kracauer: '*En passant*, if external success were an infallible sign of adaptation, the success which you are enjoying at present would betray that to the highest possible degree.'[82] He considered the theory of adaptation 'a distortion of reality – of *my* reality' that was based on ignorance and arrogance.[83] On the margins of his copy, he referred to the text as 'this emotionally laden, slanderous article of TWA, who does not shrink from telling falsehoods'.[84]

Hurt feelings and resentment aside, the issue that really separated Adorno and Kracauer was that Kracauer had only very temporarily gone along with the move from epistemology to the philosophy of history. He did not accept any kind of thinking that contradicted his individual experience. Wherever there was any doubt, he sided with experience and against theory. He was suspicious of Hegel and of all of German idealism. In philosophical terms, Kracauer remained extraterritorial. Adorno, by contrast, aimed straight at the core of concept-based philosophy in his pursuit of anti-systematic intentions. He wanted to renew philosophy from within, to unfold the historical experience of failed emancipation from within it and with it. The upshot of Adorno's project was the dialectical conception of the non-identical. Adorno felt that Kracauer was setting up experience against theory, and that his approach to critique was transcendent, not immanent.[85] On this point, too, Kracauer felt misunderstood: 'I don't believe that I failed to take pains to extrapolate the general from the extremely particular; I believe much more that it was always one of my main problems to find out how this was to be done.'[86]

Adorno also interpreted Kracauer's responses to his criticisms not in terms of substantive differences but in psychological terms: 'It almost seems to me as if the actual reason for our divergences from each other is that in your old age you have been developing an increasingly strong tendency to guide the reception of your work and the image of yourself', whereas a 'significant literary career will only survive, after all, through criticism of one's oeuvre and not through a kind of positivity which might devalue its object through an obsequious attitude towards it'.[87] Adorno thought that Kracauer was too sensitive. Just before the radio broadcast, Adorno admitted to Scholem: 'Between [concern for] the truth, the recognition of a significant potential, critique, and consideration for an excessively sensitive friend, I felt that I had to walk on eggshells.'[88] After the programme, Adorno joked with Szondi: 'I would not mind compiling a slim Suhrkamp volume of three essays under the title 'Etudes'[89]: Little Egg Dance (Kracauer), Great Bloch Band Music, Test-Your-Strength with Lukács.'[90]

Indeed, upon his eightieth birthday, Bloch did not fare much better at Adorno's hands. In his speech, Adorno could not help enlightening the guests, subcutaneously, as it were, about the birthday boy's various failings. He discussed his early experience of Bloch's *Spirit of Utopia*, this 'Heldenschatz [Treasury of the Heroic]' and 'book of magic': 'Dark as a gateway, with a muffled blare like a trumpet blast, it aroused the expectation of something vast, an expectation that quickly rendered the philosophy with which I had become acquainted as a student suspect as shallow and unworthy of its own concept.'[91] Bloch's book, by contrast, had seemed to Wiesengrund 'one prolonged rebellion against the renunciation within thought that extends even into its purely formal character'.[92] He employed the same strategy as he had with Kracauer: he located Bloch's greatness solely within his early texts and only discussed his own youthful experiences of them, for Adorno had long since dismissed Bloch as a philosopher who deals arbitrarily with this and that, and who 'sounds like a broken record'.[93] Adorno's speech concluded with a confession: that when he had 'reread' Bloch 'after more than forty years', he could not find in it what he once had found: 'It has mystically disappeared in the text. The substance of the text unfolded only in memory. It contains much more than it contains, and not only in the vague sense of potential associations. It unambiguously communicates what it unequivocally refuses to communicate. That is Bloch in a nutshell.'[94]

Adorno was very proud of this 'concluding point', which to him expressed the thought 'that the actual quality which people like us have responded to in him does not feature "with so many words" in his texts, and yet has developed from these.'[95] Bloch, too, felt he had been dealt a back-handed compliment. In a letter to Adorno on the occasion of his sixtieth birthday, he had asked: 'Now that we have grown older, what has actually happened to prevent us from being what we used to be to each other in the old days?' The remark related, on the face of it, to the history of philosophy, but it was also intended to be personal.[96] Bloch was hurt by the 'mocking tone of "Große Blochmusik" [great Bloch music]', Adorno's text on his *Traces* in the *Notes to Literature*.[97] The tangled politics of Adorno's laudatory texts recall Thomas Mann's Joseph, who innocently tells his elder brothers about his dream in which they had bowed to him. Adorno was a narcissus who acquired his brilliance, in part, by casting shadows on his friends. In his *Negative Dialectics*, Bloch and Kracauer no longer appeared, at least not explicitly. For Adorno, the tradition consisted of Plato, Aristotle, Kant, Hegel, Marx and Freud. His opponents were Heidegger and Jaspers, and his intellectual peers were Horkheimer and Benjamin.[98] Bloch and Kracauer, by contrast, had become 'Do-you-remember' philosophers.

Kracauer also contributed to Bloch's Festschrift. Apart from reports for the foundations and the preparatory work for the book on history, this was the only text he would write after 1960. Kracauer felt that it was his duty to write something for Bloch.[99] But, like Adorno, he had to find a way of dealing with the differences that existed between them. It was 'a piece that required a lot of strategy'.[100] Unlike Adorno, he mastered the task. He managed to present 'what unites and what divides our thinking' with respect and charm. He addressed 'dear Ernst' directly: 'There is a lot that separates us, and you have known this from time immemorial. You are aware of my fear and distrust of big dreams that are not written in the margins but instead intervene everywhere ... And you are aware of my tendency towards sobriety – many years ago you called it "colourful sobriety" – a tendency that often causes delays while I engage with the things and conditions around me rather than quickly interpreting them with a view to an ultimate end.' Kracauer cast himself as Sancho Panza as depicted by Kafka: a free man who serenely follows the stormy Don Quixote. Bloch dedicated a chapter in *The Principle of Hope* to Don Quixote and his 'antiquarian-utopian world' and 'poetic unconditionality'.[101] Bloch's tempestuousness sometimes takes away the breath of the Sancho Panza in him, Kracauer admitted, as he turned to discuss what united the two: '[y]our tempestuousness ... wonderfully unites utopian impatience with the ability to linger of an interpretative narrator. Although you elevate hope to the status of a principle, you do not hastily set off from what is to what is being hoped for, but instead you like to loiter around in the anterooms, questioning all those for whom hope needs to be harboured.' Kracauer remembered the pleasure Bloch took in narrating: 'Only someone who has sat up with you deep into the night knows what narrating actually means. The one who narrates, lingers; he also circles lovingly what simply is and should be changed.' Kracauer described Bloch's utopia as one that preserves, one in which 'you appear as a person'. 'In you, being here and being there come together in a way that ignites the imagination.' And following this compliment, Kracauer asked: 'Will you be offended if someone trotting after you on his donkey is not always able to follow you to every distant or deep place?'[102] The tone of Kracauer's contribution is altogether different from Adorno's: restrained, appreciative and cunning, as befits a Sancho Panza. There is nothing double-edged about it, no ingratiation, no notes to literature; it is an evaluation that works out the common philosophical ground between them: a humane interest in and care for things in the world. Bloch, for good reasons, doffed his hat to Sancho Panza, adding, with a playful wink, that Sancho probably would never have had the idea of writing *Ginster* on his own.[103]

39

Time for the Things
before the Last

Kracauer was preoccupied by the book on history, and it unsettled him. As in the case of his book on film theory, he felt that he had to use it as an opportunity to define his intellectual legacy. The process of reflecting and writing was, again, arduous and slow. And now, as a more than seventy-year-old, the ravages of time were an even more dangerous enemy for Kracauer. His work on *History: The Last Things before the Last*, as the book would come to be called, was just that: work on the last things before the final moment. And he was absolutely committed to getting it done. Chronological time, as the perhaps most important element of historiography, also became a problem in its own right for Kracauer. In September 1962, he wrote to Adorno: 'I am chasing a few really major insights but can't quite get a grip on them yet; my ineptitude is colossal. One of these involves the "Dialectic of Progress" about which you will soon be speaking, as I read.'[1] Benjamin, in his 'Theses on the Philosophy of History', had already explained that the concept of progress is tied to the chronological progression of time:

> The concept of the historical progress of mankind cannot be sundered from the concept of its progression through a homogeneous, empty time. A critique of the concept of such a progression must be the basis of any criticism of the concept of progress itself.[2]

This thought seemed plausible to Kracauer, as did Benjamin's claim that historiography needed to blast open the continuum of history and take with it what has been lost, defeated, forgotten. Kracauer did not, however, share the revolutionary and messianic utopianism of Benjamin's essay.[3]

Adorno spoke about 'progress' at the German Congress of Philosophy in 1962 in Münster. According to Adorno, there had been no progress. Adorno, who also invoked Benjamin, thought that the problem with progress is that it is tied to mankind as a whole, and thus to a totality that exists under compulsion and represents an intrinsically antagonistic unity; yet, in the absence of this unity, progress cannot even be conceived. Progress thus refers not to better and better technology but to 'the rational establishment of the whole society', including past and future generations, 'as humanity'.[4] Progress thus denotes a messianic not-yet, whereas reason has so far throughout history been tied to domination.[5] Adorno formulated the dialectic of progress as follows:

> Progress means: to step out of the magic spell, even out of the spell of progress that is itself nature, in that humanity becomes aware of its own inbred nature and brings to a halt the domination it exacts upon nature and through which domination by nature continues. In this way it could be said that progress occurs where it ends.[6]

Progress, in other words, happens when and where domination, including domination over nature, comes to an end, a domination over nature on which, however, liberated society depends. This is the same fundamental idea one finds in *Dialectic of Enlightenment*, namely that the 'enslavement to nature of people today cannot be separated from social progress'.[7]

Adorno's lecture was one of the two main papers presented at the congress, and Kracauer was very interested in it and in the other papers read at Münster, especially those by Karl Löwith, Hans Robert Jauß, Hans Blumenberg and Jürgen Habermas. In subsequent years, he would come to know all of these speakers. The question of progress was raised anew in German philosophy around 1960. As the introduction to the congress proceedings explained, the tradition of idealism and the humanities, in particular those areas of it influenced by 'Lebensphilosophie', had once faced the modern world 'with a cool, mostly critical, and often hostile and distanced attitude'; now, German philosophy needed to 'acknowledge and affirm' progress.[8] Yet, as Löwith demonstrated in the second main paper presented at the conference, which focused on 'the fate of progress', it was also necessary to explore its limits.[9] German cultural criticism had clearly been forced into a defensive position. After the caesura of 1945, the partisans of progress – the positivist and Marxist scientists and engineers – were in the stronger position; they were modern, whereas the German philosophers seemed antiquated. But the academics in the humanities disciplines defended themselves; some of them even went on the counter-attack. In the introduction to the conference proceedings, scepticism about progress was given a name: Hiroshima. It was the American atom bomb, dropped on a city 9,000 kilometres away from Münster, rather than 'Auschwitz', less than 900 kilometres away (and the centre of all of Adorno's intellectual efforts), that provided the 'sting of experience' that cast the shadow of doubt over progress.

German philosophy around 1960, however, was not only in a battle with positivist and Marxist modernists. It had its own Augean stables to clean out. In particular, scores had to be settled with the idealist, especially Hegelian, tradition, an important part of which was the 'philosophy of history'. According to Löwith, the latter was 'a systematic interpretation of universal history in accordance with a principle by which historical events and successions are unified and directed toward an ultimate meaning'.[10] Progress could constitute such a principle, but so could the absence or opposite of progress – maybe even the dialectics of progress. In any case, the real problem was the question of the principle. In that respect, Kracauer, who wanted to free history from philosophy, with its final justifications, had found an ally in Löwith:

> It is the privilege of theology and philosophy, as contrasted with the sciences, to ask questions that cannot be answered on the basis of empirical knowledge. All the ultimate questions concerning first and last things are of this character; they remain significant because no answer can silence them. They signify a fundamental quest; for there would be no search for the meaning of history if its meaning were manifest in historical events. It is the very absence of meaning in the events themselves that motivates the quest. Conversely, it is only within a pre-established horizon of ultimate meaning, however hidden it may be, that actual history seems to be meaningless.[11]

Kracauer liked passages like this: history had to be protected against a theologically charged philosophy, and this could best be achieved with philosophical means.

At the same time, however, Kracauer reacted positively to Adorno's dialectic of progress, despite its messianic overtones, because Adorno had 'recognized and clearly identified all the antinomies involved in the *idea* of progress'. Kracauer wrote to Adorno, the philosopher, that it was 'perhaps one of [his] main tasks to carry out the sublation of philosophy by philosophical means', while Kracauer himself 'rather proceed[ed] from intellectual immersion in the empirical side of history'. And he announced plans for a philosophical deepening of the dialectic within the idea of progress through a critique of chronological time.[12]

Half a year previously, Panofsky had drawn Kracauer's attention to George Kubler's *The Shape of Time* (1962).[13] Kubler was a pupil of the art historian Henri Focillon, whose work focused on the relation between art and history. He reached the conclusion that, although the history of art can often be embedded in the chronology of historical time, it is not identical with it. In ninth-century China, for example, people enjoyed *action painting*, but for a thousand years thereafter no one shared their passion until Jackson

Pollock painted, poured, dripped and squirted paint on paper in his ecstatic and abstract manner. Thus, there are forms of time that are independent of the kind of time that calendars measure, forms whose morphology needs to be investigated. Kracauer was fascinated by Kubler's history of things, and especially of artefacts, and he was intrigued by the relation of form to 'its' time.[14]

Kracauer could not stop reading: 'The material really has the power to draw you in.'[15] But in 1962 it was still too early for Kracauer himself to begin writing. Only at the beginning of 1963 did he finally have even a rough plan for how his text would be organized, 'which, however, does not quite fit yet'.[16] But he was in a position to write a first sketch for a chapter, and this he submitted as his contribution to the Festschrift for Adorno, 'Time and History': 'It treats of the concept of historical time, more precisely: the dialectic between formed times, which are created by meaningful contexts within the history of art, of political history, and (empty) chronological time, which encapsulates them all.'[17] 'Modern historiography', the corresponding chapter of *History: The Last Things Before the Last* begins, 'conceives of history as an immanent continuous process in linear or chronological time which on its part is thought of as a flow in an irreversible direction, a homogeneous medium indiscriminately comprising all events imaginable'.[18] According to Kracauer, this idea of history implies three things: first, that the time at which an event occurs contributes to its explanation; second, that attention is focused on allegedly connected sequences of events, which are seen as a unity; and third, that the historical process is viewed as a totality to which certain properties (such as, for instance, the notion of progress) are ascribed. Following Benjamin and Kubler, Kracauer challenged the power of chronology: every historical period is made up of incoherent events or groups of events. For Kracauer, however, unlike Benjamin, this does not mean that there is no place for linear time. There are factors that can only be described diachronically, and, seen from a larger perspective, even shaped times can be integrated into a stream of time. Ernst Bloch's 'non-contemporaneity of the contemporaneous' provided such a perspective. Kracauer chose the image of the 'cataract of times' in which there are '"pockets" and voids'.[19] Kracauer saw the 'antinomic character of chronological time'[20] embodied in the legendary figure of Ahasuerus, the Wandering Jew:

> How unspeakably terrible he must look! To be sure, his face cannot have suffered from aging, but I imagine it to be many faces, each reflecting one of the periods which he traversed and all of them combining into ever new patterns, as he restlessly, and vainly, tries on his wanderings to reconstruct out of the times that shaped him the one time he is doomed to incarnate.[21]

Kracauer also made reference to Marcel Proust's unique attempt at coming to terms with the complexities of time. In *In Search of Lost Time*, history does not figure as a process but as a collection of kaleidoscopic changes. Nevertheless, Proust tried to maintain the order of chronological time by retrospectively establishing temporal continuity: 'At the end of the novel, Marcel, who then becomes one with Proust, discovers that all his unconnected previous selves were actually phases or stations of a way along which he had moved without ever knowing it.'[22] Of course, Proust's solution is an artistic device that cannot be applied to historical reality. For Kracauer, the antinomy of continuous and discontinuous time cannot be resolved. The coexistence of the contemporaneous and the non-contemporaneous is irremovable. He went on to develop this central idea of his theory of history further in dialogue with others.[23]

Another central question for Kracauer's reflections on history is that of what kind of science history actually is. He had asked this question before, in a different context, at the beginning of the 1920s, in the midst of a discussion of the limits and possibilities of a scientific sociology, and more recently in his *Theory of Film*, in the course of trying to ascertain just what kinds of art film and photography actually are. The journal *History and Theory* was an important place for the discussion of such questions, questions, that is, of the philosophy of science. (It was very important for Kracauer to publish in this journal, and, shortly before his death, 'Time and History' was published in a supplement to the 1966 volume.) The first issue of the quarterly journal appeared in 1961, shortly after Kracauer's interest in the discipline of history had been sparked. The editorial board consisted of philosophically oriented sociologists and historians like Raymond Aron, Isaiah Berlin and Pieter Geyl. Kracauer struck up a dialogue with Geyl. Also on the board were Sidney Hook and Maurice H. Mandelbaum, two philosophers who were struggling with questions similar to those that were occupying Kracauer. In May 1962, Hook, a social philosopher from New York, organized a symposium on 'Philosophy and History' at New York University.[24] The historian of philosophy Morton White spoke about the logic of historical narratives and methods; Mandelbaum on objectivity in history; the historian of the French Revolution Leo Gershoy on the dual character of history as an ancient discipline combining art and science and past and present; the philosopher of science Ernest Nagel on relativism and historicism; the historian of philosophy William Dray on 'understanding' and the historical explanation of past actions; the sociologist Ernest van den Haag on history as factually oriented fiction; and Hook himself on objectivity in historiographical reconstructions. All these were themes that also interested Kracauer, and he studied the texts of these presentations carefully. Strikingly, almost all participants discussed Robin George Collingwood, the philosopher and historian who, in his famous *The Idea of History*, published posthumously in 1946, had followed Benedetto Croce in defending the thesis that history and historical truth are primarily determined by 'present interests'.[25]

All this demonstrates the significant interest there was, around 1960, in the relation between history and philosophy. In Münster the topic was the philosophy of history, and in New York it was philosophy in the writing of history.[26] The new and ambitious journal *History and Theory* explicitly pursued questions in this area, adopting a pragmatic, concrete and realist approach. It was almost as if the hermeneutically minded academics, steeped in cultural and intellectual history, had made up their minds to confront the emerging structuralist social historians.[27] The first article of the first issue, Isaiah Berlin's 'History and Theory: The Concept of Scientific History', was programmatic for the new journal (which still exists today), and it addressed a question that Kracauer had also posed in his aesthetics of film: should history – that is, what historians do – be considered a science? Berlin was of the opinion that it is a science, but not a natural science; it adopts different methods and standards and has different foundations. Still, he pointed out its similarities with the natural sciences. The 'river of time' and the 'stream of history' are metaphors that suggest the existence of certain objective patterns, and the linguistic conjunctions of historical narratives establish temporal, causal, conditional, etc., connections in such a way as to highlight regularities. Thus, there may be systematic patterns governing what people did or what befell them, patterns that are 'capable of being condensed in laws'.[28] But, on the other hand, there are differences between history and the natural sciences. 'Doctrinaire' is 'a term of abuse when applied to historians; yet it is not an insult if applied to a natural scientist' because it is the business of a scientist to reconstruct natural laws theoretically and thus to 'formulate doctrines'. Human reality, Berlin held, is too vague and complex to permit a scientifically exact investigation. A historian needs to use his or her own judgement, intuition and experience in order to develop a sense for human reality. And history is always an 'amalgam, a rich brew composed of apparently disparate ingredients' that are formed into an agreeable historical explanation. Historical explanations, he said, satisfy us if they 'accord with life as we know it and can imagine it'.[29] History is thus a science based on the a priori of human experience; hence it is a humanities discipline that is characterized by a preponderance of qualitative categories.

This line of argument was, of course, grist to Kracauer's mill. He wanted not only to liberate historical research from the straight-jacket of ultimate philosophical justifications but also to protect it against the scientific method, which had already conquered the social sciences. Following Berlin, and guided by his own thesis that film is an art form distinct from other arts, he wrote: 'If history is a science it is a science with a difference.'[30] A historian (like a film-maker) has to tell a story, but at the same time he is no mere story-teller, because he also has to explain why what happened had to happen, and thus to aim at uncovering universal historical laws. Kracauer admitted that contexts, uniformity and causal relations are parts of the historical universe; but, he added, it also contains irreducible entities, unique events and meaningless processes free of any context. As he saw it, one has to pay attention to human freedom, and to the possibility that, at any moment, something altogether novel may occur, something that simply happens to human beings. History is a double-edged affair: it is not an exact science, but, still, it should avail itself of everything that science has to offer. Historical reality is akin to our '*Lebenswelt*' [lifeworld]: it is like 'life in its fullness, life as we commonly experience it'.[31] Historical reality is not without structure; socio-economic influences, art forms, ideas, etc., bear on it, yet historical spaces are incomplete, hetero-geneous and obscure. According to Kracauer, in an 'exact analogy to the photographic approach', the 'historical approach' contains two tendencies: a realistic tendency and a formative tendency. It therefore 'comes true only if the historian's spontaneous intuition does not interfere with his loyalty to the evidence'.[32] The striving towards form, instead, has to support the realistic tendency. When a historian, as opposed to a literary writer, tells her story, she must not modify the material. The historian has to seek truth, not beauty. Next to the antinomy of historical time, this was the second main thesis informing Kracauer's reflections on history: that it is a science that 'belongs to an intermediary area' between philosophy, with its quest for ultimate justifications, and the natural sciences. Its method is, as it were, to take a photograph of the times, not in the sense of a naïve realism or historicism (capturing 'how it really was'), but – given that there are facts no one can deny – in the sense of a construction with a realistic tendency (of the sort Kracauer had attempted in his sociology of the salaried masses and in the aesthetics of film). History is the search for intermediary areas that possess a claim to their own form of knowledge; it is the search, as he put it in the introduction to his book, for 'provisional insight into the last things before the last'.[33]

Kracauer's new book on history was also motivated in part by a search for a form of humanism. This new humanism was supposed to have its roots in antiquity and to contribute to a renewal of the humanities. Most importantly, it was to involve the different disciplines entering into a dialogue with each other, and to counter the tendency towards specialization and abstraction. This was the perspective from which Kracauer viewed his work as a consultant, although he did not quite indulge in the kind of idealization of the classical good old days that was so widespread among such circles. The foundations for which Kracauer worked as an advisor were interested in an evaluation of the usefulness of various projects, such as a project for an interdisciplinary academy modelled on that of the Center for Hellenic Studies in Washington DC, and a project for an institute called 'The Residence', modelled, in turn, on the Institute for Advanced Studies at Princeton (founded in 1930). Another initiative emerging from the Bollingen Foundation was Walter R. Corti's plan for an 'artisans' lodge of the academy' near Zurich. Kracauer also discussed, with Léon Motchane, the founder of the mathematical Institut des Hautes Études Scientifiques near Paris, possibilities for fostering a new humanistic culture in the sciences. And he also attended interdisciplinary meetings in person. Beginning in 1963, he regularly attended the seminar on 'Problems of Interpretation' led by a friend, the art historian Paul Oskar Kristeller, at Columbia University. In 1964 and 1966, the research group on 'Poetics and Hermeneutics' in Germany invited Kracauer to its colloquia. These meetings gave Kracauer the opportunity to offer up his own ideas on the discipline of history for discussion. Between 1960 and 1966, he travelled to Europe every year, becoming a diplomat for the interests of the humanities and talking to countless European academics about the future of the humanities.[34] On these occasions, he talked, too, about his work on his history book. 'The mixture of working in hotels, strolling through streets, looking at pictures, and talking to people, is exactly what we love.'[35] Between 1960 and 1963, he met Isaiah Berlin, Pieter Geyl and Werner Kaegi, among others. From his conversations with them emerged important building blocks for his book. It would, in fact, be difficult to overestimate the value of these exchanges for him, as (leaving his collaborator Lili Kracauer aside) he was in these days a kind of Me-Inc., working by himself, without an academic affiliation. Kracauer also maintained his contacts with Gertrude Bing and Ernst H. Gombrich from the Warburg circle;[36] with a friend, the art historian Arnold Hauser (himself a wanderer between disciplines, nationalities and abodes); with the British scholar Herbert Butterfield (the great Cambridge critic of the 'Whig Interpretation of History');[37] with William C. Guthrie (a Scottish classical scholar from Cambridge who had written a six-volume history of Greek philosophy);[38] with Raymond Firth (an ethnologist from New Zealand based at the London School of Economics); and with Eric Robertson Dodds (an Irish Hellenist from Oxford and author of *The Greeks and the Irrational* [1951]).[39] And in France, he stayed in touch with Raymond Aron,[40] Claude Lévi-Strauss[41] and the historian Henri-Irénée Marrou.[42]

Isaiah Berlin's *The Hedgehog and the Fox* (1953) drew Kracauer's attention to the fact that literary writers may also be seen 'as historians'.[43] For Kracauer, a typical example of a literary micro-historian was Tolstoy (also Berlin's example), and he used him (apart from the historian Lewis B. Namier) for his discussion of the relationship between micro-history and macro-history. The search for God 'in the details' (Aby Warburg) was an approach which, by analogy with the close-up in film, investigated 'an endless continuum of microscopic incidents, actions, and interactions which, through their sheer accumulation, produce the macroscopic upheavals, victories, and disasters'.[44] Berlin also encouraged Kracauer to interpret Proust 'as a historian'. In this connection, Kracauer made use not only of Proust's reflections on time but also of Proust's use of the motif of alienation (Marcel and his 'strange' grandmother), something of which Kracauer had made use before, in his characterization of the photographer, and now sought to extend to the profession of the historian. Moreover, for Kracauer Proust typified the 'antiquarian interest' that pursues *lost causes*, an interest Kracauer juxtaposed with Croce's and Collingwood's 'present interests'. The antiquarian interest is evident in the déja vu elicited in Marcel by the ghostly appearance of three trees during a coach ride, which makes him aware of the fact that the 'shadows of the past' are waving at him, the child who has become an adult.

In 1962, in the pages of *History and Theory*, Pieter Geyl had launched a full-frontal attack on the cultural pessimism of the great Dutch historian Johan Huizinga. Kracauer and Geyl discussed the political background of Huizinga's historical writings and Huizinga's general approach to history, an approach with which Kracauer sympathized: Huizinga had an antiquarian interest in history and disliked schemata, systems and causal constructions. Kracauer was interested in Huizinga's concept of a 'realism of ideas'; for Huizinga, ideas are located between a nominalist consciousness and existing beings.[45] Another detail struck Kracauer: Geyl criticized Huizinga and other Dutch historians for their failure to understand and sympathize with Erasmus of Rotterdam in the dispute between Luther and the Catholic Church. The Renaissance humanist had been accused of manoeuvring between fronts without taking a position of his own, or he had been condemned for not having followed the combative Luther. Geyl, by contrast, saw Erasmus's refusal to follow either of the warring factions not as a wavering or weakness but as a strength and a courageous perseverance that resulted from his recognition that both absolute positions represented a danger to Western civilization.[46] The anti-dogmatic and humanist Erasmus was to take a prominent place in Kracauer's philosophy of the provisional.[47]

It was to Werner Kaegi that Kracauer owed the most important of all his discoveries, namely that of Jacob Burckhardt.[48] During those years, Kaegi was working on a seven-volume biography of his great predecessor in Basel, and reading it, Kracauer wrote, 'always warms me in this cold world'.[49] Beginning in 1962, Kracauer met Kaegi once a year. Alongside Marc Bloch, Herbert Butterfield, Lewis B. Namier and Leopold von Ranke, Jacob Burckhardt is one of the most oft-quoted historians in Kracauer's texts on history. At a first glance, this may seem surprising because Burckhardt was considered an anti-Semite and anti-democrat, and Kracauer had not failed to see this. But there were several ingredients in Burckhardt's historical writings that Kracauer appreciated. Burckhardt had a clear sense of the role which personal attitudes and the temperament of a historian play in the representation and understanding of the past. And for Kracauer, the man himself was an example of 'chronological exterritoriality', that is to say, a historian with a 'complex and ambivalent physiognomy' that could not simply be derived 'from the conditions under which he lived and worked'.[50] Burckhardt also disliked the chronological writing of history, general history, and the philosophy of history. Introducing his *Weltgeschichtliche Betrachtungen*, he wrote: 'We shall also do without anything systematic.'[51] For Burckhardt, history is full of contingencies, and historians have to come to terms with them. New beginnings are a permanent possibility – Burckhardt's thesis of the awakening of the individual during the Renaissance was one such substantial 'historical idea' of a new beginning.[52] Kracauer was so excited by his discovery of Burckhardt that he planned to write a lengthy separate section on him, and this he sketched in his preparatory notes for his book's concluding chapter on the 'anteroom'. 'Burckhardt's opus', it says, reflects 'the arguments offered here', that is, what he called 'anteroom thinking and conduct'. Burckhardt had recognized, and acknowledged, 'the antinomies that condition thought in the area of history'.[53] Thus, he 'brings time to a standstill and, having stemmed its flood, dwells on the cross section of immobilized phenomena which then present themselves for scrutiny. His account of them is a morphological description, not a chronological narrative. It covers a single historical period.'[54] At the same time, Burckhardt pays the chronological aspect its due and is aware of the incoherence of cultural epochs. In short, Burckhardt moves between the general and the specific in an unsystematic fashion, anxiously concerned, like Erasmus (and Kracauer himself), to avoid all fixations.[55]

The virtual intercontinental 'seminar' through which Kracauer developed his theory of history produced many new ideas and much new material. At the end of 1964, he began the process of drafting his study, which, he expected, would take him three years.

As in the case of *Theory of Film*, it was a time 'of torture and passion'. Every sentence was an effort, he said, 'probably due to the heaviness of my thoughts and my bizarre stylistic intentions'.[56] Kracauer often complained about his 'infinitely slow' writing.[57] The burden of his ambition – that this (once again) had to be 'his most important' book – was severe.[58] By October 1965, he had, at least, finished the core chapter, 'The Structure of the Historical Universe', which contains his penetrating ideas about the antinomy between micro- and macro-history.[59] He discarded macro-history on the grounds, firstly, that it rests on pseudo-essences, projections and generalizations; secondly, that it exhibits a tendency towards the most rarefied abstraction (like philosophy); and, thirdly, that it therefore moves one away from historical reality. Micro-history is where Kracauer believed the substance is, but it runs the contrary risk of disintegrating into parallel and insignificant regularities (like the natural sciences). Because open interchanges between micro and macro are limited, owing to the subjective perspectives of historians and the nature of the objects of investigation, Kracauer suggested a cinematographic solution: close-ups with the occasional panning out into long shots. By this stage in his career, Kracauer had come to consider any idea of synthesis presumptuous. (He presumably would no longer have thought of writing a 'biography of society'.) In his eyes, a film consisting entirely of close-ups would be the more realistic, but it would ultimately lack structure and would thus be difficult to watch. Even if it cannot be answered, the question of totality must not disappear from view.

An important event for Kracauer in the years after 1964 was his encountering of the 'Poetics and Hermeneutics' group. The meetings of this group would see Kracauer once again travel to Germany, and they left their traces in the chapter 'General History and the Aesthetic Approach'. The research group originated in Gießen, where Hans Robert Jauß was appointed Professor of Romance Studies in 1961 and where he met the philosopher Hans Blumenberg and the German scholar Clemens Heselhaus.[60] These three formed a group that was then supplemented by Wolf-Dieter Stempel, Wolfgang Iser, Reinhart Koselleck and Dieter Henrich, with whom Jauß had studied in Heidelberg and all of whom were now aspiring professors. Through other connections, Jacob Taubes, Max Imdahl and Peter Szondi joined them. This exclusive club was built around a common interest in the areas of aesthetics and history, or more precisely the mutually constitutive relation between the two. The result was not just some loose research network but a 'coherent and initially exclusively male circle that was organized in a rather *bündisch* way'.[61] The group represented an intellectual elite that, in publishing its work, flirted with the public, yet nevertheless pursued highly self-referential and self-reflexive academic research.

It passionately promoted reform and modernization, and was, so to speak, the humanities' response to the 'sputnik shock' of 1957/58, as Blumenberg once remarked. Its aim was to banish the 'feeling of backwardness in research' in Germany through interdisciplinary work and by garnering research funding. The group considered itself modern and forward looking (it did not, by contrast, talk about the recent past). Beginning in 1964, meetings were held at attractive and luxurious venues, such as Schloss Auel in Lohmar, near Cologne, with the support of the Volkswagen Foundation, which had been founded only three years before. The attendance policy had been thought about carefully. Hans Georg Gadamer, for instance, was not invited even once by his erstwhile pupils. Adorno was also absent. According to Jauß, the foundation of academic work was 'the interdisciplinary principle and working in dialogue' – excluding, however, politics, sociology and psychology, especially psycho-analysis. The task was the conceptual clarification of an object 'on the basis of its history, its semiotic character, or its form'; the aim was thus to achieve a philosophical, historical, linguistic or aesthetic understanding of the object. The line-up was made up exclusively of 'archons'. The group was formed by separate individuals, and yet was a proper circle in which the other members were sources of friction and providers of feedback on ideas. This allowed everyone to come into their own. And together they wanted to 'lay an egg' that none of them could have produced on their own.[62]

Kracauer came into contact with the group when he wrote to its leader, Jauß. Kracauer had admired Jauß's Proust study and had referred to it in 'Time and History'; he enclosed a copy of the article with the letter.[63] In February 1964, he received a response from Jauß, who told him that the previous autumn he had seen the collection of essays *The Mass Ornament* at the Frankfurt Book Fair and had snapped it up immediately. Kracauer's contribution to the Festschrift for Adorno, he added, was 'a special surprise and pleasure' to receive; Kracauer had opened up 'a new perspective on Proust and his relationship with history, whose full significance I had not recognized at the time'. (Jauß had focused on time as a new dimension of the novel, 'remembrance as the place of origin of beauty, and the fable of *In Search of Lost Time* as a path toward finding the self'.)[64] Jauß told Kracauer that he was currently working on various temporal processes (progress in the sciences, the cyclical development of the arts) in French seventeenth-century literature, and that he had spoken on this topic at the philosophy congress in Münster. 'Given such numerous points of contact and common problems', he said, he would very much like to get to know Kracauer personally.[65]

The two met just six months later. In spring 1964, Kracauer received an invitation from the 'Poetics and Hermeneutics' group via Jacob Taubes, whom he had met at the Columbia seminar on problems of interpretation. In July 1964, the Kracauers spent five days in Frankfurt, negotiating with Unseld and meeting Adorno; Jauß hijacked them for an afternoon in Gießen. His purpose, which was 'very important' to him, was to have a conversation with Kracauer in order to prepare him for the colloquium, for introducing a stranger to this sworn circle required care. And this stranger was a proper stranger. Kracauer was thirty years older than the young academics, many of whom had been members of the Wehrmacht during the war (not, however, Hans Blumenberg, whose maternal ancestors were Jewish), had studied after 1945, and had been appointed to professorships sometime after 1960. Kracauer was a private scholar and, apart from Kristeller's seminar, had no contact with academia at all. Most importantly, he was a Jewish emigrant who had not returned, and, from the group's perspective, it was not clear exactly what he had suffered and how much anger and hatred he might harbour towards the Germans. The meetings of the 'Poetics and Hermeneutics' group had an almost fairy-tale quality – they were gatherings of 'educated sociability', at a castle, with twelve disciples and twelve guests, so to speak. An atmosphere of elitist self-awareness was coupled with its attendees' desire for recognition, and the days of concentrated discussions were followed by meals and drinking in the evening. The intensity of these occasions meant that communication could not be controlled. Kracauer's participation created a potentially volatile situation, but it was very important to Jauß, maybe because for that very reason: he rolled out the red carpet for the Jewish émigré from New York. Kracauer felt flattered and gladly accepted Jauß's outstretched hand at being introduced into the illustrious circle. He must surely have enjoyed the fact that the finest humanities scholars of the young Federal Republic were now, subtly but unmistakeably, doffing their hats to him.[66] But one of the reasons Kracauer had not returned to Germany was that he could never be sure whose hand he was shaking, and this occasion was no different. None other than Jauß, his courteous host, had, at the beginning of the Second World War, aged seventeen, voluntarily joined the SS Dispositional Troops, the group that later became the Waffen SS. During the war, Jauß served in various SS units fighting in the Soviet Union (where he was party to the war crimes committed by the Heeresgruppe Nord [Army group North]), in Croatia (where he took part in the 'fight against partisans', which involved violent excesses aimed at the civilian population), in Czechia and, finally, in France. He reached the grade of a SS-Hauptsturmführer of the reserve, the youngest Hauptsturmführer in the Waffen SS. We do not know anything about his personal wrong-doings, but the brigades and battalions in which he served were all involved in the perpetration of war crimes. Jauß kept all this to himself. After the war, he was fined for membership of a criminal organization, but, with the skill of a clever fraudster, he systematically manipulated any information relating to his military rank and areas of employment.[67] Kracauer never learned whose hand he shook. He knew only the friendly, stimulating, educated literary scholar, with whom, according to Lili Kracauer, he had a 'human and intellectual affinity'. He accepted the invitation to Schloss Auel and, after the meeting, wrote a thank-you note: 'It is nice to be appreciated, and I was so happy at Schloss Auel.' The group of scholars had given him 'a feeling of belonging'.[68]

The colloquium was dedicated to the emergence of modern poetry in the nineteenth and early twentieth century. The hermeneutic scholars understood poetry as a genre that is paradigmatic for the turn towards modern literature.[69] After the first meeting in 1963 had, under the heading 'Imitation and Tradition', looked at the end of classical aesthetics and the tradition of *imitatio naturae*, the overall theme for the 1964 meeting was to be European cultural modernity.[70] Kracauer did not give a presentation but contributed a great deal in the debates. He summarized the contributions to the discussions and offered his comments on them, and he provided the circle with valuable observations as an external commentator. Occasionally, he adopted the role of a moderator and at times that of a provocateur, asking the immanent aestheticians 'questions external to aesthetics'. In his note in their visitors' book, Kracauer wrote

> that it is probably useful in the search for 'preliminary stages' of the novel to take into account the environmental conditions which give the novel as well as its likely preliminary stages their specific character. The *closed circuit* between poetic theory and practice, limited to the purely aesthetic, only rarely suffices as a model for a given reality.[71]

What today can be taken for granted, and what Jauß later called one of the great achievements of 'Poetics and Hermeneutics', is the importance of developing 'unexpected approaches' and 'novel questions' and the acceptance of 'sociological interests and social criticism', but this was radical thinking in Cologne at the time. Only Jacob Taubes shared Kracauer's thoughts on this score. To begin with, at least, sociological and historical contextualization remained beyond the ken of this rising racket.[72]

After his return to New York, Kracauer described the group's discussions as claustrophobic and escapist. Society had no place in this kind of hermeneutics.[73]

It is difficult to say whether Kracauer managed to leave behind a lasting impression on the young humanities scholars. Jauß later wrote to Adorno:

You know yourself that he was a highly appreciated participant at our last workshop and presented his ideas on aesthetics, on the sociology of the arts, and on the philosophy of history in our discussions. The working group owes to him not only some indispensable suggestions, but also a gradual opening of its initially immanent-aesthetic perspective on the arts toward the reality and theory of the historical, as became evident at our last meeting.[74]

That was written shortly after Kracauer's death, and of course one does not speak ill of the dead; quite apart from that, Jauß was given to rose-tinted retrospection. Others, Heselhaus for instance, felt that Kracauer's behaviour had been inappropriate.[75] Although he was not present at the meeting, Henrich remembers that he and other members of the circle had a keen interest in Kracauer, who represented a welcome contrast to the philosophical luminaries of his generation, who presented their bold claims ex cathedra. The subtle, restrained and humble manner in which he marshalled his arguments and advanced his social analyses lent Kracauer a certain charisma.[76] In any case, following the friendly 'disturbance' from the non-aesthetician, the aesthetic paradigm was soon deemed to have reached its limits. Tellingly, the title for the next meeting was 'The no longer beautiful arts'. At that meeting, Odo Marquard spoke for many of the participants when he said: 'It seems to me that the attempt to find answers through historical determinations has now entered the discussions. ... The position of the aesthetic would thus be a matter of the precise historical moment.'[77] We cannot know for certain whether Kracauer's raising of the question of the role of non-aesthetic factors was responsible here, or whether this was simply a coincidence. It certainly accompanied, and perhaps accelerated, the end of this aesthetic immanence.

Interestingly, it was one of the main representatives of 'aesthetic immanence', Hans Blumenberg, who impressed Kracauer most. Blumenberg was working on the 'problem of the origin of the modern age'. He insisted that the modern age was the beginning of a new historical epoch, separated off from the Middle Ages, and he criticized 'intellectual history' for not having paid sufficient attention to the 'functional transformations of concepts' that took place at the threshold of the modern era.[78] He developed this thesis through a critique of the concept of secularization, as it had been used by, among others, Karl Löwith. Kracauer carefully read and annotated Blumenberg's first public presentation of this thesis at the philosophy congress in Münster in 1962. According to Blumenberg, the idea of progress is not simply secularized eschatology, because 'eschatology speaks of an event breaking into history, an event that transcends and is heterogeneous to it, while the idea of progress extrapolates from a structure present in every moment to a future that is immanent in history'.[79] And, genetically, eschatology is 'an answer to the question of the meaning and course of history as a whole', while the idea of progress is originally no more than 'a structural formula for *theoretical* processes, and as such was applied to the *aesthetic* realm'.[80] Although Blumenberg did not deny that the idea of progress and religious interpretations of history overlap, he insisted on the fact that there had been a rupture in the modern age and that the concept of secularization had overlooked it:

> What actually happens in the process that is conceived of as secular-ization is not the *displacement* (transposition) of authentically theological contents into secularized alienation from their origin but rather the *reoccupation* of positions that had become vacant and as such could not be eliminated.[81]

For Blumenberg, the 'modern age' represents a radical break with all tradition, but it is also the 'result of a thoroughly theologically conditioned age' that went before it.[82]

Kracauer liked Blumenberg's erudite precision, and he appreciated how the young historian of philosophy seemed to feel 'the pulse of the concepts' (for what really matters, after all, is the evidence in the material).[83] Blumenberg's thoughts on the parallel existence of continuity and caesurae also seemed to coincide with Kracauer's own conception of the role of both chronological and shaped time in historical understanding.

This became Kracauer's 'side-by-side principle' of 'material thought', not only with regard to time but also with regard to the relation between the general and the particular. Blumenberg, in turn, thought of Kracauer's reflections on the problem of historical time as a 'fortunate coincidence' that helped him in his work on the problem of the origin of the modern age. They both saw an analogy between their ideas and quantum physics, where the complementarity between wave and particle determines the representation of the physical substratum.[84] Could it be that the attraction between Kracauer and Blumenberg also had to do with the fact that they both were Jews who had been persecuted by the Nazi regime? The sources are not much help here. Blumenberg was 'a Jew under cover';[85] that is, he did not present himself as a Jewish scholar. And although everyone knew that Kracauer was a Jewish refugee, Kracauer would probably not have seen this fact as being of particular importance. More important was their intellectual kinship. To Blumenberg, he wrote: 'Isn't it wonderful how we meet on this point [i.e. the side-by-side principle]!'[86]

In the course of preparations for the upcoming colloquium in 1966 in Lindau, Kracauer agreed to act on behalf of the group, and to ask Edgar Wind, also a Jewish emigrant from the Warburg circle, and the first professor of art history in Oxford, whether he would like to attend. To Wind, Kracauer described the group as made up predominantly of 'friends from university days', among them 'the best minds of the most recent generation of university professors, philosophers, scholars of Romance studies, Anglicists, etc.'. Hans Blumenberg, he added, was an 'unusually original and talented historian of philosophy and a philosopher as well'. Hans Robert Jauß, he said, had 'written the best analysis of Proust that I know of'. The conference at Schloss Auel had been 'really very stimulating'.[87] After Wind turned down the invitation, Kracauer, upon a request from Jauß, asked Hans Jonas and Arnold Hauser whether they would participate, but these invitations were also declined.[88] Kracauer himself was very much looking forward to the reunion with the young humanities scholars, especially to further conversations with Blumenberg and Jauß. In the summer of 1965, he met each of them separately, and he also met with Koselleck and Christian Meier for a kind of 'pre-conference' to plan the section of the conference on the writing of history and its relation to aesthetics.[89] In the summer heat, he had three 'wonderful hours' of discussion with Blumenberg, 'shirt-sleeved in the bar of Frankfurter Hof', and afterwards wrote to him: 'I eagerly await every line you will write.'[90]

Kracauer's presentation at the colloquium in Lindau illuminated the relation between the historical and the aesthetic approaches to the writing of history. He looked at the limit of the aesthetic from the opposite end of the telescope to the 'Poetics and Hermeneutics' scholars, so to speak. Whereas his focus had previously been on the relation between the writing of history, the natural sciences and philosophy, he now examined the literary aspect of history. Kracauer explained that special histories (analogous to micro-histories) aim to supplement their insights with general history (analogous to macro-history). General history, by contrast, strives for synthesis from the very beginning, because it seeks to unify its material. It is therefore dependent on artificial devices which aim at structure and composition, hence aesthetics, for its liberation from the 'cataract of times'. He further explained that, for a historian to be a great artist, it is necessary for art not so much to be the aim but a consequence of the work, for a story not to be formed in advance, and for there to be no illusion of totality. Instead, the human reality of the lifeworld must be analysed with an aesthetic sensibility:

In consequence, the saying that history is both a science and an art carries meaning only if it refers to art not as an external element but as an internal quality – art which, in a manner of speaking, remains anonymous because it primarily shows in the historian's capacity for self-effacement and self-expansion and in the import of his diagnostic probings.[91]

Kracauer's presentation, which he delivered, without stuttering, in English, was titled 'General History and the Aesthetic Approach'. It was discussed in a section on 'Aesthetics as a Limit Phenomenon of History', together with papers by Christian Meier and Reinhart Koselleck. (In his contribution, interestingly, Meier demanded that the perspective from below, that of the victim, of the 'clowns, lance corporals, tin drummers, and cyclists', should be included in political history. He did not mention Jewish expellees in his list, though. Koselleck pointed out that, in terms of conceptual history, the collective singular 'history' and the philosophy of history, as well as 'progress' in the singular, all emerged simultaneously in the eighteenth century.[92]) Kracauer's thesis about the artificial creation of consistency and the theoretical impossibility of a general history was questioned by several participants at the colloquium, partly on the grounds of the 'non-contemporaneity of the contemporaneous', which was said to have solved the problem of inconsistency, and partly on the grounds that the aesthetic formation of consistency lay already in the medium of language and even in the selection of the facts, and was therefore, in principle, ultimately unavoidable, including in the case of special histories. These fundamental reservations operate far above and far below the question of the border between aesthetics and history. The one argument runs: we have long since recognized the problem and solved it. The other says: the problem is far more general and applies to any representation of history, even to any kind of representation at all. Kracauer, by contrast, wanted to remain at the border: of course a historian selects facts, but 'it makes a big difference how one makes this selection. The selection of facts can be more or less in agreement with reality; a historian can behave more or less "aggressively" toward the reality of facts'. It is also correct, Kracauer said, that in special histories aesthetic means also play a role, but a special history 'possesses in itself already a higher degree of consistency than general history'. Unlike those putting forward their fundamental reservations, Kracauer was interested in perspectival differences and differences of degree, in the search for truth.[93] Regarding inconsistency within the events of a historical period, Kracauer suggested they speak of the 'co-existence of the contemporaneous and the non-contemporaneous' instead of the non-contemporaneousness of the contemporaneous. 'More or less', 'a higher degree of', and antinomy instead of dialectic: these formulations are suggestive of a different approach and way of thinking. When Jauß and Taubes defended Kracauer's rejection of the philosophy of history, Kracauer felt impelled to make another intervention to clarify his position, as those defending him had not represented it quite adequately:

I am not at all against any kind of philosophical consideration of history. I deal with nothing else in my book, not out of an anti-historical impulse, but – because I enjoy it so much. I depart from the antinomies of the general and the particular, and here I am indeed of the opinion that, without an understanding of this fundamental antinomy of history, universal history has today become illegitimate. The idea of a universal history must always be in the background of any special history. The question is only how we should conceive of the relation between the general of history and the specifics of special 'histories'. ... It makes a big difference whether one sets out from an idea of a universal history or not – whether, so to speak, one proceeds 'from bottom to top' or from 'top to bottom'. ... Otherwise we run the risk of falling prey to all sorts of Quixotic ideas about the general. 'Without making any boast of it, Sancho Panza succeeded in the course of years, by feeding him a great number of romances of chivalry and adventure in the evening and night hours, in so diverting from himself his demon, whom he later called Don Quixote, that his demon thereupon set out, uninhibited, on the maddest exploits, which, however, for the lack of a preordained object, which should have been Sancho Panza himself, harmed nobody. A free man, Sancho Panza philosophically followed Don Quixote on his crusades, perhaps out of a sense of responsibility, and had of them a great and edifying entertainment to the end of his days.' This would be my motto for the general in history: is it not just this Don Quixote who, like Sancho, we can follow as free men, and free from harm, only, and precisely if, we rigorously think from bottom to top?[94]

History: The Last Things Before the Last was thus intended to advance the idea of history as an intermediary area between philosophy, science and the arts. The book itself emerged within an intermediary space between structuralism and post-structuralism, between scientism and cultural relativism, and between essentialism and deconstructivism.[95] Kracauer did not forgo truth: the search for an understanding of society in its totality and of the historical transformations that affect it is not to be aborted. But the search for truth has to move into 'intermediary areas' and needs to traverse them from the bottom up. The writing of history, in particular, is such a science of intermediary spaces. In Kracauer's view, it moves between science and the arts, between chronicle and creation, between a realist and a formative tendency, between present interests and antiquarian interests, between documentation and interpretation, between facts and life experiences, between micro- and macro-dimensions, between the flow of time and those sequences which negate chronological time. Faced with these antinomies, Kracauer defined the sphere of historical reality as an anteroom: more than pure opinion, less than ultimate truth. *The Last Things before the Last.*

At the end of his visit to Europe in 1966, Kracauer had finished writing most of the seven chapters on his theory of history. An intelligent and wise book was almost complete; it drew its strength from the erudition of its author, his life experience, the careful weighing of its points, and its sometimes surprising commentaries and images.[96] Only the concluding eighth chapter, 'The Anteroom', was still a building site, with various provisional reflections that, taken together, were meant to constitute Kracauer's 'philosophy of the provisional'. Here, he sketched the anteroom he had in mind, an intermediary area between, on the one side, philosophy (which strives to uncover truths about the ultimate human concerns, and whose statements aim at the utmost generality and objective validity) and, on the other side, experiences, incidents, empirical observations, details, fleeting phenomena that cannot be captured by the general. Anteroom thinking and anteroom behaviour has, first of all, to acknowledge these antinomies, so as then to be able to discover all the things that do not yet have a name in the 'lifeworld which stretches from the everyday to the limits of philosophy proper'.[97] *History* was a tribute to contingency, with a messianic edge:

> In every generation, an old Talmudic legend had it, there are thirty-six just ones on which the existence of the world depends. In the mystical take on this sentence, they become the 'hidden just ones', that is, people part of whose essence it is to be hidden from their fellow human beings (and sometimes possibly to themselves). No one knows, no one can know, who these real saints are on whom the world rests. If their anonymity, which is part of their essence, were to be removed, they would become nothing.[98]

If their anonymity ever were removed, evil probably would find it easy to neutralize them, or even worse: these just ones would turn into terrible tyrants. Kracauer was looking for hidden truths. In order to get to this 'utopia of the in between', to this non-place – 'a terra incognita in the hollows between the lands we know' – one has to follow in the footsteps of the cunning Sancho Panza, or the wise Erasmus, or, perhaps, one just needs to read Kracauer.[99]

On 4 October 1966, the Kracauers returned to New York. Before their departure they had met with Benno Reifenberg. It was a reconciliatory meeting: 'deeply happy about the enjoyable time with your kind wife and yourself ... These were good hours in every sense.'[100] The Kracauers had enjoyed Rome very much, especially the time they spent there with Ignazio Silone and his wife, a couple with whom they had been friendly since their Paris days. To Kaegi, Kracauer reported that the book was progressing slowly;[101] he was still planning a final chapter, 'Epilogue: History Today'.[102] Then,

Kracauer caught pneumonia. The illness did not care one jot about the philosophy of history. On 27 November 1966, Leo Löwenthal received a telegram from Lili Kracauer in New York: 'Friedel passed away yesterday after a short illness.'[103]

40

After Kracauer's Death

When Rudolf Arnheim called the Kracauers on the afternoon of 27 November 1966, he was greeted 'by an unfamiliar voice instead of the expected familiar one', and he was told 'the devastating news' of Siegfried Kracauer's death.[1] He must have immediately contacted the *New York Times*, as the very next day it carried Kracauer's obituary, in which Arnheim lauded Kracauer as a social scientist and a writer.[2] The funeral took place on 29 November 1966 at the Riverside Cemetery, between Amsterdam Avenue and 76th Street. In Germany, Adorno was the first to write an obituary, having been asked by the *Frankfurter Allgemeine Zeitung* – Benno Reifenberg, an editor at the paper since 1959, could not be reached.[3] Adorno, Kracauer's oldest friend, wrote:

> His resistance – in the face of many handicaps – the resistance of someone exposed almost without any protection, to all of life's brutality, lent him a strength that bordered on heroism; his will to live increased with every threat, and finally became almost mythic. This was also expressed in his face. Extraterritorial, as if from the Far East, it acquired a certain stoniness. The fact of one's own mortality, it seemed, he was not prepared to accept; this trait exerted such a hypnotic force that his death now appears implausible.[4]

Adorno did not repeat the theory of adaptation he had proffered in 'The Curious Realist', the theory Kracauer had so forcefully rejected, and he warmly praised Siegfried Kracauer's many achievements. Nevertheless, Lili Kracauer took issue with the fact that Adorno had made such overt reference to her husband's alleged 'handicaps': 'I know only of his linguistic nervousness, and that had already disappeared completely by the time in Berlin.'[5] As Adorno's obituary was also to be included in the third volume of the 'Poetics and Hermeneutics' series, titled *Die nicht mehr schönen Künste*, she appealed to Hans Robert Jauß to press Adorno to make some changes to the text: her husband, she said, had not been exposed to 'life's brutality' any more than anyone else, and, besides, he had had a very sheltered upbringing.[6] As Lili remembered it, Kracauer had, until the very last, been an energetic, strong and healthy man, a man who protected her and made her feel secure. In her mind, there was no suggestion that he had been in a 'race against time' trying to complete the book on history. Kracauer, she said, had been full of plans, including for future book projects; his death was unexpected, both for him and for her.[7] Adorno remembered it differently. The expression 'race against time' was Friedel's own, he wrote to the widow,[8] and remarked that he had his own memories of the deceased: 'Well, I know that apart from his speech problems, Friedel also had to suffer anti-Semitic nastiness at school.' Adorno had already mentioned the bleak parental home in 'The Curious Realist', and, despite his various other dissatisfactions with the piece, Kracauer had not objected on that score. Adorno was only prepared to make minor changes to his text because, as he told Lili Kracauer, his formulations had been chosen very 'carefully' and yet had emerged out of 'a certain spontaneity', a spontaneity the obituary had to have if it were to do justice to Friedel. Adorno did not want to 'change things which simply suggested themselves to me'. He made some minor corrections, but the 'handicaps' remained, as did his thesis on his friend's 'vigorous force of resistance' and resistance as a source of Kracauer's intellectual work.[9] Adorno, it seems to me, was justified in this. Lili Kracauer idealized her partner, and they had formed a symbiotic relationship. For her, it was as though his life only began once they met. About Kracauer's adolescence she either knew very little, or she did not want to know about it – Ginster, Kracauer's alter ego, was possibly only a literary figure to her. After all they had gone through together, and because of her admiration for her husband, she did not want to accept that his self-proclaimed 'extraterritoriality' did not mean that he would avoid the problems of ageing or mortality, that it only allowed him to repress them. To outsiders, Kracauer was, very clearly, 'old, fragile and slow', or 'measured', even if such first impressions soon dissipated in the course of his lively and intellectually intense conversation.[10] To Lili, Friedel's death was an amputation: 'The incision in my life is immeasurable; the sudden end, the no longer existing, is incomprehensible.' Three months after Kracauer's death, she wrote: 'I feel no different than the first day. To be here without Friedel's presence is still incomprehensible and almost unbearable for me.' Another six months later, she told Adorno that she was still deeply shaken and was seeking treatment.[11] In the summer of 1969, during her first visit to Europe as a widow, so intensely did she miss Friedel's 'protection' and 'kindness' that she felt anxious and inhibited.[12] In her mind, he became ever greater, ever stronger, and ever more of a genius. Members of the 'Poetics and Hermeneutics' circle, in particular

Hans Robert Jauß and his wife, Helga, took care of the widow, at least. There were respectful letters of condolence from each member of the group, followed by concerned letters that sought to buoy her up; she should not isolate herself, they urged, but – in accordance with Kracauer's philosophical thinking – turn towards the here and now. During her stay in Germany in 1969, Lili Kracauer visited the Jauß and Preisendanz families in Constance; Jauß even collected her by car from Interlaken. With Jauß and his wife in particular, Lili felt she was in good hands.[13] There is, of course, something uncanny in this fact. We have to assume, however, that a friendly and caring relationship did develop between them.

Elisabeth Kracauer never really recovered after her husband's sudden death. The only thing that gave her some strength was her absolute determination to continue his work, especially to rescue the unfinished book on history. After an event for which 'no solace' was truly possible, this mission kept her going: 'One thing, however, can help to diminish the great pain of the experience: the possibility of doing something for the beloved man.'[14] Rainer Koehne, a former student of Adorno's, was entrusted with the editorial work on Kracauer's theory of history. Koehne had lived in New York since 1954 and been in fairly close contact with Kracauer. The basis for the book was the finalized 'syllabus' and the two more or less completed chapters on historical time and on the relation between history and aesthetics. Koehne's task was thus first of all to get to grips with Kracauer's ideas and to find adequate ways of formulating them – neither a mean feat. Lili Kracauer supported him by providing notes from conversations with Adorno and Blumenberg, and by pointing him towards preparatory works and earlier texts. On certain questions, Werner Kaegi was consulted, someone with whom Koehne, however, did not get on. Hans Jonas and Hermann Schweppenhäuser also helped to answer specific questions. Towards the end of the editorial work, however, an irresolvable dispute between the ghostwriter and the widow broke out. Koehne withdrew from the project; he even demanded not to be mentioned in the book as an editor. Paul Oskar Kristeller stepped in, resolving, with Lili, the final remaining questions, giving the final version his blessing, and writing a preface. The book finally appeared with Oxford University Press in 1969.[15] A German edition followed soon after: Jacob Taubes recommended Karsten Witte as a translator, and introduced him to Lili, who was immediately taken with the young man. She praised his 'great empathy, knowledge, and sense of responsibility' in all matters to do with Kracauer, and with his help *Geschichte: Vor den letzten Dingen* appeared in 1971 with Suhrkamp.[16]

The conflict with Koehne apparently concerned the placement of Kracauer's 'autobiographical note' and the 'Epilogue', which in Kracauer's manuscript consisted of no more than one sentence and a quotation from Kierkegaard. Koehne wanted to place the autobiographical note at the end of the book and add the epilogue as an 'Author's Addendum'. Lili Kracauer insisted that the book should begin with the 'autobiographical note' and that the epilogue not be treated as a mere addendum, because it contained in a nutshell everything Kracauer would have wanted to say in the ninth chapter.[17] In this case, she was right. The last lines Kracauer had written towards the *History* project were about genuineness: 'Focus on the "genuine" hidden in the interstices between dogmatized beliefs of the world, thus establishing tradition of lost causes; giving names to the hitherto unnamed.' That was the programme which the last chapter of *History* was meant to realize. The 'Kierkegaard quotation' was actually a long passage from Max Brod's biography of Kafka, in which Brod quotes Kafka quoting, in turn, Søren Kierkegaard:

> But as soon as a man with originality comes along, and consequently does not say: one must take the world as it is, but saying: whatever the world may be, I remain true to a simplicity which I do not intend to change according to the good pleasure of the world; the moment that word is heard, there is as it were a transformation in the whole of existence, as in the fairy story – when the word is said the magic castle, which has been under a spell for a hundred years, opens again and everything comes to life: in the same way existence becomes all eyes. The Angels grow busy, look about with curiosity to see what is going to happen, for that is what interests them. On the other side: dark and sinister demons who have sat idle for a long while gnawing their fingers – jump up, stretch their limbs: for, they say, 'this is something for us.'[18]

Shortly before his death, Kracauer played Chinese whispers with this convoluted chain of quotations. The message he received from Kierkegaard via Kafka, and now passed on to posterity, was: Stick to your unique self. Insist on your idiosyncrasy. Be odd, grumpy, whimsical, no matter what the world expects of you. Then, maybe, things will begin to shift, and a door to the castle might open up. What could be better than existence becoming 'all eyes'? Kracauer's epilogue amounts to an attitude in between the extremes of wanting to improve the world and adapting to the world: another intermediary realm of human possibility. Just what the angels and demons will do with it is beyond Kierkegaard's, Kafka's, Kracauer's or anyone else's influence.

The older he got, the more pronounced became Kracauer's inclination to speak in similes. In his theory of history, in fact, he deployed two metaphors to get his point across: the historical figure of Erasmus of Rotterdam and the literary figure of Sancho Panza. Erasmus, Kracauer thought, 'came as close as was possible in his situation to delineating a way of living free from ideological constraints; that in effect all that he did and was had a bearing on the humane'.[19] His 'outspokenness' was accompanied by his 'fear of all that is definitely fixed', the driving force of his intellectual endeavour.[20] Kracauer presented Erasmus as a man of conscience fighting a war of resistance against dogmatism, against those who believed they possessed the one and only truth, and as someone who did not mind, therefore, if the steadfastness of his beliefs was questioned. With this attitude, Erasmus embodied, in Kracauer's mind, true humanism.[21] Kracauer recognized a parallel here with his own thinking as a philosopher, citizen and human being. After his experiences of dictatorship, expulsion, war and genocide, he saw himself as a representative of a left humanism – a left that set itself off politically from communism and other radical movements. Academically, this group, he held, should adopt Leszek Kołakowski's definition of a humanistic left:

> By an intellectual left in the humanities I understand an attitude characterized by a radical rationalism of thinking, by a decisive rejection of all mythology in academic work, by an uncompromisingly secular world view, by strict criticism, by distrust of closed systems and doctrines, by a commitment to openness in its thinking – that is, preparedness to revise established theses, theories, and methods and to respect novel scholarly developments.[22]

Kracauer's references to Sancho Panza are also suggestive of a kind of self-portrait. In his theory of history, these references originally served as arguments against synthesizing, 'quixotic' macro-histories, those histories that are often informed by a philosophy of history. We should remind ourselves, too, that Kracauer, in 1965, sent Kafka's characterization of Sancho Panza as a *free man*, together with a text on Erasmus, to Ernst Bloch on the occasion of his birthday. These presents were ways in which Kracauer sought to explain his restraint to his friend, who harboured a life-long hope for the end of repression and fought, against all odds, to bring about the communist utopia: 'My attitude is not unlike that of the figure Kafka identified as Sancho Panza.'[23] Sancho Panza only appeared to be Don Quixote's servant, mindlessly following his master on his horse. In reality, he was, if the circumstances allowed for it, an active and autonomous human being.

Kracauer's self-stylization as an Erasmus and a Sancho Panza retrospectively legitimated his own path through life. The 'discovery' that all his activities as a writer had served the same purpose, namely 'to bring out the significance of areas whose claim to be acknowledged in their own right has not yet been recognized', served the same function.[24] Kracauer's sole interest, the argument goes, was 'the rehabilitation of objectives and modes of being which still lack a name and hence are overlooked or misjudged'.[25] Was this 'discovery' a trick in order to establish the meaning and unity of a lived life ex post facto? Had Kracauer, like Proust's Marcel, 'regained' time and reconstituted a continuity in his life of which he had known nothing while he had actually lived it?

Kracauer's thesis about 'anteroom thinking' ignores the fact that his intellectual life proceeded through qualitatively different phases. One need only read the dedications to his monographs and books to conclude as much. The text on Georg Simmel was dedicated to Margarete Susman, a symbol of a yearning for religiosity in the aftermath of war. During that phase of his life, Kracauer, under the influence of Lebensphilosophie, shared a sense of the suffering caused by capitalist and scientific modernity without, however, being able to develop a positive religiosity for himself. *Soziologie als Wissenschaft* [Sociology as a Science] made do without a dedication, because Kracauer wrote it alone, in his quiet chamber. *Der Detektiv-Roman* [The Detective Novel] is dedicated to his friend Theodor Wiesengrund-Adorno, with whom he read Kant, and then Kierkegaard; Kierkegaard was the great critic of idealism and, in particular, of Hegel who, to both Wiesengrund-Adorno and Kracauer, had not, in fact, succeeded in truly leaving idealism behind. Wiesengrund-Adorno would later argue this point in his book on Kierkegaard. During their time of 'symphilosophizing' they worked through Kierkegaard's writings, until, in 1925, they entered a new phase in which Karl Marx and ideology critique, as well as Kafka's obscure and opaque world, played important roles. The metaphysical pain eased; materialism and an attention to profane things came to the fore. In *The Salaried Masses*, Kracauer thanked Benno Reifenberg, his mentor at the *Frankfurter Zeitung* and no friend of Marxism by any stretch of the imagination; still, he provided the space for Kracauer to publish pieces expressing left-wing political views and his unusual features for the culture pages. The protagonist of *Ginster* was his alter ego, and the novel was dedicated to L., with whom Kracauer had found a new joie de vivre in Marseille. *Jacques Offenbach and the Paris of His Time* was not associated with anyone in particular – unsurprisingly, given the years of groundless existence and isolation during which it was written. Instead of a dedication, the 'biography of society' was preceded by a quotation from Charles Baudelaire: one of the first to make the fleetingness, transience and contingency of modern life a theme of his poetry. That leaves us with the 'American books': *From Caligari to Hitler* was written to combat the Germans; in the *Theory of Film*, in some ways his life's work, it says 'for my wife';

and *History: The Last Things Before the Last* was, of course, not completed by Kracauer and so remained without dedication – fitting, in a way, for a book that may be considered his legacy.

In stylistic terms, too, we may distinguish different phases of his life. In his para-religious phase, which lasted until 1925, Kracauer imitated the style of his role models Simmel and Scheler. The texts conform to a tradition of cultural criticism that belongs to the educated middle classes; they talk of 'essences and manifolds', of 'personalities and their psychological life [*Seelenleben*]', etc., and they are neither original nor in any way refined. The exact opposite is true of the numerous articles and books of his para-Marxist phase, which lasted until 1933. These are essayistic, at times aggressive and ironic, at other times allegorical and imagistic: they reveal Kracauer at the height of his powers and at his most significant. One might say that, during those years, Sancho Panza adventured with Don Quixote; the result was entertaining texts which are as intelligent as they are critically engaged, and which possess a unique tone. This forceful, witty and polemical style then paled, as a consequence of Kracauer's traumatic experience of emigration and war, but it did not disappear altogether. Kracauer's critique of society no longer pursued a positive goal; material security and making a new start were his preoccupations. After 1950, finally, Kracauer worked for many years on two academic and systematic treatises, and these sang a new and more measured melody. These two texts met with little interest. Quite a few people found Kracauer's contemplative style pedantic and boring. His theories of film and of history were subtly worked up, and their muted tone signalled a departure from his earlier writings, which were the preferred and more sought-after choices of Adorno's children, nephews and nieces. In the words of Dieter Henrich, the later Kracauer offered 'a lively conversation in a minor key'.[26]

There is plenty of diversity in Kracauer's creative output, even if he himself might not have wanted to see this. And yet it would be wrong to assume that there were no moments of unity in Kracauer's intellectual biography. They are clearly visible. Kracauer was extremely idiosyncratic, never allowed himself to be pinned down, always said 'maybe' when others demanded or pronounced a loud and clear 'yes' or 'no'. Even during his Berlin days, when he was more outspoken in his political views, he once referred to himself as the '*derrière-garde* of the avant-garde'.[27] He always moved at the margins of particular fields of knowledge, and at times was ahead of the zeitgeist. What he thought and how he wrote would often find recognition and imitators only much later. In Isaiah Berlin's terms, Kracauer was not a 'hedgehog', who knows one big thing, but a 'fox', who is familiar with many different things.[28] His philosophy of the anteroom is not a grand design like Adorno's

Negative Dialectics. Neither is it as full of determination as Bloch's
The Principle of Hope or Benjamin's theses on the philosophy of
history. But Kracauer had many irons in the fire. He 'did not belong
to any one discipline or profession' but was 'well trained in more
than one academic discipline', as Paul Oskar Kristeller emphasizes
in his foreword to *History*.[29]

Kracauer had an almost libidinal need to make contact with
'reality' and to understand it; it was as though his life – or at
least his shot at a good life – depended on it. He had an 'urge to
capture reality' [Elan zur Realiät], as he himself once put it.[30] He
was a materialist in the literal sense, an enemy of all systematic
philosophies of the subject, who – at the same time – emphasized
the subjective element in all knowledge. He could never agree with a
theory that contradicted his experience. Kracauer called his method
a 'construction out of the material', a phrase he used explicitly for
the first time in his pioneering study *The Salaried Masses*. In his
academic books from around 1960, he is clearly still pursuing this
method. In these works, he is revealed as a constructivist with a
tendency towards realism, or a constructivist realist.

Kracauer's search for the intermediary areas between philosophy,
science and the arts, a search which usually led him to areas of
the 'lifeworld' far from the large intellectual edifices and positivist
sciences, was, indeed, a peculiar driving force behind his intellectual
activity during all phases of his development. Twenty-five years ago,
Michael Schröter explained that the meaning of the term 'reality'
may undergo a shift in Kracauer's work, but the emphasis placed
on it remains constant:

> It is always the identical movement of thought and experience which
> lends Kracauer's work its dynamic: separation from reality – the
> experience of chaos – the need for a comprehensive, undeniable
> order – the recognition that such an order is impossible (because of
> historical contingency) – the critique of weak or violent systematic
> orders – a provisional occupation with dispersed but concrete
> individual elements and their cautious combination into unities at a
> medium level.[31]

This 'provisional occupation' grew into a permanent occupation
with the provisional.

Kracauer's anteroom philosophy is empathetic-mimetic rather
than critical. It neither aims at resistance, nor seeks adaptation.
It does not actively aim at resistance, nor at adaptation. But it
draws its power from the struggle against the existing conditions;
it is a declaration of love for the world in which we live, yet one
permeated by the experiences that taught Kracauer that this world
is a threatening, brutal place. For Kracauer, the rift between self and

Figure 39. Siegfried Kracauer in 1953 at Lake Minnewaska, New York.
The famous portrait was taken by Elisabeth Kracauer
Copyright: DLA Marbach. Photo: Lili Kracauer

world cannot be healed. But, precisely because of that, the *relation* with the world, the way in which subjects concern themselves with the world, has particular importance. Whether a life is a good life, that is, whether it is 'real', was for Kracauer crucially dependent on the question of whether a person's relation to reality, to things and humans, was 'resonant' (in Hartmut Rosa's sense): whether it made possible vivid experience and a life that is not alienated.[32]

What Kracauer had to say concerned concrete life. In Kracauer's peculiar face, alongside the traces of a hard life, it is still possible to discern little Friedel. But there is also present no small amount of alertness, wisdom; there is a whiff of contentedness, but also a serene melancholy. Theodor W. Adorno called him a 'curious realist', and many others have tinkered with this description, often because they were irked by the adjective 'curious' [wunderlich]. Thus, Kracauer became a 'boundless realist' (Rolf Wiggershaus), a 'critical realist' (Dagmar Barnouw) or even a 'destructive realist' (Axel Honneth).[33]

But Kracauer certainly was a 'curious realist'. It cannot be denied that he was strange, solitary and peculiar. That was also Ernst Bloch's view. In a letter to Lili Kracauer, Adolphe Lowe quoted him as saying about his recently deceased friend: 'The word "Krac" already onomatopoetically conveys something crackling-growling very well, and this is how he wanted to be understood. ... "Ginster's nightgown had a tear [Riß]" – who else was able thus to end the chapter of a novel without closing it?'[34]

Notes

1. Siegfried Kracauer – A Life

1 Transl. note: My translation. See Heinrich Heine, *The Baths of Lucca*, ch. 4, p. 312, in: *Pictures of Travel*, trans. Charles Godfrey Leland (Philadelphia: Schaefer & Koradi, 1879), pp. 302–65.
2 On the history of portraits, see Diers, 'Der Autor ist im Bilde'; the picture of Kracauer on the veranda is mentioned on pp. 585f.
3 According to Jürgen Habermas in an email to the author (7 April 2016). See also Reinold E. Thile (Westdeutscher Rundfunk) to Kracauer (29 September 1965).
4 See Kracauer to Galvin Lambert (*Sight & Sound*), 28 July 1952, or Penelope Houston (The British Film Institute, London) to Kracauer, 29 September 1961.
5 Kracauer to Adorno, 25 October 1963, in *Adorno/Kracauer, Briefwechsel*, pp. 611–13; here: pp. 611f. [Transl. note: A translation of the correspondence between Adorno and Kracauer is forthcoming from Polity. I was able to consult the draft manuscript and have used it in my translations of the passages from the letters, although with various modifications and amendments. All page references are to the German edition.]
6 Mülder-Bach, 'Schlupflöcher', p. 262.
7 See *History: The Last Things Before the Last* (Princeton: Markus Wiener Publishers, 1995), pp. 80ff.; on the extension of homelessness into an existentialist category, see Öhlschläger, '"Unheimliche Heimat"'.
8 Siegfried Kracauer, 'The Biography as an Art Form of the New Bourgeoisie', in *The Mass Ornament: Weimar Essays*, pp. 101–5; here: p. 104.
9 Siegfried Kracauer, *Jacques Offenbach and the Paris of His Time*, p. 23.
10 Siegfried Kracauer, *History: The Last Things Before the Last*, pp. 4 and 191.
11 A note on Adorno's name: up to 1942, he called himself Theodor Ludwig Wiesengrund (his father's family name); in official academic contexts, even before 1933, he called himself Wiesengrund-Adorno (adding part of his mother's maiden name, Adorno-Calvelli), and in publications from 1938 onward, he referred to himself as T. W. Adorno. When referring to him, I shall follow this pattern.
12 Transl. note: 'Paris, the Capital of the Nineteenth Century' is the title of a text by Walter Benjamin, related to the arcades project.
13 Cf. Stalder, 'Das anschmiegsame Denken', p. 47; Siegfried Kracauer, *Theory of Film*, p. xi (Kracauer is quoting Gabriel Marcel).
14 See Kracauer's thoughts on episode films in *Theory of Film*, pp. 251–61.

15 Letter from Siegfried to Rosette and Hedwig Kracauer, dated 16 March 1939.

16 SK, *Ginster*, in *Werke* 7, p. 23; Kracauer, *Georg*, p. 112.

17 Siegfried Kracauer, *History: The Last Things Before the Last*. See also Schütz, 'Der Fremde', pp. 72f.

2. Early Things: Before 1918

1 SK, *Ginster*, in *Werke* 7, p. 22.

2 Jeanette Baldes to Kracauer, 5 October 1959.

3 English edition: Soma Morgenstern, *The Son of the Lost Son*, New York, 1946. The German title, of course, alludes to the prodigal son of the New Testament.

4 Cf. Arnsberg, *Bilder aus dem jüdischen Leben*, p. 34.

5 See Kracauer to Werner Bockelmann, 28 March 1964 and to Will Brundert, 9 April 1966, two mayors of Frankfurt am Main. Kracauer thanks them as a 'Frankfurter Kind' [child of Frankfurt] for a volume by Friedrich Stoltze and for Ferdinand Happ's 'Knoppschachtel' – old familiar texts that evoked sweet memories from Kracauer's youth.

6 SK, *Ginster*, in *Werke* 7, p. 45.

7 See Spier, *Vor 1914*, p. 24.

8 Claussen, *Adorno*, pp. 16–20 and 30.

9 Spier, *Vor 1914*, p. 29.

10 Transl. note: The term 'Achtundvierziger' refers to the revolution of 1848 and the first freely elected German national assembly, which met in the Paulskirche in Frankfurt.

11 Cf. the special edition of *Gegenwart* 'Ein Jahrhundert Frankfurter Zeitung begründet von Leopold Sonnemann', in particular the preface (pp. 1f.), and Guttmann, 'Die Zeitung und das Reich', which discusses the paper's political stance during the so-called 'Gründerjahre', the founding years between 1871 and 1873.

12 See Claussen, pp. 33–4.

13 Arnsberg, *Bilder aus dem jüdischen Leben*, p. 43.

14 See Spier, *Vor 1914*, p. 30.

15 Transl. note: An allusion to Walter Benjamin's *Berlin Childhood around 1900* (Cambridge, MA: Harvard University Press, 2006).

16 SK, *Ginster*, in *Werke* 7, p. 224.

17 See Selmar Spier to Kracauer, 28 May 1930. At issue was the recognition of Kracauer's Prussian citizenship.

18 Hedwig to Siegfried Kracauer, 1 March 1939; the earlier quotations are from letters dated 15 March 1930 and 14 April 1930. At the time, she was compiling a report for the purpose of being granted an entry permit into France. According to Arnsberg, *Die Geschichte der Frankfurter Juden*, p. 254, Isidor Kracauer also studied classical philology, and in 1875 came to Frankfurt, where he was in permanent employment from 1880 onwards.

19 SK, *Ginster*, in *Werke* 7, p. 44.

20 Transl. note: 'Realschule': a secondary school that teaches eleven to sixteen-year-olds.

21 Hedwig to Siegfried Kracauer, 18 November 1933.

22 See Isidor Kracauer, *Geschichte der Juden*.

23 SK, *Ginster*, in *Werke* 7, pp. 44–5.

24 Hedwig to Siegfried Kracauer, 18 November 1933.
25 Hedwig to Siegfried Kracauer, 25 July 1930; 4 December and 17 December 1931; 30 September 1934; 21 July 1935; 20 September 1936; 11 December 1937; and 14 July and 12 December 1938.
26 SK, *Ginster*, in *Werke* 7, p. 45.
27 I would like to thank Werner Hassert-Caselli for his 'depth psychology' reading of *Ginster*.
28 Hedwig to Siegfried Kracauer, 1 March 1939.
29 SK, 'Einer, der nichts zu tun hat' [Someone with nothing to do], in *Werke* 5.3, pp. 159–61; here: pp. 159f.
30 SK, 'Die Eisenbahn' [The railway], in *Werke* 5.3, pp. 207–11; here: p. 207.
31 On Kracauer's excursions through the streets of Frankfurt, see Schopf, 'bin ich in Frankfurt der Flaneur geblieben', pp. 9–12. It was Bloch who said of Kracauer that he had something resembling a train station about him. See Ernst Bloch to Kracauer, 1 June 1932, in: Bloch, *Briefe*, vol. 1, pp. 362–5.
32 Kracauer to Gershom Scholem, 10 January 1961.
33 Spier, *Vor 1914*, p. 56.
34 Transl. note: 'Dappes' = clumsy person; 'Zores' = chaos, confusion, strife; 'Gedibber' = prattle.
35 See ibid., pp. 56–9.
36 Cf. Jay, 'The Extraterritorial Life of Siegfried Kracauer', p. 153; Linder, *Noten an den Rand des Lebens*, p. 17.
37 Arnsberg, *Bilder aus dem jüdischen Leben*, p. 11; *Ostend: Blick in ein jüdisches Viertel*, p. 20.
38 SK, *Ginster*, in *Werke* 7, p. 62.
39 Cf. Ries, 'Vor dem Ersten Weltkrieg', p. 32.
40 Ibid., p. 34.
41 Arnsberg, *Bilder aus dem jüdischen Leben*, p. 101.
42 Cf. Schlotzhauer, *Die Schule der Israelitischen Gemeinde*, p. 5.
43 Arnsberg, p. 110.
44 SK, *Ginster*, in *Werke* 7, pp. 23f.; see his diary entries for 1903, in *Marbacher Magazin*, pp. 2–5.
45 Quoted after *Marbacher Magazin*, p. 5.
46 Kracauer to the Verlag für Demoskopie (Peter Erich Neumann), 31 March 1959.
47 Cf. Kracauer library at the DLA Marbach (Krac 2).
48 Transl. note: 'Nature description' translates 'Naturbeschreibung', not commonly a school subject.
49 Transl. note: The German marks range is: 1 ('sehr gut'= very good), 2 ('gut' = good), 3 ('befriedigend' = satisfactory), 4 ('ausreichend' = adequate), 5 ('mangelhaft' = deficient), 6 ('ungenügend' = inadequate). The marks 1 to 4 count as pass marks, 5 and 6 are fails.
50 Quoted after *Marbacher Magazin*, p. 7.
51 SK, 'Ein Abend im Hochgebirge' [An evening in the high mountains], in *Werke* 5.1, pp. 10f.
52 Diary, 22 June 1907, quoted after *Marbacher Magazin*, p. 9.
53 Diary, 6 July 1907, ibid.
54 Diary, 7 July 1907, ibid.; Mann, *Tonio Kröger*, p. 5.
55 Cf. the interesting report on Kracauer's experience of reading his book as an adolescent by Andreas Bernhard, *Frankfurter Allgemeine Zeitung*, 30 October 2014. Stifter, *Indian Summer*, p. 479. Kracauer uses the quotation

in his letter of 5 April 1923 to Adorno, Adorno/Kracauer, *Briefwechsel*, pp. 9–11; here: p. 10.

56 Hesse, *Unterm Rad*, p. 118; *The Prodigy*, pp. 133 (transl. mod.) and 134.

57 Kracauer to Thomas Mann, 4 June 1935; Kracauer to Hermann Hesse, 2 February 1947.

58 See Kracauer's personal copy in his posthumous papers, DLA Marbach.

59 Cf. Mülder-Bach, 'Nachbemerkung und editorische Notiz', in *Werke* 7, pp. 649f.

60 SK, *Ginster*, in *Werke* 7, p. 24.

61 Cf. Holste, 'Vorwort', p. 8.

62 Transl. note: In this context, 'Anschaulichkeit' does not refer to ways of making something abstract visible and concrete but to a kind of intellectual intuition, that is, to the conceptual dimension in seeing. This notion is strongly associated with Goethe's concept of 'Anschauung'. Schiller once told Goethe – who had just given him an 'enthusiastic description of the metamorphosis of plants' and drawn, 'with a few characteristic strokes of the pen', a 'symbolic plant' – that his picture 'is not an observation from experience. That is an idea.' Goethe replied: 'Then I may rejoice that I have ideas without knowing it, and can even see them with my own eyes' (Goethe, 'Fortunate Encounter', p. 20).

63 Jäger, 'Kracauers Blick', p. 81.

64 Cf. Adorno, 'The Curious Realist', p. 163.

65 Diary, 20 August 1907, quoted after *Marbacher Magazin*, p. 9.

66 See *Marbacher Magazin*, pp. 7f. and 14. In the Kracauer library there is an edition of the Kant text published by Otto Hendel (Halle). It contains numerous markings and marginal notes, as well as an entry labelled 'Friedel Kracauer, stud. Arch.'.

67 Kracauer to Leo Löwenthal, 12 April 1924, in Löwenthal/Kracauer, *In steter Freundschaft*, pp. 53–5; here: p. 53.

68 Transl. note: 'TU' stands for 'Technische Universität' [Technical university]. 'Hochschule' is a generic term for educational institutions that are attended after secondary school.

69 Cf. Holste, 'Vorwort', p. 9; *Marbacher Magazin*, p. 12.

70 Kracauer to Georg Simmel, 30 November 1917.

71 Bollenbeck, *Geschichte der Kulturkritik*, pp. 205 and 256f.

72 Konersmann, *Kulturkritik*, pp. 25 and 97; *Fragments of Modernity*, pp. 3 and 6–10.

73 Diary entry for 30 October 1907, in *Marbacher Magazin*, p. 12; exchange of letters and cards between Kracauer and Simmel 1914–1918; here Kracauer to Georg Simmel, 5 July 1914; Georg Simmel to Kracauer, 26 June 1915 and 1 February 1916; in the latter Simmel offers critical remarks on Kracauer's essays and provides him with advice.

74 Cf. Mülder-Bach, 'Nachbemerkung und editorische Notiz', in *Werke* 7, p. 652.

75 The title of the dissertation was: *Die Entwicklung der Schmiedekunst in Berlin, Potsdam und einigen Städten der Mark vom 17. Jahrhundert bis zum Beginn des 19. Jahrhunderts* [The development of the art of forging in Berlin, Potsdam, and some places in the Mark from the seventeenth to the early nineteenth century] and was published in 1915 by Wormser Verlags- und Druckereigesellschaft.

76 Diary entries for 19 and 21 September 1912, quoted after *Marbacher Magazin*, pp. 17 and 20.

77 Diary entries from 1911/1912, quoted after *Marbacher Magazin*, pp. 18f.
78 As in a letter to Otto Crusius, dated 23 August 1913; cf. *Marbacher Magazin*, p. 23.
79 Cf. bundle 'Jugendgedichte' [Adolescent poems].
80 Cf. Bollenbeck, *Geschichte der Kulturkritik*, pp. 7–10.
81 SK, 'Das Leiden unter dem Wissen' [Suffering from knowledge], in *Werke* 9.1, pp. 169–397; here: p. 244.
82 Ibid., pp. 264f. and 396.
83 SK, 'Über das Wesen der Persönlichkeit' [On the nature of personality], in *Werke* 9.1, pp. 7–120; here: pp. 9, 17, 47 and 57; cf. also SK, 'Das Leiden unter dem Wissen', in *Werke* 9.1, pp. 300–4.
84 Lorenz Jäger, 'Kracauers Blick', p. 83.
85 Cf. SK, 'Das Leiden unter dem Wissen', in *Werke* 9.1, p. 237. On the fundamental experience of the separation between man and world as a point of departure and a continuous theme in Kracauer's work, cf. Schröter, 'Weltzerfall und Rekonstruktion', pp. 24f.
86 On this, see also Agard, *Kracauer*, pp. 17–26.
87 SK, 'Von der Erkenntnismöglichkeit seelischen Lebens' [On the possible knowledge of psychic life], in *Werke* 9.1, pp. 121–68; here: pp. 123, 137 and 152.
88 Ibid., pp. 157f.
89 Ibid., p. 159.
90 See SK, 'Das Leiden unter dem Wissen', in *Werke* 9.1, pp. 179 and 214.
91 See ibid., p. 306.
92 He completed the dissertation in July 1914. See Jäger, 'Kracauers Blick', especially pp. 81 and 95. Following its publication, a review of the study in the *Zentralblatt der Bauverwaltung* judged it to be a noteworthy and 'exemplary' contribution to the history of the arts and crafts in Berlin. The reviewer praised in particular the numerous sketches Kracauer had produced (no. 66, 18 August 1915, p. 436).
93 See Spier, *Vor 1914*, pp. 89f.
94 See letter from Marlene Spier to Kracauer, 5 January 1963. Marlene Spier was sorting old letters following the death of Selmar.
95 SK, *Ginster*, in *Werke* 7, pp. 37 and 80.
96 Ibid., p. 19.
97 SK, 'Vom Erleben des Kriegs' [On experiencing war], in *Werke* 5.1, pp. 11–23.
98 Cf. Kracauer's review of Scheler's *Krieg und Aufbau* (1916): 'Neue Bücher', in *Werke* 5.1, pp. 24–9.
99 SK, *Ginster*, in *Werke* 7, pp. 126f.
100 Cf. Spier, *Vor 1914*. According to the *Marbacher Magazin*, p. 27, the burial took place in September 1916.
101 SK, *Ginster*, in *Werke* 7, p. 131.
102 Ibid., p. 80.
103 Ibid., p. 112.
104 Kracauer to Georg Simmel, 30 November 1917; SK, *Ginster*, in *Werke* 7, p. 211.
105 Max Scheler to Kracauer, 1 December 1916 and 12 February 1917.
106 SK, 'Max Scheler', in *Werke* 5.3, pp. 23–8; here: p. 23.
107 Cf. *Marbacher Magazin*, p. 28.
108 Quoted after ibid., pp. 29f.
109 Kracauer, 'Georg Simmel', in *The Mass Ornament*, pp. 225–57; here: p. 227.

110 Ibid.
111 Ibid., p. 234.
112 Ibid., p. 237.
113 Ibid., p. 251 (transl. mod.).
114 Ibid., p. 257.
115 Ibid., p. 256.
116 SK, 'Georg Simmel', in *Werke* 9.2, pp. 139–280; here: pp. 145, 148, 155f., 159, 169, 174 and 176. Cf. also Kracauer's retrospective on Simmel in his letter to Kurt H. Wolff, 6 January 1957: 'For Simmel, sociology was a subsidiary subject, so to speak. During a certain period of his life, society and the many references within it offered him opportunities for demonstrating something. {I wonder whether our sociologists are aware of this "something", whether they sense the intellectual despair behind so much subtlety.}' Cf. also Wiggershaus, 'Ein abgrundtiefer Realist', pp. 285–9, and Brodersen, *Siegfried Kracauer*, pp. 36–46. [Transl. note: The passage in curly brackets is in English in the original.]
117 SK, 'Das Leiden unter dem Wissen', in *Werke* 9.1, p. 387.

3. Revolution, the *Frankfurter Zeitung* and Cultural Criticism around 1920

1 'Blut und Eisen': reference to a speech given by Otto von Bismarck on 30 September 1862, in which he said that the great questions of the day would not be decided through speeches and majority decisions but by blood and iron.
2 Bernstein, *Die deutsche Revolution*, p. 32.
3 Peukert, *Weimar Republic*, pp. 21–4; here: p. 23.
4 Cf. Nipperdey, *Deutsche Geschichte*, p. 863; Winkler, *Geschichte des Westens*, pp. 133–49; Herbert, *Geschichte Deutschlands*, pp. 177–86.
5 Cf. Diner, *Cataclysms*, pp. 59–64; Koenen, *Was war der Kommunismus?*, pp. 19f.
6 Hobsbawm, *Age of Extremes*, pp. 65–71.
7 Cf. Leonhard, *Pandora's Box*, pp. 721–5.
8 Wehler, *Deutsche Gesellschaftsgeschichte*, p. 188.
9 Rosenberg, *Geschichte der Weimarer Republik*, p. 10.
10 Cf. Wehler, *Deutsche Gesellschaftsgeschichte*, pp. 190f.
11 *Marbacher Magazin*, p. 30.
12 SK, *Ginster*, in *Werke* 7, p. 238.
13 Quoted after Schildt, 'Zur Historisierung des langen November', p. 235.
14 SK, *Ginster*, in *Werke* 7, pp. 239 and 253.
15 'Deutschnationale' after the Deutschnationale Volkspartei (DNVP), the German National People's Party, a conservative party founded in 1918 and dissolved in 1933.
16 Cf. Breuer, *Anatomie der Konservativen Revolution*, p. 1.
17 SK, 'Sind Menschenliebe, Gerechtigkeit und Duldsamkeit an eine bestimmte Staatsform geknüpft, und welche Staatsform gibt die beste Gewähr für ihre Durchführung? Eine Abhandlung' [Are philanthropy, justice, and tolerance tied to a particular kind of state, and which kind of state suits their realization best?], in *Werke* 9.2, pp. 79–136. Kracauer unsuccessfully entered this treatise for a writing competition of the Moritz-Mannheimer-Stiftung.

18 Ibid., p. 125.
19 Cf. the two texts 'Autorität und Individualismus' [Authority and individualism] (February 1921) and 'Das Wesen des politischen Führers' [The nature of political leaders] (June 1921), in SK, *Werke* 5.1, pp. 167–73 and 211–20. The following is based on these texts and the text submitted to the writing competition (see note 17).
20 Cf. Max Weber, 'Politics as a Vocation', in *Essays in Sociology*, trans. and ed. by H.H. Gerth and C. Wright Mills, London: Routledge, 1970 [1919], pp. 77–128.
21 Kracauer, *Georg*, pp. 159, 205 and 86.
22 Koenen, *Der Russland-Komplex*, esp. pp. 15–17. Lew Kopelew (ed.), *West-östliche Spiegelungen*. On Kracauer's attitude towards the young Soviet Union, cf. Belke, 'Siegfried Kracauer'.
23 Kracauer to Margarete Susman, 11 January 1920, and SK, 'Nietzsche und Dostojewski', in *Werke* 5.1, pp. 240–56.
24 Kracauer to Margarete Susman, 11 January 1920.
25 Kracauer to Margarete Susman, 10 February 1920.
26 Kracauer to Margarete Susman, 22 February 1920.
27 Kracauer to Margarete Susman, 12 October 1920.
28 Transl. note: The Spartacus League was a left-wing group that split from the Social Democratic Party in 1914 over the SPD's support for the war. It subsequently renamed itself the Kommunistische Partei Deutschlands (KPD) and joined the Comintern in 1919. Two of its founding members, Karl Liebknecht and Rosa Luxemburg, were killed on the same day (15 January 1919) by Freikorps troops following the quashed Spartacus uprising earlier that month.
29 Cf. Stalder, *Siegfried Kracauer*, pp. 27–32; Schivelbusch, *Intellektuellendämmerung*, p. 60; Becker, *Demokratie des sozialen Rechts*, pp. 7, 20–31 and 41–63; Gillesen, *Auf verlorenem Posten*, pp. 11–34.
30 Cf. Becker, *Demokratie des sozialen Rechts*, pp. 20–31, and Koszyk, *Deutsche Presse*, pp. 216–19.
31 Kracauer, *Georg*, p. 12 (transl. mod.).
32 SK, 'Die Zeitung', in *Werke* 5.1, pp. 498–500; here: p. 499.
33 SK, 'Der Wettbewerb "Hauptzollamt"' [Competition for the Hauptzollamt], in *Werke* 5.2, pp. 441–4; here: p. 444. SK, 'Deutsche Bauausstellung' [German building exhibition], in *Werke* 5.3, pp. 521–7. Cf. also von Arburg, '"Zweck-Architekturen der Verwesung"'.
34 SK, 'Über Turmhäuser' [On tower houses], 'Das Frankfurter "Hochhaus"' [The Frankfurt 'skyscraper'], in *Werke* 5.1, pp. 173–9; here: pp. 173f., 399–406 and 693–5.
35 SK, 'Der Umbau des Hauptbahnhofs' [The modification of the main train station], in *Werke* 5.1, pp. 580–3; here: p. 581.
36 SK, 'Vom Stadtbild' [On the cityscape], in *Werke* 5.1, p. 572.
37 SK, 'Das Straßenbild' [The street view], in *Werke* 5.1, p. 611.
38 SK, 'Sommerlicher Vergnügungstaumel' [Amusement frenzy in the summer], in *Werke* 5.1, pp. 669–72; here: pp. 669f.
39 Transl. note: 'Decline of the West' is, of course, a nod to the work of that name by Oswald Spengler: *Der Untergang des Abendlandes*. The first volume was published in 1918, revised in 1922, and the second volume in 1923 (*The Decline of the West*, New York: Alfred A. Knopf, 1926 and 1928).
40 Schivelbusch, *Intellektuellendämmerung*, p. 63.

41 This is how Haacke, an expert on the feuilleton, characterizes this type; quoted after Stalder, *Siegfried Kracauer*, p. 88.
42 Kracauer to Margarete Susman, 20 January 1920.
43 Reference to Ernst Bloch, *The Spirit of Utopia*, trans. Anthony A. Nassar, Stanford: Stanford University Press, 2000.
44 Mark Mazower, *Dark Continent*, pp. ixf.; Jörn Leonhard, *Pandora's Box: A History of the First World War.*
45 Claussen, *Theodor W. Adorno: One Last Genius*, pp. 66f. and 84.
46 Cf. Mai, *Europa*, pp. 7–17.
47 Leo, *Der Wille zum Wesen.*
48 Cf. Bollenbeck, *Geschichte der Kulturkritik*, pp. 215–25.
49 According to the preface to the first edition, written in December 1917.
50 Transl. note: The 'Dolchstoßlegende' (stab-in-the-back myth) refers to the claim, widespread after 1918, that responsibility for defeat lay not with the German army but with those at home, in particular those with republican convictions. 'Novemberverbrechen' (November crimes) is a phrase used to refer disparagingly to the events of the November revolution.
51 Spengler, *Decline of the West*, p. 159.
52 Ibid., p. 21.
53 Cf. the introduction to the first volume of *The Decline of the West*, pp. 1–50; Bollenbeck, *Geschichte der Kulturkritik*, p. 216; Felken, 'Nachwort' to the German edition, p. 1268.
54 SK, 'Untergang?' [Decline?], in *Werke* 5.1, pp. 704–8; here: pp. 704f. On the debates surrounding the book, see Felken, 'Nachwort', p. 1252 and Bollenbeck, *Geschichte der Kulturkritik*, p. 219.
55 SK, 'Untergang?', in *Werke* 5.1, pp. 704–8; here: pp. 704f.
56 Eßbach, 'Radikalismus und Modernität'.
57 Cf. Korol, 'Einleitung', and Ball, *Zur Kritik der deutschen Intelligenz.*
58 Oskar Negt, 'Ernst Bloch – der deutsche Philosoph der Oktoberrevolution. Mit einem Kommentar aus heutiger Zeit: Oktoberrevolution (Gesprächspartner Lenin)', in Ernst Bloch, *Vom Hasard zur Katastrophe. Politische Aufsätze, 1934–1939*. Frankfurt: Suhrkamp, 1972.
59 Bloch, *Spirit of Utopia*, p. 1.
60 Ibid.
61 Ibid., p. 3.
62 Bloch, *The Principle of Hope*, vol. 3, p. 1376.
63 Ibid., pp. 1375f.
64 Bloch, *Principle of Hope*, vol. 1, p. 6.
65 Ibid., p. 205.
66 Cf. Münster, *Ernst Bloch*, pp. 69–79.
67 Benjamin to Ernst Schoen, 19 September 1919, in *Correspondence of Walter Benjamin*, pp. 147–9; here: p. 148.
68 Cf. Müller, *Das demokratische Zeitalter*, pp. 129–33.
69 Transl. note: 'Wandervogel', literally 'wandering' or 'hiking bird', refers to a German youth movement that originated in 1896 but soon diversified into various groups. They shared the idea of getting back to nature and of freedom from the restrictions of society. The political outlook was nationalist, and the National Socialists adopted some of its elements for the Hitler Youth. The Wandervogel movement itself, along with other youth movements, was outlawed after 1933.
70 This characterization follows a lecture by Manfred Frank in Marbach (2014).

71 Cf. Vondung, *Apokalypse*, pp. 225–57.
72 This assumption was common at the time; see Lethen, *Verhaltenslehren der Kälte*.

4. Friendship (Part 1): The Jewish Renaissance in Frankfurt

1 On the uncle and aunt, cf. Schopf, 'bin ich in Frankfurt der Flaneur geblieben', pp. 9–12.
2 SK, 'Das zeugende Gespräch' [Fruitful conversations], in *Werke* 5.1, pp. 604–11.
3 Kracauer, 'Georg Simmel', in *The Mass Ornament*, pp. 225–57; here: p. 226.
4 Ibid., p. 241.
5 SK, 'Über die Freundschaft' [On friendship], in *Werke* 5.1, pp. 29–59; here: pp. 31, 37f. and 41.
6 Ibid., p. 48. Cf. also the afterword by Karsten Witte in Kracauer, *Über die Freundschaft*.
7 SK, 'Über die Freundschaft', in *Werke* 5.1, pp. 29–59; here: p. 55.
8 Ibid., p. 54.
9 Bloch, *The Principle of Hope*, vol. 3, p. 962.
10 SK, 'Über die Freundschaft', in *Werke* 5.1, pp. 29–59; here: p. 53.
11 Ibid., p. 58.
12 Ibid., p. 56.
13 The fitting title of a book by Thomas Jung and Stefan Müller-Doohm, which depicts the friendship between Adorno and Kracauer, among others.
14 Adorno, 'The Curious Realist', pp. 159–60.
15 Kracauer, *Georg*, p. 22.
16 In the novel, Fred's mother also bears a strong resemblance to Kracauer's mother, Rosette.
17 This is how Wiesengrund described his mother, according to Haselberg, 'Wiesengrund-Adorno', p. 16.
18 Jäger, *Adorno*, pp. 1–3.
19 Adorno, 'Four Hands, Once Again', p. 1.
20 Ibid., p. 3 (transl. mod.).
21 Cf. Gay, *Weimar Republic*, pp. 111–18.
22 Löwenthal, 'Recollections of Theodor W. Adorno', p. 203.
23 Horkheimer, *Jenseits der Fachwissenschaft*, p. 261. [Transl. note: I follow the translation by Rodney Livingstone in Stefan Müller-Doohm, *Adorno: A Biography*, Cambridge: Polity, 2005, pp. 18f.]
24 Cf. Classen, *Theodor Adorno*, p. 44.
25 Jäger, *Adorno*, p. 9.
26 Adorno, *Minima Moralia*, pp. 192–3.
27 Adorno, 'The Curious Realist', p. 161.
28 Löwenthal, 'Recollections of Theodor W. Adorno', p. 204.
29 Classen, *Theodor Adorno*, p. 36.
30 Adorno, 'The Curious Realist', p. 160.
31 Adorno, *Minima Moralia*, p. 18.
32 Cf. Simmel's lectures on Kant in Kracauer's library, DLA, Marbach: *Kant: Sechzehn Vorlesungen*, p. 18. Kracauer's library also contains a copy of the 1899 edition of Kant's *Critique of Pure Reason* published by Otto Henschel Verlag (Halle), which Kracauer purchased while at university.

33 Brunkhorst, *Theodor W. Adorno*, p. 46.
34 Adorno, 'The Curious Realist', p. 160.
35 Ibid.
36 Ibid. (transl. amended).
37 Ibid., p. 161.
38 See the entries for 6, 8 and 29 August 1924 in Kracauer's diary, while he was travelling to Southern Tyrol with Teddie.
39 On their joint reading of Kant, cf. Schlüpmann, *Detektiv des Kinos*, p. 15.
40 Löwenthal, 'As I remember Friedel', p. 6.
41 On the revolution in Frankfurt, cf. Claussen, *Theodor Adorno*, pp. 75–6. Löwenthal's 'Bekenntnis zur Revolution' can be found in *Das Utopische soll Funken schlagen …*, pp. 23–5.
42 Spier, *Vor 1914*, p. 61.
43 Löwenthal, *Mitmachen wollte ich nie*, pp. 15–18.
44 Ibid.
45 Ibid., p. 18.
46 Quoted after Heuberger, 'Entdeckung der jüdischen Wurzeln', p. 64; cf. Heuberger, *Rabbiner Nehemias Anton Nobel*, pp. 9–10.
47 Heuberger, *Rabbiner Nehemias Anton Nobel*, p. 50; Simon, 'N.A. Nobel als Prediger', p. 376.
48 Franz Rosenzweig, quoted after Heuberger, 'Entdeckung der jüdischen Wurzeln', p. 58.
49 Heuberger, *Rabbiner Nehemias Anton Nobel*, p. 84.
50 Ibid., p. 12.
51 Löwenthal, *Mitmachen wollte ich nie*, p. 18.
52 Quoted after Heuberger, 'Die Entdeckung der jüdischen Wurzeln', p. 62.
53 Letter of 26 December 1934 from Benjamin to Gerhard Scholem, in *The Correspondence of Walter Benjamin*, pp. 468–70; here: p. 469, and Brenner, *Jüdische Kultur*, p. 83.
54 Fromm, 'Prophets and Priests', pp. 14–15. On Fromm's time in Frankfurt, see Funk, *Erich Fromm*, pp. 32–49.
55 Cf. Heuberger, *Rabbiner Nehemias Anton Nobel*, p. 46; the quotation: p. 86; Simon, *Sechzig Jahre gegen den Strom*, pp. 24–5; Löwenthal, *Mitmachen wollte ich nie*, p. 24.
56 Quoted after Funk, *Erich Fromm*, p. 39.
57 Quoted after Simon, 'N.A. Nobel als Prediger', p. 377.
58 Ibid.
59 Cf. Glatzer, 'Das Frankfurter Lehrhaus', pp. 303–6.
60 Simon, 'Franz Rosenzweig', p. 399.
61 Two letters from Franz Rosenzweig to Kracauer, dated 25 May and 5 July 1923, DLA NL Krac. On the figure of the prophet, cf. Baumann, 'Drei Briefe'.
62 Adorno, *Jargon of Authenticity*, p. 3. Original German: GS 6, p. 415. Cf. Beck and Coomann, 'Adorno, Kracauer', pp. 11–15.
63 Cf. Hobsbawm and Ranger, 'The Invention of Tradition'.
64 Simon, 'Franz Rosenzweig', p. 401.
65 Cf. Brenner, *Jüdische Kultur*, p. 99. Some thirty years later, Kracauer could no longer recall having spoken at the institute; cf. his letter of 16 February 1957 to Selmar Spier.
66 Glatzer, 'Das Frankfurter Lehrhaus', p. 307.
67 Ibid., p. 309.
68 On the practices of the Lehrhaus, cf. Schivelbusch, *Intellektuellendämmerung*, pp. 44–51; Glatzer, 'Das Frankfurter Lehrhaus', p. 324.

69 Kracauer reviewed the books for the FZ (2 December 1922); cf. 'Der große Maggid', in *Werke* 5.1, pp. 533–7. The book appeared in English translation in 1947: *Tales of the Hasidim*, trans. Olga Marx, New York: Schocken.
70 Mosès, *The Angel of History*, p. 12.
71 Cf. Dubbels, *Figuren des Messianischen*.
72 Löwy, *Redemption and Utopia*, p. 38.
73 Millenarian followers of the character Emanuel Quint in Gerhart Hauptmann's *The Fool in Christ, Emanuel Quint: A Novel* (1911 [1910]), written between 1901 and 1910.
74 Bloch, *Thomas Münzer*, p. 240.
75 Cf. Palmier, *Walter Benjamin*, pp. 242–3.

5. Friendship (Part 2): The One Who Waits

1 Löwenthal, 'Das Dämonische', pp. 211 and 222f.
2 These are the adjectives Löwenthal used in conversation with Dubiel to describe his mood at the time; Löwenthal, *Mitmachen wollte ich nie*, p. 58.
3 Letter from Kracauer to Leo Löwenthal, dated 4 December 1921, in Löwenthal/Kracauer, *In steter Freundschaft*, pp. 31–4; here: pp. 31f.
4 On 1 March 1922, Kracauer wrote to Leo Löwenthal: 'She is a wonderful woman, and one often finds oneself sympathizing with her emotionally conditioned thinking when, in confidential conversations, one feels the genuineness and warmth of her nature. However, towards her intellectuality I always have ambivalent feelings.' Ibid., pp. 38f.; here: p. 39.
5 This is how Kracauer paraphrased Susman's description of a visit by Bloch; Kracauer to Susman, 25 May 1920, DLA Marbach, NL Susman. On Susman's relation to Bloch at this time, see Klapheck, *Margarete Susman*, pp. 52–5.
6 Kracauer to Margarete Susman, 25 May 1920.
7 Kracauer to Margarete Susman, letters of 21 and 23 July 1921.
8 SK, 'Prophetentum' [Prophetism], in *Werke* 5.1, pp. 460–9; esp. pp. 467f.
9 Kracauer to Margarete Susman, 17 September 1921.
10 Kracauer to Leo Löwenthal, 1 March 1922, in Löwenthal/Kracauer, *In steter Freundschaft*, p. 39.
11 Ernst Bloch to Kracauer, 1 September 1922, in Bloch, *Briefe*, vol. 1, pp. 265–7.
12 Bloch, 'Einige Kritiker', pp. 60f. The passage on Kracauer is only contained in the edition of 1923; in later editions, Bloch omitted it.
13 Quoted after Mülder, *Siegfried Kracauer*, p. 165.
14 Kracauer to Leo Löwenthal, 16 October 1923, in Löwenthal/Kracauer, *In steter Freundschaft*, pp. 48f.; here: p. 48.
15 Kracauer to Leo Löwenthal, 12 February 1922, in ibid., pp. 36f.
16 Wiesengrund to Leo Löwenthal, 22 August 1923, in ibid., pp. 44f.; cf. also Lessing, 'Impromptus eines Frankfurter Wunderkindes', p. 80.
17 SK, 'Gedanken über die Freundschaft' [Thoughts on friendship], in *Werke* 5.1, pp. 332–50; the following quotations are from this text.
18 Kracauer's library contains a copy of Ernst Howald, *Platons Leben* (Zurich, 1923), in which he marked passages on Eros and Mythos and on Plato's longing for friendship. However, Kracauer can only have read the book after he had written his own trilogy on friendship.

19 This is how Kracauer remembered the 'early evenings' he spent with Löwenthal in Frankfurt. Letter from Kracauer to Löwenthal, 12 April 1924, in Löwenthal/Kracauer, *In steter Freundschaft*, pp. 53–5; here: p. 53.

20 Kracauer to Leo Löwenthal, 24 January 1922, in Löwenthal/Kracauer, *In steter Freundschaft*, p. 35; the obituary from *FZ* (25 January 1922) is reprinted in SK, *Werke* 5.1, pp. 362f.

21 Transl. note: First line of a famous poem by Cäsar Flaischlen (1864–1920): 'Hab Sonne im Herzen, ob's stürmt oder schneit, ob der Himmel voll Wolken, die Erde voll Streit ... Hab Sonne im Herzen, dann komme was mag, das leuchtet voll Licht dir, den dunkelsten Tag! etc. – Carry the sun in your heart, be there storm or snow, be the sky cloudy, on earth only strife will show... Carry the sun in your heart, and then come what may, filled with light will be your darkest day'.

22 Quoted after Lesch and Lesch, 'Verbindungen zu einer anderen Frankfurter Schule', p. 177; Kracauer to Leo Löwenthal, 22 and 31 August 1923, in Löwenthal/Kracauer, *In steter Freundschaft*, pp. 44 and 46.

23 Kracauer to Margarete Susman, 10 February 1921. Max Brod's exposition of his Jewish religiosity in his 'confessional' *Heidentum, Christentum, Judentum* Kracauer, by contrast, found acceptable, but he called Martin Buber's *I and Thou* 'foppish' and 'authentic' [eigentlich], and marked up his copy with phrases like 'nebbisch' [who cares], 'Steiner' and 'Oh, Buber'.

24 Kracauer to Margarete Susman, 21 February 1920.

25 Kracauer to Leo Löwenthal, 14 January 1921, in Löwenthal/Kracauer, *In steter Freundschaft*, pp. 18–20; here: p. 19.

26 Kracauer to Leo Löwenthal, 12 April 1924, in ibid., pp. 53–5.

27 SK, 'Schicksalswende der Kunst' [A turn in the fate of the arts], in *Werke* 5.1, pp. 94–100; here: p. 95. SK, 'Universität und Geistesleben' [The universities and intellectual life], in ibid., pp. 303–8. SK, 'Das Lebensgefühl in der Epoche des Hochkapitalismus' [The feeling of life in the epoch of high capitalism], in ibid., pp. 101–8; here: p. 103. SK, 'Religiöse Versuche der Gegenwart' [Religious experiments in the present], in ibid., pp. 377–9; here: p. 377.

28 SK, 'Deutscher Geist und deutsche Wirklichkeit' [German spirit and German reality], in ibid., pp. 363–72; here: p. 370.

29 Kracauer to Margarete Susman, 20 April 1921.

30 Kracauer to Margarete Susman, 10 February 1921.

31 Kracauer to Leo Löwenthal, 1 March 1922, in Löwenthal/Kracauer, *In steter Freundschaft*, p. 39.

32 SK, 'Katholizismus und Relativismus' [Catholicism and relativism], in *Werke* 5.1, pp. 309–17; here: p. 316.

33 SK, 'Zur religiösen Lage in Deutschland' [On the religious situation in Germany], in *Werke* 5.2, pp. 154–9.

34 SK, 'Anthroposophie und Wissenschaft' [Anthroposophy and science] and 'Zum Tode Rudolf Steiners' [On the death of Rudolf Steiner], in *Werke* 5.1, pp. 256–65; here: pp. 258–60, and *Werke* 5.2, pp. 228–32; here: p. 229.

35 SK, 'Georg von Lukács' Romantheorie' [Georg von Lukács's theory of the novel], in *Werke* 5.1, pp. 282–8; here: pp. 282–3 and 288.

36 Kracauer to Margarete Susman, 12 October 1920.

37 Kracauer, 'Those Who Wait', in *The Mass Ornament*, pp. 129–40; here: p. 129.

38 Ibid., pp. 129–31.

39 Ibid., p. 138.

6. The Crisis of the Sciences, Sociology and the Sphere Theory

1 Cf. Lukács, *The Theory of the Novel*.
2 Kracauer to Margarete Susman, 11 January 1920.
3 He reports on this in his article 'Die Notlage des Architektenstandes' [The plight of the architectural profession], in *Werke* 5.1, pp. 565–71.
4 Kracauer to Margarete Susman, 2 April 1920.
5 Kracauer to Margarete Susman, 25 May 1920.
6 Kracauer to Margarete Susman, 22 February 1920.
7 Kracauer to Margarete Susman, 12 October 1920. The text 'Die Gruppe als Ideenträger' (The group as bearer of the idea) appeared in 1922 in *Archiv für Sozialwissenschaft und Sozialpolitik* (vol. 3) and was not incorporated into the book.
8 Kracauer to Margarete Susman, 4 November 1920 and 4 January 1921.
9 Kracauer to Leo Löwenthal, 9 March 1922, in Löwenthal/Kracauer, *In steter Freundschaft*, p. 42. The book appeared with the Sybillen-Verlag in Dresden as part of a series on contemporary questions and intellectual life, which also included Adolf Gunther's *Krisis der Wirtschaft und Wirtschaftswissenschaft* and Herbert Jhering's *Der Kampf ums Theater*.
10 Kracauer to Margarete Susmann, 11 January 1920.
11 SK, *Soziologie*, in *Werke* 1, pp. 9 and 32.
12 Cf. Baumann, *Vorraum*, p. 260.
13 SK, *Soziologie*, in *Werke* 1, p. 11.
14 Ibid., p. 12.
15 Ibid., pp. 15f. and 31.
16 Höffe, *Kleine Geschichte der Philosophie*, pp. 261–6; Fellmann, *Phänomenologie*, pp. 11–23.
17 SK, *Soziologie*, in *Werke* 1, pp. 37, 40 and 43f.
18 Ibid., pp. 60 and 68.
19 Ibid., pp. 77 and 98.
20 Ibid., p. 101.
21 Gerhard Colm, 'Besprechung von S. Kracauer, Soziologie als Wissenschaft', in *Zeitschrift für Politik* XIV (1925) 5, pp. 468f.
22 Eßbach, 'Die historischen Quellen soziologischen Denkens', p. 28.
23 Cf. Karl Polanyi, *The Great Transformation: The Political and Economic Origins of Our Time*.
24 On the transformations in the nineteenth century, cf. Kocka, *Geschichte des Kapitalismus*.
25 Cf. Kaesler, 'Was sind und zu welchem Ende studiert man die Klassiker der Soziologie?', pp. 21–4; Gay, *Modernism*, p. 3; Osterhammel, *Die Verwandlung der Welt*, pp. 25–7.
26 Gay, *Modernism*, pp. 69–72.
27 Cf. Frisby, *Fragments of Modernity*, pp. 11–37 and 39.
28 Lindner, *Entdeckung der Stadtkultur*, pp. 9–14.
29 Bollenbeck, *Eine Geschichte der Kulturkritik*, pp. 251f.
30 Freyer, *Soziologie*, p. 12.
31 SK, 'Der deutsche Soziologentag' [Meeting of the German sociologists], in *Werke* 5.2, pp. 133–41; here: p. 134.
32 Transl. note: 'Psychology of peoples', a science suggested by Wilhelm Wundt, who published his ten-volume *Völkerpsychologie* in 1900. According to Wundt, its aim was to establish general psychological laws that hold across all peoples, not historically or culturally specific laws.

33 Cf. Stölting, *Akademische Soziologie*, pp. 5–7, 22–5 and 105f.; Eisermann, 'Die deutsche Soziologie'; Blomert, *Intellektuelle im Aufbruch*, pp. 14–18.

34 Simmel, 'Grundfragen der Soziologie', p. 63.

35 Mannheim, *Structural Analysis of Epistemology*.

36 Kracauer to Leo Löwenthal, 1 March 1922, in Löwenthal/Kracauer, *In steter Freundschaft*, p. 38.

37 SK, '"Die Strukturanalyse der Erkenntnistheorie"' [Structural analysis of epistemology], in *Werke* 5.1, pp. 550f.

38 Freyer, *Soziologie*, p. 3.

39 Edmund Husserl to Kracauer, 14 January 1934.

40 SK, 'Die Wissenschaftskrisis' [The crisis of science], in *Werke* 5.1, pp. 591–601; here: p. 591. On Troeltsch and his reply to the academic youth ('Kierkegaards junge Herren') and their criticism of historicism, cf. Graf, *Der heilige Zeitgeist*, pp. 151–60; Baumann, *Vorraum*, pp. 266–9.

41 Cf. Koziol, 'Die Wirklichkeit ist eine Konstruktion', p. 148.

42 Weitz, *Weimar Germany*, pp. 252f.

43 Cf. Arendt, *The Human Condition*, pp. 248–68; here: p. 261 [Transl. note: Arendt is quoting Eddington: 'the former have as much resemblance to the latter as a telephone number has to a subscriber']. Blumenberg, *Legitimacy of the Modern Age*, pp. 3–12.

44 Korta, *Geschichte als Projekt und Projektion*, p. 116.

45 Boltanski, *Mysteries and Conspiracies*, pp. 5–7 and 32; SK, *Der Detektiv-Roman* [The detective novel], in *Werke* 1, p. 119.

46 Mülder, *Siegfried Kracauer*, p. 36.

47 Marquard, *Der Einzelne*, pp. 116–43.

48 SK, *Der Detektiv-Roman*, in *Werke* 1, pp. 109f.; Mülder, *Siegfried Kracauer*, p. 40; Frisby, *Fragments of Modernity*, pp. 126–8; Frisby, 'Between the Spheres'; Band, *Mittelschichten*, p. 37; Thums, 'Kracauer', p. 396.

49 SK, *Der Detektiv-Roman*, in *Werke* 1, p. 117.

50 Kracauer first described his 'spheres' in a letter to Margarete Susman, dated 22 June 1922, as 'the spheres of the highest reality, the middle reality, and of having sunk out of reality'.

51 Transl. note: The German 'Unwesen' can mean a 'monstrous state of affairs' or 'dreadfulness', as in phrases such as 'sein Unwesen treiben', which means roughly 'to carry out dreadful or monstrous deeds', 'to wreak havoc'. In the present context, however, the literal meaning – 'Un-Wesen', something in which any essence has been negated, any meaning is absent – is clearly also intended.

52 SK, *Der Detektiv-Roman*, in *Werke* 1, pp. 107 and 118.

53 Kracauer to Leo Löwenthal, 2 November 1924, in Löwenthal/Kracauer, *In steter Freundschaft*, p. 65.

54 SK, *Der Detektiv-Roman*, in *Werke* 1, pp. 144 and 147.

55 See the personal dedications in the Kierkegaard volumes, Kracauer Library, Marbach.

56 For a comparison of *The Detective Novel* and Benjamin's *The Origin of German Tragic Drama*, see Mack, 'Literature and Theory'.

57 Brodersen, *Benjamin: A Biography*, pp. 114–17; Benjamin, *Briefe an Siegfried Kracauer*, p. 10; Walter Benjamin to Gerhard Scholem, 7 July 1924, in Benjamin, *Correspondence 1910–1940*, pp. 245f.

58 The German title of Benjamin's study is *Ursprung des deutschen Trauerspiels*. The term 'Trauerspiel' is also colloquially used to mean 'a sorry state of affairs'.

59 See Brodersen, *Benjamin: A Biography*, pp. 148–50; here: p. 149.
60 See Benjamin, *Origin*, p. 177: 'The undialectic neo-Kantian mode of thought is not able to grasp the synthesis which is reached in allegorical writing as a result of the conflict between theological and artistic intentions, a synthesis not so much in the sense of a peace as a *treuga des* between the conflicting opinions.' On the failed Habilitation project, see also Palmier, *Walter Benjamin*, pp. 344–8; Van Reijen and van Doorn, *Aufenthalte und Passagen*, pp. 80–2 and 86–7.
61 Arendt, 'Walter Benjamin', p. 8.
62 Benjamin, *Origin of German Tragic Drama*, pp. 27–9; here: p. 28.
63 Adorno, 'The Curious Realist', p. 161.
64 Adorno, 'Introduction to Benjamin's *Schriften*', p. 224.
65 Cf. Benjamin, 'Critique of Violence'; Honneth, 'Zur Kritik der Gewalt', p. 193.
66 'On Language as Such and on the Language of Man' (1916) and 'The Task of the Translator' (written 1921, published in 1923). Cf. Mosès, *The Angel of History*, pp. 65–7.
67 Kracauer to Leo Löwenthal, dated 31 August 1923 and 12 April 1924, in Löwenthal/Kracauer, *In steter Freundschaft*, pp. 46 and 54.
68 Walter Benjamin to Kracauer, dated 1 March 1924, in Benjamin, *Briefe an Siegfried Kracauer*, p. 9.
69 Cf. SK, *Der Detektiv-Roman*, in *Werke* 1, pp. 130–9. See also SK, 'The Hotel Lobby', p. 176.
70 Cf. Mülder, *Siegfried Kracauer*, pp. 43f.
71 SK, *Der Detektiv-Roman*, in *Werke* 1, pp. 208f.
72 Cf. Thums, 'Kracauer und die Detektive', p. 393.

7. Friendship (Part 3): Passion and the Path towards the Profane

1 Transl. note: 'Zeugendes Gespräch': 'zeugend' may mean 'creative' or 'procreative', but also 'bearing witness'.
2 SK, 'Das zeugende Gespräch' [The fruitful conversation], in *Werke* 5.1, pp. 604–11; here: p. 604.
3 Transl. note: 'Sich unterhalten': the straightforward meaning is 'to have a conversation'. However, 'unterhalten' can also mean 'to maintain' ('Unterhalt' is 'maintenance' or 'upkeep'), or to entertain ('Unterhaltung' can mean 'entertainment' as well as 'conversation').
4 Simmel, 'The Sociology of Sociability', p. 126 (transl. amended).
5 SK, 'Das zeugende Gespräch', in *Werke* 5.1, pp. 604–11; here: pp. 605–8.
6 Kracauer, *Georg*, p. 25 (transl. mod.).
7 Ibid., p. 28.
8 Kracauer, *Georg*, p. 29 (transl. mod.).
9 Ibid.
10 Ibid., p. 30.
11 Ibid.
12 Ibid., p. 125.
13 Ibid., p. 72.
14 Ibid., p. 126.
15 Ibid., p. 136.
16 Ibid.
17 Ibid., p. 137.

18 Ibid.
19 Ibid., pp. 138f.
20 Ibid., p. 212.
21 Ibid., pp. 212f.
22 Kracauer to Adorno, 5 April 1923, in Adorno/Kracauer, *Briefwechsel*, p. 9.
23 Transl. note: The 'Bergstraße' is an old trade route running in an almost straight north–south direction along the Odenwald, a low mountain range to the south of Frankfurt.
24 SK, 'Empfindsame Suite von der Bergstraße' [A sentimental suite about the Bergstraße], in *Werke* 5.1, pp. 630–4; here: pp. 630–3.
25 Kracauer to Margarete Susman, 20 January 1920.
26 Kracauer to Leo Löwenthal, 4 December 1921, in Löwenthal/Kracauer, *In steter Freundschaft*, p. 32.
27 Cf. Reinhard Pabst, *Theodor W. Adorno*.
28 As Kracauer wrote in a piece of travel writing for the feuilleton of the *FZ* (31 August 1924).
29 SK, 'Jenseits des Brenners', *Werke* 5.2, pp. 125–9; here: pp. 127f.
30 Kracauer to Adorno, 5 April 1923, in Adorno/Kracauer, *Briefwechsel*, p. 10.
31 Kracauer to Leo Löwenthal, 12 April 1924, in Löwenthal/Kracauer, *In steter Freundschaft*, p. 54.
32 Transl. note: From 1871 onwards, §175 of the German Criminal Code made homosexual acts between men illegal. It survived, in various forms, even after the end of the Second World War, and was finally abolished in 1994.
33 Adorno to Kracauer, 29 June 1925, in Adorno/Kracauer, *Briefwechsel*, p. 88.
34 Kracauer to Leo Löwenthal, 6 June 1924, in Löwenthal/Kracauer, *In steter Freundschaft*, p. 58.
35 Cf. Steinert, *Adorno in Wien*, pp. 7f.
36 Adorno to Kracauer, 29 June 1925, in Adorno/Kracauer, *Briefwechsel*, p. 85.
37 Cf. Morgenstern, *Alban Berg*, pp. 117–24.
38 Adorno to Kracauer, 10 June 1925, in Adorno/Kracauer, *Briefwechsel*, p. 77.
39 Kracauer to Adorno, 8 August 1925, in ibid., p. 106.
40 Adorno to Kracauer, 6 August 1925, in ibid., p. 104.
41 Adorno to Kracauer, 26 August 1925, in ibid., p. 111.
42 Cf. Foucault, *History of Sexuality*, vol. 2, pp. 193–9.
43 Kracauer to Leo Löwenthal, 6 June 1924, 28 and 29 July 1924, 16 September 1924, in Löwenthal/Kracauer, *In steter Freundschaft*, pp. 57, 59 and 61.
44 Cf. *Marbacher Magazin*, p. 41.
45 SK, 'Jenseits des Brenners' [Beyond the Brenner], in *Werke* 5.2, pp. 125–9; here: p. 126.
46 SK, 'Zwischen den Zeiten' [Between the ages], in *Werke* 5.1, pp. 563f.; 'Protestantismus und moderner Geist' [Protestantism and the modern spirit], in *Werke* 5.2, pp. 51–5; 'Zur religiösen Lage in Deutschland' [On the religious situation in Germany], in *Werke* 5.2, pp. 154–9.
47 SK, 'Das Chaos als objektive Weltreligion' [Chaos as objective world religion], in *Werke* 5.2, p. 195.
48 SK, 'Hans Driesch', in *Werke* 5.2, pp. 254–61; here: p. 260.
49 SK, 'Philosophie der Gemeinschaft' [Philosophy of community], in *Werke* 5.2, pp. 148–54; here: pp. 148–50.

50 SK, 'Zum Tode Rudolf Steiners' [On the death of Rudolf Steiner], in
   Werke 5.2, pp. 228–32; here: pp. 230f.; SK, 'Der Künstler in dieser Zeit'
   [The artist in our times], in *Werke* 5.2, pp. 232–42; here: p. 233.
51 SK, 'Gestalt und Zerfall' [Form and disintegration], in *Werke* 5.2, pp.
   283–8; here: pp. 286–8.
52 On this, cf. Korta, *Geschichte als Projekt und Projektion*, pp. 130–7.

8. The Rebirth of Marxism in Philosophy

1 Cf. Eßbach, 'Radikalismus und Modernität', pp. 226–31; Niethammer,
   Kollektive Identität, pp. 136–40.
2 Quoted after Niethammer, *Kollektive Identität*. On the politicization of the
   intelligentsia, see Claussen, 'Blick zurück', p. 12.
3 Anderson, *Considerations on Western Marxism*, p. 6. And, agreeing with
   Anderson, Berlin, *Karl Marx*, pp. 28 and 37; Fetscher, *Marxismus*, pp. 43,
   46 and 49.
4 Lukács, *History and Class Consciousness*, p. 1.
5 Ibid., p. xliii.
6 Ibid.
7 Ibid., p. 10.
8 Deuteronomy 5:7, quoted after the King James Version.
9 Cf. Ryklin, *Kommunismus*; Lohmann, 'Kommunismus als Religion', p. 333.
10 Eßbach, *Marx*, and lecture by Detlev Claussen, 'Geschichte ohne
   Klassenbewusstsein', Hamburg, 11 June 2013.
11 Claussen, *Theodor Adorno*, pp. 82–4; Müller, *Das demokratische Zeitalter*,
   pp. 116–34; Jay, *Marxism and Totality*, pp. 81–127; Eßbach, 'Wer war
   Marx?', pp. 175–8; Lukács, *Verdinglichung* (introduction by the editors),
   p. 12; Henning, *Philosophie nach Marx*, pp. 11–14 and 286–302.
12 Cf. Claussen, 'Blick zurück', p. 17.
13 Cf. Claussen, *Theodor Adorno*, p. 83.
14 Cf. Arato and Breines, *The Young Lukács*, pp. 163–89; Claussen, *Theodor
   Adorno*, p. 84.
15 Cf., e.g., SK, 'Aus Zeitschriften' [From newspapers], in *Werke* 5.1, pp.
   651–5.
16 Cf. van Reijen and van Doorn, *Aufenthalte und Passagen*, p. 87.
17 Walter Benjamin to Gerhard Scholem, 16 September 1924, in *The
   Correspondence of Walter Benjamin, 1910–1940*, p. 247.
18 Cf. Palmier, *Walter Benjamin*, pp. 417–44; Lacis, *Revolutionär im Beruf*, pp.
   41–51; Moses, *The Angel of History*, p. 101.
19 Scholem, *Walter Benjamin*, p. 149 [transl. mod.]. See also Walter Benjamin
   to Gerhard Scholem, 16 September 1924, in Benjamin, *The Correspondence
   of Walter Benjamin, 1910–1940*, p. 247; Fuld, *Walter Benjamin*, p. 151;
   Witte, *Walter Benjamin*, p. 55.
20 This is how Benjamin himself referred to his dispatches to Scholem in a
   letter sent to him after his return from Capri on 22 December 1924, in *The
   Correspondence of Walter Benjamin, 1910–1940*, p. 257.
21 Walter Benjamin to Gerhard Scholem, 13 June 1924, in *The Correspondence
   of Walter Benjamin, 1910–1940*, p. 244.
22 Bloch, 'Aktualität und Utopie', pp. 615 and 621.
23 Lukács, *History and Class Consciousness*, p. 3.
24 We may draw this conclusion from a letter from Kracauer to Ernst Bloch

dated 27 May 1926 (in Bloch, *Briefe*, vol. 1, pp. 272–5) and from letters sent by Walter Benjamin to Kracauer dated 3 June and 17 June 1926 (in Benjamin, *Briefe an Siegfried Kracauer*, pp. 21–3 and 24f.).

25 Kracauer to Leo Löwenthal, 28 and 29 July 1924, in Löwenthal/Kracauer, *In steter Freundschaft*, pp. 59f.

26 Kracauer to Adorno, 16 April 1925, in Adorno/Kracauer, *Briefwechsel*, p. 47.

27 Kracauer to Ernst Bloch, 27 May and 29 June 1926, in *Briefe*, vol. 1, pp. 272 and 282f.

28 Adorno to Kracauer, 17 June 1925, in Adorno/Kracauer, *Briefwechsel*, pp. 79f.

29 As Kracauer said about the dialectical materialism of Deborin. Cf. SK, 'Marx-Engels-Archiv', in *Werke* 5.2, pp. 405–8; here: pp. 406f.

9. Kracauer Goes to the Movies: A Medium for the Masses and a Medium for Modernity

1 Kracauer, *Theory of Film*, p. xi.

2 Cf. Worschech, 'Die "lebende Photographie" in Frankfurt'.

3 Cf. Peukert, *Die Weimarer Republik*, p. 171; Kaes, 'Filmgeschichte als Kulturgeschichte', pp. 60–2; Kreimeier, *Traum und Exzess*, p. 11; more recently Hansen, in *Cinema and Experience*, has called it 'the medium of a disintegrating world' (p. 3).

4 Wehler, *Deutsche Gesellschaftsgeschichte*, pp. 234f.; Maase, 'Die soziale Konstruktion der Massenkünste', p. 271.

5 Kaes, 'Film in der Weimarer Republik', p. 39.

6 Ufa stands for Universum-Film Aktiengesellschaft, founded 18 December 1917.

7 Cf. Kreimeier, *Die Ufa-Story*, pp. 13–15; Barbian, 'Politik und Film', pp. 216 and 221–9; Korte, 'Vom Kinematographen zur Nationalen Propaganda', p. 69.

8 Prokop once called this an 'oligopol', using neo-Marxist language; cf. Prokop, *Soziologie des Films*, p. 47.

9 Cf. ibid., p. 46 and Laqueur, *Weimar*, p. 230f.

10 The figures differ from author to author; see Saldern, 'Massenfreizeitkultur', p. 21 (who gives the largest figure); Kaes, 'Film in der Weimarer Republik', p. 62; Hake, *Film in Deutschland*, p. 96. Cf. also Wehler, *Deutsche Gesellschaftsgeschichte*, pp. 480–3; Laqueur, *Weimar*, pp. 230f.

11 Cf. Korte, *Vom Kinematographen zur Nationalen Propaganda*, pp. 17f.

12 Transl. note: Freud's famous work of 1930, *Das Unbehagen in der Kultur*, has been translated into English, correctly, as *Civilization and Its Discontents*. Freud is not concerned with high (or low) culture in the modern sense, but with what you might call the self-domestication of man.

13 Sigmund Freud, *Civilization and Its Discontents*, p. 36.

14 Cf. König, *Zivilisation und Leidenschaft*; Weitz, *Weimar Germany*, p. 259. For Freud's analysis of culture, see his *Civilization and Its Discontents*.

15 Quoted after Kaes, *Shell Shock Cinema*, p. 224 (n. 51). Kracauer wrote about Stapel's anti-Semitism in 'Aus "völkischen" Kulturbezirken' [From 'völkisch' cultural areas], in *Werke* 5.2, pp. 607–9.

16 Cf. Heller, 'Massenkultur und ästhetische Urteilskraft', pp. 38f.; Happel and Michaelis, 'Wem gehört die Welt?', pp. 93–102.

17 Cf. Iske, *Die Film- und Rundfunkpolitik*; this title also contains S. Nestriepke's text, 'Wege zu neuer Filmkultur', Berlin 1927. On the 'revolutionary' appropriation of film, cf. Hake, *Film in Deutschland*, pp. 100f.
18 Georg Simmel, 'The Metropolis and Mental Life', p. 48.
19 Georg Simmel, 'Exkurs über die Soziologie der Sinne', p. 727.
20 Walter Benjamin, *The Paris of the Second Empire in Baudelaire*, p. 39.
21 Cf. Hickethier, 'Medienkultur im Wandel'; Zischler, *Kafka geht ins Kino*, pp. 12–15.
22 Ernst Bloch, 'The Anxiety of the Engineer', p. 310.
23 Transl. note: In German the two titles only vary by one letter: 'Die Großstadt und das Geistesleben' and 'Die Großstadt und das Geisterleben'.
24 Quoted after Kaes, 'Film in der Weimarer Republik', p. 62; Ehrenburg, *Die Traumfabrik*.
25 Cf. the anthology by Kaes, *Kino-Debatte*; the examples referred to are on pp. 37–9, 72–5, 133f. and 153–5.
26 Cf. Witte, 'Das Alte und das Neue', p. 10; Diederich's postscript in: Balázs, *Der sichtbare Mensch*, pp. 115–47; Schlüpmann, 'Der Gang ins Kino' p. 268.
27 Cf. Heller, 'Massenkultur und ästhetische Urteilskraft', pp. 34–7.
28 See Diderich's postscript in Balázs, *Der sichtbare Mensch*, p. 142.
29 Balázs, *Early Film Theory*, p. 5.
30 Ibid., pp. 9–13.
31 Ibid., p. 11.
32 Ibid., p. 13.
33 Ibid., p. 84.
34 Ibid., p. 4.
35 SK, 'Kleine Schriften zum Film' [Short writings on film], in *Werke* 6.1, pp. 9–12, and Kracauer, *From Caligari to Hitler*, pp. 57–60 and 125–8.
36 Transl. note: The (pejorative) term 'Tendenzfilm' marked a category of films that used stock characters and perspectives for propaganda and ideological purposes.
37 The quotations are taken from Roth, *Drei Sensationen*, pp. 11–15 and 36.
38 Ibid., p. 46.
39 Ibid., p. 158.
40 Cf. Prinzler, *Sirens & Sinners*, p. 45; Laqueur, *Weimar*, pp. 240–2.
41 Cf. Kaes, 'Film in der Weimarer Republik', pp. 60f.
42 SK, 'Die Straße' [The street] and 'Ein Film' [A film], in *Werke* 6.1, pp. 54–6 and 56–8: here: pp. 56f.
43 Transl. note: 'Entformen', literally 'to de-shape': Kracauer suggests that the powers ultimately remove all shape and form.
44 SK, 'Filmbild und Prophetenrede' [Film image and prophet's speech], in *Werke* 6.1, pp. 138–40; here: pp. 138f.
45 SK, 'Der letzte Mann', in *Werke* 6.1, pp. 119–22; here: p. 121.
46 Kreimeier, *Die Ufa-Story*, p. 171.
47 SK, 'Der letzte Mann', in *Werke* 6.1, pp. 119–22; here: p. 120. On the film, see Sadoul, *Geschichte der Filmkunst*, pp. 158–60. On the camera technique, see Kaes, 'Film in der Weimarer Republik', p. 58; Elsaesser, *Weimar Cinema*, p. 232.
48 Roth, *Drei Sensationen*, p. 137.
49 SK, 'Wetter und Retter' [Weather and saviour], in *Werke* 6.1, pp. 43f.; here: p. 43.
50 SK, 'Der verlorene Schuh' [The lost shoe], in *Werke* 6.1, pp. 51f.; here: p. 52.

51 SK, 'Spannende Romane' [Exciting novels], in *Werke* 5.2, pp. 190–5; here: p. 191; 'Edelkitsch' [Pretentious kitsch], in ibid., pp. 401f.

10. At the Feuilleton of the *Frankfurter Zeitung*

1 *Marbacher Magazin*, pp. 37–42; Stalder, *Siegfried Kracauer*, p. 83.
2 Bütow, 'Große Eschenheimer Straße 31', in a special edition of *Gegenwart*, p. 39. According to Gillesen, the doors of the editorial offices of the politics section and the feuilleton were opposite one another, and it was the economics office that was further away. That would have been a fitting arrangement. Cf. Gillesen, *Auf verlorenem Posten*, p. 20.
3 Cf. the interview with Wickenburg in Todorow, *Das Feuilleton der 'Frankfurter Zeitung'*, pp. 170 and 188.
4 Joseph Roth to Bernhard von Brentano, 19 July 1925, in Roth, *A Life in Letters*, pp. 60f. (transl. mod.).
5 Transl. note: A group formed around the journal *Die Tat*, which was founded in 1909 by the freemason Ernst Horneffer to promote Nietzschean ideas. During the Weimar Republic it was critical of the state and adopted a right-wing nationalist position. It was eventually seized by the Nazis and used as a propaganda tool.
6 On Reifenberg's network, see Bussiek, *Benno Reifenberg*, pp. 159f.
7 Cf. the portrait of Geck in the special edition of *Gegenwart*, p. 32. Gillesen, however, suggests that Roth and Brentano mocked the 'Diebolde and Gecken'; cf. Gillesen, *Auf verlorenem Posten*, p. 65. [Transl. note: The joke relates to the family names Diebold and Geck. The suffix 'bold' usually suggests something negative, as in 'Trunkenbold' = drunkard, 'Lügenbold' = liar or 'Witzbold' = buffoon. 'Geck' also means 'fop', especially in the plural form.]
8 Todorow, *Das Feuilleton der 'Frankfurter Zeitung'*, p. 91; Gillesen, *Auf verlorenem Posten*, p. 65.
9 Cf. Stalder, *Siegfried Kracauer*, pp. 32–5; on the economic profile of the *FZ*, see Koszyk, *Deutsche Presse*, pp. 216–19.
10 Knoch and Morat, 'Medienwandel und Gesellschaftsbilder', pp. 19–27.
11 Cf. Schivelbusch, *Intellektuellendämmerung*, pp. 77–94.
12 Cf. Wehler, *Deutsche Gesellschaftsgeschichte*, pp. 478f.
13 Cf. Ernst Bloch to Kracauer, 16 May 1928, in Bloch, *Briefe*, vol. 1, pp. 303–5.
14 Cf. Schivelbusch, *Intellektuellendämmerung*, p. 56.
15 Cf. Habermas, *Structural Transformation of the Public Sphere*, pp. 27–31; here: p. 27; Peukert, *Die Weimarer Republik*, pp. 163–6. On the relation between the literary field, of which newspapers formed a part, and the field of power and the world of finance, see also Bourdieu, *The Rules of Art*, pp. 214–23 and 249–52.
16 Wickenburg in the interview conducted by Todorow, *Das Feuilleton der 'Frankfurter Zeitung'*, p. 169.
17 Cf. Despoix, *Ethiken der Entzauberung*, pp. 192–4.
18 Cf. Gillesen, *Auf verlorenem Posten*, p. 64.
19 Reifenberg in his programmatic article 'Gewissenhaft' [Conscientious] in *FZ*, 1 July 1929, quoted after Stalder, *Siegfried Kracauer*, p. 104.
20 Cf. Mülder-Bach, 'Der Umschlag der Negativität', p. 359.
21 Joseph Roth to Benno Reifenberg, 17 January 1928, in Roth, *Life in Letters*, p. 114.

22 On the ambiguities surrounding the concept of the feuilleton, see Todorow, *Das Feuilleton der 'Frankfurter Zeitung'*, p. 6.
23 Roth, 'Einbruch der Journalisten in die Nachwelt', in *Ich zeichne das Gesicht der Zeit*, pp. 229–32.
24 After his return to Vienna in 1918, Roth signed his articles vor *Vorwärts* with 'Der rote Joseph', playing on his surname and red as the colour associated with left-wing politics.
25 Joseph Roth to Benno Reifenberg, 22 April 1926, in Roth, *Life in Letters*, p. 78.
26 Cf. Stalder, *Siegfried Kracauer*, p. 96.
27 On the Angerstein case, cf. Stiegler (ed.), *Tat ohne Täter*, especially Stiegler's essay on Angerstein, the reports on the trial in *Frankfurter Zeitung*, the reports and commentaries by Paul Schlesinger in *Vossische Zeitung*, the expert opinions by Richard Herbertz and Kracauer's summary article 'Tat ohne Täter' [Deed without doer], in *FZ*, 13 July 1925, in *Werke* 5.2, pp. 272–7. Also Lethen, *Verhaltenslehren der Kälte*, pp. 256–62.
28 Quoted after Stiegler, *Tat ohne Täter*, pp. 7f.
29 Freud, *Totem and Taboo*, p. 54.
30 Cf. Lethen, *Verhaltenslehre der Kälte*, pp. 256f.
31 SK, 'Die Hosenträger' [Braces], in *Werke* 5.2, pp. 482–5; here: pp. 482 and 484.
32 Walter Benjamin to Kracauer, 20 April 1926, in Benjamin, *Briefe an Siegfried Kracauer*, p. 17.
33 Transl. note: 'Mittelgebirge', usually translated as 'low mountain range'. Here, 'middling' is chosen to retain Kracauer's play on the social and physical meaning of 'Mittel-': 'Mittelstand' and 'Mittelgebirge'.
34 Transl. note: 'Alles liegt.' The German does not carry the meaning of 'telling lies'. Kracauer merely highlights the excessive, conventional use of a metaphor.
35 SK, 'Das Mittelgebirge' [Lower mountain ranges], in *Werke* 5.2, pp. 506–8; here: pp. 506f.

11. Inflation and Journeys into Porosity

1 Kracauer, *Georg*, p. 129.
2 Weber, *Economy and Society*, p. 389.
3 Cf. Simmel, *The Philosophy of Money* (1978 [1900]), and Herbert, *Geschichte Deutschlands*, p. 204.
4 Cf. Martin Geyer, *Verkehrte Welt*.
5 Cf. Peukert, *Die Weimarer Republik*, pp. 71–6; Wehler, *Deutsche Gesellschaftsgeschichte*, pp. 248f.; Herbert, *Geschichte Deutschlands*, pp. 201–13.
6 Cf. Claussen, *Theodor W. Adorno*, pp. 85f.; Münster, *Ernst Bloch*, p. 140.
7 Cf. Palmier, *Walter Benjamin*, pp. 317–20.
8 Hedwig to Siegfried Kracauer, 8 June 1930.
9 The term 'sozial freischwebende Intellektuelle', literally 'free-floating intellectuals', was coined by Alfred Weber and Karl Mannheim and intended to express the fact that intellectuals stood above social classes and that their thinking did not depend on their social background, which most often was bourgeois and rarely proletarian. Cf. Weber, 'Die Not der geistigen Arbeiter'; Mannheim, *Ideology and Utopia*, pp. 127–41. [Transl. note: in the passage from Mannheim referred to here, 'socially unattached' and 'unattachedness' rather than 'free-floating' is used.]

10 Cf. Palmier, *Walter Benjamin*, pp. 326–30; Brodersen, *Benjamin: A Biography*, pp. 120–3.
11 Benjamin, *Correspondence*, p. 216. Cf. Palmier, *Walter Benjamin*, p. 349; Wizisla, *Benjamin und Brecht*, p. 11.
12 Cf. Weber, 'Die Not der geistigen Arbeiter'.
13 Transl. note: 'Der Tausch täuscht das Bewusstsein'. Exchange and deception, in German, have a common etymological root. Sohn-Rethel's theory of exchange abstraction postulates that the assumptions implicit in the act of exchange (such as unchanging substance, abstract quantities, separation of use and exchange value, etc.) become transcendental categories of the understanding. Those who carry coins (embodying the pure commodity form) in their pockets, he says, will also carry certain abstractions in their heads, without necessarily being aware of them.
14 Cf. Hörisch, 'Die Krise des Bewusstseins', pp. 15 and 20–30. Alfred Weber's reaction to these ideas was: 'Sohn-Rethel is bonkers'.
15 Quoted after Freytag, 'Alfred Sohn-Rethel', pp. 46f. [Transl. note: the expression 'intellektuelles Wanderproletariat' is from a review of 'Jacob Job, Neapel. Reisebilder und Skizzen', in Benjamin GS III, pp. 132–5; here: p. 133. For the remainder of the passage, see Benjamin, *Correspondence*, p. 240.]
16 Cf. Brodersen, *Benjamin: A Biography*, p. 136. On the role of travels in Benjamin's work, see Palmier, *Walter Benjamin*, pp. 348–61.
17 Transl. note: Bertolt Brecht, 'changing our country more frequently than our shoes' ('öfter als die Schuhe die Länder wechselnd'). From the poem 'To Those Born Later' ('An die Nachgeborenen'), in *Poems*, pp. 318–20; here: p. 320.
18 Ernst Bloch to Kracauer, 4 October 1929, in Bloch, *Briefe*, vol. 1, p. 317.
19 Cf. Münster, *Ernst Bloch*, p. 137.
20 Cf. Markun, *Ernst Bloch*, pp. 36–8, where the passage can be found. [Transl. note: The quotation is from *Tübinger Einleitung in die Philosophie*, pp. 49f.]
21 Cf. in particular Kracauer's letter to Adorno, dated 8 August 1925, in Adorno/Kracauer, *Briefwechsel*, pp. 105–7.
22 Adorno to Berg, 12 September 1925, in *Adorno and Berg: Correspondence*, p. 14 (transl. mod.).
23 Mittelmeier, *Adorno in Neapel*, p. 34.
24 Adorno to Kracauer, 19 August 1925, in Adorno/Kracauer, *Briefwechsel*, p. 111.
25 Cf. Mittelmeier, *Adorno in Neapel*, p. 38.
26 Benjamin and Lacis, 'Naples', p. 168.
27 Cf. Bloch, 'Italy and Porosity' (1925), in *Literary Essays*, pp. 450–7; here: pp. 455f.; Brodersen, *Benjamin: A Biography*, pp. 136–42; Mittelmeier, *Adorno in Neapel*, p. 17; van Reijen and van Doorn, *Aufenthalte und Passagen*, pp. 88f.; after Kracauer's return to Germany, Sohn-Rethel published his article in the *FZ*: 'Ideal des Kaputten' (21 March 1926); it has more recently been published in Sohn-Rethel, *Das Ideal des Kaputten*; see pp. 41f.
28 Kracauer to Arthur Rosenheimer, 19 November 1944.
29 Cf. Mittelmeier, *Adorno in Neapel*, p. 86.
30 SK, 'Felsenwahn in Positano' [Rocky delusions in Positano], in *Werke* 5.2, pp. 296–303, quotations passim.
31 Adorno to Berg, 15 October 1925, in *Adorno and Berg: Correspondence*, p. 20.

12. Transitional Years: Economic Upturn, Revolt, Enlightenment

1 SK, 'Vom Institut für Sozialforschung' [News about the Institute for Social Research], in *Werke* 5.1, pp. 724–6; here: p. 726.
2 Wiggershaus, *The Frankfurt School*, pp. 24–36.
3 Cf. Zinfert, *Kracauer*, pp. 79–85.
4 SK, 'Die Revuen', in *Werke* 5.2, pp. 313–17; here: p. 313.
5 Transl. note: The German 'Abwechslung' and 'Zerstreuung' both refer to anything that takes the mind and perception off their routines. In the case of 'Zerstreuung' the emphasis is literally on the 'dispersal' of attention, without necessarily implying that the mind is distracted from something on which it should be focused. 'Unterhaltung', entertainment, and 'Abwechslung' and 'Zerstreuung' belong together. In the following, the dimension of 'dispersal' in 'distraction' (for 'Zerstreuung') should be kept in mind.
6 Kracauer, 'Cult of Distraction', pp. 327f. Löffler, *Verteilte Aufmerksamkeit*, concentrates exclusively on Kracauer's positive associations with dispersal.
7 SK, 'Ein Dokument der Zeit' [A document of the times], in *Werke* 5.2, pp. 521–4; here: pp. 521–3.
8 This is the view of Brodersen, *Siegfried Kracauer*, p. 50.
9 Cf. Handelman, 'The Forgotten Conversation', p. 235. Buber had been pursuing the plan since 1914; on the prehistory, see Lesch and Lesch, 'Verbindungen zu einer anderen Frankfurter Schule', p. 186; Jay, 'Politics of Translation'. Thirty-five years later, Buber completed the translation on his own.
10 Kracauer, 'The Bible in German', in *The Mass Ornament*, pp. 189–201; here: pp. 201 and 195. Buber's *I and Thou* and Rosenzweig's *Das dialogische Denken*. Review and underlining in the book. On Buber's concept of reality, see Lesch and Lesch, 'Verbindungen zu einer anderen Frankfurter Schule', pp. 171–82.
11 Kracauer, 'The Bible in German', in *The Mass Ornament*, pp. 189–201; here: p. 196.
12 Buber and Rosenzweig, 'Die Bibel auf Deutsch' [The Bible in German].
13 Quoted after Lesch and Lesch, 'Verbindungen zu einer anderen Frankfurter Schule', p. 183.
14 Cf. Kracauer to Leo Löwenthal, 4 December 1921, in Löwenthal/Kracauer, *In steter Freundschaft*, pp. 31–4. On Susman's perspective, see Lesch and Lesch, 'Verbindungen zu einer anderen Frankfurter Schule', pp. 187f.
15 Margarete Susman to Kracauer, 22 March 1926.
16 Ernst Simon to Kracauer, 7 May 1926, in Simon, *Sechzig Jahre*, pp. 50–4.
17 Cf. Jay, 'Politics of Translation', p. 18.
18 Benjamin, 'The Task of the Translator', p. 256.
19 Mosès, *The Angel of History*, especially pp. 68f. and 101f.
20 Walter Benjamin to Kracauer, 13 April, 13 May and 15 July 1926, in Benjamin, *Briefe an Siegfried Kracauer*, pp. 15, 20f. and 27. In a letter to Scholem, Benjamin mentions a conversation with Kracauer on the subject, prior to the publication of the review; Kracauer, he wrote, incorporated some of the things he had said in the article: Walter Benjamin to Gerhard Scholem, 29 May 1926, in *Benjamin: Correspondence*, p. 303.
21 This was Bloch's retrospective interpretation; cf. *Tagträume vom aufrechten Gang*, p. 47.
22 Ernst Bloch to Kracauer, 20 May 1926, in Bloch, *Briefe*, vol. 1, pp. 269f.
23 Kracauer to Ernst Bloch, 27 May 1925, in ibid., pp. 272 and 275.

24 See Kracauer's articles 'Lad and Bull', in *The Mass Ornament*, pp. 33–4; here: p. 34; 'Two Planes', in *The Mass Ornament*, pp. 37–9; here: p. 39; 'Stehbars im Süden' [Standing only bars in the South], in *Werke* 5.2, pp. 468–74. See also Walter Benjamin's letter to Kracauer of 5 November 1926, in which he thanks him for the 'beautiful, rich travel harvest', and mentions the places and events he recognized in the articles, in Benjamin, *Briefe an Siegfried Kracauer*, pp. 33f.

25 Cf. ibid., and Benjamin, 'Marseille', pp. 211 and 213 (transl. mod.).

26 Cf. Agard, 'Siegfried Kracauers Verhältnis zur jüdischen Identität', p. 349.

27 Kracauer to Ernst Bloch, 27 May 1925, in Bloch, *Briefe*, vol. 1, pp. 273f. Barnouw, however, is right to point out that even in the heyday of the friendship, Lukács still stood between Bloch and Kracauer. Cf. Barnouw, *Critical Realism*, p. 27.

28 Ernst Bloch to Kracauer, 6 June 1926, in Bloch, *Briefe*, vol. 1, p. 276.

29 Kracauer to Ernst Bloch, 29 June 1926, in ibid., pp. 280–4; here: pp. 280f.

30 Ernst Bloch to Kracauer, 28 September 1927, in ibid., p. 286.

31 Kracauer to Ernst Bloch, early January 1928, in ibid., pp. 288f.

32 In the end, the essay was not included.

33 Cf. Becker, 'Philosophie unterm Strich', pp. 13f.

34 Cf. the letters by Walter Benjamin to Kracauer, 17 February 1926, March 1926, 20 April 1926, 3 June 1926, 4 March 1927, in Benjamin, *Briefe an Siegfried Kracauer*, pp. 13f.; here: pp. 17, 23 and 40.

35 See Kracauer, 'The Mass Ornament', in *The Mass Ornament*, pp. 75–86.

36 Ibid., pp. 75, 79, 84 and 86. Cf. also Brodersen, *Siegfried Kracauer*, pp. 47–55; Mülder-Bach, 'Der Umschlag der Negativität'; Honneth, 'Der destruktive Realist', pp. 132–42; Hedwig to Siegfried Kracauer, 29 April 1930.

13. The Primacy of the Optical: Architecture, Images of Space, Films

1 Adolf Loos, 'Ornament and Crime', pp. 20 and 24.

2 Quoted after von Moos, 'Le Corbusier and Adolf Loos', p. 19.

3 Le Corbusier, *Towards a New Architecture*, p. 107.

4 Ibid., p. 7 (transl. mod.).

5 Quoted after Gay, *Modernism*, p. 315.

6 See ibid., pp. 281–311 and Gay, *Weimar Culture*, pp. 70–101.

7 See Gay, *Modernism*, p. 300.

8 SK, 'Stuttgarter Kunst-Sommer' [Summer of art in Stuttgart], in *Werke* 5.2, pp. 94–105.

9 See Holste, 'Kracauer als Vermittler', pp. 113–27.

10 SK, 'Stuttgarter Kunst-Sommer', in *Werke* 5.2, pp. 94–105; here: pp. 100 and 102.

11 SK, 'Die Tagung des Deutschen Werkbundes' [The congress of the German Werkbund], 'Das neue Bauen' [The new way of building], in *Werke* 5.2, pp. 106–12 and 632–40; here: pp. 108 and 637.

12 SK, 'Der Wettbewerb "Hauptzollamt"' [The competition for the 'main customs office'], in ibid., pp. 441–4, 'Deutsche Bauausstellung' [German building exhibition], in *Werke* 5.3, pp. 521–7. See also von Arburg, '"Zweck-Architekturen der Verwesung"'.

13 See Kracauer, 'Cult of Distraction: On Berlin's Picture Palaces', in *The Mass Ornament*, pp. 323–8; here: p. 352 (fn. 50).

14 Ibid., p. 323.
15 See Bernd Witte's postscript in Hessel, *Spazieren in Berlin*, p. 226 and the introduction by Moritz Reininghaus. See also Stalder, 'Hieroglyphen-Entzifferung', pp. 133–4. [Transl. note: Hessel's book recently appeared in English as *Walking in Berlin: A Flaneur in the Capital*.]
16 SK, 'Berliner Landschaft' [Berlin landscape], in *Werke* 5.3, pp. 700–2; here: p. 702.
17 See Stalder, 'Hieroglyphen-Entzifferung', p. 132; Stalder, *Siegfried Kracauer*, p. 274; Zohlen, 'Schmugglerpfad', pp. 338–41.
18 Kracauer, 'Analysis of a City Map', in *The Mass Ornament*, pp. 41–4; here: p. 44.
19 SK, 'La ville de Malakoff', in *Werke* 5.2, pp. 537–40; here: pp. 537 and 540.
20 SK, 'Erinnerung an eine Pariser Straße' [Recollection of a street in Paris], in *Werke* 5.3, pp. 358–64; here: pp. 359 and 363–4.
21 Cf. Walter Benjamin, 'Paris, the Capital of the Nineteenth Century (1935)', in *The Arcades Project*, pp. 3–13, and Rolf Tiedemann's 'Dialectics at a Standstill', ibid., pp. 929–45.
22 SK, 'Straße ohne Erinnerung' [Street without memory], in *Werke* 5.4, pp. 312–16; here: p. 316.
23 Kracauer, 'Farewell to the Linden Arcade', in *The Mass Ornament*, pp. 337–42; here: pp. 338 and 342.
24 SK, 'Über Arbeitsnachweise' [On work registries], in *Werke* 5.3, pp. 249–57; here: pp. 249–50 and 254.
25 See Gerwin Zohlen, 'Schmugglerpfad'.
26 See Schöttker, 'Siegfried Kracauer', p. 125.
27 Kracauer, 'Photography', in *The Mass Ornament*, pp. 47–63; here: p. 50.
28 Ibid., p. 61.
29 See Mülder-Bach, 'Der Umschlag der Negativität', pp. 370–3.
30 Benjamin, 'Short History of Photography', in *Selected Writings*, vol. 2, Cambridge, MA: Belknap, 1999, pp. 507–30; here: p. 512.
31 Cf. Schöttker, 'Siegfried Kracauer', p. 134.
32 SK, 'Bücher vom Film' [Books on film], in *Werke* 6.1, pp. 370–4; here: pp. 371–2.
33 Kracauer, *Georg*, pp. 259–60.
34 Sadoul, *Geschichte der Filmkunst*, p. 141.
35 Cf. Roth, *Meine Reise zu Chaplin*, p. 10.
36 Kluge, *Das fünfte Buch*, p. 206.
37 Philippe Soupault, quoted after Benjamin, 'Chaplin in Retrospect', p. 222.
38 SK, 'Chaplin', in *Werke* 6.1, pp. 269–70.
39 SK, 'Chaplin', in *Werke* 6.2, pp. 32–5; here: p. 33.
40 Kracauer, 'Two Chaplin Sketches' ('City Lights'), p. 116.
41 SK, 'Chaplin kommt an!' [Chaplin arrives!], in *Werke* 6.2, pp. 468–70; here: p. 469.
42 SK, 'Die Jupiterlampen brennen weiter' [The lamps of Jupiter continue to burn], in *Werke* 6.1, pp. 234–7; here: p. 234. Cf. Sadoul, *Geschichte der Filmkunst*, pp. 182–90; Gregor and Patalas, *Geschichte des Films*, pp. 105–13; Korte, *Film und Realität*, pp. 33–43. On montage and Pudovkin, see SK, 'Bücher vom Film', in *Werke* 6.2, pp. 118–21.
43 Bulgakowa, 'Russische Filme'.
44 Cf. Rother, 'In Deutschland entschiedener Erfolg'; Bulgakowa, 'Russische Filme', pp. 83–7.
45 Walter Benjamin, 'Reply to Oscar A.H. Schmitz', p. 17.

46 Roth, *Drei Sensationen*, pp. 175–80; here: p. 179.
47 SK, 'Die Mutter' [Mother], in *Werke* 6.1, pp. 334–6; here: p. 335.
48 SK, 'Der Eisenstein-Film' [Eisenstein films], in *Werke* 6.2, pp. 85–8; here: pp. 85–6.
49 SK, 'Sturm über Asien' [Storm over Asia], in ibid., pp. 191–5; here: p. 192.
50 Transl. note: An allusion to the game 'battleships', called 'Schiffeversenken' [to sink ships] in German.
51 See Kracauer's articles between 1926 and 1932: 'Friedrich der Große im Film' [Frederick the Great in films], in *Werke* 6.1, pp. 202–3; 'Leutnants und Liebe' [Lieutenants and love], in ibid., p. 259; 'Volk in Not' [A people in need], in ibid., pp. 272–3; 'Ein Marinefilm' [A navy film], in ibid., p. 273; 'Die versunkene Flotte' [The sunken fleet], in ibid., pp. 276–7; 'Der Emden-Film' [The Emden-film], in ibid., pp. 330–1; 'Mein Heidelberg ...' [My Heidelberg...], in ibid., p. 384; 'Primanerliebe' [High school love], in ibid., pp. 385–6; 'Der alte Fritz' [The old Fritz], in ibid., p. 430; 'Sechs Mädchen suchen Nachtquartier' [Six girls in search of a place for the night], in *Werke* 6.2, pp. 82–3; 'Der Faschingsprinz' [The carnival prince], in ibid., p. 228; 'Harry Piel', in ibid., pp. 229–30; 'Hans Albers als Don Juan' [Hans Albers as Don Juan], in ibid., p. 335; 'Ein Film nach ihrem Herzen' [A film after her heart], in ibid., p. 430; 'Der bejubelte Fridericus Rex' [The cheered Fridericus Rex], in ibid., pp. 430–4; 'Kunst und Dekoration' [Art and decoration], in ibid., pp. 551–2.
52 Kracauer, 'The Little Shopgirls Go to the Movies', in *The Mass Ornament*, pp. 291–304; here: p. 292 [original title 'Film und Gesellschaft' (Film and society), renamed in the 1963 collection of essays published by Suhrkamp, *Das Ornament der Masse*. The English translation follows the titles in that collection]. See also Kaes, 'Film in der Weimarer Republik', p. 78.
53 Kracauer, 'The Little Shopgirls Go to the Movies', in *The Mass Ornament*, pp. 291–304; here: p. 292.
54 Schröter, 'Weltzerfall und Rekonstruktion', pp. 36–7.
55 Kracauer, 'Film 1928', in *The Mass Ornament*, pp. 307–20; here: pp. 307 and 320.
56 SK, 'Bücher vom Film', in *Werke* 6.1, pp. 370–4; SK, 'Abstrakter Film' [Abstract film], in *Werke* 6.2, pp. 46–9.
57 SK, 'Wir schaffens' [We can do it], in *Werke* 6.1, pp. 411–13.
58 SK, 'Tonbildfilm' [Films with sound], in *Werke* 6.2, pp. 122–5; 'Über den Tonfilm' [On sound film], in ibid., pp. 434–6.
59 SK, 'Film-Hochsaison' [Peak season for film], in ibid., pp. 458–62.
60 SK, 'Realistische Lösung' [A realist solution], in *Werke* 6.3, pp. 97–9; here: p. 99.

14. Ginster, Georg and the Salaried Masses

1 Adorno, 'The Curious Realist', p. 171.
2 Cf. Günter, *Anatomie des Anti-Subjekts*.
3 Cf. Oschmann, *Auszug aus der Innerlichkeit*.
4 Kracauer, 'The Biography as an Art Form of the New Bourgeoisie', in *The Mass Ornament*, pp. 101–5. On the discussions surrounding the crisis of the novel, see Oschmann, *Auszug aus der Innerlichkeit*, pp. 91–2.
5 Joachim Maass, *Kölnische Zeitung* (19 July 1931), quoted after *Marbacher Magazin*, pp. 55–6.

6 Thomas Mann, *Bücherliste*, quoted after Mülder, *Siegfried Kracauer*, pp. 125–45; here: p. 133. Oschmann, *Auszug aus der Innerlichkeit*, pp. 11–17; Günter, *Anatomie des Anti-Subjekts*, pp. 9–12; Sieg, *The Ordinary in the Novel of German Modernism*, pp. 8–24; Winkler, *Über Siegfried Kracauers Roman Ginster*, pp. 298–301.

7 Cf. Inka Mülder-Bach's postscript and editorial note in *Werke* 7, pp. 648–54. 'Das Fest im Frühling' (1913), 'Die Gnade' (1913), 'Der Gast' (1926) in ibid., pp. 519–600. See also Inka Mülder-Bach, *Siegfried Kracauer*, pp. 126–7 and 132–3.

8 Kracauer to Max Tau, 13 May 1961.

9 Cf. Witte, 'Helle Trauer', pp. 307–10.

10 Cf. SK, 'Sibirien – Paris mit Zwischenstationen' [Siberia – Paris with stopovers], in *Werke* 5.2, pp. 704–7; here: pp. 704–6.

11 As Joseph Roth wrote to Benno Reifenberg; cf. *Marbacher Magazin*, p. 48.

12 Transl. note: The 'Börsenblatt' is a periodical published by the Association of the German Book Trade.

13 Ernst Bloch to Kracauer, 15 January 1928, in Bloch, *Briefe*, vol. 1, pp. 290–3; here: pp. 290–1.

14 SK, 'Buster Keaton im Krieg' [Buster Keaton in the war], in *Werke* 6.1, pp. 338–40.

15 'Junge deutsche Erzählkunst', in Volk, *Siegfried Kracauer*, pp. 55–6.

16 *Berliner Tageblatt*, 23 December 1928, DLA, Mediendokumentation, Kasten 10. Franziska Herzfeld has drawn a further parallel, apart from those to Chaplin and Schwejk, to the comedian from Munich Karl Valentin.

17 Jay, 'The Extraterritorial Life of Siegfried Kracauer', p. 197. On 'Ginsterism', see also Lau, 'Ginsterismus'.

18 Alban Berg to Kracauer, 31 December 1928.

19 Bermann Fischer to Kracauer, 9 October 1929.

20 See SK, 'Pariser Beobachtungen' [Observations in Paris] and 'Das Straßenvolk in Paris' [The people of the streets in Paris], in *Werke* 5.2, pp. 544–7 and 575–9.

21 SK, *Ginster*, in *Werke* 7, p. 252.

22 Cf. Mülder, *Siegfried Kracauer*, pp. 142–3.

23 Cf. Schröter, 'Weltzerfall und Rekonstruktion'.

24 Cf. Biebl, *Betriebsgeräusch Normalität*, pp. 81–136.

25 *Marbacher Magazin*, p. 50; Helms, 'Kolumbus', p. 77.

26 Cf. Kocka, *Die Angestellten*, pp. 12–63 and 126–40.

27 Cf. Band, *Mittelschichten und Massenkultur*, pp. 126–40. Kracauer praised Suhr's book as an 'important supplement' to his work and was on friendly terms with the Suhrs; cf. SK, 'Weibliche Angestellte' [Female employees], in *Werke* 5.3, pp. 295–7.

28 Kracauer, *Salaried Masses*, p. 29. The *terra incognita*-remark in *History: The Last Things before the Last*, p. 4.

29 *Die Neue Rundschau* (August 1929), pp. 145–61.

30 On the crisis of proletarianization, see Kocka, *Die Angestellten*, pp. 163–4.

31 Kracauer, *Salaried Masses*, p. 27.

32 Mülder, *Siegfried Kracauer*, pp. 121–2.

33 Kracauer, *Salaried Masses*, p. 32.

34 Ibid., p. 70 (transl. mod.).

35 Ibid., pp. 88 and 64.

36 Ibid., pp. 38, 49 and 91.

37 Quoted after Band, *Mittelschichten und Massenkultur*, p. 144.
38 Kracauer, *Salaried Masses*, p. 32.
39 Cf. Band, *Mittelschichten und Massenkultur*, p. 145; Schröter, 'Weltzerfall und Rekonstruktion', pp. 33–4; Hofmann, 'Kritische Öffentlichkeit', pp. 91–5; Korta, *Geschichte*, pp. 143–6.
40 Cf. Mülder, *Siegfried Kracauer*, p. 125.
41 Kracauer to Adorno, 25 May 1930, in Adorno/Kracauer, *Briefwechsel*, pp. 214–17; here: p. 215.
42 Ibid., pp. 214f.
43 Ibid., p. 215 (transl. amended).
44 *Frankfurter Zeitung*, June 1930, and *Magazin der Wirtschaft*, 28 March 1930. Ludwig Marcuse also spoke positively about the book in the *Berliner Tageblatt*, 25 May 1930. The media reactions, including the articles mentioned below, are documented in DLA Marbach.
45 Karl Mannheim to Kracauer, 2 April 1930.
46 *Beamten-Gewerkschaft* (date not known) and *Arbeit und Wirtschaft*, 15 May 1930; *Der freie Angestellte*, no. 13, 1930; *Der leitende Angestellte*, no. 11, 1930; *Sozialwissenschaftliche Rundschau. Beilage zu den ärztlichen Mitteilungen*, 15 August 1931; *Zeitschrift der GdA*, no. 5, 1930; *Deutsche Handelswacht*, 10 February 1930. DLA Marbach, Mediendokumentation.
47 Brodersen, *Benjamin*, p. 159.
48 Transl. note: GmbH stands for 'Gesellschaft mit beschränkter Haftung', a limited company.
49 Cf. Schivelbusch, *Intellektuellendämmerung*, pp. 67–76; Gillesen, *Auf verlorenem Posten*, pp. 35–75.
50 Cf. Stalder, *Siegfried Kracauer*, p. 44.
51 Cf. ibid., pp. 32–53; Breidecker, 'Das Nizza von Frankfurt', p. 40.
52 Elisabeth Kracauer, 'Erklärung an eine deutsche Behörde' [Declaration for a German authority], 8 November 1963, quoted after Zinfert, *Kracauer*, p. 85.
53 Friedrich T. Gubler to Kracauer, 3 September 1935.
54 Adorno to Elisabeth Kracauer, 1 December 1966.
55 Quoted after Bloch, *Erbschaft dieser Zeit*, p. 33.
56 Hedwig to Siegfried Kracauer, 12 May 1930.
57 Benjamin, 'An Outsider Makes His Mark', pp. 305 and 310.

15. The Idea as Bearer of the Group: The Philosophical Quartet

1 Kracauer, 'On the Writings of Walter Benjamin', in *The Mass Ornament*, pp. 259–64; here: pp. 260, 262 and 264.
2 See Scholem, *Walter Benjamin*, p. 161.
3 Transl. note: The term 'Schatzkästlein' (treasure chest) is an allusion to Johann Peter Hebel's well-known *Schatzkästlein des Rheinischen Hausfreunds* (1811), a collection of anecdotes and short stories.
4 SK, 'Ernst Bloch', in *Werke* 5.3, pp. 527f.; here: p. 527.
5 Cf. *Marbacher Magazin*, p. 64.
6 SK, 'Weltstadtjugend? – Brünstiger Zauber!' [The youth of a cosmopolitan city? – Magic in heat!], in *Werke* 5.3, pp. 308–13; here: p. 312.
7 Kracauer to Joachim Günther, 1 April 1964.
8 Kracauer to Adorno, 1 April 1964, in Adorno/Kracauer, *Briefwechsel*, pp. 658f.

9 Elisabeth Kracauer to Löwenthal, 1 December 1969.
10 Adorno to Kracauer, 23/24 August 1926 and 2 September 1926, in Adorno/Kracauer, *Briefwechsel*, pp. 129–35; here: pp. 129 and 133.
11 Adorno to Kracauer, 2 September 1926 and 29 September 1927, in ibid., pp. 131–5 and 155–7.
12 Adorno to Kracauer, 17 September 1926, in ibid., pp. 135–40.
13 Adorno to Kracauer, 20 May 1927, in ibid., pp. 145–9.
14 Adorno to Kracauer, 26 May 1927 and 15 February 1928, in ibid., pp. 150–2 and 159–61; here: pp. 151 and 160.
15 Adorno to Kracauer, 15 February 1928, in ibid., pp. 159–61; here: p. 160.
16 Adorno to Kracauer, 14 September 1929, in ibid., pp. 189–92; here: p. 189.
17 Adorno to Kracauer, 4 March 1930, in ibid., p. 194f.; here: p. 195.
18 Adorno, *Kierkegaard*, p. 86.
19 Wiesengrund-Adorno, *Kierkegaard*; SK, 'Der enthüllte Kierkegaard' [Kierkegaard unveiled], in *Werke* 5.4, pp. 486–91. See also Raulet, 'Verfallenheit ans Objekt', who identifies the 'primacy of the object' as the common denominator not only of Adorno and Kracauer but of the whole group, mentioning Simmel as their inspiration.
20 Benjamin, 'Kierkegaard', pp. 704 and 703.
21 See Adorno in *Über Walter Benjamin*, pp. 9–15; Claussen, *Theodor W. Adorno*, p. 97. [Erinnerung [Recollections of Walter Benjamin] (1964), GS 20.1, p. 173.]
22 Walter Benjamin to Kracauer, 15 February 1928, in Benjamin, *Briefe an Siegfried Kracauer*, pp. 55f.; here: p. 56.
23 Adorno, 'The Handle, the Pot, and Early Experience', p. 212.
24 Stalder, *Siegfried Kracauer*, p. 273.
25 Cf. Schiller, 'Tod und Utopie', p. 27.
26 Cf. Palmier, *Walter Benjamin*, p. 369. Asja Lacis and Gretel Karplus also took part in the conversations on Marxism; see Scholem, *Walter Benjamin*, p. 201.
27 Adorno and Benjamin, *Correspondence*, p. 18; Scholem, *Walter Benjamin*, p. 241; Brodersen, *Walter Benjamin*, pp. 198–200.
28 Hedwig to Siegfried Kracauer, 17 May 1931.
29 Adorno to Kracauer, 29 May 1931, in Adorno/Kracauer, *Briefwechsel*, pp. 274–8; here: pp. 274f.
30 Kracauer to Adorno, 7 July 1931, in ibid., pp. 280–2; here: pp. 280f.
31 Benjamin to Adorno, 17 July 1931, in Adorno and Benjamin, *Correspondence*, pp. 8–10; here: pp. 8f. (transl. mod.).
32 Ibid., pp. 9f. The passage Benjamin had in mind and quotes in the letter is the following: 'The task of philosophy is not to search for concealed and manifest intentions of reality, but to interpret unintentional reality, in that, by the power of constructing figures, or images (*Bilder*), out of the isolated elements of reality, it negates (*aufhebt*) questions, the exact articulation of which is the task of science' (Adorno, 'The Actuality of Philosophy', p. 127).
33 Adorno to Kracauer, 19 July 1931, in Adorno/Kracauer, *Briefwechsel*, pp. 285–7; here: p. 286.
34 Cf. Stadler and Wielandt, *Gesammelte Welten*, p. 149.
35 Schopf (ed.), *Adorno und seine Frankfurter Verleger*, p. 265.
36 Adorno to Kracauer, 26 May 1930, in Adorno/Kracauer, *Briefwechsel*, pp. 218–21; here: p. 218.
37 Cf. Fleck, *Erfahrung und Tatsache*. See also the article on 'Denkstil' by

Nicolas Berg in *Enzyklopädie jüdischer Geschichte und Kultur*, vol. 2, pp. 94–100.

38 Cf. Claussen, *Theodor W. Adorno*, pp. 88f.; Schiller, 'Tod und Utopie', pp. 25–7.

39 Adorno to Kracauer, 6 August 1925, in Adorno/Kracauer, *Briefwechsel*, pp. 101–5; here: p. 104.

40 Münster, *Ernst Bloch*, p. 15.

41 Radkau, *Zeitalter der Nervosität*.

42 See Adorno, 'The Curious Realist', p. 172.

43 Kluge, *Das fünfte Buch*, p. 415.

44 Cf. Brodersen, *Walter Benjamin*, pp. 71–3; Münster, *Ernst Bloch*, p. 46.

45 Bloch, in *Über Benjamin*, pp. 16–23.

46 At least according to what Ernst Bloch wrote to Adorno, 18 March 1935, in Bloch, *Briefe*, vol. 2, pp. 434–6; here: p. 435.

47 Cf. Bloch, *Heritage of Our Times*, pp. 334–7; Scholem, *Walter Benjamin*, p. 224; *Tagträume vom aufrechten Gang*, p. 48; Ernst Bloch to Kracauer, 4 February 1928, summer and early autumn 1929, and 1 June 1932, in *Briefe*, vol. 1, pp. 195–7, 316–18 and 362–5; Fischer, 'Ein Geisterseher', pp. 111–15.

48 Claussen, *Adorno*, pp. 81f.

49 Isaac Deutscher, *Der nichtjüdische Jude*.

50 Dan Diner, oral communication.

51 Cf. Benjamin, *GS* II.3, pp. 838f.

52 Cf. von Haselberg, 'Wiesengrund-Adorno', p. 12; Adorno to Kracauer, 21 May 1925, in Adorno/Kracauer, *Briefwechsel*, p. 63.

53 On this, see also Scholem, *Walter Benjamin*, pp. 97f.

54 Claussen, *Adorno*, p. 54.

55 Cf. Aschheim, 'Icons beyond the Border', p. 96; Claussen, *Theodor W. Adorno*, pp. 101f.

56 *Neue Rundschau* 76 (1954) 1. This is the only sentence in this long article which Kracauer underlined.

57 Kracauer to Adorno, 1 August 1930, in Adorno/Kracauer, *Briefwechsel*, pp. 240f.

58 SK, 'Ansichtspostkarte' [Picture postcard], in *Werke* 5.3, pp. 241f.; here: p. 242.

59 Koeppen, *Romanisches Café*, pp. 7–11.

60 On the following, see Wizisla, *Benjamin und Brecht*, pp. 115–28 and 147–51.

61 See his ms. 'Das Lied der Seeräuber-Jenny in der "Dreigroschenoper" von 1929' (which remained unpublished at the time but was later included in *Bertolt Brechts Dreigroschenbuch: Texte, Materialien, Dokument* of 1960 [pp. 195–7]), and Knopf, *Brecht*, pp. 204f.

62 Bloch, *Heritage of Our Times*, pp. 225–8 and 276.

63 Kracauer to Gershom Scholem, 23 May 1965, and Scholem, *Walter Benjamin*, p. 208. In July 1934, Kracauer wrote to Ernst Bloch from Paris, saying Benjamin had departed 'to Denmark to see his God'; Kracauer to Ernst Bloch, 5 July 1934, in Bloch, *Briefe*, vol. 1, pp. 381f.

64 Arendt, *Benjamin*, p. 15.

65 Ibid., p. 11.

66 Arendt, 'Walter Benjamin', p. 14.

67 Arendt, *Benjamin, Brecht*, p. 21 (my transl., D.S.; this sentence is not in the English text).

68 Quoted after Wizisla, *Benjamin und Brecht*, p. 21 (my transl., D.S.; but see Wizisla, *Benjamin and Brecht*, p. xiv and p. 10. The remark is from Letter 60 of the Benjamin/Karplus correspondence: 'Gerade dir ist es ja keineswegs undeutlich, daß mein Leben so gut wie mein Denken sich in extremen Positionen bewegt.' [p. 156] The English edition renders this as: 'You of all people are by no means unaware that my life, like my thinking, is characterized by extremes' [p. 105]).

69 Ernst Bloch to Kracauer, 4 February 1928, in Bloch, *Briefe*, vol. 1, pp. 295–7; here: p. 295.

70 Kracauer to Ernst Bloch, 17 January 1928, in ibid., pp. 293–5; here: p. 293.

71 Ernst Bloch to Kracauer and Friedrich T. Gubler, 28 January 1931, in ibid., pp. 351f.

72 Ernst Bloch to Kracauer, 29 April 1931, in ibid., pp. 353–5; here: p. 353.

73 Ernst Bloch to Adorno, spring/summer 1931, in Bloch, *Briefe*, vol. 2, pp. 421f.

74 Fränze Herzfelde to Kracauer, 19 May 1932.

75 Ernst Bloch to Kracauer, 25 May 1932, in Bloch, *Briefe*, vol. 1, p. 357.

76 Kracauer to Ernst Bloch, 29 May 1932, in ibid., pp. 358–61; here: pp. 360f.

77 Ernst Bloch to Kracauer, 1 June 1932, in ibid., pp. 362–5; here: pp. 362–4.

78 Kracauer to Ernst Bloch, 4 June 1932, in ibid., pp. 365–8; here: pp. 365–7.

79 Ernst Bloch to Kracauer, 24 September 1932, in ibid., pp. 369–71; here: p. 370; Barnouw, *Critical Realism*, p. 46.

80 Kracauer to Bernhard Guttmann, 16 March 1931.

81 Kracauer to Friedrich T. Gubler, 12 June 1930.

16. Berlin circa 1930: In the Midst of the Political Melee

1 On the following, see Herbert, *Geschichte Deutschlands*, pp. 259–301; Peukert, *The Weimar Republic*, pp. 258–73; Diner, *Cataclysms*, pp. 106–52.

2 Transl. note: DVP = Deutsche Volkspartei [German people's party].

3 Herbert, *Geschichte Deutschlands*, pp. 300f.

4 Peukert, *The Weimar Republic*, pp. 251–5; here: p. 255.

5 Diner, *Cataclysms*, p. 152.

6 Kracauer to Adorno, 24 August 1930, in Adorno/Kracauer, *Briefwechsel*, p. 246.

7 Ibid., pp. 246f.

8 Ibid., p. 247.

9 Ernst Bloch to Kracauer, October/November 1930, in Bloch, *Briefe*, vol. 1, p. 347.

10 As Kracauer later told Max Tau, 13 May 1961.

11 Kracauer to Bernhard Guttmann, 16 March 1931.

12 SK, 'The Biography as an Art Form of the New Bourgeoisie', p. 102.

13 SK, 'Blick auf die Nachkriegsgeneration' [A look at the post-war generation], in ibid., pp. 364–71; here: pp. 367f. and 371.

14 SK, 'Instruktionsstunde in Literatur' [Lesson of instruction in literature], in ibid., pp. 503–6; here: pp. 504 and 506; SK, 'Der "operierende" Schriftsteller' [The 'operating' writer], in *Werke* 5.4, pp. 39–42; here: p. 41.

15 Kracauer to Ferdinand Lion, 7 August 1932.

16 Kracauer, 'Franz Kafka: On his Posthumous Works', p. 267.

17 Ibid., p. 273.
18 Walter Benjamin, 'Julien Green', pp. 335f.
19 SK, 'Adrienne Mesurat', in *Werke* 5.3, pp. 47–9; here: p. 49.
20 SK, 'Angst' [Fear], in *Werke* 5.4, pp. 386–91; here: p. 386.
21 SK, 'Betrachtung zu Greens "Léviathan"' [Reflection on Green's 'Léviathan'], in *Werke* 5.3, pp. 168–72; here: pp. 168 and 172.
22 SK, 'Eroberer in Kanton' [Conquerors in Canton], in ibid., pp. 108–12; here: p. 110.
23 SK, 'Heimweh nach Sein' [Homesick for Being], in ibid., pp. 175–80; here: pp. 175, 177 and 179f.
24 SK, 'Richard Voß: "Zwei Menschen"' [Richard Voß: 'Two people'], in ibid., pp. 455–62; here: p. 455; 'Bemerkungen zu Frank Thieß' [Remarks on Frank Thieß], in ibid., pp. 508–14; here: p. 508; 'On Bestsellers and Their Audience', in *The Mass Ornament*, pp. 89–98; here: p. 95.
25 Cf. for example Löwenthal's 'On Sociology of Literature' (original title: 'Zur gesellschaftlichen Lage der Literatur') of 1932, in which the influence of the economy on the work of art is acknowledged, but this issue is only pursued in more detail via the concept of ideology, understood as the concealment of social antagonisms.
26 An independent weekly that appeared between 1920 and 1933. Between 1933 and 1940, one of the editors, Leopold Schwarzschild, published *Das Neue Tage-Buch* from his exile in Paris.
27 On anti-intellectualism in the Weimar Republic, cf. Bering, *Die Epoche der Intellektuellen*, pp. 85–129.
28 Cf. Köpke, 'Alfred Döblins Überparteilichkeit', pp. 321f.
29 Wolfgang Höpker to Kracauer, 26 August 1931. 'Ferdinand Fried' was Ferdinand Friedrich Zimmermann. In 1933, he became the editor-in-chief of the *Tägliche Rundschau*, and later of the *Münchner Neueste Nachrichten*. In 1935, Höpker also joined the *Münchner Neueste Nachrichten* as one of its editors. During the Nazi period, Zimmermann pursued a career within the SS. An anti-Semite who had been educated at the expense of a Jewish banker, he subsequently managed to have a journalistic career in the Federal Republic at the *Deutsche Allgemeine Sonntagszeitung* and *Die Welt*. Following his death, the latter said: 'He had many opponents – evil he never committed.'
30 SK, 'Aufruhr der Mittelschichten' [Revolt of the middle classes], in *Werke* 5.3, pp. 716–36; here: pp. 716, 720, 728 and 731f.
31 Kracauer to Neurath, 10 January 1932.
32 Lehmann to Kracauer, 4 October 1931.
33 SK, *Georg*, pp. 335f. (transl. amended).
34 Kracauer to André and Clara Malraux, 20 September 1932.
35 This is what Kracauer told Fritz and Annemarie Wahl, 27 July 1933.
36 Adorno to Kracauer, 2 January 1931 and Kracauer to Adorno, 12 January 1931, in Adorno/Kracauer, *Briefwechsel*, pp. 257–62; here: p. 260 and pp. 265f.; here: p. 265.
37 Frankfurter Societäts-Druckerei to Kracauer, 11 June 1930.
38 Kracauer to the Jewish Community in Berlin, 27 August 1931.
39 Kracauer to Friedrich T. Gubler, 23 January 1931.
40 Kayser to Kracauer, 14 November 1931. A fee of 80 Reichsmark per commentary had been agreed.
41 Such as *Die Camera* (Switzerland), *Der Film* (Berlin) and *Revue de Cinéma* (Paris).

42 Claassen to Kracauer, 15 July 1930.
43 In the words of Wiesengrund to Hedwig Kracauer, following a visit to the Berlin apartment; cf. Hedwig to Siegfried Kracauer, 15 January 1932.
44 Kracauer to Selmar Spier, 9 February 1933.
45 Siegfried to Elisabeth Kracauer, 18 March 1931.
46 The 'Berliner Funkstunde AG', founded in 1923, was the first German radio broadcasting corporation.
47 Nevertheless, texts by Kracauer were used for at least two broadcasts, for which he received 137 marks. Wolfgang Koeppen was the editor in Berlin who kept in contact with Kracauer. For one particular broadcast he was paid 350 Reichsmark. Cf. Funkstunde to Kracauer, 22 March 1932 and 5 July 1932.
48 Kracauer to Bernhard Guttmann, 1 January 1932 and earlier to Rudolf Geck, 29 December 1931.
49 Kracauer to Herbert Jhering, 9 February 1932.
50 Kracauer to Robert Drill, 31 January 1931.
51 Hedwig to Siegfried Kracauer, 9 December 1932.
52 Kracauer to Friedrich T. Gubler, 30 December 1929, 23 January 1930, 21 March 1930 and 13 July 1930.
53 Friedrich T. Gubler to Kracauer, 21 January 1931.
54 Kracauer to Friedrich T. Gubler, 28 November 1930, 28 January 1931, 18 October 1931 and 23 March 1932.
55 Kracauer to Friedrich T. Gubler, 5 August 1932.
56 Kracauer to Benno Reifenberg, 20 March 1933.
57 SK, 'Berliner Nebeneinander [Teil I–III], [Berlin, side-by-side (part I–III)], in *Werke* 5.4, pp. 377–81; here: p. 378. Kracauer to Hellmut Jaesrich (*Der Monat*), 10 March 1957.
58 Bussiek, *Benno Reifenberg*, pp. 211f. and 243–58.
59 Benno Reifenberg to Kracauer, 8 February 1933, 13 February 1933, 23 February 1933; Kracauer to Benno Reifenberg, 12 February 1933.
60 Kracauer to Benno Reifenberg, 18 February 1933 and 25 February 1933.
61 Herbert, *Geschichte Deutschlands*, pp. 309f.; SK, 'Rund um den Reichstag' [Around the Reichstag], in *Werke* 5.4, pp. 395f.; here: p. 395.
62 See *Marbacher Magazin*, p. 70; Breidecker, 'Das Nizza von Frankfurt', p. 43.
63 SK, 'Rund um den Reichstag' [Around the Reichstag], in *Werke* 5.4, pp. 395f.; here: p. 396.

17. The Trial

1 Kafka, *The Trial*, p. 3; 'Little Fable', p. 122.
2 Cf. SK, 'Der Prozeß' [The trial], dated 1 November 1925, in *Werke* 5.2, pp. 306–8; here: p. 306; 'Franz Kafka', from 1934, in *Werke* 5.4, pp. 501–3. [Transl. note: This text is not to be confused with the eponymous essay in *The Mass Ornament*; see the 'bibliographic information' in that volume, p. 394.]
3 SK, 'Pariser Hotel' [Paris hotel], in *Werke* 5.4, pp. 528–32; here: p. 530.
4 As on 4 January 2019.
5 Kracauer to Benno Reifenberg, 8 March 1933.
6 Kracauer to Emil Lederer, 13 July 1933.
7 Zimmermann, *Friedrich Sieburg*, pp. 115–28.

8 English edition: *Is Germany finished?*, New York: The Macmillan Company, 1932.
9 Reifenberg, 'Vorwort', in *Viénot, Ungewisses Deutschland*, pp. 7–12.
10 On the last days of the *Tage-Buch* and the beginnings of the *Neues Tage-Buch*, see Behmer, *Von der Schwierigkeit*, p. 336. On emigration to Paris in the 1920s, see Sauveur-Henn, 'Paris'. On the difficult relationships between German emigrants and the French literary scene, see Kracht, *Zwischen Berlin und Paris*, pp. 252–72; Jean Renoir to Kracauer, 27 April 1933; Wladimir von Ornesson to Kracauer, no date, 1933.
11 Benjamin to Scholem, 28 February 1933, in *Correspondence*, p. 402.
12 Hedwig to Siegfried Kracauer, 14 April 1930 and 6 March 1933; Wiggershaus, *The Frankfurter School*, pp. 127–48; Adorno to Kracauer, 15 April 1933, in Adorno/Kracauer, *Briefwechsel*, pp. 308f.; Kracauer to Selmar Spier, 20 April 1933; Kracauer to Adorno, 29 April 1933, in Adorno/Kracauer, *Briefwechsel*, pp. 312f.; Münster, *Ernst Bloch*, pp. 166f.; Ernst Bloch to Kracauer, 29 March 1933, in Bloch, *Briefe*, vol. 1, p. 373; van Reijen and van Doorn, *Aufenthalte und Passagen*, p. 138; Brodersen, *Benjamin*, p. 203; Bronsen, *Joseph Roth*, pp. 419–29; Sternburg, *Joseph Roth*, pp. 403 and 406.
13 Siegfried to Elisabeth Kracauer, 18 March 1931, 20 March 1931; Elisabeth to Siegfried Kracauer, 12 September 1932; Kracauer to Benno Reifenberg, 5 March 1933. On Elisabeth Kracauer's plans regarding photography, see the correspondence with Tau and Wallach, and see Zinfert, *Kracauer*.
14 SK, *Georg*, pp. 328f.
15 Ibid., p. 340.
16 Ibid., p. 330.

18. Europe on the Move: Refugees in France

1 Kulischer, *Europe on the Move*, p. 8.
2 Schlögel, 'Verschiebebahnhof Europa', p. 470.
3 Kulischer, *Europe on the Move*, pp. 3–7.
4 Brecht, 'Concerning the Label Emigrant', in *Poems*, p. 301.
5 Cf. on this attitude Améry, 'How much home does a person need?'.
6 See the definition by Pross, *Die deutsche akademische Emigration*, p. 18.
7 Arendt, *The Origins of Totalitarianism*, p. 267. [Transl. note: As in the case of other titles by Arendt, the English and German editions differ from each other. A more literal rendering of the German passage would run: 'Whoever was knocked out of the old three-fold unity of people-territory-state, on which the nation had rested, remained homeless and stateless; whoever had lost the rights guaranteed by citizenship, remained without rights.']
8 Cf. Bade, *Europa in Bewegung*, pp. 275–81.
9 Cf. Walter, *Asylpraxis*, p. 31.
10 Quoted after Marrus, *Die Unerwünschten*, p. 211; cf. also Walter, *Asylpraxis*, p. 38.
11 See Marrus, *Die Unerwünschten*.
12 Cf. Benz, *Flucht aus Deutschland*, p. 65; Herbert, *Geschichte Deutschlands*, p. 331.
13 Herbert, *Geschichte Deutschlands*, pp. 328–31; Friedländer, *Nazi Germany and the Jews: The Years of Persecution*, pp. 9–40 and 145–51.

14 Kulischer, *Europe on the Move*, pp. 188–92.
15 Marrus, *Die Unerwünschten*, pp. 145–9; Bade, *Europa in Bewegung*, pp. 281–4; Sauveur-Henn, 'Paris'; Unger, *Reise ohne Wiederkehr*, pp. 8–11; Benz, *Exil der kleinen Leute*; Grossmann, *Emigration*, p. 11; Vormeier, 'Frankreich', pp. 213–21.
16 Cf. Betz, *Exil und Engagement*, pp. 7–12; Franke, *Paris*, p. 19; Roussel/ Winckler, 'Exilforschung'.
17 Cf. Walter, *Asylpraxis*, p. 75.
18 Vormeier, 'Zufluchtsland Frankreich', pp. 213–17; von zur Mühlen, *Fluchtweg*, pp. 11–13 and 18–21; Franke, *Paris*, p. 20; Benz, *Das Exil der kleinen Leute*, p. 31.
19 Olden, 'Im tiefen Dunkel', pp. 112–13.
20 Silbermann, *Verwandlungen*, pp. 127–51.
21 As on 7 January 2019.
22 Franke, *Paris*, pp. 102–7, 179–80 and 229–33.
23 Margherita de Francesco to Kracauer, 15 July 1933.
24 Cf. Flusser, *Groundless*, pp. 19–22 and 41–6; German edition: *Bodenlos*, pp. 9–11 and 31–8 [Transl. note: The German and English editions differ; the quotations are from the German edition.]; Améry also speaks of his 'memory of a staggering on shaky ground', 'How much home does a person need?', p. 46.

19. The Liquidation of German Matters

1 Kracauer to Benno Reifenberg, 20 March 1933.
2 Kracauer to Benno Reifenberg, 25 March 1933 and 2 April 1933.
3 As Kracauer wrote to Selmar Spier, 6 April 1933.
4 'Street book' manuscripts and Max Tau to Kracauer, 14 March 1933.
5 Kracauer to Max Rychner, 24 March 1933; Wilhelm Hausenstein to Kracauer, 28 March 1933; Kracauer to Benno Reifenberg, 2 April 1933.
6 Cf. Benz, *Flucht aus Deutschland*, pp. 52–3; Herbert, *Geschichte Deutschlands*, p. 326.
7 Selmar Spier to Kracauer, 4 March 1933.
8 Kracauer to Selmar Spier, 6 April 1933.
9 Roóz to Kracauer, 6 June 1933.
10 Selmar Spier to Kracauer, 15 April 1933, 18 April 1933 and 27 April 1933.
11 Selmar Spier to Kracauer, 2 May 1933.
12 Kracauer to Selmar Spier, 6 May 1933.
13 Kracauer to Julius Meier-Graefe, 16 March 1934; Kracht, *Zwischen Berlin und Paris*, pp. 262 and 268f.
14 Korrodi to Kracauer, 27 April 1933; Paulhan to Kracauer, 25 April 1933; Kracauer to Margaret Goldsmith, 20 April 1933 and 4 May 1933.
15 Kracauer to Benno Reifenberg, 27 April 1933.
16 Kracauer to Selmar Spier, 6 May 1933 and 13 May 1933.
17 Hedwig to Siegfried Kracauer, 14 April 1933, 24 April 1933 and 2 May 1933.
18 *Frankfurter Zeitung*, 'Kollegiale Greuelnachricht', quoted by Kracauer in a letter to Selmar Spier, 21 May 1933.
19 Selmar Spier to Kracauer, 9 May 1933.
20 Note from Spier's files: Selmar Spier to Kracauer, 11 May 1933. Cf. Bussiek, *Benno Reifenberg*, p. 259. On the case of the Jewish musician,

see Friedländer, *Nazi Germany and the Jews: The Years of Persecution*, pp. 23f.

21 Selmar Spier to Kracauer, 12 May 1933.

22 Kracauer to Selmar Spier, 13 May 1933.

23 Rudolf Geck to Kracauer, 22 May 1933; Karl Zimmermann to Kracauer, 22 May 1933.

24 Wolf von Dewall to Kracauer, 3 May 1933.

25 Benno Reifenberg to Kracauer, 4 May 1933.

26 Bronsen, *Joseph Roth*, pp. 425f.; Brodersen, *Siegfried Kracauer*, pp. 96f.

27 Hedwig to Siegfried Kracauer, 15 October 1936.

28 Kracauer to Selmar Spier, 16 June 1933 and 27 June 1933.

29 Kracauer to Benno Reifenberg, 1 July 1933; Benno Reifenberg to Kracauer, 3 July 1933 and Selmar Spier to Kracauer, 8 July 1933; Kracauer to Joseph, no date; this letter mentions the sum of 4,000 Reichsmark.

30 Frankfurter Societäts-Druckerei to Kracauer, 22 March 1930.

31 SK, 'Mit europäischen Augen gesehen ...' [Seen with European eyes ...], in *Werke* 5.4, pp. 446–51; here: p. 448.

32 Max Tau to Kracauer, 31 August 1933; Margherita de Francesco to Kracauer, 14 July 1933.

33 Kracauer to Julius Meier-Graefe, 24 August 1933.

34 Kracauer to Selmar Spier, 11 July 1933; Selmar Spier to Kracauer, 13 July 1933; Kracauer to Benno Reifenberg, 14 July 1933; Kracauer to Selmar Spier, 14 July 1933; Selmar Spier to Kracauer, 17 July 1933 and 20 July 1933; Hedwig to Siegfried Kracauer, 22 June 1933 and 8 July 1933; Kracauer to de Francesco, 16 July 1933 and 19 July 1933.

35 Margherita de Francesco to Kracauer, 31 July 1933, 11 August 1933 and 18 August 1933.

36 Margherita de Francesco to Kracauer, no date, and 19 August 1933 and 21 August 1933.

37 Margherita de Francesco to Kracauer, 19 August 1933.

38 Hedwig to Siegfried Kracauer, 20 August 1933; Margherita de Francesco to Kracauer, 21 August 1933. De Francesco suspected Reifenberg as the benefactor, but it was probably Clementine Cramer.

39 Kracauer to Margherita de Francesco, 30 August 1933.

40 Richard Eisemann to Kracauer, 22 August 1933.

41 Benno Reifenberg to Kracauer, 8 November 1933.

42 Cf. Bussiek, *Benno Reifenberg*, p. 276; Ernst Bloch to Kracauer, 30 April 1934, in Bloch, *Briefe*, vol. 1, pp. 379f.

43 Cf. Stalder, *Siegfried Kracauer*, pp. 67–70; Wenzel, 'Nachbemerkung', p. 514.

44 Kracauer to Margherita de Francesco, 1 August 1933 and 19 August 1933.

45 Hedwig to Siegfried Kracauer, 14 October 1933.

46 Cf. the letter from Hedwig to Siegfried Kracauer, no date [1936/37].

47 SK, 'Die deutschen Bevölkerungsschichten und der Nationalsozialismus' [Strata of the German population and national socialism]; 'Über die deutsche Jugend' [On the German youth]; 'Deutsche Protestanten im Kampf' [German protestants in battle]; 'Eine intellektuelle Anpassung an den Hitlerismus' [Intellectual adaptation to Hitlerism], 'Das neue "Gesetz zur Ordnung der nationalen Arbeit"' [The new 'Work Order Act'], in *Werke* 5.4, pp. 433–44, 456–66, 474–6, 478–85 and 503–12.

48 SK, 'Die deutschen Bevölkerungsschichten und der Nationalsozialismus', in ibid., p. 443.

49 Ibid. and SK, 'Über die deutsche Jugend', in ibid., pp. 456–66.
50 SK, 'Das neue "Gesetz zur Ordnung der nationalen Arbeit"', in ibid., pp. 503–12; here: p. 504.
51 SK, 'Bestandsaufnahme' [Conclusions], in ibid., pp. 467–72; here: p. 467.
52 See Saul Friedländer, *Nazi Germany and the Jews*, Vol. 1: *The Years of Persecution: 1933–1939*, ch. 3.
53 Ibid., pp. 470 and 472.
54 Kracauer to Fritz Wahl, 12 November 1933.
55 Franzkowiak to Kracauer, 15 September 1933.
56 Kracauer to Friedrich T. Gubler, 3 May 1934.
57 Cf. Franke, 'Die Rolle der Devisenstellen', p. 81.
58 Kracauer to Reichsarbeitsgemeinschaft der Deutschen Presse, 13 January 1934. The compensation authorities of Berlin-Wilmersdorf later confirmed that Kracauer had suffered an injustice: cf. compensation file at the Entschädigungsbehörde Berlin (Berlin-Wilmersdorf), Landesamt für Bürger- und Ordnungsangelegenheiten, Abt. 1: Entschädigungsbehörde, Opfer des Nationalsozialismus, Dateneingabe MyCMDB, I A 45.
59 Kracauer to Gaston Bloch, 28 January 1934 and 15 March 1934; Kracauer to Joseph, no date; Kracauer to Landesfinanzamt Preußen, 26 January 1934.
60 Kracauer to Joseph, 19 April 1934, 10 May 1934 and 22 June 1934; Joseph to Kracauer, 6 March 1934, 17 April 1934, 21 April 1934, 5 May 1934, 14 May 1934 and 30 May 1934; Gebr. Arnhold, Dresden-Berlin to Kracauer, 2 July 1934, and Adler & Co., Banquiers, Aktien-Gesellschaft, Zürich to Kracauer, 24 July 1934. On the sale of Reichsmark from blocked accounts, which usually incurred a loss of 50 per cent, see Hilberg, *Die Vernichtung der europäischen Juden*, pp. 149f.
61 Kracauer to Julius Meier-Graefe, 16 March 1934.
62 Kracauer to Erich Franzen, 13 April 1934.
63 The fees he received from *L'Europe Nouvelle*, *Les Cahiers Juifs*, etc., were a drop in the ocean. Cf. Roger Nathan to Kracauer, 6 June 1933 (400 Francs); Piha to Kracauer, 30 August 1933 (1,213 Francs); *Cahiers Juifs* to Kracauer (220 Francs); *L'Europe Nouvelle* to Kracauer, 15 January 1934 and 31 January 1934 (190 and 1,390 Francs). Kracauer had also tried in vain to sell articles to the Netherlands; cf. Kracauer to Elsevier's Grillensteerd Maandschrift, 1 August 1933; Mautner to Kracauer, 21 July 1933 and 30 July 1933.
64 Kracauer to Karl Mannheim, 29 June 1933 and 2 November 1933; Karl Mannheim to Kracauer, 20 June 1933; Kracauer to Hendrik de Man, 27 June 1933; Kracauer to Emil Lederer, 13 July 1933; Emil Lederer to Kracauer, 16 July 1933.
65 Kracauer to James G. MacDonald, 2 December 1933.
66 Kracauer to Friedrich T. Gubler, 3 May 1934.
67 Kracauer to Ernst Bloch, 5 July 1934, in Bloch, *Briefe*, vol. 1, pp. 380–2; Kracauer to Friedrich T. Gubler, 7 June 1934. From mid-April onwards, Hedwig Kracauer reported fortnightly about the progression of the illness, assuring the Kracauers in Paris that there was no reason to worry. Hedwig to Siegfried Kracauer, 20 April 1934, 4 May 1934, 11 May 1934 and 26 May 1934.
68 S. Fischer Verlag to Kracauer, 11 August 1933; Bermann Fischer to Kracauer, 24 August 1933; cf. also Wulf, *Literatur und Dichtung*, pp. 168f.; Sternburg, *Joseph Roth*, p. 403.

69 Kracauer to Friedrich T. Gubler, 5 September 1935.
70 Kracauer, *Georg*, p. 341.
71 Ibid., p. 340.
72 Cf. Schiller, 'Verlage', pp. 1122–7; Sternburg, *Joseph Roth*, pp. 420f.
73 Kracauer to Fischer, Samuel Verlag, 16 July 1933; Kracauer to Ernst Bloch, 5 July 1934, in Bloch, *Briefe*, vol. 1, pp. 380–2.
74 SK, 'Klaus Mann sucht seinen Weg' [Klaus Mann is looking for his way], in *Werke* 5.3, pp. 560–2; here: p. 560; 'Zur Produktion der Jungen' [On the production of the young generation], in *Werke* 5.4, pp. 102–7; here: pp. 102 and 105; Klaus Mann to Kracauer, 12 May 1932 (in the bundle 'Affäre Klaus Mann').
75 Max Tau to Kracauer, 6 September 1934; Kracauer to Julius Meier-Graefe, 29 November 1934.
76 Kracauer to Thomas Mann, 29 November 1934 and 11 December 1934; Thomas Mann to Kracauer, 8 December 1934 and 15 December 1934.

20. Two Views on the Second Empire: Offenbach and the Arcades

1 In his entry on Offenbach for the *Universal Jewish Encyclopedia*; German translation in: SK, *Jacques Offenbach*, in *Werke* 8, p. 481 [my translation from the German, D.S.].
2 Karl Kraus, '"Offenbach-Renaissance". (Zum Vortrag von "Pariser Leben")', in Karl Kraus; *Schriften*, vol. 17, p. 221.
3 Benjamin, 'Karl Kraus Reads Offenbach', in *Selected Writings*, vol. 2, 1927–34, pp. 110–12. [Transl. note: 'Parisian Life' is omitted from the title in both the German *Gesammelte Werke* and the English *Selected Writings*.]
4 Adorno, 'Hoffmanns Erzählungen in Offenbachs Motiven' (1932), in *Musikalische Schriften* IV, pp. 42–6; cf. Wenzel, 'Nachbemerkung', pp. 525–7.
5 Kracauer to Margaret Goldsmith, 22 April 1934.
6 Siegfried to Hedwig Kracauer, 26 March 1938.
7 Kracauer to Max Tau, 31 October 1934.
8 Walter Benjamin to Adorno, 9 March 1934, in Adorno/Benjamin, *Correspondence*, pp. 28–9; here: p. 29.
9 Kracauer to Julius Meier-Graefe, 23 December 1934.
10 'Motion picture treatment' in English in the original.
11 Kracauer to Emil Lederer, 28 February 1936.
12 Walter Landauer to Kracauer, 16 January 1937, 25 January 1937 and 29 January 1937; Kracauer to Walter Landauer, 28 January 1937 and 1 February 1937. Before the contract with Allert de Lange was signed, an agreement had almost been reached with Oprecht and Helbling, which, however, failed because Grasset did not want to sell the copyright for foreign editions.
13 Kracauer, *Jacques Offenbach*, p. 39 (transl. mod.). [Transl. note: The text follows the convention used in the German original and puts quotations from the book on Offenbach in italics rather than quotation marks. The German passages can be found at SK, *Jacques Offenbach*, in *Werke* 8; pp. 13, 27, 55, 59, 71, 75–7, 79f., 118, 134f., 140, 157–9, 212 and 241.]
14 Ibid., p. 67 (transl. mod.).
15 Ibid., p. 157.

16 Ibid., p. 25.
17 Ibid., p. 269 (transl. amended).
18 Ibid., p. 236 (transl. mod.).
19 Ibid., p. 379.
20 Ibid., p. 89.
21 On the theory of Bonapartism and the parallels between Hitler and Napoleon III, cf. also Reil, *Siegfried Kracauers Jacques Offenbach*, pp. 51–5.
22 Kracauer, *Jacques Offenbach*, p. 151.
23 Ibid. (transl. amended).
24 Ibid., p. 152 (transl. amended).
25 Ibid., p. 134 (transl. amended).
26 Ibid., p. 94.
27 Ibid., p. 93 (transl. amended).
28 Ibid., p. 95 (transl. amended).
29 Ibid., p. 96.
30 Ibid. (transl. amended).
31 Ibid. As he confessed in a letter to Westheim (5 December 1948), Kracauer was envious of those whose home was the boulevard and looked at them with a 'longing for a lost, more beautiful world'.
32 Walter Benjamin to Adorno, 9 March 1934, in Adorno/Benjamin, *Correspondence*, p. 29.
33 Benjamin, 'Paris, the Capital of the Nineteenth Century', p. 8.
34 Benjamin, 'The Paris of the Second Empire in Baudelaire', pp. 7 and 63.
35 Ibid., p. 17.
36 Transl. note: Benjamin writes: 'Das Warenhaus ist der letzte Strich des Flaneurs' (*GS* I.2, p. 557. A 'Landstrich' is a stretch of landscape, but 'auf den Strich gehen' is an expression for street prostitution. Thus, Benjamin, in this passage, sets up a parallel between commodities, the figure of the flâneur, and prostitution.
37 Ibid., p. 31.
38 Ibid., p. 22.
39 See Tiedemann, 'Dialectics at a Standstill', pp. 938–9.
40 Wiesengrund to Benjamin, 4 May 1937, in Adorno/Benjamin, *Correspondence*, pp. 183f. (transl. amended).
41 Benjamin to Wiesengrund, 9 May 1937, in Adorno/Benjamin, *Correspondence*, pp. 184–7; here: p. 185.
42 Ibid., p. 186.
43 Ibid., p. 185.
44 Ibid., p. 187.
45 Ibid., p. 185 (transl. mod.).

21. The Disintegration of the Group

1 Ernst Bloch to Adorno, no date, in Bloch, *Briefe*, vol. 2, pp. 423–31; here: p. 424.
2 Ernst Bloch to Walter Benjamin, in ibid., pp. 652f.
3 Walter Benjamin to Gretel Adorno, 3 March 1934, and Walter Benjamin to Bertolt Brecht, 5 March 1934, in Benjamin, *Correspondence*, pp. 435–41.
4 Kracauer to Walter Benjamin, 29 November 1934, in Benjamin, *Briefe an Siegfried Kracauer*, pp. 76–7; Walter Benjamin to Adorno, 30 November

1934 and 7 January 1935, in Adorno/Benjamin, *Correspondence*, pp. 59f. and 73–6.

5 Bloch, *The Heritage of Our Times*, pp. 2f.
6 Adorno to Walter Benjamin, 17 December 1934, in Adorno/Benjamin, *Correspondence*, pp. 66–73; here: p. 71.
7 Ernst Bloch to Adorno, no date, in Bloch, *Briefe*, vol. 2, pp. 423–31; here: pp. 423–5 and 428.
8 Ernst Bloch to Walter Benjamin, 18 December 1934, in Bloch, *Briefe*, vol. 2, pp. 658f.
9 Walter Benjamin to Alfred Cohn, 19 December 1934, in *Correspondence*, pp. 464–6; here: p. 465.
10 Walter Benjamin to Gerhard Scholem, 26 December 1934, in *Correspondence*, pp. 468–70; here: p. 468.
11 Walter Benjamin to Kracauer, 15 January 1935, in Benjamin, *Briefe an Siegfried Kracauer*, pp. 80f.
12 Walter Benjamin to Alfred Cohn, 6 February 1935, in *Correspondence*, pp. 476–9; here: p. 478.
13 On this, see Palmier, *Walter Benjamin*, p. 592.
14 Bloch, *The Heritage of Our Times*, p. 1.
15 Walter Benjamin to Adorno, early April 1935, in Adorno/Benjamin, *Correspondence*, pp. 77–9; here: p. 77.
16 Walter Benjamin to Kracauer, 15 January 1935, in Benjamin, *Briefe an Siegfried Kracauer*, pp. 80f.
17 Ernst Bloch to Adorno, 18 March 1935, in Bloch, *Briefe*, vol. 2, pp. 434–6; here: p. 436.
18 Walter Benjamin to Adorno, 1 May 1935, in Adorno/Benjamin, *Correspondence*, pp. 79–82; here: p. 80.
19 Walter Benjamin to Alfred Cohn, 18 July 1935, in Benjamin, *Correspondence*, pp. 492–4; here: p. 495 (transl. amended).
20 Adorno to Kracauer, 5 July 1935, in Adorno/Kracauer, *Briefwechsel*, pp. 314–17.
21 Adorno to Walter Benjamin, 27 November 1937, in Adorno/Benjamin, *Correspondence*, pp. 227–32; Münster, *Ernst Bloch*, pp. 207–15.
22 Ernst Bloch to Walter Benjamin, 30 January 1937, 3 March 1937 and 26 April 1937, in Bloch, *Briefe*, vol. 2, pp. 664–8.
23 Ernst Bloch to Adorno, 18 September 1937, in Bloch, *Briefe*, vol. 2, pp. 438f.
24 Ernst Bloch to Adorno, 3 January 1938, in Bloch, *Briefe*, vol. 2, pp. 440f; Wiggershaus, *The Frankfurt School*, p. 190.
25 Kracauer to Ernst Bloch, 7 February 1935, in Bloch, *Briefe*, vol. 1, pp. 384–6; here: p. 385.
26 Kracauer to Walter Benjamin, 24 February 1935, in Benjamin, *Briefe an Siegfried Kracauer*, pp. 82–5; here: p. 82.
27 Adorno to Walter Benjamin, 25 April 1937 and 2 July 1937, in Adorno/Benjamin, *Correspondence*, pp. 179–82 and pp. 195–201; here: p. 180; Wiggershaus, *The Frankfurt School*, pp. 156–65.
28 Adorno to Walter Benjamin, 18 March 1936, in Adorno/Benjamin, *Correspondence*, pp. 127–34.
29 Walter Benjamin to Gerhard Scholem, 17 October 1934, in Benjamin, *Correspondence*, pp. 458–60.
30 Adorno to Walter Benjamin, 6 November 1934, in Adorno/Benjamin, *Correspondence*, pp. 52–9; here: p. 53.

31 Benjamin to Adorno, 9 March 1934, in Adorno/Benjamin, *Correspondence*, pp. 28f.; here: p. 29.

32 Adorno to Benjamin, 20 May 1935, in Adorno/Benjamin, *Correspondence*, pp. 82–7; here: p. 84 (transl. modified).

33 Ibid., p. 85.

34 Benjamin, 'Paris, the Capital of the Nineteenth Century', in *The Arcades Project*, pp. 3–13. Adorno and Gretel Karplus to Benjamin, 2 April 1935 and 5 August 1935, and Benjamin to Gretel Karplus and Adorno, 16 August 1935, in Adorno/Benjamin, *Correspondence*, pp. 104–16 and 116–19. Palmier only mentions the sharpness of the criticism; cf. Palmier, *Walter Benjamin*, pp. 463–4.

35 Walter Benjamin to Adorno, 7 January 1935, in Adorno/Benjamin, *Correspondence*, pp. 73–6.

36 Adorno to Walter Benjamin, 5 June 1935, in Adorno/Benjamin, *Correspondence*, pp. 92–5; here: p. 93 (transl. modified).

37 Walter Benjamin to Adorno, 30 June 1936 and 1 March 1937, in Adorno/Benjamin, *Correspondence*, pp. 144–5 and 168–70; here: pp. 144 and 168.

38 The goal of exploding idealism from within Adorno also took himself to share with Alfred Sohn-Rethel; Wiggershaus, *The Frankfurt School*, p. 162.

39 Adorno to Walter Benjamin, 5 December 1934, 16 December 1934 and 17 December 1934, in Adorno/Benjamin, *Correspondence*, pp. 60–5, 65f. and 66–73; here: p. 66.

40 Weigel, *Walter Benjamin*, pp. 130–63 ('Jewish Thinking in a World Without God: Benjamin's Reading of Kafka as a Critique of Christian and Jewish Theologoumena').

41 Benjamin, 'Franz Kafka', in *Selected Writings*, vol. 2, pp. 794–818; here: p. 811.

42 Cf. Palmier, *Walter Benjamin*, pp. 499–501.

43 Adorno to Kracauer, 14 March 1933, in Adorno/Kracauer, *Briefwechsel*, pp. 304f.; here: p. 304.

44 Adorno to Kracauer, 5 July 1935, in ibid., pp. 314–17; here: pp. 314f.

45 Adorno to Walter Benjamin, 13 April 1934 and 21 April 1934, in Adorno/Benjamin, *Correspondence*, pp. 42–4 and 44–8.

46 Adorno to Walter Benjamin, 6 November 1934, in Adorno/Benjamin, *Correspondence*, pp. 52–9; here: p. 56.

47 Adorno to Max Horkheimer, 23 November 1936, in Horkheimer, *Briefwechsel 1913–1936*, pp. 735–43.

48 Walter Benjamin to Adorno, 24 May 1934, in Adorno/Benjamin, *Correspondence*, pp. 50f.; here: p. 51.

49 Walter Benjamin to Bertolt Brecht, 9 January 1935, in Benjamin, *Correspondence*, pp. 473–4; Walter Benjamin to Adorno, 2 October 1937 and 2 November 1937, in Adorno/Benjamin, *Correspondence*, pp. 218–20 and 221–6; here: p. 219.

50 Walter Benjamin to Bertolt Brecht, 9 January 1935, in Benjamin, *Correspondence*, pp. 473f.; here: p. 473.

51 Walter Benjamin to Max Horkheimer, 16 October 1935, in Benjamin, *Correspondence*, pp. 508–10; cf. also Palmier, *Walter Benjamin*, pp. 553–66.

52 Adorno to Walter Benjamin, 13 May 1937, in Adorno/Benjamin, *Correspondence*, pp. 190f.; here: p. 190.

53 Walter Benjamin to Adorno, 17 May 1937, in Adorno/Benjamin, *Correspondence*, pp. 191–3; here: p. 193 (transl. mod.).

54 Adorno to Walter Benjamin, 12 May 1937, and Benjamin to Adorno, 9 May 1937, in Adorno/Benjamin, *Correspondence*, pp. 184–7 and 188f.; here: pp. 187 and 189.

55 Adorno to Kracauer, 19 May 1937, in Adorno/Kracauer, *Briefwechsel*, pp. 352–9; here: pp. 352, 354, 356 and 358f.

56 Adorno to Benjamin, 12 May 1937, in Benjamin/Adorno, *Correspondence*, pp. 188–9; here: p. 189.

57 Kracauer to Adorno, 25 May 1937, in Adorno/Kracauer, *Briefwechsel*, pp. 362–4; here: p. 362.

58 Adorno to Kracauer, 27 May 1937, in ibid., pp. 365–7; here: pp. 365 and 367; Schlüpmann, *Detektiv des Kinos*, p. 34.

22. Songs of Woe from Frankfurt

1 Hedwig to Siegfried Kracauer, 4 March 1931 and 14 July 1934.

2 Hedwig to Siegfried Kracauer, 1 March 1939.

3 Hedwig to Siegfried Kracauer, 6 February 1931, 17 May 1931 and 12 February 1932.

4 Kracauer, *Geschichte der Juden*, vol. 1, pp. 246–64 and 386–90; vol. 2, pp. 121–5 and 332–3; Wippermann, *Das Leben in Frankfurt*, pp. 21–3; Heuberger and Krohn, *Hinaus aus dem Ghetto ...*, pp. 13 and 17.

5 Hedwig to Siegfried Kracauer, 29 November 1930, 24 September 1931 and 6 February 1932.

6 Hedwig to Siegfried Kracauer, 5 July 1932.

7 Hedwig to Siegfried Kracauer, no date [spring 1933].

8 Transl. note: The 'Römerberg' is a historical square in Frankfurt's city centre. The Römer is Frankfurt's city hall, and during the Holy Roman Empire it was where imperial coronations took place.

9 Schivelbusch, *Intellektuellendämmerung*, p. 119.

10 Transl. note: 'Asphaltliteratur' was a term that had been used derogatively by the political right since 1918 to refer to literature that grew out of metropolitan life. The term came to be used in National Socialist propaganda in order to discredit the literature of certain authors as 'rootless' and without connection to 'Heimat'.

11 Wippermann, *Das Leben in Frankfurt*, pp. 53–68; Krohn, 'Im Nationalsozialismus', p. 158; Heuberger and Krohn, *Hinaus aus dem Ghetto ...*, pp. 171–6; Arnsberg, *Bilder*, pp. 144–65; Friedländer, *Nazi Germany and the Jews*, vol. 1, p. 38; Schlotzhauer, *Das Philanthropin*, pp. 98f.

12 Hedwig to Siegfried Kracauer, 9 April 1933.

13 Hedwig to Siegfried Kracauer, 26 September 1938.

14 Hedwig to Siegfried Kracauer, 14 April 1933 and 13 September 1933.

15 Hedwig to Siegfried Kracauer, 22 December 1933, 28 December 1933, 15 February 1934 and 7 September 1934.

16 Hedwig to Siegfried Kracauer, 2 May 1933, 2 June 1933, 22 June 1933 and 31 May 1934.

17 Hedwig to Siegfried Kracauer, 24 July 1934.

18 Hedwig to Siegfried Kracauer, 12 May 1935, 9 June 1935, 23 June 1935 and 30 June 1935.

19 Cf. Heuberger/Krohn, *Hinaus aus dem Ghetto ...*, pp. 184f.

20 Hedwig to Siegfried Kracauer, no date [1934], 19 January 1934, 11 May 1934 and 24 June 1934.

21 Hedwig to Siegfried Kracauer, 7 October 1934.
22 Hedwig to Siegfried Kracauer, 7 October 1934.
23 Hedwig to Siegfried Kracauer, 19 April 1936.
24 Hedwig to Siegfried Kracauer, 2 December 1934.
25 Hedwig to Siegfried Kracauer, 8 December 1935.
26 Wippermann, *Das Leben in Frankfurt*, pp. 68–83; Heuberger and Krohn, p. 177; Hedwig to Siegfried Kracauer, 13 October 1935.
27 Hedwig to Siegfried Kracauer, Whit Sunday 1936.
28 Hedwig to Siegfried Kracauer, 20 September 1936.
29 Hedwig to Siegfried Kracauer, 19 April 1936 and 9 July 1937.
30 Hedwig to Siegfried Kracauer, 16 June 1937 and 30 July 1937. The review was by Egon Kaskeline who emigrated to the USA and befriended the Kracauers in New York.
31 Kracauer to Landauer, 24 March 1937.
32 Hedwig to Siegfried Kracauer, 23 February 1937, 1 March 1937, 16 March 1937, 14 April 1937 and 20 May 1937; Siegfried to Rosette and Hedwig Kracauer, 13 March 1938.
33 On the following, see Diner, '"Vom Anschlus" zur "Kristallnacht"'; Grossmann, *Emigration*, pp. 61–6 and 111–17.
34 Grossmann, *Emigration*, pp. 111f.
35 Wippermann, *Das Leben in Frankfurt*, pp. 98–9; Krohn, 'Im Nationalsozialismus', p. 159; Heuberger and Krohn, *Hinaus aus dem Ghetto ...*, pp. 177f.; Schlotzhauer, *Das Philanthropin*, p. 111.
36 Hedwig to Siegfried Kracauer, 31 March 1938, 14 May 1938, 23 May 1938, 31 August 1938, 13 October 1938 and 3 November 1938.
37 Hedwig to Siegfried Kracauer, 10 November 1938.
38 Transl. note: 'Alljuda', roughly 'pan-Jewry': a Nazi neologism insinuating the omnipresence of Jews and the alleged international conspiracy of Jews and Judaism.
39 Hedwig to Siegfried Kracauer, 5 December 1938 and 8 December 1938.
40 Wippermann, *Das Leben in Frankfurt*, pp. 97–107; Krohn, 'Im Nationalsozialismus', p. 159; Heuberger and Krohn, *Hinaus aus dem Ghetto ...*, pp. 177–80 and 188; Schlotzhauer, *Das Philanthropin*, pp. 113f.
41 Hedwig to Siegfried Kracauer, 21 November 1938 and 28 November 1938.
42 Kracauer to Irma Oppenheimer, 15 December 1938; Robert Heinebach to Kracauer, 28 November 1938 and 5 February 1939. The Oppenheimers in America already supported a great-nephew (Irma Oppenheimer to Kracauer, 17 February 1939) and could not take on any further commitments. The Heinebachs donated a one-off payment.
43 Kracauer to Abraham Horovitz, 1 April 1939 and Abraham Horovitz to Kracauer, 12 April 1939; Siegfried to Rosette and Hedwig Kracauer, 4 March 1939 and 23 April 1939; Kracauer to Karl Müller, 24 December 1938, 7 February 1939 and 9 April 1939; Karl Müller to Kracauer, 30 December 1938 and 10 March 1939; Kracauer to Rosenthal, 11 March 1939; Kracauer to Bello, 2 February 1939; Kracauer to Paul Baerwald, 16 December 1938 and 15 January 1939; Paul Baerwald to Kracauer, 27 December 1938.
44 Hedwig to Siegfried Kracauer, 12 December 1938.
45 Hedwig to Siegfried Kracauer, 20 September 1936 and 14 July 1938.
46 Hedwig to Siegfried Kracauer, 2 January 1939, 10 January 1939 and 31 January 1939.
47 File: Emigrationsversuche Familie [Emigration attempts of the family].

48 Hedwig to Siegfried Kracauer, 23 June 1939.
49 Siegfried to Rosette Kracauer, 24 June 1939 and 23 July 1939.

23. La Vie Parisienne

1 Bernard Grasset to Kracauer, 8 April 1938.
2 Walter Landauer to Kracauer, 12 April 1937, 28 April 1937, 6 August 1937 and 18 October 1937; Knopf to Kracauer, 22 March 1939; Siegfried to Rosette and Hedwig Kracauer, 10 October 1939.
3 *Zeitschrift für Sozialforschung* 6 (1937) 3, pp. 697f.
4 Cf. Maurer Zenck, *Der hoffnungslose Radikalismus der Mitte*, pp. 18, 61, 69, 121 and 234.
5 *National-Zeitung*, 16 May 1937 and *Wiener Zeitung*, 18 May 1937.
6 Adorno/Krenek, *Briefwechsel*, p. 124.
7 Kracauer collected the following reviews: *Neuer Vorwärts*, 22 May 1937; *Das Neue Tage-Buch*, 17 July 1937; *Jüdische Rundschau*, 23 July 1937; *Neue Züricher Zeitung*, 29 December 1937; *Das Wort*, May 1938; *Pariser Tageszeitung* (in German) and *Neues Wiener Tageblatt*, no date; *Les Nouvelles Littéraires*, 12 June 1937; *Le Monde Illustré*, 19 June 1937; *La République*, 17 June 1937; *Le Journal*, 27 June 1937; *La Dépêche*, 16 June 1937; *L'OEuvre*, 23 July 1937; *Le Figaro*, 24 July 1937; *Curieux*, 24 July 1937; *La Tribune de Genève*, 29 July 1937; *Le Temps*, 30 July 1937 and 18 August 1937; *Matin*, 8 August 1937; *La Liberté*, 8 August 1937; *L'Ordre*, 9 August 1937; *The New York Times Book Review*, 23 January 1938 and 27 March 1938; *The Nation*, no date; *The New Republic*, 18 May 1938. The articles are compiled in a folder at the Mediendokumentation of the DLA Marbach. Cf. also Leo Löwenthal to Kracauer, 9 May 1938 and 31 May 1938.
8 SK, 'Alltagsleben in Paris' [Everyday life in Paris], in *Werke* 5.4, pp. 432f; here: p. 432.
9 Cf. Aubenas and Bajac, *Brassaï*.
10 Corbin, 'Die Bedeutung der Pariser Cafés'.
11 Bronsen, *Joseph Roth*, p. 593.
12 See Betz, *Exil und Engagement*, pp. 104–24; Langkau-Alex, *Volksfront für Deutschland?* and Bloch, 'Der eigentümliche Glücksfall', p. 73.
13 Kracauer to Hermann Budzislawski, 21 March 1934, 5 July 1934 and 28 April 1935; Kracauer to Wieland Herzfelde, 11 March 1935.
14 Kracauer to Nora Block, no date; Kracauer to Otto Klepper, 23 January 1936.
15 Transl. note: The former was a group that splintered off from the Socialist Party during the Weimar Republic and continued to be active in the resistance against National Socialism. His *spiritus rector* was the philosopher Leonard Nelson whose Socialism was ethical and anti-Marxist. Klepper was a German politician who fled Nazi Germany in 1933 and in 1937 founded the Deutsche Freiheitspartei while in exile in Paris. In 1947, he returned to Germany and settled in Frankfurt am Main. He was one of the co-founders of the *Frankfurter Allgemeine Zeitung*.
16 Erich Franzen to Kracauer, 28 October 1934.
17 Kracauer to Wieland Herzfelde, no date.
18 SK, 'Zur Erinnerung an Adrienne Monnier [Rue de l'Odéon]' [In remembrance of Adrienne Monnier (Rue de l'Odéon)], in *Werke* 5.4, pp. 628–31; here: pp. 628f.

19 Mülder-Bach, 'Nachbemerkung', p. 705.
20 SK, *Jacques Offenbach*, in *Werke* 8, p. 24. [Transl. note: The last paragraph of the first chapter is omitted in the English edition. It runs in full: 'As the people itself – thus, the rosy-pink glow woven around the terrors [Schrecknisse] in Paris did not emanate from the air alone, but also from the people who spread the terrors. Liberty led this people; even its darkest outbursts, therefore, were still of a human kind.']
21 Siegfried to Rosette and Hedwig Kracauer, 26 March 1938 and 29 May 1938.
22 Goldstein to Kracauer, 14 December 1935, 17 January 1936 and 31 January 1936; Kracauer to Goldstein, 2 February 1936; Lady Davis to Kracauer, 10 November 1938; Kracauer to Lady Davis, 14 May 1941.
23 Gertrud Krautheimer to Kracauer, 7 February 1936; Kracauer to Gertrud Krautheimer, 25 February 1936; Kracauer to Emil Lederer, 28 February 1936 and 10 April 1936; Emil Lederer to Kracauer, 29 March 1936 and 3 June 1936; Kracauer to New York, Graduate Faculty of Political and Social Sciences, 12 April 1936.
24 Löwenstein to Kracauer, 25 February 1939; Thomas Mann to Kracauer, 20 April 1939.
25 Siegfried to Rosette and Hedwig Kracauer, 31 March 1938.
26 Cf. Grossmann, *Emigration*, p. 11.
27 Walter Landauer to Kracauer, 7 January 1938 and 4 February 1938.
28 Siegfried to Rosette and Hedwig Kracauer, 16 April 1938.
29 Siegfried to Rosette and Hedwig Kracauer, 16 April 1939.
30 See SK, 'Pariser Filmbrief' [Letter on film from Paris], in *Werke* 6.3, pp. 229f.; Roud, *A Passion for Films*; Kracauer to Henri Langlois, 23 May 1938.
31 Siegfried to Rosette and Hedwig Kracauer, 29 June 1938, 16 July 1938, 6 September 1938, 10 October 1938 and 31 March 1939.
32 Kracauer to Thomas Mann, 1 May 1939.
33 SK, 'Bei G.W. Pabst im Atelier' [At G.W. Pabst's studio], in *Werke* 6.3, pp. 260f.; Siegfried to Rosette and Hedwig Kracauer, 18 June 1939.
34 Fritz René Allemann to Kracauer, 30 June 1938. In July 1937, the payment per line was reduced to 15 centimes, but Allemann tried to persuade the paper to make an exception in the case of Kracauer. Cf. Fritz René Allemann to Kracauer, 15 July 1939.
35 Siegfried to Rosette and Hedwig Kracauer, 15 May 1939.
36 Quoted after Bronsen, *Joseph Roth*, p. 602. See also von Cziffra, *Der heilige Trinker*, p. 138; von Sternburg, *Joseph Roth*, p. 484.
37 Siegfried to Rosette and Hedwig Kracauer, 5 June 1939.
38 Kracauer to Walter Landauer, 4 June 1939. Kracauer later wrote about Roth's final days: 'Like a seismograph he registered the coming catastrophe, which he felt, and so to speak anticipated, in every single nerve. He also saved the honour of so-called decadence. And out of fear of what was going to come, he tried quite a few false solutions.' Kracauer to Senta Zeidler, 27 August 1954.
39 Joseph Roth, *The Legend of the Holy Drinker*, trans. Michael Hofmann, London: Granta, 2000.

24. The 'Institute for Social Falsification'

1 There are conflicting stories about who was responsible for this coinage – Kracauer or Bloch. Either seems a fitting candidate.

2 Adorno to Kracauer, 1 April 1930 and 12 May 1930, in Adorno/Kracauer, *Briefwechsel*, pp. 195–8 and 206–10. Kracauer found this 'absolutely incomprehensible', as Horkheimer and Pollock had ignored the work both when it was written and after it had been published; cf. Kracauer to Adorno, 25 May 1930, in ibid., pp. 214–17.

3 Kracauer to Max Horkheimer, 22 November 1930; Max Horkheimer to Kracauer, 24 November 1930 and 1 December 1930.

4 Kracauer to Adorno, 21 December 1930, in Adorno/Kracauer, *Briefwechsel*, pp. 253–5; Adorno to Kracauer, 20 January 1931, in ibid., pp. 267–9; Kracauer to Robert Drill, 26 January 1931.

5 Wiggershaus, *Max Horkheimer*, p. 68.

6 Adorno to Kracauer, 29 January 1931, in Adorno/Kracauer, *Briefwechsel*, pp. 267–9; here: p. 269.

7 Kracauer to Adorno, 23 January 1931, in ibid., pp. 270f.; here: p. 271.

8 Cf. Wiggershaus, *The Frankfurt School*, pp. 127–48; Radkau, *Die deutsche Emigration*, pp. 39–43.

9 Kracauer to Leo Löwenthal, 3 November 1934, in Löwenthal/Kracauer, *In steter Freundschaft*, pp. 81f.

10 Kracauer to Gertrud and Richard Krautheimer, 16 May 1936.

11 Cf. Wiggershaus, *The Frankfurt School*, pp. 156–65.

12 Benjamin to Adorno, 19 October 1936, in Adorno/Benjamin, *Correspondence*, p. 155.

13 Adorno to Max Horkheimer, 12 October 1936, in Horkheimer, *GS* 15, *Briefwechsel*, pp. 662–71; here: p. 666.

14 Adorno to Walter Benjamin, 15 October 1936, Adorno/Benjamin, *Briefwechsel*, pp. 150–1; here: p. 151.

15 Adorno to Max Horkheimer, 25 June 1936 and 12 October 1936, in Horkheimer, *GS* 15, *Briefwechsel*, pp. 568–77; here: p. 571; and pp. 662–71; here: pp. 666f.

16 Kracauer to Adorno, 24 October 1936, in Adorno/Kracauer, *Briefwechsel*, pp. 319–22; here: p. 320.

17 Kracauer to Adorno, 9 October 1936, in Adorno/Kracauer, *Briefwechsel*, pp. 323–6; here: p. 324; Emil Lederer to Kracauer, 10 May 1936.

18 Kracauer to Adorno, 21 November 1936, in Adorno/Kracauer, *Briefwechsel*, pp. 328f.

19 Max Horkheimer to Adorno, 22 October 1936, in Horkheimer, *GS* 15, *Briefwechsel*, p. 689; Kracauer to Max Horkheimer, 5 February 1937 and 8 March 1937. Cf. the correspondence between Adorno and Kracauer in February and March 1937 in Adorno/Kracauer, *Briefwechsel*, pp. 334–50.

20 Max Horkheimer to Kracauer, 23 February 1937 and 3 May 1937.

21 SK, 'Totalitäre Propaganda' [Totalitarian propaganda], in *Werke* 2.2, pp. 17–173; here: pp. 31 and 36.

22 Kracauer, 'Mass and Propaganda', p. 11.

23 SK, 'Totalitäre Propaganda', in *Werke* 2.2, pp. 17–173; here: pp. 37 and 49.

24 Max Horkheimer to Kracauer, 29 October 1937 and 15 December 1937.

25 Max Horkheimer to Kracauer, 4 February 1938 and 23 February 1938.

26 Theodor W. Adorno, 'Gutachten über die Arbeit "Die totalitäre Propaganda Deutschlands und Italiens", S. 1 bis 106, von Siegfried

Kracauer' [Report on the study 'Totalitarian propaganda in Germany and Italy', p. 1 to p. 106, by Siegfried Kracauer], in SK, *Werke* 2.2, pp. 821–4; here: p. 821.

27 Adorno to Walter Benjamin, 7 March 1938, in Adorno/Benjamin, *Correspondence*, pp. 240–2; here: p. 240.

28 Leo Löwenthal to Kracauer, 9 September 1938, in Löwenthal/Kracauer, *In steter Freundschaft*, pp. 90–1.

29 See the edited article in SK, *Totalitäre Propaganda*, pp. 266 and 269, and SK, 'Totalitäre Propaganda', in *Werke* 2.2, p. 68.

30 Kracauer to Adorno, 20 August 1938, in Adorno/Kracauer, *Briefwechsel*, pp. 395–400; here: pp. 397–8.

25. Vanishing Point: America

1 Coser, *Refugee Scholars*, p. 88. Johnson was also in touch with Kracauer, because Kracauer had written a contribution on Leopold Sonnemann for the *Enzyklopädie der Sozialwissenschaften*; cf. Alvin Johnson to Kracauer, 27 June 1933; Kracauer to Alvin Johnson, 15 July 1933 and 6 May 1934.

2 Krohn, *Wissenschaft im Exil*, pp. 12f., 70 and 74–7; Coser, *Refugee Scholars*, pp. 102–9; Rutkoff and Scott, 'Die Schaffung der "Universität im Exil"', pp. 131f. [Transl. note: on the fund, see chapter 23.]

3 Krohn, *Wissenschaft im Exil*, p. 89.

4 In their letters, the Krautheimers would often enquire about Hanns Katz, who had been married to Franziska Ehrenreich. Richard Krautheimer had studied art history in Halle at the same time Elisabeth Ehrenreich was studying in nearby Leipzig.

5 Gertrud Krautheimer to Kracauer, 28 April 1936.

6 Adorno to Walter Benjamin, 4 May 1938 and 2 August 1938, in Adorno/Benjamin, *Correspondence*, pp. 248–54; here: pp. 252 and 264–9.

7 Meyer Schapiro to Kracauer, 18 January 1937.

8 It was Iris Barry who wrote: 'The film is a machine for seeing more than meets the eye', according to the dedication in Richard Griffith's *The World of Robert Flaherty* (p. v), which is in the Kracauer library.

9 Gertrud Krautheimer to Kracauer, 13 January 1937; Lynes, *Good Old Modern*, pp. 110–14 and 331.

10 Lavin, 'Panofskys Humor', p. 10; Gertrud Krautheimer to Kracauer, 13 January 1937 and 7 March 1937.

11 Max Horkheimer to Kracauer, 3 May 1937 and 24 May 1937.

12 Kracauer to Museum of Modern Art, Film Library, New York, 18 May 1937.

13 Kracauer to Ferdinand Bruckner, 29 November 1936; Gertrud Krautheimer to Kracauer, 7 March 1937; Kracauer to Gertrud Krautheimer, 7 January 1938; Wilhelm Cohnstaedt to Kracauer, 28 November 1936.

14 Gertrud Krautheimer to Kracauer, 19 December 1937 and 24 March 1938.

15 Gertrud Krautheimer to Kracauer, 23 February 1938, 8 March 1938 and 17 May 1938.

16 The memorandum is contained in 'Nachbemerkung und editorische Notiz', in SK, *Werke* 2.2, pp. 827f.

17 Max Horkheimer to Kracauer, 6 June 1938 and 30 September 1938; Pollock to Kracauer, 4 October 1938.

18 SK, 'Pariser Kunstchronik' [Paris chronicle of the arts], in *Werke* 5.4, pp. 551–3; here: p. 552; and 'Americana', in ibid., pp. 554–65; here: p. 561.
19 Kracauer to Meyer Schapiro, 7 June 1938 and 12 July 1938.
20 Meyer Schapiro to Kracauer, 31 May 1938 and 3 July 1938.
21 Kracauer to Meyer Schapiro, 11 June 1938.
22 Kracauer to Meyer Schapiro, 23 August 1938.
23 Cf. Krohn, 'Vereinigte Staaten von Amerika', p. 449.
24 Kracauer to Meyer Schapiro, 12 September 1938.
25 According to a letter from Adorno to Kracauer, 1 November 1938, in Adorno/Kracauer, *Correspondence*, pp. 403f., a view also confirmed in a letter from Gertrud Krautheimer to Kracauer, 29 October 1938.
26 Meyer Schapiro to Kracauer, 2 October 1938, 10 October 1938 and 28 October 1938; Leo Löwenthal to Kracauer, 18 October 1938 and 1 November 1938; Kracauer to Leo Löwenthal, 17 November 1938, in Löwenthal/Kracauer, *In steter Freundschaft*, pp. 95–8.
27 Kracauer to Franz L. Neumann, 17 November 1938; Kracauer to Meyer Schapiro, 17 October 1938 and 8 November 1938; Meyer Schapiro to Kracauer, 26 November 1938.
28 Meyer Schapiro to Kracauer, 6 January 1939; Gertrud Krautheimer to Kracauer, 23 January 1939; Kracauer to Meyer Schapiro, 27 January 1939.
29 Adorno to Kracauer, 6 March 1939 and 10 March 1939; Kracauer to Adorno, 24 March 1939, in Adorno/Kracauer, *Briefwechsel*, pp. 411–17; here: p. 415; Kracauer to Paul Felix Lazarsfeld, 24 March 1939 and 24 April 1939.
30 Paul Felix Lazarsfeld to Kracauer, 13 April 1939.
31 John E. Abbott to Kracauer, 19 June 1939.
32 Kracauer to Meyer Schapiro, 24 April 1939 and 15 August 1954.

26. Fleeing from France, a Last Minute Exit from Lisbon

1 Badia, 'Frankreichs Haltung', p. 20.
2 Cf. Mühlen, *Fluchtweg*, pp. 48–53; Fittko, *Mein Weg*, pp. 156–60; Fry, *Auslieferung*, pp. 148–50.
3 Koestler, *Scum of the Earth*, p. 119.
4 Cf. Mühlen, *Fluchtweg*, pp. 25f.
5 Kracauer to Borel, Ministère des Affaires Étrangères, 14 September 1939.
6 Morgenstern, *Flucht in Frankreich*, p. 26.
7 Van Reijen and van Doorn, *Aufenthalte und Passagen*, p. 190.
8 According to a letter by Herbert Levin to Kracauer, 4 January 1940, sent from Athis after Kracauer's release.
9 Morgenstern, *Flucht in Frankreich*, p. 35.
10 Herbert Levin to Kracauer, 7 August 1945. On the proper treatment of inmates in the camp, see e.g. Siegfried to Elisabeth Kracauer, 19 September 1939.
11 Kracauer to Egidius and Hedy Streiff, 25 January 1940.
12 Kracauer to Leo Löwenthal, 15 December 1939 and 25 January 1940; Leo Löwenthal to Kracauer, 20 January 1940 and 13 February 1940, in Löwenthal/Kracauer, *In steter Freundschaft*, pp. 103–6.
13 Kracauer to Leo Löwenthal, 27 March 1940, in ibid., pp. 108f.
14 Unger, *Reise ohne Wiederkehr?*, pp. 35f.; Cullin, 'An uns glaubt niemand mehr', p. 28; Vormeier, 'Einige Aspekte', pp. 35–43.

15 Cf. Meinen and Meyer, *Verfolgt von Land zu Land*, p. 8.
16 Cf. Mühlen, *Fluchtweg*, pp. 29f.; Werfel, *Gehetzt*, p. 6.
17 Leo Löwenthal to HIAS, 1 July 1940 and 14 August 1940, in Löwenthal/ Kracauer, *In steter Freundschaft*, pp. 110–12.
18 Kracauer to Paul Tillich, 9 May 1941; Kracauer to Wallach, 31 May 1944.
19 Cf. Krohn, 'Vereinigte Staaten'; Wyman, *Paper Walls*, pp. 209–13; Rutkoff and Scott, *New School*, p. 134.
20 Feuchtwanger, *The Devil in France*, p. 147.
21 Morgenstern, *Flucht in Frankreich*, p. 10.
22 Cf. Kantorowicz, *Exil in Frankreich*, pp. 110–20 and 145; Feuchtwanger, *The Devil in France*, p. 85.
23 Cf. Wunderlich, '"Feindliche Ausländer"', pp. 61–9.
24 Brecht, *Refugee Conversations*, p. 1.
25 Kantorowicz, *Exil in Frankreich*, p. 214.
26 Anna Seghers, *Transit*, p. 134.
27 Ibid., p. 91.
28 Ibid., p. 55.
29 Ibid., p. 3.
30 Ibid., p. 242.
31 Ibid., p. 161.
32 Koestler, *Scum of the Earth* – these are the titles of three of the chapters.
33 Seghers, *Transit*, p. 186.
34 SK, *Ginster*, in *Werke* 7, p. 252.
35 SK, 'Marseille', in *Werke* 5.3, pp. 198–201; here: pp. 199 and 201.
36 Cf. the anecdote related by Soma Morgenstern, according to which Benjamin said of Kracauer in Marseille that he would not commit suicide as he still 'has to finish his encyclopaedia of film'; see Puttnies and Smith, *Benjaminiana*, pp. 202f.
37 In October 1939, Kracauer had already announced that he intended to write an 'aesthetics of film that will be very strange and new'; cf. Kracauer to Hermann Linden, 17 October 1939.
38 Hansen, '"With Skin and Hair"', p. 447.
39 Ibid., p. 458.
40 Ibid., p. 457.
41 Cf. also Baumann, *Im Vorraum der Geschichte*, p. 212.
42 Hansen, '"With Skin and Hair"', p. 468.
43 SK, '"Marseiller Entwurf" zu einer Theorie des Films' [Notes toward a book on film aesthetics], quoted after Hansen, '"With Skin and Hair"', p. 437 (motto). See 'Marseiller Entwurf', in *Werke* 3, pp. 521–779; on the materialism of film, see esp. chapter IV, 'Mit Haut und Haaren' (pp. 559–91); on perception, consciousness and choc, see esp. sections E + F in chapter V (pp. 599–609).
44 Cf. Fermi, *Illustrious Immigrants*, pp. 85–7.
45 Cf. Fry, *Surrender on Demand*; Voswinckel/Berninger, *Exil am Mittelmeer*, p. 9.
46 Hasler, *Mit dem letzten Schiff*, pp. 93–8; Fry, *Surrender on Demand*, p. 215; Fermi, *Illustrious Immigrants*, p. 87.
47 Cf. Fermi, *Illustrious Immigrants*, p. 91.
48 Fry, *Surrender on Demand*, p. 189.
49 Cf. Aktives Museum, *Ohne zu zögern*, p. 172.
50 Kracauer to Ella and Friedrich T. Gubler, 27 July 1947.
51 Cf. Witte, '"Dans une situation sans issue ..."', p. 215; Brodersen, *Walter*

Benjamin, p. 257; van Reijen and van Doorn, *Aufenthalte und Passagen*, p. 224; Fittko, *Mein Weg*, pp. 139–55. After his escape, Kracauer told Eugen Wallach on 2 October 1944 about Benjamin's end: "'He could not stand the thought of what he supposed to be his fate once back in France – his mind was full of dreads of the Gestapo, and of a sinister future in America.'

52 Kracauer to E. and Friedrich T. Gubler, 27 July 1947.

53 Leo Löwenthal to HIAS, 13 November 1940, and Kracauer to Leo Löwenthal, 21 November 1940, in Löwenthal/Kracauer, *In steter Freundschaft*, p. 113.

54 Quoted after *Marbacher Magazin*, p. 97; Kracauer to Leo Löwenthal, 6 November 1940 and 7 November 1940.

55 Kracauer to Hedwig and Rosette Kracauer, 18 October 1941.

56 Fry, *Surrender on Demand*, pp. 186–7; Mühlen, pp. 36 and 42.

57 Cf. Peters, "'Abgestempelt'", p. 296.

58 Transl. note: The acronym is formed from the acronyms of three aid organizations – HIAS, the Hebrew Immigrant Aid Society (New York); ICA, Jewish Colonization Association (Paris, but a British charitable society); and Emigdirect, a Berlin-based migration. The three organizations had merged in 1927.

59 Kracauer to Leo Löwenthal, 4 March 1941, in Löwenthal/Kracauer, *In steter Freundschaft*, pp. 118–19; Mühlen, 'Die Flucht über die Pyrenäen', p. 167.

60 Vormeier, 'Einige Aspekte', p. 47.

61 Kracauer to Adorno, 28 March 1941, in Adorno/Kracauer, *Briefwechsel*, p. 427. Kracauer to Leo Löwenthal, 28 March 1941, in Löwenthal/ Kracauer, *In steter Freundschaft*, p. 121.

27. Arrival in New York

1 Quoted after Aktives Museum, *Ohne zu zögern*, p. 330. The journey seems to have been so long or boring that in Gisela Peiper's recollection it took fourteen rather than ten days.

2 *New York Herald Tribune* and *Journal America*, 25 April 1941.

3 Kracauer, 'Why France Liked Our Films', in *American Writings*, pp. 33–40; here: p. 40.

4 Kracauer to Clementine Cramer, 12 March 1940.

5 Cf. T. Szymanski, 'Das Herz der Welt', in *Tribüne* 154 (2000).

6 Roth, *The Wandering Jews*, p. 1.

7 Kracauer to Herbert and Gertrud Levin, 28 February 1942; Kracauer to Clementine Cramer, 7 September 1947; Kracauer to Friedrich T. and Ella Gubler, 10 September 1945; Aktives Museum, *Ohne zu zögern*, p. 331; Hertzberg, *Shalom Amerika!*, pp. 14–17.

8 Kracauer, 'Why France Liked Our Films', in *American Writings*, pp. 33–40; here: p. 40.

9 Ibid.

10 Kracauer, 'An American Experiment', in *American Writings*, pp. 137–8. The article appeared in the *Neue Züricher Zeitung*.

11 Siegfried to Hedwig and Rosette Kracauer, 11 August 1941. The letter to his mother and aunt, as well as, obviously, articles for German-language newspapers such as the *NZZ*, he continued to write in German.

12 Siegfried to Hedwig and Rosette Kracauer, 19 May 1941; Kracauer to Herbert Levin, 28 February 1943; Kracauer to Egidius and Hedy Streiff, 20 May 1946; Kracauer to Gunther Roth, 18 December 1955.

13 Kracauer to Max Horkheimer, 14 August 1941; Kracauer to Otto Kirchheimer, 21 July 1941.

14 Kracauer to John Marshall, 9 May 1941, and John Marshall to Kracauer, 12 May 1941. Cf. Culbert, 'The Rockefeller Foundation', pp. 495f.

15 Lazarsfeld, 'A Memoir', p. 313.

16 Cf. Bussemer, *Propaganda*, pp. 255–9, 269f. and 289; Biebl, 'Nachbemerkung und editorische Notiz', in *Werke* 2.1, pp. 504f.; Pooley, 'The New History of Mass Communication Research', pp. 49–54; Decherney, *Hollywood*, pp. 5 and 123–5.

17 Hans Speier to Kracauer, 3 June 1941; Kracauer to Max Horkheimer, 11 June 1941; Iris Barry to Kracauer, 1 July 1941. Cf. the correspondence between Barry, Marshall, Kris, Speier and Griffith, in Culbert, 'The Rockefeller Foundation'.

18 Kris and Speier, *German Radio Propaganda*, p. v; Kracauer to Hans Speier, 13 July 1941 and 1 August 1941; Kracauer to Benno Klapp, 10 March 1957.

19 Hans Speier to Kracauer, 4 June 1941.

20 Meyer Schapiro to Kracauer, 9 August 1941.

21 Kracauer to Hedwig and Rosette Kracauer, 19 May 1941.

22 Kracauer to Hans Speier, 17 July 1941.

23 Kracauer to Hedwig and Rosette Kracauer, 27 August 1941 and 18 October 1941; Kracauer to Clementine Cramer, 1 October 1941.

24 Cf. Asper, *Nachrichten aus Hollywood*, pp. 23f.; Kracauer to David, Korda Film, 17 September 1941. Levin was an ethnologist and had worked at museums. In the US, the Levins became farmers.

25 Cf. Schütz and Gurwitsch, *Briefwechsel*, p. 11.

26 Kracauer to Erwin Panofsky, 14 May 1941, in Breidecker, *Siegfried Kracauer – Erwin Panofsky*, p. 1.

27 Kracauer to Walter Friedlaender, 22 February 1943 and 15 March 1943. In this letter, Kracauer expresses his astonishment about the fact that their friendship was 'as if we had known each other since childhood'.

28 Kracauer to Max Horkheimer, 6 June 1941.

28. *Define Your Enemy*: What is National Socialism?

1 Kracauer, 'The Teutonic Mind', in *American Writings*, pp. 181–3; here: p. 181.

2 Crohn, *Wissenschaft im Exil*, pp. 70–85; Rutkoff and Scott, 'Die Schaffung der "Universität im Exil"', pp. 106–31; on the funding policies of the Rockefeller Foundation, see Fleck, *Transatlantische Bereicherungen*, pp. 9–12 and 22f.

3 Rutkoff and Scott, 'Die Schaffung der "Universität im Exil"', p. 134.

4 Cf. Speier and Kähler, *War in Our Time*.

5 Cf. Lederer, *State of the Masses*, pp. 17–20 and 98–131.

6 Biebl, 'Nachbemerkung und editorische Notiz', p. 506.

7 Pollock, 'State Capitalism'.

8 Cf. Neumann, *Behemoth*, p. 5 (on the name), pp. 39f. (on the national socialist ideology), pp. 103–9 (on anti-Semitism), pp. 181–6 (on state capitalism), pp. 382f. (on the question 'Is Germany a State?').

9 Diner, 'Aporie der Vernunft', p. 34.
10 Horkheimer, 'The Jews and Europe', pp. 225 and 226; see also Diner, 'Aporie der Vernunft' and Dubiel and Söllner, 'Die Nationalsozialismusforschung des Instituts für Sozialforschung', pp. 11f.
11 Kracauer to Max Horkheimer, 11 June 1941.
12 Cf. Diner, 'Aporie der Vernunft', esp. pp. 34 and 39; Ziege, Antisemitismus, p. 8.

29. *Know Your Enemy*: Psychological Warfare

1 Cf. Kershaw, *Fateful Choices*, pp. 382–430; Hobsbawm, *The Age of Extremes*, pp. 142–5; Tooze, *The Wages of Destruction*, pp. xxii–xxvi.
2 Hertzberg, *Shalom Amerika!*, p. 263; Slezkine, *Das jüdische Jahrhundert*.
3 Cf. Simpson, *Science of Coercion*, pp. 3–14 and 31–41; Söllner, 'Archäologie der deutschen Demokratie', p. 7; Bussemer, *Propaganda*, pp. 299–301; Pooley, 'The New History of Mass Communication Research', pp. 55–7.
4 Quoted after Hoennicke Moore, *Know Your Enemy*, p. 178.
5 Quoted after Söllner, 'Archäologie der deutschen Demokratie', p. 25.
6 Freeman, *Never Call Retreat*, pp. v and ix.
7 See Kracauer's letter of protest to the US District Court, Southern District of New York, Immigration and Naturalization Service, 5 December 1941. The court referred to the Kracauers' 'German nationality', but in his letter Kracauer declared: 'Our allegiance is only to the United States of America' (Konvolut Emigration Amerika).
8 Jay, 'The Extraterritorial Life of Siegfried Kracauer', p. 168.
9 Kracauer, 'Propaganda and the Nazi War Film', in *From Caligari to Hitler*, pp. 273–331; here: p. 274.
10 Cf. Biebl, 'Nachbemerkung und editorische Notiz', pp. 506f.
11 Cf. Bussemer, *Propaganda*, pp. 292–9. Kracauer also sent his propaganda study to the OSS and the National Film Board of Canada and offered them his services. Cf. Kracauer to Hans Speier, 9 July 1942; Office of Strategic Services, Charlton F. Scofield to Kracauer, 1 July 1942; Kracauer to John Grierson, 31 October 1942.
12 Iris Barry to Kracauer, 29 July 1942.
13 Kracauer to Erwin Panofsky, 1 August 1942, in Breidecker, *Siegfried Kracauer – Erwin Panofsky*, pp. 9f. Kracauer to Hans Speier, 16 October 1942.
14 Kracauer to Meyer Schapiro, 26 June 1942.
15 Kracauer to Hans Speier, 16 October 1942.
16 Krige and Rausch, 'Introduction', and Müller, 'Die Macht der Menschenfreunde'.
17 On the films, see Sakmyster, 'Nazi Documentaries of Intimidation', pp. 494–500. Sakmyster believes that Kracauer did not watch *Baptism of Fire* but *Campaign in Poland* (1940), a mistake, he says, that has been repeated frequently in the literature. All these films, incidentally, were shown in large cinemas in many American cities.
18 Kracauer, 'Propaganda and the Nazi War Film', in *From Caligari to Hitler*, pp. 273–331; here: p. 279.
19 Ibid., p. 293.
20 Kracauer, 'The Conquest of Europe on the Screen'.

21 Kracauer to Erwin Panofsky, 1 October 1941, in Breidecker, *Siegfried Kracauer – Erwin Panofsky*, p. 5.
22 Panofsky, 'Style and Medium in the Motion Pictures', p. 122. [Transl. note: The quotations follow a later version of Panofsky's essay, in which, however, the quoted passages are unchanged.]
23 Ibid., p. 96.
24 Ibid., p. 100.
25 Ibid., p. 123.
26 Kracauer, 'The Conquest of Europe on the Screen', p. 156.
27 Kracauer, 'Propaganda and the Nazi War Film', in *From Caligari to Hitler*, pp. 273–331; here: pp. 286–8, 290f., 293f., 297f., 300, 306f., 308f., 312 and 314f.
28 Cf. Kris and Speier, *German Radio Propaganda*, VII, p. 477.
29 Cf. Culbert, 'The Rockefeller Foundation', p. 501; Sakmyster, 'Nazi Documentaries', pp. 509f.
30 Macdonald, review of 'The Conquest of Europe on the Screen', in *Politics*, May 1944, p. 118.
31 Cf. Macdonald, *The Memoirs of a Revolutionist*, pp. vii and 319, and Sumner, *Dwight Macdonald*.
32 Farrell, *The Frightened Philistines*, p. 204.
33 Kracauer to Friedrich T. and Ella Gubler, 10 September 1945.
34 Kracauer to Erwin Panofsky, 8 November 1944, in Breidecker, *Siegfried Kracauer – Erwin Panofsky*, pp. 37f.
35 Kracauer to Eugen Schüfftan, 28 April 1946, in Asper, *Nachrichten aus Hollywood*, p. 65; and Kracauer to Herbert and Gertrud Levin, 2 September 1946. [Transl. note: In this quotation the words 'Refugees' (capitalized) and 'citizenship' are in English in the original.]
36 Kracauer to Paul Felix Lazarsfeld, 23 November 1942.
37 Erwin Panofsky to Kracauer, 18 August 1942, in Breidecker, *Siegfried Kracauer – Erwin Panofsky*, pp. 10f.
38 Cf. Erwin Panofsky to Kracauer, 2 November 1944, in Breidecker, *Siegfried Kracauer – Erwin Panofsky*, p. 36. On the wariness of the emigrants in the US regarding the thesis of the class character of National Socialism, see Radkau, *Die deutsche Emigration in den USA*, pp. 225 and 230–5.
39 Hans Richter to Kracauer, 4 October 1943.
40 Vansittart, *Black Record*, p. 16.
41 Cf. Vansittart, *Black Record*, cover text.
42 See Vansittart, *Lessons of My Life*, pp. 131 and 144.
43 Cf. Später, *Vansittart*, pp. 435–7 and 443–8.
44 Cf. Hoennicke Moore, *Know Your Enemy*, pp. 1 and 13.
45 Transl. note: Italicized passage in English in the original.
46 SK, 'Bemerkungen zur geplanten Geschichte des deutschen Films' [Remarks on a plan for a history of German film], in *Werke* 2.1, pp. 491–8; here: p. 491; on this, see also Kracauer to Herbert Levin, 28 February 1943.
47 Koffler, *Vansittartitis: A Polemic*.
48 Kracauer to Panofsky, 14 February 1944, in Breidecker, *Siegfried Kracauer – Erwin Panofsky*, p. 28.
49 Konvolut Bureau of Social Research.

30. *Fear Your Enemy*: Deportation and Killing of the Jews

1 Kracauer to Friedrich T. and Ella Gubler, 10 September 1945; Kracauer to Herbert and Gertrud Levin, 15 October 1942; Kracauer to Junghans, 7 November 1941.
2 *Und keiner hat für uns Kaddisch gesagt ...*, p. 285.
3 Herbert, *Geschichte Deutschlands*, p. 469.
4 Cf. Wippermann, *Das Leben in Frankfurt zur NS-Zeit*, pp. 139–41.
5 Kracauer to Irma Frank, 28 September 1941.
6 Kracauer to Egidius and Hedy Streiff, 3 December 1941 and 21 December 1941; *Und keiner hat für uns Kaddisch gesagt ...*, p. 283.
7 Cf. Wippermann, *Das Leben in Frankfurt zur NS-Zeit*, p. 132.
8 See the statement of Lina Katz in *Dokumente zur Geschichte der Frankfurter Juden*, pp. 507f. The Kracauers owned a copy of this documentation published in 1963.
9 *Geschichte Deutschlands*, pp. 467 and 474f.
10 Wippermann, *Das Leben in Frankfurt zur NS-Zeit*, pp. 135–7; Heuberger and Krohn, *Hinaus aus dem Ghetto ...*, p. 189, give a figure of 1,200 for the number of the deported.
11 Friedländer, *The Years of Extermination*, p. 266; Hilberg, *The Destruction of the European Jews*, vol. 2, p. 474.
12 Herbert, *Geschichte Deutschlands*, pp. 476f.
13 Hilberg, *The Destruction of the European Jews*, vol. 2, p. 424.
14 See ibid., p. 447.
15 Ibid., p. 448 [Transl. note: The quotation within the quotation is from the testimony by Staatssekretär Bühler of the Generalgouvernement, in Secretariat of the Tribunal (ed.), *Trial of the Major War Criminals*, vol. XII, p. 69. 'Bühler', Hilberg adds, 'did not believe in this fairy tale himself' (p. 448, fn 35).]
16 Friedländer, *The Years of Extermination*, p. 354.
17 Ibid.
18 Hilberg, *The Destruction of the European Jews*, vol. 2, p. 455.
19 Quoted after Herbert, *Geschichte Deutschlands*, p. 483.
20 Cf. Hilberg, *The Destruction of the European Jews*, vol. 2, pp. 474f.; Wippermann, *Das Leben in Frankfurt zur NS-Zeit*, p. 132; Kracauer to Herbert and Gertrud Levin, 15 October 1942.
21 *Dokumente zur Geschichte der Frankfurter Juden*, XIV 1, pp. 507f.
22 Siegfried and Elisabeth Kracauer to Egidius and Hedy Streiff, 25 August 1945; S. and E. Kracauer to Friedrich T. and Ella Gubler, 10 September 1945.
23 Kracauer to Herbert and Gertrud Levin, 29 October 1942 and 27 November 1942.
24 Kracauer to Gertrud Krautheimer, 16 November 1942.
25 Kracauer to Herbert and Gertrud Levin, 27 November 1942.
26 Kracauer to Herbert and Gertrud Levin, 24 July 1943, a letter written after Herbert Meyer, with whom they had both been imprisoned, had arrived in New York 'following an adventurous escape from France'; and 2 September 1946 when Willi Wolfradt arrived in New York; see also 28 December 1944.
27 Herbert, *Geschichte Deutschlands*, p. 463.
28 Gertrud Krautheimer to Kracauer, 5 November 1942.
29 Cf. Später, *Vansittart*, pp. 231–42; Greiner, *Die Morgenthau-Legende*,

pp. 48 and 121; Breitman, *Staatsgeheimnisse*, pp. 186–210; Laqueur, *The Terrible Secret*, pp. 219–38.

30 Kracauer to Egidius and Hedy Streiff, 25 August 1945.

31. *Fuck Your Enemy*: From Hitler to Caligari

1 Rotha, *Film Till Now* (1949), pp. 254–6.
2 Kracauer asked Feininger whether he knew the film, to which he answered no, adding that he had been asked that question many times before. The painting dates from 1911. Feininger also asked Kracauer whether he could watch the film at the Museum of Modern Art. Cf. Lyonel Feininger to Kracauer, 13 September 1944.
3 Kracauer to Herbert and Gertrud Levin, 1 February 1943.
4 Datus Smith to Kracauer, 10 April 1944, 15 August 1944 and 30 October 1944; Kracauer to Datus Smith, 3 November 1944; Erwin Panofsky to Kracauer, 4 August 1944, in Breidecker, *Siegfried Kracauer – Erwin Panofsky*, pp. 30f.
5 Kaes, 'Siegfried Kracauer', p. 248.
6 SK, 'Bemerkungen zur geplanten Geschichte des deutschen Films' [Remarks on a plan for a history of German film], in *Werke* 2.1, pp. 492f. and 496.
7 Kracauer, *From Caligari to Hitler*, pp. 67 and 79.
8 Ibid., p. 10 (transl. mod.).
9 Ibid., p. 160.
10 Ibid., p. 11.
11 Ibid., p. 8.
12 Ibid., p. 6.
13 Kracauer, 'The Mass Ornament', in *The Mass Ornament*, pp. 75–86; here: p. 75.
14 Kracauer, *From Caligari to Hitler*, p. 72. [Transl. note: Kracauer compares the expressionistic style to street signs such as 'Men at Work', only that its elements signal 'Soul at Work' (p. 71); hence, his use of capital letters and quotation marks.]
15 Cf. Koch, *Kracauer*, pp. 101 and 118; Elsaesser, *Weimar Cinema*, pp. 3f.; Brecht, 'Strom der Freiheit', p. 35.
16 Cf. Koch, *Kracauer*, p. 105.
17 Kracauer to Hermann Hesse, 2 February 1947.
18 See also Kaes, 'Siegfried Kracauer', p. 237.
19 Cf. Brecht, 'Strom der Freiheit', p. 11.
20 Améry, 'How Much Home Does a Person Need?', p. 50.
21 Kracauer to Herbert and Gertrud Levin, 28 April 1943.
22 Kracauer to Erwin Panofsky, 2 May 1947, in Breidecker, *Siegfried Kracauer – Erwin Panofsky*, p. 47.
23 Kracauer to Herbert and Gertrud Levin, 15 October 1942.
24 *The New York Times Book Review*, 18 May 1947 and *The New Leader*, 18 June 1947.
25 *The Hollywood Quarterly*, July 1947 and *The Nation*, 26 July 1947.
26 *New Movies* 22 (summer 1947), no. 4; *The New Republic*, 19 May 1947; *The New Leader*, 9 August 1947; *Sight & Sound* 16 (summer 1947), p. 62.
27 *Austro American Tribune* 4 (August 1947) 1; *Modern Review* 1 (August 1947), no. 6. The 'Gemeindeblatt' [community newsletter] of German

immigrants in New York, the *Aufbau*, spoke of the book in very approving and positive terms.

28 *Magazine of Art*, November 1947; *The Psychoanalytic Review* 35 (April 1948), no. 2; *Psychoanalytic Quarterly*, no date.

29 *The Film To-Day*, summer 1947.

30 Rotha, *Documentary Film*.

31 See the booklet accompanying the DVD 'Land of Promise. The British Documentary Movement 1930–1950'.

32 Kracauer to Paul Rotha, 12 July 1947.

33 *Der Monat* 1 (1948) 2, pp. 78–86 and pp. 109–11 (under the rubric 'Autoren des Monats' [Authors of the month']; here: p. 111.

34 Kracauer to Melvin Lasky, 11 September 1948 and 12 December 1948; Melvin Lasky to Kracauer, 29 April 1948 and 17 December 1948.

35 Transl. note: The German word for 'seducer' is 'Verführer', hence contains the word for *The Führer*, the 'leader', Adolf Hitler.

36 *Dionysos*, 21 May 1948. Jaesrich knew Kracauer from 'the old days in Berlin' and met with him during Kracauer's visit to Berlin in 1956. Kracauer to Hellmut Jaesrich, 10 March 1947.

37 Kracauer to Alfred Beierle, 20 December 1948.

38 Kracauer to Clementine Cramer, 1 December 1946.

39 Karl F. Borée and Kracauer, 22 January 1949 and 19 June 1949.

40 Kracauer to Herbert Demtröder, 6 November 1949.

41 Kracauer to Friedrich T. and Ella Gubler, 10 September 1945.

42 Hermann Linden to Kracauer, 24 July 1948, 5 October 1948 and 8 October 1948.

43 Kracauer to Max Niederlechner, 21 February 1949.

44 Wolfgang Weyrauch to Kracauer, 7 May 1947 and 3 September 1947, and Kracauer to Weyrauch, 13 October 1947.

45 Kracauer first enquired about Weyrauch with the social democrat Fritz Heine, who had been part of the group around Vry and had been in Lisbon with Kracauer; cf. Fritz Heine to Kracauer, 27 March 1948. He also asked Hermann Linden about Weyrauch; see Hermann Linden to Kracauer, 9 June 1948.

46 Bernard Guttmann to Kracauer, 17 August 1949. Another case in which Kracauer initiated correspondence was that of Karl Walther Klüger, who was much younger than Kracauer. Klüger had also published a contribution in *Der Monat* and Kracauer liked his views and writing style very much; see Kracauer to Karl W. Klüger, 31 July 1949 and 31 August 1949. Following their first positive exchanges, Kracauer began asking Klüger questions regarding German film. Klüger, however, died soon afterwards from a heart attack.

47 Kracauer to Datus Smith, 20 October 1948.

48 The first of such requests came from the publisher Bruno Henschel und Sohn from East Berlin; Harald Henschel to Kracauer, 17 March 1948; Lieselotte Glaue to Kracauer, 20 September 1948.

32. Cultural Critic, Social Scientist, Supplicant

1 The work was translated into Italian (1954), Spanish, Polish (1958) and German.

2 Kracauer to Hans Richter, 12 July 1947.

3 Kracauer to Adorno, 24 April 1947, in Adorno/Kracauer, *Briefwechsel*, p. 439.

4 Kracauer to Datus Smith, 30 September 1950.

5 Kracauer to Erwin Panofsky, 19 December 1945, in Breidecker, *Siegfried Kracauer – Erwin Panofsky*, p. 42; Kracauer to Herbert and Gertrud Levin, 25 July 1945; Hadley Cantril to Kracauer, 6 July 1945.

6 Kracauer to Horkheimer, 30 March 1945; Horkheimer to Kracauer, 12 October 1946. Fleck and Stiegler, 'Nachbemerkung und editorische Notiz', in SK, *Werke* 2.2, pp. 849–54. On the project for this film, cf. Koch, *Die Einstellung*, pp. 54–94. On research on prejudice by the IfS and AJC, Ziege, *Antisemitismus*, pp. 229–84. The books and articles on prejudice research from the perspective of sociology or social psychology in the Kracauer library in Marbach are covered with annotations, for instance a copy of *Anatomy of Racial Intolerance*, New York, 1946.

7 Kracauer to Friedrich T. and Ella Gubler, 20 May 1946; Kracauer to Fritz Heine, 23 May 1948.

8 Kracauer to Friedrich T. and Ella Gubler, 10 September 1945.

9 Cf. Kracauer's file at the Entschädigungsbehörde Berlin [Office for compensation], in Berlin-Wilmersdorf, Landesamt für Bürger- und Ordnungsangelegenheiten, Abt. 1: Entschädigungsbehörde, Opfer des Nationalsozialismus [victims of National Socialism], Dateneingabe MyCMDB, I A 45.

10 Kracauer to Horace M. Kallen, 2 March 1946.

11 Kracauer, 'The Revolt against Rationality', in *American Writings*, pp. 51–4.

12 Kracauer, 'On Jewish Culture', in *American Writings*, pp. 54–6. I do not know why it was not included.

13 Kracauer, 'Psychiatry for Everything and Everybody', in *American Writings*, pp. 62–72.

14 Kracauer, 'The Decent German', in *American Writings*, pp. 157–61; here: p. 159.

15 Ibid., p. 160.

16 Kracauer to William Dubois, 17 November 1948.

17 Cf. income tax declaration of 22 December 1954 in Kracauer's compensation file at the Entschädigungsbehörde Berlin in Berlin-Wilmersdorf, Landesamt für Bürger- und Ordnungsangelegenheiten, Abt. 1: Entschädigungsbehörde, Opfer des Nationalsozialismus, Dateneingabe MyCMDB, I A 45.

18 Kracauer to Herbert and Gertrud Levin, 19 November 1947.

19 Transl. note: 'Unter dem Strich': beginning with the French Revolution, articles on cultural matters became part of newspapers, and were printed – beginning with the front page – below a line that separated them from news and debate. German papers adopted this practice, and it was common until the mid-1920s.

20 Kracauer, 'Psychiatry for Everything and Everybody', in *American Writings*, pp. 62–72; here: p. 68, and 'Pictorial Deluge', in *American Writings*, pp. 192–5.

21 Cf. Gregor and Patalas, *Geschichte des Films*, pp. 310–12.

22 Herman G. Weinberg to Kracauer, 6 June 1947 and 13 July 1949.

23 Robert J. Flaherty to Kracauer, 9 January 1948. Flaherty produced the first full-length American documentary film, *Nanook of the North* (1922).

24 Cf. the joint reviews of the two books by David T. Bazelon, 'The Hidden

Movie', in *Commentary* 4 (1947) 2 and Thomas J. Fitzmorris, 'Films Psychoanalyzed', in *America*, 16 August 1947; *The New York Times Book Review*, 18 May 1947; also Parker Tyler to Kracauer, 17 April 1950.

25 Quoted after MacDonald, *Cinema* 16, pp. 128–30; here: p. 130; cf. also pp. 1–35.

26 Kracauer, 'The Eternal Jew', in *American Writings*, pp. 162–5.

27 Amos Vogel to Kracauer, 27 April 1948 and 25 October 1948; 29 September 1958.

28 Kracauer, 'Hollywood's Terror Films', in *American Writings*, pp. 41–7; here: p. 46.

29 Kracauer, 'The Mirror Up to Nature', in *American Writings*, pp. 105–8; here: p. 106.

30 Kracauer, 'Paisan', in *American Writings*, pp. 150–6; here: p. 152.

31 Farrell, by contrast, thought the scene in which a resistance fighter does not betray his comrades while being tortured was not only unrealistic, but also akin to Stalinist hero-worshipping. Cf. James T. Farrell to Kracauer, 4 September 1946, 14 October 1946 and 26 August 1948.

32 Kracauer, 'Paisan', in *American Writings*, pp. 150–6; here: p. 155.

33 Kracauer to Friedrich T. and Ella Gubler, 10 September 1945; Kracauer to Herbert and Gertrud Levin, 28 April 1945, 25 July 1945 and 28 April 1946. Kracauer to Ludwig Hardt, 23 November 1945.

34 Else Staudinger to Kracauer, 6 December 1945 and 20 December 1945.

35 National Institute of Arts and Letters to Kracauer, 28 December 1945 and 26 April 1946.

36 Kracauer to Herbert and Gertrud Levin, 13 July 1947.

37 Kracauer to Leo Löwenthal, 21 February 1947 and Leo Löwenthal to Kracauer, 25 February 1947 and 12 August 1947, in Löwenthal/Kracauer, *In steter Freundschaft*, pp. 132–5.

38 Else Staudinger to Kracauer, 1 December 1948.

39 Social Studies Association to Kracauer, 13 July 1948.

40 Kracauer to Harold Mantell, 3 June 1948; Kracauer to Salman Schocken, 14 September 1947; Kracauer to Slesinger, American Film Center, 30 January 1945; Kracauer to Henry Blanke, 8 September 1947; Kracauer to H. William Fitelson, 27 August 1947; Kracauer to Luther H. Evans, January/February 1946; Kracauer to Samuel H. Flowerman, 3 March 1949 and 26 April 1949; David M. Levy to Kracauer, 11 June 1947; Kracauer to Charles P. Holmes, United Nations, 24 June 1947. On the evaluation of *Crossfire*, see Koch, *Die Einstellung*, pp. 94–113. In this context, in the summer of 1947, he again met the usual suspects in mass communication research: Herta Herzog, Marie Jahoda, Ernst Kris, Leo Löwenthal, Paul Lazarsfeld, Margaret Mead, Robert K. Merton. On Kracauer's criticism of *Crossfire*, see his letter to Leo Löwenthal of 5 October 1947, in Löwenthal/Kracauer, *In steter Freundschaft*, pp. 136–8.

41 Kracauer to Herbert and Gertrud Levin, 13 July 1947.

42 Kracauer to Herbert and Gertrud Levin, 21 November 1948.

43 Kracauer to Herbert and Gertrud Levin, 23 May 1949.

44 Kracauer to Herbert and Gertrud Levin, 21 November 1948 and 1 December 1949.

45 Moltke and Rawson, 'Introduction', p. 12. [Transl. note: Moltke and Rawson paint the opposite picture, using the term 'missing link': 'In retrospect and for reasons we outline below, we are tempted to see in

Kracauer the missing link between the Frankfurt School and the New York Intellectuals.']

46 Kracauer to Leo Löwenthal, 5 August 1951, in Löwenthal/Kracauer, *In steter Freundschaft*, pp. 139–41; here: p. 141.

47 Kracauer to Herbert and Gertrud Levin, 21 September 1947.

48 Kracauer to Egidius and Hedy Streiff, 20 May 1946.

49 Kracauer to Gregory Bateson, 16 November 1947.

50 Kracauer to Clyde Kluckhohn, 23 February 1948, 27 February 1948, 2 March 1948 and 18 May 1948. On Kluckhohn and his work on psychological warfare during the Cold War, see Müller, *Krieger und Gelehrte*, pp. 113–16.

51 Kracauer to Hadley Cantril, 24 February 1948, 25 March 1948, 3 April 1948, 19 April 1948, 1 May 1948 and 21 November 1948.

52 Kracauer received $250 for it. Hadley Cantril to Kracauer, 1 May 1948; Kracauer to Paul Schrecker, 3 July 1948. Kracauer, 'National Types as Hollywood Presents Them', in *American Writings*, pp. 81–104.

53 Adolph Lowe to Kracauer, 11 February 1949 and 2 May 1949. On the Institute of World Affairs, see Krohn, *Wissenschaft im Exil*, pp. 156–67, and Rutkoff and Scott, *New School*, pp. 137–43.

54 Kracauer to Paul Fejos, 11 September 1948, 15 September 1948 and 29 March 1949.

55 Kracauer to Otto Klineberg, 10 September 1948.

56 Kracauer to Leo Löwenthal, 5 August 1951, in Löwenthal/Kracauer, *In steter Freundschaft*, pp. 139–41; here: p. 141.

33. The Aesthetics of Film as Cultural Studies

1 Kracauer to Adorno, 12 February 1949, in Adorno/Kracauer, *Briefwechsel*, pp. 444–7; here: pp. 444f.

2 Newhall, *The History of Photography*, pp. 103–18. Newhall was in charge of the Museum of Modern Art's photography section, which he had created himself. His *History of Photography* was Kracauer's essential point of reference regarding matters of photography.

3 SK, 'Vorläufige Angaben zu einer Untersuchung über die Ästhetik des Films' [Preliminary remarks on an investigation of the aesthetics of film], in *Werke* 3, pp. 819–21.

4 SK, 'Vorläufige Übersicht über ein Buch zur Ästhetik des Films' [Preliminary synopsis of a book on the aesthetics of film], in *Werke* 3, pp. 826–43; here: p. 827.

5 Ibid., p. 843. I believe the omission of the words 'it from' in Kracauer's manuscript is a mistake, as it is unlikely that he thinks violence and terror should be rescued. [Transl. note: In German, the word omitted is just a single one ('von'), making a slip of the pen a likely explanation.]

6 Koch, *Die Einstellung*, p. 130. Cf. also Mülder-Bach, 'Die umschlagende Negativität'; Kimmich and Grunert, *Denken durch die Dinge*, pp. 7–10.

7 Proust, *The Guermantes Way*, p. 157. Kracauer came across the Proust passage in May 1949; cf. Kracauer to Beaumont Newhall, 30 May 1949.

8 Kracauer to Erwin Panofsky, 12 December 1948 and 23 January 1949, in Breidecker, *Siegfried Kracauer – Erwin Panofsky*, pp. 48 and 50. Other recipients of the grant before Kracauer included Hermann Broch, Max

Raphael (1945) and Erich Kahler (1947), and, following Kracauer, Hans Kelsen (1952), Meyer Schapiro (1954), Anton Ehrenzweig (1957), Irving Howe, Alfred Kazin and Walther R. Corti (1959).

9 Cf. Belke, 'Kracauers letzte Lebensjahre', pp. 443–51.

10 Adorno to Kracauer, 22 December 1942, in Adorno/Kracauer, *Briefwechsel*, p. 428.

11 Adorno to Kracauer, 7 February 1942, in ibid., pp. 442f.

12 Kracauer to Adorno, 12 February 1949, in ibid., pp. 444–6.

13 Adorno to Kracauer, 17 October 1950, in ibid., p. 453.

14 Cf. Arnheim, *Zauber des Sehens*, pp. 13, 18f., 68 and 87; Arnheim, *Visual Thinking*, pp. v–vii; Arnheim, 'Zur Psychologie der Kunst', p. 204.

15 Cf. Arnheim, *Zauber des Sehens*, pp. 8, 21f. and 52–4.

16 Rudolf Arnheim to Kracauer, *Briefwechsel* 1949–1953 (DLA Marbach, NL Kracauer); especially: no date, spring 1949; 26 September 1949, 23 October 1949, 13 November 1949, 30 December 1949, 8 August 1950 and 19 August 1950, 14 September 1951, 23 October 1953, 25 October 1953 and 3 November 1953. Kracauer to Leo Löwenthal, 26 October 1955, in Löwenthal/Kracauer, *In steter Freundschaft*, p. 157.

17 Warshow, *The Immediate Experience*, p. xli.

18 Transl. note: 'Mit Haut und Haaren', meaning 'the whole person is fully committed'. In the Marseille Notebooks, the expression was the title of the chapter that became 'The Spectator' in *The Theory of Film*.

19 Hansen, *Cinema and Experience*, pp. 255–8; here: p. 258.

20 Ibid., p. 27.

21 Erwin Panofsky to Philip Vaudrin, copy sent to Kracauer, 17 October 1949.

22 Breidecker, '"Ferne Nähe"'. In 'Vom Eisen zum Film', Breidecker identifies this closeness in the shared search for an anonymous, non-idealist art history of modernity, adding the architect Giedion as a third kindred spirit in this regard.

23 Panofsky, *Meaning in the Visual Arts*, 'Introduction: The History of Art as a Humanistic Discipline', p. 23.

24 Cf. Breidecker, '"Ferne Nähe"', pp. 132–8.

25 Rutkoff and Scott, *New School*, pp. 153–71.

26 Kracauer to Erwin Panofsky, 1 October 1941, 3 October 1941, 1 August 1942, 16 October 1942, 23 December 1942 and 4 February 1947.

27 Even earlier, Kracauer had written an article on 'Stage vs. Screen Acting' for *Studies in Philosophy and Social Sciences*, the journal of the Institute for Social Research. However, it did not appear because the journal was discontinued at the end of 1941. Kracauer managed to place another article on silent film comedies (1951) in *Sight & Sound*.

28 Kracauer, 'The Photographic Approach', in *American Writings*, pp. 204–13; here: p. 209. See also the section on 'The Photographic Approach', in *Theory of Film*, pp. 13–18. On the basic aesthetic principle, see *Theory of Film*, pp. 12–13.

29 Panofsky, *Meaning in the Visual Arts*, 'Introduction: The History of Art as a Humanistic Discipline', pp. 7 and 24; Panofsky, *Meaning in the Visual Arts*, 'Iconography and Iconology: An Introduction to the Study of Renaissance Art', pp. 26–54.

30 Schöttker, 'Bild, Kultur und Theorie', pp. 125 and 138f.; Breidecker, '"Ferne Nähe"', pp. 151–6 and 163.

34. Two Boxes from Paris

1 Kracauer to Adorno, 1 October 1950, in Adorno/Kracauer, *Briefwechsel*, pp. 447–50; here: p. 449.
2 Ibid., p. 448.
3 Kracauer to Adorno, 4 July 1951, in ibid., pp. 455–8; here: p. 456.
4 Ibid., p. 455.
5 Kracauer to Adorno, 28 August 1954, in ibid., pp. 469–71; here: p. 469.
6 Max Stettiner to Kracauer, no date (1950).
7 Kracauer to Leo Löwenthal, 5 August 1951, in Löwenthal/Kracauer, *In steter Freundschaft*, pp. 139–42; here: p. 140.
8 Kracauer to Alfred Beierle, no date and 20 December 1948.
9 Annemarie and Fritz Wahl to Siegfried and Elisabeth Kracauer, 18 February 1950.
10 Kracauer to Willy Haas, 14 September 1952.
11 Siegfried and Elisabeth Kracauer to Annemarie and Fritz Wahl, 10 September 1950.
12 Ella Gubler to Siegfried and Elisabeth Kracauer, 22 January 1946, 20 January 1947 and 8 June 1953.
13 Kracauer to Annemarie and Fritz Wahl, 18 February 1950, 19 February 1950, 10 September 1950, 17 December 1950 and 22 December 1950.
14 Elisabeth Kracauer to Benno Reifenberg, 22 February 1967.
15 Bernhard Guttmann to Kracauer, 3 November 1954.
16 Kracauer to William S. Schlamm, 10 September 1950; e.g. Gertrud and Richard Krautheimer to Siegfried and Elisabeth Kracauer, 29 October 1950.
17 Kracauer to Friedrich T. and Ella Gubler, 4 September 1953.
18 Kracauer to William S. Schlamm, 10 September 1950.

35. Working as a Consultant in the Social Sciences and Humanities

1 Cf. Jansen, *Das Utopische*, pp. 141f.
2 Lazarsfeld, 'A Memoir', p. 314. On the foundations of 'content analysis' from today's perspective, see Berelson, *Content Analysis*.
3 Lasswell, 'Psychological Policy Research and Total Strategy', p. 491.
4 Fleck and Siegler, 'Nachbemerkung und editorische Notiz', pp. 856f.; Neurath, 'Paul Lazarsfeld', pp. 79–83; Ritsert, *Inhaltsanalyse*, p. 14; Kracauer to Leo Löwenthal, 5 May 1951, in Löwenthal/Kracauer, *In steter Freundschaft*, p. 141; Kracauer to William S. Schlamm, 10 September 1950; Kracauer to Herbert and Gertrud Levin, 30 June 1951. At that point, Kracauer's age ruled out permanent employment by the Bureau of Applied Social Research.
5 Cf. Stöver, *Der Kalte Krieg*, pp. 89–116.
6 Müller, *Krieger und Gelehrte*, pp. 59–68.
7 Kracauer and Berkman, *Satellite Mentality*, p. 15.
8 Ibid., p. 51.
9 Cf. Kaes, 'Siegfried Kracauer', pp. 264–6.
10 Cf. Haury, 'Zur Logik des bundesdeutschen Antizionismus', pp. 138–41; Später, '"Kein Frieden mit Israel"', pp. 248f.
11 Quoted after Dan Diner, *America in the Eyes of the Germans*, p. 149 (transl. modified). On the rejection of communism 'across ideological

divides', including among Marxist sociologists, see Horovitz, 'Zwischen der Charybdis des Kapitalismus und der Szylla des Kommunismus'.

12 Kracauer to Erika Lorenz, 1 March 1962.

13 Ibid.

14 Kracauer and Berkman, *Satellite Mentality*, p. 2.

15 Ibid., p. 6.

16 Wheatland, *The Frankfurt School in Exile*, p. 191.

17 Cf. ibid., pp. 191–203.

18 Merton, *On the Shoulders of Giants*; Neurath, 'Paul Lazarsfeld', pp. 78–83.

19 Neurath, 'Paul Lazarsfeld', pp. 83–99; Glock, 'Organizational Innovation', pp. 28f.

20 Cf. Adorno's and Lazarsfeld's memories of the time of their joint research in Newark, New Jersey in Fleming and Bailyn, *The Intellectual Migration*.

21 He assured Adorno of their fundamental agreement after having read Adorno's 'Sociology and Empirical Research': see letter of 22 April 1958, in Adorno/Kracauer, *Briefwechsel*, p. 492. His reservations regarding Adorno's knowledge of empirical methods he only mentioned to Löwenthal. Kracauer to Löwenthal, 3 May 1958, in Löwenthal/Kracauer, *In steter Freundschaft*, p. 205. [Transl. note: Adorno's paper can be found in *The Positivist Dispute in German Sociology*, London, 1976, pp. 68–86.]

22 Cf. Ritsert, *Inhaltsanalyse*, pp. 19–21; Fleck and Stiegler, 'Nachbemerkung und editorische Notiz', p. 858; Alfred Schütz to Kracauer, 18 April 1953. On Adorno's position, cf. his 'Sociology and Empirical Research' (fn. 20). Kracauer to Leo Löwenthal, 3 May 1958, in Löwenthal/Kracauer, *In steter Freundschaft*, p. 206. On Merton and his imperatives regarding the social sciences, cf. Kaesler, 'Was sind und zu welchem Ende studiert man die Klassiker der Soziologie?', pp. 18–20.

23 Leo Löwenthal to Kracauer, 8 October 1959 and Kracauer to Löwenthal, 31 October 1959. Kracauer agreed with Löwenthal's judgment. Löwenthal/Kracauer, *In steter Freundschaft*, pp. 218–20.

24 Kracauer, 'A Statement on the Humanistic Approach', in *American Writings*, pp. 124–7; here: p. 126; 'The Challenge of Qualitative Analysis', p. 641.

25 Diplomarbeit Erika Lorenz, *Siegfried Kracauer als Soziologe* (Prof. Th.W. Adorno, April 1962), DLA Marbach, NL Kracauer, 80.

26 Erich Auerbach, 'In the Hotel de la Mole', *The Partisan Review*, May 1951, pp. 265–303.

27 Shahar, 'Auerbach's Scars', p. 608.

28 Kracauer to Erich Auerbach, 4 July 1951; Auerbach to Kracauer, 6 July 1951; Kracauer to Auerbach, 29 September 1951; Auerbach to Kracauer, 1 September 1953.

29 Cf. Löwenthal, *Literature and the Image of Man*, pp. ix–xv; *Literature, Popular Culture, and Society*, pp. xi and 1–13.

30 Kracauer to Leo Löwenthal, 3 April 1956, in Löwenthal/Kracauer, *In steter Freundschaft*, pp. 168–71.

31 On the concept of 'Textgelehrter' [textual scholar], see Berg and Burgdorf, 'Textgelehrsamkeit'.

32 See Coser, *Refugee Scholars*, p. 10; Krohn, *Wissenschaft im Exil*, p. 8; Söllner, 'Vom Völkerrecht zur *science of international relations*', p. 164. On the influence of German emigrants on the social sciences and art history, see Pross, *Die deutsche akademische Emigration*, pp. 59–65.

33 See Wheatland, *The Frankfurt School*, p. 203.
34 According to Franz Neumann; cf. Coser, *Refugee Scholars*, p. 12.
35 Kracauer to Erika Lorenz, 4 February 1962.
36 Quoted after Coser, *Refugee Scholars*, p. 10.
37 Cf. Shahar, 'Auerbach's Scars', pp. 616f. On the particular style of the emigrants, see Heilbut, *Kultur ohne Heimat*, p. 9. On the area between the 'sciences' and 'humanities', see Breidecker, '"Ferne Nähe"', pp. 163–5.
38 Kracauer to Egon Kaskeline, 27 June 1957.
39 Kracauer to Charles Y. Glock, 23 November 1957.
40 Kracauer and John W. Bennett, various letters from 1957 to 1959
41 Kracauer to Leo Löwenthal, 13 March 1951, in Löwenthal/Kracauer, *In steter Freundschaft*, pp. 143f.; here: p. 144.
42 Kracauer to Bernhard Guttmann, 29 August 1954; Kracauer to David Riesman, 8 June 1958.
43 Kracauer to Elihu Katz, 6 March 1955.
44 Kracauer to Paul Rotha, 12 March 1953 and 7 May 1953.
45 According to Anderson, 'Siegfried Kracauer', p. 25, Meyer Schapiro had recommended him.
46 Kracauer to Rainer Koehne, 8 April 1956; Belke, 'Nachbemerkung und editorische Notiz', in SK, *Werke* 4, pp. 443–51; Brooks to Kracauer, 1 February 1952.

36. Mail from Germany, Letters from the Past, Travels in Europe

1 Kracauer to Herbert and Gertrud Levin, 7 August 1949 and 19 June 1950.
2 Kracauer to Friedrich T. and Ella Gubler, 27 August 1955.
3 Kracauer to Leo Löwenthal, 17 July 1955, in Löwenthal/Kracauer, *In steter Freundschaft*, p. 151.
4 Charles W. Eiseman to Kracauer, 27 April 1954.
5 Cf. *Marbacher Magazin*, p. 112; Kracauer to Mina Kirstein Curtiss, 22 February 1956 and 9 November 1958; Curtiss, *Bizet*, p. x.
6 Entschädigungsakte Kracauer [Compensation file Kracauer] at the Entschädigungsbehörde Berlin in Berlin-Wilmersdorf, Landesamt für Bürger- und Ordnungsangelegenheiten, Abt. 1: Entschädigungsbehörde, Opfer des Nationalsozialismus, Dateneingabe MyCMDB, I A 45; Kracauer to Friedrich T. and Ella Gubler, 2 June 1953.
7 Ibid. See also Brunner, Frei and Goschler, 'Komplizierte Lernprozesse', pp. 14f.
8 Correspondence between Kracauer and Fritz Wahl, 27 May 1953, 2 January 1954 and 19 December 1954.
9 Kracauer to Friedrich T. Gubler, 28 August 1954.
10 Kracauer to Richard Eisemann, 20 February 1955.
11 Brunner, Frei and Goschler, 'Komplizierte Lernprozesse', pp. 24–7.
12 Kracauer to Marta Salomon-Mierendorff, 13 May 1956.
13 See Kracauer to Antoine P.J. Kroonenburg, correspondence 1948–53; Kracauer to Hein Kohn, correspondence 1952/53.
14 Kracauer to Maria Horch, 28 June 1955, 1 November 1955, 19 November 1955; Kracauer to Marta Salomon-Mierendorff, 13 May 1956.
15 Wolfgang Weyrauch to Kracauer, 17 November 1951, 10 December 1952, 5 October 1955.
16 Enno Patalas to Kracauer, 19 September 1955. Cf. also the correspondence

of 1957 with Benno Klapp, who was writing a dissertation on 'realism in film' and contacted Kracauer upon the advice of Patalas.

17 Adorno to Kracauer, 22 October 1962, in Adorno/Kracauer, *Briefwechsel*, pp. 552f. 'Oberhausen group' is the name for the signatories of the Oberhausen Manifesto of 28 February 1962, in which those involved in the film industry called for a shift in the political orientation of film-making, a new German film, and a new culture of film that distanced itself from the time before 1945.

18 Kracauer to Leo Löwenthal, 28 October 1956, in Löwenthal/Kracauer, *In steter Freundschaft*, pp. 182f.

19 Kracauer to Leo Löwenthal, 29 September 1957, in ibid., p. 197.

20 Cf. Kracauer, *Von Caligari bis Hitler* (1958); Witte, 'Nachwort des Herausgebers', in SK, *Werke* 2, pp. 611f.; Brodersen, *Siegfried Kracauer*, p. 127.

21 Kracauer to Joseph Christ, 18 June 1956.

22 Rainer Koehne to Kracauer, 1 September 1956.

23 Ella Gubler to Kracauer, 30 July 1956.

24 Transl. note: 'Stolpersteine' are 10 cm by 10 cm brass plates inserted in the pavement that are inscribed with the names and biographical data of victims of the Nazi crimes. They mark the last residence of the victims and can be found in many German and Austrian cities, as well as in other European countries. The German artist Gunter Demnig initiated the project in 1992.

25 Kracauer to Ernst Bloch, 21 October 1959, in Bloch, *Briefe*, vol. 1, pp. 393f.

26 Kracauer to Leo Löwenthal, 28 October 1956, in Löwenthal/Kracauer, *In steter Freundschaft*, pp. 182–4; here: pp. 182f.

27 Selmar Spier and Kracauer, 3 September 1956, 19 September 1956 and 14 October 1956.

28 Kracauer to Selmar Spier, 16 February 1957, 3 May 1957, 26 January 1958 and 5 March 1962.

29 Marlene Spier to Kracauer, 26 December 1964.

30 Kracauer to Leo Löwenthal, 28 October 1956, in Löwenthal/Kracauer, *In steter Freundschaft*, pp. 182–4; here: p. 183.

31 Kracauer to David Riesman, 10 October 1957; Luther P. Eisenhart to Kracauer, 10 December 1957; Kracauer wrote a report for Luther P. Eisenhart, 7 December 1958.

32 London, British Academy to Kracauer, 10 July 1958; Paul Rotha to Kracauer, 12 February 1958 and 25 June 1958.

33 Fritz Kempe to Kracauer, 9 May 1958.

34 The passages in italics are in English in the original.

35 Kracauer to Leo Löwenthal, 27 October 1958, in Löwenthal/Kracauer, *In steter Freundschaft*, pp. 211–13; here: p. 212.

36 Dahrendorf, *Society and Democracy in Germany*; Herbert, 'Liberalisierung als Lernprozess', p. 29.

37 Kracauer to Everett C. Hughes, 11 December 1958.

38 Ella Gubler to Kracauer, 19 September 1953; Rainer Koehne to Kracauer, 20 January 1955.

39 See Arendt, 'The Aftermath of Nazi Rule: Report from Germany'.

40 Kracauer to Leo Löwenthal, 27 October 1958, in Löwenthal/Kracauer, *In steter Freundschaft*, pp. 211–13.

41 Kracauer to Rainer Koehne, 19 March 1956 and 7 July 1956.

42 Hans G. Helms to Kracauer, 5 December 1958 and 14 December 1958.
43 Kracauer to Leo Löwenthal, 27 October 1958, in Löwenthal/Kracauer, *In steter Freundschaft*, pp. 211–13; here: p. 212; Kracauer to Max Niederlechner, 21 February 1949.
44 *Cinema tedesco* (1918–33), *Biblioteca Montadori* (1954); Guido Aristarco to Kracauer, 7 May 1958.
45 Kracauer to Adorno, 15 February 1959, in Adorno/Kracauer, *Briefwechsel*, p. 503.
46 Rudolf Arnheim to Kracauer, 3 November 1953.
47 Guido Aristarco to Kracauer, 26 October 1954.
48 Kracauer to David Riesman, 3 June 1958.
49 Kracauer to Paul Rotha, no date [January/February 1958]; Kracauer to Henri Langlois, 9 January 1958 and 1 February 1958.
50 Erich P. Neumann to Kracauer, 23 July 1958 and 24 September 1958.
51 Transl. note: The English edition opts for yet another subtitle: 'Duty and Distraction in Weimar Germany'.
52 Neumann, 'Einführung'. The planned series was discontinued after only three volumes, among them the famous Marienthal study by Jahoda and Lazarsfeld. Cf. Kracauer and Hughes, 19 November 1958 and 29 November 1958; Kracauer to Verlag für Demoskopie, 16 January 1960.
53 Kracauer to Leo Löwenthal, 15 February 1960, in Löwenthal/Kracauer, *In steter Freundschaft*, pp. 227f.
54 See Kracauer to David Riesman, 1 October 1958; Kracauer to Leo Löwenthal, 27 October 1958, in Löwenthal/Kracauer, *In steter Freundschaft*, pp. 211–13.

37. The Practice of Film Theory and the Theory of Film

1 Kracauer to Guido Aristarco, 27 November 1954.
2 Kracauer to Rainer Koehne, 17 January 1956.
3 Kracauer, *Theory of Film*, p. xiv.
4 Kracauer to Paul Rotha, 15 January 1956, 12 February 1956 and 8 December 1957. Paul Rotha to Kracauer, 18 February 1953, 23 November 1957 and 24 March 1958. Rotha, *Rotha on the Film*, p. 22. On 'Umberto D.', cf. Gregor and Patalas, *Geschichte des Films*, pp. 330–3.
5 Kracauer to Adorno, 27 August 1955, in Adorno/Kracauer, *Briefwechsel*, p. 478.
6 Arnheim, 'Melancholy Unshaped', p. 291.
7 Mülder-Bach, 'Nachbemerkung und editorische Notiz', in SK, *Werke* 3, p. 861.
8 Kracauer to Guido Aristarco, 25 January 1958; Kracauer to Adorno, 13 May 1958, in Adorno/Kracauer, *Briefwechsel*, p. 496; Philip Vaudrin to Kracauer, 7 July 1950.
9 Kracauer to Paul Rotha, 10 August 1959 and 24 September 1959.
10 Kracauer to Leo Löwenthal, 12 February 1956, in Löwenthal/Kracauer, *In steter Freundschaft*, p. 165.
11 Kracauer to Peter Suhrkamp, 27 October 1957.
12 See Kracauer's letter to The Chapelbrook Foundation of 3 March 1954, where he says that he had been thinking about a new *Ginster* for the past ten years.

13 Kracauer, *Theory of Film*, p. 108.
14 Ibid.
15 Kracauer to Rudolf Arnheim, 16 October 1960.
16 Kracauer, *Theory of Film*, p. ix.
17 Ibid., p. 18.
18 Ibid., p. 60.
19 This idea came from his friend, the art historian Arnold Hauser; cf. Hauser, *Philosophie der Kunstgeschichte*, p. 401: 'Film is the only art form which leaves significant parts of reality unchanged. Of course, it interprets them, but the interpretation remains a photographic interpretation.'
20 Kracauer, *Theory of Film*, p. 202.
21 Ibid., p. xi.
22 Kracauer to Barbara Deming, 9 February 1961.
23 Kracauer, *Theory of Film*, p. 294.
24 Frisby, *Fragments of Modernity*, p. 20.
25 Kracauer, *Theory of Film*, pp. 300 and 305f.
26 Kracauer, *Theory of Film*, p. 169.
27 Husserl, *The Crisis of European Sciences*, p. 156.
28 See the introduction to Ludwig Landrebe in Schütz and Gurwitsch, *Briefwechsel*, pp. xxxvii–xxxviii. Jay, 'The Extraterritorial Life of Siegfried Kracauer', p. 179, argues that Kracauer now 'wholeheartedly' accepted the notion of life he once criticized in Simmel.
29 Husserl, *The Crisis of European Sciences*, p. 140.
30 Adorno, *Against Epistemology*, p. 48. See the copy of Adorno, *Zur Metakritik der Erkenntnistheorie*, p. 57 in the Kracauer library. See also the copy of Husserl, *Die Krisis der europäischen Wissenschaften*, in which numerous passages relating to the problem of the 'lifeworld', as part of the general problem of the objective sciences, are marked.
31 Berlin, *The Hedgehog and the Fox*, p. 19.
32 Schlüpmann, *Ein Detektiv des Kinos*, p. 107. On the expulsion from paradise, see Konersmann, *Kulturkritik*, p. 122.
33 Kracauer, *Theory of Film*, p. 171.
34 Ibid., p. 290.
35 Ibid., p. 305.
36 Ibid., p. 306.
37 Ibid.
38 See Koch, *Die Einstellung*, pp. 127–32; Koch, '"... noch nirgends angekommen"'.
39 Witte, 'Das Alte und das Neue', p. 11.
40 Cf. Lethen, *Der Schatten des Fotografen*, pp. 71 and 75; Lethen, 'Sichtbarkeit', p. 196.
41 Koch, *Kracauer*, p. 135.
42 Ibid., p. 137.
43 Schlüpmann, *Ein Detektiv des Kinos*, p. 125; and Lethen, 'Sichtbarkeit', p. 197.
44 'Der Philosoph vor der Leinwand', in *Frankfurter Allgemeine Zeitung* (10 April 1965).
45 Koch, *Kracauer*, p. 255. Cf. also Schlüpmann, *Ein Detektiv des Kinos*, p. 10.
46 Hansen, *Cinema and Experience*, p. 3.
47 Cf. ibid., p. 254; Agard, *Kracauer*, pp. 258–62. That was particularly the reaction in Germany: cf. *Film-Telegramm*, 15 December 1964; Hans-Dieter Roos wrote in *Süddeutsche Zeitung* (30 April 1964) that Kracauer's film

theory was only in part systematic, was permeated by dogmatic premises and was written in a wearying prose.

48 Macdonald in December 1960 in his column on film in the men's magazine *Esquire*; Arlene Croce in *The Commonweal* (13 January 1961); Vernon Young in *The Hudson Review*, summer 1961; Wallace Markfield in *Commentary* 31 (1961) 3; Richard Schickel in the *New York Times*, 14 March 1965. The articles are chosen from the Mediendokumentation at DLA Marbach.

49 Kael, 'Is There a Cure for Film Criticism?', p. 243.

50 Ibid., p. 246.

51 Ibid., p. 260.

52 Ibid., p. 263.

53 Kracauer to Leo Löwenthal, 29 November 1959; Kracauer to Paul Rotha, 3 April 1960.

54 David Riesman to Kracauer, 6 July 1961.

55 Cf. Despoix, 'Geschichtsschreibung', p. 106.

56 Read, in *BJA* 2 (1962) 2, pp. 190f.; Siepman in *POQ* 25 (1961) 1, pp. 153f.; cf. also Despoix, 'Geschichtsschreibung', p. 106.

57 Sitney (ed.), *Film Culture Reader*; Kracauer to Jonas Mekas, 12 July 1959; Kracauer to Enno Patalas, 12 October 1955.

58 Kracauer to Mina Kirstein Curtiss, 22 February 1956; Kracauer to Paul Rotha, 8 April 1956 and 3 June 1956; Kracauer to Adorno, 16 December 1956, in Adorno/Kracauer, *Briefwechsel*, p. 489.

59 Kracauer to Ernst Callenbach, founder and editor of the *Film Quarterly*, 12 May 1962.

60 Flyer of 'cinema frontiers', in Mediendokumentation DLA Marbach.

61 On the new generation after 1960, see Gregor and Patalas, *Geschichte des Films*, pp. 447–68.

62 Susan Sontag, 'Film and Theatre', p. 26.

63 Kracauer to Guido Aristarco, 29 December 1962; Kracauer to Michel Cimet, 23 May 1965.

38. Talks with Teddie and Old Friends

1 As Kracauer wrote to Wolfgang Weyrauch, 4 June 1962.

2 Kracauer, *History: The Last Things before the Last*, pp. 3f.

3 Kracauer to Adorno, 15 February 1959, in Adorno/Kracauer, *Briefwechsel*, pp. 503f.

4 Kracauer to Leo Löwenthal, 15 February 1960, in Löwenthal/Kracauer, *In steter Freundschaft*, p. 227.

5 Transl. note: The sentence following the colon in English in the original.

6 Kracauer to Leo Löwenthal, 10 February 1961, in *Marbacher Magazin*, p. 118.

7 Kracauer, 'Photography', pp. 49–50.

8 Kracauer, *History: The Last Things Before the Last*, p. 4.

9 As Ernst Bloch puts it in his letter to Kracauer, 12 September 1959, in Bloch, *Briefe*, vol. 1, p. 392.

10 Claussen, *Theodor Adorno*, pp. 281f.

11 Cf. Münster, *Ernst Bloch*, pp. 219–33.

12 Cf. Markun, *Ernst Bloch*, pp. 99f.

13 Cf. Schopf (ed.), *Adorno und seine Frankfurter Verleger*, p. 298.

14 Kracauer to Adorno, 15 February 1959, in Adorno/Kracauer, *Briefwechsel*, pp. 503f.

15 Cf. Kracauer to Ernst Bloch, 10 June 1962, in Bloch, *Briefe*, vol. 1, pp. 396f.

16 Kracauer to Leo Löwenthal, 29 October 1960, in Löwenthal/Kracauer, *In steter Freundschaft*, p. 230.

17 Kracauer to Adorno, 18 March 1964, in Adorno/Kracauer, *Briefwechsel*, p. 655 (transl. amended).

18 Kracauer to Ernst Bloch, 17 June 1963, in Bloch, *Briefe*, vol. 1, pp. 398f.; Bloch, *Tübinger Einleitung*, pp. 118–53; Münster, *Ernst Bloch*, pp. 331–5.

19 'Talk with Teddie', in *American Writings*, pp. 127–32; here: p. 127.

20 Ibid., p. 128.

21 Ibid., p. 130.

22 Ibid., p. 131. [Transl. note: Kracauer's notes on the 'Talk' can also be found in Adorno/Kracauer, *Briefwechsel*, pp. 514–17.]

23 Jay, 'Adorno and Kracauer', p. 226.

24 Kracauer, *History: The Last Things Before the Last*, p. 201.

25 Adorno, *Negative Dialectics*, p. 5.

26 Ibid.

27 Ibid., pp. 31 (emphasis added), 33 and 37.

28 Ibid., p. 3.

29 Kracauer to Leo Löwenthal, 15 February 1960, in Löwenthal/Kracauer, *In steter Freundschaft*, pp. 226–8; here: pp. 227f.

30 Kracauer to Adorno, 16 October and 11 December 1960, in Adorno/Kracauer, *Briefwechsel*, pp. 513 and 522f.; here: p. 522.

31 Kracauer to Adorno, 15 February 1963, in ibid., p. 581.

32 Adorno to Kracauer, 4 June 1962, in ibid., p. 526.

33 Schweppenhäuser, *Kierkegaards Angriff*, pp. 9f.

34 Kracauer to Adorno, 12 October 1962, in Adorno/Kracauer, *Briefwechsel*, pp. 549–51; here: p. 549.

35 Schmidt, *The Concept of Nature in Marx*, pp. 45f.

36 See the editorial notes to letter no. 241 in Adorno/Kracauer, *Briefwechsel*, p. 659. In *History: The Last Things before the Last*, Kracauer refers to an article by Schmidt in a Suhrkamp volume that deals with the relationship between existentialism and Marxism. In the spring of 1963, Kracauer exchanged letters with Schweppenhäuser in connection with the Festschrift for Adorno's sixtieth birthday. Schweppenhäuser contributed some aphorisms; Kracauer liked them. See Kracauer to Schweppenhäuser, 24 November 1963.

37 Transl. note: The words in italics in English in the original. – 'Spleen' refers to Benjamin's specific use of the term, taken from Baudelaire: '"Spleen et idéal" – in the title of this first cycle of poems in *Les Fleurs du mal*, the oldest loanword in the French language was joined to the most recent one. For Baudelaire, there is no contradiction between the two concepts. He recognizes in spleen the latest transfiguration of the ideal; the ideal seems to him the first expression of spleen.' *Arcades Project* ('Paris, the Capital of the Nineteenth Century'), p. 22.

38 Kracauer to Rolf Tiedemann, 21 February 1966.

39 Adorno to Kracauer, 5 November 1963; Kracauer to Adorno, 1 April 1964, in Adorno/Kracauer, *Briefwechsel*, pp. 619 and 658f.

40 Kracauer to Karl Heinz Haag, 26 April 1963; Kracauer to Adorno, 16 January 1964, in Adorno/Kracauer, *Briefwechsel*, pp. 638–41; here: p. 641. On Heidegger's speech and Haag's interpretation, see ibid., p. 643 (notes).

41 Transl. note: A university lecturer teaching individual courses who has no permanent contract.
42 Kracauer to Karl Heinz Haag, 12 December 1964.
43 According to an email from Habermas, 7 April 2016. See also the letters from Kracauer to Jürgen Habermas, 7 November 1964 and 21 March 1965.
44 Adorno to Kracauer, 4 September 1963 and Kracauer to Adorno, 23 December 1963, in Adorno/Kracauer, *Briefwechsel*, pp. 607 and 632–4.
45 Ibid., p. 608.
46 Kracauer to Peter Szondi, 18 March 1965; Bernhard Heidtmann to Kracauer, 23 July 1965.
47 Cf. Adorno, 'Vorrede', p. 7; Sparr, 'Peter Szondi', pp. 428–30.
48 Kracauer to Adorno, 22 August 1962, in Adorno/Kracauer, *Briefwechsel*, pp. 535f.; here: p. 536.
49 Kracauer to Alexander Kluge, 24 December 1962.
50 Kracauer to Adorno, 10 December 1962, in Adorno/Kracauer, *Briefwechsel*, pp. 568–71; here: p. 570.
51 From the introduction to Erika Lorenz, 'Siegfried Kracauer als Soziologe', unpublished Diplomarbeit (Prof. Th.W. Adorno, April 1962), in NL Kracauer at the DLA Marbach.
52 Kracauer to Erika Lorenz, 22 October 1961 and 31 March 1962.
53 Kracauer to Erika Lorenz, 22 October 1961.
54 Kracauer to Erika Lorenz, 15 February 1962 and 1 March 1962.
55 Kracauer to Erika Lorenz, 9 May 1962.
56 Otto Stammer and Kracauer, 28 November 1962 and Kracauer to Stammer, 2 December 1962.
57 Kracauer to Adorno, 22 August 1962, 4 September 1962, 9 December 1962, 10 December 1962 and 15 February 1963, in Adorno/Kracauer, *Briefwechsel*, pp. 535–7, 538f., 568–73 and 581–3. The dedication, incidentally, served as a pretext to remove Kracauer's review of Wiesengrund's book on Kierkegaard from the volume. The real reason was that Adorno disliked the gentle 'patronizing undertones', as he saw them, of Kracauer's text. See *Adorno und seine Verleger*, p. 424.
58 Adorno to Kracauer, 7 December 1962, in Adorno/Kracauer, *Briefwechsel*, pp. 565f.; Kracauer to Wolfgang Weyrauch, 28 March 1960.
59 Kracauer to Adorno, 15 February 1963, in Adorno/Kracauer, *Briefwechsel*, pp. 581–3. And 26 March 1963, pp. 589–91; here: p. 590.
60 Siegfried Unseld to Kracauer, 2 January 1964.
61 Kracauer to Adorno, 23 December 1963, in Adorno/Kracauer, *Briefwechsel*, pp. 632–4; here: p. 634.
62 Kracauer to Marie Swarzenski, 2 January 1963.
63 Kracauer to Adorno, 3 August 1963, in Adorno/Kracauer, *Briefwechsel*, pp. 604f.; here: p. 604.
64 Siegfried Unseld to Kracauer, 2 January 1964 and Kracauer to Unseld, 7 January 1964; see Adorno/Kracauer, *Briefwechsel*, p. 653 (note).
65 Quoted after Claussen, *Theodor Adorno*, p. 283 (transl. amended).
66 Adorno to Kracauer, 11 November 1960, in Adorno/Kracauer, *Briefwechsel*, pp. 518–20; here: p. 519.
67 Adorno to Kracauer, 20 September 1963, in ibid., pp. 608f.
68 Adorno, 'The Curious Realist', pp. 174f.
69 Adorno to Kracauer, 23 February 1955 and 1 September 1955, in Adorno/Kracauer, *Briefwechsel*, pp. 475 and 482.
70 Adorno to Kracauer, 3 February 1959, in ibid., p. 500.

71 Adorno to Kracauer, 18 October 1963, 3 February 1964 and 28 October 1964, in ibid., pp. 610, 644f. and 672.

72 Kracauer to Adorno, 16 January 1964, in ibid., pp. 638–41; here: p. 638.

73 Adorno, 'The Curious Realist', p. 161.

74 Ibid., p. 163 (transl. amended).

75 Transl. note: A line from Brecht's poem 'Of Poor B.B', in *Poems*, p. 107.

76 Ibid., p. 171.

77 Ibid., p. 174.

78 Ibid., p. 177.

79 Kracauer to Adorno, 15 October 1964, in Adorno/Kracauer, *Briefwechsel*, pp. 669–71; here: p. 670.

80 On this, see the chapter 'The Palimpsest of Life', in Claussen, *Theodor W. Adorno: One Last Genius*.

81 Kracauer to Adorno, 15 October 1964, in Adorno/Kracauer, *Briefwechsel*, pp. 669–71.

82 Kracauer to Adorno, 3 November 1964, in ibid., pp. 676–9.

83 Kracauer to Adorno, 21 November 1964, in ibid., pp. 684–6; here: p. 685.

84 Note on a copy of 'The Curious Realist', quoted after Jay, 'Adorno and Kracauer', p. 235. See also Barnouw, 'An den Rand geschriebene Träume', pp. 2–5.

85 Cf. Claussen, *Theodor W. Adorno*, pp. 285 and 297; Adorno to Kracauer, 22 July 1963, in Adorno/Kracauer, *Briefwechsel*, pp. 601–3; here: p. 602.

86 Kracauer to Adorno, 3 November 1964, in Adorno/Kracauer, *Briefwechsel*, pp. 676–8; here: p. 678.

87 Adorno to Kracauer, 13 November 1964, in ibid., pp. 680–3; here: p. 682.

88 Adorno to Scholem, 22 January 1964, in Adorno and Scholem, *Correspondence*, p. 217 (transl. amended).

89 Transl. note: The titles for Bloch and Lukács are plays on words: 'Blochmusik' instead of 'Blechmusik' (brass band music), and 'Hau den Lukas', the funfair game known in English as a 'high striker'.

90 Szondi, *Briefe*, p. 146.

91 Adorno, 'The Handle, the Pot, and Early Experience', p. 211.

92 Ibid., p. 212.

93 Adorno to Kracauer, 5 February 1965, in Adorno/Kracauer, *Briefwechsel*, pp. 687–9; here: p. 689.

94 Adorno, 'The Handle, the Pot, and Early Experience', p. 219.

95 Adorno to Kracauer, 21 December 1965, in Adorno/Kracauer, *Briefwechsel*, pp. 708f.

96 Quoted after Claussen, *Theodor Adorno: One Last Genius*, p. 268. Claussen rejects the personal reading of the remark, but then goes on to mention all the quarrels that were not philosophically or politically motivated.

97 Ernst Bloch to Adorno, 2 September 1965: 'Your remembrance of the pot has truly moved me, although the *pars pro toto* seems friendlier in it than the *totum in parte*.' Bloch, *Briefe*, vol. 2, p. 454. [Transl. note: Adorno's 'Ernst Bloch's *Spuren*' in the *Notes to Literature* was originally published under the title 'Große Blochmusik' in *Neue Deutsche Hefte* 69 (1960/61), pp. 14–26.]

98 Claussen, *Theodor Adorno: One Last Genius*, p. 272.

99 Kracauer to Leo Löwenthal, 28 October 1962, in Löwenthal/Kracauer, *In steter Freundschaft*, pp. 238f.; Kracauer to Arnold Hauser, 22 December 1964.

100 Kracauer to Friedrich T. and Ella Gubler, 20 January 1965.

101 Bloch, *The Principle of Hope*, vol. 3, pp. 1034–57; here: pp. 1042 and 1044.
102 SK, 'Zwei Deutungen in zwei Sprachen' [Two interpretations in two languages], passim.
103 Ernst Bloch to Kracauer, 11 September 1965, in Bloch, *Briefe*, vol. 1, p. 404.

39. Time for the Things before the Last

1 Kracauer to Adorno, 11 September 1962, in Adorno/Kracauer, *Briefwechsel*, pp. 539–41; here: p. 540.
2 Benjamin, 'Theses on the Philosophy of History' (Thesis XIII), p. 251.
3 Kracauer to Rolf Tiedemann, 21 February 1966. Baumann (*Im Vorraum der Geschichte*, pp. 272–82) discusses the way in which Kracauer digested Benjamin's theses on historicism and progress in a preparatory collection of arguments, the 'Guide to History' (see Baumann, p. 19).
4 Adorno, 'Progress', p. 144.
5 See the chapter 'The Concept of Enlightenment', in Horkheimer and Adorno, *Dialectic of Enlightenment*, pp. 1–34.
6 Ibid., p. 150.
7 Horkheimer and Adorno, *Dialectic of Enlightenment*, p. xvii. See Adorno, 'Progress', pp. 144–6.
8 Cf. Kuhn and Wiedmann, 'Vorwort', pp. 9–12.
9 Cf. Löwith, 'Das Verhängnis des Fortschritts', esp. p. 27.
10 Löwith, *Meaning in History*, p. 1.
11 Ibid., pp. 3f.
12 Kracauer to Adorno, 27 November 1962, in Adorno/Kracauer, *Briefwechsel*, pp. 561–4; here: p. 562.
13 Erwin Panofsky to Kracauer, 7 March 1962, in Breidecker, *Siegfried Kracauer – Erwin Panofsky*, p. 67.
14 Cf. Kubler, *The Shape of Time*, pp. 96–122; esp. pp. 120 and 122, and the introduction by Gottfried Boehm in the German edition, *Die Form der Zeit*, pp. 7–26; see also Kracauer to Erwin Panofsky, 31 March 1962, in Breidecker, *Siegfried Kracauer – Erwin Panofsky*, pp. 68f.
15 Kracauer to Werner Kaegi, 4 January 1963.
16 Kracauer to Arnold Hauser, 26 November 1962.
17 Kracauer to Werner Kaegi, 18 February 1963.
18 Kracauer, *History: The Last Things Before the Last*, p. 139; see also 'Time and History', pp. 65 and 66.
19 Ibid., p. 199.
20 Ibid., p. 160 ('Time and History', p. 75).
21 Ibid., p. 157 ('Time and History', p. 74).
22 Ibid., p. 162 ('Time and History', p. 77).
23 Cf. Kreuzer, 'Augenblick und Zeitraum'.
24 Cf. Hook, *Philosophy and History*.
25 Collingwood, *The Idea of History*, p. 203; see especially the chapter 'History as Re-Enactment of Past Experience', pp. 282–301.
26 Further books consulted by Kracauer were *Theories of History* (1959; edited by Patrick Gardiner, a collection of canonical texts from Vico to Collingwood with commentaries by established scholars such as Berlin, Geyl and Mandelbaum); *The Philosophy of History in Our Time* (1959; edited by Hans Meyerhoff, a similar, but thematically arranged anthology

in which two of the future editors of *History and Theory*, Aron and Berlin, were represented); J.H. Hexter's *Reappraisals in History* (1961; Kracauer met with Hexter and prepared for their conversation by drawing up a list of eleven points to be addressed. See the note in his copy of the book in the Kracauer library); and, finally, *Philosophy and History*, ed. by Klibansky and Paton, a re-edition of the Festschrift for Ernst Cassirer of 1936.

27 Iggers, *Neue Geschichtswissenschaft*, p. 49. The first five volumes of *History and Theory* contain numerous articles that Kracauer used for his book on history.

28 Berlin, 'History and Theory', p. 5.

29 Ibid., p. 24.

30 Kracauer, *History: The Last Things Before the Last*, pp. 29f.

31 Ibid., p. 58. Kracauer thought Blumenberg's use of the 'Lebenswelt' concept remarkable, underlining Blumenberg's characterization of it in the special edition of 'Lebenswelt und Technisierung unter Aspekten der Phänomenologie' (*Edizioni die Filosofia*, Turin, 1965) '[a]s the perennially inexhaustible reserve of what is unquestionably present, familiar, and – precisely because familiar – unknown'.

32 Ibid., p. 56.

33 Ibid., p. 16.

34 See the reports 'About the State of the Humanities' and 'A Statement on the Humanistic Approach', in *American Writings*, pp. 117–27; and John Marshall to Kracauer, 7 January 1963, who had asked Kracauer whether it would make sense to provide financial support for the humanities to allow them to pursue research freely, independent of the context of the university.

35 Kracauer to Arnold Hauser, 26 November 1962.

36 Cf. Breidecker's compilation of letters 'Siegfried Kracauer "under the spell of the living Warburg tradition"', in Breidecker, *Siegfried Kracauer – Erwin Panofsky*, pp. 93–128.

37 Butterfield, a Cambridge historian, was not only the greatest living authority on historiography. He also took a particular interest in the debates over the right balance between micro- and macro-history. He especially liked to engage in fierce discussions with Lewis B. Namier over this question. Cf. the correspondence between Butterfield and Kracauer, 1960–4.

38 Kracauer read Guthrie's *The Greek Philosophers (from Thales to Aristotle)* very closely.

39 Correspondence between Raymond Firth and Kracauer, 1960; between Eric Robertson Dodds and Kracauer, 1962.

40 Kracauer meticulously read the first chapter ('La philosophie de l'histoire' [The philosophy of history]) of Aron's *Dimensions de la conscience historique* [Dimensions of historical consciousness], especially with regard to the scientificity of history, relativism and the Marxist philosophy of history.

41 Kracauer shared Lévi-Strauss's critique of temporally continuous representations of history, which Lévi-Strauss discarded as a method and considered a myth: 'History is a discontinuous set composed of domains of history, each of which is defined by a characteristic frequency and by a differential coding of *before* and *after*' (Lévi-Strauss, *The Savage Mind*, pp. 359f.). For Lévi-Strauss, the 'savage mind' was fundamentally

characterized by the principle of affinity, an engagement in never-ending constructions out of the given material, rather than by a search for something that might lie behind the things or be their foundation. The given material has priority. This also applies to Kracauer's constructions out of the given material. Cf. Kracauer to Claude Lévi-Strauss, 18 December 1963.

42 Kracauer to Henri-Irénée Marrou, 18 May 1964. Marrou emphasized the uniform flow of time. Kracauer defended Kubler and Lévi-Strauss, but also agreed with Marrou, pointing to the antinomies of time. Kracauer adopted the image of the historian setting out on a journey from Marrou's *L'Histoire et ses méthodes* [History and its methods] (Paris, 1961). In the summer of 1961, Kracauer also tried to arrange a meeting with Fernand Braudel, but Braudel was not in Paris at the time; cf. Gérard Lagneau to Kracauer, 25 September 1961.

43 Kracauer to Isaiah Berlin, 31 May 1962. Cf. Belke, 'Kracauers letzte Lebensjahre', p. 470. Even earlier, Gardiner, in his *Theories of History* (pp. 166–87), had made Tolstoy part of his canon of classics in historical writing.

44 Kracauer, *History: The Last Things Before the Last*, p. 107.

45 Kracauer's library contains Huizinga's collection of essays *Men and Ideas* (1959) and *Im Bann der Geschichte* (1943), both with a great deal of underlining and numerous annotations.

46 Geyl, 'Huizinga', p. 258. Cf. the correspondence between Geyl and Kracauer in 1963. Kracauer also studied Geyl's *Debates with Historians and Encounters in History*, a kind of episodic history of 'history' on the basis of individual great historians or themes.

47 Transl. note: See Kracauer's definition of his goal in *History: The Last Things Before the Last*, namely 'to establish the intermediary area of history as an area in its own right – that of provisional insight into the last things before the last', p. 16.

48 Kracauer to Werner Kaegi, 18 February 1963 and 4 June 1963.

49 Kracauer and Werner Kaegi, *Correspondence 1962–1966*; here: 4 June 1963.

50 Kracauer, *History: The Last Things Before the Last*, pp. 68f.

51 Burckhardt, *Weltgeschichtliche Betrachtungen*, p. 4, underlined by Kracauer.

52 Kracauer, *History: The Last Things Before the Last*, p. 97.

53 Ibid., p. 207.

54 Ibid., p. 151.

55 See ibid.

56 Kracauer to Rudolf Grossmann, 28 November 1964; Kracauer to Arnold Hauser, 22 December 1964.

57 Kracauer to Werner Kaegi, 5 June 1965.

58 Kracauer to Siegfried Unseld, 13 February 1966.

59 Kracauer to Raymond Aron, 17 October 1965. Cf. Ginzburg, 'Details, Early Plans, Microanalysis: Thoughts on a Book by Siegfried Kracauer'.

60 On the following, see Wagner, 'Anfangen' and Boden, 'Arbeit an Begriffen'.

61 Julia Wagner, 'Anfangen', p. 56. [Transl. note: The 'Bündische Jugend' was a youth movement in the Weimar Republic that developed out of the Wandervogel movement.]

62 Thus Jauß in his epilogue on the research group in 1998, quoted after Boden, 'Arbeit an Begriffen', p. 103. The term 'archons' was used by Aleida

Assmann, 'to lay an egg' by Manfred Frank at the Marbach meeting on 'Poetics and Hermeneutics' in January 2014.

63 Cf. Belke, 'Kracauers letzte Lebensjahre', pp. 486–9.

64 Cf. Jauß, *Zeit und Erinnerung*, pp. 13f.

65 Hans Robert Jauß to Kracauer, 4 February 1964; Jauß, 'Ursprung und Bedeutung der Fortschrittsidee'.

66 Kracauer to Hans Blumenberg, 23 January 2016.

67 Cf. the documentation by Jens Westermeier, *Jugend, Krieg und Internierung*.

68 Kracauer to Hans Robert Jauß, 19 January 1965 and 18 September 1964.

69 Cf. the preface in Iser (ed.), *Immanente Ästhetik*, pp. 9f.

70 Cf. Erhart, '"Wahrscheinlich haben wir beide recht"', p. 84; Jauß (ed.), *Nachahmung und Illusion*, pp. 7f.

71 Cf. Iser (ed.), *Immanente Ästhetik*, pp. 418 and 446.

72 Cf. Erhart, '"Wahrscheinlich haben wir beide recht"', pp. 80–91.

73 In a note on the 1963 colloquium Kracauer wrote: 'Changes of theory are almost always stated without reference to extramural environmental changes, social or otherwise. [...] The social climate is practically nonexistent in the colloquy.' Konvolut Kolloquium 'Nachahmung und Illusion'. Cf. also Ahlrich Meyer, *NZZ*, 23 January 2016.

74 Hans Robert Jauß to Adorno, 4 January 1967, in NL Kracauer (file on Poetik und Hermeneutik), quoted after Wagner, 'Anfangen', p. 57.

75 Cf. Boden, 'Vom Umgang mit Dissens und Kontroversen', p. 303.

76 Oral communication by Dieter Henrich, June 2016.

77 Cf. Jauß (ed.), *Die nicht mehr schönen Künste*, pp. 630–4; here: pp. 633f.

78 Cf. Belke, 'Kracauers letzte Jahre', pp. 503f.

79 Blumenberg, *Legitimacy of the Modern Age*, p. 30.

80 Blumenberg, '"Säkularisation"', p. 243.

81 Ibid., p. 250. See also *Legitimacy of the Modern Age*, p. 65.

82 Cf. ibid., p. 265, and *The Legitimacy of the Modern Age*.

83 Kracauer to Hans Blumenberg, 31 October 1964. (Blumenberg's letters are part of the file on the colloquium 'Nachahmung und Illusion'.)

84 Hans Blumenberg to Kracauer, 22 December 1964.

85 According to Assmann at the Marbach meeting of 'Poetics and Hermeneutics' in January 2014.

86 Kracauer to Hans Blumenberg, 17 January 1965. Cf. Baumann, *Im Vorraum der Geschichte*, pp. 285–97; Blumenberg, '"Säkularisation"'.

87 Kracauer to Edgar Wind, 3 March 1965.

88 Kracauer to Hans Robert Jauß, 24 December 1965.

89 Hans Robert Jauß to Kracauer, 22 February 1965, and Kracauer to Hans Robert Jauß, 5 May 1965.

90 Kracauer to Hans Blumenberg, 18 December 1965.

91 Kracauer, *History: The Last Things Before the Last*, p. 178.

92 Cf. Jauß (ed.), *Die nicht mehr schönen Künste*, pp. 559–81. The following quotations are from pp. 568f. and 577. The Sancho Panza idea had been brewing in Kracauer's mind since at least the end of 1963; cf. Kracauer to Adorno, 23 December 1963, in Adorno/Kracauer, *Briefwechsel*, pp. 632–4; here: p. 633. Koselleck had first presented his thesis in *Kritik und Krise* (1959); see pp. 105–15 of the 1973 edition.

93 Cf. Barnouw, 'An den Rand geschriebene Träume', pp. 8f.

94 Jauß (ed.), *Die nicht mehr schönen Künste*, p. 577. The English translation of Kafka's text, 'The Truth About Sancho Panza', is taken from Franz Kafka, *Collected Stories*, p. 397.

95 On the development from historicism to structural history (especially social history) and to recent cultural history, see especially Raphael, *Geschichtswissenschaft*, pp. 14f. and Iggers, *Neue Geschichtswissenschaft*, pp. 7–15.

96 Cf. the nice appreciation by Barnouw, 'An den Rand geschriebene Träume', p. 9. Also Despoix, 'Geschichtsschreibung'; Ginzburg, 'Details, Early Plans, Microanalysis: Thoughts on a Book by Siegfried Kracauer'; Kessler, 'Entschleiern und Bewahren'.

97 The concept of the anteroom had probably been developing in Kracauer's mind for quite some time. In his copy of Raymond Aron's *Dimensions de la conscience historique* (Paris, 1961), the concept appears several times as a marginal annotation. I do not know, however, when he actually read this essay.

98 SK, *Geschichte*, in *Werke* 4, p. 22. Kracauer asked Gershom Sholem about the legend of the thirty-six just ones, which had preoccupied him since his childhood: Kracauer to Gershom Scholem, 10 January 1961 and 18 January 1961. [Transl. note: In the English edition of the book on history, the corresponding passage runs as follows: 'An old Jewish legend has it that there exist in every generation thirty-six just men who uphold the world. Without their presence the world would be destroyed and perish. Yet nobody knows them; nor do they themselves know that it is because of their presence that the world is saved from doom. The impossible quest for these hidden just ones – are there really as many as thirty-six in every generation? – seems to me one of the most exciting adventures on which history can embark.' *History: The Last Things Before the Last*, p. 15.]

99 Kracauer, *History: The Last Things Before the Last*, pp. 191–217; here: p. 217.

100 Kracauer to Benno Reifenberg, 8 October 1966.

101 Kracauer to Werner Kaegi, 29 October 1966.

102 Elisabeth Kracauer to Sheldon Meyer, 17 November 1968; cf. Baumann, *Im Vorraum der Geschichte*, p. 314.

103 Elisabeth Kracauer to Leo Löwenthal, 27 November 1966, in Löwenthal/ Kracauer, *In steter Freundschaft*, p. 262.

40. After Kracauer's Death

1 Rudolf Arnheim to Elisabeth Kracauer, 27 November 1966.

2 *The New York Times*, 28 November 1966, 'Dr. Siegfried Kracauer Is Dead; A Social Scientist and Author'. Cf. Breidecker, '"Ferne Nähe"', p. 152.

3 Benno Reifenberg to Elisabeth Kracauer, 1 December 1966.

4 *Frankfurter Allgemeine Zeitung*, 1 December 1966. Reprinted with minor changes in Jauß (ed.), *Die nicht mehr schönen Künste*, pp. 6f.

5 Elisabeth Kracauer to Adorno, 19 March 1967. However, the fact that 'linguistic inhibitions' were mentioned in connection with the teaching appointment at the YMHA in New York, when Schapiro and Adorno tried to bring Kracauer to the United States in the autumn of 1938, contradicts this claim. Cf. Adorno/Kracauer, *Briefwechsel*, pp. 403–7.

6 Elisabeth Kracauer to Hans Robert Jauß, 18 April 1968. These claims are also contradicted, in this case by *Ginster* and Adorno's recollections.

7 Elisabeth Kracauer to Adorno, 27 March 1967, and Elisabeth Kracauer to Leo Löwenthal, 31 August 1967.

8 This is very likely correct, as Kracauer also wrote to Löwenthal about a 'race against time', Kracauer to Löwenthal, 28 October 1962, in Löwenthal/Kracauer, *In steter Freundschaft*, p. 238. Kracauer's obsession with his 'exterritoriality' also speaks in favour of rather than against, the fact that the passing of his lifetime was a problem for him.

9 Adorno to Elisabeth Kracauer, 20 June 1967 and 4 February 1969.

10 Personal communications to the author from Jürgen Habermas (7 April 2016) and Ferdinand Fellmann (20 May 2016); see also Adorno to Elisabeth Kracauer, 1 December 1966.

11 Elisabeth Kracauer to Adorno, 7 January 1967, 19 March 1967 and 17 October 1967.

12 Elisabeth Kracauer to Ernst and Karola Bloch, 26 February 1970.

13 Hans Robert Jauß to Elisabeth Kracauer, 8 December 1966 and 11 March 1967; Elisabeth Kracauer to Hans Robert Jauß, 20 February 1968. See also the letters from Henrich, Koselleck, Ritter and Taubes.

14 Elisabeth Kracauer to Gretel Adorno, 12 August 1969, following the death of Theodor W. Adorno.

15 Paul Oskar Kristeller to Elisabeth Kracauer, 26 March 1969 and 2 April 1969.

16 Jacob Taubes to Elisabeth Kracauer, 8 August 1970; Elisabeth Kracauer to Hans Robert Jauß, 9 January 1971. Dieter Henrich offered to check the translation, but that was not necessary; cf. Dieter Henrich to Elisabeth Kracauer, 5 November 1969.

17 Cf. Baumann, *Im Vorraum der Geschichte*, pp. 15–18; Belke, 'Nachbemerkung und editorische Notiz', in SK, *Geschichte*, in *Werke* 4, pp. 619f.

18 Kracauer, *History: The Last Things Before the Last*, p. 219. SK, *Geschichte*, in *Werke* 4, p. 239. Schweppenhäuser looked for and found the original quotation for Lili in Kierkegaard's diaries: Sören Kierkegaard, *Tagebücher*, Wiesbaden, 1947, pp. 200f.: 'Sobald jedoch ein Mensch erscheint [...] denn da gibt es etwas für uns, sagen sie.' Kracauer took the quotation from Brod, *Franz Kafka. A Biography*, New York, 1963 [1937]. The German edition of *History* uses the translation in Brod's *Über Franz Kafka*, Fischer Verlag (1966).

19 Kracauer, *History: The Last Things Before the Last*, p. 9.

20 Ibid., p. 10.

21 On the question of Erasmus's character, Kracauer primarily consulted the introduction by Walther Köhler to an edition of Erasmus's letters, published by Carl Schünemann Verlag in 1956.

22 Kołakowski, *Der Mensch ohne Alternative*, p. 22. Kracauer highlighted this, as his note calls it, 'definition of humanistic left' in his copy of the book and added exclamation marks.

23 SK, 'Zwei Deutungen in zwei Sprachen' [Two interpretations in two languages], p. 145.

24 Kracauer, *History: The Last Things Before the Last*, p. 4.

25 Ibid.

26 Henrich in a telephone conversation with the author, end of May 2016.

27 Adorno, 'The Curious Realist', p. 164.

28 Cf. Berlin, *The Hedgehog and the Fox*.

29 Kristeller, 'Preface', in *History: The Last Things Before the Last*, p. xii.

30 Kracauer to Adorno, 25 May 1930, in Adorno and Kracauer, *Briefwechsel*, pp. 214–17; here: p. 215.

31 Schröter, 'Weltzerfall und Rekonstruktion', pp. 37 and 22.

32 Cf. Rosa, *Resonance*.

33 Wiggershaus, 'Ein abgrundtiefer Realist'; Barnouw, *Critical Realism*; Honneth, 'Der destruktive Realist'. Similar attempts at such re-labelling are: 'metaphysical materialist' (Inka Mülder-Bach) and 'modernist materialist' (Miriam Bratu Hansen); cf. Mülder, *Siegfried Kracauer*, p. 18; Hansen, *Cinema and Experience*, p. 17. Still of a special elegance is Arnheim's characterization of Kracauer's philosophy as 'melancholy unshaped': Kracauer's realism, he writes, seeks to depict 'the world … as an unbound, loosely knit continuum'. Arnheim, 'Melancholy Unshaped', p. 294.

34 Adolph Lowe to Elisabeth Kracauer, 6 May 1967.

Bibliography

Works by Siegfried Kracauer

Before Kracauer was forced into exile, he published in German. After his arrival in the US, he published in English. There are English translations of his early works, as well as German translations of his later works. The following bibliography lists his works in chronological order. The original publication is followed by the translation(s).

In the endnotes, Kracauer's English texts, and English translations of his texts originally written in German, are referenced 'Kracauer, + title'. References to German works are given as 'SK, + title'. Abbreviated titles that do not use the beginning of the full title are given in square brackets below.

The German complete edition of Kracauer's writings is:

Werke, 9 vols., Inka Mülder-Bach and Ingrid Belke (eds), Berlin, 2004–12.
Vol. 1 *Soziologie als Wissenschaft. Der Detektiv-Roman. Die Angestellten.*
  Soziologie als Wissenschaft: Eine erkenntnistheoretische Untersuchung, pp. 9–101.
Der Detektiv-Roman: Eine Deutung, pp. 107–209.
Die Angestellten: Aus dem neuesten Deutschland, *Werke* 1, pp. 213–310.
Vol. 2.1 *Von Caligari zu Hitler.*
Vol. 2.2 *Studien zu Massenmedien und Propaganda.*
Vol. 3 *Theorie des Films: Die Errettung der äußeren Wirklichkeit.*
Vol. 4 *Geschichte – Vor den letzten Dingen.*
Vol. 5.1 *Essays, Feuilletons, Rezensionen 1906–1923.*
Vol. 5.2 *Essays, Feuilletons, Rezensionen 1924–1927.*
Vol. 5.3 *Essays, Feuilletons, Rezensionen 1928–1931.*
Vol. 5.4 *Essays, Feuilletons, Rezensionen 1932–1965.*
Vol. 6.1 *Kleine Schriften zum Film 1921–1927.*
Vol. 6.2 *Kleine Schriften zum Film 1928–1931.*
Vol. 6.3 *Kleine Schriften zum Film 1932–1961.*
Vol. 7 *Romane und Erzählungen.*
Ginster, pp. 9–256.
Georg, pp. 257–516.
Vol. 8 *Jacques Offenbach und das Paris seiner Zeit.*
Vol. 9.1 and 9.2 *Frühe Schriften aus dem Nachlaß.*

Die Angestellten: Aus dem neuesten Deutschland, Frankfurt am Main, 1930.
Die Angestellten: Eine Schrift vom Ende der Weimarer Republik, Bonn, 1959.
Die Angestellten: Aus dem neuesten Deutschland, Frankfurt am Main, 1971.
Die Angestellten. Aus dem neuesten Deutschland, in *Werke* 1, pp. 213–310.
The Salaried Masses: Duty and Distraction in Weimar Germany, trans. Quentin Hoare, London, 1998.
'Mass and Society' [1936], *Film Studies*, Volume 16 (Spring 2017), pp. 6–15.
Jacques Offenbach und das Paris seiner Zeit. Amsterdam, 1937.
Jacques Offenbach und das Paris seiner Zeit, Munich, 1962.
Jacques Offenbach and the Paris of His Time, trans. Gwenda David and Eric Mosbacher, New York, 2016.
'Propaganda and the Nazi War Film', in *From Caligari to Hitler: A Psychological History of the German Film*, Princeton, NJ, 1947, pp. 273–331. (Originally published as: *Propaganda and the Nazi War Film*, New York, 1942.)
'The Conquest of Europe on the Screen: The Nazi Newsreel, 1939–1940', in *Social Research* 82(1) (2015), pp. 153–74. (Originally published in *Social Research: An International Quarterly of Political and Social Science* 10(3) (1943), pp. 337–57.)
From Caligari to Hitler, Princeton, NJ, 1947.
Von Caligari bis Hitler: Ein Beitrag zur Geschichte des deutschen Films, Hamburg, 1958.
Von Caligari zu Hitler: Eine psychologische Geschichte des deutschen Films, Frankfurt am Main, 1979.
Von Caligari zu Hitler, in *Werke* 2.1, Berlin, 2012, pp. 7–427.
'The Challenge of Qualitative Content Analysis', *The Public Opinion Quarterly* 16(4), Special Issue on International Communications Research (Winter 1952–3), pp. 631–42.
Kracauer, Siegfried and Paul L. Berkman, *Satellite Mentality: Political Attitudes and Propaganda Susceptibilities of Non-Communists in Hungary, Poland and Czechoslovakia*, New York, 1956.
Theory of Film: The Redemption of Physical Reality, New York, 1960.
Theorie des Films. Die Errettung der äußeren Wirklichkeit, Frankfurt am Main, 1964.
Theorie des Films. Die Errettung der äußeren Wirklichkeit, in *Werke* 3, Frankfurt am Main, 2005, pp. 11–493.
Straßen in Berlin und anderswo, Frankfurt am Main, 1964.
Streets in Berlin & Elsewhere, Cambridge, 2007.
Das Ornament der Masse, Frankfurt am Main, 1963.
The Mass Ornament, trans. Thomas Y. Levin, Cambridge, MA, 1995.
Ginster, Frankfurt am Main, 1963.
'Time and History', in Horkheimer (ed.), *Theodor W. Adorno zum sechzigsten Geburtstag*, Frankfurt am Main, 1963, pp. 50–64. [Here quoted after: 'Time and History', *History and Theory* 6, Supplement 6: History and the Concept of Time (1966), pp. 65–78.]
'Zwei Deutungen in zwei Sprachen', in *Ernst Bloch zu ehren: Beiträge zu seinem Werk*, Siegfried Unseld (ed.), Frankfurt am Main, 1965, pp. 145–55.
History: The Last Things Before the Last, New York, 1969.
History: The Last Things Before the Last, Princeton, NJ, 1995.
Der Detektiv-Roman: Ein philosophischer Traktat, Frankfurt am Main, 1971.
Georg, Frankfurt am Main, 1977.
Georg, in *Werke* 7, pp. 257–516.
Georg, New York, 2016.

Über die Freundschaft: Essays, Frankfurt am Main, 1986.

Straßen in Berlin und anderswo, Berlin, 1987.

Berliner Nebeneinander: Ausgewählte Feuilletons 1930–33, Andreas Volk (ed.), Zurich, 1996.

Frankfurter Turmhäuser: Ausgewählte Feuilletons 1906–30, Andreas Volk (ed.), Zurich, 1997.

'Two Chaplin Sketches' ('City Lights' and 'Chaplin's Triumph'), *The Yale Journal of Criticism* 10(1) (1997), pp. 115–20.

Siegfried Kracauer's American Writings: Essays on Film and Popular Culture, Berkeley, 2012 [quoted as *American Writings*].

Totalitäre Propaganda, Berlin, 2013.

General Bibliography

Adorno: Eine Bildmonographie, Theodor W. Adorno Archiv (ed.), Frankfurt am Main, 2003.

Adorno, Theodor W., 'Große Blochmusik', *Neue Deutsche Hefte* 69 (1960/61), pp. 14–26.

Adorno, Theodor W., 'Scientific Experiences of a European Scholar in America', in Fleming and Bailyn (eds), *The Intellectual Migration*, 1969, pp. 338–70.

Adorno, Theodor W., 'Vorrede', in Tiedemann, *Studien zur Philosophie Walter Benjamins*, 1973, pp. 7–11.

Adorno, Theodor W., *The Jargon of Authenticity*, trans. Knut Tarnowski and Frederic Will, Evanston, IL, 1973 [1964].

Adorno, Theodor W., 'Sociology and Empirical Research', in *The Positivism Dispute in German Sociology*, trans. Glyn Adey and David Frisby, London, 1976, pp. 68–86.

Adorno, Theodor W., 'The Actuality of Philosophy', in *Telos* 31 (1977), pp. 113–33.

Adorno, Theodor W., *Kierkegaard: Construction of the Aesthetic*, trans. Robert Hullot-Kentor, Minneapolis, 1989 [1933].

Adorno, Theodor W., 'The Curious Realist', in *New German Critique* 54 (1991), pp. 159–77.

Adorno, Theodor W., 'Ernst Bloch's Spuren', in *Notes to Literature*, vol. 1, trans. Shierry Weber Nicholson, New York, 1992, pp. 200–15.

Adorno, Theodor W., 'The Handle, the Pot, and Early Experience', in *Notes to Literature*, vol. 2, trans. Shierry Weber Nicholson, New York, 1992, pp. 211–19.

Adorno, Theodor W., 'Introduction to Benjamin's *Schriften*', in *Notes to Literature*, vol. 2, trans. Shierry Weber Nicholson, New York, 1992, pp. 220–32.

Adorno, Theodor W., *Gesammelte Schriften* (GS), 20 vols, ed. by Rolf Tiedemann, Frankfurt am Main, 2003.

Adorno, Theodor W., 'Hoffmanns Erzählungen in Offenbachs Motiven', in GS 17, pp. 42–6.

Adorno, Theodor W., *Negative Dialectics*, trans. E.B. Ashton, London, New York, 2004.

Adorno, Theodor W., *Minima Moralia: Reflections on A Damaged Life*, London, 2005.

Adorno, Theodor W., 'Progress', in *Critical Models: Interventions and Catchwords*, trans. Henry W. Pickford, New York, 2005, pp. 143–60.

Adorno, Theodor W., 'Four Hands, Once Again', *Cultural Critique* 60 (2005), pp. 1–4.

Adorno, Theodor W., *Against Epistemology: A Metacritique*, trans. Willis Domingo, Cambridge, 2013 [1956].

Adorno, Theodor W. and Walter Benjamin, *Theodor W. Adorno and Walter Benjamin: The Complete Correspondence, 1928–1940*, trans. Nicholas Walker, Cambridge, 1999.

Adorno, Theodor W. and Alban Berg, *Correspondence 1925–1935*, trans. Wieland Hoban, Cambridge, 2005.

Adorno, Theodor W. and Siegfried Kracauer, *Briefwechsel 1923–1966*, ed. by Wolfgang Schopf, Frankfurt am Main, 2008.

Adorno, Theodor W. and Siegfried Kracauer, *Correspondence: 1923–1966*, ed. by Wolfgang Schopf, Cambridge, 2020.

Adorno, Theodor W. and Ernst Krenek, *Briefwechsel*, Frankfurt am Main, 1974.

Adorno, Theodor W. and Gerschom Scholem, *Correspondence: 1939–1969*, ed. by Asaf Angermann, Cambridge, 2020.

Agard, Olivier, 'Siegfried Kracauers Verhältnis zur jüdischen Identität', in *Akten des XI. Internationalen Germanistenkongresses*, Paris, 2005, vol. 12, pp. 347–54.

Agard, Olivier, *Kracauer: Le chiffonnier mélancolique*, Paris, 2010.

Aktives Museum (ed.), *Ohne zu zögern: Varian Fry, Berlin-Marseille-New York*, Berlin, 2007.

Améry, Jean, 'How Much Home Does a Person Need?', in *At the Mind's Limits*, trans. Sidney Rosenfeld and Stella P. Rosenfeld, Bloomington, 1980, pp. 41–61.

Anatomy of Racial Intolerance, compiled by George B. de Huszar, New York, 1946.

Anderson, Mark M., 'Siegfried Kracauer and Meyer Schapiro: A Friendship', in *New German Critique* 54 (1991), pp. 18–29.

Anderson, Perry, *Considerations on Western Marxism*, London, 1979 [1976].

Arato, Andrew and Paul Breines, *The Young Lukács and the Origins of Western Marxism*, New York, 1979.

Arburg, Hans-Georg von, '"Zweck-Architekturen der Verwesung": Siegfried Kracauers Roman *Ginster* im Kontext von Friedhofsreform, Denkmalstreit und Neuem Bauen in der Weimarer Republik', *Jahrbuch zur Kultur und Literatur der Weimarer Republik* 6 (2001), pp. 73–105.

Arendt, Hannah, 'The Aftermath of Nazi Rule: Report from Germany', *Commentary* 10 (1950), pp. 342–53.

Arendt, Hannah, *The Origins of Totalitarianism*, London, 1951.

Arendt, Hannah, 'Introduction: Walter Benjamin, 1892–1940', in Walter Benjamin, *Illuminations: Essays and Reflections*, trans. Harry Zohn, New York, 1968, pp. 1–55.

Arendt, Hannah, *Walter Benjamin, Bertolt Brecht: Zwei Essays*, Munich, 1971.

Arendt, Hannah, *Die verborgene Tradition: Essays*, Frankfurt am Main, 1976.

Arendt, Hannah, 'Die verborgene Tradition', in *Die verborgene Tradition*, pp. 50–79.

Arendt, Hannah, 'Juden in der Welt von gestern', in *Die verborgene Tradition*, pp. 80–94.

Arendt, Hannah, *The Human Condition*, Chicago, 1998 [1958].

Arendt, Hannah, 'Besuch in Deutschland', in *Zur Zeit: Politische Essays*, ed. by Marie Luise Knott, Hamburg, 1999, pp. 43–70.

Aristarco, Guido, *Marx, das Kino und die Kritik des Films*, Munich, Vienna, 1981.

Arnheim, Rudolf, 'Melancholy Unshaped', *The Journal of Aesthetics and Art Criticism* 21(3) (1963), pp. 291–7.

Arnheim, Rudolf, *Visual Thinking*, Berkeley, 1969.

Arnheim, Rudolf, *Film als Kunst*, Munich, 1974.

Arnheim, Rudolf, 'Zur Psychologie der Kunst und ihrer Geschichte', in *Kunsthistoriker in eigener Sache: Zehn autobiographische Skizzen*, ed. by Martina Sitt, Berlin, 1990, pp. 201–20.

Arnheim, Rudolf, 'The Two Authenticities of the Photographic Media', *The Journal of Aesthetics and Art Criticism* 51(4) (1993), pp. 537–40.

Arnheim, Rudolf, *Zauber des Sehens* (Gespräch mit Ingo Hermann in der Reihe 'Zeugen des Jahrhunderts'), ed. by Ingo Hermann, Göttingen, 1993.

Arns, Alfons, '"Ex Kino lux": Siegfried Kracauer, Frankfurt am Main und das Kino', in *Lebende Bilder einer Stadt: Kino und Film in Frankfurt am Main*. Ausstellungskatalog des Deutschen Filmmuseums, Frankfurt am Main, 1995, pp. 90–117.

Arnsberg, Paul, *Bilder aus dem jüdischen Leben im alten Frankfurt*, Frankfurt am Main, 1970.

Arnsberg, Paul, *Die Geschichte der Frankfurter Juden seit der Französischen Revolution*, vol. 1: *Der Gang der Ereignisse*, Darmstadt, 1983.

Arnsberg, Paul, *Die Geschichte der Frankfurter Juden seit der Französischen Revolution*, vol. 3: *Biographisches Lexikon der Juden in den Bereichen, Wissenschaft, Kultur, Bildung, Öffentlichkeitsarbeit*, Frankfurt am Main, 1983.

Aron, Raymond, *Dimensions de la conscience historique*, Paris, 1962.

Aron, Raymond, *Die deutsche Soziologie der Gegenwart: Systematische Einführung in das soziologische Denken*, Stuttgart, 1969.

Aschheim, Steven E., *Brothers and Strangers: The East European Jew in German and German Jewish Consciousness, 1800–1923*, Madison, WI, 1982.

Aschheim, Steven E., *Culture and Catastrophe: German and Jewish Confrontations with National Socialism and other Crises*, London, 1996.

Aschheim, Steven E., 'Icons beyond the Border', in *Beyond the Border: The German-Jewish Legacy Abroad*, Princeton, NJ, 2007, pp. 81–118.

Asper, Helmut G. (ed.), *Nachrichten aus Hollywood und anderswo: Der Briefwechsel Eugen und Marlise Schüfftans mit Siegfried und Lili Kracauer*, Trier, 2003.

Aubenas, Sylvie and Quentin Bajac, *Brassaï: Le flaneur nocturne*, Paris, 2012.

Auerbach, Erich, *Mimesis: The Representation of Reality in Western Literature*, Princeton, NJ, 2013 [1946].

Bade, Klaus J., *Europa in Bewegung: Migration vom späten 18. Jahrhundert bis zur Gegenwart*, Munich, 2000.

Badia, Gilbert, 'Frankreichs Haltung gegenüber dem deutschsprachigen Emigranten', in Sauveur-Henn (ed.), *Fluchtziel Paris*, 2002, pp. 29–40.

Balázs, Béla, *Der sichtbare Mensch oder die Kultur des Films*. With an afterword by Helmut H. Diederichs, Frankfurt am Main, 2001.

Balázs, Béla, *Early Film Theory: Visible Man and the Spirit of Film*, trans. Rodney Livingstone, New York, 2010.

Band, Henri, *Mittelschichten und Massenkultur: Siegfried Kracauers publizistische Auseinandersetzung mit der populären Kultur und der Kultur der Mittelschichten in der Weimarer Republik*, Berlin, 1999.

Barbian, Jan-Pieter, 'Politik und Film in der Weimarer Republik', in *Archiv für Kulturgeschichte* 80 (1998), pp. 213–45.

Barck, Karlheinz and Martin Treml, 'Einleitung: Erich Auerbachs Philologie als Kulturwissenschaft', in Barck and Treml (eds), *Erich Auerbach*, Berlin, 2007, pp. 9–29.

Barkai, Avraham, *Das Wirtschaftssystem des Nationalsozialismus*, Frankfurt am Main, 1995.

Barnouw, Dagmar, 'An den Rand geschriebene Träume: Kracauer über Zeit und Geschichte', in Kessler and Levin (eds), *Siegfried Kracauer*, pp. 1–15.

Barnouw, Dagmar, *Critical Realism: History, Photography, and the Work of Siegfried Kracauer*, Baltimore, 1994.

Barnouw, Dagmar, 'Vielschichtige Oberflächen: Kracauer und die Modernität von Weimar', in Grunert and Kimmich (eds), *Denken durch die Dinge*, pp. 13–27.

Barry, Iris, *Let's Go to the Movies*, New York, 1972.

Baumann, Stephanie, 'Drei Briefe: Franz Rosenzweig an Siegfried Kracauer', in *Zeitschrift für Religions- und Geistesgeschichte* 63(2) (2011), pp. 166–76.

Baumann, Stephanie, *Im Vorraum der Geschichte: Siegfried Kracauers 'History – The Last Things before the Last'*, Konstanz, 2014.

Bauschulte, Manfred, *Religionsbahnhöfe der Weimarer Republik: Studien zur Religionsforschung 1918–1933*, Marburg, 2007.

Beck, Max and Nicholas, Coomann, 'Adorno, Kracauer und die Ursprünge der Jargonkritik', in *Sprachkritik als Ideologiekritik: Studien zu Adornos Jargon der Eigentlichkeit*, Würzburg, 2015, pp. 7–27.

Becker, Ralf, 'Philosophie unterm Strich', in Bloch, *Der unbemerkte Augenblick*, pp. 9–66.

Becker, Werner, *'Demokratie des sozialen Rechts': Die politische Haltung der Frankfurter Zeitung, der Vossischen Zeitung und des Berliner Tageblatts 1918–1924*, Dissertation, Munich, 1965.

Behmer, Markus, *Von der Schwierigkeit, gegen Illusionen zu kämpfen: Der Publizist Leopold Schwarzschild – Leben und Werk vom Kaiserreich bis zur Flucht aus Europa*, Münster, 1997.

Belke, Ingrid, 'Siegfried Kracauer als Beobachter der jungen Sowjetunion', in Kessler and Levin (eds), *Siegfried Kracauer*, pp. 17–38.

Belke, Ingrid, 'Kracauers letzte Lebensjahre (1959–1966) und sein Buch *Geschichte*', in Kracauer, *Werke*, vol. 4, pp. 435–627.

Benjamin, Walter, 'Theses on the Philosophy of History', in *Illuminations*, trans. Harry Zohn, New York, 1969, pp. 253–64.

Benjamin, Walter, *Gesammelte Schriften* (GS), 17 vols, ed. by Rolf Tiedemann and Hermann Schweppenhäuser, Frankfurt am Main, 1972–99.

Benjamin, Walter, 'Das Kunstwerk im Zeitalter seiner technischen Reproduzierbarkeit. Dritte Fassung', in GS I.2, pp. 471–508.

Benjamin, Walter, 'Charles Baudelaire. Tableaux parisiens', in GS IV.1, pp. 7–63.

Benjamin, Walter, *Briefe*, 2 vols., ed. and with annotations by Gershom Scholem and Theodor W. Adorno, Frankfurt am Main, 1978.

Benjamin, Walter, 'Marseille', in *One-Way Street and Other Writings*, trans. Edmund Jephcott and Kingsley Shorter, London, 1979, pp. 209–14.

Benjamin, Walter, *Briefe an Siegfried Kracauer: Mit vier Briefen von Siegfried Kracauer an Walter Benjamin*, ed. by Theodor W. Adorno Archiv, Marbach am Neckar, 1987.

Benjamin, Walter, *The Correspondence of Walter Benjamin, 1910–1940*, trans. Manfred R. Jacobson and Evelyn M. Jacobson, Chicago, IL, 1994.

Benjamin, Walter, 'On Language as Such and on the Language of Man', in *Selected Writings*, Vol. 1, Cambridge, MA, 1996, pp. 62–74.

Benjamin, Walter, 'Critique of Violence', in *Selected Writings*, Vol. 1, trans. Edmund Jephcott, Cambridge, MA, 1996, pp. 236–52.

Benjamin, Walter, 'The Task of the Translator', in *Selected Writings*, Vol. 1, Cambridge, MA, 1996, pp. 253–63.

Benjamin, Walter, *The Origin of German Tragic Drama*, trans. John Osborne, New York, 1998.

Benjamin, Walter, *The Arcades Project*, trans. Howard Eiland and Kevin McLaughlin, Cambridge, MA, 1999.

Benjamin, Walter, 'Paris, the Capital of the Nineteenth Century' (1935), in *The Arcades Project*, pp. 3–13.

Benjamin, Walter, 'Little History of Photography', in *Selected Writings*, Vol. 2, trans. Rodney Livingstone et al., Cambridge, MA, 1999, pp. 507–30.

Benjamin, Walter, 'Julien Green', in *Selected Writings*, Vol. 2, trans. Rodney Livingstone et al., Cambridge, MA, 1999, pp. 331–6.

Benjamin, Walter, 'Reply to Oscar A.H. Schmitz', in *Selected Writings*, Vol. 2, trans. Rodney Livingstone et al., Cambridge, MA, 1999, pp. 16–19.

Benjamin, Walter, 'Chaplin in Retrospect', in *Selected Writings*, Vol. 2, trans. Rodney Livingstone et al., Cambridge, MA, 1999, pp. 222–4.

Benjamin, Walter, 'An Outsider Makes His Mark', in *Selected Writings*, Vol. 2, trans. Rodney Livingstone et al., Cambridge, MA, 1999, pp. 305–11.

Benjamin, Walter, 'Kierkegaard', in *Selected Writings*, Vol. 2, trans. Rodney Livingstone et al., Cambridge, MA, 1999, pp. 703–5.

Benjamin, Walter, 'Karl Kraus Reads Offenbach', in *Selected Writings*, Vol. 2, trans. Rodney Livingstone et al., Cambridge, MA, 1999, pp. 110–12.

Benjamin, Walter, 'On Language as Such and on the Language of Man', in *Selected Writings*, Vol. 1, trans. Rodney Livingstone et al., Cambridge, MA, 1999, pp. 62–74.

Benjamin, Walter, 'Franz Kafka', in *Selected Writings*, vol. 2, trans. Rodney Livingstone et al., Cambridge, MA, 1999, pp. 794–818.

Benjamin, Walter, 'Arcades' and 'The Arcades of Paris', in *The Arcades Project*, trans. Howard Eiland and Kevin McLaughlin, Cambridge, MA, 1999, pp. 871–84.

Benjamin, Walter, 'The Paris of the Second Empire in Baudelaire', in *Selected Writings*, Vol. 4, Cambridge, MA, 2003, pp. 3–92.

Benjamin, Walter and Gretel Karplus, *Correspondence 1930–1940*, trans. Wieland Hoban, Cambridge, 2008.

Benjamin, Walter and Asja Lacis, 'Naples', in *Reflections: Essays, Aphorisms, Autobiographical Writings*, trans. Edmund Jephcott, New York and London, 1978, pp. 163–73.

Benz, Wolfgang (ed.), *Das Exil der kleinen Leute: Alltagserfahrungen deutscher Juden in der Emigration*, Munich, 1991.

Benz, Wolfgang, *Flucht aus Deutschland: Zum Exil im 20. Jahrhundert*, Munich, 2001.

Berelson, Bernard, *Content Analysis in Communications Research*, New York, 1971.

Berg, Nicolas and Dieter Burdorf (eds), *Textgelehrte: Literaturwissenschaft und literarisches Wissen im Umkreis der Kritischen Theorie*, Göttingen, 2014.

Berg, Nicolas and Dieter Burdorf, 'Textgelehrsamkeit. Ein Denkstil und eine Lebensweise zwischen Wissenschaft und Literatur', in *Textgelehrte:*

Literaturwissenschaft und literarisches Wissen im Umkreis der Kritischen Theorie, Göttingen, 2014, pp. 9–35.

Berg, Ronald, *Die Ikone des Realen: Zur Bestimmung der Photographie im Werk von Talbot, Benjamin und Barthes*, Munich, 2001.

Berghahn, Volker, *Europa im Zeitalter der Weltkriege: Die Entfesselung und Entgrenzung der Gewalt*, Frankfurt am Main, 2002.

Bering, Dietz, *Die Epoche der Intellektuellen, 1989–2001: Geburt, Begriff, Grabmal*, Berlin, 2010.

Berlin, Isaiah, 'History and Theory. The Concept of Scientific History', *History and Theory* 1(1) (1961), pp. 1–31.

Berlin, Isaiah, *The Hedgehog and the Fox: An Essay on Tolstoy's View of History*, London, 1992.

Bernstein, Eduard, *Die deutsche Revolution von 1918/19: Geschichte der Entstehung und ersten Arbeitsperiode der deutschen Republik*, Bonn, 1998.

Betz, Albrecht, *Exil und Engagement: Deutsche Schriftsteller im Frankreich der dreißiger Jahre*, Munich, 1986.

Biebl, Sabine, 'Nachbemerkung und editorische Notiz', in Kracauer, *Werke* 2.1, pp. 499–532.

Biebl, Sabine, *Betriebsgeräusch Normalität: Angestelltendiskurs und Gesellschaft um 1930*, Berlin, 2013.

Birnbaum, Nathan, *Gottes Volk*, Vienna, Berlin, 1918.

Bloch, Ernst, 'Einige Kritiker', in *Durch die Wüste: Frühe kritische Aufsätze*, Frankfurt am Main, 1964, pp. 60–71.

Bloch, Ernst, *Thomas Münzer: Als Theologe der Revolution*, Frankfurt am Main, 1967 [1921].

Bloch, Ernst, 'Aktualität und Utopie: Zu Lukács' "Geschichte und Klassenbewußtsein"', in *Philosophische Aufsätze zur objektiven Phantasie*, Frankfurt am Main, 1969, pp. 598–621.

Bloch, Ernst, *Tagträume des aufrechten Ganges: Sechs Interviews mit Ernst Bloch*, ed. and with an introduction by Arno Münster, Frankfurt am Main, 1977.

Bloch, Ernst, *Geist der Utopie. Unveränderter Nachdruck der bearbeiteten Neuauflage der zweiten Fassung von 1923*, 3rd edn, Frankfurt am Main, 1980.

Bloch, Ernst, 'Der eigentümliche Glücksfall. Über "Jacques Offenbach" von Siegfried Kracauer', *Text + Kritik* 68 (1980), pp. 73–5.

Bloch, Ernst, *Briefe 1903–1975*. Vol. 1 + 2, ed. by Karola Bloch et al., Frankfurt am Main, 1985.

Bloch, Ernst, *Tübinger Einleitung in die Philosophie*, Frankfurt am Main, 1985.

Bloch, Ernst, *The Principle of Hope*, vols 1–3, trans. Neville Plaice, Stephen Plaice, Paul Knight, Cambridge, MA, 1986.

Bloch, Ernst, *The Heritage of Our Times*, trans. Neville Plaice and Stephen Plaice, Cambridge, 1991.

Bloch, Ernst, 'The Anxiety of the Engineer', in *Literary Essays*, trans. Andrew Joron et al., Stanford, 1998, pp. 304–14.

Bloch, Ernst, 'Italy and Porosity', in *Literary Essays*, trans. Andrew Joron et al., Stanford, 1998, pp. 450–7.

Bloch, Ernst, *The Spirit of Utopia*, trans. Anthony A. Nassar, Stanford, 2000.

Bloch, Ernst, *Traces*, trans. Anthony A. Nassar, Stanford, 2006.

Bloch, Ernst, *Der unbemerkte Augenblick: Feuilletons für die 'Frankfurter Zeitung' 1916–1934*, Frankfurt am Main, 2007.

Bloch, Marc, *Apologie der Geschichte oder Der Beruf des Historikers*, Stuttgart, 1974.

Blomert, Reinhard, *Intellektuelle im Aufbruch: Karl Mannheim, Alfred Weber, Norbert Elias und die Heidelberger Sozialwissenschaften der Zwischenkriegszeit*, Munich, Vienna, 1999.

Bloom, Alexander, *Prodigal Sons: The New York Intellectuals and their World*, New York, Oxford, 1986.

Bluestone, George, *Novels into Film*, Berkeley, CA, 1957.

Blumenberg, Hans, '"Säkularisation": Kritik einer Kategorie historischer Illegitimität', in Kuhn and Wiedmann (eds), *Die Philosophie*, pp. 240–65.

Blumenberg, Hans, *The Legitimacy of the Modern Age*, trans. Robert M. Wallace, Cambridge, MA, 1985.

Boden, Petra, 'Arbeit an Begriffen. Zur Geschichte von Kontroversen in der Forschungsgruppe "Poetik und Hermeneutik"', *Internationales Archiv für die Sozialgeschichte der Literatur* 35 (2010), pp. 103–21.

Boden, Petra, 'Vom Umgang mit Dissens und Kontroversen. Ein Forschungsbericht über das Projekt *Arbeit an Begriffen. Zur Geschichte von Kontroversen in der Forschungsgruppe "Poetik und Hermeneutik" (1966–1984)*', *Internationales Archiv für die Sozialgeschichte der Literatur* 38(2) (2013), pp. 281–314.

Boden, Petra, 'Vom Protokoll zum idealen Gespräch. Einblicke in die Werkstatt von Poetik und Hermeneutik', *Zeitschrift für Germanistik. Neue Folge* 23(2) (2013), pp. 359–73.

Bollenbeck, Georg, *Eine Geschichte der Kulturkritik: Von Rousseau bis Günther Anders*, Munich, 2007.

Boltanski, Luc, *Mysteries and Conspiracies: Detective Stories, Spy Novels, and the Making of Modern Societies*, Cambridge, 2014.

Bourdieu, Pierre, *The Rules of Art: Genesis and Structure of the Literary Field*, trans. Susan Emanuel, Stanford, CA, 1995.

Braunstein, Dirk, *Adornos Kritik der politischen Ökonomie*, Bielefeld, 2011.

Brecht, Bertolt, *Flüchtlingsgespräche*, Frankfurt am Main, 1961.

Brecht, Bertolt, *Poems 1913–1956*, London, 1976.

Brecht, Bertolt, *Bertolt Brecht's Refugee Conversations*, London, 2019.

Brecht, Bertolt and Siegfried Unseld (eds), *Bertolt Brechts Dreigroschenbuch: Texte, Materialien, Dokument*, Frankfurt am Main, 1960.

Brecht, Christoph, 'Strom der Freiheit und Strudel des Chaos. Ausblicke auf Kracauers Caligari-Buch', *Marbacher Magazin* 105, pp. 5–52.

Brecht, Christoph, *Im Reich der Schatten. Siegfried Kracauers 'From Caligari to Hitler'*, Marbach, 2004.

Breidecker, Volker (ed.), *Siegfried Kracauer – Erwin Panofsky. Briefwechsel 1941–1966*, Berlin, 1996.

Breidecker, Volker, '"Ferne Nähe". Kracauer, Panofsky and "the Warburg Tradition"', in Breidecker (ed.), *Siegfried Kracauer – Erwin Panofsky*, pp. 129–226.

Breidecker, Volker, 'Vom Eisen zum Film', in Holste, *Kracauers Blick*, pp. 159–84.

Breidecker, Volker, 'Das Nizza von Frankfurt', *Zeitschrift für Ideengeschichte* 5(3) (2011), pp. 33–44.

Breitman, Richard, *Staatsgeheimnisse: Die Verbrechen der Nazis – von den Alliierten toleriert*, Munich, 1999.

Brenner, Michael, *Jüdische Kultur in der Weimarer Republik*, Munich, 2000.

Breuer, Stefan, *Anatomie der Konservativen Revolution*, Darmstadt, 1995.

Brod, Max, *Heidentum, Christentum, Judentum: Ein Bekenntnisbuch*, Munich, 1921.

Brod, Max, *Über Franz Kafka*, Frankfurt am Main, 1966.

Brodersen, Momme, *Benjamin: A Biography*, trans. Malcolm R. Green and Ingrida Ligers, London, 1996.

Brodersen, Momme, *Siegfried Kracauer*, Reinbek bei Hamburg, 2001.

Bronsen, David, *Joseph Roth: Eine Biographie*, Cologne, 1974.

Brunkhorst, Hauke, *Theodor W. Adorno: Dialektik der Moderne*, Munich, 1990.

Brunkhorst, Hauke, *Adorno and Critical Theory*, Cardiff, 1999.

Buber, Martin, *I and Thou*, trans. Ronald Gregor Smith, London, 2013.

Buber, Martin, *Tales of the Hasidim*, trans. Olga Marx, New York, 1947.

Buber, Martin and Franz Rosenzweig, 'Die Bibel auf Deutsch. Zur Erwiderung', in Buber and Rosenzweig, *Die Schrift und ihre Verdeutschung*, Berlin, 1936, pp. 276–291.

Bulgakowa, Oksana, 'Russische Filme in Berlin', in Bulgakowa (ed.), *Die ungewöhnlichen Abenteuer des Dr. Mabuse im Lande der Bolschewiki*, Berlin, 1995, pp. 81–94.

Burckhardt, Jacob, *Weltgeschichtliche Betrachtungen*, Stuttgart, 1946.

Bussemer, Thymian, *Propaganda: Konzepte und Theorien*, 2nd revised edn, Wiesbaden, 2008.

Bussiek, Dagmar, *Benno Reifenberg 1892–1970: Eine Biographie*, Göttingen, 2011.

Bütow, Hans, 'Große Eschenheimer Straße 31', *Gegenwart. Sonderheft zur Frankfurter Zeitung*, 1956, p. 39.

Claussen, Detlev, 'Blick zurück auf Lenin', in Claussen (ed.), *Blick zurück auf Lenin: Georg Lukács, die Oktoberrevolution und die Perestroika*, Frankfurt am Main, 1990, pp. 7–41.

Claussen, Detlev, *Adorno: One Last Genius*, trans. Rodney Livingstone, Cambridge, MA, 2008.

Claussen, Detlev, 'Im Spiegel eines Dritten: Hannah Arendt und Theodor W. Adorno', in Liliane Weissberg (ed.), *Affinität wider Willen? Hannah Arendt, Theodor W. Adorno und die Frankfurter Schule*, Frankfurt am Main, 2011, pp. 67–83.

Collingwood, Robin George, *The Idea of History: With Lectures 1926–1928*, Oxford, 1993 [1946].

Corbin, Anne-Marie, 'Die Bedeutung der Pariser Cafés für die geflohenen deutschsprachigen Literaten', in Sauveur-Henn (ed.), *Fluchtziel Paris*, 2002, pp. 88–101.

Coser, Lewis A., *Refugee Scholars in America: Their Impact and their Experiences*, New Haven, CT, 1984.

Culbert, David, 'The Rockefeller Foundation, the Museum of Modern Art Film Library, and Siegfried Kracauer, 1941', *Historical Journal of Film, Radio and Television* 13(4) (1993), pp. 495–511.

Cullin, Michel, '"An uns glaubt niemand mehr." Zur Situation des deutschsprachigen Exils in Frankreich 1940', in Werfel (ed.), *Gehetzt*, pp. 9–30.

Curtiss, Mina, *Bizet and His World*, London, 1959.

Cziffra, Géza von, *Der heilige Trinker: Erinnerungen an Joseph Roth*, Berlin, 2006.

Dahrendorf, Ralf, *Society and Democracy in Germany*, New York, 1979.

Dannemann, Rüdiger, *Georg Lukács: Eine Einführung*, Wiesbaden, no year.

Decherney, Peter, *Hollywood and the Culture Elite: How the Movies Became American*, New York, 2005.

Despoix, Philippe, *Ethiken der Entzauberung: Zum Verhältnis von ästhetischer, ethischer und politischer Sphäre am Anfang des 20. Jahrhunderts*, Bodenheim, 1998.

Despoix, Philippe, 'Geschichtsschreibung im Zeitalter fotografischer und filmischer Reproduzierbarkeit. Siegfried Kracauer vor den letzten Dingen', in Robnik et al. (eds), *Film als Loch in der Wand*, pp. 103–15.

Deutscher, Isaac, *Die ungelöste Judenfrage: Zur Dialektik von Antisemitismus und Zionismus*, Berlin, 1977.

Deutscher, Isaac, *Der nichtjüdische Jude*, Berlin, 1991.

Diers, Michael, 'Der Autor ist im Bilde. Idee, Form und Geschichte des Dichter- und Gelehrtenporträts', in *Jahrbuch der Deutschen Schillergesellschaft* 51 (2007), pp. 551–86.

Diner, Dan (ed.), *Zivilisationsbruch: Denken nach Auschwitz*, Frankfurt am Main, 1988.

Diner, Dan, 'Aporie der Vernunft. Horkheimers Überlegungen zu Antisemitismus und Massenvernichtung', in Diner, *Zivilisationsbruch*, pp. 30–53.

Diner, Dan, *America in the Eyes of the Germans: An Essay on Anti-Americanism*, Princeton, NJ, 1996.

Diner, Dan, 'Vom "Anschluss" zur "Kristallnacht" – das Krisenjahr 1938', in Jüdisches Museum Berlin (ed.), *Heimat und Exil*, Frankfurt am Main, 2006, pp. 22–30.

Diner, Dan, *Cataclysms: A History of the Twentieth Century from Europe's Edge*, Madison, WI, 2008.

Dostojewski, Fjodor M., *Die Brüder Karamasow. Fünftes Buch*, Leipzig, 1975.

Dubbels, Elke, *Figuren des Messianischen in Schriften deutsch-jüdischer Intellektueller 1900–1933*, Berlin, 2011.

Dubiel, Helmut and Alfons Söllner, 'Die Nationalsozialismusforschung des Instituts für Sozialforschung – ihre wissenschaftliche Stellung und ihre gegenwärtige Bedeutung', in Horkheimer et al., *Wirtschaft, Recht und Staat im Nationalsozialismus*, pp. 7–31.

Ehrenburg, Ilja, *Die Traumfabrik*, Berlin, 1931.

Eisermann, Gottfried, 'Die deutsche Soziologie im Zeitraum von 1918 bis 1933', in Eisermann, *Bedeutende Soziologen*, Stuttgart, 1968, pp. 26–43.

Eisner, Lotte H., *The Haunted Screen: Expressionism in the German Cinema and the Influence of Max Reinhardt*, Berkeley, CA, 2008 [1952].

Eksteins, Modris, 'The Frankfurt Zeitung, Mirror of Weimar Democracy', in *Journal of Contemporary History* 4 (1971), pp. 3–28.

Elsaesser, Thomas, *Das Weimarer Kino – aufgeklärt und doppelbödig*, Berlin, 1999.

Elsaesser, Thomas, *Weimar Cinema and After: Germany's Historical Imaginary*, London, New York, 2000.

Enzensberger, Hans Magnus, *Einzelheiten I*, Frankfurt am Main, 1962.

Erhart, Walter, '"Wahrscheinlich haben wir beide recht". Diskussion und Dissens unter "Laboratoriumsbedingungen". Beobachtungen zu "Poetik und Hermeneutik" 1963–1966', *Internationales Archiv für die Sozialgeschichte der Literatur* 35 (2010), pp. 77–102.

Eßbach, Wolfgang, 'Radikalismus und Modernität bei Jünger und Bloch, Lukács und Schmitt', in Manfred Gangl and Gérard Raulet (eds), *Intellektuellendiskurse in der Weimarer Republik: Zur Politischen Kultur einer Gemengelage*, Frankfurt am Main, 2007, pp. 219–32.

Eßbach, Wolfgang, 'Wer war Marx? Bilder eines Intellektuellen', in Richard Faber (ed.), *Was ist ein Intellektueller? Rückblicke und Vorblicke*, Würzburg, 2012, pp. 163–82.

Eßbach, Wolfgang, 'Die historischen Quellen soziologischen Denkens, Aus welchen Traditionen entwickelt sich die Soziologie ?', in Jörn Lamla et al. (eds), *Handbuch der Soziologie*, Konstanz, Munich, 2014, pp. 25–44.

Farrell, James T., *The League of Frightened Philistines*, New York, 1945.

Felken, Detlef, 'Nachwort', in Spengler, *Untergang*, pp. 1250–70.

Fellmann, Ferdinand, *Phänomenologie zur Einführung*, Hamburg, 2006.

Fermi, Laura, *Illustrious Immigrants: The Intellectual Migration from Europe 1930–41*, Chicago, IL, 1968.

Fetscher, Iring, *Der Marxismus: Seine Geschichte in Dokumenten, Philosophie, Ideologie, Ökonomie, Soziologie, Politik*, Munich, Zurich, 1983.

Feuchtwanger, Lion, *Exil*, Berlin, 1956.

Feuchtwanger, Lion, *The Devil in France: My Encounter with Him in the Summer of 1940*, trans. Elisabeth Abbott, New York, 1941.

Fittko, Lisa, *Mein Weg über die Pyrenäen: Erinnerungen 1940/41*, Munich, 2008.

Fleck, Christian, *Transatlantische Bereicherungen: Zur Erfindung der empirischen Sozialforschung*, Frankfurt am Main, 2007.

Fleck, Christian and Bernd Stiegler, 'Nachbemerkung und editorische Notiz', in Kracauer, *Werke* 2.2, pp. 827–64.

Fleck, Ludwik, *Erfahrung und Tatsache: Gesammelte Aufsätze*, Frankfurt am Main, 1983.

Fleming, Donald and Bernard Bailyn (eds), *The Intellectual Migration: Europe and America 1930–1960*, Cambridge, MA, 1969.

Flusser, Vilém, *Groundless*, trans. Rodrigo Maltes Novaes, no place, 2017.

Foucault, Michel, *The History of Sexuality*, vol. 2 (The Uses of Pleasure), trans. Robert Hurley, New York, 1990.

Franke, Christoph, 'Die Rolle der Devisenstellen bei der Enteignung der Juden', in Katharina Stengel (ed.), *Die staatliche Enteignung der Juden im Nationalsozialismus*, Frankfurt am Main, 2007, pp. 80–93.

Franke, Julia, *Paris – eine neue Heimat? Jüdische Emigranten aus Deutschland 1933–1939*, Berlin, 2000.

Freeman, Joseph, *Never Call Retreat*, New York, Toronto, 1943.

Freud, Sigmund, *Totem and Taboo: Resemblances between the Psychic Life of Savages and Neurotics*, trans. A.A. Brill, New York, 1919.

Freud, Sigmund, *Civilization and Its Discontents*, trans. James Strachey, New York, 1962.

Freund, Gisele, *The World in My Camera*, New York, 1974.

Freyer, Hans, *Soziologie als Wirklichkeitswissenschaft: Logische Grundlegung des Systems der Soziologie*, Leipzig, Berlin, 1930.

Freytag, Carl, 'Alfred Sohn-Rethel in Italien, 1924–1927', in Alfred Sohn-Rethel, *Das Ideal des Kaputten*, Bremen, 2008.

Friedländer, Saul, *Nazi Germany and the Jews: The Years of Persecution 1933–1939*, London, 1998.

Friedländer, Saul, *Nazi Germany and the Jews: The Years of Extermination, 1939–1945*, New York, 2007.

Frisby, David, *Fragments of Modernity: Theories of Modernity in the Work of Simmel, Kracauer, and Benjamin*, Cambridge, 1985.

Frisby, David, 'Between the Spheres: Kracauer and the Detective Novel', *Theory, Culture & Society* 9 (1992), pp. 1–22.

Fromm, Erich, 'Prophets and Priests', in *On Disobedience: Why Freedom Means Saying 'No' to Power*, New York, 1981, pp. 13–39.

Fromm, Erich, *Die Furcht vor der Freiheit*, Munich, 1990.

Fry, Varian, *Surrender on Demand*, London, 1999.

Fuld, Werner, *Walter Benjamin: Eine Biographie*, Reinbek bei Hamburg, 1979.

Funk, Rainer, *Erich Fromm: His Life and Ideas*, trans. Ian Portman and Manuela Kunkel, New York, 2000.

Gardiner, Patrick (ed.), *Theories of History*, Glencoe, IL, 1959.

Gay, Peter, *Weimar Culture: The Outsider as Insider*, New York, 2001.

Gay, Peter, *Modernism: The Lure of Heresy – From Baudelaire to Becket and Beyond*, New York, 2008.

Gemünden, Gerd and Johannes von Moltke (eds), *Culture in the Anteroom: The Legacies of Siegfried Kracauer*, Ann Arbor, MI, 2012.

Gerhardt, Christina, 'On Natural History. Concepts of History in Adorno and Kracauer', in Gemünden and von Moltke (eds), *Culture in the Anteroom*, pp. 229–43.

Geyer, Martin H., *Verkehrte Welt: Revolution, Inflation und Moderne, München 1914–1924*, Göttingen, 1998.

Geyl, Pieter, *Debates with Historians*, Groningen, 1955.

Gillesen, Günther, *Auf verlorenem Posten: Die Frankfurter Zeitung im Dritten Reich*, Berlin, 1986.

Ginzburg, Carlo, 'Details, Early Plans, Microanalysis: Thoughts on a Book by Siegfried Kracauer', in *Threads and Traces: True False Fictive*, trans. Anne C. Tedeschi and John Tedeschi, Berkeley, CA, 2012, pp. 180–92.

Glatzer, Nahum N., 'Das Frankfurter Lehrhaus', in *Der Philosoph Franz Rosenzweig (1886–1929)*, vol. 1: *Die Herausforderung jüdischen Lernens*, ed. by Wolfdietrich Schmied Kowarzik, Freiburg, Munich, 1988, pp. 303–26.

Glock, Charles Y., 'Organizational Innovation for Social Science Research and Training', in Merton (ed.), *Qualitative and Quantitative Social Research*, pp. 23–36.

Goebel, Eckart and Sigrid Weigel (eds), *'Escape to Life'. German Intellectuals in New York: A Compendium in Exile after 1933*, Berlin, Boston, 2012.

Goethe, Johann Wolfgang, 'Fortunate Encounter', in *The Collected Works*, vol. 12, ed. and trans. by Douglas Miller, Princeton, NJ, 1995.

Graf, Friedrich Wilhelm, *Der heilige Zeitgeist: Studien zur Ideengeschichte der protestantischen Theologie in der Weimarer Republik*, Tübingen, 2011.

Gregor, Ulrich and Enno Patalas, *Geschichte des Films*, Gütersloh, 1962.

Greiner, Bernd, *Die Morgenthau-Legende: Zur Geschichte eines umstrittenen Plans*, Hamburg, 1995.

Griffith, Robert, *The World of Robert Flaherty*, London, 1953.

Grob, Norbert and Karl Prümm (eds), *Die Macht der Filmkritik: Positionen und Kontroversen*, Munich, 1990.

Große Kracht, Klaus, *Zwischen Berlin und Paris: Bernhard Groethuysen (1880–1946): Eine intellektuelle Biographie*, Tübingen, 2002.

Grossmann, Kurt R., *Emigration: Geschichte der Hitler-Flüchtlinge 1933–1945*, Frankfurt am Main, 1969.

Grunert, Frank and Dorothee Kimmich (eds), *Denken durch die Dinge: Siegfried Kracauer im Kontext*, Munich, 2009.

Günter, Manuela, *Anatomie des Anti-Subjekts: Zur Subversion autobiographischen Schreibens bei Siegfried Kracauer, Walter Benjamins und Carl Einstein*, Würzburg, 1996.

Guthrie, W.K.C., *The Greek Philosophers (from Thales to Aristotle)*, London, 1968 [1950].

Guttmann, Bernhard, 'Die Zeitung und das Reich', in *Gegenwart*. Special Issue. *Ein Jahrhundert Frankfurter Zeitung begründet von Leopold Sonnemann*, 1956, pp. 3–5.

Haag, Karl Heinz, *Kritische Philosophie: Abhandlungen und Aufsätze*, Bad Langensalza, 2012.

Haag, Karl Heinz, 'Kritik der neueren Ontologie', in *Kritische Philosophie*, pp. 7–93.

Haag, Karl Heinz, 'Das Unwiederholbare', in *Kritische Philosophie*, pp. 97–107.

Habermas, Jürgen, *The Structural Transformation of the Public Sphere: An Inquiry into a Category of Bourgeois Society*, trans. Thomas Burger (with the assistance of Frederick Lawrence), Cambridge, 1989.

Hake, Sabine, *Film in Deutschland: Geschichte und Geschichten seit 1895*, Reinbek bei Hamburg, 2004.

Handelman, Matthew, 'The Forgotten Conversation. Five Letters from Franz Rosenzweig to Siegfried Kracauer, 1921–1923', in *Scientia Poetica* 15 (2011), pp. 234–51.

Hansen, Miriam, '"With Skin and Hair", Kracauer's Theory of Film, Marseille 1940', in *Critical Inquiry* 19(3) (1993), pp. 437–69.

Hansen, Miriam, *Cinema and Experience: Siegfried Kracauer, Walter Benjamin and Theodor W. Adorno*, Berkeley, CA, 2012.

Happel, Reinhold and Margot Michaelis, 'Wem gehört die Welt? – Filme der Arbeiterbewegung in der Weimarer Republik', in *Film und Realität in der Weimarer Republik*, pp. 93–243.

Haselberg, Peter von, 'Wiesengrund-Adorno', in *Text + Kritik*, special issue, Munich, 1977, pp. 7–21.

Hasler, Eveline, *Mit dem letzten Schiff: Der gefährliche Auftrag von Varian Fry*, Munich, 2013.

Hauptmann, Gerhart, *The Fool in Christ, Emanuel Quint: A Novel*, trans. Thomas Seltzer, New York, 1911.

Haury, Thomas, 'Zur Logik des bundesdeutschen Zionismus', in Léon Poliakov, *Vom Antizionismus zum Antisemitismus*, Freiburg, 1992, pp. 125–59.

Hauser, Arnold, *Philosophie der Kunstgeschichte*, Munich, 1958.

Heilbut, Anthony, *Exiled in Paradise: German Refugee Artists and Intellectuals in America, from the 1930s to the Present*, New York, 1983.

Heim, Susanne, '"Polizeilich organisierte Gesetzeslosigkeit". Zur Situation der jüdischen Flüchtlinge in Frankreich und den Niederlanden', in *Heimat und Exil*, pp. 59–71.

Heller, Heinz B., 'Massenkultur und ästhetische Urteilskraft. Zur Geschichte und Funktion der deutschen Filmkritik vor 1933', in Grob and Prümm, *Die Macht der Filmkritik*, pp. 25–45.

Hellige, Hans Dieter, 'Generationskonflikt, Selbsthaß und die Entstehung antikapitalistischer Positionen im Judentum: Der Einfluß des Antisemitismus auf das Sozialverhalten jüdischer Kaufmanns- und Unternehmersöhne im Deutschen Kaiserreich und in der K. u. K.-Monarchie', in *Geschichte und Gesellschaft* 5/4 (1979), pp. 476–518.

Helms, Hans G., *Die Ideologie der anonymen Gesellschaft: Max Stirners 'Einziger' und der Fortschritt des demokratischen Selbstbewußtseins vom Vormärz bis zur Bundesrepublik*, Cologne, 1966.

Helms, Hans G., '*Kolumbus mußte seiner Theorie nach in Indien landen, er entdeckte Amerika*: Siegfried Kracauers Bemühen um die Reflexion konkreter Wirklichkeit und sein polit-ökonomischer Ansatz', in Kessler and Levin (eds), *Siegfried Kracauer*, pp. 77–86.

Henning, Christoph, *Philosophie nach Marx: 100 Jahre Marxrezeption und die normative Sozialphilosophie der Gegenwart in der Kritik*, Bielefeld, 2005.

Herbert, Ulrich, 'Liberalisierung als Lernprozess', in Herbert (ed.),

Wandlungsprozesse in Westdeutschland: Belastung, Integration, Liberalisierung 1945–1980, Göttingen, 2002, pp. 7–49.

Herbert, Ulrich, *Geschichte Deutschlands im 20. Jahrhundert*, Munich, 2014.

Hertzberg, Arthur, *Shalom, Amerika! Die Geschichte der Juden in der Neuen Welt*, Munich, 1992.

Heß, Tillmann, 'Zur Architektur in Kracauers Stadtbildern', in Volk (ed.), *Siegfried Kracauer*, pp. 111–55.

Hesse, Hermann, *Unterm Rad*, Frankfurt am Main, 1972.

Hesse, Hermann, *The Prodigy*, trans. W. J. Strachan, London and Chester Springs, 2002 [1961].

Hessel, Franz, *Walking in Berlin: A Flaneur in the Capital*, trans. Amanda DeMarco, Cambridge, MA, 2017.

Heuberger, Rachel, 'Die Entdeckung der jüdischen Wurzeln. Leo Löwenthal und der Frankfurter Rabbiner Nehemias Anton Nobel', in Jansen (ed.), *Das Utopische soll Funken schlagen ...*, pp. 47–67.

Heuberger, Rachel, *Rabbiner Nehemias Anton Nobel: Die jüdische Renaissance in Frankfurt am Main*, Frankfurt am Main, 2005.

Heuberger, Rachel and Helga Krohn, *Hinaus aus dem Ghetto ... Juden in Frankfurt am Main 1800–1950*, Frankfurt am Main, 1988.

Hexter, Jack H., *Reappraisals in History*, Aberdeen, 1961.

Hickethier, Knut, 'Medienkultur im Wandel', in Werner Faulstich (ed.), *Die Kultur im 20. Jahrhundert im Überblick*, Munich, 2011, pp. 221–39.

Hilberg, Raul, *Die Vernichtung der europäischen Juden*, 2 vols., Frankfurt am Main, 1990.

Hobsbawm, Eric, *Age of Extremes: The Short Twentieth Century 1914–1991*, London, 1995.

Hobsbawm, Eric, 'The Influence of Marxism 1880–1914', in *How to Change the World: Reflections on Marx and Marxism*, New Haven, 2011, pp. 211–60.

Hoennicke Moore, Michaela, *Know Your Enemy: The American Debate on Nazism, 1933–1945*, New York, 2010.

Höffe, Otfried, *Kleine Geschichte der Philosophie*, Munich, 2001.

Hofmann, Martin Ludwig, 'Georg Simmel (1858–1918): Theorie der Extravaganz als Kulturtheorie der Moderne', in Hofmann et al. (eds), *Culture Club*, pp. 31–47.

Hofmann, Martin and Tobias Korta, *Siegfried Kracauer – Fragmente einer Archäologie der Moderne*, Sinzheim, 1997.

Hofmann, Martin Ludwig, Tobias F. Korta and Sibylle Niekisch (eds), *Culture Club: Klassiker der Kulturtheorie*, Frankfurt am Main, 2004.

Hofmann, Martin Ludwig, Tobias F. Korta and Sibylle Niekisch (eds), *Culture Club II: Klassiker der Kulturtheorie*, Frankfurt am Main, 2006.

Hogen, Hildegard, *Die Modernisierung des Ich: Individualitätskonzepte bei Siegfried Kracauer, Robert Musil und Elias Canetti*, Würzburg, 2000.

Holste, Christine (ed.), *Kracauers Blick: Anstöße zu einer Ethnographie des Städtischen*, Hamburg, 2006.

Holste, Christine, '"Wenn der Mensch aus dem Glas steigt" – Siegfried Kracauer als Vermittler einer neuen Formensprache der Architektur', in Holste (ed.), *Kracauers Blick*, pp. 103–57.

Honneth, Axel, '"Zur Kritik der Gewalt"', in Lindner (ed.), *Benjamin-Handbuch*, pp. 193–210.

Honneth, Axel, 'Der destruktive Realist. Zum sozialphilosophischen Erbe Siegfried Kracauers', in Honneth, *Vivisektionen eines Zeitalters*, Berlin, 2014, pp. 120–42.

Hook, Sidney (ed.), *Philosophy and History: A Symposium*, New York, 1963.

Horkheimer, Max, 'Beginnings of the Bourgeois Philosophy of History' [1930], in *Between Philosophy and Social Science: Selected Early Writings*, Cambridge, MA, 1993, pp. 313–88.

Horkheimer, Max (ed.), *Zeugnisse: Theodor W. Adorno zum sechzigsten Geburtstag*, Frankfurt am Main, 1963.

Horkheimer, Max, 'Jenseits der Fachwissenschaft: Adorno zum 60. Geburtstag', in *Gesammelte Schriften*, vol. 7: *Vorträge und Aufzeichnungen 1949–1973*, Frankfurt am Main, 1985, pp. 261–4.

Horkheimer, Max, 'The Jews and Europe', in Eduardo Mendieta (ed.), *The Frankfurt School on Religion*, New York, London, 2005, pp. 225–41.

Horkheimer, Max and T. W. Adorno, *Dialectic of Enlightenment: Philosophical Fragments*, trans. Edmund Jephcott, Stanford, CA, 2002.

Horkheimer, Max et al., *Wirtschaft, Recht und Staat im Nationalsozialismus: Analysen des Instituts für Sozialforschung 1939–1942*, ed. by Helmut Dubiel und Alfons Söllner, Frankfurt am Main, 1981.

Horkheimer, Max et al., *Studien über Autorität und Familie: Forschungsberichte aus dem Institut für Sozialforschung*, Lüneburg, 1987.

Horovitz, Irving Louis, 'Zwischen der Charybdis des Kapitalismus und der Szylla des Kommunismus, Die Emigration deutscher Sozialwissenschaftler 1933–1945', in Srubar (ed.), *Exil, Wissenschaft, Identität*, pp. 37–63.

Horstkotte, Silke, '"Steinchen eines Mosaiks": Siegfried Kracauer als Bildgelehrter', in Berg and Burdorf (eds), *Textgelehrte*, pp. 103–8.

Huizinga, Johan, *Im Bann der Geschichte. Betrachtungen und Gestaltungen*, Basel, 1943.

Huizinga, Johan, *Men and Ideas: History, the Middle Ages, the Renaissance*, New York, 1959.

Husserl, Edmund, *The Crisis of European Sciences and Transcendental Phenomenology: An Introduction to Phenomenological Philosophy*, trans. David Carr, Evanston, IL, 1970.

Idel, Moshe, *Alte Welten, neue Bilder: Jüdische Mystik und die Gedankenwelt des 20. Jahrhunderts*, Berlin, 2012.

Iggers, Georg G., *Neue Geschichtswissenschaft: Vom Historismus zur Historischen Sozialwissenschaft*, Munich, 1978.

Iggers, Georg G., *Geschichtswissenschaft im 20. Jahrhundert*, Göttingen, 1993.

Iggers, Georg G., Q. Edward Wang and Supriya Mukherjee, *Geschichtskulturen: Weltgeschichte der Historiografie von 1750 bis heute*, Göttingen, 2013.

Illustrierte Geschichte der deutschen Revolution, Berlin, 1929.

Isenberg, Noah, 'This Pen for Hire: Siegfried Kracauer as American Cultural Critic', in Gemünden and von Moltke (eds), *Culture in the Anteroom*, pp. 29–41.

Iser, Wolfgang (ed.), *Immanente Ästhetik: Ästhetische Reflexion. Lyrik als Paradigma der Moderne. Kolloquium Köln 1964, Vorlagen und Verhandlungen*, Munich, 1966.

Jacob, Heinrich Eduard, *Blood and Celluloid*, London, 1930.

Jacob, Joachim, 'Undurchdringlichkeit. Oder: Über Kracauer und die "Fruchtbarkeit des gegenständlichen Widerstandes" in der deutschen Kulturphilosophie der 1920er Jahre', in Grunert and Kimmich, *Denken durch die Dinge*, pp. 103–18.

Jacobsen, Wolfgang, Anton Kaes and Hans Helmut Prinzler (eds), *Geschichte des deutschen Films*, Stuttgart, Weimar, 1993.

Jäger, Lorenz, *Adorno: A Political Biography*, New Haven, CT, 2004.

Jäger, Lorenz, 'Kracauers Blick. Überlegungen zu seiner Dissertation "Die Entwicklung der Schmiedekunst"', in Holste, *Kracauers Blick*, pp. 81–102.

Jansen, Peter-Erwin (ed.), *Das Utopische soll Funken schlagen ... Zum hundertsten Geburtstag von Leo Löwenthal*, Frankfurt am Main, 2000.

Jasper, Willi, *Deutsch-jüdischer Parnass: Literaturgeschichte eines Mythos*, Berlin, 2004.

Jauß, Hans Robert, 'Ursprung und Bedeutung der Fortschrittsidee in der "Querelle des Anciens et des Modernes"', in Kuhn and Wiedmann (eds), *Die Philosophie und die Frage nach dem Fortschritt*, pp. 51–72.

Jauß, Hans Robert (ed.), *Die nicht mehr schönen Künste: Grenzphänomene des Ästhetischen*, Munich, 1968.

Jauß, Hans Robert (ed.), *Nachahmung und Illusion: Kolloquium Gießen, Juni 1963, Vorlagen und Verhandlungen*, Munich, 1969.

Jauß, Hans Robert, *Zeit und Erinnerung in Marcel Prousts 'A la recherche du temps perdu': Ein Beitrag zur Theorie des Romans*, Frankfurt am Main, 1986.

Jay, Martin, *The Dialectical Imagination: A History of the Frankfurt School and the Institute for Social Research 1923–1950*, Berkeley, CA, 1973.

Jay, Martin, 'Politics of Translation. Siegfried Kracauer and Walter Benjamin on the Buber-Rosenzweig Bible', *Yearbook Leo Baeck Institute* 21 (1976), pp. 3–24.

Jay, Martin, *Marxism and Totality: The Adventures of a Concept from Lukács to Habermas*, Cambridge, 1984.

Jay, Martin, *Permanent Exiles: Essays on the Intellectual Migration from Germany to America*, New York, 1986.

Jay, Martin, 'The Extraterritorial Life of Siegfried Kracauer', in *Permanent Exiles*, pp. 152–97.

Jay, Martin, 'Adorno and Kracauer: Notes on a Troubled Friendship', in *Permanent Exiles*, pp. 217–36.

Jedlicki, Jerzy, *Die entartete Welt: Die Kritiker der Moderne, ihre Ängste und Urteile*, Frankfurt am Main, 2007.

Jhering, Herbert, *Filmkritiker: Mit Kritiken und Aufsätzen von Herbert Ihering. Essay von Karin Herbst-Meßlinger*, Munich, 2011.

Jüdisches Museum Berlin (ed.), *Heimat und Exil: Emigration der deutschen Juden nach 1933*, Frankfurt am Main, 2006.

Jüdisches Museum Frankfurt (ed.), *Ostend: Blick in ein jüdisches Viertel: Begleitbuch zur Ausstellung im Jüdischen Museum*, Frankfurt am Main, 2000.

Jumonville, Neil, *Critical Crossings: The New York Intellectuals in Postwar America*, Berkeley, CA, 1991.

Kael, Pauline, 'Is There a Cure for Film Criticism? Or, Some Unhappy Thoughts on Siegfried Kracauer's Theory of Film: The Redemption of Physical Reality', in *I Lost it at the Movies*, Boston, 1965, pp. 269–92.

Kaes, Anton (ed.), *Kino-Debatte: Literatur und Film 1909–1929*, Tübingen, 1978.

Kaes, Anton, 'Filmgeschichte als Kulturgeschichte, Reflexionen zum Kino der Weimarer Republik', in *Filmkultur zur Zeit der Weimarer Republik*, ed. by Uli Jung and Walter Schatzberg, Munich, 1992, pp. 54–64.

Kaes, Anton, 'Film in der Weimarer Republik. Motor der Moderne', in Jacobsen, Kaes and Prinzler (eds), *Geschichte des deutschen Films*, pp. 39–100.

Kaes, Anton, *Shell-Shock Cinema: Weimar Culture and the Wounds of War*, Princeton, NJ, 2011.

Kaes, Anton, 'Siegfried Kracauer, The Film Historian in Exile', in Goebel and Weigel, *'Escape to Life': German Intellectuals in New York. A Compendium in Exile after 1933*, pp. 236–69.

Kaesler, Dirk, *Die frühe deutsche Soziologie 1909 bis 1934 und ihre Entstehungsmilieus: Eine wissenschaftssoziologische Untersuchung*, Opladen, 1984.

Kaesler, Dirk, 'Was sind und zu welchem Ende studiert man die Klassiker der Soziologie?', in Kaesler, *Klassiker der Soziologie*, vol. 1, Munich, 2012, pp. 11–38.

Kafka, Franz, 'The Truth About Sancho Panza', trans. Willa and Edwin Muir, in *Collected Stories*, London, 1993.

Kafka, Franz, *The Trial*, London, 2015.

Kafka, Franz, 'Little Fable', in *The Burrow: Posthumously Published Short Fiction*, trans. Michael Hofmann, London, 2017, p. 122.

Kantorowicz, Alfred, *Exil in Frankreich: Merkwürdigkeiten und Denkwürdigkeiten*, Frankfurt am Main, 1986.

Katz, Elihu, 'With what Effect? The Lessons from International Communications Research', in Merton (ed.), *Qualitative and Quantitative Social Research*, pp. 299–318.

Kaube, Jürgen, *Max Weber: Ein Leben zwischen den Epochen*, Berlin, 2014.

Kershaw, Ian, *Fateful Choices: Ten Decisions that Changed the World 1940–1941*, London, 2007.

Kessler, Michael, 'Entschleiern und Bewahren. Siegfried Kracauers Ansätze für eine Philosophie und Theologie der Geschichte', in Kessler and Levin (eds), *Siegfried Kracauer*, pp. 105–28.

Kessler, Michael and Thomas Y. Levin (eds), *Siegfried Kracauer: Neue Interpretationen*, Tübingen, 1990.

Kesten, Hermann (ed.), *24 neue deutsche Erzähler*, Berlin, 1929.

Kimmich, Dorothee, 'Überleben im Niemandsland oder die Entdeckung raumzeitlicher *interzones*. Siegfried Kracauers *Abschied von der Lindenpassage*', in Berg and Burdorf (eds), *Textgelehrte*, pp. 109–22.

Klapheck, Elisa, *Margarete Susman und ihr jüdischer Beitrag zur politischen Philosophie*, Berlin, 2014.

Klein, Richard, Johann Kreuzer and Stefan Müller-Doohm (eds), *Adorno-Handbuch. Leben – Werk – Wirkung*, Stuttgart, 2011.

Klemperer, Victor, *Munich 1919: Diary of a Revolution*, Cambridge, 2017.

Klibansky, Raymond and Herbert J. Paton (eds), *Philosophy and History: The Ernst Cassirer Festschrift*, New York, 1963.

Kluge, Alexander, *Lebensläufe*, Frankfurt am Main, 1986.

Kluge, Alexander, *Das fünfte Buch: Neue Lebensläufe. 402 Geschichten*, Berlin, 2012.

Knoch, Habbo and Daniel Morat (eds), 'Medienwandel und Gesellschaftsbilder 1880–1960. Zur historischen Kommunikologie der massenmedialen Sattelzeit', in Knoch and Morat (eds), *Kommunikation als Beobachtung: Medienwandel und Gesellschaftsbilder 1880–1960*, Munich, 2003, pp. 9–33.

Knopf, Jan, *Bertolt Brecht: Lebenskunst in finsteren Zeiten*, Munich, 2012.

Koch, Gertrud, '"… noch nirgends angekommen": Über Siegfried Kracauer', in Diner (ed.), *Zivilisationsbruch*, pp. 99–110.

Koch, Gertrud, *Die Einstellung ist die Einstellung: Visuelle Konstruktionen des Judentums*, Frankfurt am Main, 1992.

Koch, Gertrud, *Kracauer zur Einführung*, Hamburg, 1996.

Kocka, Jürgen, *Die Angestellten in der deutschen Geschichte 1850–1980: Vom Privatbeamten zum angestellten Arbeitnehmer*, Göttingen, 1981.

Kocka, Jürgen, *Geschichte des Kapitalismus*, Munich, 2013.

Koenen, Gerd, *Der Russland-Komplex: Die Deutschen und der Osten 1900–1945*, Munich, 2005.

Koenen, Gerd, *Was war der Kommunismus?*, Göttingen, 2010.

Koeppen, Wolfgang, *Romanisches Café: Erzählende Prosa*, Frankfurt am Main, 1972.

Koestler, Arthur, *Scum of the Earth*, New York, 1941.

Koffler, Dosio, *Vansittartitis: A Polemic*, London, 1943.

Köhn, Eckhardt, 'Die Konstruktion des Intellekts: Zum Verhältnis von gesellschaftlicher Erfahrung und literarischer Darstellung in Kracauers Romanen', *Text + Kritik* 68 (1980), pp. 41–54.

Kołakowski, Leszek, *Der Mensch ohne Alternative: Von der Möglichkeit und Unmöglichkeit, Marxist zu sein*, Munich, 1960.

Konersmann, Ralf (ed.), *Kulturphilosophie*, Leipzig, 1996.

Konersmann, Ralf, *Kulturkritik*, Frankfurt am Main, 2008.

König, Helmut, *Zivilisation und Leidenschaft: Die Masse im bürgerlichen Zeitalter*, Reinbek bei Hamburg, 1992.

Kopelew, Lew, *West-östliche Spiegelungen*, Munich, 2009.

Köpke, Wulf, 'Alfred Döblins Überparteilichkeit', in Thomas Koebner (ed.), *Weimars Ende*, Frankfurt am Main 1982, pp. 318–29.

Korsch, Karl, *Marxismus und Philosophie*, Leipzig, 1923.

Korta, Tobias F., *Geschichte als Projekt und Projektion: Walter Benjamin und Siegfried Kracauer zur Krise des modernen Denkens*, Frankfurt am Main, 2001.

Korta, Tobias F., 'Siegfried Kracauer (1889–1966). "Long Shots" und "Close-ups" der materialen Wirklichkeit', in Hofmann, Korta and Niekisch (eds), *Culture Club II*, pp. 38–60.

Korte, Helmut, 'Vom Kinematographen zur Nationalen Propaganda. Zur Entwicklung des frühen deutschen Films', in Korte, *Film und Realität in der Weimarer Republik*, Munich, Vienna, 1978, pp. 13–89.

Koselleck, Reinhart, *Kritik und Krise*, Frankfurt am Main, 1973.

Koszyk, Kurt, *Deutsche Presse 1914–1945*, *Geschichte der deutschen Presse*, Part III, Berlin, 1972.

Koziol, Klaus, 'Die Wirklichkeit ist eine Konstruktion. Zur Methodologie Siegfried Kracauers', in Kessler and Levin (eds), *Siegfried Kracauer*, pp. 147–58.

Kracauer, Isidor, *Geschichte der Juden in Frankfurt a. M.*, 2 vols, Frankfurt am Main, 1925 and 1927.

Kraus, Karl, '"Offenbach-Renaissance" (Zum Vortrag von "Pariser Leben")', in Karl Kraus, *Schriften*, ed. by Christian Wagenknecht, 20 vols, Frankfurt am Main, 1986–1994, vol. 17: *Die Stunde des Gerichts: Aufsätze 1925–1928* (1992), pp. 220–9.

Kreimeier, Klaus, *Die Ufa-Story: Geschichte eines Filmkonzerns*, Munich, Vienna, 1992.

Kreimeier, Klaus, *Traum und Exzess: Die Kulturgeschichte des frühen Kinos*, Vienna, 2011.

Kreuzer, Johann, 'Augenblick und Zeitraum. Zur Antinomie geschichtlicher Zeit', in Kessler and Levin (eds), *Siegfried Kracauer*, pp. 159–70.

Krige, John and Helke Rausch (eds), *American Foundations and the Coproduction of World Order in the Twentieth Century*, Göttingen, 2012.

Krige, John and Helke Rausch, 'Introduction – Tracing the Knowledge-Power Nexus of American Philanthropy', in Krige and Rausch (eds), *Foundations*, pp. 7–34.

Kris, Ernst and Hans Speier, *German Radio Propaganda: Report on Home Broadcasts During the War*, London, 1944.

Kristeller, Paul Oskar, *Renaissance Thought and the Arts: Collected Essays*, Princeton, NJ, 1990.

Kristeller, Paul Oskar, 'Foreword to the first edition', in Siegfried Kracauer, *History – The Last Things Before the Last*, Princeton, NJ, 1995, pp. xi–xvi.

Krohn, Claus-Dieter, *Wissenschaft im Exil: Deutsche Sozial- und Wirtschaftswissenschaftler in den USA und die New School for Social Research*, Frankfurt am Main, 1987.

Krohn, Claus-Dieter, 'Vereinigte Staaten von Amerika', in Krohn et al. (eds), *Handbuch der deutschsprachigen Emigration*, pp. 446–66.

Krohn, Claus-Dieter et al. (eds), *Handbuch der deutschsprachigen Emigration 1933–1945*, Darmstadt, 2008.

Krohn, Helga, 'Im Nationalsozialismus. Einführung zu biographischen Beiträgen', in *Ostend: Blick in ein jüdisches Viertel*, Frankfurt am Main, 2000, pp. 158–61.

Kubler, George, *The Shape of Time: Remarks on the History of Things*, New Haven, CT, 1962.

Kuhn, Helmut and Franz Wiedmann (eds), *Die Philosophie und die Frage nach dem Fortschritt*, Munich, 1964.

Kulischer, Eugene M., *Europe on the Move*, New York, 1948.

Külpe, Oswald, *Einleitung in die Philosophie*, 4th revised edn, Leipzig, 1907.

Lacis, Asja, *Revolutionär im Beruf: Berichte über proletarisches Theater, über Meyerhold, Brecht, Benjamin und Piscator*, ed. by Hildegard Brenner, Munich, 1971.

Landauer, Gustav, *Aufruf zum Sozialismus*, 4th edn, Cologne, 1923.

Langkau-Alex, Ursula, *Volksfront für Deutschland?*, vol. 1: *Vorgeschichte und Gründung des 'Ausschusses zur Vorbereitung einer deutschen Volksfront', 1933–1936*, Frankfurt am Main, 1977.

Laqueur, Walter, *Weimar: A Cultural History*, London, 2017 [1974].

Laqueur, Walter, *The Terrible Secret: Suppression of the Truth about Hitler's 'Final Solution'*, New York, 1998 [1980].

Laskin, David, *Partisans*, New York, 2000.

Lasswell, Harold D., 'Psychological Policy Research and Total Strategy', *The Public Opinion Quarterly* 16(4), Special Issue on International Communications Research (1952–3), pp. 491–500.

Lau, Jörg, '"Ginsterismus": Komik und Ichlosigkeit. Über filmische Komik in Siegfried Kracauers erstem Roman "Ginster"', in Volk (ed.), *Siegfried Kracauer*, pp. 13–42.

Lavin, Irving, 'Panofskys Humor', in Panofsky, *Die ideologischen Vorläufer*, pp. 7–16.

Lazarsfeld, Paul F., 'An Episode in the History of Social Research. A Memoir', in Fleming and Bailyn (eds), *The Intellectual Migration*, pp. 270–337.

Le Corbusier, *Towards a New Architecture*, trans. Frederick Etchells, New York, 1986.

Lederer, Emil, *State of the Masses: The Threat of the Classless Society*, New York, 1967.

Leo, Per, *Der Wille zum Wesen: Weltanschauungskultur, charakterologisches Denken und Judenfeindschaft in Deutschland 1890–1940*, Berlin, 2013.

Leonhard, Jörn, *Pandora's Box: A History of the First World War*, trans. Patrick Camiller, Cambridge, MA, 2018.

Lesch, Martina and Walter Lesch, 'Verbindungen zu einer anderen Frankfurter Schule: Zu Kracauers Auseinandersetzung mit Bubers und Rosenzweigs Bibelübersetzung', in Kessler and Levin (eds), *Siegfried Kracauer*, pp. 171–93.

Lessing, Wolfgang, 'Impromptus eines Frankfurter Wunderkindes', in Wolfram Schütte (ed.), *Adorno in Frankfurt*, Frankfurt am Main, 2003, pp. 77–84.

Lethen, Helmut, 'Sichtbarkeit. Kracauers Liebeslehre', in Kessler and Levin (eds), *Siegfried Kracauer*, pp. 195–228.

Lethen, Helmut, *Verhaltenslehren der Kälte: Lebensversuche zwischen den Kriegen*, Frankfurt am Main, 1994.

Lethen, Helmut, *Die Schatten des Fotografen: Bilder und ihre Wirklichkeit*, Berlin, 2014.

Lévi-Strauss, Claude, *The Savage Mind*, Oxford, 2004 [1966].

Lichtblau, Klaus, *Georg Simmel*, Frankfurt am Main, 1997.

Linder, Christian, *Noten an den Rand des Lebens: Portraits und Perspektiven*, Berlin, 2011.

Lindner, Burkhard (ed.), *Benjamin-Handbuch: Leben – Werk – Wirkung*, Stuttgart, Weimar, 2006.

Lindner, Rolf, *Die Entdeckung der Stadtkultur: Soziologie aus der Erfahrung der Reportage*, Frankfurt am Main, 1990.

Lipset, Seymour Martin, *Soziologie der Demokratie*, Neuwied am Rhein, Berlin-Spandau, 1962.

Löffler, Petra, *Verteilte Aufmerksamkeit: Eine Mediengeschichte der Zerstreuung*, Zurich, Berlin, 2014.

Lohmann, Hans Martin, 'Kommunismus als Religion', in Lukács et al., *Verdinglichung*, pp. 331–8.

Loos, Adolf, 'Ornament and Crime', in Ulrich Conrads (ed.), *Programs and Manifestos on 20th-Century Architecture*, trans. Michael Bullock, Cambridge, MA, pp. 19–24.

Lorenz, Erika, *Siegfried Kracauer als Soziologe*, unpublished Diplomarbeit, supervised by Prof. Th. W. Adorno, April 1962.

Löwenthal, Leo, 'Zur gesellschaftlichen Lage der Literatur', *Zeitschrift für Sozialforschung* 1(1) (1932), pp. 85–102.

Löwenthal, Leo, *Literature, Popular Culture, and Society*, Englewood Cliffs, NJ, 1961.

Löwenthal, Leo, *Literatur und Gesellschaft: Das Buch in der Massenkultur*, Neuwied am Rhein, 1964.

Löwenthal, Leo, *Mitmachen wollte ich nie: Ein autobiographisches Gespräch mit Helmut Dubiel*, Frankfurt am Main, 1980.

Löwenthal, Leo, 'Recollections of Theodor W. Adorno', in *An Unmastered Past: The Autobiographical Reflections of Leo Löwenthal*, Berkeley, CA, 1987, pp. 201–15.

Löwenthal, Leo, *Falsche Propheten: Studien zum Autoritarismus*, Frankfurt am Main, 1990.

Löwenthal, Leo, 'Das Dämonische. Entwurf einer negativen Religionsphilosophie', in Löwenthal, Leo, *Schriften*, vol. 5: *Philosophische Frühschriften*, Frankfurt am Main, 1990, pp. 207–23.

Löwenthal, Leo, 'As I remember Friedel', in *New German Critique* 54, Special Issue on Siegfried Kracauer (1991), pp. 5–17.

Löwenthal, Leo, *Literature and the Image of Man*, London, 2017.

Löwenthal, Leo, 'On Sociology of Literature', in *Literature and Mass Culture* (*Communication in Society*, vol. 1), London, 2017, pp. 255–67.

Löwenthal, Leo and Siegfried Kracauer, *In steter Freundschaft: Leo Löwenthal – Siegfried Kracauer. Briefwechsel 1921–1966*, ed. by Peter-Erwin Jansen and Christian Schmidt, Springe, 2003.

Löwith, Karl, *Meaning in History: The Theological Implications of the Philosophy of History*, Chicago, IL, 1949.

Löwith, Karl, 'Das Verhängnis des Fortschritts', in Kuhn and Wiedmann (eds), *Die Philosophie*, pp. 15–29.

Löwy, Michael, *Redemption and Utopia — Jewish Libertarian Thought in Central Europe: A Study in Elective Affinity*, trans. Hope Heaney, London, 2017.

Lukács, Georg, *The Theory of the Novel*, Cambridge, MA, 1971.

Lukács, Georg, *History and Class Consciousness: Studies in Marxist Dialectics*, trans. Rodney Livingstone, Cambridge, MA, 1971.

Lukács, Georg et al., *Verdinglichung, Marxismus, Geschichte: Von der Niederlage der Novemberrevolution zur kritischen Theorie*, ed. and with an introduction by Markus Bitterolf and Denis Maier, Freiburg, 2012.

Lynes, Russell, *Good Old Modern: An Intimate Portrait of the Museum of Modern Art*, New York, 1973.

Maase, Kaspar, 'Die soziale Konstruktion der Massenkünste. Der Kampf gegen Schmutz und Schund 1907–1918. Eine Skizze', in Martin Papenbrock et al. (eds), *Kunst und Sozialgeschichte*, Pfaffenweiler, 1995, pp. 262–78.

Maase, Kaspar, *Grenzenloses Vergnügen: Der Aufstieg der Massenkultur 1850–1970*, Frankfurt am Main, 1997.

Maase, Kaspar and Wolfgang Kaschuba (eds), *Schund und Schönheit: Populäre Kultur um 1900*, Cologne, 2001.

Macdonald, Dwight, *The Memoirs of a Revolutionist: Essays in Political Criticism*, New York, 1957.

Macdonald, Dwight, 'Review of "The Conquest of Europe on the Screen: the Nazi Newsreel, 1939–1940"', *Politics*, May 1944, p. 118.

MacDonald, Scott, *Cinema 16: Documents Toward a History of the Film Society*, Philadelphia, PA, 2002.

Mack, Michael, 'Literature and Theory, Siegfried Kracauer's Law, Walter Benjamin's Allegory and G.K. Chesterton's *The Innocence of Father Brown*', *Orbis Litterarum* 54 (1999), pp. 399–423.

Mai, Gunther, *Europa 1918–1939: Mentalitäten, Lebensweisen, Politik zwischen den Weltkriegen*, Stuttgart, 2001.

Makropolous, Michael, *Theorie der Massenkultur*, Munich, 2008.

Malraux, André, *The Conquerors*, trans. Stephen Becker, Chicago, IL, 1992.

Mann, Thomas, 'Tonio Kröger', in *Die Erzählungen*, Frankfurt am Main, 1986, pp. 298–374.

Mann, Thomas, *Death in Venice, Tonio Kröger, and Other Stories*, New York, 1999.

Mannheim, Karl, *Ideology and Utopia: An Introduction to the Sociology of Knowledge*, New York, London, 1954.

Mannheim, Karl, 'Structural Analysis of Epistemology', in *Essays on Sociology and Social Psychology*, London, 1969 [1953], pp. 15–73.

Marbacher Magazin 47 (1988), *Siegfried Kracauer 1889–1966*, ed. by Ingrid Belke and Irina Renz.

Markun, Silvia, *Ernst Bloch*, Reinbek bei Hamburg, 1977.

Marquard, Odo, *Der Einzelne: Vorlesungen zur Existenzphilosophie*, Stuttgart, 2013.

Marrus, Michael R., *Die Unerwünschten: Europäische Flüchtlinge im 20. Jahrhundert*, Berlin, 1999.

Maurer Zenck, Claudia (ed.), *Der hoffnungslose Radikalismus der Mitte: Der Briefwechsel Ernst Krenek – Friedrich T. Gubler, 1928–1939*, Vienna, Cologne, 1989.

Mazower, Mark, *Dark Continent*, London, 1998.

Meinen, Inka and Alrich Meyer, *Verfolgt von Land zu Land: Jüdische Flüchtlinge in Westeuropa 1938–1944*, Paderborn, 2013.

Menke, Bettine, '"Ursprung des deutschen Trauerspiels"', in Lindner (ed.), *Benjamin-Handbuch*, pp. 210–29.

Merleau-Ponty, Maurice, *Die Abenteuer der Dialektik*, Frankfurt am Main, 1974.

Merton, Robert K. et al. (eds), *Qualitative and Quantitative Social Research: Papers in Honor of Paul F. Lazarsfeld*, New York, London, 1979.

Merton, Robert K., *On the Shoulders of Giants*, Chicago, IL, 1993.

Meyerhoff, Hans (ed.), *The Philosophy of History in Our Time*, London, 1985.

Mittelmeier, Martin, *Adorno in Neapel: Wie sich eine Sehnsuchtslandschaft in Philosophie verwandelt*, Munich, 2013.

Moltke, Johannes von, 'Manhattan Crossroads: *Theory of Film* between the Frankfurt School and the New York Intellectuals', in Gemünden and von Moltke (eds), *Culture in the Anteroom*, pp. 42–60.

Moltke, Johannes von and Kristy Rawson (eds), *Siegfried Kracauer's American Writings: Essays on Film and Popular Culture*, Berkeley, CA, 2012.

Moltke, Johannes von and Kristy Rawson, 'Introduction: Affinities', in Moltke and Rawson (eds), *Siegfried Kracauer's American Writings*, pp. 1–26.

Moos, Stanislaus von, 'Le Corbusier and Adolf Loos', in Max Risselada (ed.), *Raumplan versus Plan Libre*, Delft, 1988, pp. 17–26.

Morgenstern, Soma, *Alban Berg und seine Idole: Erinnerungen und Briefe*, Berlin, 1999.

Morgenstern, Soma, *Flucht in Frankreich*, Berlin, 2000.

Mosès, Stéphane, *The Angel of History: Rosenzweig, Benjamin, Scholem*, trans. Barbara Harshav, Stanford, CA, 2008.

Mühlen, Patrik von zur, *Fluchtweg Spanien – Portugal: Die deutsche Emigration und der Exodus aus Europa 1933–1945*, Bonn, 1992.

Mühlen, Patrik von zur, 'Die Flucht über die Pyrenäen und der Exodus aus Europa', in Werfel (ed.), *Gehetzt*, pp. 145–68.

Mülder, Inka, *Siegfried Kracauer – Grenzgänger zwischen Theorie und Literatur: Seine frühen Schriften 1913–1933*, Stuttgart, 1985.

Mülder-Bach, Inka, 'Der Umschlag der Negativität. Zur Verschränkung von Phänomenologie, Geschichtsphilosophie und Filmästhetik in Siegfried Kracauers Metaphorik der "Oberfläche"', in *Deutsche Vierteljahresschrift für Literaturwissenschaft und Geistesgeschichte* 61 (1987), pp. 359–73.

Mülder-Bach, Inka, 'Schlupflöcher. Die Diskontinuität des Kontinuierlichen im Werk Siegfried Kracauers', in Kessler and Levin (eds), *Siegfried Kracauer*, pp. 249–66.

Mülder-Bach, Inka, 'Nachbemerkung und editorische Notiz', in Kracauer, *Werke* 5.4, pp. 697–716.

Müller, Jan-Werner, *Das demokratische Zeitalter: Eine politische Ideengeschichte Europas im 20. Jahrhundert*, Berlin, 2013.

Müller, Tim B., *Krieger und Gelehrte: Herbert Marcuse und die Denksysteme im Kalten Krieg*, Hamburg, 2010.
Müller, Tim B., 'Die Macht der Menschenfreunde – Die Rockefeller Foundation, die Sozialwissenschaften und die amerikanische Außenpolitik im Kalten Krieg', in Krige and Rausch (eds), *American Foundations*, pp. 146–72.
Müller-Doohm, Stefan, *Adorno: A Biography*, trans. Rodney Livingstone, Cambridge, 2005.
Müller-Doohm, Stefan and Wolfgang Schopf, 'Die Freundschaft zwischen Adorno und Kracauer', in Thomas Jung and Stefan Müller-Doohm (eds), *Prekäre Freundschaften: Über geistige Nähe und Distanz*, Munich, 2011, pp. 73–88.
Münster, Arno, *Ernst Bloch: Eine politische Biographie*, Berlin, Vienna, 2004 [2001].
Negt, Oskar, 'Ernst Bloch – der deutsche Philosoph der Oktoberrevolution. Mit einem Kommentar aus heutiger Zeit: Oktoberrevolution (Gesprächspartner Lenin)', in *Bloch Almanach* 34/2017, Bielefeld, 2017, pp. 53–72.
Neumann, Erich Peter, 'Einführung', in Kracauer, *Die Angestellten* (1959), pp. xi–xviii.
Neumann, Franz, *Behemoth: The Structure and Practice of National Socialism*, London, 1942.
Neumeyer, Harald, *Der Flaneur – Konzeptionen der Moderne*, Würzburg, 1999.
Neurath, Paul, 'Paul F. Lazarsfeld and the Institutionalization of Empirical Social Research', in Robert B. Smith, *An Introduction to Social Research*, Cambridge, MA, 1983.
Neurath, Paul, 'Paul Lazarsfeld und die Institutionalisierung der empirischen Sozialforschung, Ausfuhr und Wiedereinfuhr einer Wiener Institution', in Srubar (ed.), *Exil, Wissenschaft, Identität*, pp. 67–105.
Neurath, Paul, 'In memoriam Paul F. Lazarsfeld: Paul F. Lazarsfeld and the Institutionalization of Empirical Social Research', in Burkhart Holzner et al. (eds), *Realizing Social Science Knowledge*, Heidelberg and Berlin, 1983, pp. 13–28.
Newhall, Beaumont, *The History of Photography, from 1839 to the Present Day*, The Museum of Modern Art (ed.), New York, 1949.
Niethammer, Lutz, *Kollektive Identität: Heimliche Quellen einer unheimliche Konjunktur*, Reinbek bei Hamburg, 2000.
Nipperdey, Thomas, *Deutsche Geschichte: 1866–1918*, vol. 2: *Machtstaat vor Demokratie*, Munich, 1992.
Öhlschläger, Claudia, '"Unheimliche Heimat": Literarische Positionen und Reflexionen zur Psychologie des Exils', in Werfel (ed.), *Gehetzt*, pp. 169–90.
Olden, Rudolf und Ilka, *'Im tiefen Dunkel liegt Deutschland'. Von Hitler vertrieben – Ein Jahr deutsche Emigration*, ed. and with an introduction by Charmian Brinson and Marian Malet, Berlin, 1994.
Orth, Karin, *Die NS-Vertreibung der jüdischen Gelehrten: Die Politik der Deutschen Forschungsgemeinschaft und die Reaktionen der Betroffenen*, Göttingen, 2016.
Oschmann, Dirk, *Auszug aus der Innerlichkeit: Das literarische Werk Siegfried Kracauers*, Heidelberg, 1999.
Oschmann, Dirk, 'Erzählendes Denken – Denkendes Erzählen. Ernst Blochs *Spuren*', in Berg and Burdorf (eds), *Textgelehrte*, pp. 65–79.
Pabst, Reinhard (ed.), *Theodor W. Adorno: Kindheit in Amorbach: Bilder und Erinnerungen*, Frankfurt am Main, 2003.
Palmier, Jean-Michel, *Walter Benjamin: Lumpensammler, Engel und bucklicht*

Männlein: Ästhetik und Politik bei Walter Benjamin, Frankfurt am Main, 2009.

Panofsky, Erwin, 'Introduction: The History of Art as a Humanistic Discipline', in *Meaning in the Visual Arts*, London, 1983 [1955], pp. 1–25.

Panofsky, Erwin, 'Iconography and Iconology: An Introduction to the Study of Renaissance Art', in *Meaning in the Visual Arts*, London, 1983 [1955], pp. 26–54.

Panofsky, Erwin, 'Style and Medium in the Motion Pictures', in *Three Essays on Style*, Cambridge, MA, 1995, pp. 91–123.

Perivolaropoulou, Nia, 'Zeit der Geschichte und Zeit des Films bei Siegfried Kracauer', in Robnik et al. (eds), *Film als Loch in der Wand*, pp. 146–59.

Peters, Dietlinde, '"Abgestempelt", Der Fluchtweg des Ehepaars Lili und Siegfried Kracauer', in Aktives Museum (ed.), *Ohne zu zögern*, pp. 297–302.

Peukert, Detlev, *The Weimar Republic: The Crisis of Classical Modernity*, trans. Richard Deveson, New York, 1993.

Polanyi, Karl, *The Great Transformation: The Political and Economic Origins of Our Time*, Boston, MA, 2001 [1944].

Pollock, Friedrich, 'State Capitalism: Its Possibilities and Limitations', in Andrew Arato and Eike Gebhardt, *The Essential Frankfurt School Reader*, New York, 1982, pp. 71–94.

Pooley, Jefferson, 'The New History of Mass Communication Research', in David W. Park and Jefferson Pooley (eds), *The History of Media and Communication Research: Contested Memories*, New York, 2008, pp. 43–69.

Prinzler, Hans Helmut, *Sirens & Sinners: A Visual History of Weimar Film*, New York, London, 2013.

Prokop, Dieter, *Soziologie des Films*, Darmstadt, Neuwied, 1974.

Proust, Marcel, *The Guermantes Way*, trans. C.K. Scott Moncrieff, London, 2000.

Prümm, Karl, 'Filmkritik als Medientransfer. Grundprobleme des Schreibens über Filme', in Grob and Prümm, *Die Macht der Filmkritik*, pp. 9–24.

Puttnies, Hans and Gary Smith, *Benjaminiana*, Gießen, 1991.

Rabinbach, Anson, *In the Shadow of Catastrophe: German Intellectuals between Apocalypse and Enlightenment*, Berkeley, CA, 1997.

Radkau, Joachim, *Die deutsche Emigration in den USA: Ihr Einfluß auf die amerikanische Europapolitik 1933–1945*, Dusseldorf, 1971.

Radkau, Joachim, *Das Zeitalter der Nervosität: Deutschland zwischen Bismarck und Hitler*, Munich, Vienna, 1998.

Raphael, Lutz, *Geschichtswissenschaft im Zeitalter der Extreme: Theorien, Methoden, Tendenzen von 1900 bis zur Gegenwart*, Munich, 2010.

Rapsch, Alexandra, *Soziologie der Freundschaft: Historische und gesellschaftliche Bedeutung von Homer bis heute*, Stuttgart, 2004.

Raulet, Gérard, 'Verfallenheit ans Objekt. Zur Auseinandersetzung über eine Grundfigur dialektischen Denkens bei Adorno, Benjamin, Bloch und Kracauer', in Grunert and Kimmich (eds), *Denken durch die Dinge*, pp. 119–34.

Raulff, Ulrich, *Kreis ohne Meister: Stefan Georges Nachleben*, Munich, 2009.

Reifenberg, Benno, 'Erinnerung an Joseph Roth', in Reifenberg, *Lichte Schatten*, Frankfurt am Main, 1953.

Reijen, Willem van and Herman van Doorn, *Aufenthalte und Passagen: Leben und Werk Walter Benjamins. Eine Chronik*, Frankfurt am Main, 2001.

Reil, Harald, *Siegfried Kracauers Jacques Offenbach: Biographie, Geschichte, Zeitgeschichte*, New York, 2003.

Richter, Gerhard, *Thought-Images: Frankfurt School Writer's Reflections from Damaged Life*, Stanford, CA, 2007.

Ries, Ludwig, 'Vor dem Ersten Weltkrieg. Erinnerungen eines Schülers', in *Das Philanthropin zu Frankfurt am Main: Dokumente und Erinnerungen*, Frankfurt am Main, 1964, pp. 32–5.

Ritsert, Jürgen, *Inhaltsanalyse und Ideologiekritik: Ein Versuch über kritische Sozialforschung*, Frankfurt am Main, 1972.

Robnik, Drehli, Amália Kerikes and Katalin Teller (eds), *Film als Loch in der Wand: Kino und Geschichte bei Siegfried Kracauer*, Vienna, Berlin, 2013.

Rosa, Hartmut, *Resonance: A Sociology of Our Relationship to the World*, Cambridge, 2019.

Rosenberg, Arthur, *A History of the German Republic*, trans. Ian F. D. Morrow and L. Marie Sieveking, London, 1936.

Rosenzweig, Franz, *Der Stern der Erlösung: Mit einer Einführung von Reinhold Mayer und einer Gedenkrede von Gershom Scholem*, 4th edn, Frankfurt am Main, 1993.

Roth, Joseph, *Briefe 1911–1939*, ed. and with an introduction by Hermann Kesten, Cologne, 1970.

Roth, Joseph, *Flight Without End*, trans. David Le Vay, London, 1977.

Roth, Joseph, *The Wandering Jews*, trans. Michael Hofmann, New York, 2001.

Roth, Joseph, *'Ich zeichne das Gesicht der Zeit': Essays, Reportagen, Feuilletons*, ed. and annotated by Helmuth Nürnberger, Göttingen, 2010.

Roth, Joseph, *Joseph Roth: A Life in Letters*, trans. Michael Hofmann, London, 2012.

Roth, Joseph, *Drei Sensationen und zwei Katastrophen: Feuilletons zur Welt des Kinos*, Göttingen, 2014.

Roth, Joseph, *The Hundred Days*, trans. Richard Panchyk, New York, 2016.

Roth, Patrick, *Meine Reise zu Chaplin*, Frankfurt am Main, 1997.

Rotha, Paul, *Documentary Film*, London, 1938.

Rotha, Paul, *Rotha on the Film*, London, 1958.

Rotha, Paul and Richard Griffith, *The Film Till Now: A Survey of World Cinema*, London, 1949.

Rother, Rainer, 'In Deutschland entschiedener Erfolg: Die Rezeption sowjetischer Filme in der Weimarer Republik', in *Die rote Traumfabrik: Meschrabpom-Film und Prometheus 1921–1936*, ed. by Günter Agde and Alexander Schwarz, Berlin, 2012, pp. 10–23.

Roud, Richard, *A Passion for Films: Henri Langlois and the Cinémathèque Française*, London, 1983.

Roussel, Hélene and Lutz Winckler, 'Exil in Frankreich. Selbstbehauptung, Akkulturation, Exklusion – über einige Themen der Forschung', *Exilforschung* 30 (2012), pp. 166–91.

Rutkoff, Peter M. and William B. Scott, 'Die Schaffung der "Universität im Exil"', in Srubar (ed.), *Exil, Wissenschaft und Identität*, pp. 106–41.

Rutkoff, Peter M. and William B. Scott, *New School: A History of the New School for Social Research*, New York, London, 1986.

Ryklin, Michail, *Kommunismus als Religion: Die Intellektuellen und die Oktoberrevolution*, Frankfurt am Main, 2008.

Sadoul, Georges, *Geschichte der Filmkunst*, Frankfurt am Main, 1982.

Sakmyster, Thomas, 'Nazi Documentaries of Intimidation, "Feldzug in Polen" (1940), "Feuertaufe" (1940) und "Sieg im Westen" (1941)', *Historical Journal of Film, Radio and Television* 16(4) (1996), pp. 485–514.

Saldern, Adelheid von, 'Massenfreizeitkultur im Visier', *Archiv für Sozialgeschichte* 33 (1993), pp. 21–58.

Saß, Anne-Christin, *Berliner Luftmenschen: Osteuropäisch-jüdische Migranten in der Weimarer Republik*, Göttingen, 2012.

Sauveur-Henn, Anne Saint (ed.), *Fluchtziel Paris: Die deutschsprachige Emigration 1933–1940*, Berlin, 2002.

Sauveur-Henn, Anne Saint, 'Paris in den dreißiger Jahren, Mittelpunkt des europäischen Exils?', in Sauveur-Henn (ed.), *Fluchtziel Paris*, 2002, pp. 14–28.

Scheible, Hartmut, *Theodor W. Adorno*, Reinbek bei Hamburg, 1989.

Schildt, Axel, 'Der lange November – zur Historisierung einer deutschen Revolution', in Alexander Gallus (ed.), *Die vergessene Revolution von 1918/19*, Göttingen, 2010, pp. 223–44.

Schiller, Dieter, 'Verlage', in Krohn et al. (eds), *Handbuch der deutschsprachigen Emigration*, pp. 1122–44.

Schiller, Hans-Ernst, 'Tod und Utopie, Ernst Bloch, Georg Lukács', in Klein, Kreuzer and Müller-Doohm (eds), *Adorno Handbuch*, pp. 25–35.

Schivelbusch, Wolfgang, *Intellektuellendämmerung: Zur Lage der Frankfurter Intelligenz in den zwanziger Jahren*, Frankfurt am Main, 1982.

Schlaffer, Hannelore, 'Der engagierte Flaneur', in Volk (ed.), *Siegfried Kracauer*, pp. 43–56.

Schlaffer, Heinz, 'Denkbilder. Eine kleine Prosaform zwischen Dichtung und Gesellschaftstheorie', in *Poesie und Politik: Zur Situation der Literatur in Deutschland*, ed. by Wolfgang Kuttenkeuler, Stuttgart, 1982, pp. 137–54.

Schlotzhauer, Inge, *Das Philanthropin 1804–1942: Die Schule der Israelitischen Gemeinde in Frankfurt am Main*, Frankfurt am Main, 1990.

Schlüpmann, Heide, 'Der Gang ins Kino – ein Ausgang aus selbstverschuldeter Unmündigkeit. Zum Begriff des Publikums in Kracauers Essayistik der Zwanziger Jahre', in Kessler and Levin (eds), *Siegfried Kracauer*, pp. 267–95.

Schlüpmann, Heide, *Ein Detektiv des Kinos: Studien zu Siegfried Kracauers Filmtheorie*, Frankfurt am Main, 1998.

Schmidt, Alfred, 'Zum Verhältnis von Geschichte und Natur im dialektischen Materialismus', in *Existentialismus und Marxismus: Eine Kontroverse zwischen Sartre, Garaudy, Hyppolite, Vigier und Orcel*, Frankfurt am Main, 1965, pp. 103–55.

Schmidt, Alfred, *The Concept of Nature in Marx*, trans. Ben Fowkes, London, New York, 2014.

Schoeck, Helmut, *Die Soziologie und die Gesellschaften: Problemsicht und Problemlösung von Beginn bis zur Gegenwart*, Freiburg, Munich, 1964.

Scholem, Gershom, 'Zum Verständnis der messianischen Idee im Judentum', in Scholem, *Judaica*, Frankfurt am Main, 1963, pp. 7–74.

Scholem, Gershom, *Walter Benjamin: The Story of a Friendship*, New York, 1981.

Schopf, Wolfgang (ed.), *Adorno und seine Frankfurter Verleger: Der Briefwechsel mit Peter Suhrkamp und Siegfried Unseld*, Frankfurt am Main, 2003.

Schopf, Wolfgang, *'bin ich in Frankfurt der Flaneur geblieben …': Siegfried Kracauer und seine Heimatstadt*, Berlin, 2013.

Schöttker, Detlev, 'Bild, Kultur und Theorie, Siegfried Kracauer und der Warburg-Kreis', in *Leviathan* 34(1) (2006), pp. 124–41.

Schroer, Markus, 'Unsichtbares sichtbar machen. Visualisierungsstrategien bei Siegfried Kracauer', in Grunert and Kimmich (eds), *Denken durch die Dinge*, pp. 169–88.

Schröter, Michael, 'Weltzerfall und Rekonstruktion. Zur Physiognomik Siegfried Kracauers', *Text + Kritik* 68 (1980), pp. 18–40.

Schulte, Christoph, 'Messias und Identität. Zum Messianismus im Werk einiger deutsch-jüdischer Denker', in *Messianismus zwischen Mythos und Macht: Jüdisches Denken in der europäischen Geistesgeschichte*, ed. by Eveline Goodman-Thau and Wolfdietrich Schmied-Kowarzik, Berlin, 1994, pp. 197–209.

Schütte, Wolfram (ed.), *Adorno in Frankfurt: Ein Kaleidoskop mit Texten und Bildern*, Frankfurt am Main, 2003.

Schütz, Alfred, 'Der Fremde. Ein sozialpsychologischer Versuch', in Schütz, *Relevanz und Handeln 2: Gesellschaftliches Wissen und politisches Handeln*, Konstanz, 2011, pp. 59–74.

Schütz, Alfred and Aron Gurwitsch, *Briefwechsel 1939–1959: Mit einer Einleitung von Ludwig Landgrebe*, ed. by Richard Grathoff, Munich, 1985.

Schweppenhäuser, Hermann, *Kierkegaards Angriff auf die Spekulation: Eine Verteidigung*, Frankfurt am Main, 1967.

Secretariat of the Tribunal (ed.), *Trial of the Major War Criminals*, Nuremberg, 14 November 1945–1 October 1946, vol. XII, Proceedings 18 April 1946–2 May 1946 (International Military Tribunal: Nuremberg, 1947); available at: https://www.loc.gov/rr/frd/Military_Law/pdf/NT_Vol-XII.pdf

Seghers, Anna, *Transit*, trans. Margit Bettauer Dembo, New York, 2013.

Seidel, Alfred, *Bewußtsein als Verhängnis*, from posthumous papers ed. by Hans Prinzhorn, Bonn, 1927.

Sesterhenn, Raimund (ed.), *Das Freie Jüdische Lehrhaus – eine andere Frankfurter Schule*, Munich, Zurich, 1987.

Shahar, Galili, 'Auerbach's Scars: Judaism and the Question of Literature', *The Jewish Quarterly Review* 101(4) (2011), pp. 604–30.

Sieg, Christian, *The Ordinary in the Novel of German Modernism*, Bielefeld, 2011.

Silbermann, Alphons, *Verwandlungen: Eine Autobiographie*, Bergisch-Gladbach, 1989.

Simmel, Georg, *Kant: Sechzehn Vorlesungen*, Leipzig, 1905.

Simmel, Georg, 'The Metropolis and Mental Life', in *Classic Essays on the Culture of Cities*, David Sennett (ed.), Englewood Cliffs, NJ, 1969, pp. 47–60.

Simmel, Georg, *The Philosophy of Money*, trans. David Frisby, London, 1978.

Simmel, Georg, 'Exkurs über die Soziologie der Sinne', in *Soziologie, Gesamtausgabe*, vol. 11, Frankfurt am Main, 1992, pp. 722–42.

Simmel, Georg, 'The Sociology of Sociability', in *Simmel on Culture: Selected Writings*, London, 1997, pp. 120–9.

Simmel, Georg, 'Grundfragen der Soziologie', in *Georg Simmel Gesamtausgabe*, vol. 16, Frankfurt am Main, 1999, pp. 59–87.

Simon, Ernst, *Brücken: Gesammelte Aufsätze*, Heidelberg, 1965.

Simon, Ernst, 'N.A. Nobel als Prediger', in Simon, *Brücken*, pp. 375–80.

Simon, Ernst, 'Franz Rosenzweig und das jüdische Bildungsproblem', in Simon, *Brücken*, pp. 393–406.

Simon, Ernst, *Sechzig Jahre gegen den Strom: Briefe von 1917–1984*, ed. by Leo Baeck Institut Jerusalem, Tübingen, 1998.

Sitney, P. Adams (ed.), *Film Culture Reader*, New York, 1970.

Slezkine, Yuri, *Das jüdische Jahrhundert*, Göttingen, 2006.

Sohn-Rethel, Alfred, *Das Ideal des Kaputten*, Freiburg, 2018.

Söllner, Alfons, 'Archäologie der deutschen Demokratie. Eine

Forschungshypothese zur theoretischen Praxis der Kritischen Theorie im amerikanischen Geheimdienst', in *Zur Archäologie der Demokratie in Deutschland*, vol. 1: *Analysen von politischen Emigranten im amerikanischen Geheimdienst 1943–1945*, Frankfurt am Main, 1986, pp. 7–40.

Söllner, Alfons, 'Vom Völkerrecht zur *science of international relations*. Vier typische Vertreter der politikwissenschaftlichen Emigration', in Srubar (ed.), *Exil, Wissenschaft, Identität*, pp. 164–80.

Sontag, Susan, 'Film and Theatre', *The Tulane Drama Review* 11(1) (1966), pp. 24–37.

Sparr, Thomas, 'Peter Szondi: *Über philologische Erkenntnis*', in Berg and Burdorf, *Textgelehrte*, pp. 427–38.

Später, Jörg, *Vansittart: Britische Debatten über Deutsche und Nazis, 1902–1945*, Göttingen, 2003.

Später, Jörg, '"Kein Frieden mit Israel": Zur Rezeptionsgeschichte des Nahostkonflikts durch die deutsche Linke', in BUKO (ed.), *radikal global: Bausteine für eine internationalistische Linke*, Berlin, 2003, pp. 245–59.

Speier, Hans (ed.), *War in Our Time*, New York, 1939.

Spengler, Oswald, *The Decline of the West*, vols 1 & 2, New York, 1926 and 1928.

Spier, Selmar, *Vor 1914: Erinnerungen an Frankfurt geschrieben in Israel*, Frankfurt am Main, 1961.

Spoerhase, Carlos, 'Rezeption und Resonanz. Zur Faszinationsgeschichte der Forschungsgruppe "Poetik und Hermeneutik"', *Internationales Archiv für die Sozialgeschichte der Literatur* 35 (2010), pp. 122–42.

Srubar, Ilja (ed.), *Exil, Wissenschaft, Identität: Die Emigration deutscher Sozialwissenschaftler 1933–1945*, Frankfurt am Main, 1988.

Stadler, Ulrich and Magnus Wieland, *Gesammelte Welten: Von Virtuosen und Zettelpoeten*, Würzburg, 2014.

Stalder, Helmut, 'Hieroglyphen-Entzifferung und Traumdeutung der Großstadt: Zur Darstellungsmethode in den "Stadtbildern" Siegfried Kracauers', in Volk (ed.), *Siegfried Kracauer*, pp. 131–83.

Stalder, Helmut, *Siegfried Kracauer: Das journalistische Werk in der 'Frankfurter Zeitung' 1921–1933*, Würzburg, 2003.

Stalder, Helmut, 'Das anschmiegende Denken: Kracauers Erotik der Wirklichkeit', in Grunert and Kimmich, *Denken durch die Dinge*, pp. 47–84.

Steinert, Heinz, *Adorno in Wien: Über die (Un-) Möglichkeit von Kunst, Kultur und Befreiung*, Münster, 2003.

Steinmeyer, Georg, *Siegfried Kracauer als Denker des Pluralismus: Eine Annäherung im Spiegel Hannah Arendts*, Berlin, 2008.

Sternburg, Wilhelm von, *Joseph Roth: Eine Biographie*, Cologne, 2009.

Stiegler, Bernd (ed.), *Tat ohne Täter: Der Mordfall Fritz Angerstein*, Konstanz, 2013.

Stifter, Adalbert, *Indian Summer*, New York, 1985.

Stölting, Erhard, *Akademische Soziologie in der Weimarer Republik*, Berlin, 1986.

Stöver, Bernd, *Der Kalte Krieg: Geschichte eines radikalen Zeitalters 1947–1991*, Munich, 2007.

Sumner, Gregory D., *Dwight Macdonald and the* Politics *Circle: The Challenge of Cosmopolitan Democracy*, Ithaca, NY, 1996.

Susman, Margarete, *Ich habe viele Leben gelebt: Erinnerungen*, Stuttgart, 1964.

Szondi, Peter, 'Benjamins Städtebilder', in Szondi, *Lektüren und Lektionen*.

Versuche über Literatur, Literaturtheorie und Literatursoziologie, Frankfurt am Main, 1973, pp. 134–49.

Szondi, Peter, *Theory of the Modern Drama*, Minneapolis, MN, 1987.

Szondi, Peter, *Briefe*, ed. by Christoph König and Thomas Sparr, Frankfurt am Main, 1993.

Talbot, Daniel (ed.), *Film: An Anthology*, Berkeley, CA, 1969.

Thums, Barbara, 'Kracauer und die Detektive, Denk-Räume einer "Theologie im Profanen"', *Deutsche Vierteljahresschrift für Literaturwissenschaft und Geistesgeschichte* 84(3) (2010), pp. 390–406.

Tiedemann, Rolf, *Studien zur Philosophie Walter Benjamins*, Frankfurt am Main, 1973.

Tiedemann, Rolf, 'Einleitung des Herausgebers', in Benjamin, *Das Passagen-Werk*, pp. 9–41.

Tiedemann, Rolf, 'Dialectics at a Standstill: Approaches to the *Passagen-Werk*', in *The Arcades Project*, trans. Howard Eiland and Kevin McLaughlin, Cambridge, MA, pp. 929–45.

Tillich, Paul, 'The Totalitarian State and the Claims of the Church', *Social Research* 1(4) (1934), pp. 405–33.

Todorow, Almut, *Das Feuilleton der 'Frankfurter Zeitung' in der Weimarer Republik: Zur Grundlegung einer rhetorischen Medienforschung*, Tübingen, 1996.

Tooze, Adam, *The Wages of Destruction: The Making & Breaking of the Nazi Economy*, London, 2006.

Traverso, Enzo, *Siegfried Kracauer: Itinéraire d'un intellectuel nomade*, Paris, 2006.

Treml, Martin and Karlheinz Barck (eds), *Erich Auerbach: Geschichte und Aktualität eines europäischen Philologen*, Berlin, 2007.

Tyler, Parker, *The Hollywood Hallucination*, New York, 1944.

Tyler, Parker, *Magic and Myth of the Movies*, New York, 1947.

Über Walter Benjamin: Mit Beiträgen von Theodor W. Adorno, Ernst Bloch et al., Frankfurt am Main, 1968.

'Und keiner hat für uns Kaddisch gesagt …': Deportationen aus Frankfurt am Main 1941 bis 1945, Frankfurt am Main, 2004.

Unger, Corinna R., *Reise ohne Wiederkehr? Leben im Exil 1933 bis 1945*, Darmstadt, 2009.

Unseld, Siegfried (ed.), *Ernst Bloch zu Ehren: Beiträge zu seinem Werk*, Frankfurt am Main, 1965.

Vansittart, Robert, *Black Record: Germans Past and Present*, London, 1941.

Vansittart, Robert, *Lessons of My Life*, London, 1943.

Vialon, Martin, 'Über Bilder, Mimesis, ein Gespräch über den Roman und den Film – Erich Auerbach und Siegfried Kracauer', in *Konvergenzen: Studien zur deutschen und europäischen Literatur*, ed. by Michael Ewert and Martin Vialon, Würzburg, 2000, pp. 157–67.

Viénot, Pierre, *Ungewisses Deutschland: Zur Krise seiner bürgerlichen Kultur*, Frankfurt am Main, 1931.

Vogt, Jochen, 'Nicht nur Erinnerung, "Hitlers Gewalt": Ernst Blochs Beitrag zur Faschismustheorie', *Text + Kritik*, special issue (1985), pp. 98–123.

Volk, Andreas (ed.), *Siegfried Kracauer: Zum Werk des Romanciers, Feuilletonisten, Architekten, Filmwissenschaftlers und Soziologen*, Zurich, 1996.

Vondung, Klaus, *Die Apokalypse in Deutschland*, Munich, 1988.

Vormeier, Barbara, 'Frankreich', in Krohn, Mühlen, Paul and Lutz (eds), *Handbuch der deutschsprachigen Emigration*, Darmstadt, 2012, pp. 213–50.

Vormeier, Barbara, 'Einige Aspekte zur Lage der Ausländer, Juden und Emigranten in Vichy-Frankreich (Juni 1940–Sommer 1942)', in Werfel (ed.), *Gehetzt*, pp. 31–50.

Voswinckel, Ulrike and Frank Berninger, *Exil am Mittelmeer: Deutsche Schriftsteller in Südfrankreich von 1933–1941*, Munich, 2005.

Wagner, Julia, 'Anfangen. Zur Konstitutionsphase der Forschungsgruppe "Poetik und Hermeneutik"', *Internationales Archiv für die Sozialgeschichte der Literatur* 35 (2010), pp. 53–76.

Wald, Alan M., *The New York Intellectuals: The Rise and Decline of the Anti-Stalinist Left from the 1930s to the 1980s*, Chapel Hill, NC, 1987.

Walter, Hans-Albert, *Asylpraxis und Lebensbedingungen in Europa: Deutsche Exilliteratur 1933–1950*, Darmstadt, Neuwied, 1972.

Warshow, Robert, *The Immediate Experience: Movies, Comics, Theatre & Other Aspects of Popular Culture*, Cambridge, MA, 2001.

Wasson, Haidee, *Museum Movies: The Museum of Modern Art and the Birth of Art Cinema*, Berkeley, CA, 2005.

Weber, Alfred, 'Die Not der geistigen Arbeiter', *Schriften des Vereins für Sozialpolitik* 163 (1923), pp. 165–84.

Weber, Max, 'Politics as a Vocation', in *Essays in Sociology*, trans. and ed. by H.H. Gerth and C. Wright Mills, London, 1970 [1919], pp. 77–128.

Weber, Max, *Economy and Society*, ed. and trans. by Keith Tribe, Cambridge, MA, 2019.

Wehler, Hans-Ulrich, *Deutsche Gesellschaftsgeschichte*, vol. 4: *Vom Beginn des Ersten Weltkrieges bis zur Gründung der beiden deutschen Staaten, 1914–1949*, Munich, 2003.

Weigel, Sigrid, *Walter Benjamin: Images, the Creaturely, and the Holy*, Stanford, CA, 2013.

Weitz, Eric D., *Weimar Germany*, Princeton, NJ, 2007.

Wenzel, Mirjam, 'Nachbemerkung und editorische Notiz', in Kracauer, *Werke* 8, pp. 509–49.

Wenzel, Mirjam, 'Von Buchstaben, Träumen und Vorräumen. Die "Close-Up-Perspektive" Siegfried Kracauers', in Berg and Burdorf (eds), *Textgelehrte*, pp. 91–101.

Werfel, Ruth (ed.), *Gehetzt: Südfrankreich 1940. Deutsche Literaten im Exil*, Zurich, 2007.

Westermeier, Jens, *Jugend, Krieg und Internierung: Wissenschaftliche Dokumentation über Hans Robert Jauß*, Geiselhöring, 2015.

Wheatland, Thomas, *The Frankfurt School in Exile*, Minneapolis, MN, 2009.

Wickenburg, Erik G., 'Rudolf Geck', in *Gegenwart*, special issue on the *Frankfurter Zeitung*, 1956, pp. 31–2.

Wiggershaus, Rolf, *The Frankfurt School: Its History, Theories and Political Significance*, trans. Michael Robertson, Cambridge, 2010.

Wiggershaus, Rolf, 'Ein abgrundtiefer Realist. Siegfried Kracauer, die Aktualisierung des Marxismus und das Institut für Sozialforschung', in Kessler and Levin (eds), *Siegfried Kracauer*, pp. 285–95.

Winkler, Heinrich August, 'Einsichten eines Außenseiters. Eduard Bernstein und die Weimarer Republik', in Bernstein, *Die deutsche Revolution*, pp. 7–24.

Winkler, Heinrich August, *The Age of Catastrophe: A History of the West 1914–1945*, trans. Stewart Spencer, New Haven, CT, 2015.

Winkler, Michael, 'Über Siegfried Kracauers Roman *Ginster*, mit einer Coda zu *Georg*', in Kessler and Levin (eds), *Siegfried Kracauer*, pp. 297–306.

Wippermann, Wolfgang, *Das Leben in Frankfurt zur NS-Zeit I: Die nationalso-zialistische Judenverfolgung*, Frankfurt am Main, 1986.

Witte, Bernd, 'Das Alte und das Neue', in Witte (ed.), *Theorie des Kinos*, Frankfurt am Main, 1973, pp. 7–12.

Witte, Bernd, *Walter Benjamin*, Reinbek bei Hamburg, 1985.

Witte, Bernd, '"Dans une situation sans issue ...". Exil und Tod des Schriftstellers Walter Benjamin', in Werfel (ed.), *Gehetzt*, pp. 191–214.

Witte, Bernd, 'Nachwort', in Franz Hessel, *Spazieren in Berlin*, Berlin, 2011, pp. 223–32.

Witte, Karsten, 'Nachwort des Herausgebers', in Siegfried Kracauer, *Schriften*, vol. 2: *Von Caligari zu Hitler*, Frankfurt am Main, 1979, pp. 605–15.

Witte, Karsten, 'Nachwort', in Kracauer, *Über die Freundschaft*, pp. 99–105.

Witte, Karsten, 'Helle Trauer. Siegfried Kracauer als Literaturkritiker', in Kessler and Levin (eds), *Siegfried Kracauer*, pp. 307–24.

Wizisla, Erdmut, *Benjamin and Brecht: The Story of a Friendship*, trans. Christine Shuttleworth, London, 2016.

Worschech, Thomas, 'Die "lebende Photographie" in Frankfurt. Zur Frühgeschichte eines neuen Mediums, 1896–1914', in *Lebende Bilder einer Stadt: Kino und Film in Frankfurt am Main*. Exhibition catalogue, Deutsches Filmmuseum, Frankfurt am Main, 1995, pp. 24–51.

Wunderlich, Heinke, '"Feindliche Ausländer" – Literaten in Frankreich auf der Flucht', in Werfel (ed.), *Gehetzt*, pp. 51–76.

Wyman, David S., *Paper Walls: America and the Refugee Crisis 1938–1941*, Boston, MA, 1968.

Young-Bruehl, Elisabeth, *Hannah Arendt: Leben, Werk und Zeit*, Frankfurt am Main, 1991.

Zerlang, Martin, 'Ernst Bloch als Erzähler. Über Allegorie, Melancholie und Utopie in den "Spuren"', *Text + Kritik*, special issue (1985), pp. 61–75.

Ziege, Eva-Maria, *Antisemitismus und Gesellschaftstheorie: Die Frankfurter Schule im amerikanischen Exil*, Frankfurt am Main, 2009.

Zimmermann, Harro, *Friedrich Sieburg – Ästhet und Provokateur: Eine Biographie*, Göttingen, 2015.

Zinfert, Maria (ed.), *Kracauer: Fotoarchiv*, Zurich, Berlin, 2014.

Zischler, Hanns, *Kafka geht ins Kino*, Reinbek bei Hamburg, 1996.

Zohlen, Gerwin, 'Text-Straßen. Zur Theorie der Stadtlektüre bei S. Kracauer', *Text + Kritik* 68 (1980), pp. 62–72.

Zohlen, Gerwin, 'Bilder der Leere. Anmerkungen zu Kracauers "Straßen in Berlin und anderswo"', in Siegfried Kracauer, *Straßen in Berlin und anderswo*, Berlin, 1987.

Zohlen, Gerwin, 'Schmugglerpfad. Siegfried Kracauer, Architekt und Schriftsteller', in Kessler and Levin (eds), *Siegfried Kracauer*, pp. 325–44.

Index